W9-BAT-492

London, British Library, Royal MS 18 B. xxii, f. 34^r
William Worcester, *The Boke of Noblesse*, revised by the author, 1475
Reproduced by permission of the British Library

WILLIAM WORCESTER

THE BOKE OF NOBLESSE

AND

THE ENGLISH TEXTS FROM ITS CODICIL

———————

EARLY ENGLISH TEXT SOCIETY
O.S. 362

2023

de Premierfait	Laurent de Premierfait, *Livre de vieillesse*, ed. Stefania Marzano (Turnhout, 2009)
De sen.	Cicero, *Cato Maior de senectute*, ed. J. G. F. Powell, Cambridge Classical Texts and Commentaries, 28 (Cambridge, 1987)
DIMEV	Linne R. Mooney, Daniel W. Mosser, and Elizabeth Solopova, with Deborah Thorpe and David Hill Radcliffe, *A Digital Index of Middle English Verse* <www.dimev.net>
DMF	*Dictionnaire du Moyen Français (1330–1500)*, version 2020 (Nancy, 2020) <http://www.atilf.fr/dmf/>
DMLBS	*Dictionary of Medieval Latin from British Sources*, ed. Richard Ashdowne, David Howlett and Ronald Latham (Oxford, 2018) <http://clt.brepolis.net/dmlbs/Default.aspx>
EETS	Early English Text Society
OS	original series
ES	extra series
SS	supplementary series
EHR	*English Historical Review*
Foedera	*Foedera, Conventiones, Litterae et cujuscunque generis Acta Publica*, ed. Thomas Rymer, 10 vols. (The Hague, 1739–45)
.FP	Fastolf Papers (at OMA)
Froissart	Jean Froissart, *Chroniques de Jean Froissart*, ed. Siméon Luce, Gaston Raynaud, Léon Mirot and Albert Mirot, 15 vols. (Paris, 1869–1975)
Gairdner	*The Paston Letters*, ed. James Gairdner, 6 vols. (London, 1904)
Giles' Chronicle	*Incerti Scriptoris Chronicon Angliae de Regnis Trium Regum Lancastriensium*, ed. J. A. Giles (London, 1848)
GCF	*Les Grandes chroniques de France*, cited by the French king's reign and chapter
GCF-1476-7	*Chroniques de France*, 3 vols. (Paris: Pasquier Bonhomme, 16 Jan. 1476/77; *ISTC* ic00483000)
Hearne	*Thomæ de Elmham Vita et Gesta Henrici Quinti Anglorum Regis*, ed. Thomas Hearne (Oxford, 1727)
ISTC	*Incunabula Short Title Catalogue* <https://data.cerl.org/istc/_search>
Itineraries	William Worcestre, *Itineraries*, ed. John H. Harvey (Oxford, 1969)
Julius	BL, Cotton MS Julius F. vii
Laennec	Christine Moneera Laennec, 'Christine *antygrafe*:

ABBREVIATIONS

LIST OF ILLUSTRATIONS

CONTENTS

ACKNOWLEDGEMENTS

We thank the many librarians and archivists who allowed us access to their materials, often during the difficult conditions caused by the Covid-19 pandemic. We are very grateful to Richard Beadle for copious advice and to James Carley, John Colley, Anne Curry, Hannes Kleineke, Tristan Major, J. R. Mattison, Rebecca Menmuir, David Rundle, Christopher Tilmouth, Cameron Wachowich, and Shelley Williams for sharing work prior to publication or answering queries. We especially thank Sheri Chriqui for helping us to gather images of manuscripts at the start and Michael Angerer for helping us to check references at the end.

OXFORD

UNIVERSITY PRESS

Great Clarendon Street, Oxford, OX2 6DP,
United Kingdom

Oxford University Press is a department of the University of Oxford.
It furthers the University's objective of excellence in research, scholarship,
and education by publishing worldwide. Oxford is a registered trade mark of
Oxford University Press in the UK and in certain other countries

British Library Cataloguing in Publication Data

Data available

ISBN 978-0-19-889451-3

Typeset by John Waś, Oxford
Printed in Great Britain
on acid-free paper by
TJ Books Limited, Padstow, Cornwall

MIX
Paper from
responsible sources
FSC® C013056

WILLIAM WORCESTER
THE BOKE OF NOBLESSE
AND
THE ENGLISH TEXTS FROM ITS CODICIL

EDITED BY

CATHERINE NALL

AND

DANIEL WAKELIN

Published for
THE EARLY ENGLISH TEXT SOCIETY
by the
OXFORD UNIVERSITY PRESS
2023

	Authorship and Self in the Prose Works of Christine de Pizan with an Edition of B.N. Ms. 603 *Le Livre des Fais d'Armes et de Chevallerie*', 2 vols. (PhD diss., Yale, 1988)
LALME	M. Benskin, M. Laing, V. Karaiskos, and K. Williamson, *An Electronic Version of A Linguistic Atlas of Late Mediaeval English* (Edinburgh, 2013) <http://www.lel.ed.ac.uk/ihd/elalme/elalme.html>
LPL	London, Lambeth Palace Library
Nichols	*The Boke of Noblesse*, ed. John Gough Nichols (London, 1860)
MED	*Middle English Dictionary*, ed. Robert E. Lewis and others <http://quod.lib.umich.edu/m/middle-english-dictionary>
OCD	*The Oxford Classical Dictionary*, ed. Simon Hornblower, Antony Spawforth, and Esther Eidinow, 4th edn. (Oxford, 2012)
ODNB	*Oxford Dictionary of National Biography*, ed. H. C. G. Matthew, Brian Harrison, and Lawrence Goldman (Oxford, 2004) <https://www.oxforddnb.com/>
OED	*The Oxford English Dictionary*, ed. James A. H. Murray and others, 3rd edn., 20 vols. (Oxford, 2022) <https://oed.com>
OMA	Oxford, Magdalen College Archives
OMC	Oxford, Magdalen College Library
PL	*Paston Letters and Papers of the Fifteenth Century*, ed. Norman Davis (i–ii), ed. Richard Beadle and Colin Richmond (iii), EETS ss 20–2, 3 vols. (2005–7)
PROME	*The Parliament Rolls of Medieval England*, ed. Chris Given-Wilson and others, 16 vols. (London, 2005)
Royal	BL, Royal MS 13 C. i
RS	Rolls Series
s.n.	*sub nomine*
Sumption	Jonathan Sumption, *The Hundred Years War*, 4 vols. (London, 1990–2015)
Taylor and Roskell	*Gesta Henrici Quinti*, ed. and trans. Frank Taylor and John S. Roskell (Oxford, 1975)
Titus	BL, Cotton MS Titus A. xxiv (Part 2)
TNA	London, The National Archives
Tulle	*Caxton: Tulle of Olde Age: Textuntersuchung mit Literarischer Einführung*, ed. Heinz Susebach (Halle, 1933)
Viard	*Les Grandes chroniques de France*, ed. Jules Viard,

	Société de l'histoire de France, 10 vols. (Paris, 1920–53), cited by volume and page
Wars in France	*Letters and Papers Illustrative of the Wars of the English in France during the Reign of Henry VI, King of England*, ed. Joseph Stevenson, 2 vols., RS 22 (London, 1861–4)
Williams	*Henrici Quinti, Angliæ Regis, Gesta*, ed. Benjamin Williams (London, 1850)
WW	William Worcester
Wylie and Waugh	J. H. Wylie and W. T. Waugh, *The Reign of Henry the Fifth*, 3 vols. (Cambridge, 1914–29)

OTHER ABBREVIATIONS

c.	century
interl.	interlineate(s/d), interlineation
l., ll.	line(s)
marg.	margin/marginal (note)
PDE	Present Day English
rel.	relative
scr.	scribe/scribal
siden(n).	sidenote(s)

INTRODUCTION

On 15 June 1475, William Worcester, pen in hand, put finishing touches to a revision of his political treatise *The Boke of Noblesse*. He hoped to give it, apparently along with a multilingual Codicil of political and military documents evidencing some of its claims, to Edward IV, then invading France. The treatise is a strange one, composed of examples as much as precepts, taken from a diverse combination of sources. It draws on older Latin and French chronicles and annals—about the Saxons, Danes, Normans, Plantagenets. With some pretension at the renewed vogue for the classics, the *studia humanitatis* or humanism, it makes scattered allusion to various classical or pseudo-classical sources—Boethius, Ovid, Livy, Nonius Marcellus—and part is based on Cicero's *De senectute*. Much of that learning is taken from French intermediaries, from Laurent de Premierfait, Alain Chartier, and Christine de Pizan, revealing the reading in French typical of educated layfolk in England at this time. Finally, these bookish sources are spiced up with the recent military history of the wars in France under Henry V and Henry VI, including eyewitness reports by Worcester's former employer, the veteran Sir John Fastolf (1380–1459). It mixes from these ingredients a unique blend of ideas: Francophilic urbanity and Francophobic nationalism; Cicero's political theory and soldiers' practical policy; royal prerogatives and the *res publica*, or *comon wele* or *comon profit*, a harbinger of the monarchical republic of Tudor society.

The Boke of Noblesse has often been used as a near-contemporary record of fifteenth-century military history and of political attitudes after the English defeats in France. Those attitudes might in the twenty-first century hold a negative fascination, for they show the specious justifications that people develop for invading another country. But the positive fascination of *The Boke of Noblesse* is that it shows how exactly a writer built those justifications. That is possible because Worcester left traces of his reading almost without parallel in fifteenth-century England. Beyond *The Boke* and its Codicil, there survive his separate, full translation of Cicero's *De senectute* and two works by other people that he revised or to which he contributed in autograph, as well as twenty-three other manuscripts annotated by him and seven miscellanies containing works he annotated or notes he compiled. From those riches, one can reconstruct the intellectual journey that led to *The Boke of Noblesse*. Moreover, unusually, *The Boke* and its Codicil survive in fair copies to which Worcester added revisions in autograph. They therefore offer a rare chance to see a fifteenth-century author at work, in some cases from annotating sources to compiling notebooks to composing a work and then rethinking his words.[1] There is no writer in English of this period whose intellectual formation can be traced as thoroughly.

As a result, the textual notes of this edition are designed to show the stages of Worcester's work, and the Explanatory Notes are more detailed than is customary, in order to show the links between Worcester's reading and *The Boke of Noblesse*. The Notes are also extensive because *The Boke of Noblesse* requires some explanation. Worcester's copious references are sometimes imprecise in detail yet precise in implication, and both aspects need careful explication. The text has been printed before, for the Roxburghe Club in 1860, but fuller annotation makes its complexity more evident. It is also useful to bring together *The Boke of Noblesse* with some of the Codicil of probative documents that Worcester apparently and, after his death, his son definitely prepared to accompany it, and which were previously printed separately. Together they illuminate the intellectual life and political and military ideologies of the fifteenth century.

AUTHORSHIP

J. G. Nichols, printing *The Boke of Noblesse* in 1860, did not identify Worcester as the author.[2] It was George F. Warner, editing *The Epistle of Othea* by Stephen Scrope (d. 1472), who first recognized Worcester's handwriting in the 1475 revisions to the manuscript of *The Boke* and so argued for his authorship of those revisions and for a large part of the remainder.[3] In addition, the prologue by Worcester's son to the Codicil describes what must be *The Boke of Noblesse* as a work by his father.[4] Worcester's handwriting appears too in the Codicil, adding titles and revisions to its copies of older documents. The two works were evidently meant to accompany each other, and Worcester's role as author and compiler is indisputable.

[1] On the rarity of this, see Olivier Delsaux, *Manuscrits et pratiques autographes chez les écrivains français de la fin du moyen âge* (Paris, 2013), 185.

[2] Nichols, p. i.

[3] Stephen Scrope, *The Epistle of Othea to Hector*, ed. George F. Warner (London, 1904), pp. xliii–xlvi; confirmed by K. B. McFarlane, 'William Worcester: A Preliminary Survey', in J. Conway Davies (ed.), *Studies Presented to Sir Hilary Jenkinson* (London, 1957), 196–221 at 210–13.   [4] See C1/34.

That said, Warner also suggested Scrope's involvement in the first version of *The Boke*. That is theoretically possible, as Worcester served in Fastolf's household, and Scrope was Fastolf's stepson, but there is no positive evidence for it. Warner suggested too that the translation from a French intermediary of Cicero's *De senectute*, printed by William Caxton and described by him as dedicated to Fastolf, could also be by Scrope, for he suspected that Worcester was only learning French in 1458, a year before Fastolf's death.[5] But that suspicion is contradicted by Worcester's work for Fastolf in Normandy in the early 1440s and his notes dated to the 1440s, 1450, and 1453 from manuscripts in French; and it adds an unnecessary second translation of *De senectute* alongside that which Worcester claims to have given to William Waynflete on 10 August 1472.[6] There are also verbal echoes between the translation of *De senectute* printed by Caxton and *The Boke of Noblesse*,[7] so it seems certain that Worcester wrote both works.

The lineaments of William Worcester's life (1415–*c*.1480×85) can be reconstructed.[8] His literary works, marginalia, and miscellanies reveal much. There also survive twenty-three autograph letters or petitions by him, three more of his letters extant in copies by others,[9] and at least forty-two letters or memoranda supposedly composed by others but in fact copied or corrected in Worcester's handwriting, in thirty-six cases as amanuensis for his employer, Fastolf.[10] He also passed among people—notably, the legalistic Paston family and William Waynflete, an Oxford college's founder—who preserved letters and the administrative records that reveal his life and milieu.[11]

---

[5] Scrope, *Epistle of Othea*, ed. Warner, pp. xliii–xlvi. Warner misinterprets WW's French lessons reported in *PL*, no. 574, ll. 17–25, dated 27 Aug. 1458 (on which see n. 28 below), as basic teaching, but studying French alongside 'poetré' sounds like a more advanced or literary education.

[6] See *Itineraries*, 252; McFarlane, 'William Worcester', 200, on trips to Normandy; and Titus, introduced below, pp. lxxi–lxxii, and our Explanatory Notes *passim*. C&A, 39, are cautious about Worcester's ability in French.

[7] See 1803–11n. to 2138–51n. in general.

[8] *ODNB, s.n.* Worcester [Botoner], William, gives an up-to-date survey by Nicholas Orme, with references to 2004. The fullest biography is McFarlane, 'William Worcester'.

[9] For lists, see *PL*, ii, p. xxxii, and iii, p. xxiv: nos. 496, 498, 506, 529, 535, 537, 540, 558–9, 566, 571–2, 576, 604 (in a copy by Richard Calle), 727 (original lost), 780, 883–4, 888, 899, 912–13, 1030, 1046, 1049 (OMA, FP 84, on the scribe of which see pp. xxiv–xxvi below), 1050.

[10] For lists, see *PL*, ii, p. xxxiii, and iii, p. xxv: nos. 457, 507, 509, 523, 526, 531, part of 538, 541, 554–5, 579, 587–8, 877, 887, 955–6, 960, 901.B, 981–3, 986, part of 987, 988–91, 993–6, 1005–6, 1009, 1011, 1015, 1017, 1022, 1027, 1034, 1043.

[11] Alison Hanham, 'The Curious Letters of Friar Brackley', *Historical Research*, 81 (2008), 28–51, quotes many of the (often harsh) descriptions of Worcester in *PL*.

Worcester himself recorded some family history in a notebook that includes a detailed topographical account of Bristol and other anti-quarian jottings, now edited and titled as *Itineraries*. He was born in 1415 in St James's parish, Bristol, the son of an elder William Worcester and his wife Elizabeth, née Botoner, whose maiden name the younger William often used. On 5 July 1417, the family moved to a property belonging to his mother's family in Broadmead, Bristol.[12] His father seems to have been of secure income, owning and renting various build-ings and gardens around the city; and there was a connection with the clergy through his mother's brother, who was chaplain to one of the four chantry priests of a wealthy lay guild known as the Kalendars.[13] Worcester attended a grammar school in a room above Newgate, Bris-tol, where he was taught by Robert Londe. The life of the school at the time Worcester attended can be reconstructed from a notebook, includ-ing evocative *vulgaria*, owned in the late 1420s by a senior pupil or junior master, Thomas Schort.[14] In 1432 Worcester began studying at the University of Oxford, and from soon after survives his astronomical notebook, with most entries dated between 1438 and 1440.[15]

Rather than enter the Church, Worcester entered secular service, working for Sir John Fastolf, formerly a distinguished military com-mander in English-occupied Normandy, under the late John, duke of Bedford (1389–1435), for whom Fastolf acted as an executor. In 1439 Fastolf returned from campaigning in France to live largely at Fastolf Place, his house in Southwark, and set about extending and maintaining his landholdings in the West Country and East Anglia, including at Caister Castle in Norfolk, which he fortified in 1443 and to which he retired in 1454.[16] Worcester was surveyor or receiver of Fastolf's estates at Castle Combe, not far from Bristol, as early as May

[12] *Itineraries*, 310–11.

[13] William Worcestre, *The Topography of Medieval Bristol*, ed. Frances Neale, Bristol Record Society, 51 (Bristol, 2000), 14–15, 42–3, 56–7, 104–7, 122–3, 256–9; on the guild, see 210–11, and Nicholas Orme, 'The Guild of Kalendars, Bristol', *Transactions of the Bris-tol and Gloucestershire Archaeological Society*, 96 (1978), 32–52 at 46. For reference to a 'younger' William Worcester renting land in St James's parish in 1415, see Alfred E. Hudd, 'Bristol Merchant Marks', *Proceedings of the Clifton Antiquarian Club*, 7 (1912), 97–194 at 132.

[14] Worcestre, *Topography*, 28–9, 286; and Oxford, Lincoln College, MS Lat. 129 and MS Lat. 130, discussed by Nicholas Orme, 'A Grammatical Miscellany of 1427–1465 from Bristol and Wiltshire', *Traditio*, 38 (1982), 301–26 at 302, 306–7, 309, 311; Nicholas Orme, *Education in the West of England, 1066–1548* (Exeter, 1976), 38–40.

[15] BodL, MS Laud misc. 674, ff. 42^r, 74^r.

[16] *PL*, no. 83, ll. 4–5. This letter suggests that Stephen Scrope also resided with him there.

1438 and he served Fastolf as administrator, legal researcher, and secretary from some point by 1440 then throughout the 1440s and 1450s.[17] He might also have provided astrological or medical advice.[18] Some of his literary activity seems to have been intended for Fastolf, as were the works of Fastolf's stepson, Stephen Scrope.[19] Working for the apparently authoritarian, opinionated, and financially mean Fastolf cannot have been easy: Worcester himself complained of it in his letters, though with humorous detachment.[20] After Fastolf's death on 5 November 1459, Worcester and Fastolf's other executors, especially John Paston I, fought at length over what Fastolf's intentions and legal will were; Worcester ultimately failed. In 1470, Caister Castle was granted to the Pastons and the rest of the estate to William Waynflete, bishop of Winchester, to endow his recent establishment of Magdalen College, Oxford. Worcester was busy until 1474 transferring the estate.[21] Then, in his last few years, Worcester travelled widely through England pursuing his studies and otherwise lodged at Pockthorpe near Norwich.

Worcester reports in one letter that it was thirty years before he mixed with women's 'company' or made a woman 'of my councelle', so he perhaps married at over thirty years of age (that is, after 1445).[22]

---

[17] See Beadle and Richmond's headnote to *PL*, 955, a letter by Fastolf in WW's handwriting datable between 1436 and 1440. Also, WW later recorded that he had been 'tunc superuisor' at Castle Combe during a court session on 29 May 1438: BL, Add. MS 28208, f. 9[r], printed in *Itineraries*, 405–6. G. Poulett Scrope, *History of the Manor and Ancient Barony of Castle Combe, in the County of Wiltshire* (London, 1852), 170–2, 192–261, and Anthony Robert Smith, 'Aspects of the Career of Sir John Fastolf (1380–1459)' (D.Phil. thesis, Oxford, 1982), 64–5, describe WW's management of Fastolf's estates there.

[18] See BodL, MS Bodley 179, a French medical text with Fastolf's ownership recorded on the paste-down: it is possible that some but not all of the short English glosses on ff. i[r]–iii[v] might be by WW.

[19] For Scrope's biography, see Scrope, *History of Castle Combe*, 262–88; Scrope, *Epistle of Othea*, ed. Warner; Stephen Scrope, *The Dicts and Sayings of the Philosophers*, ed. Curt F. Bühler, EETS 211 (1941); Stephen Scrope, *The Epistle of Othea*, ed. Curt F. Bühler, EETS 264 (1970).   [20] *PL*, nos. 506, ll. 6–14 and 566, ll. 1–18.

[21] Narrated most fully in Colin Richmond, *The Paston Family in the Fifteenth Century: Fastolf's Will* (Cambridge, 1996). Jonathan Rose, 'Medieval Estate Planning: The Wills and Testamentary Trials of Sir John Fastolf', in Susanne Jenks, Jonathan Rose, and Christopher Whittick (eds.), *Laws, Lawyers and Texts: Studies in Medieval Legal History in Honour of Paul Brand* (Leiden, 2012), 299–326, provides a helpful list of sources. Hanham, 'Curious Letters', 34–8, 43–4, 50, presents a less positive view of Worcester's role in this business than does Richmond.

[22] *PL*, no. 780, ll. 13–15; Norman Davis, 'The Epistolary Usages of William Worcester', in D. A. Pearsall and R. A. Waldron (eds.), *Medieval Literature and Civilization: Studies in Memory of G. N. Garmonsway* (London, 1969)', 249–74 at 250.

His wife was called Margaret, and she was the daughter of Isabel, sister of Thomas Howes, chaplain to Fastolf and head of his household at Caister.[23] Worcester and Howes were evidently close friends, though they later quarrelled over Fastolf's will.[24] Worcester and his wife had at least one daughter and two sons, one with the initial 'R', perhaps the Robert about whose education at Lincoln's Inn Worcester worried; and one of these sons composed a prologue to the Codicil to *The Boke of Noblesse* (printed as C1 below) dedicating the Codicil to Richard III.[25] From that prologue, it is evident that Worcester had died some time between his last dated entry in one of his notebooks in 1480 and the end of Richard III's reign on 22 August 1485; in September 1485 Norwich city records referred to a woman as 'vxore nuper Willelmi Wyssetor' or 'recently' his wife, implying that he had only lately died.[26]

While some hard biographical facts are missing, what can be vividly reconstructed is Worcester's intellectual life. His annotations, miscellaneous notebooks, and letters to, from, and about him give telling details of the swapping of expertise, and books or bookish gifts such as 'a penner *and* an hynkehorn'.[27] In 1458 he was reported to be in London studying alongside the Italian merchant Carlo Gigli, 'to lern and to be red in poetré or els in Frensh'.[28] He read classical literature in Latin and in French translation; he dabbled briefly in Greek and Hebrew; he gathered information on English history; he took detailed notes on topography and architecture; he did work in astronomy.[29] Many of

---

[23] *PL*, no. 925, ll. 6–16: in a declaration in her name after Worcester's death.

[24] See respectively *PL*, nos. 516, ll. 3–4 and 888, ll. 22–3, on which Richmond, *The Paston Family . . . Fastolf's Will*, 84, 89, 94.

[25] See *PL*, no. 780, ll. 7–15, about 'Robert' (1 Mar., probably 1478), and a letter by his son 'R' in CCCC, MS 210, pp. 39, 41–2, printed in *Itineraries*, 386 (Lent, probably 1478), which mentions a brother and sister. See C1/34, where the author of the prologue to the Codicil claims Worcester as father, and C1/31, where he calls himself *lege-man*, i.e. not the daughter. No figure is identifiable as Worcester's son in Sir John Baker, *The Men of Court 1440 to 1550: A Prosopography of the Inns of Court and Chancery and the Courts of Law*, 2 vols. (London, 2012). [26] *Itineraries*, p. ix.

[27] *PL*, no. 969, ll. 20–9, on which see Daniel Wakelin, *Humanism, Reading, and English Literature 1430–1530* (Oxford, 2007), 96, 103, and in the Explanatory Notes below 70–1n., 750–2n. and 1596–9n.; and *PL*, no. 970, l. 7.

[28] *PL*, no. 574, ll. 17–25 (on which see n. 5 above); N. R. Havely, *Dante's British Public: Readers and Texts, from the Fourteenth Century to the Present* (Oxford, 2014), 5–6; *England's Immigrants 1330–1550* <www.englandsimmigrants.com>, *s.n.* Carlo de Giliis [31375]. Hanham, 'Curious Letters', 37 n. 46, suggests that Worcester's unapologetic passion for poetry, reported in *PL*, no. 574, was 'secretive'.

[29] McFarlane, 'William Worcester'; Catherine Nall, *Reading and War in Fifteenth-Century England: From Lydgate to Malory* (Cambridge, 2012), 39–41, 53–8, 66–74; Wakelin, *Humanism*, 93–125, 152–9.

his polymathic interests, along with the military concerns of his former employer Fastolf, coalesce in *The Boke of Noblesse* and its Codicil.

MANUSCRIPTS

1. London, British Library, Royal MS 18 B. xxii

This is the only manuscript of *The Boke of Noblesse*.[30]

Binding

The binding (290 mm×207 mm) is an early nineteenth-century style typical of the then British Museum. It is in brown leather stamped in gold with the royal arms, motto, and date 1757, the date of the transfer of the Royal collection to the Museum, the Royal shelfmark, allocated in the early eighteenth century,[31] and 'PLUT. XIII. D', signalling which shelf (*pluteus*) it was stored on at the Museum after 1824.[32] Interior paste-downs of marbled papers are glued to the first, front flyleaf f. i[r] and the last, rear flyleaf f. xii[v].[33]

Foliation and Flyleaves

The manuscript consists of ff. i–vi+1–45+vii–xii. The pencil foliation, probably late nineteenth-century, includes the quires containing *The Boke of Noblesse* and two fifteenth-century letters bound with them. No flyleaves are foliated.

Folios i–iii at the front and ff. x–xii at the rear are modern card. Folios iv–v at the front and ff. viii–ix at the rear are each a bifolium of parchment, slightly smaller (*c.*270 mm×200 mm) than the main quires,

[30] For descriptions, see J. P. Gilson and George F. Warner, *Catalogue of Western Manuscripts in the Old Royal and King's Collections*, 4 vols. (London, 1921), ii. 294–5; Anne F. Sutton and Livia Visser-Fuchs, 'Richard III's Books: XII. William Worcester's *Boke of Noblesse* and his Collection of Documents on the War in Normandy', *The Ricardian*, 115 (1991), 154–65, and their *Richard III's Books: Ideals and Reality in the Life and Library of a Medieval Prince* (Stroud, 1997), 291–3, and fig. 37, which illustrates ff. 14[v]–15[r].

[31] Warner and Gilson, *Catalogue*, i, p. xi.

[32] On the BL's foliation and shelfmarks, see Andrew Prescott, 'What's in a Number? The Physical Organization of the Manuscript Collections of the British Library', in A. N. Doane and Kirsten Wolf (eds.), *Beatus Vir: Studies in Early English and Norse Manuscripts in Memory of Philip Pulsiano* (Tempe, AZ, 2006), 471–525 at 475, 513.

[33] In Dec. 2020, the spine was coming loose, and the upper and lower boards were detached and kept in place by string. In May 2022 the MS underwent extensive conservation work by BL conservator Heather Marshall, including renewing or rebacking the spine with new leather. We thank Janet Portman and Charmaine Fagan for information about this process.

with follicle marks and many plaques; of these leaves, ff. iv^r and ix^v were formerly paste-downs. In the centre of the top edge and near the top of the fore-edge of ff. iv–v and ff. viii–ix are consistent small holes with discolouration, perhaps caused by metal furniture from a former binding.

The next front flyleaf f. vi is a singleton of medieval parchment that wraps round quire I, emerging as an irregular stub after f. 12^v, with pen-trials on it. On flyleaf f. vi^r are late fifteenth- or sixteenth-century strapwork majuscules and scribbles, now faded, including perhaps a name 'heinesey'. Glued to f. vi^r is a rectangular fragment of faded red or pink leather, perhaps from an earlier binding, on which fragment is written roughly 'Edward wych ys' in early sixteenth-century secretary handwriting, as well as scribbled letters and perhaps the word 'bold' in a different hand. Overleaf on f. vi^v, are pen-trials and scribbles, many illegible, and 'Symond Samson' (on whom see 'Provenance', pp. xxx–xxxi below).

The rear flyleaf f. vii is a singleton of early modern paper, not cognate with the mount f. 45; it is marked with a pencil collation note.

Materials

The main quires are 284 mm×207 mm, made from paper. Chain-lines run horizontally, about 60 mm apart. In all four quires, half the pairs of cognate leaves (except where leaves are lost) have across their gutters a watermark of scissors, with points 20 mm apart, below a flower with five rounded petals. It seems identical to a paper stock attested in Genoa in 1472, which accords loosely with other evidence of the date of this manuscript.[34] Different watermarks of scissors occur in Worcester's letters, miscellanies, and a copy of the Latin *Gesta Henrici Quinti* annotated by Worcester, but none is identical to this.[35]

---

[34] *Briquet Online* <https://briquet-online.at/> (consulted 28 June 2022), no. 3725. In *Wasserzeichen-Informationssystem* <https://www.wasserzeichen-online.de> (consulted 28 June 2022), there are similar but not identical specimens in Germany in 1478 (no. DE4215-PO-122540) and northern Italy in the early 1480s (nos. IT5235-PO-122542, IT6780-PO-122543).

[35] e.g. BL, Add. MS 34888, ff. 49, 53 (*PL*, nos. 989, 994), and OMA, FP Add. 2 (*PL*, no. 991); BL, Cotton MS Julius E. iv, ff. 113–15, 119, 121, 123–25; Arundel, ff. 29, 329, 331 and ff. 141, 144–6, 150, 151, 194–5. Deborah Thorpe, 'Writing and Reading in the Circle of Sir John Fastolf (d. 1459)' (PhD thesis, York, 2012), 216–17, notes some of the earlier watermarks.

Collation

The quires are constructed: I–II¹², III¹² (2 wanting after f. 25ᵛ, 11–12 wanting after f. 33ᵛ, all with loss of text), IV¹² (11–12 cancelled after f. 43ᵛ, probably with no loss of text).

Quiring is revealed by clear string between central bifolia, sewn with seven holes through each gutter. Leaf signatures occur: in quire I, on ff. 3ʳ, 5ʳ, 6ʳ, both Indo-Arabic numerals 3, 5, and 6 and roman numerals +*iij*, +*v*, and +*vj*;³⁶ in quire II, on ff. 13ʳ–18ʳ, *a* and roman numerals, in a mid-fifteenth-century secretary hand, perhaps the scribe's; in quire III, on ff. 24ʳ–29ʳ, *b* and Indo-Arabic numerals, with some irregularities, in a fifteenth-century hand but perhaps not that of the signatures in quire II;³⁷ and in quire IV, on ff. 34ʳ–39ʳ, *c* and Indo-Arabic numerals in a fifteenth-century hand. There are no catchwords.

Following the main quires, two mid-fifteenth-century missive letters are bound in as singletons. Folio 44 is a letter, oriented landscape fashion (210 mm×248 mm), bound into this MS with a flap of 50 mm on its right-hand side folded inwards to fit the width of the binding. It is on paper with no visible watermarks. It was formerly folded into a packet (60 mm×74 mm) and had an address on the dorse (f. 44ᵛ), now oriented upside down. Folio 45 is a letter also formerly oriented landscape fashion (145 mm×270 mm) but now rotated 90° for binding, so that the writing runs vertically. A small amount of text is trimmed off at the right-hand side, now the top. There are no signs of folding nor any address on the dorse. It is mounted on a stub of paper.

Contents

f. viʳ⁻ᵛ: flyleaf, with jottings (see above) and added name (see 'Provenance' below).

ff. 1ʳ–42ʳ: William Worcester, *The Boke of Noblesse*.

f. 42ᵛ: various added names (see 'Provenance' below), one also adding a bookplate in three couplets (*DIMEV* 1896/5) and anti-feminist couplet (*DIMEV* 132/3), both widely attested;³⁸ added phrases as pen-trials (some from the reign of a king and one from the reign of Mary I); and added doodles.

---

³⁶ WW's marginal addition on f. 4ʳ obscures any signatures there; Nichols, p. lv, could see other roman numerals on ff. 1ʳ, 2ʳ.

³⁷ BL, Royal MS 18 B. xxii, f. 27ʳ, has no 'b .4.' but a trimmed different note at the foot; f. 28ʳ has some erasure under '.b.5.'

³⁸ *DIMEV* incorrectly records the folio as f. 44ᵛ. *DIMEV* 2318/1, is said to be in this MS, f. 64ᵛ, but there is no such folio or couplet in this MS.

f. 43[r]: pen-trials of French and English words, repeated letters, and a face.

f. 44[r]: letter in French from Thomas Appulton, captain of Pont-d'Ouve and La Haye-du-Puits, to Fastolf, from La Haye-du-Puits, 31 May, datable to 1436.[39]

f. 45[r]: letter in English from the bailiffs of Winchester to an officer of the exchequer, dated 8 May, without year; in handwriting of the second half of the fifteenth century.

Scribe

There are textual revisions and corrections in Worcester's handwriting in brown ink. Prior to his intervention, the manuscript was a fair copy by a separate scribe. That fair copy can be dated c.1474–5, given datable references in the text, and certainly before 15 June 1475, the date given by Worcester for his autograph revisions. (See below, pp. lv–lvii.) The handwriting is freehand without ruling and is generally level but varies slightly in module; it shifts between current execution and slower, almost calligraphic touches: for instance, minims on **m** and **n** are formed with one 'zigzag' stroke but on **u** are set separately. The model is a kind of secretary script typical of the third quarter of the 1400s. In each case, distinctive letterforms include one-compartment **a** with horns and broken strokes top-left; broken strokes creating an extra diagonal at the bottom-left of the bowl of **b**; sloping, almost curled, ascenders of **b**, **h**, and **l**; **d** with a long left-leaning looped ascender; line-final **d** with an otiose curve; horned **e**; sloping **f** and long **s**; flat-topped **g** with a pronounced horn top-right and very perfunctory tail; word-final long **r** with a curl for abbreviation of ⟨e⟩; a mixture of two kinds of final **s**, with occasional sigmoid shape akin to anglicana **s** but a stronger preference for secretary's kidney-shaped **s** with many broken strokes; **st** ligature that tapers at its top; a tall stem of **t** above its crossbar sloping forwards; **v** with a broken stroke at its foot; the same element in the formation of the second part of **w**, while the first part is notably taller than the x-height; an occasional alternative rounded **w** evocative of anglicana; a rightward curl in the tail of **y**. Overall, the frequent broken strokes, especially on **a**, **d**, and **e**, typical of French-influenced secretary handwriting, are balanced by a slightly rounded aspect more akin to anglicana. That suggests that the scribe was probably not trained in France—otherwise a possibility in Fastolf's household.

---

[39] This and the next item printed by Nichols, p. lvi; summarized by Gilson and Warner, *Catalogue*, ii. 294–5.

Similar kinds of handwriting occur in other manuscripts datable from the third quarter of the century and from similar milieux, notably in copies of the works of Stephen Scrope, Fastolf's stepson.[40] That suggests the typicality or appropriateness of this style of script for English philosophical prose at this time and place. Similar but more French-influenced styles of secretary occur in other texts Worcester owned.[41] Some notes and documents copied for Worcester do, however, seem to be in the same hand as Royal MS 18 B. xxii:

- BL, Cotton MS Julius F. vii, ff. 6^r–13^v: a list of chapter titles from the French *Ovide moralisé en prose II*, with space left for reproducing the illustrations; annotated by Worcester.[42]
- BL, Cotton MS Julius F. vii, f. 23^{r-v}: a list of Latin incipits to Ovid's works in Latin.
- OMA, FP 70/1: English list of property received by William Yelverton after Fastolf's death; completed and retranscribed by Worcester.[43]

The recurrence suggests that this scribe was somebody whom Worcester could call on frequently, for pay or for favours, for large jobs or small. There were many such figures in and around Fastolf's household. For instance, *c.*1460 it was reported that one John Bussard had been copying a chronicle of Jerusalem and a work on the deeds of Fastolf for Worcester, using more than twenty quires of paper, and had also copied 'bill*ys* or ded*ys* or ony o*p*er evydens' for him.[44] It is tempting to wonder whether the list of property received by Yelverton

---

[40] For example, very similar is Longleat House, MS 253, e.g. f. 22^v, printed as frontispiece to Scrope, *Epistle of Othea*, ed. Warner. Looser likenesses are in BodL, MS Bodley 943, on which see Scrope, *Dicts*, pp. xx–xxi, xxix–xxxv; Cambridge, Emmanuel College, MS I.2.10, e.g. f. 73^r (with annotation by WW), printed as frontispiece to Scrope, *Dicts*; and Cambridge, St John's College, MS H.5, e.g. f. 34^r, printed as frontispiece to Scrope, *Epistle*, ed. Bühler.

[41] e.g. Julius, ff. 67^r–69^r, 103^r–104^r, 165^r–166^v, 167^r, 172^r–174^r, 186^r–200^v; Royal, ff. 181^r–184^v; Arundel, ff. 47^r–52^v, 174^r–179^r, 208^r–209^v, 220^r–224^r, 236^r–269^r, 286^r–288^r, 339^r–340^r.

[42] The French *Ovide moralisé en prose II* was also the source for Caxton's translation: see William Caxton, *The Middle English Text of Caxton's Ovid: Book I*, ed. Diana Rumrich, Middle English Texts, 43 (Heidelberg, 2010), pp. ix, xliv–xlv.

[43] Thorpe, 'Writing and Reading', 297–8; Richmond, *The Paston Family . . . Fastolf's Will*, 97. Worcester says that his copy of this list in OMA, FP 70/2, 'extrascribitur de billa manu propria Thome howys', presumably meaning that that the exemplar was in Howes's hand, but OMA, FP 70/1 is not in Howes's hand, which is different and identified by Davis in BL, Add. MS 27444, f. 54^r (*PL*, no. 564) and BL, Add. MS 34888, f. 69^r (*PL*, no. 1008).

[44] *PL*, no. 602, ll. 6–15. McFarlane, 'William Worcester', 209, notes that OMA, FP 72, records that Worcester gave money to the ill, impoverished Bussard at this time.

after Fastolf's death (OMA, FP 70/1) could be one of the 'bill*ys*' copied by Bussard—and, therefore, whether Bussard could be scribe of *The Boke*.[45] But that can only be speculation. Any of the people in this network whose handwriting remains unnamed could be this scribe.

In addition, there is similar but not identical handwriting in other copying from this milieu in the 1450s to the 1470s:

- Arundel, ff. 194^r–195^r, 210^r–215^r, 284^{r-v}, 339^r–340^r: transcriptions of various historical documents, in a compilation annotated in places by Worcester.[46]
- London, College of Arms, MS M.9, ff. 31^r–66^r: *Basset's Chronicle*.[47]
- OMA, FP 48, first scribe: a petition in the name of Fastolf, dated 7 February 1453.[48]
- OMA, FP 49: draft of a document on the same subject, annotated by Worcester.
- OMA, FP 84: a petition in the name of Worcester to James Goldwell, bishop of Norwich, seeking his assistance in carrying out Fastolf's original intentions, and in recouping his costs as executor; revised by Worcester.[49]
- OMA, FP 87 (part i): an account of Fastolf's will, so dated after 5 November 1459, supplemented by Worcester.[50]

This other scribe's handwriting is of the same kind and date as that of *The Boke of Noblesse*, but not identical—although the conventions and recurrent spellings for different languages and the different grades of formality or currency for different genres might lead to different aspects of the handwriting. There are likenesses in many letterforms, but this handwriting often has a more elaborate tail on **g**, a more *v*-shaped form of short **r**, or a greater frequency of the trailing form of word-final sig-

---

[45] See OMA, FP 70/1 in n. 43 above. Worcester's second version of this document calls it a 'billa' (OMA, FP 70/2).

[46] Arundel, f. 339^r, is reproduced and discussed in C&A, 17.

[47] Printed in C&A, with the MS described fully, 10–18.

[48] Reproduced by Thorpe, 'Writing and Reading', 296, 349, and Deborah Thorpe, 'Documents and Books: A Case Study of Luket Nantron and Geoffrey Spirleng as Fifteenth-Century Administrators and Textwriters', *Journal of the Early Book Society*, 14 (2011), 195–216 at 200–1, 213; C&A, 11–14.

[49] *PL*, no. 1049, and Richmond, *The Paston Family . . . Fastolf's Will*, 69–71, date it '[p]robably 1472'; but McFarlane, 'William Worcester', 201–3, dates it *c*.1477, and Richmond, at 256, also suggests 'a year or two earlier' than 1477. See also K. B. McFarlane, 'The Investment of Sir John Fastolf's Profits of War', *Transactions of the Royal Historical Society*, 7 (1957), 91–116 at 105, 108; Rose, 'Medieval Estate Planning', 317.

[50] Richmond, *The Paston Family . . . Fastolf's Will*, 69.

moid **s**. In aspect this handwriting has spikier, hairline strokes, and a less rounded execution, while also, conversely, lacking the broken strokes on the top left of **a**. Moreover, in OMA, FP 84, and Arundel, ff. 131^r–138^r, there are some instances of long **r** typical of the anglicana script of scribes trained in England. But many likenesses, including less prominent, imitable, or stylized elements (e.g. the base of **b**) and the proportions, make it possible that the scribe of *The Boke of Noblesse* copied these documents too, and make it probable that he was trained and worked in the same milieu.

It has been suggested that many of these similar specimens and one seemingly identical specimen (OMA, FP 70/1) are in the handwriting of Luket Nantron.[51] If true, that would make him the scribe of *The Boke of Noblesse*. Nantron, according to reports by Worcester, was born in Paris and died in London on 4 October 1471.[52] He had done clerical work for Fastolf and continued to work as a scribe for various of Fastolf's executors after his death.[53] His handwriting was recognizable, as members of this circle mention documents 'writen of Luket*tes* hande' or 'writon by Luket'.[54] We do not, however, identify this similar scribe as Nantron, nor link all the specimens together. First, it looks certain that this version of *The Boke* was copied *c*.1474–5 (see below, pp. lv–lvii), after Nantron's reported death. Likewise, one document ascribed to Nantron and in handwriting similar but not perfectly identical to *The Boke*, a petition to James Goldwell as bishop of Norwich (OMA, FP 84), cannot be by Nantron, as the document must date after 16 July 1472, when Goldwell was appointed to this bishopric; but, as mentioned, Nantron is reported to have died the previous year.[55] Most importantly, Nantron

[51] C&A, 9–18; Thorpe, 'Writing and Reading', 47, 232–3, 292–5, 348. For the other identifications as Nantron, see ibid. 47–8, 230–1, 285–6, 293–8, 325–6, 349, and Thorpe, 'Documents and Books', 200–1, 204–5, 213, 215. Some MSS there ascribed to Nantron seem different again and not similar to the scribe of *The Boke*: (i) BL, Add. MS 39848, ff. 19^r (*PL*, no. 1016), 26^r (*PL*, no. 520), 35^r (*PL*, no. 538), 38^r (*PL*, no. 542), letters by Fastolf dated between 20 July 1454 and 12 February 1456; (ii) BL, Sloane MS 4, ff. 29^r–35^v, a Latin medical text, corrected by Worcester; (iii) BodL, MS Bodley 179, ff. ii^r–viii^r, a table of contents added to a medical treatise in French, owned by Fastolf.

[52] London, College of Arms, MS M.9, f. 31^r (C&A, 181); *Itineraries*, 254–5.

[53] *PL*, nos. 116, ll. 38–9 and 906, l. 105; McFarlane, 'William Worcester', 207–8; and most fully Thorpe, 'Writing and Reading', 47–8, 254, 285–6, 293–300, 325–6; and Thorpe, 'Documents and Books', 195–216.   [54] *PL*, nos. 569, ll. 3–4 and 574, ll. 7–8.

[55] *ODNB*, *s.n.* Goldwell, James. Thorpe, 'Writing and Reading', 293, and in her contribution to C&A, 16, notes this problem with dating. It is possible that WW writing *Itineraries*, 254, in *c*.1479–80 from memory erred in dating Nantron's death; the rest of that page includes entries about 1472 and 1475, and Worcester says that Nantron's death occurred while Worcester was with the bishop of Winchester at Waltham Manor, and he

has been identified as a scribe solely from a title added by Worcester to *Basset's Chronicle*, yet Worcester there names Nantron as one of three men alongside himself by whom *Basset's Chronicle* was 'compilatus'. K. B. McFarlane, interpreting Worcester's title, merely surmised that Nantron, being a native speaker of French and a clerk, 'likely' was 'responsible for the actual composition', that is, composing the words; the title does not claim that Nantron made the copy.[56] This scribe, who did a lot of copying for Worcester and whose hand is similar but probably not identical to that of *The Boke of Noblesse*, seems unlikely to be Nantron.

Correction

The main scribe makes few corrections: he adds *quam* in the margin (71) and a few interlined letters (565, 730, 737), but otherwise makes six small changes over unerased errors of a letter or two; twenty-three more such corrections written over unerased text cannot be apportioned to the scribe or to Worcester securely.

By far most uses of the techniques of correcting are by Worcester. Just over half a dozen times he writes single words over erasures, which were difficult to make on paper but not impossible. As the paper is little damaged but the ink is a little fuzzy, Worcester might have removed the text with water (e.g. f. 4ᵛ, *tho* 238). Just over two dozen times he alters spellings or mechanical errors by writing over the text, which is left unerased. (In the resulting mess it is not always easy to be sure whether the scribe or Worcester was responsible.) More often, he interlines something, about 115 times, or adds something at the end of the line, about thirty-five times. (Some interlined additions are also too small to apportion to him or to the main scribe securely.) He also makes several longer additions around the margins. But he most often uses these techniques not for correction but for revision (as discussed below, pp. lxii–lxiv).

Several corrections alter one allograph of **a** (264, see n., etc.) or **r** (204, see n., etc.) to another. It is difficult to apportion such tiny changes but a few seem to be in Worcester's handwriting, one of them made to one of his own marginal additions (204, 2076, 2085, 2446).

elsewhere on the same page (*Itineraries*, 252: all from CCCC, MS 210, p. 321) reports that he was with the bishop of Winchester at Esher on 10 Aug. in 1472.

[56] McFarlane, 'William Worcester', 208. Louise Campbell and Francis W. Steer, *A Catalogue of Manuscripts in the College of Arms* (London, 1988), 129, suggest only that Nantron was 'possibly' the scribe of London, College of Arms, MS M.9.

Punctuation

The scribe uses the *punctus* . most commonly, well over a thousand times. It usually either begins or ends, or both, roman numerals (and has been reproduced as variably used thus in this edition). It is also used to separate units of syntax, sometimes whole new 'sentences' as parsed today, but also smaller phrasal groups or subclauses. The scribe uses the double *punctus*, a mark like the modern colon : forty-six times but not the similar *punctus elevatus* or *punctus versus*. This double *punctus* introduces units of sense dependent on what precedes the mark.[57] The virgule / is uncommon, occurring only sixteen times in its own right, though frequently used as a prompt for paraphs.

The paraph ¶ is very common, used nearly 500 times, for diverse purposes. Some paraphs mark what would be paragraphs in Present Day English: shifts in the topic and ideas. Others helpfully pace the run of longer 'sentences' with multiple clauses, break up lists, and introduce authorities or quotations. But they are not applied consistently in any of their tasks, and some seem misplaced entirely so that they interrupt the syntax (e.g. f. 15ᵛ, *It is fulle gret* ¶ *iupardie* 923). Often the scribe wrote prompts like two virgules // for a paraph, which he supplied in colour later; and somebody consistently made a black dot in the left margin adjacent to the line where black paraphs, but not red ones, should occur. In a few places, the scribe omitted to supply the paraph (e.g. f. 7ʳ, after *oriflamble* 372). In addition, fourteen paraphs were added in a further stage of checking between the lines or squeezed tightly between words, in paler red, by Worcester as he supplied the red sidenotes (on which see below, pp. lxiv–lxvi).

Layout

The main text quires have a frame-ruling only (178 mm × 123 mm), as is common for manuscripts in English on paper in the second half the 1400s; the frame is in a pale lilac hue, which was fashionable often for more elaborate ruling patterns in the third quarter of the 1400s. The frame continues on ff. 42ᵛ–43ᵛ, which were otherwise left blank by the main scribe (but now contain jottings).

Chapter titles are by the main scribe in a larger display script, underlined in black ink; somebody then added a red paraph before them and redrew the underlining in red. The red underlining often continues

[57] e.g. BL, Royal MS 18 B. xxii, f. 2ʳ, *namely* 65 or *but* 69, or f. 4ʳ, contrasting numbers *Thre of them bene of right* : *and the other tweyn of vallente* 166–7.

erroneously into the chapter itself for the rest of the line or a subsequent one or two lines.

Chapters usually, but not always (e.g. ff. 8ʳ–12ᵛ, 13ᵛ–14ʳ, 18ʳ), begin with lombardic capitals either two lines high (to f. 4ᵛ) or one line high (from f. 7ᵛ), in pale red ink over guide letters by the scribe.

In the text, there is underlining in red of some names (e.g. f. 1ʳ, *Kayus* 10; f. 5ʳ, *Edmonde Irensede* 254), quotations (f. 2ʳ, '*Sed . . . querele*' 71) and numbers (e.g. f. 21ᵛ, *Mˡ. CCCClj*.1272; f. 22ᵛ, *Mˡ. CCCCiij* 1332–3).

In addition, Worcester added a heading and subheading on f. 1ʳ (1–4, 17) in red ink and on most pages (except ff. 1ʳ–3ʳ, 15ʳ, 18ᵛ, 40ʳ⁻ᵛ, 41ᵛ–42ʳ) he added sidenotes of text in red, as well as several prompts for such notes in black; he also added a distinctive abstract symbol on several pages. (The incidence and meaning of the symbols and sidenotes and their presentation in this edition are discussed below, pp. lxiv–lxvii and cvii–cviii.)

Readers' Marginalia

There are marginalia by at least two readers with handwriting of the late fifteenth or early sixteenth century (identified in the textual notes as readers 1 and 2).

Reader 1 writes forty-six marginalia, heavily in the first half of the text and intermittently after f. 21ᵛ, commenting on both the main scribe's copy and Worcester's revisions. Twenty of the marginalia are page headings (e.g. ff. 12ᵛ–13ʳ, 15ʳ⁻ᵛ, 17ʳ). Reader 1 writes currently, sometimes untidily, with frequent abbreviation, in an anglicana script typical of the late 1400s, and some marginalia are datable to the reign of Henry VII. One of the marginalia glosses *youre predecessoure* as Henry VI (f. 3ʳ, 121), and although such a comment might seem to come from the reign of Edward IV, the need to clarify the reference instead suggests that it dates from a later reign. Another marks a description of Henry VI's coronation in Paris as useful *pro titulo Regis henrici vij* (f. 9ᵛ, 556) and others highlight the royal title to lands in France (e.g. ff. 11ʳ⁻ᵛ, 17ᵛ–19ᵛ, 20ᵛ). In addition, reader 1 makes one identifiable interlinear addition to the text (f. 1ᵛ, 31; see textual notes): he adds that the ancient Celtic language of Brutus's line flows *yn your most noble persone*, which would apply best to Henry VII, who was of Welsh descent. This same reader also changed the dedication from Edward IV to Henry VII, though his modification was later undone by another unidentified reader in turn (2n.). Also, where one of

Worcester's additions mentions the ordinances of the duke of Bedford, reader 1 remarks 'Inquire pro libro illo . bonum est' (f. 15^r, 917); this might have been relevant in 1489–92, when Henry VII was planning to invade France and commissioned Caxton's translation of Christine de Pizan's military treatise—one of Worcester's other sources—and Richard Pynson's statutes of war (1492). William Paston II bought a copy of the latter.[58]

Reader 2 annotates only the first half of the work, up to f. 17^v (1070), commenting on both the main scribe's copy and Worcester's revisions (e.g. f. 8^r, 426). This reader is well-informed, at least once adding a detail not given by *The Boke of Noblesse* itself (388). He corrects reader 1's marginal note referring to the title of Henry VII to France to note that the annotated passage refers to Henry VI (f. 9^v, 556; see textual notes). Reader 2 has handwriting predominantly modelled on secretary script but with a few letterforms influenced by humanist *littera antiqua*, notably an occasional caroline **a**, an upright, unhooked, and unlooped ascender on **h** and less often **l**, and a full figure-of-eight form of word-final **s**. Such influences occur in some other specimens of secretary script from the 1470s onwards, in educated circles where people had encountered humanist books.[59] The height of the stem of **t** above its crossbar and the trailing head of word-final sigmoid **s** are more typical of the 1500s than earlier.

A few readers' notes are too small to apportion to one of these hands (e.g. f. 4^v, 212; f. 11^r, 644; f. 13^r, 772). There are also other pen-trials in sixteenth-century hands, some indistinct, others including two notes on the Latin verb *esse* and an alphabet doodled (ff. 9^r, 12^v, 19^r).

Provenance

Names added in BL, Royal MS 18 B. xxii, ff. vi^v, 1^r, 35^r, and 42^v, suggest the circles among which it circulated in the fifteenth and sixteenth centuries.

The possibility that the book remained in the Fastolf circle is sug-

[58] William Caxton, trans., *The Book of Fayttes of Armes and of Chyualrye*, ed. A. T. P. Byles, EETS 189 (1932), and Richard Beadle and Lotte Hellinga, 'William Paston II and Pynson's *Statutes of War* (1492)', *The Library*, 7th ser., 2 (2001), 107–19. In addition, John Paston II earlier owned statutes of war in BL, Lansdowne MS 285: G. A. Lester, *Sir John Paston's 'Grete Boke': A Descriptive Catalogue, with an Introduction, of British Library MS Lansdowne 285* (Cambridge, 1984), 167–72.

[59] Cf. e.g. humanistic influences in the handwriting of BL, Add. MS 60577, from Winchester cathedral priory: *The Winchester Anthology: A Facsimile of British Library Additional Manuscript 60577*, ed. Edward Wilson (Cambridge, 1981), 4. For Winchester connections with the provenance of *The Boke*, see p. xxxi below.

gested by the fact that an original letter addressed to Fastolf is now bound into the manuscript (f. 44^{r-v}). The earliest name jotted in the manuscript, to judge by the handwriting, which seems late fifteenth-century, is 'Symond Samson' (f. vi^v). Simon Sampson, as elsewhere spelled, was on the edge of the Paston and Fastolf circles. A 'Sampson' is described as John Paston II's 'cosyn' in 1471 and referred to as a friendly associate of his sons John and William Paston II in 1471 and 1487.[60] There is also a connection to John Fastolf of Oulton (d. 1446), cousin of Worcester's employer Sir John. The cousin John's widow, Katherine, married a second time one John Sampson (d. c.1456).[61] Some time between 1456 and 1460, one 'Symon Sampson' and William Bedingfield sued for continued use of the lands at Oulton of the late Katherine Fastolf.[62] Between 1475 and 1480 'Simond Sampson' and Bedingfield were still recorded as feoffees to the use of these lands.[63] But by some point between 1504 and 1512 'Simond Sampson' had died, for his son and heir and his widow Alice, by then remarried to Robert Hoddys, defended that claim against Richard Hughson, a merchant of Norwich, son and heir to the late Nicholas Hughson, a lawyer at Clement's Inn (d. 1512).[64] Given these connections, Simon Sampson, an adult by 1460 at the latest and dead by 1512 at the latest, is plausibly the 'Symond Samson' in the manuscript.

The name recurs on blank page at the rear (f. 42^v) but in a different spelling, 'Symeon Sampson', and in handwriting that differs subtly; that handwriting, judging from the pious phrases written in the same hand on that page, seems typical of a generation or so later in the early to mid-sixteenth century. It is possible that this is a second Simon Sampson, also from Suffolk (1498/99–1563), who was a lawyer from the 1520s and perhaps at the Inner Temple, where the manuscript circulated later (as

[60] *PL*, respectively nos. 264, ll. 13–16 and 270, ll. 47–8 (on which see Richmond, *The Paston Family . . . Fastolf's Will*, 243–4), 358, ll. 41–2 and 409, ll. 47–56.

[61] *PL*, no. 557, ll. 23–5, by John Brackley, datable to 29 June 1456, with the address in WW's handwriting, reporting John Sampson's recent death. See Colin Richmond, *The Paston Family in the Fifteenth Century: The First Phase* (Cambridge, 1990), 222–3; McFarlane, 'Investment', 100.

[62] TNA, C 1/26/608 (formerly C1/26/375). He addressed his complaint to William Waynflete in his capacity from 1456–60 as chancellor, but so would many people do while Waynflete held that office. This probably has no bearing on the later links between Waynflete and Worcester.

[63] TNA, C 1/53/87

[64] TNA, C 1/324/41 and 42; TNA, C 1/360/60. The dates are determined by the various Lord Chancellors addressed in these documents. Baker, *Men of Court*, ii. 906, suggests that Nicholas Hughson died without male heir, but a faded passage of TNA, C 1/324/41, seems to call Richard his 'son and here'.

noted below).[65] This younger Simon Sampson was one heir—perhaps the son—of another lawyer, Robert Sampson (d. 1519/20), who leased land in Wokingham.[66]

There is a connection with Wokingham for another surname on the same rear blank page: one 'Iohn Twychener' in an early Tudor handwriting (f. 42ᵛ), which also added extracts of verse. John Twychener of Wokingham (1502–c.1546), entered Winchester College aged 13 in 1515, studied at Oxford, and returned to Winchester as *informator* or headmaster in 1526–31; his syllabus survives—one typical of an early Tudor school, lightly classicizing.[67] The Winchester connection is strengthened because the manuscript also has bound into it (f. 45ʳ) a draft of a letter from the bailiffs of Winchester to an officer of the exchequer, dated 8 May in an unspecified year in late fifteenth-century handwriting (described above, p. xxii). There are also sixteenth-century pen trials on ff. 9ʳ, 12ᵛ, and 19ʳ of the Latin verb *esse* and an alphabet, which could be made by many novice readers but would be common in a school too.

Two other names do not allow such precise suggestions. An early sixteenth-century hand wrote the name 'Thomas claspam' in the margin of one page (f. 26ʳ). He has not yet been identified. 'Rycharde Dyconson' (f. 42ᵛ), written on the rear blank page in an early Tudor hand, is too common a name to be identified securely. One 'Dyckonson' without a recorded forename gained an Oxford MA by incorporation in 1524 and so would have been a close contemporary at Oxford with the younger John Twychener.[68] A Richard 'Deconson' was at Cambridge 1539–51.[69]

Two other names in the manuscript are too common to identify securely but suggest that the manuscript circulated among the Inns of Court and Chancery from the 1540s to the 1570s. 'Robert Savylle' in a margin (f. 35ʳ) in a perhaps mid-Tudor hand could be the Robert Savile,

[65] Baker, *Men of Court*, ii. 1358, disentangles two men named Simon Sampson from the records.   [66] Ibid., ii. 1357–8; TNA, PROB 11/19/368.

[67] A. B. Emden, *A Biographical Register of the University of Oxford A.D. 1500–1540* (Oxford, 1974), 582; Thomas Frederick Kirby, *Winchester Scholars* (London, 1888), 102, 114; A. F. Leach, 'History of Schools', in *The Victoria County History: Hampshire and the Isle of Wight*, ii (Westminster, 1903), 250–408 at 296–300. In addition, a 'clerk' of that name was party to a dispute about a marriage agreement involving property of the former abbey of Chertsey in Surrey between 1537 and 1544: see TNA, C 1/706/32 (datable by its address to Thomas Audley as Chancellor and the dissolution of Chertsey Abbey in 1537). John's brother Richard Twychener enrolled at Winchester College in 1518, as had another Richard Twychener of Farnborough in 1475 (Kirby, *Winchester Scholars*, 84, 109).

[68] Emden, *Biographical Register . . . Oxford A.D. 1500–1540*, 180.

[69] John Venn and J. A. Venn, *Alumni Cantabrigiensis*, 10 vols. (Cambridge, 1922–54), i, part 2, 40.

probably of Pilham, Lincolnshire, admitted to Lincoln's Inn *c*.1544 and dead *c*.1576.[70] The signature in the manuscript is in an earlier style of script and different from a signature in BL, Egerton MS 2429, dated 1577, of one 'Roberte Savyle', from Poolham, Lincolnshire, received into the Inner Temple in 1560.[71] A continued circulation at the Inns of Court and Chancery is probable, because the manuscript also has the name 'Edward Jones of Clementes in the' in Elizabethan secretary hand-writing (f. 42ᵛ). Among the Inns of Chancery for more junior lawyers, Clement's Inn was one of those affiliated to the Inner Temple, where the younger Robert Savile is recorded.[72] An Edward Jones of Plas Cadogan, Denbighshire, entered the Inner Temple in 1578,[73] and would probably have done so from Clement's Inn or one of two other affiliated Inns. He and the younger Savile overlapped at the Inner Temple.

After circulating among the Inns of Chancery and Court, the manuscript was later owned by collectors of older manuscripts: Edward Banyster (1540–*c*.1606), who signs the foot of f. 42ᵛ in the gutter, was an antiquary and bibliophile. His will, dated 27 March 1600 but proved 24 November 1606, mentions an unspecified number of books not to be sold but to be kept at his house in Idsworth for his son, also Edward, when he came of age. It also names Sir Robert Cotton (1571–1631), the distinguished manuscript collector, as a landlord from whom he leased a house in Putney.[74] (As is noted below, there is reason to suspect that the manuscript of the Codicil passed through Cotton's hands.) Banyster owned at least seven pre-Reformation manuscripts, including *The Boke of Noblesse*. He also made his own copies of Middle English romances in 1564, distinguished by their illustrations adapted from woodcuts.[75]

---

[70] Baker, *Men of Court*, ii. 1368. For the possible connection of Worcester's son to Lincoln's Inn, see p. xviii above.

[71] BL, Egerton MS 2429, f. 45ʳ; William Henry Cooke, *Students Admitted to the Inner Temple* (London, 1878), 38 (who gives the place as 'Poolsham').

[72] For the institution's history, see e.g. *Pension Book of Clement's Inn*, ed. Cecil T. Carr, Selden Society, 78 (London, 1960), pp. xviii–xxii.

[73] Cooke, *Students Admitted to the Inner Temple*, 86. The handwriting in BL, Royal MS 18 B. xxii, f. 42ᵛ, is several generations too late in date to be that of another Edward Jones of the Inner Temple in 1497 (Baker, *Men of Court*, ii. 952).

[74] TNA, PROB 11/108/430, ff. 294ᵛ–296ʳ.

[75] M. C. Seymour, 'MSS Douce 261 and Egerton 3132A and Edward Banyster', *Bodleian Library Record*, 10 (1980), 162–5, notes variation between Banyster's hand across his MSS. For discussion, see Maldwyn Mills, 'EB and His Two Books: Visual Impact and the Power of Meaningful Suggestion. Reading the Illustrations in MSS Douce 261 and Egerton 3132A', in Stephen Kelly and John J. Thompson (eds.), *Imagining the Book* (Turnhout, 2005), 173–91. BodL, MS Douce 261, was copied by Banyster in 1564 (ff. 25ᵛ, 48ᵛ). The

Banyster's seven known pre-Reformation manuscripts, including *The Boke of Noblesse*, later passed to John, Baron Lumley (1533–1609), who owned one of the largest private libraries of Elizabethan England.[76] The name Lumley appears in an italic hand at the bottom of f. 1^r, where Lumley customarily signed his books. In addition, the 1609 catalogue of Lumley's library lists a 'Chronicle in English called the booke of noblesse dedicated to Kinge Edwarde the 4th incitinge the English to warre in France. manuscript'.[77] Lumley also referred to *The Boke of Noblesse* on the flyleaf of a fifteenth-century manuscript of Honoré Bouvet's *L'Arbre des batailles*.[78]

After Lumley's death on 11 April 1609, his books were gifted to form a library for Prince Henry Frederick, eldest son of James I. On Prince Henry's death in 1612, his books joined the Royal collection proper, with which was founded the British Museum's library.[79]

2. London, Lambeth Palace Library, MS 506

This is the sole fifteenth-century manuscript of the Codicil.[80]

name 'Banister' appears in a different 16th-c. hand in the margin of BL, Harley MS 3943, f. 85^v (*Troilus and Criseyde*).

[76] BL, Royal MS 5 F. xvii, Royal MS 7 D. iii, Royal MS 8 C. xiv, Royal MS 8 E. v, Royal MS 17 B. xvii, and Royal MS 17 C. xxxviii also went from Banyster to Lumley. None contains an obvious connection to Worcester. In addition, Lumley signed BL, Royal MS 17 A. viii, f. 17^r, a 14th-c. collection of English medical remedies, with added remedies in 15th-c. hands, including on f. 83^v one to cure 'all wondes' with the note 'per monsieur Iohannem fastolf'. George R. Keiser in his editorial introduction to 'Epilepsy: The Falling Evil', in *Popular and Practical Science of Medieval England*, ed. Lister M. Matheson (East Lansing, MI, 1994), 219–44 at 221–2, suggests that the MS spent time in Fastolf's 'circle'. It contains no trace of WW's handwriting. Lumley also acquired Holbein's painting of Erasmus from Banyster: see Susan Foister, *Holbein in England* (London, 2006), 25 (no. 14).

[77] Gilson and Warner, *Catalogue*, i, pp. xix, xlii (no. 161); Sears Jayne and Francis R. Johnson (eds.), *The Lumley Library: The Catalogue of 1609* (London, 1956), 131 (no. 1024). See Kathryn Barron, 'The Collecting and Patronage of John, Lord Lumley (c.1535–1609)', in Edward Chaney (ed.), *The Evolution of English Collecting: Receptions of Italian Art in the Tudor and Stuart Periods* (New Haven, 2003), 125–58 at 128–9.

[78] Jayne and Johnson, *The Lumley Library*, 12. For Lumley's note, see BL, Royal MS 20 C. viii, flyleaf f. iii^r, discussed by Nichols, p. iv; Jennifer Summit, *Lost Property: The Woman Writer and English Literary History, 1380–1589* (Chicago, 2000), 77–8. Lumley probably acquired this from his brother-in-law Humphrey Llwyd (Jayne and Johnson, *The Lumley Library*, 6–8).

[79] Jayne and Johnson, *The Lumley Library*, 13–17, correcting Gilson and Warner, *Catalogue*, i, p. xix.

[80] For descriptions, see M. R. James, *A Descriptive Catalogue of the Manuscripts in the Library of Lambeth Palace*, 5 parts in 1 vol. (Cambridge, 1930–2), 710–14; O. S. Pickering and V. M. O'Mara, *The Index of Middle English Prose Handlist XIII: Manuscripts in Lam-*

Binding

The binding (c.265 mm×c.160 mm) is of boards covered with brown leather tooled in gold with three framing lines round the edge and on the centre a shield bearing three lions, the arms of George Carew (1555–1629). It has the remnants of two lost clasps. The same gold tooling appears on London, Lambeth Palace Library, MS 264, a prose *Brut* chronicle of the late fifteenth century, also owned by Carew,[81] although the clasps on the lower boards differ on MS 264. The spine, bearing the Lambeth shelfmark, has been replaced.

Foliation and Flyleaves

The manuscript consists of ff. i–ii+1–65+1–11+iii–iv.

Paste-downs, front flyleaves ff. i–ii and rear flyleaves ff. iii–iv are modern paper.[82] A third front flyleaf, foliated as f. 1, is a parchment singleton, formerly a paste-down, with a late fifteenth-century note of contents on f. 1^v.

We follow a modern librarian's foliation in pencil, which covers only the leaves with fifteenth-century writing, as 2–7, 8–50, 51–60. That foliation takes account of a fifteenth-century former paste-down f. 1 (but *1* is not written onto it) but ignores two blank leaves between ff. 7 and 8, three blank leaves between ff. 50 and 51, and the 11 late sixteenth- or early seventeenth-century parchment leaves. (For consistency, our description below notionally foliates the later additions as [61]–[71].)

There was already a late sixteenth- or early seventeenth-century foliation in ink 1–54 on what are now (as above) ff. 8^r–59^r, i.e. ignoring Worcester's son's prologue (text C1 below). Cross-references to that ink foliation were added in the margins of the prologue on ff. 2^r–6^v, and that ink foliation is used in the late sixteenth- or early seventeenth-century contents list (f. 7^{r-v}) and digests of content added at the end (ff. [62^r]–[64^v], [67^r]–[71^v]). That ink foliation was subsequently extended in pencil onto the final fifteenth-century leaf, f. 60^r, and the late sixteenth- or early seventeenth-century added leaves.

---

beth Palace Library (Cambridge, 1999), 45–6; P. R. Robinson, *A Catalogue of Dated and Datable Manuscripts c. 888–1600 in London Libraries* (London, 2003), 53–5, and pl. 140, 212; and that of Aaron Hope, completed Sept. 2011, in LPL's online catalogue <https://archives.lambethpalacelibrary.org.uk>.

[81] James, *Lambeth*, 710, and 410–11, notes LPL, MS 264.

[82] This differs from the early modern paper paste-downs and flyleaves in LPL, MS 264.

Materials

The main quires are parchment, $c.258$ mm×$c.150$ mm. There are few defects. Some leaves in quire I are 3–4 mm shorter at the foot than other leaves. Ff. 30–4 seem to have shrunk and deformed from a rectangular shape.

Collation

The quires are constructed in three fifteenth-century booklets:

(1) I^8=ff. 2^r–7^v,+2 blank unfoliated leaves
(2) II–IV^8, V^8 (wants 7, 8), VI–VII^8=ff. 8^r–50^v,+3 blank unfoliated leaves
(3) VIII^6, IX^4 (misbound: the current innermost bifolium should be the outermost)=ff. 51^r–60^v.

They are followed by one late sixteenth- or early seventeenth-century booklet:

(4) X^4 (wants 4, perhaps blank), XI^2, XII^4, XIII^2.

Blank leaves and quire signatures suggest that booklets (2) and (3) were constructed in separate campaigns, although they share scribes and elements of layout and were combined early on.

Quiring is revealed by visible stitching within formerly or still central bifolia, in blue thread in the first booklet (between f. 5^v and f. 6^r) and in white thread in the second and third booklets (between ff. 11^v and 12^r, 19^v and 20^r, 35^v and 36^r, 41^v and 42^r, 49^v and 50^r, 53^v and 54^r). Stitching is not visible in quire IV, but a pattern of follicles at the foot of ff. 27^v–28^r suggests that those leaves are one, therefore central, bifolium. Stitching is not visible in the final, misbound quire IX nor in the fourth, much later booklet.

In booklet (1), what may be remnants of a leaf signature, since trimmed off, are visible at the foot of f. 5^r.

In booklet (2) there is one set of leaf signatures, mixing Indo-Arabic and roman numerals, in a fifteenth-century hand and pale ink, and then a further set of marks emending some of them:

- quire II: on ff. 8^r–11^r, *c, c ij, c3, c4*; a further mark, like majuscule *A*, is then written twice close to the fore-edge on the first leaf (f. 8^r)
- quire III: on ff. 16^r–19^r, *d j, d ij, d3, d4*, with *B* written over *d* on the first leaf (f. 16^r)

- quire IV: on ff. 24^r–31^r, *e j* to *e vij* and *e8*; the numerals in the leaf signatures *e v* to *e8* are written over unerased numerals *j, ij, iij*, and *4*; and on the first leaf, *e* might have been overwritten to form majuscule *C*
- quire V: on ff. 33^r–35^r, only *b ij, b3, b4* visible; but on the first leaf f. 32^r in orange ink a majuscule, perhaps *G*, written three times
- quire VI: on ff. 39^r–41^r, only *a ij, a iij, a iiij* visible; but on the first leaf f. 38^r in faint orange ink a majuscule, perhaps *E*
- quire VII: ff. 46^r–49^r: *a ix, a x, a xi, a xiij* [*sic*]; but on the first leaf, *ff* (i.e. the equivalent of a majuscule *F*) is added (f. 46^r)

The first set of leaf signatures, with minuscule letters and a mixture of roman and Indo-Arabic numerals, was evidently added after or as Worcester corrected the texts, as the erroneous signature *a xiij* (for *a xij*) on f. 49^r is not in the customary position near the fore-edge, but is further left, because Worcester's long addition to the text (C5/1–21 below) had already used that space. This first set was then modified into a new sequence, as the quires were reordered. (See 'Revisions to the Codicil' below.)

In booklet (3), a marking *d*, large enough perhaps to be considered an equivalent to majuscule *D*, is on the first four of six leaves of quire VIII (ff. 51^r–54^r), but four minims, perhaps a number *iiij*, are on the second leaf (f. 52^r) and something is trimmed from the third (f. 53^r). On what was formerly (before misbinding) the third of four leaves of quire IX (f. 60^r), there is a marking like *e* and four minims below, as well as an abbreviated word *smp* (?).

In booklet (4) of the late sixteenth- or early seventeenth-century, only a modern librarian's pencil enumeration marks the quires' boundaries.

Contents

f. 1$^{r–v}$: blank apart from a fifteenth-century note 'Declaracion de Iohan duc de bedford des ordonnancez de france' (f. 1^v)

ff. 2^r–6^v: William Worcester's son's prologue to the Codicil; English; copied by scribe A;=text C1 below

f. 7$^{r–v}$: a list of the contents in a late sixteenth- or early seventeenth-century italic hand (see 'Provenance' below)

two unfoliated leaves

ff. 8^r–11^r: the household and retinue of John, duke of Bedford, in France, 1422–35, and the knights and men-at-arms in Aquitaine,

1422–37; Latin; copied by scribe B, with modifications by scribe C and modifications and a French heading by Worcester;=Appendix 1 below

ff. 11ʳ–23ᵛ: lists in Latin relating to the war in France under John, duke of Bedford: list of French allies and those who served under John, duke of Bedford (ff. 11ʳ–12ᵛ); estimated receipts from English-held lands in France, 1 October 1427–30 September 1438 (ff. 12ᵛ–13ᵛ); estimated payments made by the regent of France, Michaelmas 1427–Michaelmas 1428 (ff. 13ᵛ–14ᵛ); payments made to officers in the Parlement of Paris (ff. 14ʳ–15ᵛ); payments to captains, Michaelmas 1427–Michaelmas 1428 (ff. 15ᵛ–16ᵛ); garrisons and retinues in Normandy, Michaelmas 1433–Michaelmas 1434 (ff. 16ᵛ–20ʳ); receipts from Normandy (f. 20ʳ⁻ᵛ); payments and expenses relating to Normandy (f. 21ʳ); annual value of Maine, Michaelmas 1433–Michaelmas 1434 (f. 21ᵛ); lands and tenements rewarded to combatants at the battle of Verneuil (f. 22ʳ); expenses relating to Maine (ff. 22ᵛ–23ʳ); Latin; copied by scribe B, with annotations and some headings by Worcester;=*Wars in France*, ii. 529–52

ff. 23ʳ–24ʳ: annual value of the counties of Harcourt and Dreux and other lands in the hands of the regent; Latin; copied by scribe B and, from the top of f. 24ʳ, Worcester;=*Wars in France*, ii. 553-5

ff. 24ʳ–25ᵛ: payments and expenses for counsellors of law and armed men (f. 24ʳ⁻ᵛ); various other payments (ff. 24ᵛ-25ᵛ); Latin; copied by Worcester;=*Wars in France*, ii. 555–9

ff. 26ʳ–27ᵛ: estimate of expenses relating to Normandy, 1 October 1433–30 September 1434 (ff. 26ʳ–27ʳ); list of ordinary gifts and presents (f. 27ʳ⁻ᵛ); French; copied by scribe C, with Latin heading and 'e*xaminatur*' added by Worcester;=*Wars in France*, ii. 559–65

ff. 28ʳ–31ʳ: list of garrisons and retinues in Normandy under Richard, duke of York, after the Truce of Tours (28 May 1444), and probably over 1444–6; Latin; copied by scribe B, with heading and modifications by Worcester=Appendix 2 below

f. 31ᵛ: blank

ff. 32ʳ–37ʳ: inventory of munitions of war found in Rouen castle upon the death of John, duke of Bedford (ff. 32ʳ–37ʳ); Latin; copied by scribe B, with heading and modifications by Worcester;=*Wars in France*, ii. 565–74

ff. 37ᵛ: blank

ff. 38ʳ–50ʳ: instructions on the wars in France: Fastolf's articles relating to the congress of Arras, 1435 (ff. 38ʳ–43ᵛ); articles of the council of Richard, duke of York, 1440 (ff. 44^r–47^r); Fastolf's instructions to Edmund Beaufort, duke of Somerset, March 1448 (ff. 47^v–48^v); Fastolf's advice on relieving the duke of Somerset, 1450 (ff. 49^r–50^r); English; copied by scribe B, with some headings and a few modifications by Worcester;=texts C2 to C5 below, and *Wars in France*, ii. 575–97

f. 50^v and three unfoliated leaves: blank, apart from a late sixteenth-century note identifying 'Sir Ihon Falstoffe knight Baron of &c' on the verso of the final unfoliated leaf, facing f. 51^r

ff. 51^r–55^r: demands made by the French at the council of Calais, 1439; French; copied by scribe C, with a Latin heading by Worcester; edited from another manuscript containing a longer text in 'Documents Relating to the Anglo-French Negotiations of 1439', ed. C. T. Allmand, *Camden Miscellany XXIV*, Camden Society (London, 1972), 79–149 at 135–9.

ff. 55^r–56^v: petition from the inhabitants of Maine, 1452; French; copied by scribe C, with an additional note by Worcester;=*Wars in France*, ii. 598–603

f. 57^r and f. 58^{r-v} (ff. 57 and 58 misbound out of order; f. 57^v blank): incomplete letter from the English council at Rouen to Henry VI, 1441; French; copied by scribe C;=*Wars in France*, ii. 603–7

f. 59^r: blank

f. 59^v: notes on the duke of Bedford and men serving under him, notably at the battle of Verneuil; Latin; written by Worcester;=part of Appendix 3 below

f. 60^r: blank

f. 60^v: notes on various other figures; Latin; written by Worcester;=part of Appendix 3 below

unfoliated f. [61^{r-v}]: blank

unfoliated ff. [62^r]–[64^v]: digests in English of information from the Codicil, occasionally keyed to an older foliation (which had excluded the prologue, etc.); in a late sixteenth- or early seventeenth-century mixed italic and secretary hand

unfoliated ff. [65^r]–[66^v]: blank

unfoliated ff. [67^r]–[71^v]: digests in English of information from the Codicil; in a late sixteenth- or early seventeenth-century mixed italic and secretary hand

Scribes

The fifteenth-century parts of the Codicil are by four scribes.

Scribe A of ff. 2^r–6^v, Worcester's son's prologue (text C1 below), uses a variety of anglicana script, with a simplified **w**, as is common in the late 1400s, and occasional open-tailed secretary **g** (e.g. f. 2^r, l. 6 'belongyng', l. 7 'god', l. 8 'legeaunce'; f. 2^v, l. 18 'seyng', l. 19 'vegesius'). The great depth of long **r** and of the limb of **h** looped below the baseline, relative to the *x*-height of letters above the baseline, is typical of the last quarter of the 1400s. The slightly rigid upright aspect, the smallness of the top compartment of **a** relative to the bottom compartment, and the heavy horizontal splay on word-final sigmoid **s** show incipient tendencies that typify anglicana when it fossilizes into various legal hands in the mid-1500s; these features might suggest a scribe with legal training. This scribe tends to use majuscule letters for initial **C**, **R**, and to some extent **E** and **G** at the start of words for no apparent emphasis or syntactical clarity; this is typical of later fifteenth-century scribes.[83]

Scribe B of the Latin and English on ff. 8^r–23^v, 28^r–37^r, and 38^r–50^r uses a variety of late fifteenth-century secretary script, but with the closed-tail **g** more typical of anglicana. This handwriting is of a loosely similar kind, in its aspect and repertoire of letterforms, to the handwriting of *The Boke of Noblesse* in BL, Royal MS 18 B. xxii, but it is not the same. As well as the closed-tail **g** not found there, the overall ductus differs: this scribe B prefers broken strokes at various points: in the bowl of **a**; at the top of ascenders, which create hooks rather than loops; in the ligature **st**; and between **w** and its approach stroke. The style is, though, suggestive of the same period in the third quarter of the 1400s as the style of BL, Royal MS 18 B. xxii.

Scribe C copies French documents on ff. 26^r–27^v and adds a few corrections to other documents by scribe B, some noted in the textual notes to the Appendices below (e.g. f. 10^v, Appendix 1/148). This scribe employs a variety of *cursiva* used in the later fifteenth century by scribes trained in northern France and the southern Netherlands (and so the term 'secretary' is less conventional). One similar specimen was used by a student of the University of Paris, Jehan Pelhisser, 'seruiteur' of Edward IV, to copy heraldic extracts and French military financial accounts in London in 1477 for Walter Bellengier, Ireland King of Arms, an associate of Worcester (on whom see 517–18n.,

---

[83] Albert Derolez, *The Palaeography of Gothic Manuscript Books* (Cambridge, 2003), 138, 150.

917–21n.).[84] Typical features of scribe C are the perfunctory tail of **g**; frequent use of majuscule **R** word-initially in a form that bifurcates at the top; the use of sigmoid final **s** that ends in a trailing stroke; and a tall stem on **t** that curves to the right. But in scribe C's work two instances of two-compartment **a** used mid-word might suggest that he had English training or influences.[85] A similar hand appears in a copy of the surrender of the garrison at Bayeux in one of Worcester's notebooks.[86]

Scribe C copies the French documents on ff. 51^r–57^r and 58^{r-v}. Most of these leaves are written more slowly and formally than ff. 26^r–27^v, probably because this section consists not of accounts but of extended formal prose; leaf signatures also suggest that this was a separate campaign of copying. At first two consistently different graphs are used in ff. 51^r–55^r: an unlooped ascender on **d** and kidney-shaped rather than sigmoid final **s**. However, the other letterforms have the same structure, and the proportions and angles of strokes seem the same. And from f. 55^r onwards the looped **d** and sigmoid **s** resume interchangeably with the other allographs, and the letterforms become gradually more current.

Scribe D is William Worcester, who wrote all of ff. 24^r–25^v, completing a text by scribe B; who added headings and corrections throughout pages by scribes B and C; and who made rough notes on ff. 59^v and 60^v. Worcester also added the costs in the margin of some lists of charges (ff. 12^v–16^v, 21^v, 22^v–23^v, ff. 34^r–35^v), though it is difficult to identify the handwriting of brief numbers categorically. Changes in the colour of his ink and size and haste of his handwriting suggest that he worked in more than one stint. He also wrote the abbreviation for 'examinatur' throughout the accounts copied by scribes B and C, at the end of quires (ff. 15^v, 23^v), the foot of pages ff. 26^r–27^r, or mid-page adjacent to tallies (e.g. ff. 16^v twice, 21^r, 22^v, 23^r, etc.), and 'examinatur vsque hic' at the foot of f. 36^v, before the final tally in scribe

---

[84] BL, Add. MS 4101, ff. 1^r–56^v, with accounts on ff. 46^r–51^v. Reproduced by Andrew G. Watson, *Catalogue of Dated and Datable Manuscripts c.700-c. 1600 in the Department of Manuscripts, the British Library*, 2 vols. (London, 1979), no. 1, pl. 793. See other loosely similar specimens in e.g. Watson, *Dated and Datable Manuscripts . . . British Library*, no. 815, pl. 701 (France, 1467), or no. 940, pl. 874 (Malines, modern Mechelen, Belgium, 1492); and Andrew G. Watson, *Catalogue of Dated and Datable Manuscripts c. 435-1600 in Oxford Libraries*, 2 vols. (Oxford, 1984), no. 477, pl. 591 (Paris, 1461), or no. 611, pl. 718 (La Chaise-Dieu, France, 1473).

[85] LPL, MS 506, f. 26^v, ll. 15 ('par'), 22 ('notaire').

[86] Arundel, ff. 321^r–322^r (*Wars in France*, ii. 730–5). Others more loosely alike in kind include Arundel, ff. 180^r–183^r, 185^r–191^r.

B's accounts. This activity echoes his tallying of financial records from Fastolf's estates.[87]

There are also additions made in the very late sixteenth or early seventeenth centuries. Folio 7[r–v] has a list of the contents in a looser, 'Crescian' style of italic with clubbed ascenders, which appears from the late 1580s or 1590s and thrives in some literary milieux in the early seventeenth century.[88] Folios [62[r]]–[64[v]], [67[r]]–[71[v]] have digests of the information from the original Codicil. The writing here begins in italic and is perhaps by the same scribe as the contents list on f. 7[r–v], but it soon begins to incorporate secretary features and then to switch back and forth between italic and secretary. Such mixed hands are commoner in the early seventeenth century.[89] The list of contents and the digests of information were copied into London, Society of Antiquaries, MS 41 (see below), in an early seventeenth-century secretary hand.

Layout

The layout varies between the booklets.

Booklet (1), a single quire by scribe A, has frame-ruling in black ink, creating a text area of c.170 mm×c.100 mm. Initial majuscules are often splashed in red, and the first words of syntactical units and some other keywords, such as proper nouns and philosophical concepts, are underlined in red. Folio 2[r] begins with a majuscule **M** in a blue lombardic capital with red tracery (in a style different from that of BL, Royal MS 18 B. xxii, f. 1[r]). A late sixteenth- or early seventeenth-century hand has added folio-references linking the *précis* of contents in this prologue to the leaves that follow.

Booklets (2) and (3), mostly by scribes B and C (ff. 8[r]–50[v]+3 unfoliated blanks, ff. 51[r]–60[v]), share frame-ruling in red ink, creating a text area of c.180 mm×90 mm.

The prose works copied by scribes B and C are set as paragraphs with spaces between them. Scribe B's prose works have red initials only at the start of sequences of prose, but scribe C's prose works have a red initial at the start of most paragraphs within a sequence, for which space was

[87] e.g. OMA, FP 42, FP 43 (e.g. f. 6[v]), FP 51, FP 69, FP 78 (1b), FP 87 (ii), FP 87 (iv).

[88] For this style, see Jonathan Gibson, 'From Palatino to Cresci', in James Daybell and Andrew Gordon (eds.), *Cultures of Correspondence in Early Modern England* (Philadelphia, 2016), 29–47 at 40–6; and e.g. Giles E. Dawson and Laetitia Kennedy-Skipton, *Elizabethan Handwriting 1500–1650: A Manual* (New York, 1966), 108, and pl. 41, datable c.1625.

[89] Gibson, 'From Palatino to Cresci', 46; Dawson and Kennedy-Skipton, *Elizabethan Handwriting*, 110, 112, and pl. 42–3, datable c.1630.

left of differing heights, between one and three lines in depth, no matter how large the red initial is. For both scribes, the initials are in 'dusky' red; all the initials on scribe C's work and one on scribe B's (f. 12^v) seem to be written over erased markings seemingly in text ink, in some cases formerly decorated in 'tomato' red.

The other texts, as appropriate, are set out as lists or accounts, each item starting on a new line. Where those lists include financial details on the right, the tally ('Summa') is given at the end of the list or its sub-sections or at the end of each page, usually indented, as is common in fifteenth-century accounts. On both scribe B and scribe C's lists, there is underlining in 'tomato' red of the headings, the first few words of items, the tallies, and in a few places the financial details on the right.

Through prose and lists alike there are intermittent paraphs in 'tomato' red, some eleven on scribe B's work (ff. 28^v–30^r, 31^r) and sixteen on scribe C's work (ff. 51^v–54^r, 55^r–56^r). Somebody then added more, but still intermittent, paraphs in a 'dusky' red on both scribe B's work (ff. 8$^{r–v}$, 11^r–12^v, 15$^{r–v}$, 29^r, 32$^{r–v}$, 38^v, 45$^{r–v}$, 47$^{r–v}$, 49^v–50^r) and the first stint of scribe C's work (f. 26$^{r–v}$) in booklet (2). Three of the four 'dusky' red paraphs on scribe B's work on f. 29^r overlay earlier 'tomato' red paraphs. These booklets were evidently rubricated twice.

Worcester often adds headings in space left blank at the start of items (e.g. f. 47^v, C2/1–24), or in the top margin, sometimes spilling down the margin (e.g. f. 44^r, C3/1–10); he also sometimes lightly crosses out a previous heading. His heading on f. 22^r and tally on f. 24^v are in a bright 'tomato' red, which raises the possibility that he added the first stage of 'tomato' red rubrication to scribe B and scribe C's work.

Booklet (4) of the late sixteenth- or early seventeenth-century has no ruling. The digests of information are tabulated in complex layouts.

Provenance

After the addition of the prologue by William Worcester's son between 1483 and 1485, the next evidence for the Codicil's provenance is the likelihood that it was the source for some notes made by Edward VI, probably in 1552, in London, British Library, Cotton MS Nero C. x, ff. 94^r–97^r. Most of that manuscript contains a record in the handwriting of Edward VI of his daily affairs,[90] along with his notes on the Order of

---

[90] BL, Cotton MS Nero C. x, edited most recently as *The Chronicle and Political Papers of King Edward VI*, ed. W. K. Jordan (London, 1966), 185–90. Jordan, pp. xxxi–iii, suggests that Edward VI also consulted BL, Harley MS 782, ff. 49^v, 52^v; but that MS is later than Edward VI's death, as it is in the handwriting of Robert Glover (1543/4–88); and among

the Garter (ff. 98^r–101^r, 102^r–107^r, 108^r–111^v), and other political writings (ff. 113^r–117^v). It also includes information from the Codicil, as follows:

f. 94^r: number of knights, etc., under John, duke of Bedford≅LPL, MS 506, ff. 8^r–11^r≅Appendix 1

f. 94^r: number of allied men of France≅LPL, MS 506, ff. 11^r–12^v≅ *Wars in France*, ii. 529–32

f. 94^r: revenues from France against costs≅LPL, MS 506, ff. 12^v–16^v≅ *Wars in France*, ii. 532–40

f. 94^v: revenue of Normandy in 1433≅LPL, MS 506, f. 20^{r-v}≅ *Wars in France*, ii. 547–8

f. 94^v: cost of defending Normandy, and further calculations≅LPL, MS 506, f. 21^r≅ *Wars in France*, ii. 548–9

f. 95^r: revenue from Maine in 1434≅LPL, MS 506, f. 21^v≅ *Wars in France*, ii. 549–50

f. 95^r: cost of defending Maine≅LPL, MS 506, f. 22^v≅ *Wars in France*, ii. 551–2

f. 95^r: gifts of land for service≅LPL, MS 506, f. 22^r≅ *Wars in France*, ii. 550–1

ff. 95^v–96^r: a brief and selective paraphrase of the English text found in LPL, MS 506, ff. 38^r–43^v (perhaps skipping f. 41^{r-v}), headed 'Sir Ihon Fastols councel'≅C2

ff. 96^v–97^r: a brief and selective paraphrase of the English text found in LPL, MS 506, ff. 44^r–47^r≅C3

The notes look like a collection of practical advice for war in France. Edward might also have had an interest in John, duke of Bedford, as his courtiers were attentive to the Regent as a predecessor who had ruled during a royal minority.[91] The text is paraphrased in brief, but as the paraphrase is of disparate documents that occur together only in the Codicil, mostly in the order in which they appear there,[92] and includes

the pages that Jordan proposes were copied from BL, Harley MS 782, are its ff. 52^v–53^v, which had been transcribed from LPL, MS 506, ff. 8^r–11^r (i.e. Appendix 1 below), but not printed in *Wars in France*, which edition Jordan reports as his source. BL, Cotton MS Nero C. x, was also printed in *Literary Remains of King Edward VI*, ed. John Gough Nichols (London, 1857), 555–60. Although Nichols noted the resemblance of Edward VI's notes to London, Society of Antiquaries, MS 41, he did not link them to LPL, MS 506, or identify them with the Codicil accompanying *BkNob*.

[91] Stephen Alford, *Kingship and Politics in the Reign of Edward VI* (Cambridge, 2002), 49–50, 92.

[92] The exception is that on BL, Cotton MS Nero C. x, f. 95^r, information from LPL, MS 506, f. 22^v precedes that from f. 22^r.

details that Worcester had added to LPL, MS 506,[93] evidently the Codicil or some copy made from it was accessible to Edward VI in the period 1547–53.

This need not mean that the extant manuscript of the Codicil was in royal ownership, for there is evidence that it was in the hands of heralds after Edward VI read it; earlier heralds might have either obtained it from or shared it with the king. A short section of the Codicil was translated and appears in London, British Library, Harley MS 782, a collection of records gathered by Robert Glover (1543/4–1588), Somerset Herald, and owned from at least 1604 by Ralph Brooke (c.1553–1625), York Herald. Most of the collection concerns the reign of Edward III, but one section considers the fifteenth-century wars in France. It includes information from the so-called *Basset's Chronicle*, to which Worcester contributed, which was also in the hands of heralds then, as now,[94] and a translation (ff. 52ᵛ–53ᵛ) of two lists from the Codicil (LPL, MS 506, ff. 8ʳ–11ʳ=Appendix 1). The translation is close: it omits some details, usually by abbreviating longer entries in the lists, but must descend from the Codicil's version of these lists, for it incorporates some of Worcester's and scribe C's additions and deletions.[95] And some visual details suggest that the Codicil was the direct exemplar for the translation. On f. 53ᵛ the translator once misunderstands *N* (for *nomen*) and a space at the start of a new entry (Codicil, f. 9ʳ) and so runs this entry onto the end of the previous entry (Appendix 1/63); and twice the translator leaves a blank space for a forename, as does the Codicil (ff. 10ᵛ, 11ʳ=Appendix 1/145, Appendix 1/165). The fact that the translation omits some text that is partly, though not entirely, obliterated by a dark substance on the page of the Codicil might suggest that the translator consulted the Codicil manuscript directly and found it already damaged. Overall, London, British Library, Harley MS 782

---

[93] e.g. the ascription of some articles to Fastolf, added to LPL, MS 506, f. 38ʳ (C2/2), also in BL, Cotton MS Nero C. x, f. 96ʳ; or the date of Richard, duke of York's commission, added to LPL, MS 506, f. 44ʳ (C3/8–10), also in BL, Cotton MS Nero C. x, f. 96ᵛ.

[94] BL, Harley MS 782, ff. 49ᵛ–50ᵛ, and maybe ff. 49ʳ, 50ʳ, 51ᵛ–52ʳ. On the scribe of this MS and provenance of this MS and of *Basset's Chronicle* (i.e. London, College of Arms, MS M.9), see C&A, 134–8, who mention that BL, Harley MS 782 'may reflect the use of' LPL, MS 506; *ODNB, s.n.* Glover, Robert (1543/4–88); *ODNB, s.n.* Brooke (Brookesmouth), Ralph. See also *A Catalogue of the Harleian Manuscripts in the British Museum*, 4 vols. (London, 1808), i. 436.

[95] Some of the revisions not translated might have been omitted because they were incomplete (e.g. Worcester adding *capitaneus de* but no placename: Appendix 1/120, 1/121).

suggests that the Codicil circulated among the heralds in the second half of the 1500s.

By some route unknown, it then moved from the heralds or the royal household to Sir Robert Cotton's circle or George Carew. (Cotton did acquire books formerly in royal ownership.)[96] It was supplemented with a list of contents on f. 7^{r-v}, in late sixteenth- or early seventeenth-century italic handwriting, described by M. R. James as written 'by or for' the great collector Sir Robert Cotton (1571–1631), and by P. R. Robinson as 'by' Cotton.[97] The provision of such contents tables was common in Cotton's library by Richard James (1591–1638), the librarian after 1625; by another scribe with what Colin G. C. Tite calls a 'stylized hand'; by William Dugdale; by Cotton himself; and by Cotton's son.[98] We cannot ascribe the list in the Codicil with confidence to a particular one of these people, but it is laid out similarly to other such lists from that milieu.[99] After that material was added, the Codicil with some of the additions of c.1600 was transcribed extensively in handwriting of the early 1600s (London, College of Antiquaries, MS 41, described below).

That it might have passed through Cotton's circle makes sense, for it bears a binding with the arms of George Carew (as noted above, p. xxxiv), earl of Totnes from 1605, a military leader in England's colonization in Ireland and a courtier with antiquarian interests.[100] Carew was a member of Cotton's circle, but whether it went from Cotton to Carew or vice versa is unclear. Some books moved from Carew's ownership to Cotton's,[101] but equally Carew borrowed manuscripts from Cotton, and Cotton identified some of them as never returned.[102] Carew wrote to Cotton twice c.1611 for assistance in finding evidence about

[96] James P. Carley, 'The Royal Library as a Source for Sir Robert Cotton's Collection: A Preliminary List of Acquisitions', *British Library Journal*, 18 (1992), 52–73. In addition, Colin G. C. Tite, *The Early Records of Sir Robert Cotton's Library: Formation, Cataloguing, Use* (London, 2003), 98, suggests that BL, Cotton MS Julius E. iv, the *Gesta Henrici Quinti* annotated by Worcester, might have come to Cotton from Prince Henry, who (see p. xxxiii above) acquired *The Boke of Noblesse* from Lumley.

[97] James, *Lambeth*, 411; Robinson, *Dated and Datable Manuscripts . . . London*, 53.

[98] Tite, *The Early Records of Sir Robert Cotton's Library*, 14–15.

[99] Cf. the reproductions ibid., pl. 3a–4b; Colin G. C. Tite, '"Lost or stolen or strayed": A Survey of Manuscripts Formerly in the Cotton Library', in C J. Wright (ed.), *Sir Robert Cotton as Collector: Essays on an Early Stuart Courtier and his Legacy* (London, 1997), 262–306, figs. 2–5.

[100] *ODNB*, s.n. Carew, George, earl of Totnes.

[101] Tite, *Early Records*, 93, 178, 195, 200; Tite, '"Lost or stolen or strayed"', 270, 272–3.

[102] Tite, *Early Records*, 35, 37, 64, 196, 215, 223; Colin G. C. Tite, 'A Catalogue of Sir Robert Cotton's Printed Books?', in C. J. Wright (ed.), *Sir Robert Cotton as Collector: Essays on an Early Stuart Courtier and his Legacy* (London, 1997), 183–93 at 189, 192n.

Henry V.[103] The Codicil could have served similar interests in the wars under Henry VI, and a loan not returned could then have followed other of Carew's books to Lambeth Palace Library.

Unlike Carew's other medieval manuscript at Lambeth (MS 264), the Codicil has not been identified on a list of Carew's books, mostly on Irish affairs, acquired by Gilbert Sheldon (1598–1677), archbishop of Canterbury, and then bequeathed to Lambeth Palace Library.[104] Carew seems, however, the likeliest provenance. Some of his manuscripts went to his protégé and perhaps illegitimate son Sir Thomas Stafford (d. 1655), who drew on them for his history of the wars in Ireland. Stafford's widow reportedly sold them through a bookseller Cornelius Bee; eventually one Lady Shirley, probably the widow of the antiquary Sir Thomas Shirley (c.1590–1654), is recorded sending them to Sheldon in 1664 after his appointment as archbishop.[105] Her husband's nephew, the royalist Sir Robert Shirley (1629–56), had sheltered Sheldon during the Interregnum. He bequeathed his books to Lambeth Palace Library, which they reached after a legal battle in 1683.[106]

3. London, Society of Antiquaries, MS 41

There is also an early seventeenth-century transcription of most but not all of the Codicil, including the late sixteenth- or early seventeenth-century additions to it but excluding texts in French and some additional notes by Worcester (printed as Appendix 3).[107] It is of use in establishing the text only where the fifteenth-century manuscript of the Codicil is obliterated by a stain (e.g. Appendix 1/65–6); however, it is of use in tracing the circulation of the Codicil in the sixteenth and early seventeenth centuries.

---

[103] BL, Cotton MS Julius C. iii, ff. 68^r, 69^r; Tite, *Early Records*, 98.

[104] James, *Lambeth*, 714; M. R. James, 'The History of Lambeth Palace Library', *Transactions of the Cambridge Bibliographical Society*, 3 (1959), 1–31 at 15. In the sequence of shelfmarks at Lambeth it (LPL, MS 506) precedes other Carew–Sheldon books (LPL, MSS 507 to 522).

[105] M. R. James, 'The Carew Manuscripts', *EHR* 42 (1927), 261–7 at 264–6; *ODNB, s.n.* Shirley, Sir Thomas, and Stafford, Sir Thomas; Sir Thomas Stafford, *Pacata Hibernia: Ireland Appeased and Reduced, or, An Historie of the Late Warres of Ireland* (London, 1634), sig. A3.

[106] Richard Palmer, 'Sancroft Versus Sheldon: A Case of Books', *The Library*, 7th ser., 18 (2017), 271–91 at 284, 286–7; *ODNB, s.n.* Sheldon, Gilbert.

[107] For a full description, see Pamela J. Willetts, *Catalogue of Manuscripts in the Society of Antiquaries of London* (Woodbridge, 2000), 20.

Binding

It is bound in brown leather with blind-tooled decorations. The paste-downs and unfoliated endpapers are bifolia of eighteenth-century marbled paper. Glued inside the front paste-down is a bookplate of the Society of Antiquaries, with a pencil note 'i' above '187 F', which partly overlaps another bookplate of 'T. Morell D.D. F.R.S. & S.A.' (on whom see 'Provenance' below). On the verso of the unfoliated flyleaf of marbled paper is '2155' in pencil.

Foliation and Flyleaves

The manuscript consists of one leaf of unfoliated marbled paper cognate with a paste-down+ff. i–iii+1–63+unfoliated iv–v+another leaf of unfoliated marbled paper cognate with a paste-down. There is foliation in red in the gutter, seemingly of the same hue as the frame-ruling added after writing; that foliation is repeated in pencil at the top of the fore-edge.

Materials

Folios 1–63 are early modern paper.

Collation

The collation is impossible to determine. Pamela J. Willetts describes the book as being constructed in 'quarto',[108] so it might be constructed of sixteen quires of four.

Contents

It consists of a transcription, with some local errors or omissions, of most of the Latin and all of the English fifteenth-century contents of the Codicil, and of the late sixteenth- or early seventeenth-century additions to that manuscript. The transcription also includes several passages crossed out but legible in that exemplar (e.g. those in the textual notes to Appendix 2/1–3 and Appendix 2/2–3).

ff. 1^r–4^v:=LPL, MS 506, ff. 2^r–6^v;=text C1 below
f. 5^{r-v}: a list of the contents, copied from LPL, MS 506, f. 7^{r-v}
ff. 6^r–9^r:=LPL, MS 506, ff. 8^r–11^r;=Appendix 1 below
ff. 9^v–23^r:=LPL, MS 506, ff. 11^r–25^v;=*Wars in France*, ii. 529–59;
    Worcester's title from LPL, MS 506, f. 11^r is omitted, and there is a

---

[108] Ibid. 20.

note on f. 9ᵛ in an early seventeenth-century hand in pencil, partly
trimmed and erased, '⟨?⟩h lacketh the ⟨?⟩ in the ⟨mar⟩gent'

f. 23ʳ: Worcester's Latin heading to LPL, MS 506, f. 26ʳ; and a note in an
early seventeenth-century hand in pencil 'He [*sic*] wanteth diuerse
paiementes which were written in French contayneing three sides of
a leafe and a halfe', then recopied by a near-contemporary hand in
brown ink

ff. 23ᵛ–24ᵛ: blank

ff. 25ʳ–27ᵛ:=LPL, MS 506, ff. 28ʳ–31ʳ;=Appendix 2 below

ff. 28ʳ–32ᵛ:=LPL, MS 506, ff. 32ᵛ–37ʳ;=*Wars in France*, ii. 565–74

ff. 33ʳ–43ᵛ:=LPL, MS 506, ff. 38ʳ–50ʳ;=texts C2 to C5 below, and *Wars
in France*, ii. 575–97

f. 44ʳ: a note in an early seventeenth-century hand in pencil 'Here
wanteth ~~ix~~ ·viij leafes which was written in French containeing peti-
ciones ex parte Ambassatorum Caroli septimi aduersarij Regis Angli
Colore pacis facte tunc non concesse tam apud Arras quam apud
Calix'

ff. 44ᵛ–49ᵛ: blank

ff. 50ᵛ–52ᵛ: digests in English of information from the Codicil, copied,
in places page by page, from LPL, MS 506, ff. [62ʳ]–[64ᵛ][109]

f. 53ʳ⁻ᵛ: blank

ff. 54ʳ–58ᵛ: digests in English of information from the Codicil; copied
from LPL, MS 506, ff. [67ʳ]–[71ᵛ]

ff. 59ʳ–63ᵛ: blank.

This manuscript, however, does not transcribe the following sections of
the Codicil:

the bottom half of f. 23ʳ and all of ff. 23ᵛ–24ᵛ are left blank and omit
documents in French from LPL, MS 506, ff. 26ʳ–27ᵛ;=*Wars in France*,
ii. 559–65

ff. 44ʳ–49ᵛ are left blank and omit documents in French from LPL, MS
506, ff. 51ʳ–57ʳ and f. 58ʳ⁻ᵛ;='Documents Relating to the Anglo-French
Negotiations of 1439', ed. Allmand, and *Wars in France*, ii. 598–607

ff. 44ʳ–49ᵛ also omit Worcester's rough notes in Latin from LPL, MS 506,
ff. 59ᵛ and 60ᵛ;=Appendix 3

The omissions of texts in French were noted by a seventeenth-century
reader (as recorded above).

---

[109] Willetts, *Catalogue*, 20, suggests that ff. 50ᵛ–52ᵛ, 54ʳ–58ᵛ, are not in LPL, MS 506,
but they are.

Scribe

The manuscript has been variously dated from its handwriting as sixteenth-century and seventeenth-century.[110] The handwriting is in secretary script typical of the very late sixteenth or early seventeenth century.[111] The handwriting evidently dates after the additions to the Codicil in the hand associated with Sir Robert Cotton's circle, for the transcriber copies into this manuscript (here ff. 5^{r-v}, 50^v–52^v, 54^r–58^v) the list of contents and English digests which had been added to the Codicil (there ff. 7^{r-v}, 62^r–64^v, 67^r–71^v); as some of those additions to the Codicil show features of handwriting typical of the early seventeenth century, we date this transcription to that period likewise.

Layout

The pages were originally frame-ruled in pale grey pencil, and text in ink is aligned to that frame, with the first letter of each line over the top of the left pencil vertical. Somebody then drew a second frame-ruling in red over the top, wider than that in pencil, to enclose all the approach-strokes, ascenders, and descenders of the script and to close off areas of blank space.

Provenance

The notes in early seventeenth-century hands on f. 23^r, which record the passages omitted from the transcription of London, Lambeth Palace Library, MS 506, suggest that this transcription remained available for comparison with MS 506 after the scribe had finished making it, and before that manuscript entered Lambeth Palace Library later in the seventeenth century.

In MS 41, f. 1^r has the signature, crossed out, of Brian Fairfax the younger (1676–1749), an antiquary. After his death, his library of 2,343 volumes was offered for auction in April 1756, but it was purchased en bloc for £2,000 by the banker Sir Francis Childs (1735–63) for his newly remodelled library at Osterley.[112] In the catalogue for the proposed auction, it is difficult to identify this volume exactly; it might be 'The Rates

[110] Cf. James, *Lambeth*, 714, and Willetts, *Catalogue*, 20.

[111] e.g. Jean F. Preston and Laetitia Yeandle, *English Handwriting, 1400–1650: An Introductory Manual* (Binghamton, NY, 1992), pl. 23 and 24 (each dated *c.*1600); Robinson, *Dated and Datable Manuscripts . . . London*, pl. 302 (1597), pl. 304 (1598).

[112] *ODNB*, in the entry for Fairfax, Brian (1633–1711), viz. his father; William Younger Fletcher, *English Book Collectors* (Frankfurt, 2020), 115–16; John Nichols, *Literary Anecdotes of the Eighteenth Century*, 6 vols. (London, 1812), v. 326–7.

of Wages and Expences of Officers in Peace and Warre' or 'Histoire de les Gurres entre Anglois & François, durant les Regnes des Henry 4, 5 & 6 d'Angleterre', but neither description fits exactly.[113] The Childs family commissioned a catalogue by Dr Thomas Morell, FSA (1703–84), printed in 1771, but this manuscript cannot readily be identified in that catalogue, nor do manuscripts mentioned in 1756 seem to be listed again in 1771.[114]

By whatever means, this manuscript came into the possession of Morell himself, as it contains his bookplate on a flyleaf (described above). Morell donated it and five other manuscripts to the Society of Antiquaries on 31 May 1781.[115]

THE CIRCULATION OF *THE BOKE*
OF NOBLESSE AND THE CODICIL

It emerges from Worcester's son's prologue to it (printed as C1) that the Codicil was designed to complement *The Boke of Noblesse*.[116] He describes his father writing *this boke . . . aftir the seyng of the masters of philosophie*, named as Vegetius, Frontinus, and *a new a`u'ctoure* called *The Tree of Batayles* (C1/37–42), and the deictic *this* implies that he is referring to something that the reader has to hand alongside the Codicil in which he writes this prologue. The list of philosophers sounds like *The Boke of Noblesse*, where Vegetius and *The Tree of Batayles* are cited by name, if not accurately (152, 614, 789, 850, 1671). The next lines contrast the theoretical advice of *the seide auctours* with *the experiense of men* in practice which *preuaylethe moste* (C1/42–5), as though the Codicil's practical tactics supplement, even surpass, the philosophy of *The Boke*.

A *Codicelle* (C1/48, C1/214), as the prologue twice calls it, was commonly an addition to a will, as, for instance, in the Paston letters.[117] The Paston and Fastolf circle letters show an interest in this sort of docu-

---

[113] John Prestage, *A Catalogue of the Entire and Valuable Library of the Honourable Bryan Fairfax Esq., One of the Commissioners of His Majesty's Customs, Deceased* (London, 1756), 68.

[114] Mark Purcell, *The Country House Library* (New Haven, 2017), 217–18. See Thomas Morell, *Catalogus librorum in bibliotheca Osterleiensi* (London, 1771).

[115] Anon., 'Presents to the Society since the Publication of the last Volume of the Archaeologia', *Archaeologia*, 6 (1782), 400–4 at 402. The date is given by Willetts, *Catalogue*, 20.

[116] Scrope, *Othea*, ed. Warner, pp. xliii–xlvi, first noted the connection.

[117] e.g. *PL*, 1042, ll. 4–9.

mentary proof as a supplement to their communications.[118] Worcester talks in *The Boke* itself of having recently presented to Edward IV the *statutes* of John, duke of Bedford (see 917–21n. and below, p. lvi), and it would be in keeping with such activity to present the documents in the Codicil too. Teasingly, an unidentified fifteenth-century person wrote the title 'Declaracion de Iohan duc de bedford des ordonnancez de france' on the flyleaf facing the prologue,[119] which makes the Codicil sound like the *statutes* Worcester presented to Edward IV. That said, the use of the first person (*I take vpon me . . . in this litill Codicelle* C1/47–8) in the prologue might suggest that it was Worcester's son who made the decision to add the Codicil to *The Boke*; that is possible.

Most of the contents of the Codicil are accessible in Stevenson's volume on *The Wars in France* published for the Rolls Series between 1861 and 1864 (as listed above, pp. xxxvi–xxxviii). For completeness of record, we print as Appendices 1 to 3 those documents which Stevenson excluded. For convenience of comparing them with *The Boke of Noblesse*, we also print the Codicil's prologue (C1) and its advisory texts in English (C2 to C5). The advisory texts are all either directly attributed to Fastolf or the product of a Council of which he was a part; all share concerns with *The Boke* and each other, sometimes almost *verbatim* (as shown in the Explanatory Notes below). They are in quires VI and VII, now signed E and *ff*, but originally both signed *a*; so they began the Codicil at some stage. Worcester added *Explicit ad presens hoc opusculum* (C5/82) after the last of the four English documents, treating them as a single small work in itself.

There is, however, no definite evidence that the extant manuscripts of *The Boke* and the Codicil circulated together or reached their royal dedicatees.[120] First, the provenance (sketched above) of *The Boke* in London, British Library, Royal MS 18 B. xxii makes it unlikely that this copy reached Edward IV, for it only entered the royal collection in 1609. Second, the provenance of the Codicil in London, Lambeth Palace Library, MS 506 is evidently different. The notes made by Edward VI suggest that he had access to the text of the Codicil in some copy *c.*1552, but there is no evidence that the surviving copy of it was in royal ownership earlier, say, during Richard III's reign, nor the copy of *The Boke*

---

[118] e.g. *PL*, 935, ll. 49; 936, ll. 26; and 961, ll. 73.

[119] LPL, MS 506, f. 1ᵛ.

[120] Sutton and Visser-Fuchs, *Richard III's Books*, 97, 291–3, consider why Worcester's son would dedicate *BkNob.* and its Codicil to Richard III but refrain from a definite assertion that these extant copies reached him.

in Edward IV's. Neither contains an obvious number from the inventory of holdings consolidated at Westminster around 1550, soon before Edward VI took his notes from the Codicil; nor does either obviously appear in inventories of books at Richmond Palace in 1535 or Westminster Palace in 1542.[121]

Moreover, even allowing for trimming by binders, the proportions of BL, Royal MS 18 B. xxii and LPL, MS 506 are different; their materials and decor differ. They are not obviously 'a set'. Next, neither extant copy seems smart enough for presentation to royalty. The script of each was a specimen of secretary script of only middling grade, in a period when a high-grade French-influenced bastard secretary flourished; there is only slight decoration. Books made for Edward IV in Flanders about this time are more calligraphic and better decorated.[122] The script, scale, and, for *The Boke of Noblesse*, use of paper are comparable rather with the so-called *Basset's Chronicle* produced in Fastolf's household. That said, before Worcester's heavy revisions, the manuscript of *The Boke* seems to have been first planned as a fair copy and perhaps at a quality suitable for presentation to somebody humbler than the king.

One entirely speculative suggestion is that Worcester might have envisaged presenting the text in some form to William Waynflete, bishop of Winchester. In the painful negotiations about Fastolf's will, Waynflete triumphed, and between 1470 and 1474 Worcester assisted him in using Fastolf's estate to endow Magdalen College in Oxford. During this period, Worcester's letters and notebooks record frequent dealings with Waynflete and three gifts of books to the bishop, no doubt seeking favour.[123] He gave his own translation of Cicero's *De senectute* to Waynflete on 10 August 1472, for which he got no reward.[124] He gave the bishop another book, a twelfth-century manuscript, on 16

[121] See *The Libraries of Henry VIII*, ed. James P. Carley, Corpus of British Medieval Library Catalogues, 7 (London, 2000). On the Westminster inventory, see Carley, 'Royal Library as a Source', 52. On books owned by Edward IV, see Janet Backhouse, 'Founders of the Royal Library: Edward IV and Henry VII as Collectors of Illuminated Manuscripts', in Daniel Williams (ed.), *England in the Fifteenth Century: Proceedings of the 1986 Harlaxton Symposium* (Woodbridge, 1987), 23–41 at 39–41.

[122] Warner and Gilson, *Catalogue*, i, pp. xii–xiii; Backhouse, 'Founders of the Royal Library', 24–31.

[123] He dealt with Waynflete on 4 Oct. 1471 and on 10 Aug. 1472 (*Itineraries*, 252, 254), in Dec. 1473 and 4 Feb. 1474 (OMA, FP 101; the typescript catalogue kept at OMA misdates this a year later), on 21 Aug. 1474 (*PL*, no. 1050) and on 28 Aug. and 7 Oct. 1478 (*Itineraries*, 34, 40). For the whole story, see e.g. *PL*, nos 569, ll. 36–9; 570, l. 2; 574, ll. 3–10; 948, ll. 40–2, and Richmond, *The Paston Family . . . Fastolf's Will*, 213–22, 255–6.

[124] *Itineraries*, 252; Virginia Davis, *William Waynflete: Bishop and Educationalist* (Cambridge, 1993), 93–4, 131–9.

December 1473.[125] And Worcester's son 'R', perhaps Robert, wrote in an undated letter to Worcester, bound into a notebook of the late 1470s, that he had delivered 'youre boke' to Winchester, perhaps to Bishop Waynflete.[126] Could some iteration of *The Boke* have been presented to Waynflete? That can only be a speculation.

Either way, Worcester's plans for the surviving manuscripts of *The Boke of Noblesse* and its Codicil appear to have changed. Like the manuscript of *Basset's Chronicle*, those of *The Boke* and its Codicil were revised by Worcester, turning a formerly fair copy, if an incomplete one for the Codicil, into a second draft.[127] In *The Boke* itself, the revision included modifying pronouns from *oure* to `y'oure* or adding additional *your* to strengthen the address to Edward IV directly; such visible alterations might have been embarrassing if not incorporated silently in a neater copy.[128] The manuscript of the Codicil had space left for headings or illustrations; and in his additions to the Codicil, Worcester seems to be finalizing the text for recopying, with headings that clarify the nature and purpose of the documents. For instance, on f. 28[r] he deleted two previous headings and added a better one (Appendix 2/1–3); the replication would be confusing were this manuscript not recopied before presentation. Some of his additions seem like directions to a future copyist to alter the text (e.g. 'vacant iste .iij. linee' on f. 23[r]) or add headings or change the layout (e.g. the abbreviation for 'capitulum' on ff. 10[v], 11[r], 12[v], 22[r–v]). Likewise, Worcester's holograph revisions all over *The Boke of Noblesse* itself altered the text in ways that he presumably thought improved it, but they marred the appearance. So each extant manuscript probably was reimagined as an exemplar for a more formal dedicatory copy now lost or never made.[129]

[125] OMC, MS Lat. 26, f. ii[v], discussed by Wakelin, *Humanism*, 97. WW also received from Waynflete OMC, MS Lat. 198, as recorded on f. ii[v].

[126] CCCC, MS 210, pp. 39, 41–2, printed in *Itineraries*, 386. On 'R' or Robert, see p. xviii above.

[127] On this phenomenon, see Gilbert Ouy, 'Manuscrits autographes en France au temps des premiers humanistes', in Olivier Delsaux and Tania Van Hemelryck, *Les Manuscrits autographes en français au Moyen Âge: Guide de recherches* (Turnhout, 2014), 157–95 at 172, 185.

[128] See 219 (and n.), 2239–40, 2309, 2362. See also added address to Edward IV at 234 (and n.).

[129] What Delsaux, *Manuscrits*, 2, calls a 'manuscrit d'édition'.

The Boke of Noblesse is centrally concerned with the loss of the Lancastrian lands in France, from the eventual delivery of Maine to the French in 1448, to the fall of Bordeaux, in the *Boke*'s account, in June 1451. It is with disbelief that Worcester states, not inaccurately, that the French king, Charles VII, managed to conquer Normandy *bethyn the space of xv. monithes* (52–3). For Worcester, the conditions that led to this were an unfortunate tendency, evident through the centuries, for the English to trust the French when it came to truces, a particular issue because the Truce of Tours of 1444, in Worcester's view, allowed Charles VII to regroup; and, more concretely, the lack of provision for castles, fortresses, and garrisons and the covetous behaviour and dishonest practice of particular, unnamed, captains.

The questions that animate Worcester's text were ones that were posed urgently in the period from Charles VII's first successes in Normandy in the summer of 1449 to the first battle of St Albans in May 1455. When parliament met in November 1449, shortly following the fall of the capital of Lancastrian Normandy, Rouen, on 29 October, the business of assigning blame for the deteriorating situation in France began. By the parliament's second session, the commons had identified William de la Pole, duke of Suffolk, as responsible.[130] He had conspired with the French and had even encouraged Charles VII to invade England.[131] Those who marched on London in June and July 1450 named others as responsible and meted out their own justice.[132] Worcester, politicly, does not name individuals in *The Boke of Noblesse*. But when reading in his notebook of the examples of the ancient traitors Calchas and Curion, taken from Alain Chartier's *Le Livre de l'espérance*, he was reminded of the duke of Suffolk, murdered by sailors on his way to exile in the Low Countries in May 1450, and William Aiscough, bishop of Salisbury, hacked to death as he fled from London to Sherborne in June, two others who found 'leur mort ou ilz querioent leur seurte'.[133]

The rivalry between Richard, duke of York, and his replacement as lieutenant of France, Edmund Beaufort, duke of Somerset, shaped the

[130] For events, see Ralph A. Griffiths, *The Reign of King Henry VI: The Exercise of Royal Authority, 1422–1461* (London, 1981), 676–712.
[131] *PROME*, xii. 92–106. [132] Even Sir John Fastolf was blamed: see 2072–87n.
[133] Royal, f. 138ᵛ, annotating extracts from Alain Chartier, *Le Livre de l'espérance*, ed. François Rouy (Paris, 1989), Pr. III. 94–101. On these extracts, see n. 224 below.

politics of these years, and the loss of Normandy was one important part of that rivalry.[134] In a series of articles, York accused Somerset of engaging in financial corruption, withholding soldiers' wages, lessening the power of garrisons in Normandy—all of which led to the ease with which Normandy had fallen.[135] Documents now in one of Worcester's notebooks relate to this, asserting, for example, that castles and towns, rather than being delivered because of siege, assault, mines, lack of victuals, or 'Faute' of men, were delivered 'for lucre of good'.[136] A repeated charge in these materials concerned the misappropriation of the money that was supposed to compensate those dispossessed by the cession of Maine.[137] This lack of compensation is a particular concern of *The Boke of Noblesse*, often articulated through the voice of those dispossessed, of those *dolorous parsones suffring intollerabill persecucions and miserie* (1492–3), and no doubt of special interest for Worcester because his employer had owned substantial lands in Maine for which he, too, had not been compensated.[138]

These are the circumstances that *The Boke* most clearly addresses, but quite when Worcester began writing it is less clear. When he completed it is, by contrast, known definitely and more precisely than for most other English literary works of the fifteenth century. In a colophon in his own handwriting, Worcester dates his revisions to *the xv. day of Iune the yeere of Crist M^l iiij^C lxxv.* or 15 June 1475 (2580–1). His revisions had been occasioned by a new invasion of France, led by King Edward IV himself, whose aim, at least ostensibly, was to recover both the French throne and those lands in France which had been lost in the early 1450s.[139] The king's intention to lead such an expedition had been announced to parliament in May 1468, but the events of 1469–71—the rebellion of the earl of Warwick and the duke of Clarence, Edward IV's exile, the Readeption of Henry VI, and Edward IV's recovery of the throne—meant that it was not until 1472 that preparations began in

[134] M. K. Jones, 'Somerset, York and the Wars of the Roses', *EHR* 104 (1984), 285–307.

[135] York's 1452 articles, printed in the Introduction to Gairdner, i. 103–9.

[136] 'Aduertirimentes' (*sic*: see 2391n.), in Arundel, f. 324^r.

[137] 'The questions to be asked of Somerset concerning his misconduct', in Arundel, ff. 323^{r-v}, 328^r; 'Aduertirimentes' in Arundel, f. 325^v; York's 1452 articles in the Introduction to Gairdner, i. 108.

[138] One of Fastolf's complaints against the Crown concerned lack of compensation for his barony of Sillé-le-Guillaume: BL, Add. MS 27444, f. 38^r, in WW's hand.

[139] For debate about Edward IV's war aims, see J. R. Lander, 'The Hundred Years War and Edward IV's 1475 Campaign in France', in A. J. Slavin (ed.), *Tudor Men and Institutions* (Baton Rouge, LA, 1972), 70–100; Charles Ross, *Edward IV*, 2nd edn. (New Haven, 1997), 205–37.

earnest.[140] Various materials promoting this new campaign survive.[141] In particular, the speech for the opening of parliament in October 1472 shares with *The Boke of Noblesse*, as others have noted, reference to the Punic wars and to past English kings to guide and inspire warfare. Superficial classical allusions were becoming more common in political writing at this time.[142] But, on the whole, the emphases of these materials are different from those of *The Boke*: they tend to present an invasion more directly as a defensive move, to prevent the French from attacking England, and to present the making of war outward as a salve to civil war. Neither of these are particular focuses of *The Boke of Noblesse*.[143] The army that eventually left England in the June and July of 1475 was the largest to cross to France in the fifteenth century.[144] But within weeks, on 29 August 1475, Edward IV and Louis XI had agreed a seven-year truce at Picquigny.[145]

That many of Worcester's holograph revisions were made just before or on 15 June 1475 is corroborated by one of the revised lines where he added a reminder that he had presented Fastolf's copy of the military ordinances of John, duke of Bedford, to his reader, *your hyghnes*, Edward IV, *the day before your departyng owt of London* (920), that is 29 May 1475, just over two weeks beforehand.[146] The date of early June 1475 for Worcester's revisions implies, of course, that the rest of the text must date *before* that. The question is how much before, and whether what existed before these known dates had already gone through intermediate iterations not visible in the once fair copy. Not-

---

[140] *PROME*, xiv. 2–5, 14–21, 85–91, 230–48, 309–17; Ross, *Edward IV*, 217. The 'Annales' in Arundel, f. 19ʳ (*Wars in France*, ii. 789), record that the king made the announcement to parliament himself ('declarauit ore suo proprio').

[141] e.g. the charge given to commissioners, TNA, C 49/36/6, discussed in D. A. L. Morgan, 'The Political After-Life of Edward III: The Apotheosis of a Warmonger', *EHR* 112 (1997), 856–881 at 871; letters requesting money for the war, e.g. *The Politics of Fifteenth-Century England: John Vale's Book*, ed. M. L. Kekewich and others (Stroud, 1995), 145–7; *The Coventry Leet Book*, ed. M. D. Harris, EETS os 134, 135, 138, 146 in one vol. (1907–13), 409–11.

[142] *Literae Cantuarienses: The Letter Books of the Monastery of Christ Church, Canterbury*, ed. J. B. Sheppard, 3 vols., RS 85 (London, 1887–9), iii. 279, 282–3, on which see Wakelin, *Humanism*, 64, 120.

[143] That said, Worcester does urge the king *to clothe you in armoure of defen`s'e ayenst youre ennemies* (582–3).

[144] Lander, 'The Hundred Years War', 70–100; Anne Curry, *The Hundred Years War*, 2nd edn. (Basingstoke, 2003), 102; Ross, *Edward IV*, 221.

[145] Ross, *Edward IV*, 233.

[146] The ordinances were originally issued at Caen on 10 Dec. 1423; they are printed by B. J. H. Rowe, 'Discipline in the Norman Garrisons under Bedford, 1422–35', *EHR* 46 (1931), 194–208 (201–6).

ably, the fair copy, before the revisions completed on 15 June, did not acknowledge Edward IV's plans. There is a suggestion that the shame incurred to *ye worshipfull men of Englisshe nacion . . . by youre said aduersaries of Fraunce . . . may be in goodely hast remedied* (228–34), but the verb *may* suggests that a plan to recover England's lost territories is not yet definite. It was only in his autograph revision in June 1475 that Worcester added *as youre hyghnesse now entendyth* to that suggestion (234). Indeed, the rest of *The Boke* seems less a justification of an invasion that was already in prospect than an attempt to persuade the king to act, to undertake a new campaign to claim his *auncien enheritaunce* (688).

In the edition for the Roxburghe Club, J. G. Nichols, while not realizing that Worcester was the author of *The Boke of Noblesse*, noted the connection to Sir John Fastolf and stated that 'it seems not at all improbable that the substance' of *The Boke* was written while Fastolf was still alive, that is, before 1459.[147] At issue here is the degree of influence Fastolf had on *The Boke*'s existence and its content. Worcester does credit Fastolf as his source of information (452–3, 1961, 2062–3, and 2332–3), but these are all in the additions, which are dated to 1475.[148] Other advice contained in *The Boke* certainly echoes that given by Fastolf in other contexts (see 223n., 456–7n., and 892–902n.), and Worcester would unsurprisingly reflect some of the thinking of the man he served in life and death for decades, though he nowhere in *The Boke* explicitly names Fastolf as its patron. An instructive comparison is the chronicle in French covering the English wars in France between 1415 and 1429, which Worcester himself said was compiled 'ad nobilem virum Iohannem Fastolf' (where Latin 'ad' implies 'for') and in the year 1459 'anno quo dictus Iohannes Fastolf obijt'.[149] People were composing works under Fastolf's direction or for his enjoyment in the 1450s. Yet the editors of that chronicle convincingly argue that it was left incomplete at Fastolf's death in 1459. Whatever *The Boke of Noblesse*'s condition at that time, it evidently was open for revision afterwards.

K. B. McFarlane, too, favoured an earlier date of initial composition for *The Boke*, suggesting that it was originally composed 'soon after 1451' and then 'bears traces of two successive but imperfect attempts at revision' in the 1470s, the first revision before Worcester's second

---

[147] Nichols, p. i, gives 1460, rather than 1459, as the year of Fastolf's death.

[148] WW's black sidenote on f. 37^v (2332) also clarifies that his source for the material in 2332–40 was Fastolf.

[149] *Basset's Chronicle*, f. 31^r (C&A, 181); and on the date, see C&A, 44.

visible changes of 1475.[150] There is some textual evidence in support of
a date for a first draft of 1451. A passage describing how *many of youre
saide trew liege-peple* were forced to become subjects of Charles VII is
introduced as *now in the yere of Crist M^l. iiij^C. lj.* (1156–62). 1451 is on
another occasion called *this yere* (1272). The chronologically last territorial loss Worcester mentions is that of Bordeaux in June 1451; he does
not mention its recovery the following year, and what would turn out to
be its permanent loss in 1453, nor does he mention the Battle of Castil-
lon of July that year.[151] These might point to a date of composition of
parts of the text, at least, in 1451. Certainly, as early as 1453, there is evidence of Worcester's interest in political writing, for it is his hand that
copies—and, one wonders, perhaps composes—a petition to the Privy
Council in the name of the duke of Norfolk complaining of the lack
of justice received by those responsible, namely the duke of Somerset,
for the loss of Normandy and Aquitaine.[152] *The Boke of Noblesse* seems
plausibly first begun in 1451.

  Yet the text as it survives in the fair copy was certainly redrafted after
the accession of Edward IV on 4 March 1461. On two occasions (56,
2432), Edward IV's Lancastrian predecessor, Henry VI, is described as
named king, i.e. as king in name only and not in legal right; and this is
in text copied by the main scribe.[153] Henry VI is consistently described
as *youre predecessour* (e.g. 746) or *youre antecessoure* (e.g. 55), and the
kin relationships are, as McFarlane commented, correct for Edward IV;
for instance, Richard, duke of York, is called *youre father* (1238).[154]
Moreover, the date of an interim draft captured in the fair copy can
be narrowed further. The watermark of the paper used in Royal MS 18

[150] McFarlane, 'William Worcester', 211–12. For other discussions of dating, see Sutton
and Visser-Fuchs, 'Richard III's Books: XII'; Christopher Allmand, 'France-Angleterre à
la fin de la guerre de cent ans: Le "Boke of Noblesse" de William Worcester', in *La France
anglaise au moyen âge* (Paris, 1988), 103–11; Christopher Allmand and Maurice Keen,
'History and the Literature of War: *The Boke of Noblesse* of William Worcester', in Christopher Allmand (ed.), *War, Government and Power in Late Medieval France* (Liverpool,
2000), 92–105 at 96, 104.

[151] Cf. 'John Benet's Chronicle for the Years 1400 to 1462', ed. G. L. and M. A. Harriss,
Camden Miscellany XXIV, Camden Society, 4th ser., 9 (London, 1972), 151–233 at 205,
208, 209.

[152] Gairdner, no. 230, from BL, Add. MS 34888, f. 90^r. Colin Richmond, 'John Fastolf,
the Duke of Suffolk, and the Pastons', in Linda S. Clark (ed.), *Rule, Redemption and Representations in Late Medieval England and France* (Woodbridge, 2008), 73–103 at 92, notes
that Richard Beadle identified this document as being in Worcester's handwriting.

[153] There is one example of *named* (810) alone being added by WW at the time of his
revision to the text; the remaining three occurrences in WW's hand (734, 918, 2072) are
part of his longer additions to the text.

[154] See also 1325n. and McFarlane, 'William Worcester', 211.

B. xxii seems to date from 1472, suggesting a date that year at the earli-est or within a few years after. (See p. xx above.) And in the text itself, while some allusions suggest a date of 1451, others suggest c.1474 or the first half of 1475. First, the text in fair copy says that *it is rather in defaute of exercising of armes, left this .xxiiij. yere day, that the londes were lost* (865–6), which implies the loss of lands in France twenty-four years previously; from 1450 or 1451 this would be 1474 or 1475. Two other calculations imply that Worcester was writing particular sections in, and counting backwards from, 1474 or 1475. He says that due to the marriage of Matilda to Geoffrey Plantagenet in 1127 (see 666–71n.), her son was *right enheritour and seised of* Plantagenet lands in France *continued this .iij^C. xlvij. yere* (675–7). Some 347 years after 1127 would be 1474. Third and finally, he writes that since the marriage of Henry II to Eleanor of Aquitaine *aboute* 1146 (notably loosely), *youre noble pro-genitours haue continuelly be possessid and seased of this .iij^C xxviij yere complete* (708, 717–8). Some 328 years after 1146 would be 1474. Given these dates, and the evidence from watermarks, it seems likely that the text in the fair copy was produced in 1474 or 1475.

WORCESTER'S EARLIER REVISION

Beyond such datable references to people and moments, it is difficult to pinpoint what might have been added or altered in a second draft in the reign of Edward IV, though it is possible to speculate. One hypothesis is that *The Boke* began life around 1451 as a useful collection of practical and legal advice and historical precedent, perhaps more like its Codicil of probative documents. It would also have looked, as the Codicil still does, more like other compilations of such texts that circulated in fifteenth-century England. Other collectors gathered the sorts of docu-ments that were among Worcester's sources or that made points akin to his. Some were grand in presentation, others humbler, often in similar kinds of secretary script to the fair copy of *The Boke*. People collected copies or translations of documents such as the treaties of Brétigny and Troyes to which Worcester refers (e.g. 1102, 1169, 1225) or accounts of the congress of Arras, on which the Codicil offers advice (C2).[155] They collected royal genealogies, like those that Worcester explains (e.g. 40–7, 663–77).[156] They collected lists of loyal garrisons, like that

[155] Compare e.g. BL, Harley MS 861, ff. 30^r–33^r, 88^v–90^r; BL, Harley MS 4763, ff. 41^r–43^r, 57^v–59^v, 135^r–141^v; BodL, MS Bodley 885, ff. 45^r–51^v.

[156] Compare e.g. BL, Harley MS 861, ff. 27^r, 67^r; BL, Harley MS 4763, ff. 33^r, 35^r; BodL, MS Bodley 885, ff. 37^r, 38^r.

in the Codicil (Appendix 2).[157] They collected financial accounts of the wars, like those in the Codicil.[158] They gathered articles of advice making points like those in *The Boke* or its Codicil, such as advice to ambassadors (C2).[159] Much of *The Boke of Noblesse* resembles this kind of material redacted into prose form, and supplemented by the Codicil of just such documents.

Then, however, Worcester expanded his vision of what might make his treatise more persuasive, perhaps, as P. S. Lewis proposed, under the inspiration of French works on the wars with more literary flair.[160] The miscellanies of documents in England often included some literary works on the wars, such as Petrarch's twelfth eclogue and *Le Songe du Verger*.[161] Even in the document that Worcester copied or composed in the name of the duke of Norfolk in 1453, there is an allusion to Honoré Bouvet's *L'Arbre des batailles* to bolster an argument; this is a work named in *The Boke of Noblesse*, albeit there confused with Christine de Pizan's *Livre des fait d'armes* (152: see n.).[162] This might be a sign that Worcester was already reading widely, or might have been a spur to do so, in dressing up the plain advice of *The Boke* with more such literary allusions.

One hypothesis is that *The Boke* was revised to fit the growing fashion for classical allusions, like those used before parliament in 1472, for one passage that looks as though it could have been added separately is that adapted from Cicero's *De senectute*. The preceding lines of *The Boke* describe good governance with *sententiae* and examples from John of Wales's *Communiloquium* (1596–9, 1732–89), the kind of source found in other English political treatises in the early to mid-1400s;[163] and among those sayings and stories are several that John of Wales ascribes

[157] Compare e.g. BL, Harley MS 861, ff. 59ʳ–62ᵛ; BL, Harley MS 4763, ff. 170ʳ–172ʳ.

[158] Compare e.g. BL, Add. MS 4101, ff. 41ʳ⁻ᵛ, 46ʳ–51ᵛ: see pp. xxxix–xl above.

[159] Compare e.g. BL, Harley MS 861, ff. 124ʳ; BL, Harley MS 4763, ff. 248ʳ–252ʳ, 265ᵛ–269ʳ; BodL, MS Bodley 885, ff. 53ʳ–58ᵛ, 80ʳ–91ᵛ.

[160] P. S. Lewis, 'War Propaganda and Historiography in Fifteenth-Century France and England', *Transactions of the Royal Historical Society*, 15 (1965), 1–21 at 14–15. On French recognition of the need for persuasive writing in diplomacy, see Craig Taylor, 'War, Propaganda and Diplomacy in Fifteenth-Century France and England', in Christopher Allmand (ed.), *War, Government and Power in Late Medieval France* (Liverpool, 2000), 70–91 at 83–4.

[161] e.g. BL, Harley MS 861, ff. 67ʳ–72ʳ, 86ʳ–88ʳ; BL, Harley MS 4763, ff. 35ʳ–41ʳ, 55ʳ–57ᵛ; BodL, MS Bodley MS 885, ff. 4ʳ–7ᵛ.

[162] See Gairdner, no. 230 in n. 152 above.

[163] e.g. *Four English Political Tracts of the Later Middle Ages*, ed. Jean-Philippe Genet Camden Society, 4th ser., 18 (London, 1977), 43–4.

to Cicero, including two from *De senectute*.[164] Then in *The Boke* comes the long section translated fairly closely from Laurent de Premier-fait's French translation of Cicero's *De senectute* (1803–2151), offering examples of good governance by Roman heroes. The phrasing that first introduces these examples is not woven smoothly into the preceding clauses, as it switches from *wolde haue a verray parfit loue*, following *wolde* with a verb without *to*, as is idiomatic, to a construction *and to folow the pathis*, with *to*, as is not idiomatic (1792–3). And that phrase then introduces the Ciceronian chapters with a clause left incomplete (that Worcester noted in 1475, adding a verb *ys* at 1799, to improve but not perfect the transition):

And so wolde the mightifull God that euery gouernoure wolde haue a verray parfit loue to the gouernaunce of a comon wele by wise and goode counceile; and to folow the pathis and weies and examples of the noble senatours of Rome, . . ., as I shall in example put here in remembraunce and is founden writen in diuers stories, as of one among othir 'ys' (1791–9)

Worcester explains that he will *put* the Ciceronian material *here*, and the join between the text based on John of Wales and *diuers stories* from Cicero's work seems visible. And after the long passage based on *De senectute*, Worcester reverts to one of the practical topics of the earlier part of *The Boke of Noblesse*, the paying of soldiers' wages (2156–2251; cf. e.g. 877–910). One can speculate that John of Wales's citations from Cicero might have prompted Worcester to seek out Cicero's work to add it here. *De senectute* was circulating in his milieu in Latin, for Worcester took notes summarizing it in one of his miscellanies that contains materials gathered between 1462 and 1475. Worcester reported that he had translated *De senectute* ('per me translatum in anglicis') and had given a copy to Waynflete on 10 August 1472.[165] It would make sense if Worcester added this material from *De senectute* to *The Boke of Noblesse* after 1451, while or after making his fuller translation.

Those interim revisions can only be guessed at, but the visible revisions, finished on 15 June 1475, offer a rare insight into the processes

---

[164] See 1732-6n., 1738-43n., 1751-4n., 1768-72n., and 1773—86n.

[165] Julius, f. 72^{r-v}; *Itineraries*, 252. Also, in an inventory datable between 1475 and 1479, in *PL*, no. 316, ll. 24–5, WW's associate John Paston II had a copy of it in an unspecified language ('in quayerys Tully de Senectute in d⟨. . .⟩ wheroff ther is no more cleere wretyn ⟨. . .⟩').

by which authors drafted and redrafted their works.[166] They are typical of Worcester's world and work elsewhere. He often provided postscripts to his letters, written left of and below the subscription,[167] or in the margin.[168] The process of drafting emerges clearly in a letter from Fastolf in Worcester's hand in May or June 1444, with a few lines of an alternative draft crossed out, as Fastolf or Worcester pondered how to broach matters.[169] The process of ongoing revision emerges too in various documents. For instance, one of Fastolf's declarations to the Crown of his grievances exists in three stages: a rough version by Worcester, a fair copy with further revisions by Worcester, and a final fair copy by another scribe, to which Worcester adds a final detail.[170] Likewise, Fastolf's will survives in multiple versions: a Latin first draft, with a few interlinear revisions, then an expanded English version of that in Worcester's hand with multiple interlinear revisions that make the text very challenging to read, and finally a fair copy by another scribe, who smooths some syntactical complexities but does not capture all Worcester's revisions.[171] This messy draft and its copy suggest the sort of complex layers of revisions that might have been in Worcester's exemplar for the fair copy of *The Boke* and might explain some of its more baffling passages. Worcester was also, on other occasions, willing to make further revisions to fair copies, as he did, for instance, to a petition to the bishop of Norwich.[172] These are the same methods of drafting, copying, and revising found in *The Boke of Noblesse*.

Worcester made nearly two hundred changes to the fair copy of *The Boke of Noblesse*. All use the techniques of correcting such as erasures overwritten with new words; interlineations, often keyed to the text with caret marks; and additions in the margins, often keyed with *signes de renvoi*. A few changes are indeed corrections, but most of them are better considered as revisions. His preferred technique is interlineation,

---

[166] For other examples, see Richard Beadle, 'English Autograph Writings of the Later Middle Ages: Some Preliminaries', in Paola Chiesa and Lucia Pinelli (eds.), *Gli autografi medievali: Problemi paleografici e filologici* (Spoleto, 1994), 249–68 at 256–7.

[167] *PL*, nos. 558, 566, 780, 883, 899.

[168] *PL*, no. 780: WW to John Paston II on 1 Mar. prob. 1478 in BL, Add. MS 34889, f. 152[r].   [169] *PL*, no. 956, in OMA, FP 40.

[170] Gairdner, no. 310, in stages as BL, Add. MS 27444, ff. 40[r], 41[r], then f. 39[r], then BL, Add. MS 34888, ff. 125[v]–126[r]. See similarly Gairdner, no. 309, in stages as BL, Add. MS 27444, f. 38[r], then BL, Add. MS 34888, ff. 123[v]–124[r].

[171] Respectively OMA, FP 63, FP 64, and FP 65 (see p. xcvii below). There was also a brief Latin abstract of its provisions, OMA, FP 66. John Paston I later created a revised, purportedly nuncupative will: *PL*, no. 54

[172] e.g. *PL*, no. 1049, in OMA, FP 84. On this scribe, see pp. xxiv–xxvi above.

which he uses over 110 times. About thirty-five short additions occur at the end of a line and sometimes also at the start of the next. In these continuations of lines, the decision to revise might have been opportunistic, prompted by the marginal space. Worcester used the margins also for much longer additions, sometimes beginning interlineally where the addition must be inserted.

Except for a few words grammatically essential (e.g. *vppon* 222), many of Worcester's additions between or at the ends of lines predominantly add an extra detail, a clarification or short phrases or adjectives to change the emotional effect. The longer supplements add significant new information, usually drawn from a different source of information. Many of the longest and most evocative marginal additions recount contemporary history, from Duke Humphrey's gifts to Oxford to the use of guard-dogs at Harfleur; these details are apparently drawn from first-hand accounts (as phrases such as *as yt ys seyd* betray).[173] The other longer additions cite books, some of them still extant and identifiable: Ralph de Diceto, Alain Chartier, Nonius Marcellus.[174] Seeing these sources adduced in a way circumscribed by the space of the margins suggests how other works of learned *compilatio* might have grown when composed in manuscript. Other additions supply little new information but finesse the style by adding adjectives, always optional for syntax and sense,[175] or by elaborating a single noun into a doublet, triplet, or list: *prince* into `*kyng or*' *prince*, or *roiaume* into `*an empyre or*' *roiaume*.[176] These continuations thereby make the prose style more 'amplified' or 'copious' according to the canons of taste of rhetorical manuals. What emerges from Worcester's revisions is his investment in *The Boke of Noblesse* not only as political advice but as a display of erudition and an exercise in style.

These revisions were evidently made after the book was already prepared in quires, whether ready for loose tacketing or formal binding, for on f. 15^r Worcester's marginal addition (917–21) ends with a short line that might intentionally avoid the signature *a iij*, and on f. 34^r the leaf signature *c1* is covered by letters *gr* of *grace* in Worcester's marginal addition (2087). There is also evidence that the revisions, though seemingly dated precisely, were not all made in one campaign, nor in the sequence in which they occur in the text. One longer addition that

---

[173] Quoting 1378–9, 1400, and see also e.g. 189–206, 426–56, 536–8, 917–21, 1961–74, 2059–87, 2332–3.   [174] e.g. 680, 732, 1733.

[175] e.g. 189, 2410.

[176] Quoting 169–70 and 2446; see also 239, 297, 840, 842, 1663, 1755.

runs down the margin had to be squeezed around an addition of a doublet ('*hys armee and*' *his power*) that is on a later line of the text, but that had evidently already been made and protruded into the margin (290–5, 297: see nn.). Another long marginal passage betrays signs of starting as a short interlineation and then being extended down the margin later, with an interruption in syntax and shift in the spelling of *Harfleur* (426–56: see n.). Just as *The Boke of Noblesse* had gone through at least two drafts before the fair copy, likewise Worcester revised the fair copy more than once.

That makes it difficult to judge how this process of revision fitted into the preparation of a presentation copy for a patron, such as the imagined reader Edward IV. First, as when he emended *The Dicts and Sayings of the Philosophers* by Stephen Scrope, in March 1473,[177] Worcester turned what was at first a fair copy into a visual mess.[178] He perhaps envisaged treating this extant manuscript as the exemplar of a presentation copy. That seems possible, even though he added sidenotes that seem to 'dress up' the page. Worcester added the sidenotes to *The Boke* in two colours of ink, suggesting two stages of annotation. Throughout the manuscript he added seventy-five sidenotes in black ink commenting on the text. He then duplicated nineteen of the black sidenotes in red ink, sometimes in more expansive wording (ff. 7[v], 8[v], 10[r]–11[v], 14[r], 18[r], 19[r], 24[r–v]), extended three of the black sidenotes with additional words in red at their start or end (f. 26[v], 1570SN, 1576SN; f. 28[r], 1666SN), and then added 162 new red sidenotes commenting on the text further. Worcester clearly wrote the black sidenotes before the red ones, as he used red ink to duplicate or adorn the less prominent black ones. Some are underlined, boxed, and once corrected (f. 21[v], 1287SN) in red.

The red sidenotes with wording are evidently designed for presentation, the black not obviously so; but the black might have been prompts for such red decoration, as scribes often left such prompts unerased in manuscripts.[179] Some black sidenotes were further adorned by underlining in an even blacker ink, as though being re-evaluated to become part of the final page design. It seems that Worcester developed the page design as he developed the text itself, in more than one 'draft'. (For this reason, this edition reproduces the black and red sidenotes alike, as they

[177] Scrope, *Dicts*, ed. Bühler, pp. xxiii–xxv, xxxvi–xxxvii, 292.

[178] For example, he twice extended chapter titles by writing over the scribe's decorative red line-fillers: see 318 (f. 6[r]), 423 (f. 7[v]).

[179] For such prompts, see Daniel Wakelin, *Designing English: Early Literature on the Page* (Oxford, 2017), 75–8.

were evidently part of Worcester's intended layout of text and paratext for *The Boke*: see below, pp. cvii–cviii.)

The sidenotes assist a reader by summarizing the story or commending the key points with 'Nota bene' or 'Notandum' or similar, and some contribute more content: four add facts not mentioned in the text (490SN, on which see 490n.; 832SN, on which see 833–4n.; 1191SN, on which see 1188–96n.; 1751SN, on which see 1751–4n.); one adds information on Christine de Pizan (1666SN); a few compare passages to the works of Alain Chartier (750SN, 759SN, 799SN, 976SN). The content of a few suggests that Worcester might have made the sidenotes only after revising the text, or at least after revising the page in question. One red sidenote highlights information only mentioned in one of Worcester's additions, including detail taken from the local source in *Les Grandes Chroniques de France*, albeit detail that could have been common knowledge (291SN, on which see 290–5n.); a second sidenote mentions a person, Matthew Gournay, only named in an interlinear addition, albeit one of puzzling date (406SN, on which see 417–18n.); and a third highlights not Worcester's praise for a Roman hero in the main text but his retraction of that praise in a later addition (1944SN, and 1961–74). Another supplies a correct date that is emended wrongly in the main text (520SN, on which see 517–18n.). But overall the form of the red sidenotes suggests that they followed revision. A few are written in anomalous positions, where the revisions had already taken up the margin: one is at the head of the page rather than parallel with the text (426–56, f. 8ʳ); another naming Caen and its defenders (838SN) is interrupted by a revision expanding a doublet a few lines below ('*sodeyn iorneys and' sharpe recountres* 840, f. 14ʳ); another black sidenote is indistinguishable from a revision, except that it is in Latin, but its opening words were added later in red, squashed awkwardly (*Notandum est quod* 1666SN). The red ink of the sidenotes is a paler shade than that used by the main scribe and it was also used for some additional paraphs that seem to have been supplied by Worcester, squeezing them between words in the main text.[180] One of these paraphs had to be placed between the lines, as a textual correction by Worcester had already used the space.[181] A few textual revisions include paraphs in pale red or underlining in red.[182] Worcester's tasks

---

[180] For added red paraphs, see e.g. BL, Royal MS 18 B. xxii, f. 25ᵛ, before *and sithe* and *and also* 1503–4. [181] BL, Royal MS 18 B. xxii, f. 4ʳ, *of* 170: see 165–76n.
[182] e.g. red paraphs twice on BL, Royal MS 18 B. xxii, f. 11ᵛ, e.g. before *And the noble actys* 678, six times on f. 32ᵛ, e.g. before *how that there be* 1962, and seven times on f. 34ʳ,

of revising, punctuating, and annotating seem to have unfolded in one continual process of polishing the text. He described this process in his reworking of Scrope's *Dicts and Sayings*, which he claimed to have 'correctid . . . and perrafed also': these tasks go intellectually hand in hand in *The Boke of Noblesse* too.[183]

In addition to the sidenotes, Worcester added a distinctive abstract symbol in the margin. He added it seventy-seven times in black ink close to the fore-edge. Three of those symbols seem to be included inside a box drawn round longer sidenotes (f. 20ᵛ, 1179SN, 1190SN, 1203SN). Worcester then underlined five of those black symbols in red (ff. 33ʳ, 34ᵛ, 35ʳ⁻ᵛ, and 36ᵛ, 1995SN, 2117SN, 2143SN, 2179SN, 2243SN); and he added two more of them in red (ff. 34ʳ and 35ᵛ, 2101SN, 2193SN), all within one late section of *The Boke*. A similar but not identical symbol appears in Worcester's signature, where it functions like the *paraphe final* that French royal secretaries used to authenticate their work.[184] But the version in *The Boke of Noblesse* is different in design: here it only has a single vertical line in the centre and not a double one, as elsewhere, and here it sometimes has a horizontal crossbar and at other times does not (e.g. two different versions adjacent to 2447 on f. 39ᵛ). That other, similar symbol with the vertical stroke doubled has in the past been identified as an astronomical sign for Saturn or for Jupiter, but that is closer to Worcester's astrological sign for Cancer.[185] He uses it in a list of the zodiac signs that govern various cities; in a horoscope next to a reference to the zodiac sign Cancer; and, curiously, at the start of a medical remedy for 'cancrum' or 'Canker' in the mouth.[186] But the sym-

---

e.g. before *And that policie* 2066; red underlining on f. 32ᵛ, *manlye* and *hardye* 1963–4, and on f. 34ʳ, *Bastyle of Seynt Antonye off Parys* 2073.

[183] Scrope, *Dicts*, ed. Bühler, 292.

[184] For WW's signature, see e.g. BL, Add. MS 34888, f. 132ʳ (reproduced in *PL*, pl. XVI). Compare Claude Jeay, *Signature et pouvoir au moyen âge* (Paris, 2015), 344–56, 412–22.

[185] For identification as Saturn, see Davis's note to *PL*, no. 506 (with an illustration in his pl. XVI), following Harvey's suggestion in his edition of *Itineraries*, 300; for Jupiter, see Hanham, 'Curious Letters', 51. Another symbol appears on the addresses of WW's letters in BL, Add. MS 27444, ff. 37ᵛ, 42ᵛ (*PL*, nos. 535, 558).

[186] Respectively BodL, MS Laud misc. 674, f. 43ʳ; CCCC, MS 210, p. 223 (text but not symbol printed in *Itineraries*, 300); BL, Sloane MS 4, f. 57ʳ. Other cities' zodiac signs in BodL, MS Laud misc. 674, f. 43ʳ, are explained in a Latin translation of an Arabic meteorological and astrological treatise, *Tractatus pluviarum*, which was known in 15th-c. England, but not the signs for the cities to which WW gave this symbol: ed. in Charles Burnett, 'Weather Forecasting, Lunar Mansions and a Disputed Attribution: The *Tractatus pluviarum et aeris mutationis* and *Epitome totius astrologiae* of "Iohannes Hispalensis"', in Wim Raven and A. Akasoy (eds.), *Islamic Thought in the Middle Ages: Studies in Text, Transmission and Translation, in Honour of Hans Daiber* (Leiden, 2008), 219–65

bol in the manuscript of *The Boke* might not allude to the zodiac sign for Cancer, for it has a simpler form with single vertical lines. This version is used in the margins of his later notebooks, and the editor of one notebook suggested that there it might abbreviate *questio* or *query*.[187] The symbol could also be **q** followed by a flourish for Latin *quid* or *quod*. So our textual notes call it simply his 'symbol'.

The purpose of this abstract symbol is difficult to determine but seems different from that of the sidenotes. It is written most often close to the fore-edge, sometimes partly trimmed off, so that it superficially resembles the black prompts for sidenotes. But because only five of these seventy-seven symbols were then adorned in red, they do not usually seem to be a prompt for designing the layout for other readers. Instead, they seem in most cases (except the few decorated) like Worcester's private response to his work. (Therefore this edition records the black symbols in the textual notes at the foot of the page; only those adorned in red or accompanying text are presented as part of Worcester's design for sidenotes: see below, pp. cvii–cviii.)

THE REVISIONS TO THE CODICIL

In the Codicil too there is evidence of multiple stages of compilation, composition, revision, and response. In particular, two quires by scribe C look like a separate booklet (in codicological terms), as they have different leaf signatures and form a separate body of works, viz. French diplomatic prose (ff. 51ʳ–57ʳ, 58ʳ⁻ᵛ). However, scribes B and C evidently worked in close proximity in another booklet, for both appear in the middle of quire IV (ff. 24ʳ–31ʳ) and even on the same, central bifolium (ff. 27ᵛ–28ʳ). Moreover, scribe C added to the work of scribe B (e.g. Appendix 1/22, Appendix 1/70), and the work of both scribes was checked (with 'examinatur', etc.) and supplemented by Worcester.

The current arrangement of the Codicil seems to have changed during copying and subsequently by misbinding. Most importantly, the leaf signatures suggest that the quires were originally in a different order: quires VI and VII (both signed *a*), quire V (signed *b*), quires II, III,

at 245–6. Among MSS of *Tractatus pluviarum* in England, one of them, Cambridge, Trinity College, MS O.2.40, f. 110ʳ, which contains a different excerpt, also contains notes on longitude and latitude (f. 109ᵛ) seemingly from the same source as Worcester's list in BodL, MS Laud misc. 674, f. 74ʳ.

[187] e.g. Julius, e.g. ff. 33ᵛ, 60ᵛ, 77ᵛ–78ʳ, 94ᵛ; CCCC, MS 210, e.g. pp. 100, 103, 107, 111 (*Topography*, 38, 48–50, 58). Interpreted by Neale, editing *Topography*, 284.

and IV (signed *c*, *d*, and *e*). The Codicil evidently began with f. 38^r, one of the English prose works (C2 below), which had the largest red initial in scribe B's work and the largest space left blank, two thirds of the page, for a title or picture to be supplied. (Worcester added a title, C2/1–24, in his customary handwriting less suited to display.)

The unusual process of signing what were originally the first two quires, now VI and VII, both as *a* with enumeration running up to *a xiij* (visible on ff. 39^r–41^r, 46^r–49^r, listed on p. xxxvi above) might suggest that these quires were expanded after the rest of the alphabetical sequence of signatures was already established. One possibility is that some of the English texts in these quires (C2 to C5) were added as a 'prequel' to the largely financial and military records, and that these added opening texts proved longer than envisaged. The first text (C2) finishes late in the formerly first quire, now VI (viz., on its sixth verso, f. 43^v); texts C3, C4, and C5 might have been added later, expanding into an extra quire, now VII (signed *a ix* to *a xiij*). That is one possible change of plan for the Codicil.

A possible error in execution and another possible change of plan are revealed by quire IV. The second half of quire IV (ff. 29^r–31^v) had leaf signatures *e j* to *e4*, like the other quires in this booklet; these leaves were, therefore, formerly the first half of the quire. They contained work by scribe B, which ended on the recto of the fourth leaf (f. 31^r), leaving its verso (f. 31^v) and the four other leaves, the second halves of each bifolium, blank. Then those four bifolia were folded back in the opposite direction, so that they became the leaves in the second half of the quire. The leaf signatures were started afresh in the new first half *e j* to *e iiij* (ff. 24^r–27^r) and those in what had become the second half were modified to *e v* to *e8*. The blank leaves in what had become the first half were then filled, the first two by Worcester (ff. 24^r–25^v), continuing a list of moneys received, each line beginning 'Item receptum', which scribe B had been writing at the end of the previous quire (quire III, signed *d*). Worcester seems to have realized that scribe B had mistakenly started quire IV (signed *e*) with a new text, a list of troops, rather than completing the list from the previous quire; so he folded the quire backwards to use the blank leaves to complete the previous text. Then on the final remaining blank leaves, now mid-quire, scribe C added more financial records (ff. 26^r–27^v).

Moreover, as this quire, now IV, was formerly the sixth and last (signed *e*, after others signed *a*, then *a* again, then *b*, *c*, *d*), so scribe C's addition was probably the last thing done to this booklet. And scribe

C's two quires VIII and IX, which, as they stand now, could look like a separate booklet, were probably made as a later expansion by him after filling two blank leaves in the former booklet.

There were then two further changes. At some point after scribe C's quire VIII was complete and still placed after IV, the quires were rearranged so that the three quires signed *a* twice and *b* were moved later in the book. (It is not clear where scribe C's small, damaged quire IX was placed.) The evidence for this is the leaf signature on the first leaf of each quire, which was replaced or overwritten to form a new sequence of majuscule letters *A* to *G*, including scribe C's added quire as *d*. This was the order of the quires when Worcester's son wrote the prologue of *c*.1483–5 with a descriptive *précis* of the Codicil in this order:

- C1/88–90, C1/113–35: the contents of quires II–IV, formerly signed *c*, *d*, and *e* but later *A*, *B*. and *C* (ff. 8^r–27^v), very briefly summarized.
- C1/136–50: list of garrisons and retinues in Normandy under Richard, duke of York (ff. 28^r–31^r); in the rest of quire IV, formerly signed *e* but later *C*, which quire had been refolded and finished by scribe C.
- C1/151–75: demands made by the French at the council of Calais; in scribe C's later quire VIII signed *d* (ff. 51^r–55^r).
- C1/176–83 (describing *the laste partye of this Codycelle*): Fastolf's 1435 articles on the congress of Arras (ff. 38^r–43^v, text C2); copied by scribe B, in quire VI, the first of the two formerly signed *a*, but later signed *E*.
- C1/192–205 (describing *the latter partie of this writyng*): articles of the council of Richard, duke of York (ff. 44^r–47^r, text C3); runs across quires VI and VII, both formerly signed *a* but later signed respectively *E* and *F*.
- C1/206–213 (adding *Also ys here specyfied*): inventories of military equipment (ff. 32^r–37^r); in quire V formerly signed *b* but later *G*.
- C1/214–222 (adding *Also yn this Codycelle ys made mencyon*): two sets of instructions to Edmund, duke of Somerset (ff. 47^v–50^r, texts C4 and C5); now in quire VII, the second of two quires formerly signed *a*, later signed *F*.

The prologue's confusing references to the *laste partye* and *latter partie* warn that his *précis* might not be a wholly accurate reflection of the order of the text at the time, and the final item reflects neither the current order nor the order suggested by either set of leaf signatures. But this summary mostly suggests that the quires had been reordered from the first sequence of leaf signatures to the second before or as the prologue was written in *c*.1483–5. The addition of that prologue, bound at the front in an added extra quire, was the last fifteenth-century change to the Codicil.

Then at some point after this, scribe C's quire VIII, then with the marking *d* (ff. 51^r–56^v), formerly slotted in after quire IV, was misbound in its current later location. (Any movement of scribe C's other quire IX cannot be determined.) This had happened before or with the provision of the current binding with the arms of George Carew and before the very late sixteenth- or early seventeenth-century hand added foliation, a contents list, and a digest of further material.

THE SOURCES

Bookish sources are common in other English political treatises of the fifteenth century, such as Sir John Fortescue's *The Governance of England*, but *The Boke of Noblesse* has an unusual number of them, and an unusual emphasis on classical or pseudo-classical ones. Moreover, Worcester's learned sources can in many cases be traced to his surviving miscellanies or to other manuscripts he annotated. This makes *The Boke* a rare opportunity to study how an English author used and transformed his reading. The Explanatory Notes set out the details, but the background and a few patterns can be summarized.

First, Worcester's reading is evident in seven miscellanies that have been identified as his: three predominantly contain his own handwritten notes—truly his notebooks; four also contain works or notes copied by others but belonging to or annotated by Worcester.[188] The miscellanies are:

- CCCC, MS 210: mostly Worcester's handwritten notes; largely the topography of Bristol and of Britain; contains items dated 1477–80 (here cited as '*Itineraries*').
- BL, Cotton MS Julius F. vii: a mixture of Worcester's handwrit-

---

[188] To the list in Daniel Wakelin, 'William Worcester Writes a History of His Reading', *New Medieval Literatures*, 7 (2005), 53–71 at 71, we add BL, Cotton MS Titus A. xxiv (Part 2) but omit BL, Add. MS 28208. The latter contains Worcester's hand and is a codex but primarily consists of estate records. A full list of his documentary papers is a desideratum.

ten notes and others' texts and notes; largely grammar, classics, and history; contains items dated variously between 1462 and 1475 (here 'Julius').

- BL, Cotton MS Titus A. xxiv (Part 2): Worcester's handwritten notes; history and French literature; dated 1443–4 (here 'Titus').
- BL, Royal MS 13 C. i: mostly others' texts and notes, with some annotations by Worcester and some of Worcester's handwritten notes; largely history and French literature; contains items dated 1453 (here 'Royal').
- BL, Sloane MS 4: a mixture of others' texts and notes and Worcester's handwritten notes; largely medicine; contains items dated variously between 1460 and 1478.
- London, College of Arms, MS Arundel 48: mostly others' texts and notes, with some annotations and handwritten notes by Worcester; largely history, including recent military events, and documents; contains items variously datable at times after 1434, 1446, and 1450 (here 'Arundel').
- BodL, MS Laud misc. 674: Worcester's handwritten notes; astronomy; texts dated variously to April 1438 and to 1440, with additions in 1463.

Only the first has been printed, misleadingly as though it were a finished work,[189] but five of the others have long been recognized and cited as Worcester's collections.[190]

One notebook on this list, BL, Cotton MS Titus A. xxiv (Part 2), has not hitherto been recognized as Worcester's (and therefore needs a brief description). It consists of fifteen sheets of paper, all roughly 200 mm × 150 mm, all now mounted on conservators' guards, so of unclear original structure. They are bound as Part 2 with other unrelated manuscripts in a miscellany compiled in the Cotton library in the seventeenth century. Whether this sheaf of notes was intended as a self-standing quire, perhaps tacketed loosely, or as a booklet within a larger miscellany is not clear. The handwriting is unmistakable as Worcester's, especially on one more current and cramped page (f. 76^r). The handwriting is in places a little neater than that in some other notebooks; it resembles his red sidenotes, perhaps a neat 'display script', in the manuscript of

---

[189] In a nonetheless convenient edition, *Itineraries*, which we cite, but always checking the arrangement of the MS itself, as the edition rearranges the text.

[190] Sometimes it is not clear whether all of a miscellany's contents were in it when Worcester owned it. In such cases, the Explanatory Notes describe materials 'now in' Worcester's miscellanies.

The Boke of Noblesse, and is closest to the extended copying in his astronomical notebook, BodL, MS Laud misc. 674, dated to April 1438. This neatness might reflect the earlier period of his life, before increasing pressure of duties or decreasing sight, for one leaf is dated 1443 and another apparently 1444 (ff. 65^r, 67^r), though that second date is partly trimmed off. The notebook contains transcriptions and summaries from: a French translation of Marco Polo (f. 64^r); Josephus in Latin (f. 65^{r-v}); notes in French on the genealogies of the kings of Troy, Rome, and England taken from Brunetto Latini, *Li Livres dou tresor* (ff. 67^r–68^v); further notes in French on Trojan history (ff. 67^r–72^r, 73^{r-v}, seemingly disarranged); notes on Trojan, French and Norman history, and the origins of the Hundred Years War (ff. 73^v–78^v) taken from and ascribed, on f. 77^r, to *Les Grandes Chroniques de France*.

This notebook confirms features of Worcester's reading that led to *The Boke of Noblesse*. Three of the works are sources for *The Boke* (as the Explanatory Notes record), and that suggests how long-standing was Worcester's blend of interests in classical, French, and English history. In particular, it confirms that Worcester at some early date had access to *Les Grandes Chroniques de France*, a hitherto unrecognized source for much of *The Boke*.[191] The identification of this dated notebook shows that he knew *Les Grandes Chroniques* early enough to draft parts of *The Boke* in 1451 (as proposed above, p. lviii). He could have accessed the French works in Fastolf's Caister Castle in Norfolk, for *Les Grandes Chroniques*, Josephus, and French histories of the classical world often ascribed to Orosius are among the books listed in an inventory of Caister made in October 1448;[192] or he could have accessed them on trips to sort out Fastolf's business in Normandy in 1440 and again c.1441–2.

Throughout his life, Worcester had no shortage of reading material. He took notes from an array of books belonging to other people or institutions and often, helpfully for posterity, recorded whose books he was using, where and when.[193] From these notes one can identify over one hundred texts, as well as a dozen liturgical books or martyrologies, to which he had access, and over eighty people or institutions who gave him access. Moreover, beyond the newly identified notebook, his astro-

---

[191] See n. 200 below.

[192] OMA, FP 43, f. 10^r, printed as Gairdner, no. 389, and contextualized by Richard Beadle, 'Sir John Fastolf's French Books', in Graham D. Caie and Denis Renevey (eds.), *Medieval Texts in Context* (London, 2008), 96–112 at 99 (and see 1565nn. below).

[193] Wakelin, 'William Worcester Writes', traces his bibliographical and autobiographical impulses.

nomical notebook and his topographical notebook, Worcester's other miscellanies generally combine his own note-making with copies of complete, excerpted, or summarized works made by others. He evidently had frequent access to many copyists (including those who made *The Boke of Noblesse* and its Codicil). The density of allusion, quotation, and borrowing in *The Boke of Noblesse* reflects his bookish social network.

That impression of ready access to books is extended by some twenty-three books, beyond those he composed or revised, which Worcester annotated.[194] These come in three overlapping categories. Eight contain Worcester's name, usually recording that he owned, donated, or received them. Two of those and twelve further ones contain what David Rundle has identified as *cotes* or shelfmarks from an institutional library. Rundle argues convincingly that these books were gathered by Worcester to form a library for the college of learned priests that Fastolf wanted to establish at Caister in Norfolk, but this foundation was redirected to support Magdalen College in Oxford, where all bar one of these books with *cotes* now survives. Worcester obtained many or all of them in the 1460s after Fastolf's death, continuing until the early 1470s, when he marked them up before transfer to Waynflete.[195] Finally, thirteen books, some from these two categories and some without Worcester's name or cataloguing, contain further annotations by him. Some have just one or two notes, others many.

Gathering texts and information was part of Worcester's work for Fastolf; that day-to-day gathering might inspire the mode of composing *The Boke*—more than the scholastic literary model of *compilatio* perhaps—and some of the kind of information Fastolf sought appears in *The Boke*. Worcester and other members of the Fastolf and Paston

[194] For lists see Wakelin, 'William Worcester Writes', 71, extended by David Rundle, 'William Worcestre, Sir John Fastolf and Latin Learning', *The Library*, forthcoming (2024). We are grateful to David Rundle for allowing us to draw on his identification of further MSS handled by WW, in advance of the publication of those identifications. The editors of 'The Chronicle of John Somer, OFM', ed. Jeremy Catto and Linne Mooney, in *Camden Miscellany XXXIV: Chronology, Conquest and Conflict in Medieval England*, Camden Society 5th ser., 10 (Cambridge, 1997), 197–285 at 213–14, and N. R. Ker, A. J. Piper, and Andrew G. Watson, *Medieval Manuscripts in British Libraries*, 5 vols. (Oxford, 1969–2002), iv. 494–5, record WW's copying of a calendar in a Book of Hours now at St Peter's Church, Tiverton, which we have not seen. In addition, Catto and Mooney, 205, query whether an annotation to John Somer's chronicle in BL, Cotton MS Domitian A. ii, f. 1ʳ, might be by WW; it is. Also, on f. 4ʳ, WW added 'qui sepelitur apud haylys postea' to Richard of Cornwall (1209–72) and 'coronatur' to the date of Henry III's first coronation, and on f. 5ʳ added 'Petrus' to 'Gau'e'ston', 'Rex Anglie' to Edward III, and 'Gilbertus' to 'Comes Glouc'.   [195] Rundle, 'Worcestre'.

circles gathered historical documents such as pedigrees and records to support legal claims (e.g. 'many olde and mony record*es* writon by som Frenshman'),[196] and some of that fed into *The Boke*. They also gathered information about news ('As for nouueltés none couth, but yt ys seyd . . ', 'as to nouueltees . . .'), which could be useful for a landowner, such as Fastolf, with land to defend and alliances to mend; it could also be a subject of nervous or prurient curiosity, then as now.[197] This suggests that when *The Boke of Noblesse* covers events in the lifetime of Worcester or his associates, the information might come not from written sources but from hearsay, as in the many additions of information *as yt ys seyd* and so on (noted above, p. lxiii). A few other details of the wars in France cannot be corroborated from written sources and so might come from Fastolf's or others' memory. Most importantly, the Codicil that accompanied *The Boke of Noblesse* mostly consists of military records and diplomatic documents that can only have been gathered from networks including the original soldiers and political leaders. This practical and first-hand information fed directly into Worcester's other literary activity, notably the so-called *Basset's Chronicle* or *Soldiers' Chronicle* of the recent French wars, in whose composition he was involved somehow in 1459.[198] That chronicle, however, highlights the contrasting features of *The Boke*: the chronicle has a tone of triumphalism, perhaps to cheer the old soldier Fastolf in his decline, *The Boke* a tone of lament; the chronicle recounts fact, *The Boke* uses facts to form opinions.

The difference emerges because *The Boke of Noblesse* addresses its immediate political moment and the practical needs of that by drawing not only on recent English military experience but also on learned authorities. The first sets of authorities are chronicles in Latin and French on English history and the related Norman and French histories.[199] Worcester read Geoffrey of Monmouth, Ralph de Diceto, Ranulph Higden; more than one life of Henry V; *Les Grandes Chroniques de France* and Froissart's history; chronicles of Normandy; both belle-lettristic chronicles and collections of short 'annals' or mere lists of dates. He loves dates—though often gets them wrong. Sometimes the facts in *The Boke* could come from any of several sources, as their content is common, for instance, in general assertions about the Trojan

---

[196] e.g. *PL*, nos. 574, ll. 11–16, and 747, ll. 7–19.

[197] Quoting e.g. *PL*, nos. 572, ll. 39–54 and 883, ll. 25–31.

[198] *Basset's Chronicle*, f. 31ʳ (C&A, 181). On Worcester's contribution, see C&A, 30–8, and on personal testimony, see C&A, 49–50.

[199] A good overview is Allmand and Keen, 'History and the Literature of War'.

or Danish ancestors of the English, but also for details of particular wars or campaigns, where Worcester had access to, and took information from, several different chronicle accounts of the same events. At other times *The Boke* hews closely to *Les Grandes Chroniques*.[200] The choice was a surprising one by this point in the fifteenth century,[201] but the work's compendiousness seems to be what made it useful to Worcester.

Compendiousness is the keynote when Worcester blends recent English and French history with the histories of ancient Rome, Carthage, Greece, and the Holy Land, as though continuous or comparable, in the manner of 'universal history'. Some of the books that Worcester saw suggest the general taste for such universal history that pervades *The Boke*: Nicholas Trevet's French *Cronicles*, from which some details of *The Boke* might come, switch back and forth between each empire, offering a 'convergence of the national and the universal';[202] so does Wauchier de Denain's deceptively named *Histoire ancienne jusqu'à César*, from which Worcester took notes.[203] Honorius's Latin *Imago mundi*, which he saw, ends with a survey of biblical and Greek rulers conquering each other in sequence, including figures such as Rehoboam and Hannibal, named in *The Boke* from other texts.[204] A sense of history as one failed empire after another pervades too Giovanni Boccaccio's *De casibus virorum illustrium*, which Worcester owned.[205]

---

[200] See notes on 27–9, 211–14, 277–81, 286–399, 644–55, 693–704, 989–97, 1064–81, 1188–96, 2457–64, and perhaps 1287–94, 2417–20. Fastolf's ownership is recorded in OMA, FP 43, f. 10ʳ; Gairdner, no. 389, and explained by Beadle, 'Fastolf's French Books', 102. WW copied extracts of *GCF* in Titus, ff. 73ᵛ–78ʳ, and owned other sections in Arundel, ff. 159ʳ–167ʳ, 220ʳ⁻ᵛ. The version WW used is close to that printed by Viard, apart from some details, and some dates which correspond to those in the textual tradition printed as *Chroniques de France*, 3 vols. (Paris: Pasquier Bonhomme, 16 Jan. 1476/77), here abbrev. as *GCF-1476-7*: see 338–48n., 341–5n., 345n., 377–8n., 387—90n.

[201] On its readership then, see Anne D. Hedeman, *The Royal Image: Illustrations of the Grandes chroniques de France, 1274–1422* (Berkeley, 1991), 179–81.

[202] OMC, MS Lat. 45 (identified by Rundle, 'Worcestre'), as cited in notes on 250–3, 261–5, 644–50, 1279–86. Worcester took notes from this text in Julius, f. 39ʳ. On universal history, see Suzanne Conklin Akbari, 'Historiography: Nicholas Trevet's Transnational History', in Suzanne Conklin Akbari and James Simpson (eds.), *The Oxford Handbook of Chaucer* (Oxford, 2020), 368–85, quoting 369–70, and e.g. Emily Steiner, *John Trevisa's Information Age: Knowledge and the Pursuit of Literature, c.1400* (Oxford, 2021), 2, 5.

[203] See 1565n. For an edition, see *The Histoire ancienne jusqu'à César: A Digital Edition*, ed. Hannah Morcos and others (London, 2022) <http://www.tvof.ac.uk/textviewer/>, and for analysis of its circulation, see Jane Gilbert, Simon Gaunt and William Burgwinkle, *Medieval French Literary Culture Abroad* (Oxford, 2020), 122–93.

[204] OMC, MS Lat. 8, ff. 27ᵛ–33ʳ. Contrast 762–72n., 1787–9n. Other geography and history seen by WW included Solinus (OMC, MS Lat. 50, identified by Rundle, 'Worcestre') and Diodorus Siculus (Oxford, Balliol College, MS 124, ff. 151ʳ–242ᵛ).

[205] OMC, MS Lat. 198, with an ownership note on f. iiᵛ.

And other works copied or bound into his miscellanies and more of his own notes gather lists of rulers, realms, and their dates.[206] *The Boke of Noblesse* fits English history into this wider melancholic view of history.

Yet *The Boke* uses that history to offer lessons, often encapsulated in quotations from wise authorities. He is not alone in this: works translated for Fastolf by his stepson, Stephen Scrope, dispense many dicts and sayings of philosophers, and Worcester shared a liking for such *sententiae*; indeed, he revised one of Scrope's works in March 1473, just before revising *The Boke*.[207] A taste for sententious *auctores* is attested in books Worcester handled and in his own notes on dicta of the philosophers, at least one of which is quoted in *The Boke*.[208] For instance, he saw a copy of Seneca's letters that ended with pages of wise sayings, many broadly akin to exhortations in *The Boke* to learn from adverse fortune how to turn it to good, others expressing praise for old age, for instance, as Worcester does. His whole work could be summarized, for example, in one saying from this book: 'Calamitas . uirtutis occasio est'.[209] Vexingly, even with these riches, we have not identified sources for all the *sententiae* he cites, not least as the source is sometimes obscured by his English translation of it. However, similar ideas can be found in different wording, or ascribed to different authors, elsewhere in his notes or in books he knew. The ideas were widely shared, in sayings meant for sharing, and they give much of his work the authority of what might have seemed to his readers like common-sense wisdom. As he exhorted princes and military men to serve the common weal, such commonness was a virtue.

These experiential, historical, and sententious sources show up in many fifteenth-century English works, but two other kinds of source are notable for their prominence in Worcester's work. First, as well as dicta of dubious pedigree and histories from universal compendia, Worcester turns often to the classical texts from which such material had originally come. This engagement with classical sources is notable not as a complete novelty, for many writers do it a little; but he does it a lot, in a way that might reflect the influence of the *studia humanitatis* or so-called

---

[206] e.g. Arundel, ff. 22ʳ–30ᵛ, 33ʳ–42ʳ, 43ʳ–44ᵛ, 47ʳ–52ᵛ, 55ʳ–57ʳ, 69ʳ–82ᵛ, 86ʳ–93ʳ, 94ᵛ–95ᵛ, 99ʳ–109ᵛ, 112ʳ–119ʳ; Royal, ff. 147ʳ–151ʳ, 153ʳ–154ʳ, 155ʳ–170ᵛ.

[207] Scrope, *Dicts*, ed. Bühler, pp. xxi–xxiv, xxxvi–xlvi. For comparable topics, see 2048–58 (and n.).

[208] See 1763–4n. For other learned sayings, see e.g. Julius, ff. 47ʳ–48ᵛ, 74ʳ–91ᵛ, 115ʳ⁻ᵛ; OMC, MS Lat. 22 (see next n.).

[209] Quoting OMC, MS Lat. 22 (identified by Rundle, 'Worcestre'), f. 125ᵛ.

humanism. From the 1430s increasingly many patrons, scholars, and readers in England turned to ancient history and philosophy, as well as grammar, rhetoric, and poetry, with renewed zeal. Worcester was one of them in his reading, if not in his own Latin or handwriting. He collected classical books from others, including Greek texts, and read and took notes from many more Roman texts.[210] Some works might have inspired *The Boke of Noblesse* in vaguer ways: for instance, Worcester handled Cassiodorus' *Variae*, which, as letters to rulers, might have modelled his own rhetoric for addressing powerful men on matters of policy; and he saw some of Cicero's rhetorical works on the art of public persuasion.[211] In one copy of Cicero's works in a humanist hand, the scribe marks in red in the margins classical characters (e.g. Lucius Junius Brutus) or set-piece exclamations ('exclamatio' and similar) that are then used in *The Boke* and highlighted there by Worcester's own red and black sidenotes.[212] Such annotated humanist books might be one of Worcester's general models for his page design. Other works are invoked in *The Boke* directly: for example, Worcester saw Cicero's *De divinatione* in a copy in humanist script and then referred to it by name in *The Boke*; and most strikingly, from a copy in humanist script of Nonius Marcellus' *De Compendiosa doctrina*, Worcester annotated and then transcribed mostly excerpts of Cicero's lost *De republica*, which again he mentioned as a model in *The Boke*.[213] Both form and content of his treatise, then, reflect enthusiasm for the classics in his milieu.

Yet it is notable that in *The Boke of Noblesse* not all of the professed sources are genuinely classical, for Worcester drew many citations from second-hand intermediaries, sometimes John of Wales, but more often French translations from the classics. That is an index of the ongoing use of French books among the educated laity of fifteenth-century England, which others have traced,[214] but the fact that Worcester often claims or implies that he is reading the original suggests the declining prestige of French in favour of the Latin *studia humanitatis* as badges of sophistication in this period. Worcester draws in *The Boke* on Pierre Bersuire's French translation of Livy, cites Vegetius second-hand from Christine de Pizan's *Livre des faits d'armes*, and read and perhaps loosely recalled a compilation of classical history known as *Li Fet des*

---

[210] Wakelin, *Humanism*, 93–125, gives details.   [211] OMC, MS Lat. 166.

[212] e.g. OMC, MS Lat. 206, e.g. f. 4^r (Cicero, *De Oratore*, I. ix. 37), as in 2138–51 (see n.).

[213] Respectively, OMC, MS Lat. 62 (identified by Rundle, 'Worcestre'), on which see 1527–8n.; and OMC, MS Lat. 206, ff. 113^r–273^v, on which see 1732–6n.

[214] In particular, Julia Rice Mattison, 'Cest livre est a moy: French Books and Fifteenth-Century England' (PhD thesis, Toronto, 2021).

Romains.[215] In particular, he translated about a fifth of *The Boke* from Laurent de Premierfait's French translation of Cicero's *De senectute*, which he had separately translated in full by 1472 (as discussed above, pp. lx–lxi).[216] Many of these French works were owned by Fastolf, probably acquired from the French royal library by John, duke of Bedford, one of whose executors Fastolf was.[217] The copies in Fastolf's collection seldom survive, although other French books from the household do.[218] But some sense of them can be guessed from comparable copies with textual variants that must have recurred in copies Worcester saw or with other English owners. For instance, Fastolf's manuscript of Pierre Bersuire's Livy, a text Worcester used, was almost certainly illustrated, for most copies were.[219] The taste for these French versions of the classics was widespread in England, Burgundy, and France in this period: for instance, the dauphin Louis de Guyenne (1397–1415) was advised to read Bersuire's Livy, *Les Grandes Chroniques de France* and Boethius, all invoked by Worcester.[220]

Yet Worcester also read French literature beyond translations, notably the works of Christine de Pizan and Alain Chartier. Both were popular among English, as among French and Burgundian, patrons, found in the same libraries or even in miscellanies alongside copies of other of Worcester's sources. Among Christine de Pizan's many works read and translated in England, her *Epître d'Othéa à Hector* was owned by Fastolf in a deluxe copy and translated by Scrope.[221] *The Boke of Noblesse* directly translates parts of Christine's *Le Livre des faits*

---

[215] See respectively 769n., 1622–65n., and 2515–71n. (Livy); 850–5n. (Vegetius); and 1670–85n. and 2273–9n. (*Li Fet*). Vegetius is also cited from John of Wales: see 614–24n.

[216] See 1803–11n. to 2138–51n. This seems to be the trans. ed. by Susebach (*Tulle*), originally printed as *Tullius de senectute* (Westminster: William Caxton, 1481; *STC* 5293), though differences between *BkNob.* and *Tulle* would merit full analysis.

[217] Beadle, 'Fastolf's French Books'.

[218] For other French books owned by Fastolf or Worcester, see e.g. BodL, MS Laud misc. 570, and CUL, MS Add. 7870, on which see Wakelin, *Humanism*, 103; Catherine Nall, 'Ricardus Franciscus Writes for William Worcester', *Journal of the Early Book Society*, 11 (2008), 207–16; Mattison, 'Cest livre est a moy', 200–1; and BodL, MS Bodley 179, analysed by Mattison, 'Cest livre est a moy', 105–6 and nn. 18 and 51 above.

[219] See 1622–65n., and on illustrated MSS see Jessica Berenbeim, 'The Past of the Past: Historical Distance and the Medieval Image', *New Medieval Literatures*, 21 (2021), 191–220 at 206–7.

[220] Berenbeim, 'The Past of the Past', 204–5. She also notes French and Burgundian nobility who owned Bersuire's translation alongside *GCF*.

[221] Respectively BodL, MS Laud misc. 570 and Scrope, *Epistle*, ed. Bühler. From the large literature on Christine's English reception, see most recently Misty Schieberle, *Feminized Counsel and the Literature of Advice in England, 1380–1500* (Turnhout, 2014), 139–92.

THE SOURCES lxxix

d'armes.[222] Alain Chartier's *Le Livre de l'espérance* and *Le Quadrilogue invectif* were translated and read in England.[223] Worcester annotated a set of extracts and summaries of these two works of Chartier,[224] and although Chartier was a direct source for only a few passages of *The Boke*, in his sidenotes Worcester points out where Chartier's works corroborated the statements and sentiments of *The Boke*.[225] But it is possible to speculate that, in a more substantial way, Worcester's encounter with Chartier's works might have influenced his transformation of his 1451 draft of *The Boke of Noblesse* from something practical and parochial into something more imaginative and erudite (as argued above, p. lx) in its classical exempla, philosophical concepts, and heightened rhetorical address, such as his use of *prosopopoeia*.[226] It is this use, combination, and range of sources that makes *The Boke of Noblesse* a work of not only military, but literary, ambition.

THE STYLE

French and Latin writing offered looser models for Worcester's style too. The most distinctive feature of his style is his use of elaborate chains of clauses, extended in length, each dependent on another, yet with ambiguous or loose connections. This style reflects the influence both of administrative 'curial' prose and to a lesser extent of Latin periodic style. The curial style came from documents in French and Latin—

---

[222] See 151–85, 762–807, 850–5, 1666–700, and nn.

[223] Blayney, ii. 1–4; Catherine Nall, 'William Worcester Reads Alain Chartier: *Le Quadrilogue Invectif* and its English Readers', in Emma Cayley and Ashby Kinch (eds.), *Chartier in Europe* (Cambridge, 2008), 135–47.

[224] WW annotated another scribe's extracts from *Le Quadrilogue invectif*, in Royal, ff. 136ʳ–138ᵛ (ed. Bouchet, the 1st being 5, ll. 10–12, the last 82, l. 20–83, l. 6), and from *Le Livre de l'espérance* (ed. Rouy, the 1st being Pr. II. 142–52, the last Pr. XIV. 24–175), in Royal, ff. 134ʳˑᵛ, 138ᵛ–141ʳ (where f. 134ʳˑᵛ should come after f. 140ᵛ). Although the extracts abridge and alter, those from *Le Livre de l'espérance* are textually close to BL, Cotton MS Julius E. v, even in glosses, orthography, and capitalization. That MS is in textual branch *i* of *Le Livre de l'espérance* (see Rouy, pp. cxxv–cxxvi), along with BnF, MS fr. 126, a MS that also includes de Premierfait's translation of *De senectute* (described in ed. Rouy, pp. xvi, xxi, xxiv, xxxvii), which WW also knew. WW's annotations of extracts of Chartier refer to events of 1450, an earliest possible date for his reading (see Royal, f. 138ᵛ, in n. 133 above).

[225] See borrowings at 732–8n., 1576–83n., 2503–8n., 2509–14n. and perhaps 2273–9n. and 2417–20n.; and contrast sidenotes at 750SN, 759SN, 799SN, 976SN, discussed in 750–2n., 752–6n., 762–72n., 799–807n., 972–80n., 2413–16n.

[226] See Catherine Nall, 'Moving to War: Rhetoric and Emotion in William Worcester's *Boke of Noblesse*', in Stephanie Downes, Andrew Lynch, and Katrina O'Loughlin (eds.), *Emotions and War: Medieval to Romantic Literature* (London, 2015), 117–32 at 120.

letters, petitions, records—that then fed into literary French and into documentary and literary writing in English as well. The style offered, as J. D. Burnley defined it, 'precision in reference and ceremony of tone', though as Burnley noted there was over time a 'tendency towards elaboration at the expense of clarity'.[227] That seems a fair characterization of Worcester's style, with some attempts at precision, some at grandiloquence, and some at the expense of clarity. Burnley felt that the curial style had little effect on literary, as opposed to technical, prose in fifteenth-century English, but *The Boke of Noblesse*, written by someone alongside his day job as secretary, does show its influence.[228]

The concern with precision in reference helps to explain one of Worcester's stylistic tics. He is notably fond of phrases in apposition, glossing one phrase by another. Co-ordinative apposition with *and* or *or* is common in legal or expository prose, where it clarifies the referent (and is also a rhetorical trick, *correctio*).[229] And synonymic apposition without an explicit co-ordinator is typical of 'informational written registers', where it is marked in speech by intonation, in print by commas (or parentheses): consider *Charles* [rising intonation; pause] *king of France* [falling intonation; pause] *rode into battle* or *Charles, king of France, rode into battle*.[230] This often occurs where proper nouns are followed by other noun-phrases which serve as descriptive epithets, a syntactical pattern still common in English. This can require untangling when these appositional phrases pile up: for instance, in the phrase *Iohn, duc of Bedfor[d], the erle of Marche, your moste noble antecessour, accompanyed wyth many othyr nobles wyth a puissaunt armee of shyppis, fought* (435–7), the subject of the verb is plural, two people, (i) *Iohn* who was *duc of Bedfor[d]* and also (ii) *the erle of Marche* who is the addressee's *moste noble antecessour* (see 436n.). With customary epithets apposition is less confusing, but this continual provision of

[227] J. D. Burnley, 'Curial Prose in England', *Speculum*, 61 (1986), 593–614 at 595–6. By contrast, John H. Fisher, 'Chancery and the Emergence of Standard Written English in the Fifteenth Century', *Speculum*, 52 (1977), 870–99 at 886–7, found control and clarity in hypotactic bureaucratic prose modelled on French.

[228] Cf. Burnley, 'Curial Prose', 611, 613.

[229] Päivi Pahta and Saara Nevanlinna, 'Re-phrasing Early English: The Use of Expository Apposition with an Explicit Marker from 1350 to 1710', in Matti Rissanen, Merja Kytö, and Kirsi Heikkonen (eds.), *English in Transition: Corpus-based Studies in Linguistic Variation and Genre Styles* (Berlin, 1997), 121–83 at 147–8.

[230] Quoting Douglas Biber and Bethany Gray, 'Grammatical Change in the Noun Phrase: The Influence of Written Language Use', *English Language and Linguistics*, 15 (2011) 223–50 at 233. On intonation and punctuation, see Saara Nevanlinna and Päivi Pahta, 'Middle English Nonrestrictive Expository Apposition with an Explicit Marker', in Jacek Fisiak (ed.), *Studies in Middle English Linguistics* (Berlin, 1997), 373–402 at 374.

supplementary information can make Worcester's sentences congested, as in this account of the Third Crusade:

King Richarde the First, clepid Cuer de Lion, whiche in a croiserie went into the Holy Londe, and Baldewyn, archebisshop of Caunterburie, Hubert, bisshop of Salisburie, Randolf, the erle of Chestre, Roberd Clare, erle of Gloucestre, and werreied vppon the hethen paynemys in the companie of King Phelip Dieudonne of Fraunce, whiche King Richard conquerid and wanne by roiall power vppon the Sarrasyns (270–7)

Some customary epithets (*the erle of . . .*) and relative clauses (*whiche in a croiserie . . .*) cause no problems, but there are so many names and epithets that they need disentangling, and the effect is confused by a later *whiche* clause (*whiche King Richard conquerid . . .*) that is not describing the just-mentioned Philippe Dieudonné but is a delayed gloss on Richard. The effect is exacerbated because, like other fifteenth-century scribes of English, the scribe of *The Boke* does not have a consistent punctuation for lists. (Our edition, therefore, requires the heavy use of commas and sometimes semicolons in long lists of names with extra epithets: e.g. 375–86.) The phenomenon makes sense in bureaucratic and legal prose of a 'curial' kind as a quest for ever more information and precision of reference, which, conversely, makes clauses harder to parse, referents harder to disentangle.

There is also a subset of cases that could be apposition of a clarifying, even emphatic, kind, but which could be error. (This feature presents temptations for the editor to emend, challenges for the reader to parse, and so needs explanation.) This is the occurrence of two or three verbs or common nouns in apposition without any co-ordinating conjunction. Other appositions are less staccato as they include accompanying function words (e.g. *of here spiritis, of egre courages* 95–6, *as the gouernoure, the maister, auisithe hem* 1776), but in *The Boke* this also happens with two or three common nouns on their own:

reaume, dukedoms 23
piteous complaintes, dolorous lamentacions 57–8
iustice, title 221
quantite of, mesure of 770
finaunce, 'wagyngys' 871 (one word added by Worcester)
defalking, abbregging 908
pilleris, robberis, extorcioneris 928 < Fr. 'Robeurs et pillars'
nouches, ringis 940
sacrement, othes, promisses 1180–1

> *armurs, wepyns* 2070 (within an addition by Worcester)
> *bribe, rewarde* 2181
> *obeissaunce, `lawes'* 2224 (one word added by Worcester)
> *senatours, counceilours* 2569 < Fr. 'li consul'

And it happens with verbs:

> *vapour, sprede out* 104–5
> *apparteine, be meinteined vnder* 173–4
> *meoued, excited* 220
> *fought, `beseged'* 835–6 (one word added by Worcester)
> *leiethe . . . rehersithe* 1671, 1673
> *manassed, beten* 2211

It could simply be that the scribe omits the words *and* or *or* at such points; Worcester does favour doublets, and scribes often omit small function words; but it seems implausible that the scribe should err so often in this one way. It could also be that Worcester erred by shifting his construction part way through: for example, in the list *to take no bribe, rewarde, or defalke the kingis wagis* (2180–1), the first two items sound like the start of a rhetorical tricolon of objects for the verb *take*, requiring a third noun, say, *bribe, rewarde* and perhaps *defalcacion*, as in another list a few lines previously (*bribe, defalcacion or abreggement* 2173), but the third item shifts to a verb *defalke* with a direct object. The apparent asyndeton in *bribe, rewarde* could be a feature of style that has misfired.

But other examples suggest they are a deliberate feature of style. In three appositional pairs (*fought, `beseged'; finaunce, `wagyngys'; obeissaunce, `lawes'*) Worcester added the second word in his own handwriting, so they seem to reflect authorial intention. They could still be errors as incomplete revisions, forgetting to supply a conjunction, or to delete a word he was replacing. If that were so, other examples might have been similar incomplete revisions by Worcester in a now lost exemplar that the scribe has reproduced faithfully. (That would invite emendation, though it would be difficult to decide whether Worcester's intention were to form a doublet with a forgotten conjunction or to replace one half of the appositional pair with the other.) But these words in apposition sometimes balance a more Latinate or French-derived word with a plainer one. Such glossing was a common use for apposition.[231]

---

[231] Nevanlinna and Pahta, 'Middle English Nonrestrictive Expository Apposition', 379–80.

For instance, *lawes* glosses French-derived *obeissaunce* and creates a stylish parallel between this non-finite clause and the next one, which also ends with *lawes* (cf. *lyuyng vnder youre obeissaunce, 'lawes'* and *youyng and yelding to youre lawes*, 2224–5). They also bring lexical variety and with it persuasive force, a recognized aspiration of rhetorical instruction.[232] That might be the goal of the appositive tricolon *pilleris, robberis, extorcioneris* (928) rebuking the pursuit of war booty, or of *any sacrement, othes, promisses, made by youre aduersarie* (1180–1) piling up in condemnation the vows the enemy has broken. In addition, some pairs bring greater precision: for instance, *beseged* is more accurate than *fought* for what John, duke of Somerset, did to Harfleur in 1440 (835–6), *wagyngys* more specific than *finaunce* (871). These nouns or verbs in apposition clarify the meaning, the reference, of the words, which is one goal of curial prose.

Related to this clarification of referent is Worcester's fondness for the term *the said X*, and related variants *your said X* and so on. *The said*, in various spellings, occurs some 240 times; *said* after *your* or *his* thirty-one times; and *(be)foresaid* seven times: in total, about once every hundred words. Indeed, Worcester thrice adds the adjective *seyd* clarifying a noun as something already mentioned (='aforesaid', 554, 812, 1337). This is wordy but adds clarity. Less clear is the desire to tie clauses together with subordinating conjunctions. These words—*which, that*—are often ambiguous and pleonastic in this period in general,[233] and so they prove in Worcester's prose. Here *which* connects clauses not strictly with a noun as referent, but more loosely with a sense little stronger than 'and also' (e.g. 508, 1344–5). Sometimes, *which* does work as a subordinating conjunction, but the chain of clauses becomes so long so that it is more comprehensible to the twenty-first-century reader to intrude a full stop (e.g. 1118, 1481, 1505, 1858). Likewise, what seems like a needless or pleonastic use of subordinating *that* is a marker of learned style—as it has been shown to be in medical texts, where it is commoner in translations than in practical remedies.[234] Each clause has a precise reference, and one is glossed somehow by another, but the syntactical links between them

[232] For an example in WW's letters, ending one on a resounding note, see *PL*, no. 1046, l. 154: 'aftyr my grete labours troubles' (as clearly written without revision in OMA, FP 96).

[233] Olga Fischer, *The Syntax of Early English* (Cambridge, 2000), 101–3.

[234] Javier Calle Martín, '"When that Wounds Are Evil Healed": Revisiting Pleonastic *That* in Early English Medical Writing', *Studia Anglistica Posnaniensia*, 52 (2017), 5–20 at 13.

are loose. The provision of more information is more important than the connection between pieces of information, in a way that Burnley identified as typical of curial prose.[235]

Curial prose does have one stylistic benefit, though: orotundity. A 'ceremony of tone' (as Burnley put it) required the stretching of syntactical chains to a size that befits the occasion. This is the other distinctive feature of Worcester's prose. Any page will reveal how Worcester, with several parenthetical phrases, which might include several subclauses, interrupts or supplements the main clause; which subclauses, with whatever delay, are themselves extended by further clauses, often not expanded into finite verb clauses but condensed into non-finite participial clauses, phrases in grammatical apposition, synonyms, some with uncertain subjects or objects or their relationship difficult to infer; which, extending over many lines, can be difficult for readers to follow, so that it is fair to say that Worcester often overreaches, seeming to forget how these lengthy sentences started, until he, by the end of these long sentences, loses control, repeating or omitting key parts of speech, or which have uncertain referents. Such syntax, marked by anacoluthon and pleonasm, might reflect speech,[236] and the loose links are less confusing when one reads aloud, quickly, or for gist.[237] (Editors might be tempted, as Phillipa Hardman has proposed for John Lydgate's verse, not to punctuate.)[238]

This bureaucratic style is supplemented by another model, albeit one not imitated exactly: florid rhetoric in Latin and the Latin periodic sentence familiar from Cicero. Worcester's notebooks show him transcribing or taking notes from various works on Latin grammar and rhetoric, and he at some point had access to an extensive commentary on Cicero's *Rhetorica ad Herennium* and to other of Cicero's rhetorical works.[239] Among them were Cicero's *Orator*, which set out how in epideictic rhetoric—like the praise and blame of which *The Boke of Noblesse* consists—one should write 'in that style of encircling reach, so that the speech might run as though enclosed in an orb, because it stops

[235] Burnley, 'Curial Prose', 596–7.   [236] Fischer, *Syntax of Early English*, 90.

[237] For this point, see e.g. Cristina Suárez-Gómez, 'Clause Linkage across Time and Genres in Early English: A Preliminary Approach to Relative Clauses', *Studia Neophilologica*, 84 (2012), 138–50 at 139.

[238] Phillipa Hardman, 'Lydgate's "Uneasy" Syntax', in Larry Scanlon and James Simpson (eds.), *John Lydgate: Poetry, Culture, and Lancastrian England* (Notre Dame, IN, 2007), 12–35.

[239] e.g. Julius, ff. 48ᵛ, 67ʳ–68ᵛ, 71ʳ–73ʳ, 97ᵛ (notes on Cicero); OMC, MS Lat. 82 (identified by Rundle, 'Worcestre'), f. iiᵛ (see 736–40n.).

with the single phrases complete and perfect' ('more illa circumscrip-
tione ambituque ut tanquam in orbe inclusa currat oratio quod insistat
in singulis perfectis absolutisque sentencijs').[240] Some of Worcester's
letters have a periodic style of balance and contrast, circular move-
ments, patterning of sound.[241] The origins of the style are evident in *The
Boke of Noblesse* when Worcester uses it for a quotation from St Jerome:
'*If we haue not*', seiethe he, '*know God in welthe and prosperite, then at
the leest let vs know hym in oure aduersite*' (2296–8). The patterning was
also a feature of *sententiae* that Worcester read or transcribed.[242]

Worcester uses such patterning often, as here, to create a neat complement, contrast, or connection. It happens on a small scale in doublets
(*hors-mete and mannys mete* 899), but also on a large scale in pairs
of balancing but contrasting clauses (*mysfortune among vs here and
priuacion of . . . contreis ther* 1562–3), which exploit the length of his
sentences to good effect. The parallels can be created by repeating single
words, perhaps in slightly different senses (*turned* in *turned to the gret
vndoing . . . that they haue turned theire hertis frome vs* 2186–8), or
by constructions with more abstract parallels. For instance, this phrase
seems loose of construction: *ye in youre hertis may bring to mynde and
remember the vengeaunce of hard offensis to this roiaume shewed, and to
the recuuere of the worship of the roiaume late lost* (2472–4). But the pattern repeated is: prepositional phrase (*in youre, to the*)+word starting
re- involving restoration (*remembre, recuuere*)+noun phrase including
roiaume+passive participle (*shewed, lost*). There is evidence that this
stylistic tic is deliberate when Worcester strengthens one parallelism by
adding extra words *shall be* into each clause: *that ʻshall beʼ men of soude
and of armes, as well tho that ʻshallʼ be vndre youre lieutenauntis . . . may
be duely paide* (2168–70). Worcester does not handle it well: in his first
that ʻshall beʼ men his elliptical *that* without *tho* (meaning 'those who')
obscures the parallel with the second *tho that ʻshallʼ be*. But extended
parallelism seems to be the intention, even if it falls short in execution.

Worcester also turns to rhetorical figures favoured by Latin treatises
for a very specific goal of 'the arousal of specific emotions'.[243] One of
Worcester's favoured rhetorical tricks is exclamation or *apostrophe*,
often beginning with an interjection *Heʻhʼ, He, A* or *allas* (1241, 1281,

---

[240] OMC, MS Lat. 206, f. 97ʳ (Cicero, *Orator*, 207).

[241] e.g. *PL*, no. 506, ll. 1–5, no. 558, ll. 20–1, no. 1046.

[242] e.g. a set of sayings after Seneca's letters in OMC, MS Lat. 22 (identified by Rundle,
'Worcestre'), e.g. f. 128ᵛ, 'Bona mors est; uitę quę extinguit mala', or f. 131ᵛ, 'Malus est
uocandus; qui sua causa est bonus'.   [243] Nall, 'Moving to War', 118–20.

1410, 1492, 2223, 2273, 2487). Such *exclamatio* is highlighted by
Worcester's sidenotes in *The Boke*, as it is by a scribal annotation in
a manuscript of Cicero's rhetorical works that he handled.[244] Moving
speeches are also a staple of classical histories, such as Livy's; *The Boke*
translates one of Livy's speeches from a French intermediary version
(e.g. 2539–53). Another model might have been rhetorically elaborate
laments in the Vulgate, whence other English writing of this period
borrows such exclamations, such as the *dolorous lamentacions vpon the
prophesie of Iooell* (2295–8).[245] Worcester uses these exclamations to
express his own or elicit his readers' emotional responses to England's
woes, as here:

He, allas! We dolorous parsones suffring intollerabill persecucions and miserie,
as well in honoure lost as in youre lyuelode there vnrecompensid as in oure
meueable goodes bereued! What shalle we doo or say? Shalle we in this doloure, anguisshe and heuynesse contynew long thus? Nay, nay! God defend that
suche intrusions, grete wrongis and tiranye shuld be left vnpunisshed, and so
gret a losse vnpunysshed and not repared! (1492–8)[246]

Such emotional excesses suggest that Worcester, though he often
muddled his language, had attempted to fit it for rhetorical purposes. He borrowed from Latin prose some features of an emotionally
persuasive style to complement his curial prose.

He also borrows from Latin prose two kinds of compressed syntax
typical of that language. The first is a tendency to echo the Latin ablative absolute: a noun phrase modified by passive or past participles of the
verb of which it would be the object, were there a full finite clause; they
condense a subordinate idea into few words. This construction becomes
more common in the late 1300s as English prose imitates Latin, for
instance, in the Wycliffite versions of the Vulgate, and is common in
the 1400s, notably in the Paston letters.[247] These phrases explain what
has already happened while or before the main action and main verb of
an adjacent clause. So in the lines *Prince Edwarde . . . had the bataile . . .
ayenst the Bastarde Henry . . . and, hym descomfit, voided the feelde*, the

[244] OMC, MS Lat. 206, f. 98ᵛ ('pulchra exclamatio' on Cicero, *Orator*, 225), and cf.
WW's sidenotes at e.g. 226SN, 1241SN, 1454SN, 1492SN, 2200SN, 2223SN, 2400SN.

[245] On interjections as echoes of the Vulgate, see Irma Taavitsainen, 'Exclamations in
Late Middle English', in Jacek Fisiak (ed.), *Studies in Middle English Linguistics* (Berlin,
1997), 573–608 at 589, 601.

[246] For other exclamations and rhetorical questions, see e.g. 759, 1241–5, 1410, 2223–
32, 2487–92.

[247] Tauno F. Mustanoja, *A Middle English Syntax: Part I, Parts of Speech* (Helsinki,
1960), 114–17.

phrase *hym descomfit* refers to Enrique de Trastámara who has been defeated before his opponent, Edward the Black Prince, *voided the feelde* (400–4). Or in the lines *the armee taried . . . almost a quarter of a yere . . . and the cite of Burdeux lost in the meanetyme*, the phrase *the cite of Burdeux lost* describes what happened while the army tarried in England (1273–5). The absolute clause can modify the object of the main verb, but it can also modify the subject: St Louis, for example, *suffrethe* in various ways, for instance, *he and his knightis ouerthrow and take prisoneris*, or having been overthrown and taken prisoner (1287–91). Sometimes the subject and object of Worcester's absolute phrases are unclear: in *good corage and comfort taken to theyme, they were made conquerours*, it is unclear whether *they*, the Maccabees, had *good corage* 'given' to them by God, in an old sense of *taken*, or they 'took it to themselves' (i.e. *theyme*, the unemphatic relative pronoun), before *they were made conquerours* (1284–5).[248] Perhaps the exact sense is less important than the general provision of more information in a compact, compendious form.

Comparable is a feature that Norman Davis noted as one of the verbal tics in Worcester's letters: giving a verbal noun or gerund after its object noun, a construction much commoner in earlier centuries than in the fifteenth.[249] This habit might also be a faint echo of some dense Latin construction with a gerund. It occurs about twenty times in *The Boke of Noblesse*:

sieges keping 362
sieg(e/i)s l(ie/ey)eng 425, 462, 1231, 1368
batailes yeueng 457
othe-making 1142
trewes-taking 1185
trewes-keping 1243
iustice-keping 1328, 1621, 2159 (but see n.)
corage gyuyng 1408
werre-making 155, 1645
counceile-yeuyng 1924
prouidence vsing 1977
rentis-paieng 2217
armes lernyng 2306–7

---

[248] This is exacerbated by the multiple senses of the verb: see *MED, taken, v.*, e.g. 9a.(a), 31a.(a).

[249] Davis, 'Epistolary', 261–2, citing comparanda from Mustanoja, *Syntax*, 574–5; e.g. *PL*, no. 540, l. 10.

courtis-halding 2348
shiris-halding 2349
practik vsing 2370

It also occurs in one of the English texts in the Codicil, which might suggest Worcester's authorship of that text.[250] The frequency of such constructions in Worcester's writing is a personal tic, but it is of a piece with his tendency to use condensed constructions akin to Latin. (This edition hyphenates only those hyphenated by *The Oxford English Dictionary*, because they have become widely established collocations,[251] or those treated in the syntax of *The Boke of Noblesse* as single nouns.)

THE LANGUAGE

Worcester's reading in French and to a lesser extent Latin shapes some other aspects of his language. In his lexis, his borrowings from Latin are not numerous, though there are some: he uses half a dozen words with roots in Latin for the first recorded time, notably four adverbs (e.g. *aduersarily* 1532, *dispositiflie* 1542, *vulgarilie* 1692, *accustumablie* 2162: see nn.),[252] and half a dozen other Latinate words in specific senses not recorded earlier (e.g. *consules* 1761, *caus(e/i)s naturell* 1815, 1831, *principales* 1827–8, *importunyte* 2444: see nn.).[253] But he is not fond of Latin 'inkhorn' terms, unlike some other authors of the 1400s and 1500s. Rather, he enriches his diction with vocabulary from French, both directly drawn from his sources and from a knowledge of the language in general. This is at once the most striking feature of his diction, and also something shared with other English prose of the late 1400s. French was the language of much polite and educated reading, and of many sources Worcester read. The Explanatory Notes identify several words or specific senses of words that lexicographers have only hitherto

[250] See *appointement breking* C4/19–20, *iustice-keping* C4/37.
[251] Cf. e.g. *trewes-taking* 1185, hyphenated as in *OED*, *truce*, *n.*, and in *MED*, *treu(e, n.*(1), but also *trewes-keping* 1243 hyphenated only by analogy.
[252] One of his letters is also the first cited user of another Latinate adverb which recurs in *BkNob.*, *MED*, *notorili, adv.*: see 90n. For other first citations, see also *defalcacion* 2173 and *coherted* 1160n., 2078–9n., the latter discussed by Davis, 'Epistolary', 263.
[253] Davis, 'Epistolary', 263–6, identifies first citations or antedatings in Worcester's letters, but the completion of *MED* and revision of *OED* have removed some. For other first citations of words or particular uses not from Lat. or Fr., see nn. on e.g. *meo'u'ed* 1648, *falle* 2003, *mildewis* 2051, *bere out* 2348, *bobauncees* 2419 and the coinage from a formerly Fr.-derived v. *wele-defensid* 1134.

recorded in English first in *The Boke of Noblesse* or in some cases later and that might be modelled on cognate words or senses in French.[254]

On some occasions, Worcester uses these words or senses for the first time in passages with identifiable French sources, so that they seem like clear borrowings—in effect, calques. For instance, in the lengthy section adapted from Laurent de Premierfait's French version of Cicero's *De senectute*, half a dozen words and senses are recorded in English for the first time and come from de Premierfait's French, in some cases with errors.[255] Two adjectives thus calqued (*terrien, mondeyn*) even appear postposed, after the noun, as they would in French (as do other adjectives noted below).

The French borrowings are, though, more extensive and more varied in origin than these from translation. First, even in passages with a French source, some apparently new French-derived words or senses are not attested in the immediate source;[256] they show, instead, how saturated by the French language was military, political, and philosophical prose in English. Second, while the limits of lexicography must not suggest that these words or senses were definitely new, conversely nor must dictionaries dismiss the possibility that words recorded in writing somewhere else before *The Boke of Noblesse* might nonetheless have been unknown to Worcester except as French words and have felt to him or to his readers like novelties.[257] This might have been the effect for him of words that, although not used here in English for the first time, were taken directly from the source. For instance, in one passage of about 125 words translated from Christine de Pizan's *Livre des faits d'armes et de chevalerie*, about nineteen words are close equivalents to those in the French. Though Worcester could have encountered all of them in English somewhere, his particular choice of them is closely guided by Christine's use.[258] He sometimes alters the syntax and so uses

---

[254] See nn. on *preferryng* 3, *reual(e/i)d* 64, 230, *cote-armes* 506, `liures' turneis* 948, *complisses* 1187, *conduit* 1897, *entreprennoure* 1939, *patised* 2219, *archedenes* 2257, *aduertisementis* 2391, *employ* 2484.

[255] See nn. on e.g. *angures* 1814 < misreading Fr. 'augure'; *desert* 1898 < mistranslating Fr. 'desertés'; *folehardiesse* 1910–11 < Fr. 'folle hardiesse'; *viellars* 1936 < Fr. 'vieillars'; *terrien* 2096 < Fr. 'terrienne'; *mondeyn(e)* 2117, 2121 < Fr. 'mondaine'; *beneurte* 2121 < Fr. 'bieneurté'.

[256] e.g. in the passage largely taken from de Premierfait, e.g. *conduit* 1897, *entreprennoure* 1939, *charged* 1951, *labouragis* 1986 (but cf. < Fr. 'laboureur'), *approwementis* 1986, *frank and quite* 1996, *ale`y'ed* 2107.

[257] e.g. *desteined* 230, *seneschalcie* 1145, *Highe Fraunce* 1590, *vaillauntnesse* 1309.

[258] In 166–76 from Christine, *Livre des faits d'armes*, I. 4 (BL, Royal MS 15 E. vi, f. 406ʳ; Laennec, ii. 26), see *principall* < 'principaulx' (both as postposed adj.), *vallente* <

a different part of speech in English from that in the French (e.g. the noun 'vengence' becomes *to be venged*), but even then he uses cognate words that evoke the vocabulary of the source.

As well as this Frenchified lexis, on occasion Worcester imports French word-order and even inflections. In particular, several adjectives derived from French, especially from French translations of classical sources, are placed after their nouns as they would be in French. As Norman Davis observed, it is a habit in his correspondence too, most common in certain set phrases.[259] The noun-adjective order was a possibility in English of this period under certain conditions, one of them being that the adjective was a 'learned' one derived from French.[260] Sure enough, in *The Boke of Noblesse* it occurs in phrases derived from French or (where signalled below) from Worcester's immediate French sources:[261]

> *causes principall* 166 < Fr. 'mouuemens principaulx'
> *cos(i/y)ns-germa(i/y)ns* 377 < Fr. 'cousins germains', and repeated at 1325, 1392
> *knightis banerettis* 382 < Fr. 'chevaliers bannerez'
> *subgettis obeisauntes* 541
> *payne resonable* 914
> *men of armes cheualerous* 929 < Fr. 'hommes darmes et cheualereux'
> *seigniourie terrien* 2096 < Fr. 'seignorie terrienne'
> *ricchesse roiall* 2103
> *felicite / beneurte mondeyn(e)* 2117, 2121 < Fr. 'felicité mondaine', 'bieneurté mondaine'
> *noblesse roiall* 2118
> *tymes oportune* 2119
> *officers roiall* 2179, 2252

'volente', *susteyne* < 'soustenir', *iustice* < 'Iustice', *defoule, grief and oppresse* < 'fouler greuer et oppresser', *contre* < 'contree', *recuuer* < 'recouurer', *seignories* < 'seignouries', *rauisshed* < 'ravies', *vsurped* < 'vsurpees', *prince* < 'prince', *subgett`ys' shuld apparteine* < 'subgettz deussent appartenir', *to be venged* < 'vengence', *grief* < 'grief', *conquere* < 'conquerir', *strange* < 'estranges'.

[259] Davis, 'Epistolary', 262; e.g. *PL*, no. 540, l. 3.

[260] Olga Fischer, 'Syntax', in Norman Blake (ed.), *The Cambridge History of the English Language*, ii: *1066–1476* (Cambridge, 1992), 207–408 at 214; Fischer, *The Syntax of Early English*, 80.

[261] By contrast, *pease finall* 397 and *caus(e/i)s naturell* 1815, 1831 evoke common phrases in Lat. (see nn.). But *naturell* is also found in Fr., which might be echoed here with ⟨e⟩ rather than ⟨a⟩ in the final syllable. See *OED*, *natural, adj.* and *adv.*, headnote on etymology.

seruice honourable 2322
goodis meueable 2521

The postposing of adjectives recurs in some of these and other phrases in the Codicil too.[262] The influence of French is suggested by two postposed adjectives that are also inflected with ⟨s⟩ in the plural, as would be common in that language (*banerettis, obeisauntes*).[263] This was an occasional sign of the influence of French in fifteenth-century English.[264] That combination of postposing and, where relevant, plural ⟨s⟩ happens frequently on one further word: on all bar one use of *Romayn(e)* as an adjective postposed after nouns referring to people, *citesyn/citezin, consul(l), nobles, prince(s),* or *senatour(s).*[265] However, when the same adjective modifies the non-human nouns *batailes/batellis, contreis, (h)o(o)st(e/es/is), lawes,* and *stories* it is placed before the noun and not inflected with ⟨s⟩.[266] Similar inconsistency occurs with *roiall, finall,* and *obeisauntes,* which recur elsewhere preceding the noun.[267] Rather than a grammatical rule, this seems like a stylistic affectation of Francophone flavour.

Beyond the curial syntax and some French lexis, Worcester's language is otherwise typical for the third quarter of the 1400s. While *The Boke of Noblesse* and the English items in the Codicil are for the most part copied by other scribes, presumably imposing their own spelling and dialect, Worcester checked each copy, so each carries to some degree his imprimatur. They can also be compared with many English letters in his handwriting, some composed by him, some supposedly composed, perhaps dictated, by others but in Worcester's handwriting. Those letters, the subject of a thorough study by Norman Davis, confirm features of his language discernible in *The Boke* and Codicil.

In orthography, one habit consistent across the letters and *The Boke of Noblesse* might be an index of style more than dialect. Davis noted

[262] See *officers royall* C1/115, C1/118, *profites ordinarie* C1/121, *reason vaylable* C1/191, *trux generalle* C2/10, *homage lyege* C2/17 (a set phrase), and *pees finall* C2/52. See also in WW's letters 'desyres resonable' (*PL,* no. 1046, l. 101).

[263] The plural inflection ⟨s⟩ also occurs on *lieges-men* 122, but not on the other five uses of *liege* in a compound, and on *othres certaine lordes* 374, *others barouns* 700, and *othirs officers* 1763.   [264] Mustanoja, *Syntax,* 277.

[265] See 1602, 1619, 1626, 1660, 1803–4, 1853, 1943, 2029, 2032, 2033, 2044, 2123–4. In the *Romayns stories* 1624 and *Romayns condicions* 1646, final ⟨s⟩ seems to mark a plural genitive (=PDE the Romans' stories).

[266] e.g. 769, 1519, 1521, 1566, 1631, 1676, 1806, 1945, 1946, 1976–7, 1989.

[267] Cf. preposing *royal* (in various sp.) on 178, 187, 277, 320, 461, 476, 1434, and C1/88; preposing *final* on 68, 1000, 1092, 1099, 1108, 1113, 1168, 1173, 1482, and C1/19 (cf. see 397n.); and *obeissauntes subgettis* on 895.

that etymological ⟨b⟩ is common in words such as *doubt* in the letters, 'in which case Worcester was more modern than his contemporaries'.[268] This preference is preserved by the scribe of *The Boke* too, who spells *doubte* and cognate words eight times with medial ⟨b⟩ (304, 1248, etc.) and never without it. Likewise, he uses ⟨c⟩ in *auctor, auctorite*, and cognates twelve times (10, 25, etc.), ⟨c⟩ in *fructis* and *fructufull* (1702, 2107), and ⟨b⟩ again in *subtile* four times (53, 111, etc.), with only one use of *sotill* (1249). This etymological spelling might be intended not as 'more modern' but more ancient, for it reflects the Latin etymological root of such words and so might reflect Worcester's interest in classical models. The spelling *fruct-* with ⟨c⟩, in particular, is rare and is found in a few contexts with classical influence.[269]

In dialect, the orthography is relatively colourless, as is common by the late 1400s. There is only once some self-consciousness about orthography: twice where the scribe had written *liche*, he or once perhaps Worcester corrected it to *like* (630, 737). There is little distinctively evocative of Bristol, where Worcester grew up. The orthography with ⟨eo⟩ in the verb *meoue* (='move' 26, 148, etc.) or more rarely *moeu(e/ithe)* (163, 209) is typical of Worcester's correspondence and documents and might reflect some dialectal colouring.[270] But other distinctive features occur only as minor variants. For instance, Worcester's letters use ⟨f⟩ for the voiced sound /v/, which Davis suggested might reflect a Bristol dialect, but this occurs only eight times in *The Boke*,[271] whereas forms with ⟨u⟩, the medial positional allograph for the sound /v/, are far more common.[272] Likewise, Worcester's letters use the earlier spelling ⟨d⟩ for what eventually became sound /ð/ in words such as *fader*,[273] but while this occurs in *The Boke* three times (*moder* 673, 713, *faderis* 1644),

---

[268] Davis, 'Epistolary', 270.

[269] This is the only use of that sp. thus cited in *MED, fruitful, adj.*; only two occur in *MED, fruit, n.*, one of them translated from Lat. in a bilingual MS. See also Daniel Wakelin, 'England: Humanism beyond Weiss', in David Rundle (ed.), *Humanism in Fifteenth-Century Europe*, Medium Ævum Monograph Series (Oxford, 2012), 265–305 at 303, for humanist influence.

[270] See also OMA, FP 76 ('to meofe', 'meoved') and FP Add. 2 ('meoffe'); *PL*, nos 509, l. 21; 530, l. 18 (and Davis's headnote); 1046, l. 75. Cf. the spelling *goed(e)* in Gloucestershire just north of Bristol in *LALME*, dot map 155.

[271] See *gife*='give' 1603; *lefe*='leave' 625; *lifelode*='livelihood' 947, 1895; *lofe*='love' 1604 (added by WW); *abofe*='above' 1552; *behofefull*='behoveful' 1779 (but cf. *behofe*= 'behove' 2432, which is the more common spelling for *OED, behoof, n.*); *excessife*='excessive' 2051.

[272] Too common to list: see e.g. *yeue*, etc.='give' 457, 1316, etc.; *leue*='leave' 2250, 2289, etc.; *liuelode*='livelihood' 2210, 2442; *loue(d)*=love' 124, 621, etc.

[273] Davis, 'Epistolary', 268.

medial ⟨th⟩ occurs twenty times. (There are also four spellings with ⟨d⟩ in the Codicil, including *brodyr*: C1/34, C1/38, C1/196, C2/51.) And the only vocabulary that might be marked as south-western is *bethyn* and *bethout*; these prepositions recur in Worcester's correspondence, including a petition by a scribe like that of *The Boke*, and in his son's prologue to the Codicil, but they are otherwise rare; *bethout* twice causes the scribe some confusion.[274] There are few other distinctive traces of Worcester's Bristol origins.

Equally, there are no signs of the distinctive spelling system that had thrived in Norfolk and died out late in the 1400s (such as ⟨x⟩ for PDE ⟨sh⟩). In general, as Davis observed, among equally acceptable variant spellings Worcester's letters use the form that with hindsight has survived (e.g. ⟨sh⟩ over ⟨sch⟩).[275] The same tendencies hold in *The Boke of Noblesse*. He avoids the obsolescent graphemes ⟨þ⟩ and ⟨ȝ⟩, which never appear in *The Boke* and occur only once in one of his handwritten revisions to the Codicil (*knyȝt* C5/14); they are rare in Worcester's correspondence too.[276]

Likewise, in morphology there is little that is exceptional (beyond the adjectives inflected for the plural, noted above). Just a few noteworthy features occur in the inflection for the possessive case, which is spelled in a variety of ways. Most plurals and possessives have the common inflection ⟨s⟩, often with a preceding vowel as ⟨es⟩, ⟨is⟩, or ⟨ys⟩. The spelling ⟨es⟩ appears just over half of the time, ⟨is⟩ just under, and ⟨ys⟩ only about 5 per cent of the time (many inflections in ⟨ys⟩ being in Worcester's handwriting). There are, though, some uncommon spellings for this final sibilant (*baleese* 1653) and in particular ⟨z⟩, which occurs as a plural marker ten times, mostly on nouns derived from French.[277] There are also four or five places where the scribe was perhaps confused about the plural mark ⟨z⟩, as the graph z could readily be confused with the 'round' or zetoid shape

<hr />

[274] e.g. 52, 112, 176, 192, 221, 223, 426, 449, etc., and the Codicil, C1/135, and for scribal confusion, 52n. and 223n. Cf. *PL*, e.g. nos 566, l. 3 (with n. by Davis), 579, ll. 8, and 1005, ll. 9–10 (where WW interl. it), and no. 1049, l. 94 (from OMA, FP 84, on which see pp. xxiv–xxvi above). See Glossary, s.v. **bethyn, bethout**; *MED*, *bithin*(*ne, prep*.; *OED, bythout* | *bythinne, n*. [*sic*], and for the geographical distribution of *bithout*(*en*) in Gloucestershire, north of Bristol, see *LALME*, dot map 295.

[275] Davis, 'Epistolary', 267–8.

[276] Davis, 'Epistolary', 268. Also ⟨þ⟩ appears only twice in the son's prologue to the Codicil (C1/162, C1/199) and ⟨ȝ⟩ once, perhaps over erasure (C1/183).

[277] See *ducheez* 21 (but cf. *duchees* 1030, 1334, 1463), *lieutenauntz* 89, *counteez* 283, 1117, 1118, 1485, *alliez* 1243, 1392, 1501, *aduocatz* 1909.

of **r**.[278] They suggest that the spelling with ⟨z⟩ was not this scribe's preference, but was something he found in his exemplar, perhaps one in Worcester's hand. For Worcester himself interlineates some plural inflections with ⟨z⟩ (*entreprise`z'*, *place`z'*, *goode`z'*, *meene`z'* 842, 843, 934, 992, 2288), and marking plural or possessive with ⟨z⟩ is common in letters by Worcester or in his handwriting, again mostly on words derived from French.[279] In addition, there are a few anomalous forms of the possessive inflection. Twenty-two possessives are rendered with a genitive separated from the noun, usually *is* or once *his* (785) or, in Worcester's own handwriting, *ys*. All bar one of the separated genitives accompany human possessors, male or plural (e.g. *the kyng ys grete councell(e)* 2067, C5/8 *Troian is blode* 1299), and in a majority of cases proper nouns and/or group genitives (e.g. *the erle of Warwik is sonne* 410–11). (The non-human exception is *cow ys hede* 440 in Worcester's handwriting.) This separated genitive was emerging in the mid and later 1400s and probably still an orthographical variant, rather than reflecting speakers' reanalysis as a form of the pronoun (as arguably happened in the late 1500s). But it does occur as a variant in south-western England, where Worcester grew up, and in Norfolk where he worked, including in the letters of the closely connected Paston and Fastolf circles, some in Worcester's handwriting (e.g. 'the Kyng ys hand').[280] (As many examples in *The Boke of Noblesse* and Codicil give the opportunity to observe an author's autograph usage, our edition, despite the slight unfamiliarity for readers now, preserves the word division for these separated genitives. This

[278] See textual notes to *bataile*[z] 61, *duchee*[z] 113, 283, 314, *duchie*[z] 1125, and see Explanatory Notes on 61 and 113. For other possible confusion or concern about the graphs r and z, see *marcher* 1371n., *allie`s'* 141n., 1505, 1515.

[279] e.g. *PL*, nos. 496, l. 5; 540, l. 4; 982, l. 11; 960, l. 6; 960, l. 13; 982, l. 21; 996, l. 31; 996, l. 47, as well as letters by others in Fastolf's household: e.g. *PL*, nos. 958, l. 7 and 958, l. 21. But cf. words continuing from Old English: *PL*, no. 540, l. 4 'frendz'; 982, l. 15 'londz'; 982, l. 27 'handz'. Anomalous is WW's use on a v.: *PL*, no. 996, l. 41 'nedz most'.

[280] Quoting *PL*, no. 1009, l. 85. See also e.g. *PL*, no. 960, l. 5, no. 981, l. 21, no. 994, l. 27, etc.; and Davis, 'Epistolary', 270. For geographical distribution to *c.*1450, see *LALME*, dot map 420 ('Detached genitive'), and for debate on its significance, see e.g. Cynthia L. Allen, *Genitives in Early English: Typology and Evidence* (Oxford, 2008), 243–52; Teo Juvonen, 'Variation in the Form and Function of the Possessive Morpheme in Late Middle and Early Modern English', in Kersti Börjars, David Denison & Alan Scott (eds.), *Morphosyntactic Categories and the Expression of Possession* (Amsterdam, 2013), 35–55 at 43–9. The citations in *OED*, *his*, *adj.*, II.5, and *MED*, *his*, *pron.*(1), suggest a tendency to use this form on nouns referring to people, especially proper nouns. But unlike the dictionaries, we do not take a view on whether to interpret the separated genitive as the pronoun *his*; it appears in our Glossary, s.v. **his**, solely because the Glossary alphabetizes by the variant spelling that comes first in the alphabet.

also follows practice in the latest edition of the Paston and Fastolf letters.)[281]

Elsewhere, the possessive is often unmarked on proper nouns, on a few instances of *predecessor* and *antecessor* and, as now, on plurals already ending in ⟨s⟩.[282] The unmarked singular is a relatively rare feature that, though, recurs in some texts from Norfolk.[283]

Otherwise, *The Boke of Noblesse* shows changes traceable elsewhere in writing in English of the late 1400s. The third person plural pronouns for the most part reflect the change from forms beginning with the sound /h/ to forms beginning with the sound /ð/. For the third person plural pronoun in the oblique cases there are almost equal numbers of the older *hem* and the newer *the(y)m*.[284] The third person plural possessive is *her* or *here*, with the final ⟨e⟩ abbreviated with a pronounced curl, about a third of times, but it is *theire* and once *their* about two thirds of times. And the subject is always *they* (or four times *thei*). That variation reflects the transition between forms in the later 1400s, as the shift to the pronunciation with /ð/ spread through the nominative, possessive, and finally oblique cases in turn.[285] Interestingly, in Worcester's autograph letters, Davis found a similar pattern, but fewer instances of *them*, instead of *hem*; and when he surveyed Worcester's letters chronologically, from 1444 to 1474 he found 'a slight move towards *th-* forms from about 1457'.[286] It is consistent with such a move that *The Boke of Noblesse*, revised in 1474 or early 1475 and corrected in June 1475, has an even higher proportion of *th-* spellings.

Similarly, Worcester's verbal inflections witness the shifts that befell English in this period. The infinitives of verbs are formed without final ⟨n⟩ for the most part, with just two exceptions,[287] and verbs in the third person plural are usually unmarked without ⟨n⟩ likewise, especially *haue* or the modal auxiliaries.[288] *The Boke of Noblesse* preserves

---

[281] e.g. *PL*, no. 25, l. 51, no. 48, l. 21, no. 53, l. 8, etc. (and Allen, *Genitives*, cites *PL*, no. 742, ll. 20, 21).

[282] e.g. *Kayus son* 10 (= 'Caius' son'), *Saxons bloode* 33, 40 (= 'Saxons' blood'), and *predecessoure obedience*, e.g. 121. See also *the king of Spayne doughter* 704.

[283] Davis, 'Epistolary', 262, citing Mustanoja, *Syntax*, 71; e.g. *PL*, no. 558, l. 12.

[284] Both *hem* and *them* also serve as the reflexive pronoun, but *hemsilfe*, a relatively new construction in the late 1400s, also appears seven times (624, 1106, etc.).

[285] Roger Lass, 'Phonology and Morphology', in Norman Blake (ed.), *The Cambridge History of the English Language*, ii: *1066–1476* (Cambridge, 1992), 23–155 at 120.

[286] Davis, 'Epistolary', 273. Davis did not discuss the subject pron. *they*.

[287] See *to seene* 618, *wolde yelden* 1679. Davis, 'Epistolary', 272, notes that WW uses final ⟨n⟩ on only four or five of about 425 infinitives in his autograph letters.

[288] e.g. *they haue* 908, 1311, etc., *they m(i/y)ght* 619, 1250, etc. Likewise, Davis, 'Epis-

the third person plural ending ⟨n⟩ only twenty-one times in the present tense, six in the past.[289] It does, however, distinctively preserve the present tense, third person plural inflection ⟨th⟩ some twenty-four times.[290] This was a marker of southern dialects, which became increasingly rare in the 1400s even as far south as London.[291] Yet the scribe or his exemplar evidently found it possible to switch back and forth between forms in ⟨th⟩ and forms in ⟨n⟩, as in one clause: *rennen, halithe or clymethe* (1781). Likewise, he uses the customary inflection ⟨ithe⟩ for the plural or polite imperative (*leuithe* 73, *puttithe* 2400, etc.), interchangeably with a form inflected in ⟨en⟩: *Comythe, therfor, and approchen* (140). The language of *The Boke of Noblesse* reflects these changes under way in English pronouns and morphology in the late 1400s.

TEXTUAL PROBLEMS

The Boke of Noblesse might be expected to have few textual problems, as the fair copy has been read by the author, and as the author's final revisions exist in his handwriting on that copy. Unfortunately, the scribe makes some errors that suggest incomprehension of an exemplar containing an earlier stage of revisions by Worcester. The text had gone through at least two drafts, of 1451 and 1474 or early 1475, before this fair copy (as argued above), and one hypothesis is that some redrafting was visible in the exemplar, as further revisions are in the fair copy, squeezed between or at the ends of lines or in the margins, and unclearly or incorrectly keyed to the main text. It is often noted that authorial revisions risked illegibility in the exemplars for future copyists.[292] The problem can be seen in one of Worcester's letters, dated 7 February 1460, which survives in a copy by Richard Calle, which gives a sense of

tolary', 272, notes that in his letters 80 uninflected forms outnumber 8 forms of the pr. 3 pl. inflected with ⟨n⟩.

[289] See pr. 3 pl. *ben(e)*, 24, 39, etc., *haunten* 99, *accorden* 1530, *writen* 1731, *rennen* 1781, *labouren* 1785, *fauten* 1827, *dwellin* 2264; and pa. 3 pl. *foughten* 1954, *vsurpen* 2260, *halden* 2218, 2384, *saiden* 2532 and *seiden* 2533. See also the pr. 1 pl. *hauen* 2545; the pr. 2 pl., including uses with sg. addressee for politeness, *ye ben(e)* 42, 709, 863.

[290] See pr. 3 pl. *vsithe* 100, *witnessithe* 586, *concernithe* 863–4, *takethe* 888, *departhethe* 890, *reignithe* 924, 1598, 1659, 2449, *enforcethe* 980, *sounethe* 1531, *com(e/y)the* 1532, 1534, *fallithe* 1534, *halithe* 1774, 1781, *goithe* 1775 (twice), *nedithe* 2190, *wastithe* 2192, *destroiethe* 2192, *rehersithe* 2273, *apparteynithe* 2403, *belongithe* 2403.

[291] Lass, 'Phonology and Morphology', 97, 137; Jacek Fisiak, *A Short Grammar of Middle English* (Warsaw, 1968), 92–4; and on WW's usage, Davis, 'Epistolary', 271.

[292] Delsaux, *Manuscrits*, 191.

how challenging it was to copy Worcester's compositions.[293] Similarly, Fastolf's will survives in a messy draft by Worcester, which the scribe making the final version improved silently while copying.[294]

Whatever the cause in *The Boke of Noblesse*, the scribe frequently errs. Like all scribes, he omits small, closed-class function words (e.g. *of* 1221, 1772, 1778, 1789, *by* 1759, 2054) or switches them when they sound alike (e.g. *and* for *an* 695, 2118). Emendations of such errors are frequent but seldom controversial. More troublingly, the scribe also seems to omit whole halves of sentences, leaving a subclause without any main clause, or leaving a clause incomplete. In some passages, that might be part of Worcester's involuted and delaying style, but other such passages were evidently judged as errors by Worcester—whether his or the scribe's—for he corrects them, if not always well, by finishing an incomplete clause (e.g. 1266–7) or supplying the main clause to balance a subclause (e.g. 1318). That the scribe can omit the bulk of a clause raises the question of whether some other puzzles in the syntax, where a new clause changes the grammatical subject suddenly, might be things that Worcester could have identified as errors. It would be very tempting to emend the syntax throughout *The Boke of Noblesse* by supplying more closed-class words to clarify the meaning. But while many of Worcester's revisions include their own evident errors (e.g. dittography *the the*: 2066: see textual notes), and he leaves some evident errors uncorrected (e.g. repetition in *chirche of Saint Andrieu chirche* 1127: see textual note), he has corrected what look like larger omissions, and so it would be intrusive to emend his syntax and style too heavy-handedly.

The problems caused by Worcester's revision are teasing, however, as the author's handwriting might seem to give authority to everything he writes, and more authority than most other English manuscripts of this period that are scribal copies. But one cannot trust Worcester's handiwork entirely, if one seeks a readable text—and one can assume that readability was Worcester's intention, whatever his execution. English and French authors of the fifteenth century could also be sporadic or careless in their attention when copying or correcting their own work, perhaps expecting the roughness to be smoothed out by further copying.[295] Worcester makes duplications and omissions, and there is

[293] *PL*, no. 604, on which see Davis's headnote: 'Calle has clearly been unable to read Worcester's rather crabbed hand.'
[294] OMA, FP 64 and FP 65, mentioned on p. lxii above.
[295] See e.g. John M. Bowers, 'Hoccleve's Two Copies of *Lerne to Dye*: Implications for

a lack of syntactical precision—or a style of syntax more effusive than analytical. He perhaps expected his revised manuscript to be recopied more legibly in syntax and page design for presentation.

This edition takes on the role of fair copyist and incorporates Worcester's revisions smoothly, signalling them only lightly with 'primes' (or for an insertion into an insertion "double primes") and in the textual notes below. When Worcester obviously duplicates the adjacent words of the fair copy at the start or end of his addition, we delete what is obviously dittography (e.g. in the textual notes *famous Clerk of Eloquence* 732–6n.; *act* 655n.; *and that* 921n.; *to* in *kepe hospitalitee for to* 2271n.). Some duplication occurs around a line break or page break that would readily cause confusion (e.g. *.M^l. Cxxxj.* 270n.; *Peyters* 351n.).[296] (The manuscript readings in the textual notes at the foot of the page preserve the word division and capitalization of the manuscript, which differ from the regularized edited text.) But when we can imagine a possible stylistic reason for the duplication, we keep it: this most often affects certain pairs of words in grammatical apposition (as discussed above, pp. lxxx–lxxxiii). As this edition is based on a partly autograph manuscript, we have been cautious about emending if we can find any reason for preserving seeming oddities.

Despite this caution, sometimes the scribe's copy of a much-revised text and Worcester's further hasty revisions need emendation to be comprehensible. For example, in 901–2 the original prepositional phrase *by lak of simple payment* explains why soldiers were not paid, but he adds a new clause *caused the rather the ducdom of Normandy to be lost*. The addition completes the thought, the cause and effect: this lack of payment is ultimately why Normandy was lost. But it makes the grammar incomplete, as the new verb *caused* lacks a subject. On the page (f. 15^r) the placement of the interlineation is signalled clearly with a caret mark after *lak of payment*; but as it is long, the interlineation's first word *caused* falls above a use of the word *and* earlier in the line, and it might be that Worcester was imagining an *and* before the clause; more customary for him would have been the use of *which* to tack on a subclause. Rather than preserve his incomplete syntax, we emend by supplying *which*.

Textual Critics', *Papers of the Bibliographical Society of America*, 83 (1989), 437–72; and in general Delsaux, *Manuscrits*, 193–4.

[296] Worcester also duplicates words at line breaks in the middle of his longer revisions: *Seyntclow* 196n.; *yt yt* and *ser ser* 428n. So does the main scribe over a page break: *And after* 391.

Besides confused syntax, the text also contains errors of fact, especially incorrect dates and names. Some of these errors perhaps arose from the scribe miscopying Worcester's exemplar, given the probable complexity of it (as just hypothesized). Many errors, however, seem explicable as Worcester's: some occur here in his handwriting; some recur repeatedly here; and some recur in other writings, notebooks and annotations by Worcester or in books or sources he handled. Given this authorial involvement, again this edition is cautious about emending these errors and leaves them as records of his or his scribe's state of knowledge. The Explanatory Notes and the Index clarify them.

EDITORIAL CONVENTIONS

Conventions of Transcription

The main scribe of *The Boke of Noblesse* is unusual in that most of the time he distinguishes **u** and **n** clearly, unlike some scribes of this period (such as the scribes of the Codicil). In instances where the distinction is unclear, the edition follows the spelling most likely in context or most common in his usage elsewhere (e.g. five instances of *auncien(t)* with uncertain minims in the first syllable, as opposed to twenty-one where the distinction **un** is clear). The clear letterforms **n** and **u** sometimes reveal surprising spellings or errors, especially in French or classical names and terms: e.g. *Erle Nauson* 380 = count of Nassau; *Amyeus* 1045 = Fr. Amiens; *angures* 1814 = PDE 'auguries' < Fr. 'augure' < Lat. *augur*; *Corninus* 2123 < Lat. Corvinus; *Cornicanus* and *Cornicanois* 1833, 1839 = Lat. Coruncanius; *Aruus* = Lat. Aruns 2139–48. The edition leaves these errors in the use of **n** and **u** unemended, as it does Worcester's or the scribe's other errors of fact. (They are explained in the Explanatory Notes and Index.) The exception is the name *Aniou*, spelled four times with a clear final **u** (664, 676, 1024, 1340) but five times with a letterform similar to the curled **n** favoured in word-final position (284, 384, 671, 707, 715). As the scribe clearly knows that the name ends with a vowel, and more often spells it *Angew* (ten times: 266, 662, etc.), we ignore and silently treat as **u** the five inconsistent uses of the form similar to **n**. Worcester does not correct these errors with **n** and **u**.

The manuscript's distribution of **u** and **v** and **i** and **j** usually represent not different sounds, for in each pair both forms can be either vowel or consonant, but positional allographs of one conceptual graph (as with different shapes of **s**). However, we follow the common editorial convention with English of this period to preserve a manuscript's distribution of these allographs **u** and **v** and **i** and **j**. This also captures the few instances of the nascent shift to a different distribution of these allographs as separate graphs with a phonological distinction, as found in Worcester's autograph revisions in particular.

With minuscule **i** and **j**, the forms are easily distinguished. The unambiguous minuscule **j** is only used at the end of the names of months *Ianuarij* (130, 1082) and *Maij* (110, 134, etc.) derived from Latin genitive forms ending *ii*.[297] This seems done by analogy with the use of **j** for the final position in roman numerals, where it prevented people from modifying the number. This use of minuscule **j** as the final minim in roman numerals also occurs throughout the text, rendered in this edition as *j*.[298] But in *The Boke* often initially and on eleven occasions medially in French-derived words (*Aniou* 284, 384, etc., and *donioune* 335, *enioie* 2396; see also *donion* C2/253) a majuscule form is used that is indistinguishable as **I** or **J**. However, as it is identical to minuscule **i** in function and position, appearing initially or medially (whereas **j** appears finally, except as the roman numeral for one), therefore, in all cases at the start or in the middle of words this edition interprets the ambiguous majuscule **I/J** as **I**. Then, as the edition adjusts capitalization to Present Day English conventions, it converts many instances of that majuscule, understood as **I**, to *i*. In addition, majuscule **I** is used for the roman numeral for one (that is, when it stands alone, presumably to avoid ambiguity), on two occasions in the manuscript of *The Boke* (394, 1464) and nineteen in the manuscript of Appendix Text 2; again, we standardize the capitalization, therefore printing *i*. This policy differs from Davis, Beadle, and Richmond's edition of the Paston letters and papers,[299] where the majuscule **I** or **J** is interpreted as either majuscule **I** or long **j** when the word would not now be capitalized.

Several patterns suggest that majuscule **I** is not a reanalysis of the allograph as a new grapheme **J** or **j**. First, it can appear as a vowel still: in the main text of *The Boke of Noblesse* itself, there are 12 uses of majuscule **I** for the first-person singular pronoun and 43 on **In**. There are 92 uses of it at the start of names, including all uses of **Ia**, **Ie**, **Ih**, and

---

[297] The minuscule long **j** is also used in Latin passages for ablative inflections ending *ijs* 12, 1732 and 1747 and in some sidenotes at 1546sn, 1861sn, and 1923sn.

[298] Minuscule *j* is twice used for the roman numeral for one in the sidenotes at 603sn, 617sn; and somebody unidentifiable changed the first element in the roman numeral *.ix.* to *.'j'x.* 495, suggesting uncertainty about the convention.

[299] See *PL*, i, p. lxxxi.

68 of 76 cases of **Io** and six of **Iu**; here it seems simply a tendency to use majuscules for proper nouns.[300] Excluding names or words after paraphs, capitalized anyway, 45 on **Iu** and 32 on **In** prevent minim confusion from **iu** and **in**, as suggested by a correction of **iu** to **Iu** and **in** to **In** once each.[301] And the uses of **Iu** and eight of **Io** co-exist with the minuscule in 22 of **iu** and eight of **io**, often on the same words, which suggest which minuscule letter is the equivalent.[302] For these reasons, we treat majuscule **I** always as *i* or *I*, depending on Present Day English capitalization, and never as *j* or *J*.

We do not add accents to French words that would now receive them (e.g. *Phelip Dieudonne* 275, 1199 for Modern French 'Dieudonné') or to accented final **e** in English (e.g. *duche* 51=PDE 'duchy').

For numbers, the manuscripts use a mixture of verbal forms, Indo-Arabic numerals, and roman numerals, and the edition leaves them as they appear. The scribes are inconsistent about whether and where they place a *punctus* before and/or after numerals; we follow this varying practice. Numerals often are accompanied by superscript abbreviations for the verbal form. The edition does not expand these abbreviations in numbers, except when the remainder of the word is written with letters (*millions* 398). When a number is part of a monarch's name, it is capitalized, whether it is in numerals or words.

Punctuation

The edition adjusts all capitalization to Present Day English conventions. Following the conventions of series such as Oxford Medieval Texts, titles such as *King*, *Duke*, and *Bishop* are capitalized only when they introduce a proper noun directly, including instances where the text omits *of* (e.g. *Erle Vendosme* 379), but not when they introduce a place name with *of* (e.g. cf. *King Knowt* 39–40 but *king of Iherusalem*

---

[300] e.g. *Ianuarij* 130, 1082, *Iaques* 376, *Iames* 694; *Ieroyme* 2295, *Ierem(y/i)e* 2390, 2392; *Iherusalem* 44–5, etc., the abbreviation **Ihc** for *Ihesus* 952, etc. and **Ihu** for *Ihesu* 2273; *Iob* 146, etc., *Ioh(a)n* 321, etc., *Iooell* 2296, *Ioachym* 2390; *Iune* 720, 2580, *Iuile / Iuilly* (='July') 1087, 1128, *Iudas* 1280, *Iudee* 1722, *Iuda* 2390.

[301] See textual notes on 'i'ustice 905 and 'i'nordynat 927. A majuscule in **Iu** appears on a limited range of words: *iusticer* 39, *iustice* 154, etc., *iust(er)* 162, etc., *iu(p/b)ardie* 923, etc., *iuelx / iuellis* 940, etc., *iugement(is)* 944, etc., *iuge(d)* 1262, etc.; Lat. *iusticie* 1747, Lat. *iudices* 1753, Lat. *iusta* 1754. While 8 uses of the majuscule in **Io** are all on *io(u)rney* 500, etc., which might suggest that the letterform is differentiating the pronunciation, *iourneis* is also twice written **io** without differentiation 1153, 1350.

[302] Viz. a minuscule in **io** on *iourneis* 1153, 1350 (see previous n.), as well as *ioyned* 764, 2117, *ioifull* 1662, *ioly* 1901, *ioieust* 2110, *ioie* 2122; **iu** on Eng. *iust* 80, etc., *iustice* 167, etc., *iustly* 907, *iugement(is)* 1549; and Lat. *iusticia* 1742.

44–5; or cf. *Erle Dorset* 427 but *erle of Dorset* 836–7). Words such as *city*, *county*, or *duchy* are not capitalized, even when they form elements of place names (e.g. *counte of Mayne* 22), nor is *battle* when it prefaces a specific place name. Other capitalization follows *The Oxford English Dictionary*'s preference (e.g. *Saras`y′nes, Holy Land* 268, but *croiserie* 271). French place names are given the hyphens and apostrophes of the present forms where possible. Pronouns referring to the deity are not capitalized. Word division and hyphenation follow *The Oxford English Dictionary* in most cases, except where it seemed unclear in context (e.g. *harde-hert* 2002) and in a few of Worcester's common compounds with the present participle (noted above, pp. lxxxvii–lxxxviii). The edition follows the practice in the recent edition of the Paston and Fastolf letters and papers in printing the separated genitives, favoured especially by Worcester, with word division (e.g. *the duke is son* 123, as explained above, pp. xciv–xcv).

The edition replaces the manuscript's punctuation (described above, p. xxvii) with modern punctuation. However, the edition does not use apostrophes to mark the possessive, whether the manuscript forms it by an inflection or a separated genitive or leaves it unmarked.

Editing a work by Worcester's associate, Stephen Scrope, Curt Bühler noted that 'the rules of modern usage were found inadequate',[303] and that is the case with *The Boke of Noblesse* in places. Four aspects of the syntax particularly challenge Present Day English punctuation. First, clauses are often linked in long sequences by the relative conjunction *which*, used in diverse ways, including some more like a co-ordinating conjunction; therefore, this edition sometimes uses a full stop before *which* to start a new sentence, solely to give the reader pause (e.g. 808, 1026). Second, Worcester frequently changes grammatical subject without stating the new subject clearly in a noun or pronoun and yet tying the new clause with a conjunction; in such cases, a semicolon registers the blend of connection and disconnection. Third, many sentences are extended by non-finite or absolute clauses (as discussed above, pp. lxxxvi–lxxxvii), modifying an uncertain or changing referent; for clarity, this edition sometimes separates them with a semicolon, rather than a comma (e.g. before *beyng also* 1353). Fourth, even without those ambiguities of connection, many clauses are conjoined in longer sequences than is customary in Present Day English, so that while a co-ordinating conjunction such as *and* might require only a comma, a semicolon or full stop is helpful to separate the

[303] Scrope, *Dicts*, ed. Bühler, p. lxiii.

ideas. In addition, to clarify other serpentine digressions and caveats within clauses, the edition makes slightly heavier use of parenthetical commas than many editions do. To counterbalance that, prepositional phrases with an adverbial function marking dates (e.g. he *expelled . . . owt of Parys cytee the yeere of Crist M^l. iiii^C. xij and slow many* 190–2) have not been 'bracketed off' with further commas, and the 'Oxford comma' has not been used.

The manuscript of *The Boke* itself is written as one continuous block of prose, excepting the corrections and revisions in the margins, and breaks on f. 1^r and f. 42^r where Worcester supplies a subtitle and colophon (17, 2580–2). The edition, however, divides the prose into paragraphs, sometimes following the paraphs (described above, p. xxvii), but not only or always so. Chapter titles are run into the block of prose in the manuscript without line breaks, but the edition sets them on a separate line.

Chapter titles and a few other words are underlined for prominence in the manuscript of *The Boke of Noblesse*; they are sometimes written in a slightly larger display script. In the edition, chapter titles marked thus are rendered in bold. Other uses of display script or underlining are not placed in bold, though they often are given an equivalent Present Day English punctuation (e.g. speech marks for quotations). The scribe sometimes begins or ends this marking of a chapter title too late (as noted above, pp. xxvii–xxviii); the edition ignores these errors. Likewise, in the Prologue to the Codicil, the scribe often follows his punctuation marks of paraphs or virgules with a horizontal line under one or more subsequent words (e.g. ¶ *and inasmoche* C1/27, *and I as* C1/31); this marking too is ignored as part of the punctuation that we have modernized.

The manuscripts of *The Boke* and its Codicil occasionally use an enlarged initial at the start of a chapter or other section. The edition prints these at the same size as the rest of the text.

Abbreviations

Abbreviations are expanded silently. In the Latin texts in the Appendices, they are frequent but conventional. In the English texts, only one is frequent, whereas the extent of others is more controversial. There is a small number of unusual abbreviations to particular words, usually echoing practice in copying Latin or French: e.g. *Iherusalem* 294, *seigniour* 1143, *seigniouries* 1485–6 (see nn.). The abbreviation for the honorific is expanded *Ser* in *The Boke of Noblesse* and for consistency whenever written in Worcester's handwriting in the Codicil (see C3/5), for this how it is spelled when written in full in *The Boke* (e.g. 373, 376).[304] It is written as *Sire*, with an abbreviation of the final ⟨e⟩, the few times it occurs in those parts of the Codicil which are by a different scribe (C3/21, C4/5).

For the plural or possessive inflections ⟨s⟩ there are very few abbreviations, all using the conventional mark (a circle with a tail). The main scribe of *The Boke* spells this inflection in full only slightly more often with ⟨es⟩ (as noted above), scribe B of most of the Codicil uses ⟨es⟩ and ⟨is⟩ equally. We therefore expand their rare abbreviations of these inflections following each scribe's preferred spelling of the word in question. As it happens, in the work of the main scribe for *The Boke* and scribe B of the Codicil for most of texts C2 to C5 this abbreviation is therefore mostly expanded as *-is* (except for *homages* 1136, *sterlinges* 542, *places* C4/53, but see n.). The Codicil's scribe A for text C1 prefers the inflection ⟨es⟩ about four fifths of the time, which we follow except on *a(u/v)ertisementis* (C1/193, C1/198), which he elsewhere spells in full with ⟨is⟩ (C1/199).

The superscript **a**, conventionally abbreviating ⟨ra⟩, also abbreviates only ⟨a⟩, as used rarely by the scribe of *The Boke of Noblesse* and often by scribe A of the Codicil before ⟨un⟩, giving ⟨aun⟩ in words derived from French. Scribes A and B of the Codicil also use it for ⟨au⟩ (*lyeutenaunte* C1/217 and repeatedly *auaunc-* by scribe A; *auauntage* and *lieutenaunt* C2/103, C4/2 by scribe B). Worcester consistently uses this abbreviation for ⟨au⟩. All the scribes almost exclusively use spellings with ⟨aunce⟩ and ⟨aunt⟩ in French-derived words spelled ⟨anc⟩ and ⟨ant⟩ in Present Day English.[305]

As in many English manuscripts of the fifteenth century, flourishes and crossbars in word-final position are of ambiguous significance: they could signify an abbreviated final ⟨e⟩, often with no clear etymological or phonological rationale, or could be otiose.[306] Curt Bühler noted that it is impossible to be sure which final-word flourishes are otiose in handwriting of the later fifteenth century.[307] This edition treats as otiose

[304] This follows the practice of expansion for WW's *Ser* in *PL*, e.g. nos 529, l. 9, 535, l. 4, 956, l. 16.

[305] Exceptions are *habundantlie* 2556 (perhaps reflecting a difference in syllable stress) and, by scribe B of the Codicil, *puissantly* C2/97, C2/180, C2/198. Proper nouns are more various in spelling of this syllable.

[306] On this problem, see recently *Sir Bevis of Hampton*, ed. Jennifer Fellows, EETS 349–50, 2 vols. (2017), ii, pp. lxxvii–lxxviii.

[307] Scrope, *Dicts*, ed., Bühler, pp. lxii–lxiii. Bühler in his earlier edition of Scrope, *Dicts*,

most of these flourishes and crossbars that other editors, including the Victorian editor of *The Boke of Noblesse*, have expanded with a final ⟨e⟩. In this, the edition follows the practice of editions of the Paston letters and papers and of Scrope's *Epistle of Othea*.[308]

There is often a tail on word-final **d**, curling at variable angles and of variable length to the right, and slightly downwards. This especially seems a flourish when it occurs in line-final position, where it can even help to 'justify' the ragged margin of the prose, and it complements other elongated strokes on the tops, bottoms, and right margins of pages in fifteenth-century manuscripts: e.g. f. 2ᵛ, bottom l. *contynued~* 114; f. 3ʳ, l. 12 *manhod~* 124–5; f. 3ᵛ, l. 3 *kindelid~* 143; f. 3ᵛ, l. 22 *shuld~* 159. These flourishes also appear in diverse syntactical and phonological positions. The edition therefore treats all such flourishes on word-final **d** as otiose.

There are crossbars on most word-final instances of **ll** and consonantal clusters including **h** or **l**. Although some words thus marked can be found elsewhere spelled with final ⟨e⟩, the scribe's orthography, like that of many scribes of fifteenth-century English, is not consistent even when unabbreviated. Very rarely a crossbar occurs in medial position with an abbreviating function of a different sort: e.g. f. 26ʳ, l. 32, *singłer*, here edited as *singuler* 1558. But there are also crossbars on **h** or **l** where it would be difficult to add an additional vowel: e.g. f. 2ʳ, l. 18, *lamentabłe* printed as *lamentable* 74; f. 39ᵛ, l. 26, *mightie* printed as *mightie* 2451. In ignoring these marks, the edition follows Norman Davis's practice in editing the related corpus of the Paston letters and the practice in other editions of comparable kinds of later fifteenth-century English prose.[309]

The edition also treats as otiose a macron over word-final instances of **n**, as such macrons seem to be simply diacritics to guide the interpretation of the two minims as **n** and not **u** (e.g. *Agamenon* 593, *Anthen* 604).[310]

---

used record type to record the ambiguous strokes rather than interpret them editorially; in his later edition, Scrope, *Epistle*, he ignored most of them.

[308] *PL*, i, pp. lxxxii–lxxxiii; Scrope, *Epistle*, ed. Bühler, p. xxix.

[309] *PL*, i, pp. lxxxii–lxxxiii; Blayney, i, p. xii; Scrope, *Epistle*, ed. Bühler, p. xxix. *A Late-Medieval History of the Ancient and Biblical World*, ed. Cosima Clara Gillhammer, 2 vols. (Heidelberg, 2022), ii, pp. lxxvii–lxxx, disentangles different uses of flourishes on **h** and **l**.

[310] As argued convincingly by Anya Adair, 'The Otiose Labour of William Darker: Some Light on Ambiguous Strokes in Fifteenth- to Sixteenth-Century English Manuscripts', *Review of English Studies*, 71 (2020), 630–51. This use, as a diacritic to parse minims, is also proposed in *PL*, i, p. lxxxii.

However, curls on word-final **r** are expanded as an abbreviated ⟨e⟩. Editions of the Paston letters and papers and works by Scrope vary in their treatment of this ambiguous marking. But in line with many editions, this edition does treat the marks on final **r** as an abbreviation.[311]

As Davis noted of the Paston letters, the crossed **p** can be expanded as either *par* or *per*, depending on context; that contextual interpretation is followed here. Crossed **p** occurs in *The Boke* only six times, five by the scribe and one by Worcester (*emperour* 447), for words spelled in full elsewhere or in Latin as *per*.[312] It occurs eight times, all in Worcester's autograph additions, for the same or related words spelled in full elsewhere only as *par* (e.g. *parforme* 293, cf. unabbreviated *parfourmed* 399). The syllable is spelled in full sixty-four times as *per*, 140 as *par*, even where Present Day English prefers *per* (e.g. *parsonelly* 1230, *parsecuted* 1259). That confirms for Worcester's milieu the preference observed by Davis for *par*, even in words that Davis was wary of expanding thus such as *parson(e)(s)* (=PDE 'person'), unabbreviated with *par* eight times (e.g. 129, 514, etc.).[313] In the English texts of the Codicil, again the crossed **p** is expanded both ways, following the spelling of the same words in full elsewhere (e.g. *experience* C1/59, *parfourmed* C3/14).[314] There is the full spelling *person(e)(s)* three times but *parsone(s)* four, all by scribe B of the Codicil, so four uses of crossed **p** in this word, all by scribe A instead, in text C1, could be either; the preference across both *The Boke* and the Codicil suggests *parson(e)(s)*.

In his autograph additions, Worcester's habits of abbreviation are often slightly different from the other scribes'; they are interpreted and explained individually if problematic (e.g. *shyppis* 437; see n.).

---

[311] See similarly Davis in *PL*, i, p. lxxxii. That said, in a headnote to *PL*, no. 154, Davis records that John Paston III from 1460 begins using a curl on word-final **r** habitually, and while some instances must signify abbreviations, e.g. for a necessary final syllable spelled ⟨e⟩, others seem less meaningful and so Davis ignored them 'Unless . . . the curve is exceptionally strong' (i. 258, n. 4). Bühler, editing Scrope, *Dicts*, p. lxii, treats the mark on **r** as ambiguous, but editing Scrope, *Epistle*, p. xxix, twenty-five years later, expands **r** and a curl as ⟨re⟩.

[312] There is no comparison in *The Boke* for *perseuered* 2406. As well as abbreviated *persecucions* 1493, 2201, spelled unabbreviated as *persecucion* 2053, the first syllable of cognate words varies when spelled in full: *persecutours* 1721, *parsecuted* 1259.

[313] Davis in *PL*, i, p. lxxxi.

[314] There is no comparison in the Codicil for scribe A's *temperaunce* C1/10–11, C1/105 nor for scribe A's and WW's *perpetuall*, *-ell(e)* C1/73, C1/91, C2/10; but *BkNob.* has the cognates *temper'at'* 2374 and *perpetuell(y)* 592, 2006 and cognate *perpetuite* 8 (and only once *parpetuite* 1976), which suggest the expansions. The abbreviation is also used once in scribal error: C2/98 textual note.

Diacritics for Stages of Correction and Revision

All additions and changes in the manuscript are enclosed in ˋprimes´ in this edition. When further additions or changes are made to added or changed passages, they are enclosed in ˋˋdouble primes˝. The textual notes at the foot of the page specify where and how the additions or changes were made, and whether the main scribe of the text in question made the changes or Worcester (abbreviated as WW) or another person did. Where it is impossible to be confident who made a change, then it is not said who made it. The aim of marking Worcester's revisions in detail is to allow analysis of the stages of composition and to allow comparison with his revisions to Stephen Scrope's *The Dicts and Sayings of the Philosophers*.[315] The textual notes also record the interventions by early readers. Deletions from the texts, made by crossing out or erasure, are recorded only in the textual notes.

Worcester's Sidenotes

Worcester himself supplied marginal annotations in the manuscript of *The Boke of Noblesse* itself, written neatly in red, or less neatly in black, some with prompts. The sidenotes seem integral to his plans for how the work should be presented and read (as noted above, pp. lxiv–lxvi). As such, his sidenotes are included in this edition and are presented to the side of the page, inset into the text. It should be recognized that their printed position inset into the text differs from Worcester's positioning of them in the margins in the manuscript. (Textual annotation on the sidenotes is keyed to the number of the first line that the sidenote accompanies, followed by the initials SN.)

The edition does not distinguish black prompts for missing red sidenotes from those, far more numerous, completed in red. Worcester's additional black prompts, which he did then duplicate with red sidenotes, are only recorded in the textual notes, specified as having been wholly or partly duplicated by the printed red sidenote, as they are presumed not part of the final ˋpolished´ page design; those of his black prompts that he did not, however, duplicate in red are included inset into the text, presumed as intended parts of the page design that were never fully completed in manuscript.

For similar reasons, Worcester's symbols in the margin are included among the sidenotes (printed as §) only in the rare cases that they are

---

[315] Scrope, *Dicts*, ed. Bühler, p. lxiv. Bühler prints them in his apparatus in bold type for ready comparison.

drawn or underlined in red or accompany text. The presence of others is recorded in the textual notes at the foot of the page as 'WW symbol'.

The punctuation and capitalization of Worcester's red and black sidenotes are modernized and standardized as in the main text. Emendations (recorded in the textual notes) are made to ensure that Worcester's Latin notes are legible (e.g. *Fr[a]ncie* 1066SN) but not to correct his spelling or grammar (e.g. *efectum* 1092SN).

Readers' Marginalia

Conversely, later readers' annotations (described above, pp. xxviii–xxix) are recorded only in the textual notes at the foot of the page; their presentation is not standardized. This edition thereby separates Worcester's sidenotes from these readers' marginalia, from the reign of Henry VII at the earliest, post-dating Worcester's death; in this respect, this edition differs considerably from the edition of Nichols, which conflates Worcester's sidenotes and readers' annotations.

Editorial History

The textual notes do not record where previous printed editions by Nichols or, for the texts from the Codicil, by Stevenson diverge from this edition. In particular, ignoring ambiguous strokes makes many words differ in orthography. Some textual cruces where this edition and Nichols diverge in substantives are discussed in the Explanatory Notes.

BIBLIOGRAPHY

MANUSCRIPTS

Brussels, KBR, MS 9009–11
Cambridge, Corpus Christi College, MS 210
Cambridge, Emmanuel College, MS I.2.10
Cambridge, Pembroke College, MS 215
Cambridge, St John's College, MS H.5
Cambridge, Trinity College
  MS B.3.28
  MS O.2.40
Cambridge, University Library, MS Add. 7870
Chantilly, Musée Condé, MS 769
Eton College
  MS 21
  MS 22
  MS 23
Harvard, Houghton Library, MS Richardson 32
Longleat House, MS 253
London, British Library
  Add. MS 4101
  Add. MS 11612
  Add. MS 27444
  Add. MS 28208
  Add. MS 34888
  Add. MS 34889
  Add. MS 39848
  Add. MS 40007
  Add. MS 60577
  Cotton MS Claudius E. iii
  Cotton MS Domitian A. ii
  Cotton MS Julius C. iii
  Cotton MS Julius E. iv
  Cotton MS Julius E. v
  Cotton MS Julius F. vii
  Cotton MS Nero C. x
  Cotton MS Titus A. xxiv (Part 2)
  Egerton MS 2429
  Harley MS 782
  Harley MS 861

Harley MS 3943
Harley MS 4205
Harley MS 4605
Harley MS 4763
Harley MS 6166
Lansdowne MS 285
Royal MS 5 F. xvii
Royal MS 7 D. iii
Royal MS 8 C. xiv
Royal MS 8 E. v
Royal MS 13 C. i
Royal MS 15 E. vi
Royal MS 16 G. vii
Royal MS 17 A. viii
Royal MS 17 B. xvii
Royal MS 17 C. xxxviii
Royal MS 17 F. ii
Royal MS 18 B. xxii
Royal MS 19 B. xviii
Royal MS 20 C. i
Royal MS 20 C. viii
Sloane MS 4
London, College of Arms
   MS Arundel 48
   MS M.9
London, Lambeth Palace Library
   MS 264
   MS 506
London, National Archives
   C 1/26/608
   C 1/53/87
   C 1/324/41
   C 1/360/60
   C 1/706/32
   E 36/188
   E 36/189
   PROB 11/19/368
   PROB 11/108/430
London, Society of Antiquaries, MS 41
Manchester, John Rylands Library, MS Eng. 1
Oxford, Balliol College, MS 124
Oxford, Bodleian Library
   MS Bodley 179

MS Bodley 885
MS Bodley 943
MS Canon. misc. 438
MS Douce 148
MS Douce 261
MS Laud misc. 570
MS Laud misc. 638
MS Laud misc. 674
MS Rawl. C.447
MS Tanner 407
Oxford, Lincoln College
MS Lat. 129
MS Lat. 130
Oxford, Magdalen College Archives
FP 40
FP 42
FP 43
FP 48
FP 49
FP 51
FP 63
FP 64
FP 65
FP 66
FP 69
FP 70/1
FP 70/2
FP 72
FP 76
FP 78
FP 84
FP 87
FP 96
FP 101
FP Add. 2
Oxford, Magdalen College Library
MS Lat. 8
MS Lat. 22
MS Lat. 26
MS Lat. 45
MS Lat. 50
MS Lat. 62
MS Lat. 65

MS Lat. 82
MS Lat. 166
MS Lat. 198
MS Lat. 206
New Haven, Beinecke Library, MS Takamiya 86
Paris, Bibliothèque nationale de France
MS fr. 246
MS fr. 251
MS fr. 1243
MS fr. 2606
MS fr. 2619
MS fr. 2813
MS fr. 20350
Paris, Bibliothèque Sainte-Geneviève, MS fr. 777

PRINTED PRIMARY SOURCES

Adæ Murimuth Continuatio chronicarum Robertus de Avesbury de Gestis mirabilibus regis Edwardi Tertii, ed. Edward Maunde Thompson, RS 93 (Oxford, 1889).

Annual Report of the Deputy Keeper of the Public Records, 41 (London, 1880).

Aristotle, *Nichomachean Ethics*, trans. H. Rackham (Cambridge, MA, 1934).

St Augustine, *De civitate Dei*, ed. Bernhard Dombart and Alfons Kalb, 5th edn., 2 vols. (Turnhout, 1981, repr. 1993).

'Bale's Chronicle', in *Six Town Chronicles of England*, ed. Ralph Flenley (Oxford, 1911), 114–53.

'John Benet's Chronicle for the Years 1400 to 1462', ed. G. L. Harriss and M. A. Harriss, *Camden Miscellany XXIV*, Camden Society, 4th ser., 9 (London, 1972), 151–233.

Boethius, *De consolatione philosophiae; Opuscula theologica*, ed. Claudio Moreschini (Munich, 2000).

Calendar of Inquisitions Post Mortem, xiv: *Edward III*, ed. A. E. Stamp, J. B. W. Chapman, Cyril Flower, M. C. B. Dawes, and L. C. Hector (London, 1952).

Calendar of the Patent Rolls: Edward III, xi: *1358–61* (London, 1911).

Calendar of the Patent Rolls: Henry VI, vi: *1446–1452* (London, 1909).

Capgrave, John, *Liber de illustribus Henricis*, ed. Francis Charles Hingeston, RS 1 (London, 1858).

Caxton, William, *Caxton: Tulle of Olde Age: Textuntersuchung mit literarischer Einführung*, ed. Heinz Susebach (Halle, 1933).

—— trans., *The Book of Fayttes of Armes and of Chyualrye*, ed. A. T. P. Byles, EETS 189 (1932).

—— *The Game and Playe of Chesse*, ed. Jenny Adams (Kalamazoo, MI, 2008).

—— *The Middle English Text of Caxton's Ovid: Book I*, ed. Diana Rumrich, Middle English Texts, 43 (Heidelberg, 2010).

—— *The Prologues and Epilogues of William Caxton*, ed. W. J. B. Crotch, EETS 176 (1928).

Chartier, Alain, *Le Livre de l'espérance*, ed. François Rouy (Paris, 1989).

—— *Le Quadrilogue invectif*, ed. Florence Bouchet (Paris, 2011).

Chartier, Jean, *Chronique de Charles VII, roi de France*, ed. Vallet de Viriville, 3 vols. (Paris, 1858).

Chaucer, Geoffrey, *The Riverside Chaucer*, ed. Larry D. Benson, 3rd edn. (Boston, 1987).

Christine de Pizan, *The Book of Peace*, ed. and trans. Karen Green, Constant J. Mews, Janice Pinder, and Tania van Hemelryck (University Park, PA, 2008).

The Chronicle and Political Papers of King Edward VI, ed. W. K. Jordan (London, 1966).

Chronicles of London, ed. Charles Lethbridge Kingsford (Oxford, 1905).

A Chronicle of London from 1089–1483, ed. N. H. Nicolas and E. Tyrell (London, 1827).

Chronicon anonymi Cantuariensis: The Chronicle of Anonymous of Canterbury 1346–1365, ed. and trans. Charity Scott-Stokes and Chris Given-Wilson (Oxford, 2008).

Chronicon Galfridi le Baker de Swynbroke, ed. Edward Maunde Thompson (Oxford, 1889).

Chroniques de France, 3 vols. (Paris: Pasquier Bonhomme, 16 Jan. 1476/77; *ISTC* ic00483000).

Chroniques des cordeliers, in *La Chronique d'Enguerran de Monstrelet en deux livres avec pièces justificatives 1400–1444*, ed. L. Douët-d'Arcq, 6 vols. (Paris, 1857–62), vi. 191–327.

Chronique de Mont-Saint-Michel (1343–1468), ed. Siméon Luce, 2 vols. (Paris, 1879–83).

Cicero, *Cato Maior de senectute*, ed. J. G. F. Powell, Cambridge Classical Texts and Commentaries, 28 (Cambridge, 1987).

—— *Rhetorica ad Herennium*, trans. Harry Caplan (Cambridge, MA, 1954).

—— *Tullius de senectute* (Westminster: William Caxton, 1481; *ISTC* ic00627000).

Collection générale des documents français en Angleterre, ed. J. Delpit (Paris, 1847).

Courtecuisse, Jean, *Sénèque des III vertus: La Formula Honestae Vitae de Martin de Braga (pseudo-Sénèque)*, ed. Hans Haselbach (Bern, 1975).

The Coventry Leet Book, ed. M. D. Harris, EETS os 134, 135, 138, 146 in one vol. (1907–13).

Debating the Hundred Years War: Pour ce que plusieurs (La Loy Salique) and A declaration of the trew and dewe title of Henrie VIII, ed. Craig Taylor, Camden Society, 5th ser., 29 (Cambridge, 2008).

'Documents Relating to the Anglo-French Negotiations of 1439', ed. C. T. Allmand, *Camden Miscellany 24*, Camden Society, 4th ser., 9 (1972), 79–149.

'The Earliest English Sailing Directions', ed. Geoffrey A. Lester, in Lister M. Matheson (ed.), *Popular and Practical Science of Medieval England* (East Lansing, MI, 1994), 331–67.

English Suits before the Parlement of Paris, 1420–1436, ed. C. T. Allmand and C. A. J. Armstrong, Camden Society, 4th ser., 26 (1982).

'Epilepsy: The Falling Evil', ed. George R. Keiser, in Lister M. Matheson (ed.), *Popular and Practical Science of Medieval England* (East Lansing, MI, 1994), 219–44.

Fifteenth-Century Translations of Alain Chartier's Le Traité de l'Esperance and Le Quadrilogue Invectif, ed. Margaret S. Blayney, EETS 271, 280, 2 vols. (1974–80).

Flores historiarum, ed. Henry Luard, 3 vols., RS 95 (London, 1890).

Foedera, Conventiones, Litterae et cujuscunque generis Acta Publica, ed. Thomas Rymer, 10 vols. (The Hague, 1739–45).

Fortescue, John, *The Governance of England*, ed. Charles Plummer (Oxford, 1885).

Four English Political Tracts of the Later Middle Ages, ed. Jean-Philippe Genet, Camden Society, 4th ser., 18 (London, 1977).

Froissart, Jean, *Chroniques de Jean Froissart*, ed. Siméon Luce, Gaston Raynaud, Léon Mirot, and Albert Mirot, 15 vols. (Paris, 1869–1975).

Geoffrey of Monmouth, *The History of the Kings of Britain*, ed. Michael D. Reeve, trans. Neil Wright (Cambridge, 2007).

Gesta Henrici Quinti, ed. and trans. Frank Taylor and John S. Roskell (Oxford, 1975).

The Gesta Normannorum ducum of William of Jumièges, Orderic Vitalis, and Robert of Torigni, ed. and trans. Elisabeth M. C. Van Houts, 2 vols. (Oxford, 1992).

Les Grandes Chroniques de France, ed. Jules Viard, Société de l'histoire de France, 10 vols. (Paris, 1920–53).

Les Grandes Chroniques de France: Chronique des règnes de Jean II et de Charles V, ed. R. Delachenal, 4 vols. (Paris, 1910–20).

'Grants of Arms, etc. from the Reign of Edward IV', ed. W. H. St John Hope, *Proceedings of the Society of Antiquaries*, 2nd ser., 16 (1897), 340–56.

Hall's Chronicle, ed. H. Ellis (London, 1809).

Hardyng, John, *The Chronicle of John Hardyng, together with the Continuation by Richard Grafton*, ed. Henry Ellis (London, 1812).

Henrici Quinti, Angliæ regis, gesta, ed. Benjamin Williams (London, 1850).

Higden, Ranulph, *Polychronicon*, ed. Churchill Babington and J. Rawson Lumby, 9 vols., RS 41 (London, 1865–86).

The Histoire ancienne jusqu'à César: A Digital Edition, ed. Hannah Morcos and others [London, 2022], http://www.tvof.ac.uk/textviewer/.

Hoccleve, Thomas, *Complaint and Dialogue*, ed. J. A. Burrow, EETS 313 (1999).

—— *The Regement of Princes*, ed. Frederick J. Furnivall, EETS ES 72 (1897).

Incerti Scriptoris Chronicon Angliae de Regnis Trium Regum Lancastriensium, ed. J. A. Giles (London, 1848).

Jean de Waurin, *Recueil des croniques et anchiennes istories de la Grant Bretaigne, a present nomme Engleterre, 1422–1431*, ed. William Hardy and Edward L. C. P. Hardy, 5 vols., RS 39 (London, 1864–91).

[Jerome] Hieronymus, *Commentarii in prophetas minores*, ed. M. Adriaen, Corpus Christianorum Series Latina, 76 and 76A, 2 vols. (Turnhout, 1969–70).

Joan of Arc: La Pucelle, ed. and trans. Craig Taylor (Manchester, 2006).

John of Wales, *Summa collationum, sive Communiloquium* (Cologne: Ulrich Zel, c.1472; ISTC ij00328000).

—— *Summa collationum, sive Communiloquium* (Augsburg: Anton Sorg, 1475; ISTC).

Journal de Clément de Fauquembergue, greffier du Parlement de Paris, 1417–1435, ed. Alexandre Tuetey and Henri Lacaille, 3 vols. (Paris, 1903–15).

Journal du siège d'Orléans, 1428–1429, ed. Paul Charpentier and Charles Cuissard (Orléans, 1896).

Journal d'un bourgeois de Paris, ed. Alexandre Tuetey (Paris, 1881).

Knighton's Chronicle 1337–1396, ed. and trans. G. H. Martin (Oxford, 1995).

A Late-Medieval History of the Ancient and Biblical World, ed. Cosima Clara Gillhammer, 2 vols. (Heidelberg, 2022).

Latini, Brunetto, *Li Livres dou tresor*, ed. Francis J. Carmody (Berkeley and Los Angeles, 1948).

Laurent de Premierfait, *Livre de vieillesse*, ed. Stefania Marzano (Turnhout, 2009).

Letters and Papers Illustrative of the Wars of the English in France during the Reign of Henry VI, King of England, ed. Joseph Stevenson, 2 vols., RS 22 (London, 1861–4).

Letters, Orders and Musters of Bertrand du Guesclin, 1357–1380, ed. Michael Jones (Woodbridge, 2004).

Lettres de rois, reines et autres personnages des cours de France et d'Angleterre, ed. J. J. Champollion-Figeac, 2 vols. (Paris, 1839–47).

The Libraries of Henry VIII, ed. James P. Carley, Corpus of British Medieval Library Catalogues, 7 (London, 2000).

Libri commentariorum, ed. J. Migne, Patrologia Latina, 25 (Paris, 1845).

Li Fet des Romains, ed. L.-F. Flutre and K. Sneyders de Vogel, 2 vols. (Paris, 1937–8).

Literae Cantuarienses: The Letter Books of the Monastery of Christ Church, Canterbury, ed. J. Brigstocke Sheppard, 3 vols., RS 85 (London, 1887–9).

Literary Remains of King Edward VI, ed. John Gough Nichols (London, 1857).

Le Livre des hommages d'Aquitaine: Restitution du second livre noir de la connétable de Bordeaux, ed. Jean-Paul Trabut-Cussac (Bordeaux, n.d.).

Livy, *Ab urbe condita*, ed. and trans. B. O. Foster and others, 14 vols. (Cambridge, MA, 1919–59).

Lydgate, John, *Troy Book*, ed. Henry Bergen, 4 vols., EETS ES 97, 103, 106, 126 (1906–35).

Narratives of the Expulsion of the English from Normandy: MCCCCXLIX–MCCCCL, ed. Joseph Stevenson, RS 32 (London, 1863).

On the Properties of Things: John Trevisa's Translation of Bartholomaeus Anglicus, De Proprietatibus Rerum: A Critical Text, ed. M. C. Seymour, 3 vols. (Oxford, 1975–87).

Ordonnances des roys de France de la troisième race, vi, ed. D. F. Secousse (Paris, 1741).

The Parliament Rolls of Medieval England, ed. Chris Given-Wilson and others, 16 vols. (London, 2005).

The Paston Letters, ed. James Gairdner, 6 vols. (London, 1904).

Paston Letters and Papers of the Fifteenth Century, ed. Norman Davis (I–II), ed. Richard Beadle and Colin Richmond (III), 3 vols., EETS SS 20–2 (2005–7).

Pension Book of Clement's Inn, ed. Cecil T. Carr, Selden Society, 78 (London, 1960).

The Politics of Fifteenth-Century England: John Vale's Book, ed. M. L. Kekewich and others (Stroud, 1995).

Proceedings and Ordinances of the Privy Council, ed. N. H. Nicolas, 7 vols. (London, 1834–7).

Procès de condamnation et de réhabilitation de Jeanne d'Arc dite la Pucelle, ed. Jules Quicherat, 5 vols. (Paris, 1841–9).

Prosatori latini del Quattrocento, ed. Eugenio Garin (Milan, 1952).

Prose e rime de' due Buonaccorsi da Montemagno, con annotazioni, ed alcune rime di Niccolò Tinucci, ed. Giovambattista Casotti (Florence, 1718).

Rabil, Albert Jr (ed. and trans.), *Knowledge, Goodness, and Power: The Debate over Nobility among Quattrocento Italian Humanists*, MRTS 88 (Binghamton, NY, 1991).

Ralph of Diceto, *The Historical Works of Master Ralph de Diceto, Dean of London*, ed. William Stubbs, 2 vols., RS 68 (London, 1876).

Roger of Hoveden, *Chronica*, ed. William Stubbs, 4 vols., RS 51 (London, 1868–71).

Scrope, Stephen, *The Dicts and Sayings of the Philosophers*, ed. C. F. Bühler, EETS 211 (1941).

—— *The Epistle of Othea*, ed. C. F. Bühler, EETS 264 (1970).

—— *The Epistle of Othea to Hector*, ed. George F. Warner (London, 1904).

'A Short English Chronicle', in *Three Fifteenth-Century Chronicles with Historical Memoranda by John Stowe*, ed. James Gairdner (London, 1880), 1–80.

Sir Bevis of Hampton, ed. Jennifer Fellows, 2 vols., EETS 349–50 (2017).

A Soldiers' Chronicle of the Hundred Years War: College of Arms Manuscript M9, ed. Anne Curry and Rémy Ambühl (Cambridge, 2022).

'The Chronicle of John Somer, OFM', ed. Jeremy Catto and Linne Mooney, in *Camden Miscellany XXXIV: Chronology, Conquest and Conflict in Medieval England*, Camden Society 5th ser., 10 (Cambridge, 1997), 197–285.

Stafford, Sir Thomas, *Pacata Hibernia: Ireland Appeased and Reduced, or, An Historie of the Late Warres of Ireland* (London, 1634).

Thomæ de Elmham Vita et Gesta Henrici Quinti Anglorum Regis, ed. Thomas Hearne (Oxford, 1727).

Tractatus pluviarum et aeris mutationis, ed. Charles Burnett in 'Weather Forecasting, Lunar Mansions and a Disputed Attribution: The *Tractatus pluviarum et aeris mutationis* and *Epitome totius astrologiae* of "Iohannes Hispalensis"', in Wim Raven and A. Akasoy (eds.), *Islamic Thought in the Middle Ages: Studies in Text, Transmission and Translation, in Honour of Hans Daiber* (Leiden, 2008), 219–65.

'A Treatise on the Elections of Times', ed. Lister M. Matheson and Ann Shannon, in Lister M. Matheson (ed.), *Popular and Practical Science in Medieval England* (East Lansing, MI, 1994), 23–59.

Treaty Rolls Preserved in the Public Record Office, ii: *1337–1339*, ed. John Ferguson (London, 1972).

Vegetius, *The Earliest English Translation of Vegetius' De Re Militari*, ed. Geoffrey Lester, Middle English Texts, 21 (Heidelberg, 1988).

La Vie du Prince Noir by Chandos Herald, ed. Diana B. Tyson (Tübingen, 1975).

Walsingham, Thomas, *The St. Albans Chronicle. The Chronica Maiora of Thomas Walsingham*, ii: *1394–1422*, ed. and trans. John Taylor, Wendy R. Childs, and Leslie Watkiss (Oxford, 2011).

Walter of Châtillon (Galteri de Castellione), *Alexandreis*, ed. Marvin L. Colker (Padua, 1978).

—— *Alexandreis*, trans. David Townend (Philadelphia, 1996).

The Winchester Anthology: A Facsimile of British Library Additional Manuscript 60577, ed. Edward Wilson (Cambridge, 1981).

[Worcester, William], *The Boke of Noblesse*, ed. John Gough Nichols (London, 1860).

Worcestre, William, *Itineraries*, ed. John H. Harvey (Oxford, 1969).

—— *The Topography of Medieval Bristol*, ed. Frances Neale, Bristol Record Society, 51 (Bristol, 2000).

SECONDARY SOURCES

Adair, Anya, 'The Otiose Labour of William Darker: Some Light on Ambiguous Strokes in Fifteenth- to Sixteenth-Century English Manuscripts', *Review of English Studies*, 71 (2020), 630–51.

Akbari, Suzanne Conklin, 'Historiography: Nicholas Trevet's Transnational

History', in Suzanne Conklin Akbari and James Simpson (eds.), *The Oxford Handbook of Chaucer* (Oxford, 2020), 368–85.

Alford, Stephen, *Kingship and Politics in the Reign of Edward VI* (Cambridge, 2002).

Allan, Alison, 'Yorkist Propaganda: Pedigree, Prophecy and the "British History" in the Reign of Edward IV', in Charles Ross (ed.), *Patronage, Pedigree and Power in Later Medieval England* (Gloucester, 1979), 171–92.

Allen, Cynthia L., *Genitives in Early English: Typology and Evidence* (Oxford, 2008).

Allmand, Christopher, 'France-Angleterre à la fin de la guerre de cent ans: Le "Boke of Noblesse" de William Worcester', in *La France anglaise au moyen âge* (Paris, 1988), 103–11.

—— *Henry V* (New Haven, 1997).

—— 'The Lancastrian Land Settlement in Normandy, 1417–50', *Economic History Review*, NS 21 (1968), 461–79.

—— *Lancastrian Normandy, 1415–1450: The History of a Medieval Occupation* (Oxford, 1983).

—— and Maurice Keen, 'History and the Literature of War: *The Boke of Noblesse* of William Worcester', in Christopher Allmand (ed.), *War, Government and Power in Late Medieval France* (Liverpool, 2000), 92–105.

Ambühl, Rémy, *Prisoners of War in the Hundred Years War: Ransom Culture in the Late Middle Ages* (Cambridge, 2013).

Anglo-Norman Dictionary, ed. William Rothwell and others, 2nd edn. (Aberystwyth, 2022), https://anglo-norman.net.

Anon., 'Presents to the Society since the Publication of the Last Volume of the Archaeologia', *Archaeologia*, 6 (1782), 400–4.

Anselme, Père, *Histoire généalogique et chronologique de la maison royale de France*, 3rd edn. (Paris, 1712–33).

Les Archives de littérature du Moyen Âge (ARLIMA), https://www.arlima.net/.

Ayton, Andrew, and Philip Preston, *The Battle of Crécy, 1346* (Woodbridge, 2005).

Backhouse, Janet, 'Founders of the Royal Library: Edward IV and Henry VII as Collectors of Illuminated Manuscripts', in Daniel Williams (ed.), *England in the Fifteenth Century: Proceedings of the 1986 Harlaxton Symposium* (Woodbridge, 1987), 23–41.

Baker, Sir John, *The Men of Court 1440 to 1550: A Prosopography of the Inns of Court and Chancery and the Courts of Law*, 2 vols. (London, 2012).

Barron, Kathryn, 'The Collecting and Patronage of John, Lord Lumley (c.1535–1609)', in Edward Chaney (ed.), *The Evolution of English Collecting: Receptions of Italian Art in the Tudor and Stuart Periods* (New Haven, 2003), 125–58.

Bates, David, *Normandy before 1066* (London and New York, 1982).

—— *The Normans and Empire* (Oxford, 2013).

Bazin, J. Louis, *Brancion: Les seigneurs, la paroisse, la ville* (Paris, 1908).

Beadle, Richard, 'English Autograph Writings of the Later Middle Ages: Some Preliminaries', in Paola Chiesa and Lucia Pinelli (eds.), *Gli autografi medievali: Problemi paleografici e filologici* (Spoleto, 1994), 249–68.

—— 'Sir John Fastolf's French Books', in Graham D. Caie and Denis Renevey (eds.), *Medieval Texts in Context* (London, 2008), 96–112.

—— and Lotte Hellinga, 'William Paston II and Pynson's *Statutes of War* (1492)', *The Library*, 7th ser., 2 (2001), 107–19.

Bell, Adrian R., Anne Curry, Andy King, and David Simpkin (eds.), *The Soldier in Later Medieval England* (Oxford, 2013).

Berenbeim, Jessica, 'The Past of the Past: Historical Distance and the Medieval Image', *New Medieval Literatures*, 21 (2021), 191–220.

Biber, Douglas, and Bethany Gray, 'Grammatical Change in the Noun Phrase: The Influence of Written Language Use', *English Language and Linguistics*, 15 (2011), 223–50.

Billanovich, G., 'Petrarch and the Textual Tradition of Livy', *Journal of the Warburg and Courtauld Institutes*, 14 (1951), 137–208.

Bogner, Gilbert, 'Military Knighthood in the Lancastrian Era: The Case of Sir John Montgomery', *Journal of Medieval Military History*, 7 (2009), 104–26.

Bowers, John M., 'Hoccleve's Two Copies of *Lerne to Dye*: Implications for Textual Critics', *Papers of the Bibliographical Society of America*, 83 (1989), 437–72.

Briquet Online, https ://briquet-online.at/.

Brown, Elizabeth A. R., 'Eleanor of Aquitaine Reconsidered: The Woman and Her Seasons', in Bonnie Wheeler and John Carmi Parsons (eds.), *Eleanor of Aquitaine: Lord and Lady* (New York, 2002), 1–54.

Brundage, James A., 'The Canon Law of Divorce in the Mid-Twelfth Century: Louis VII c. Eleanor of Aquitaine', in Bonnie Wheeler and John Carmi Parsons (eds.), *Eleanor of Aquitaine: Lord and Lady* (New York, 2002), 213–21.

Burnley, J. D., 'Curial Prose in England', *Speculum*, 61 (1986), 593–614.

Calle Martín, Javier, '"When that Wounds Are Evil Healed": Revisiting Pleonastic *That* in Early English Medical Writing', *Studia Anglistica Posnaniensia*, 52 (2017), 5–20.

Campbell, Louise, and Francis W. Steer, *A Catalogue of Manuscripts in the College of Arms* (London, 1988).

Carley, James P., 'The Royal Library as a Source for Sir Robert Cotton's Collection: A Preliminary List of Acquisitions', *British Library Journal*, 18 (1992), 52–73.

A Catalogue of the Harleian Manuscripts in the British Museum, 4 vols. (London, 1808).

Chadwick, Henry, *Boethius: The Consolations of Music, Logic, Theology, and Philosophy* (Oxford, 1990).

Clark, Linda (ed.), *The House of Commons 1422–1461*, 7 vols. (Cambridge, 2020).

Collins, Hugh, *The Order of the Garter, 1348–1461: Chivalry and Politics in Late Medieval England* (Oxford, 2000).

—— 'Sir John Fastolf, John Lord Talbot and the Dispute over Patay: Ambition and Chivalry in the Fifteenth Century', in Diana Dunn (ed.), *War and Society in Medieval and Early Modern Britain* (Liverpool, 2000), 114–40.

Contamine, Philippe, 'L'Idée de guerre à la fin du Moyen Age; aspects juridiques et éthiques', *Comptes rendus des séances de l'Academie des Inscriptions et Belles-Lettres*, 123/1 (1979), 70–86.

Cooke, William Henry, *Students Admitted to the Inner Temple* (London, 1878).

Coopland, G. W., *Nicole Oresme and the Astrologers: A Study of his Livre de Divinacions* (Liverpool, 1952).

Crouch , David, *The Normans: The History of a Dynasty* (London, 2002).

Curry, Anne, *The Battle of Agincourt: Sources and Interpretations* (Woodbridge, 2000).

—— 'The Battle Speeches of Henry V', *Reading Medieval Studies*, 34 (2008), 77–97.

—— 'The Coronation Expedition and Henry VI's court in France 1430–32', in Jenny Stratford (ed.), *The Lancastrian Court* (Donington, 2003), 29–52.

—— 'The Garrison Establishment in Lancastrian Normandy in 1436 according to Surviving Lists in Bibliothèque Nationale de France manuscrit français 25773', in Gary P. Baker, Craig L. Lambert, and David Simpkin (eds.), *Military Communities in Late Medieval England: Essays in Honour of Andrew Ayton* (Cambridge, 2018), 237–69.

—— 'Henry V's Harfleur: A Study in Military Administration, 1415–1422', in L. J. Andrew Villalon and Donald J. Kagay (eds.), *The Hundred Years War (Part III): Further Considerations* (Leiden, 2013), 259–84.

—— *The Hundred Years War*, 2nd edn. (Basingstoke, 2003).

—— 'John, Duke of Bedford's Arrangements for the Defence of Normandy in October 1434: College of Arms MS Arundel 48, folios 274r–276v', *Annales de Normandie*, 62 (2012), 235–51.

—— 'The Military Ordinances of Henry V: Texts and Contexts', in Chris Given-Wilson, Ann Kettle, and Len Scales (eds.), *War, Government and Aristocracy in the British Isles, c.1150–1500: Essays in Honour of Michael Prestwich* (Woodbridge, 2008), 214–49.

Cust, Lady Elizabeth, *Some Account of the Stuarts of Aubigny, in France, 1422–1672* (London, 1891).

Davis, Norman, 'The Epistolary Usages of William Worcester', in D. A. Pearsall and R. A. Waldron (eds.), *Medieval Literature and Civilization: Studies in Memory of G. N. Garmonsway* (London, 1969), 249–74.

—— 'Margaret Paston's Uses of *Do*', *Neuphilologische Mitteilungen*, 73 (1972), 55–62.

Davis, Virginia, *William Waynflete: Bishop and Educationalist* (Cambridge, 1993).

Dawson, Giles E., and Laetitia Kennedy-Skipton, *Elizabethan Handwriting 1500–1650: A Manual* (New York, 1966).

Delsaux, Olivier, *Manuscrits et pratiques autographes chez les écrivains français de la fin du moyen âge* (Paris, 2013).

Denifle, H., *La Désolation des églises, monastères et hopitaux en France pendant la Guerre de cent ans*, 2 vols. (Paris, 1897–9).

Derolez, Albert, *The Palaeography of Gothic Manuscript Books* (Cambridge, 2003).

DeVries, Kelly, *Joan of Arc: A Military Leader* (Stroud, 2003).

Douët d'Arcq, L., 'Inventaire de la Bastille de l'an 1428', *Revue archéologique*, 12 (1855–6), 321–49.

Dubosc, F., 'Manuscrit inédit tiré des archives de la maison de Matignon', *Journal des Savants de Normandie* (Rouen, 1844), 52–61, 209–18.

An Electronic Version of A Linguistic Atlas of Late Mediaeval English, ed. M. Benskin, M. Laing, V. Karaiskos and K. Williamson (Edinburgh, 2013), http://www.lel.ed.ac.uk/ihd/elalme/elalme.html.

Emden, A. B., *A Biographical Register of the University of Cambridge to 1500* (London, 1963).

——*A Biographical Register of the University of Oxford A.D. 1500–1540* (Oxford, 1974).

England's Immigrants 1330–1550, www.englandsimmigrants.com.

Fisiak, Jacek, *A Short Grammar of Middle English* (Warsaw, 1968).

Fisher, John H., 'Chancery and the Emergence of Standard Written English in the Fifteenth Century', *Speculum*, 52 (1977), 870–99.

Fischer, Olga, 'Syntax', in Norman Blake (ed.), *The Cambridge History of the English Language*, ii: *1066–1476* (Cambridge, 1992), 207–408.

——*The Syntax of Early English* (Cambridge, 2000).

Fletcher, William Younger, *English Book Collectors* (London, 1902; repr. Frankfurt, 2020).

Flutre, Louis-Fernand, *Les Manuscrits des Faits des Romains* (Paris, 1932).

Foister, Susan, *Holbein in England* (London, 2006).

Fowler, Kenneth, 'Sir John Hawkwood and the English Condottieri in Trecento Italy', *Renaissance Studies*, 12 (1998), 131–48.

Fryde, E. B., 'Edward III's Wool Monopoly of 1337: A Fourteenth-Century Royal Trading Venture', *History*, NS 37 (1952), 8–24.

The Gascon Rolls Project (1317–1468), www.gasconrolls.org.

Gibson, Jonathan, 'From Palatino to Cresci', in James Daybell and Andrew Gordon (eds.), *Cultures of Correspondence in Early Modern England* (Philadelphia, 2016), 29–47.

Gilbert, Jane, Simon Gaunt, and William Burgwinkle, *Medieval French Literary Culture Abroad* (Oxford, 2020).

Gillingham, John, *Richard I* (New Haven, 1999).

Gilson, J. P., and George F. Warner, *Catalogue of Western Manuscripts in the Old Royal and King's Collections*, 4 vols. (London, 1921).

Given-Wilson, Chris, *Henry IV* (New Haven, 2016).

—— and Françoise Bériac, 'Edward III's Prisoners of War: The Battle of Poitiers and its Context', *EHR* 116 (2001), 802–33.

Goodman, Anthony, *John of Gaunt: The Exercise of Princely Power in Fourteenth-Century Europe* (Harlow, 1992).

Green, David S., 'The Household and Military Retinue of Edward the Black Prince', 2 vols. (Ph.D. thesis, Nottingham, 1998).

Greenway, Diana E., 'Historical Writing at St Paul's', in Derek Keene, Arthur Burns, and Andrew Saint (eds.), *St Paul's: The Cathedral Church of London, 604–2004* (New Haven, 2004), 151–6.

—— 'The Succession to Ralph de Diceto, Dean of St Paul's', *Historical Research*, 39 (1966), 86–95.

Griffiths, Ralph A., *The Reign of King Henry VI: The Exercise of Royal Authority, 1422–1461* (London, 1981).

Grummitt, David, *The Calais Garrison: War and Military Service in England, 1436–1558* (Woodbridge, 2008).

Guard, Timothy, *Chivalry, Kingship and Crusade: The English Experience in the Fourteenth Century* (Woodbridge, 2013).

Hagger, Mark S., *Norman Rule in Normandy, 911–1144* (Woodbridge, 2017).

Hanham, Alison, 'The Curious Letters of Friar Brackley', *Historical Research*, 81 (2008), 28–51.

Hardman, Phillipa, 'Lydgate's "Uneasy" Syntax', in Larry Scanlon and James Simpson (eds.), *John Lydgate: Poetry, Culture, and Lancastrian England* (Notre Dame, IN, 2007), 12–35.

Harriss, G. L., 'Fictitious Loans', *Economic History Review*, NS 8 (1955), 187–99.

—— *King, Parliament, and Public Finance in Medieval England to 1369* (Oxford, 1975).

—— 'Marmaduke Lumley and the Exchequer Crisis of 1446–9', in J. G. Rowe (ed.), *Aspects of Late Medieval Government and Society* (Toronto, 1986), 143–78.

Havely, N. R., *Dante's British Public: Readers and Texts, from the Fourteenth Century to the Present* (Oxford, 2014).

Hawkyard, Alasdair, 'Sir John Fastolf's "Gret Mansion by me late edified": Caister Castle, Norfolk', in Linda Clark (ed.), *Of Mice and Men: Image, Belief and Regulation in Late Medieval England*, The Fifteenth Century, 5 (Woodbridge, 2005), 39–67.

Hedeman, Anne D., *The Royal Image: Illustrations of the* Grandes chroniques de France, *1274–1422* (Berkeley, 1991).

Hudd, Alfred E., 'Bristol Merchant Marks', *Proceedings of the Clifton Antiquarian Club*, 7 (1912), 97–194.

Hughes, Jonathan, *Arthurian Myths and Alchemy: The Kingship of Edward IV* (Stroud, 2002).

James, M. R., 'The Carew Manuscripts', *EHR* 42 (1927), 261–7.

—— *A Descriptive Catalogue of the Manuscripts in the Library of Lambeth Palace*, 5 parts in 1 vol. (Cambridge, 1930–2).

—— 'The History of Lambeth Palace Library', *Transactions of the Cambridge Bibliographical Society*, 3 (1959), 1–31.

Jayne, Sears, and Francis R. Johnson (eds.), *The Lumley Library: The Catalogue of 1609* (London, 1956).

Jeay, Claude, *Signature et pouvoir au moyen âge* (Paris, 2015).

Jefferson, Lisa, 'Fragments of a French Prose Version of Gautier de Châtillon's *Alexandreis*', *Romania*, 115 (1997), 90–117.

—— 'MS Arundel 48 and the Earliest Statutes of the Order of the Garter', *EHR* 109 (1994), 356–85.

Johnson, P. A., *Duke Richard of York, 1411–1460* (Oxford, 1988).

Jones, M. K., 'The Battle of Verneuil (17 August 1424): Towards a History of Courage', *War in History*, 9 (2002), 375–411.

—— 'The Beaufort Family and the War in France, 1421–1450' (PhD thesis, Bristol, 1982).

—— 'The Relief of Avranches (1439): An English Feat of Arms at the End of the Hundred Years War', in Nicholas Rogers (ed.), *England in the Fifteenth Century* (Stamford, UK, 1994), 42–55.

—— 'Somerset, York and the Wars of the Roses', *EHR* 104 (1984), 285–307.

Juvonen, Teo, 'Variation in the Form and Function of the Possessive Morpheme in Late Middle and Early Modern English', in Kersti Börjars, David Denison & Alan Scott (eds.), *Morphosyntactic Categories and the Expression of Possession* (Amsterdam, 2013), 35–55.

Keen, Maurice, 'Chaucer's Knight, the English Aristocracy and the Crusade', in V. J. Scattergood and J. W. Sherborne (eds.), *English Court Culture in the Later Middle Ages* (London, 1983), 45–61.

—— *The Laws of War in the Late Middle Ages* (London, 1965).

—— *Origins of the English Gentleman: Heraldry, Chivalry and Gentility in Medieval England c.1300–c.1500* (Stroud, 2002).

—— and M. J. Daniel, 'English Diplomacy and the Sack of Fougères in 1449', *History*, 59 (1974), 375–91.

Ker, N. R., A. J. Piper, and Andrew G. Watson, *Medieval Manuscripts in British Libraries*, 5 vols. (Oxford, 1969–2002).

Kieckhefer, Richard, *Magic in the Middle Ages* (Cambridge, 1989).

Kirby, Thomas Frederick, *Winchester Scholars* (London, 1888).

Lachaud, Frédérique, 'The Knowledge and Use of the "Teachings of Saint Louis" in Fourteenth-Century England', in Hannah Skoda, Patrick Lantschner, and R. L. J. Shaw (eds.) *Contact and Exchange in Later Medieval Europe: Essays in Honour of Malcolm Vale* (Woodbridge, 2012), 189–209.

Laennec, Christine Moneera, 'Christine *antygrafe*: Authorship and Self in the Prose Works of Christine de Pizan with an Edition of B.N. Ms. 603 *Le Livre des Fais d'Armes et de Chevallerie*', 2 vols. (PhD diss., Yale, 1988).

Lander, J. R., 'The Hundred Years War and Edward IV's 1475 Campaign in France', in A. J. Slavin (ed.), *Tudor Men and Institutions* (Baton Rouge, LA, 1972), 70–100.

Lass, Roger, 'Phonology and Morphology', in Norman Blake (ed.), *The Cambridge History of the English Language*, ii: *1066–1476* (Cambridge, 1992), 23–155.

Leach, A. F., 'History of Schools', in *The Victoria County History: Hampshire and the Isle of Wight*, ii (Westminster, 1903), 250–408.

Lester, G. A., *Sir John Paston's 'Grete Boke': A Descriptive Catalogue, with an Introduction, of British Library MS Lansdowne 285* (Cambridge, 1984).

Lewis, P. S., 'War Propaganda and Historiography in Fifteenth-Century France and England', *Transactions of the Royal Historical Society*, 15 (1965), 1–21.

Litt, Thomas, *Les Corps célestes dans l'univers de saint Thomas d'Aquin* (Louvain, 1963).

Mann, Nicholas, *Petrarch Manuscripts in the British Isles*, Italia medioevale e umanistica, 18 (Padua, 1975).

Massey, R., 'The Lancastrian Land Settlement in Normandy and Northern France, 1417–1450' (PhD thesis, Liverpool, 1987).

Mattison, Julia Rice, 'Cest livre est a moy: French Books and Fifteenth-Century England' (PhD diss., Toronto, 2021).

McFarlane, K. B., 'The Investment of Sir John Fastolf's Profits of War', *Transactions of the Royal Historical Society*, 7 (1957), 91–116.

—— 'William Worcester: A Preliminary Survey', in J. Conway Davies (ed.), *Studies Presented to Sir Hilary Jenkinson* (London, 1957), 196–221.

McKenna, John W., 'Piety and Propaganda: The Cult of King Henry VI', in Beryl Rowland (ed.), *Chaucer and Middle English Studies: In Honour of Rossell Hope Robbins* (London, 1974), 145–62.

Mills, Maldwyn, 'EB and His Two Books: Visual Impact and the Power of Meaningful Suggestion. Reading the Illustrations in MSS Douce 261 and Egerton 3132A', in Stephen Kelly and John J. Thompson (eds.), *Imagining the Book* (Turnhout, 2005), 173–91.

Milner, John D., 'The Battle of Baugé, March 1421: Impact and Memory', *History*, 91 (2006), 484–507.

Mitchell, R. J., *John Tiptoft (1427–1470)* (London, 1938).

Molinier, Émile, *Étude sur la vie d'Arnoul d'Audrehem, maréchal de France (130.–1370)* (Paris, 1883).

Mombello, Gianni, 'Notizia su due manoscritti contenenti "l'Epistre Othea" di Christine de Pizan ed altre opere non identificate', *Studi francesi*, 31 (1967), 1–23.

Morell, Thomas, *Catalogus librorum in bibliotheca Osterleiensi* (London, 1771).

Morgan, D. A. L., 'The Political After-Life of Edward III: The Apotheosis of a Warmonger', *EHR* 112 (1997), 856–81.

Morgan, Philip, 'Historical Writing in the North-West Midlands and the Chester Annals of 1385–88', in James Bothwell and Gwilym Dodd (eds.), *Fourteenth Century England IX* (Woodbridge, 2016), 109–29.

Mustanoja, Tauno F., *A Middle English Syntax: Part I, Parts of Speech* (Helsinki, 1960).

Nall, Catherine, 'Moving to War: Rhetoric and Emotion in William Worcester's *Boke of Noblesse*', in Stephanie Downes, Andrew Lynch, and Katrina O'Loughlin (eds.), *Emotions and War: Medieval to Romantic Literature* (London, 2015), 117–32.

—— *Reading and War in Fifteenth-Century England: From Lydgate to Malory* (Cambridge, 2012).

—— 'Ricardus Franciscus Writes for William Worcester', *Journal of the Early Book Society*, 11 (2008), 207–16.

—— 'William Worcester Reads Alain Chartier: *Le Quadrilogue invectif* and its English Readers', in Emma Cayley and Ashby Kinch (eds.), *Chartier in Europe* (Cambridge, 2008), 135–48.

—— and Daniel Wakelin, 'Le Déclin du multilinguisme dans *The Boke of Noblesse* et son Codicille de William Worcester', *Médiévales*, 68 (2015), 73–91.

Nevanlinna, Saara, and Päivi Pahta, 'Middle English Nonrestrictive Expository Apposition with an Explicit Marker', in Jacek Fisiak (ed.), *Studies in Middle English Linguistics* (Berlin, 1997), 373–402.

Nichols, John, *Literary Anecdotes of the Eighteenth Century*, 6 vols. (London, 1812).

Nichols, John Gough, 'An Original Appointment of Sir John Fastolfe to be Keeper of the Bastille of St Anthony at Paris in 1421', *Archaeologia*, 44 (1873), 113–22.

Ogilvie, R. M., *A Commentary on Livy Books 1–5* (Oxford, 1965).

Orme, Nicholas, *Education in the West of England, 1066–1548* (Exeter, 1976).

—— 'A Grammatical Miscellany of 1427–1465 from Bristol and Wiltshire', *Traditio*, 38 (1982), 301–26.

—— 'The Guild of Kalendars, Bristol', *Transactions of the Bristol and Gloucestershire Archaeological Society*, 96 (1978), 32–52.

Ormrod, W. M., *Edward III* (New Haven, 2011).

—— 'A Problem of Precedence: Edward III, the Double Monarchy, and the Royal Style', in J. S. Bothwell (ed.), *The Age of Edward III* (York, 2001), 133–53.

Ouy, Gilbert, 'Manuscrits autographes en France au temps des premiers humanistes', in Olivier Delsaux and Tania Van Hemelryck, *Les Manuscrits autographes en français au Moyen Âge: Guide de recherches* (Turnhout, 2014), 157–95.

Pahta, Päivi, and Saara Nevanlinna, 'Re-phrasing Early English: The Use of

Expository Apposition with an Explicit Marker from 1350 to 1710', in Matti Rissanen, Merja Kytö, and Kirsi Heikkonen (eds.), *English in Transition: Corpus-based Studies in Linguistic Variation and Genre Styles* (Berlin, 1997), 121–83.

Palmer, Richard, 'Sancroft Versus Sheldon: A Case of Books', *The Library*, 7th ser., 18 (2017), 271–91.

Perry, Guy, *The Briennes: The Rise and Fall of a Champenois Dynasty in the Age of the Crusades, c. 950–1356* (Cambridge, 2018).

Phillips, Seymour, *Edward II* (New Haven, 2010).

Pickering, O. S., and V. M. O'Mara, *The Index of Middle English Prose Handlist XIII: Manuscripts in Lambeth Palace Library* (Cambridge, 1999).

Pollard, A. J., *John Talbot and the War in France, 1427–53* (London, 1983).

Powicke, F. M., *The Loss of Normandy, 1189–1204: Studies in the History of the Angevin Empire*, 2nd edn. (Manchester, 1960).

Prescott, Andrew, 'What's in a Number? The Physical Organization of the Manuscript Collections of the British Library', in A. N. Doane and Kirsten Wolf (eds.), *Beatus Vir: Studies in Early English and Norse Manuscripts in Memory of Philip Pulsiano* (Tempe, AZ, 2006), 471–525.

Prestage, John, *A Catalogue of the Entire and Valuable Library of the Honourable Bryan Fairfax Esq., One of the Commissioners of His Majesty's Customs, Deceased* (London, 1756).

Preston, Jean F., and Laetitia Yeandle, *English Handwriting, 1400–1650: An Introductory Manual* (Binghamton, NY, 1992).

Prestwich, Michael, *Edward I* (New Haven, 1997).

Purcell, Mark, *The Country House Library* (New Haven, 2017).

Reno, Christine, 'The Manuscripts of the *Livre des fais d'armes et de chevalerie*', *Digital Philology: A Journal of Medieval Cultures*, 6/1 (2017), 137–62.

Richard, Jean, *Saint Louis: Crusader King of France*, ed. Simon Lloyd, trans. Jean Birrell (Cambridge, 1983).

Richmond, Colin, 'John Fastolf, the Duke of Suffolk, and the Pastons', in Linda S. Clark (ed.), *Rule, Redemption and Representations in Late Medieval England and France* (Woodbridge, 2008), 73–103.

—— *The Paston Family in the Fifteenth Century: Fastolf's Will* (Cambridge, 1996).

—— *The Paston Family in the Fifteenth Century: The First Phase* (Cambridge, 1990).

Robinson, P. R., *A Catalogue of Dated and Datable Manuscripts c. 888–1600 in London Libraries* (London, 2003).

Rogers, Clifford J., 'By Fire and Sword: *Bellum Hostile* and "Civilians" in the Hundred Years War', in Mark Grimsely and Clifford J. Rogers (eds.), *Civilians in the Path of War* (Lincoln, NE, 2002), 33–78.

—— 'Gunpowder Artillery in Europe, 1326–1500: Innovation and Impact', in Robert S. Ehlers Jr., Sarah K. Douglas, and Daniel P. M. Curzon (eds.), *Tech-

nology, Violence, and War: Essays in Honor of Dr. John F. Guilmartin, Jr. (Leiden, 2019), 37–71.

—— *War Cruel and Sharp: English Strategy under Edward III, 1327–1360* (Woodbridge, 2000).

Rose, Jonathan, *Maintenance in Medieval England* (Cambridge, 2017).

—— 'Medieval Estate Planning: The Wills and Testamentary Trials of Sir John Fastolf', in Susanne Jenks, Jonathan Rose, and Christopher Whittick (eds.), *Laws, Lawyers and Texts: Studies in Medieval Legal History in Honour of Paul Brand* (Leiden, 2012), 299–326.

Roskell, J. S., Linda Clark, and Carole Rawcliffe (eds.), *The House of Commons, 1386–1421*, 4 vols. (Stroud, 1993).

Ross, Charles, *Edward IV*, 2nd edn. (New Haven, 1997).

Rowe, B. J. H., 'Discipline in the Norman Garrisons under Bedford 1422–35', *EHR* 46 (1931), 194–208.

Rundle, David, 'William Worcestre, Sir John Fastolf and Latin Learning', *The Library*, forthcoming (2024).

Sammut, Alfonso, *Unfredo duca di Gloucester e gli umanisti italiani* (Padua, 1980).

Schieberle, Misty, *Feminized Counsel and the Literature of Advice in England, 1380–1500* (Turnhout, 2014).

Scholderer, V., 'The Early Editions of Johannes Vallensis', *National Library of Wales Journal*, 3 (1944), 76–9.

Scrope, G. Poulett, *History of the Manor and Ancient Barony of Castle Combe, in the County of Wiltshire* (London, 1852).

Seymour, M. C., 'MSS Douce 261 and Egerton 3132A and Edward Banyster', *Bodleian Library Record*, 10 (1980), 162–5.

Skinner, Quentin, *The Foundations of Modern Political Thought*, 2 vols. (Cambridge, 1978).

Smith, Anthony Robert, 'Aspects of the Career of Sir John Fastolf (1380–1459)' (D.Phil. thesis, Oxford, 1982).

The Soldier in Later Medieval England Online Database, www.medievalsoldier.org#.

Steel, Anthony, 'Mutua per talliam, 1399–1413', *Historical Research*, 13 (1935), 73–84.

Steiner, Emily, *John Trevisa's Information Age: Knowledge and the Pursuit of Literature, c.1400* (Oxford, 2021).

Stratford, Jenny, *The Bedford Inventories: The Worldly Goods of John, Duke of Bedford, Regent of France, 1389–1435* (London, 1993).

Strohm, Paul, *Politique: Languages of Statecraft between Chaucer and Shakespeare* (Notre Dame, IN, 2005).

Suárez-Gómez, Cristina, 'Clause Linkage across Time and Genres in Early English: A Preliminary Approach to Relative Clauses', *Studia Neophilologica*, 84 (2012), 138–50.

Summit, Jennifer, *Lost Property: The Woman Writer and English Literary History, 1380–1589* (Chicago, 2000).

Sumption, Jonathan, *The Hundred Years War*, 4 vols. (London, 1990–2015).

Sutton, Anne, and Livia Visser-Fuchs, *Richard III's Books: Ideals and Reality in the Life and Library of a Medieval Prince* (Stroud, 1997).

—— 'Richard III's Books: XII. William Worcester's *Boke of Noblesse* and his Collection of Documents on the War in Normandy', *The Ricardian*, 115 (1991), 154–65.

Swanson, Jenny, *John of Wales: A Study of the Works and Ideas of a Thirteenth-Century Friar* (Cambridge, 1989).

Syme, Ronald, *The Augustan Aristocracy* (Oxford, 1986).

Taavitsainen, Irma, 'Exclamations in Late Middle English', in Jacek Fisiak (ed.), *Studies in Middle English Linguistics* (Berlin, 1997), 573–608.

Taylor, Craig, 'Edward III and the Plantagenet Claim to the French Throne', in James Bothwell (ed.), *The Age of Edward III* (Woodbridge, 2001), 155–69.

—— 'War, Propaganda and Diplomacy in Fifteenth-Century France and England', in Christopher Allmand (ed.), *War, Government and Power in Late Medieval France* (Liverpool, 2000), 70–91.

Tester, S. J., *A History of Western Astrology* (Woodbridge, 1987).

Thompson, Guy Llewelyn, *Paris and its People under English Rule: The Anglo-Burgundian Regime 1420–1436* (Oxford, 1991).

Thomson, Rodney M., and James G. Clark (eds.), *The University and College Libraries of Oxford*, 2 vols., Corpus of British Medieval Library Catalogues, 16 (London, 2015).

Thorpe, Deborah, 'Documents and Books: A Case Study of Luket Nantron and Geoffrey Spirleng as Fifteenth-Century Administrators and Textwriters', *Journal of the Early Book Society*, 14 (2011), 195–216.

—— 'Writing and Reading in the Circle of Sir John Fastolf (d. 1459)' (PhD thesis, York, 2012).

Tilmouth, Christopher, *Passion's Triumph over Reason: A History of the Moral Imagination from Spenser to Rochester* (Oxford, 2007).

Tite, Colin G. C., 'A Catalogue of Sir Robert Cotton's Printed Books?', in C J. Wright (ed.), *Sir Robert Cotton as Collector: Essays on an Early Stuart Courtier and his Legacy* (London, 1997), 183–93.

—— *The Early Records of Sir Robert Cotton's Library: Formation, Cataloguing, Use* (London, 2003).

—— '"Lost or stolen or strayed": A Survey of Manuscripts Formerly in the Cotton Library', in C. J. Wright (ed.), *Sir Robert Cotton as Collector: Essays on an Early Stuart Courtier and his Legacy* (London, 1997), 262–306.

Vale, M. G. A., *English Gascony, 1399–1453* (Oxford, 1970).

—— 'The Last Years of English Gascony, 1451–1453', *Transactions of the Royal Historical Society*, 5th ser., 19 (1969), 119–38.

Vaughan, Richard, *Philip the Bold: The Formation of the Burgundian State* (London, 1962).

—— *Philip the Good: The Apogee of Burgundy* (London, 1970).

Venn, John, and J. A. Venn, *Alumni Cantabrigiensis*, 10 vols. (Cambridge, 1922–54).

Vernier, Richard, *The Flower of Chivalry: Bertrand du Guesclin and the Hundred Years War* (Woodbridge, 2003).

Voigts, Linda Ehrsam, 'A Doctor and his Books: The Manuscripts of Roger Marchall (d. 1477)', in Richard Beadle and A. J. Piper (eds.), *New Science out of Old Books: Studies in Manuscripts and Early Printed Books in Honour of A. I. Doyle* (Aldershot, 1995), 249–301.

Wachowich, Cameron, 'On *Ormesta*', *Quaestio insularis*, 22 (2021), 107–62.

Wakelin, Daniel, *Designing English: Early Literature on the Page* (Oxford, 2017).

—— 'England: Humanism beyond Weiss', in David Rundle (ed.), *Humanism in Fifteenth-Century Europe*, Medium Ævum Monograph Series (Oxford, 2012), 265–305.

—— *Humanism, Reading, and English Literature, 1430–1530* (Oxford, 2007).

—— *Scribal Correction and Literary Craft: English Manuscripts 1475–1510* (Cambridge, 2014).

—— 'William Worcester Reads Chaucer's *Boece*', *Journal of the Early Book Society*, 5 (2002), 177–80.

—— 'William Worcester Writes a History of His Reading', *New Medieval Literatures*, 7 (2005), 53–71.

Walker, Simon, *The Lancastrian Affinity, 1361–1399* (Oxford, 1990).

Walther, Hans, *Proverbia sententiaeque latinitatis medii aevi*, 6 vols. (Göttingen, 1963–9).

Wasserzeichen-Informationssystem, https://www.wasserzeichen-online.de.

Watson, Andrew G., *Catalogue of Dated and Datable Manuscripts c. 435–1600 in Oxford Libraries*, 2 vols. (Oxford, 1984).

—— *Catalogue of Dated and Datable Manuscripts c.700–c. 1600 in the Department of Manuscripts, the British Library*, 2 vols. (London, 1979).

Watts, John, *Henry VI and the Politics of Kingship* (Cambridge, 1996).

Wheeler, Everett L., 'Christine de Pizan's *Livre des fais d'armes et de chevalerie*: Gender and the Prefaces', *Nottingham Medieval Studies*, 46 (2002), 119–61.

Whiting, Bartlett Jere, and Helen Wescott Whiting, *Proverbs, Sentences and Proverbial Phrases: From English Writings Mainly before 1500* (Cambridge, MA, 1968).

Willetts, Pamela J., *Catalogue of Manuscripts in the Society of Antiquaries of London* (Woodbridge, 2000).

Wolffe, Bertram, *Henry VI* (New Haven, 2001).

Wright, Laura, 'Bills, Accounts, Inventories: Everyday Trilingual Activities in the Business World of Later Medieval England', in D. A. Trotter (ed.), *Multilingualism in Later Medieval Britain* (Cambridge, 2000), 149–56.

Wright, Nicholas, 'Ransoms of Non-combatants during the Hundred Years War', *Journal of Medieval History*, 17 (1991), 323–32.

Wylie, J. H., and W. T. Waugh, *The Reign of Henry the Fifth*, 3 vols. (Cambridge, 1914–29).

THE BOKE OF NOBLESSE

'*The Boke of Noblesse*, compiled to the most hygh
and myghty prince Kyng Edward the IIIJ^{the} for the
auauncyng and preferryng the comyn publique
of the royaumes of England and of Fraunce'

First, in the worship of the Holy Trinite, bring to mynde to calle, in the ₅
begynnyng of euery good work, for grace.

And sithe this litill epistle is write and entitled to courage and comfort noble men in armes to be in perpetuite of remembraunce for here
noble dedis, as right conuenient is soo to bee, and as it is specified by
auctorite of the noble cenatoure of Rome, Kayus son, in these termes ₁₀
foloweng: 'Hoc igitur summum est nobilitatis genus: posse maiorum
suorum egregia facta dicere; posse eorum beneficijs petere honores pu-
blicos; posse gloriam rei publice hereditareo quodam iure vendicare;
posse insuper sese eorum partes vocare et clarissimas in suis vultibus
ymagines ostendere, quos enim appellat vulgus, nisi quod nobilissimi ₁₅
parentes genuere.'

'De remedio casus rei publice.'

Here folowethe the evident examples and the resons of comfort for a
reformacion to be had vppon the piteous complaintes and dolorous
lamentacions made for the right grete, outragious and most greuous ₂₀
losse of the royaume of Fraunce, ducheez of Normandie, of Gascoyne
and Guyen, and also the noble counte of Mayne and the erledom of Pontif. And, for releuyng and geting ayen the said reaume, dukedoms, vndre
correccion of amendement ben shewed the exortacions and mocions,
be auctorite, example of actis in armes, bothe by experience and other- ₂₅
wise, purposid, meoued and declared to corage and comfort the hertis
of Englisshe nacion—hauyng theire first originall of the nacion of the
noble auncient bloode of Troy more than .M^l. yere before the birthe
of Crist.

1–4 *The Boke of Noblesse* . . . Fraunce] *WW in top marg. in red*   2 Ed-
ward] *reader 1 adds* harry *after l. end in lighter brown ink;* harry *then crossed out in
darker brown ink*   IIIJ^{the}] *reader 1 alters* iiij *to* vij *in lighter brown ink;* iiij *and
its alteration then crossed out in darker brown ink and* iiij *interl.*   17 De . . .
publice] *WW in blank space in red*   27 Englisshe nacion] *reader 2 in marg.*
Anglorum natio (*corrected from* natione) originem sumpsit ex natione troianorum

f. 1ᵛ   In token and profe wherof, the auncient | langage of the Brutes bloode
31   at this day remayne'th' bothe in the princedome of Walis and in the
     auncient prouynce and dukedom of Cornewaile, whiche was at tho
     daies called corrupt Greke. And next after, the mighty Saxons bloode,
     otherwise called a prouynce in Germayne, that the vaileaunt Duke Cer-
35   dicius arriued in this reaume; whiche whan, Arthur, king of the Breton
     bloode, made mighty werre and suffred hym to inhabit here. And tho
     Saxons, as it is writen in Berthilmew in his *Booke of Propreteis*, also were
     decendid of the nacion of Grekis. And next after came the feers manly
     Danys nacion, also of Grekis bene decendid, that the gret iusticer, King
40   Knowt, this land subdued 'and' the Saxons bloode. And sithen the noble
     Normannes, also of the Danys nacion descendid, be William Conquer-
     our of whome ye ben lyniallie descendid, subdued this lande. And last
     of alle, the victorius bloode of Angeuyns, by mariage of that puissaunt
     Erle Geffrey Plantagenet, the son and heire of Fouke, king of Iherus-
45   alem, be mariage of Dame Maude, emperes, soule doughter and heire
     to the king of grete renoune Henry the First of Inglond, and into this
     day lineally descendid in most prowes.
         And whiche said Englisshe nacion ben sore aston'y'ed and dulled for
     the repairing and wynnyng ayen, vppon a new conquest to be hadde,
50   for youre verray right and true title in the enheritaunce of the saide
     reaume of Fraunce and the duche of Normandie. Of whiche duchie we
     haue in the yere of oure Lorde Mˡiiijᶜ. l., lost as bethyn the space of
     xv. monithes, be put out wrongfullie thoroughe subtile wirkingis con-
     spired and wrought be the Frenshe partie vndre the vmbre and coloure
55   of trewis late taken betwixt youre antecessoure King Harry the Sext,
     then named king, and youre grete aduersarie of Fraunce, Charles the
f. 2ʳ VIJᵗʰᵉ. And whereas the saide piteous complaintes, dolorous | lamenta-
     cions, of youre verray true obeisaunt subgectis for lesing of the said
     countreis may not be tendrid ne herde, many daies haue had but litill
60   comfort; nether the anguisshes, troubles and diuisions here late before
     in this reaume be cyuyle bataile[z] to be had may not preuaile them
     to the repairing and wynnyng of any soche manere outrageous losses

     30 langage] *reader 2 in marg.* jᵒ Nota quod lingua britonum adhuc vsitatur in wallia et
     Cornibea que lingua vocabatur corrupta greca   31 remayne'th'] th *over uneras.* n
     bothe] *before* bothe *reader 1 interl.* yn your most noble persone and   33 Saxons]
     reader 2 in marg. ijᵒ Lingua Saxonum alias lingua germanorum   34–5 Cerdicius]
     reader 2 in marg. Dux Cerdicius applicuit in britannia tempore Regis Arthuri et sic per
     fauorem regis inhabitauit et iret (?) ex natione grecorum.   39 Danys] *reader 2 in
     marg., directly after previous note,* iijᵒ Lingua danorum ex natione grecorum Rex danorum
     knott conquestum fecit   40 and] WW *interl.*   48 aston'y'ed] WW y *over
     uneras.* i   61 batailez] Batailer

to this reaume, whiche hathe thoroughe sodein and variable chaunces
of vnstedfast fortune so be reualed and ouerthrow. The tyme of relief
and comfort wolde not be despendid ne occupied so, namely withe 65
theym whiche that haue necessite of relief and socoure of a grettir
auauntage and a more profitable remedie for theire auauncement to a
new conquest, or by a good tretie of a finall peace for the recouere of
the same. But to folow the counceile of the noble cenatoure of Rome,
Boicius, in the second prose of his first booke *Of Consolacion* seieng, 70
'Sed medicine', inquid, 'tempus est 'quam' querele.'

Therfor, alle ye louyng liege-men, 'both' youre noble alliaunces and
frendis, leuithe suche idill lamentacions, put away thoughte and gret
pensifnes of suche lamentable passions and besinesse, and put ye hem
to foryetefulnesse. And doo not away the recordacion of actis and dedis 75
in armes of so many famous and victorious kingis, princes, dukis, erles,
barounes and noble knyghtis, as of full many other worshipfull men
haunting armes, whiche as verray trew martirs and blissid soules haue
taken theire last ende by werre, some wounded and taken prisonneris,
in so iust a title and conquest vppon youre enheritaunce in Fraunce 80
and Normandie, Gasquyn and Guyen; and also by the famous king and
mighty prince, King Edwarde the Thrid, first heriter to the said royaume of Fraunce, and by Prince Edwarde, his eldist son, and all his
noble bretherin pursued his title and right be force of armes; as was
of late tyme sithe the yere of Crist .M^l. iiij^{C}xv. done | and made a new f. 2^v
conquest, in conquering bothe the saide reaume of Fraunce and duche 86
of Normaundie, by the prince of blissid memorie King Harry the V^{the},
also be the eide of tho thre noble prynces, his bretherne, and be other of
his puissaunt dukes and lordis being lieutenauntz for the werre in that
parties, as it is notorily knowen thoroughe alle Cristen nac'y'ons to the 90
gret renomme of worship of this reaume.

How euery good man of 'worshyp yn' armes shulde in the werre be resembled to the condicion of a lion.

And therfor in conclusion, euery man in hymsilf, let the passions of
dolours be turned and empressid into 'bys'nes of here spiritis, of egre 95
courages of manlinesse and feersnesse, after the condicion of the lion

71 quam] *scr. in marg.*   72 both] *scr. over eras. of shorter word*   90 nac'y'ons]
WW y *over uneras.* e   92 worshyp yn] WW *at end of one l. and start of*
next l.   shulde] *followed by eras. of perhaps 2 letters, covered with line-filler*
95 empressid] emperressid, *with unnecessary* er *abbrev. on* p   'bys'nes] bys *over uneras.*
e⟨?⟩t

resembled in condicions vnto. For as ire, egrenesse and feersnesse is
holden for a vertu in the lion, so in like manere the said condicions is
taken for a vertue and renomme of worship to alle tho that haunten
100 armes, that so vsithe to be egre, feers vppon his aduers partie, and not
to be lamentable and soroufull after a wrong shewed vnto theym, and
thus withe coragious hertis putting forthe theire prowes in dedis of
armes. So that all worshipfull men whiche ought be stedfast and holde
togider may be of one intencion, wille and comon assent to vapour,
105 sprede out, according to the floure-de-lice and auaunce hem forthe be
feernesse of strenght and power to the verray effect and dede ayenst
the vntrew reproches of oure auncien aduersaries halding vppon the
Frenshe partie, whiche of late tyme, by vniust dissimilacions vndre the
vmbre and coloure of trewis and abstinence of werre late hadde and
110 sacred at the cite of Tairs the .xxviij. day of Maij the yere of Crist M^l. iiij^C
xliiij^{to}, haue by intrusion of soche subtile dissimilacion wonne vppon
vs, bethyn .v. yeres next foloweng withyn the tyme of 'the last' trieux,
the said reaume and duchee[z]. So that in the meane tyme and sethe
f. 3^r contynued | forthe the saide trewes frome yere to yere to this land grete
115 charge and cost, till they had conspired and wrought theire auauntage, as it approuethe dailie of experience; and vnder this, they being
assailours vppon this lande and begynneris of the trewes breking.

How the Frenshe partie began first to offende and brake the trewis.

120 First, by taking of youre shippis and marchaundises vpon the see,
keping men of noble birthe vndre youre predecessoure obedience and
diuers other true lieges-men prisoneris vnder arest; as that noble and
trew knight Ser Gilis, the duke is son of Bretaine, whiche, for his grete
trouthe and loue he hadde to this youre royame-warde, ayenst all man-
125 hod vngoodely entretid, died in prison; and also, before the taking of
Fugiers, Ser Simon Morhier, knight, the prouost of Paris, a lorde also of
youre partie and chief of the kingis counceile, take prisoner by Deepe
and paieng a grete raunson or he was deliuerid; and sone after, one
Mauncell, a squier comyng fro Rone with xx. parsones in his company
130 to Deepe pesibly, in the monythe of Ianuarij next before the taking of
Fugiers, were in Deepe taken prisoneris wrongfullie vndre the vmbre

112 the last] *WW interl.*   113 ducheez] ducheer   121 predecessoure]
reader 1 in marg. Tempore Regis Henrici vj^{ti}

of trewis; and sithen the Lord Faucomberge, take prisoner by subtile
vndew meanys of `a cautel', taken vnder safconduct of youre aduersarie
at Pountelarge the xv day of Maij the yere of Crist M^l. iiij^{C}xlix; and
also the said forteresse of Pountlarge, take the said day be right vndew   135
meanys taken vppon the said Lorde Faucomberge, contrarie to the
said trewis, forging here colourable matieris in so detestable vniust
quarellis. For reformacion of whiche gret iniuries conspired, shewed
and doone, alle ye put to youre handis to this paast and matier!

  Comythe, therfor, and | approchen, bothe kyn, affinitees, frendis,   f. 3^v
subgectis, allie`s' and alle welle-willeris. Now at erst the irnesse be   141
brennyng hote in the fire thoroughe goode courage. The worke is ouermoche kindelid and begonne thoroughe oure dulnesse and sleuthe
slommering many day. For be the sheding of the bloode of good
Cristen people, as hathe be done in youre predecessours conquest that   145
now is lost, is said be the wordis of Iob, 'Criethe and bewailethe in the
feelde, frendis and kyn, take heede pitously to youre bloode.'

Notandum. **A question of grete charge and wight meoued first
to be determyned: whethir for to make werre vppon Cristen
bloode is laufull.**   150

But first ther wolde be meoued a question, whiche Dame Cristyn
makithe mencion of in the seconde chapitre of *The Tree of Batailles*:
whethir that werres and batailes meintenyng and vsing ben laufull
according to iustice, or no. And the oppinion of many one wolde
vndrestond that haunting of armes and werre-making is not lefull ne   155
iust thing, for as moche in haunting and vsing of werre be many infinite
damages and extorsions done, as mourdre, slaughter, bloodesheding,
depopulacion of contrees, castell, citees and townes brennyng, and
many suche infinite damages. Wherfor it shuld seme to, meintenyng of
werre is a cursid deede, not dew to be meyntened.   160

  As to this question, if it may be answerd, that entreprinses and werris taken and founded vppon a iust cause and a trew title is suffred of
God, for Dame Cristen seiethe and moeuithe in the first booke of *The
`A'rbre of Bataile*, how it is for to haue in consideracion why that princes
shuld maynteyne werre | and vse bataile. And the saide Dame Cristin   f. 4^r

---

133 a cautel] *WW over eras.*   137 so] *followed by eras. of perhaps 4 letters, covered
with line-filler*   141 allie`s'] s *over uneras.* z   151 But] *WW symbol at fore-edge*
156 infinite] infinitee   164 `A'rbre] A *over eras. of perhaps 1 letter and an uneras.* e

166 saiethe .v. causes principall. Thre of them bene of right, and the other
      Prima. tweyn of vallente. The first cause is to susteyne right and iustice.
      ij.^{da}. The second is to withestande all soche mysdoers the whiche wold
      defoule, grief and oppresse the peple of the contre that the 'kyng or'
170 iiij.^d. prince is gouernoure 'of'. The thrid is for to recuuer landes, sei-
      gnories and goodes be other vnrightfully rauisshed, taken away be force
      or vsurped, whiche shulde apperteine to the 'kyng and' prince of the
      same seigniorie, or ellis to whome his subgett'ys' shuld apparteine, be
      meinteined vnder. And the othre tweyn be but of violen'c'e, as for to
175 be venged for dammage or grief done by another; the othir to conquere
      straunge countrees bethat any title of right, as King Alexaundre con-
      querid vppon the Romayn; whiche tweine last causes, they the conquest
      or victorie by violence or by roiall power sownethe worshipfull in dede
      of armes, yet ther ought no Cristen prince vse them.
180   And yet in the first thre causes, before a prince 'to' take an entreprise,
      it most be done be a iust cause, and hauyng right gret deliberacion by
      the conduyt and counceile of the most sage, approuued men of a reaume
      or countre that the prince is of. And so for to vse it in a iust quarell, it
      is the right execucion of iustice, [as iustice] requirithe, whiche is one
185 of the principall .iiij. cardinall vertues. And if that vsing of armes and
      haunting of werre be doone rather for magnificence, pride and wilful-
      nesse to destroie roiaumes and countreis by roiall gret power, as whan
      tho that wolde avenge haue noo title but sey 'Viue le plus fort' (is 'to sey',
      'Let the 'grettest' maistrie haue the feelde')—'lyke as when the duc off
190 Burgoyn by cyvyle bataylles by maisterdom expelled the duc of Orly-
      ance partie and hys frendes owt of Parys cytee the yeere of Crist M^l.
      iiii^C. xij and slow many "thowsandes and" hondredes bethout title of
      iustice, but to be venge a synguler querel betwene both princes for the
      deth of the duc off Orlyance, slayn yn the vigille of Seynt Clement by
195 Raulyn Actovyle of Normandye yn the yeer of Crist M^l. iiij^C. vij°; and
      the bataylle of Seynt-Clow besyde Parys, by the duc of Burgoyn wyth
      help of capteyns of England, owt of England waged by the seyd duc,
      was myghtly foughten and had the feelde ayenst theyr aduerse partye,
      albeyt the duc of Orlyance waged another armee sone aftyr owt of Eng-

    169 kyng or] *WW at end of one l. and start of next l.*   170 of] *WW in
space between words*   172 kyng and] *WW at end of one l. and start of next l.*
173 subgett'ys'] *WW ys over scr's abbrev. for es*   174 violen'c'e] *top of t eras.
to form c*   180 to] *WW at l. end*   184 iustice, as iustice requirithe] iustice
requirithe (*see n.*)   188 to sey] *WW over eras.*   189 grettest] *WW at l. end*
189–206 lyke as when . . . the seyd yere] *WW in marg.*   192 thowsandes and] *WW
interl. into marg. addn*   196 Seynt-Clow] Seyntclow *duplic. at end of one l. and
start of next*

land to relyeve the ovyrthrow he had at Seynt-Clowe; and the dyvysyon 200
betwene the duc of Orlyance and the duc of Burgoyn dured yn Fraunce
contynuelly by xj. yeer day, as to the yeere of Crist .M^l. iiij^C xviij., yn
whych yeere Phelip, duc of Burgoyn, a greet frende to thys land, was
pyteousely slayn at Motreaw; an"d" the cyte of Pa"r"ys ayen taken by
the Burgonons, Lord L'Ysel-Adam pryncipall capteyn; and the erle of 205
Armonak, conestable, sleyn by the comyns the seyd yere'—in soche
vndew entreprises theire can be thought no grettir tiranny, extorcion
ne cruelte 'by dyvysyons'.

How Seint Lowes exorted and counceiled his | sonne to moeue no werre ayenst Cristen peple.

f. 4^v
210

Seynt Lowys. And the blissid king of Fraunce, Seint Lowes, exhorted and
comaunded in his testament writen of his owne hand that he made
1270. the tyme of his passing out of this worlde the yere of Crist M^l.
CClxx. to his sonne Philip that reigned after hym, that he shulde kepe
hym well to meoue no werre ayenst no Cristen man, but if he had gre- 215
uously done ayenst hym; and if he seke waies of pece, of grace and
mercie thou oughtest pardon hym and take soche amendis of hym as
God may be pleasid. But as for this blissid kingis counceile: it is notorily and openly knowen thorcughe alle Cristen royaumes that 'y'oure
aduerse party hathe meoued, excited, werre and batailes bothe by lond 220
and see ayenst this noble royaume bethout any iustice, title, and bethout
waies of pease shewed. And as for to defende them assailours 'vppo'n
youre true title may be 'be'thout note of tiranye, to put yow in youre
deuoire to conquere youre rightfull enheritaunce without that a bettir
m'o'y'e'ne be had. 225

Exclamacio. A exortacion of a courageous disposicion for a reformacion of a wrong done.

O then, ye worshipfull men of Englisshe nacion, whiche bene descendid
of the noble Brutis bloode of Troy, suffre ye not than youre highe,
auncien couragis to be reualid ne desteined by youre said aduersaries 230

204 an"d"] WW interl. d   Pa"r"ys] short r overwritten with long r   208 by
dyvysyons] WW at end of one l. and start of next l.   212 that] unidentified reader
annot. nota   219 'y'oure] WW y interl.   222 'vppo'n] WW vppo over eras.
223 'be'thout] WW interl. be   225 m'o'y'e'ne] o over uneras. e and an additional
e interl.

of Fraunce at this tyme, neither in tyme to come; ne in this maner to
be rebuked and put abak to youre vttermost deshonoure and reproche
in the sight of straunge nacions—without that it may be in goodely
hast remedied, 'as youre hyghnesse now entendyth'—whiche ye haue be
235 conquerours of, as ye to be yolden and ouercomen in deffaute of goode
and hasty remedie, thoroughe lak of prouision, of men of armes, tresour and finaunce, of suffisaunt nombre of goodes in season and tyme
couenable to wage and relief them. For were ye not somtyme 'tho' that,
f. 5ʳ thoroughe youre gret 'prowesse,' | corages, feersnes, manlinesse and of
240 strenght, ouerleid and put in subgeccion the gret myght and power of
the feers and puissaunt figheters of alle straunge nacions that presumed
to set ayenst this lande?

How many worthi kinges of this lande haue made gret con-
questis in ferre contrees in the Holy Lande, and also for the
245 **defence and right of this lande and for the duche of Normandie.**

Arthure. And for an example and witnes of King Arthur, whiche dis-
comfit and sleine was vndre his banere the emperoure of Rome in
bataile; and conquerid the gret part of the regions be west of Rome.
And many othre conquestis hathe be made before the daies of the said
250 Brenus. Arthur be many worthi kinges of this roiaume, as by Brenus,
King Belynus brother, a puissaunt chosen duke that was before the
Incarnacion wanne and conquerid to Rome, except the Capitoile of
Rome; and sithen of other victorious kinges and princes, as
Edmundus Irenside. Edmonde Irensede had many gret bataile, desconfited the
255 Willelmus Conquestor. Danes to safe Englond. And what victorious dedis William
Conqueroure did: gret actis in bataile vppon the Frenshe
Henricus Primus, fundator plurimorum castrorum. partie '"in" conquestys'. And also his son 'Kyng' Harry
after hym defendid Normaundie, bilded and fortified
many a strong castell in his londe to defende his duke-
260 Robertus, frater Henrici Primi, electus rex de Ieru- salem, sed renuit. dome ayenst the Frenshe partie. And how victoriouslie
his brother Roberd did armes vppon the conquest of the
Holy Londe, that for his gret prowesse there was elect to
be king of Iherusalem and refusid it for a singuler couetice
to be duke of Normandie, 'returned home' 'a'nd neuer had grace of

234 as . . . entendyth] WW interl.   238 tho] WW over eras.   239 prowesse]
WW at l. end   257 '"in" conquestys] WW interl.; ma and tail of y eras. to leave minims
as in   Kyng] WW interl.   264 returned home] WW over longer eras.; followed by
a line-filler   'a'nd] one-compartment a changed to two-compartment a

victorie after. And to bring to mynde how the noble werriour Fouke, 265

Fulco, comes de Angou, rex Ierusalem. erle of Angew, father to Geffrey Plantagenet, youre noble auncetour, left his erledom to his sonne and made werre vppon the Saras`y'nes in the Holy Land, and for his noble

1131. dedis was made king of Iherusalem `the yeer' *anno Christi*

De Ricardo Rege Primo in Terra Sancta. .M^l. | Cxxxj. As how King Richarde the First, clepid Cuer f. 5^v de Lion, whiche in a croiserie went into the Holy Londe, 271

Archiepiscopus Cantuariensis. and Baldewyn, archebisshop of Caunterburie, Hubert,

Comes Chestre. bisshop of Salisburie, Randolf, the erle of Chestre, Roberd

Robertus Clare, comes Gloucestrie. Clare, erle of Gloucestre, and werreied vppon the hethen paynemys in the companie of King Phelip Dieudonne of 275

Philippus, rex Francie, vocatus Deodatus, in Terra Sancta. Fraunce, whiche King Richard conquerid and wanne by roiall power vppon the Sarrasyns in the yere of Crist M^l. C.

iiij^xx vij° and toke the king of Cipres and many other gret prisonneris; also put the londe of Surie in subieccion; the isle of Cipres and the gret cite of Damask wanne be assaut; slow the king of Spayne clepid 280 Ferranus. And the said King Richard kept and defendid frome his aduersarie Philip Dieudonne, king of Fraunce, be mighty werre made to hym, the duchee[z] of Normandie, Gascoigne, Gyen, the counteez of Aniou and Mayne, Tourayne, Pontyue, Auuerne and Champaigne, of alle whiche he was king, duke, erle and lorde as his enheritaunce, and 285

Edwardus Rex Primus. as his predecessours before hym did. Also in like wise King Edward First after the Conquest, being prince in ab`ou't the yere of Crist M^l. ij^C. lxx., put hym in gret laboure and auenture amongis the Sarrasins in the count`r'e of Aufrik; was at the conquest of the gret cite of the roiaume of Thunes—`yn whych cuntree that tyme 290

Sanctus Lodowi- cus, rex Francie, obijt in viagio antequam per- uenit ad Terram Sanctam. and yeere Seynt Lowys, kyng of Fraunce, dyed, and the croyserye grete revaled by hys trespassement, had not the seyd Prince Edward ys armee be redye there to parforme that holye voyage to Iherusalem, as he dyd wyth many

noble lordes off England'; also full noblie ententid about the defence 295 and saufegarde of the gret cite of Acres in the lond of Sirie that had be lost and yolden to the Sarrazins, had not `hys armee and' his power bee, and by an hole yere, osteyng and abiding there, in tyme of gret pestilence and mortalite reigning there and by whiche his peple were

---

268 Saras`y'nes] *WW* y *over uneras.* i 269 the yeer] *WW interl.* 270 .M^l. [f. 5^v] Cxxxj] *WW duplic.* Cxxxj. *in marg. at foot of f.* 5^r *and* .M^l. *in marg. at top of f.* 5^v King] *WW symbol at fore-edge* 273SN Comes Chestre] *MS places after next siden.* Robertus . . . Gloucestrie 283 ducheez] ducheer 287 ab`ou't] *two minims written over* at *altering them to* ou 289 count`r'e] *WW interl.* r 290-5 yn whych cuntree . . . England] *WW interl. and continues in marg.* 297 hys armee and] *WW at l. end*

300 gretely wastid; where he was be treason of a vntrew messaunger Sar-
rasin wounded hym in his chambre almost to dethe, that the souldone
of Babiloyne had waged hym to doo it, becaus of sharpe and cruell
werre the seid Edwarde made vppon the Sarrasines, of gret fere and
doubte he had of the said Prince Edward and of his power (whiche

f. 6ʳ processe ye may more groundly see in the *Actis* of the said | Prince
306 Edwarde is laboure). And his father King Harry Thrid decesid while
his son was in the Holy Londe warring vppon the Sarasines. And

Ricardus, how worshipfullie Richard, emperoure of Almaine and
imperator Ale-
mannie et comes brother to the said King Henry, did gret actis of armes
310 Cornewayle. in the Holy Londe vppon the Sarasines and in the yere of

Edwardus Crist M^l. ij^C. xl. And ouermore, the said King Edwarde
Primus Rex.
 First kept vnder subieccion bothe Irelond, Walis and
Scotlond, whiche were rebellis and wilde peple of condicion; and also
protectid and defendid the duchee[z] of Gascoigne and Guyen, his
315 rightfull enheritaunce.

How King Edward Thrid had the victorie at the bataile of Scluse and gate Cane by assaut and, hauyng the victorie at the batelle of Cressye, ʻwanne Calix by sege.ʼ

And sithen, ouer that, how that the most noble famous knight of
320 renomme, King Edwarde the Thrid, the which withe his roiall power
the yere of Crist M^l. CCC xl. ʻthe day of Seynt Iohn Baptisteʼ wanne
the gret bataile vppon the see at Scluse ayenst Philip de Valoys, calling
hym the Frenshe king, and his power and alle his gret nauye of shippis
destroied to the nombre of .xxv. M^l. men and .CCxxx^{ti}. shippis and
325 barges. And also after that in the yere of Crist .M^l. iij^C xlvj. the said
King Philip purposid to haue entred into Englond and had waged a
gret noumbre of Genues shippis and othre nauyes. And the said King
Edward Thrid thought rather to werre withe hym in ʻthatʼ countre;
rather tooke his viage to Cane withe .xij^C. shippis; passed into Nor-
330 mandie by The Hagge, wynnyng the contrees of Constantine ʻfrom
Chyrburghʼ tʻyʼlle he came to Cane, and by grete assautes entred and

314 ducheez] ducheer 318 wanne Calix by sege] WW and . . . sege *at
l. end over an uneras. red line-filler, duplic.* and *by scr.* 321 the day . . . Bap-
tiste] WW *at l. end after* wanne (*see n.*) 327–8 King Edward Thrid] *reader 1 in
marg.* De Rege Edwardo iij^{cij}. (*sic*) et eius factis 328 that] WW *over eras* countre]
WW *symbol at fore-edge* 330 Constantine] *an additional* C *interl. before* Constantine *in pale ink, perhaps eras.;* WW Ca⟨?⟩ *trimmed at fore-edge* 330–1 from
Chyrburgh] WW *interl.* 331 tʻyʼlle] WW y *over uneras. letter*

gate the towne and fought withe the capitaine and burgeises fro midday
Comes de Ew captus. till night; where the erle of Eu, connestable of Fraunce,
Comes Tanker-vyle captus. the erle of Tancaruille and others, knightis and squiers,
'were' take prisoneris. But the castell and donioune held 335
still, where the bisshop of Baieux and othre kept hem. | And than the f. 6ᵛ
king departed thens, for he wolde not lese his peple 'by segyng yt';
and after that the yere of Crist .Mˡ. iij^C. xlvj. descomfit the said King
Philip and wanne the feelde vppon hym at the dolorous and gret bataile
Cressye. of Cressy in Picardie, the .xxvj. day of August the said yere, 340
where the king of Beame was slayne, the son of Henry the emperoure,
and alle the gret part of the noble bloode of Fraunce, of dukes, erlis
and barons, as the erle of Alaunson, king of Fraunce is brother, the
duke of Lorraine, the erle of Bloys, the erle of Flaundres, the erle of
Harecourt, the erle of Sancerre, the erle of Fennes, to the nombre of .l. 345
knightis sleyne, as well as to othre gret nombre of his liege-peple (as
in the .39. chapitre of the *Actis* of the said King Philip more plainly is
Comes Derbye. historied). And also the full noble erle of Darby, hauyng
⟨Gu⟩yen. rule vnder the said King Edwarde in the duchie of Guyen,
hostied the said tyme and yere and put in subieccion fro the towne of 350
Saint-Iohn-Euangelist vnto the citee of Peyters, whiche he wanne also
be the said erle of Derbye is entreprises.

How Dauid, king of Scottis, was take prisoner.

And in the said King Edward tyme, Dauid, king of Scottis, was take
prisoner, as I haue vndrestond, at the bataile beside De'r'am vpon the 355
Marchis of Scotlond. And also the said king kept Bretaine in gret subiec-
⟨B⟩reteyn. cion, had the victorie vppon Charles de Bloys, duke of Breteine,
and leid a siege in Breteine to a strong forteresse clepid Roche-Daryon
and kept be his true subgectis. After many assautes and grete escarmisshes and a bataile manly foughten, the said duke was take and, 360
hauyng .vij. woundes, was presentid to the said King Edward. And he
⟨C⟩alix. also wanne Calix after, by a long and puissaunt sieges keping
by see and be londe—and they, enfamyned, couthe haue no socoure of

---

332 burgeises] *WW symbol at fore-edge*   335 were] *WW interl.*   337 by
segyng yt] *WW at l. end*   351 Peyters] Pey|ters *split over a l. break; WW duplic.* ters
at end of 1st l. and ters *crossed out on 2nd l.*   354 Dauid] *reader 2 in marg.* Dauid
Rex scotorum captus est apud deraham   355 De'r'am] *short* r *overwritten with*
long r   357 Charles] *reader 2 in marg.* Karolus dux Britannie captus est per Edwardum iijᵐ   362 Calix] *reader 2 in marg.* Calicia capta (*corr. from* Calicius captus) est
eodem tempore per Edwardum iijᵐ

f. 7ʳ King Philip and so for faute of vitaile | yeldid Calix vp to King Edwarde
365 the iiij. day of August in the yere of Crist Mˡ. CCCxlvij—and also put
Nor⟨mandie⟩. Normandie, gret part of it, in subgeccion.

And therto in his daies his eldist sonne Edward, prince of Walis, the
xix day of Septembre the yere of Crist Mˡ. iijᶜlvj. had a gret discomfi-
Peyters. ture afore the cite of Peyters vppon Iohn, calling hym king of
370 Fraunce, where the said king was taken prisoner, and in whiche bataile
was slaine the duke of Bourbon, the duke of Athenes, the Lord Clermont, Ser Geffrey Chauny that bare the baner of the oriflamble, and
also take withe King Iohn, Ser Philip 'le Hardye', duc of Bourgoine,
his yongist sonne; and for whois raunson and othres certaine lordes
375 King Edwarde rewarded the prince .xx. Mˡ. liures sterlinges. Also taken
that day: Ser Iaques de Bourbon, erle of Pontieu, Charles his brothir,
erle of Longville, the kingis cosins-germains; Ser Iohn Meloun, erle of
Tancaruile; Ser William Meleum, archebisshop of Sens; the Erle Dampmartyn; the Erle Vendosme; the Erle Vaudemont; the Erle Salebruce;
380 the Erle Nauson; Ser Arnolde of Doneham, mareshall of Fraunce; and
many other knightis and gentiles to the nombre of Mˡ. vijᶜ. prisoneris; of whiche were taken and 'sl'eine .lij. knightis banerettis. And the
kingis eldist sonne Charlis, calling hym duc of Normandie; the duc of
Orliauns, the kingis brother; the duc of Aniou; the erle of Peiters, that
385 after was clepid 'Iohn', the duc of Berrie; the erle of Flaundris; withe a
few other lordis withedrew hem and escaped from the seide bataile.

And sone after, the yere of Crist Mˡ. iijᶜlvij. the xvj day of Aprill the
said Prince Edward with King Iohn tooke the see at Burdeux to Englond
and londed the .iiij. day of Maij and came to London the xxiiij day of
390 Maij, the said King Edwarde, his father, meting withe King Iohn in the
f. 7ᵛ feelde, doing hym gret honoure and reuerence. | And after in the yere
De redempcione of Crist .Mˡ. iijᶜ lxvij the 'month' of Maij the said King
Iohannis, di-
centis regem Iohn was put to finaunce and raunson of thre millions of
Francie. scutis of golde (that two of hem be worthe .i. noble), of

364 Calix] *reader 2 in marg.* Calicia reddita est in manus Regis Edwardi iij
367 Edward] *reader 2 in marg.* Edwardus princeps cepit Iohannem vocantem se
Regem Francie 'anno domini' Mˡᵒ CCCᵒ lvjᵒ   373 le Hardye] *WW interl.; caret
placed after* duc (*see n.*)   375 Edwarde] *reader 2 in marg.* Edwardus Rex anglie
iijᵘˢ retribuit xx Mˡ libros Edwardo principi filio suo   382 'sl'eine] *scr.* sl *over
partially eras.* C   383 Charlis] *reader 2 in marg.* karolus filius Regis Iohannis
francie ac nominando se pro duce Normandie captus est   385 Iohn] *WW interl.*
388 Prince Edward] *reader 2 in marg.* Edwardus princeps nauim ascendit cum Iohanne
nominando se pro Regi Francie ac applicuerunt prope dover iiijᵒ die Maij anno domini
Mˡᵒ etc.   391 And after] *duplic. at foot of f. 7ʳ and top of f. 7ᵛ*   392SN De . . .
Francie] *red siden. duplic. black* ⟨r⟩edempcio   392 month] *WW over eras.*

whiche was paied sex hondred thousand scutis be the said King Iohn,   395
comyng to Calix. And in certein yeris after was obliged vnder gret seurtees, as it is declared in the articulis of the pease finall made betwene
bothe kingis, to be paied 400000, till the said thre hondred millions
were fullie paied—whiche, as it is said, was not parfourmed.

And after that, the said Prince Edwarde and Harry, that noble duke   400
De bello de   of Lancastre, had the bataile of Nazar in Spaine withe King
Nazar.   Petir ayenst the Bastarde Henry, calling hym king of Spaine,
haueng .lxiij. M^l. fighting men in his host; and, hym descomfit, voided
the feelde. And many a noble knighte of Englonde and of Gascoigne and
Guyen, withe many othre worshipfulle gentiles, quite hem right manlie.   405

Chandos, Beauchamp Comes,   And amongis many goode men of cheualrie,
Dominus Hastyngys, Dominus   Ser Iohn Chandos auaunced hym chief in that
Nevyle, Dominus Rays,
Radulphus Hastyngys cheualier,   bataile 'havyng the auauntgard', for he had in
Thomas Felton, Robertus
Knolles, Courteneys, Tryvett,   his retenu M^l. ij^C. penons armed and x. M^l.
Matheu Gournay et quamplures
alij milites, hic nimis diu ad   horsmen. And Ser William Beauchampe, the   410
inscribendum.   erle of Warwik is sonne; Lorde Hue Hastinges;

Lord Neuyle; Lorde Rais, a Breton; lorde 'of' Aubterre; withe many
Gascoignes there also, Ser Raufe Hastingis, Ser Thomas Felton, Ser
Roberd Knolles, withe many other notable of the cheualrie of Inglonde,
passed the streit highe 'monteyns' of Pirone by Runcyuale in the contre   415
of Pampilon, going from the cite of Burdeux into Spaine; and Ser Hughe
Courtney, Ser Philip Courtnay, Ser Iohn Tryuet, 'Matheu Gournay de
Bertilmus Clekyn, locu-   comitatu Somerset'. And there was take Ser Barthil-
mtenens aduerse partis,
captus et prisonarius   mew Clekyn, the Frenshe kingis lieutenaunt for the
werre, prisoner; also the mareshall of Fraunce; the Besque; withe many   420
othre notable lordis; whiche bataile of Nazar was in the yere of Crist M^l.
iij^{C}lxvj., the thrid day of Aprill.

How King Henry the .V. conquerid 'Normandy and Fraunce'.

And sithe now late the noble 'prince', Henry the .Vte, how in his daies
withyn the space of .vij. yere and .xv. daies thoroughe | sieges lieng   f. 8^r

---

401SN De . . . Nazar] *red siden. duplic. black* nazare nomina armorum   406SN Has-
tyngys] *red siden. partly duplic. black* hastyngys   408 havyng the auauntgard]
WW interl.   412 of] *WW over eras.*   415 monteyns] *WW at l. end*
416 and Ser] and ser *(crossed out)* and ser   417–18 Matheu . . . Somerset]
WW interl.   423 Normandy and Fraunce] *WW at l. end over an uneras. red
line-filler*   424 And sithe] *reader 2 in marg.* De Henrico quinto   prince] *WW over
eras.*   425 sieges] *reader 1 at top of p.* De nobili fama Regis Henrici .V^{ti}. et fratrum
suorum

426 *De extrema defencione ville* 'wan the towne of Harflete bethyn xl. days, made
Harflue contra potestatem
Francie, et de fame ibidem. Thomas Beauford, then Erle Dorset, hys oncle,
capteyn of yt; and the seyd erle made Ser Iohn Fastolf, cheualier, hys
lieutenaunt wyth .M^l v^C. sudeours and the baron of Carew wyth .xxxiij.
430 knyghtys; contynuelly defended the seyd toune ayenst the myghty
power of Fraunce b"y" the space of one yere and half aftyr the seyd
prince, Herry .Vte., departed from Hareflue.

And the seyd towne was beseged by the Frensh partye by lond and
also by see wyth a grete navye of carekys, galeyes and shyppis off Spayn,
435 tille that yn the meenetyme Iohn, duc of Bedfor[d], the erle of Marche,
your moste noble antecessour, accompanyed wyth many othyr nobles
wyth a puissaunt armee of shyppis, fought wyth tho carekys; and shyppis lyeng at Seyn-Hede before Hareflue were taken, and manye one
sleyn and drowned; and so vytailled Harflue, yn grete famyn that a
440 wreched cow ys hede was sold for vj s viij d sterlyng and the tong
for xl. d; and dyed of Englysh soudeours mo then .v^C. yn defaut of
sustenaunce. And the second voyage after wythynne the tyme before-
seyd, Iohn, erle of Huntydon, was made chieff admyrall of a new armee
to rescue Harflue, beseged of the new wyth a grete navy of shyppys and
445 carekys of the Frensh partye, were foughten wyth and ovyrcom throw
myghty fyghtyng, and of the new vitailled Hareflue, the seyd Erle Dorset
then beyng yn England at the emperour commyng hedre, called Sygemendus. I brieffly title thys incident to th'entent not to be foryete how
such tweyn myghty batailles were foughten vppon the see bethyn one
450 yere and half, and how the seyd toune of Hareflue was deffended and
kept ayenst the puyssaunt power of Fraunce, beseged as yt were by the
seyd tyme. And as for wach and ward yn the wynter nyghtys, I herd the
seyd Ser Iohn Fastolf sey that euery man kepyng the scout-wach had
a masty hound at a lyes to berk and warn, yff ony aduerse partye were
455 commyng to the dykes or to aproch the towne for to scale yt.

And the seyd prince, Herry .V^{the}., ' albeit that it consumed gretlie his
peple, and also by batailes yeueng, conquerid 'the towne of Harflete'
and wanne bothe the saide duchie of Normandie first and after the
roiaume of Fraunce, conquerid and brought in subieccion and wanne
460 be his gret manhode, withe the noble power of his lordis and helpe
of his comonys, and so ouerleid the mightie roiall power of Fraunce

426–56 wan . . . Herry .V^{the}'] *WW interl. then continues in marg., then at foot of p.*
426 Harflete] *reader 2 in marg. Nota quomodo Rex Henricus V^{us} obtinuit Harefleet*
428 yt] yt yt *duplic. across l. break*   Ser] ser ser *duplic. across l. break*   431 b"y"]
WW y *over uneras. letter*   435 Bedford] Bedfor   436 your] wyth your, *with*
wyth *crossed out*   457 the towne of Harflete] *WW interl.*

be the seide sieges lieng, first, in his first viage at Harflete; and in the
second viage he made, manly besegid Cane, the cite of Rone, Falleise,
Argenten, Maunt, Vernon-sur-Seyne, Melun, Meulx-en-Brie and at
many other castellis, forteressis, citeis and townes to long to rehers; 465

Bell'um' super also had gret batailes on the see ayenst many grete carekkis
mare contra *lez*
carrikes. and shippes that besieged Hareflue after it was Englisshe;

Agyn⟨court⟩. and had a gret discomfiture at the bataile of Agincourt in
the yere of Crist .M^l. iiij^{C}xv. at his first viage, where many dukes, erlis
and lordis and knightis were slaine and take prisoneris, that bene in 470
remembraunce at this day of men yet liuyng; and after allied hym to the
Frenshe King Charlis VJ^{te}. is doughter. Because of whiche alliaunce,
gret part of the roiaume of Fraunce were yolden vnto his obeisaunce
and now also, in the said noble conquest, hathe be kept vndre the
obediaunce of Englisshe nacion; from the begynnyng of the said late 475

Nota. conquest by xxxv. yeris `b'e continued and kept by roiall power;
as first, be the noble and famous prince, Iohn, duke of Bedforde, regent
and gouernoure of the roiaume of Fraunce, by .xiij. yeris, withe the eide
and power of the noble lordis of this londe, bothe youre said royaume
of Fraunce and duchie of Normandie was kept, and the ennemies kept 480
ferre of, in gret subieccion.

How that in Iohn, duke of Bedforde, tyme, [he], be his lieu-tenaunt, erle of Salisburie, had the victorie at the batell of Crauant.

In profe wherof, how and in the first | yere of the reigne of King Harry f. 8^v
the Sext, at whiche tyme his seide vncle toke vppon hym the charge 486
and the name of regent of the roiaume of Fraunce that had the vic-
Bellum de Cravant. torie at the bataile of Crauant, whereas at that tyme
Thomas Montagu, comes Thomas Montagu, the noble erle of Salisburie, the
Sarum.
Willelmus Pole, comes erle of Suffolk, the marchall of Bourgoine, the Lord 490
Suffolchie.
Dominus Willughby. Willoughebie, withe a gret power `of' Phelip, the
duke of Bourgoine is host, holding the partie of the said Iohn, regent

---

462 first] *reader 2 in marg.* Nota qualiter per ciuitates (*corrected from* ciuitas) et
mare obtinuit   466SN Bell'um'] *WW writes* u *and abbrev.* m *over uneras. letter*
468 Agincourt] *reader 2 in marg.* Nota de bello apud Agincourt   471 allied] *reader
2 in marg.* Henricus Rex duxit in vxorem filiam Regis Francie   473 his] hym his
476 `b'e] b *over uneras.* h   482 Iohn] *reader 2 in marg.* Iohannes dux bedforde
he, be his] be his   487 had] *two-letter word eras. before* had   488 bataile]
WW indistinct black siden., perhaps duplic. by red sidenn. on this p.   491 of] *WW
interl.*

of Fraunce, duc of Bedforde, withe the eide and helpe of the trew subgettis of this lande had the ouerhande of the ennemies assembled to
495 the nombre of .ʼjʼx. M¹ Frenshemen and Scottis at the said bataile of
Crauant in the duchie of Bourgoine. There were slayne of the ennemies
to the nombre of .iiij. M¹. beside .ij. M¹. prisonneris take, of whiche
gret part of them were Scottis, the Erle Bougham being chief capitein
ouerthrow; whiche late before were the cause of the male-infortuned
500 Vindicacio   iourney at Bougee, where the famous and victorious knight
mortis ducis
Clarencie.   Thomas, duc of Claraunce, youre nere cousyn, for the right
of Fraunce, withe a smale company of his side, withe the Scottis to a
grete nombre there ʼassembledʼ, among hem in the feelde was ʼslaynʼ,
withe many a noble lorde, baron, knightis, squyers of Englond, that
505 neuer so gret an ouerthrow of lordes and noble bloode was seene in
no mannys daies as it was then, aboute the nombre of . ij^C. l. cote-armes
slaine and take prisoneris, ʼas yt was seydʼ, be the saide Scottis halding withe youre aduerse party of Fraunce. Whiche God of his infinite
goodeʼnesʼ, sone after at the saide batelle Crauant and after at the bateile
510 Secunda vice   of Vernell was sent a chastisement vpon the saide Scottis for
punicio mortis
ducis Clarencie. theire cruellʼteeʼ, vengeable and mortalle dethe of the said
victorious prince, duke of Claraunce, and of other of his noble lordis
and knightis.

How Iohn, duke of Bedforde, had yn his owne parsone the batell
515 **of Vernelle.** |

f. 9ʳ Also in the said daies, sone after the saide batell of Cravant, in the yere
.1423., batelle of Crist M¹. iiij^C. xxiii, the .iij yere of King Harry the Sext,
of Cravant.   the .xvij. day of August, the said Iohn, duke of Bedford,
had a gret descomfiture and the victorie vpon youre aduersaries of
520 Batell of   Fraunce and of Scottis at the batell of Vernell-en-Perche,
Vernoyle,
.1424.   whereas Iohn, cleping hym duc of Alaunson, lieutenaunt
for the Frenshe partie, was take prisoner that day. And the said Erle
Bougham of Scotlonde, marchall of Fraunce, whiche was cause of that
noble prince, Thomas, duke of Claraunce, dethe, was in the said bataile
525 ouerthrow and sleyne; and the Erle Douglas, made duc of Tourayne,

---

495 .ʼjʼx.] .ix. *with* i *changed to* j   496 There] *were* there *with* were *crossed out*
503 assembled] *WW interl.*   slayn] *WW interl.*   507 as yt was seyd] *WW interl.*
509 goodeʼnesʼ] *WW interl.* nes   511 cruellʼteeʼ] *WW* tee *over uneras. otiose flour-*
ish   516 Also] *at top of p., 16th-c. note on Lat. verb* esse   517 xxiii] *minims*
retouched in iii; *followed by eras. of.* j

as well as his sonne and heire, that was in the feelde at Shrewisburie
ayenst King Henry the IIIJ^{the}, and another tyme, being ayenst the said
Iohn, duc of Bedford, at Homeldon Hill in Scotlond, was also slaine
at the said batell, withe many other grete lordis of the Frenshe partie
slayne and taken prisoneris at the said bataile.   530

How that the grettir part of the counte of Mayne, the cite of Mauns, withe many other castellis were yolden.

And ouermore not long after, youre auncien enheritaunce in the counte
Mayn. of Mayne, the cite of Maunce, conquerid and brought be the said
regent, duc of Bedforde, withe the power of his lordis and helpers in   535
subgeccion, 'by the erle of Salysbery, Lord Scalys, Ser Iohn Fastolf, Ser
Iohn Popham, Ser N. Mongomery, Ser William Oldhall, cheualiers, and
many othyr noble men of worshyp'.

And whiche counte of Mayne was accustomed sithen to be in valeu
yerely to the eide and helpe of the werres of Fraunce and to the releue 540
of the 'kyng ys' subgettis obeisauntes lyuyng vppon the werre for the
furtheraunce of that conquest, .x. M^l liures sterlinges.

Also the said regent of Fraunce with the power of youre noble bloode
and lordes wanne the feeld at the forseid grete bataile of Vernell-in-
Perche ayenst the power of the Frenshe aduerse party of Fraunce | being   f. 9^v
assembled to the nombre of xl. M^l. fighters of the Frenshe partie. And   546
there Iohn, cleping hymsilf duke of Alaunson, lieutenaunt to Charles
the VIJ., calling hym Frenshe king, taken prisonner withe many other

Redempcio Iohannis, dicentis
ducem de Allaunson, pro Clx.
M^l salux, bene solutis, vltra alia
onera suarum exspensarum.
lordis, barons and knightes and noble men of
worship, whiche paied to the said regent, duc of   550
Bedforde, for his raunson and finaunce allone
.Clx M^l. salux, beside his other grete costis and charges, whiche was a
gret relief and socoure to the eide of the conquest; whiche bataile was
in the yere of Crist M^l. iiij^C xxii'ij', the 'seyd .iij^d.' yere of the reigne of
King Henry Sext.   555

536–8 by the erle . . . worshyp] WW interl., continuing in right marg.   541 kyng
ys] WW interl.   545 Fraunce] at foot off. 9^r, 15th-c. pen-trial Ryght   554 xxii'ij']
ij over uneras. j   seyd .iij^d.] WW over eras.

How that Henry the Sext was crouned king be the might of grete lordes.

And he also for a gret act of remembraunce to be had in writing was crouned king of Fraunce in the noble citee of Paris in the yere of Crist
560 .M^l. iiij^{C}xxix, the ix yere of his reigne, withe right gret solennyte amongis the Lordis Spirituell and Temporell, and be the gret might and power as well in goodes and richesse of his graunt-oncle Henry, cardinalle of Englande, ʼbysshop of Wynchesterʼ, and by the gret might and power of his vncle Iohn, regent of the roiaum of Fraunce, duc of Bedforde,
565 being present at that tyme to thʼeʼir grettist charge and cost to resist theire gret aduersarie of Fraunce calling hym Dolphin. For, sethen the roiaume of Englonde first began to be inhabite withe peple, was neuer so worshipfulle an act of entreprise done in suche a case, the renoume of whiche coronacion spradde thoroughe alle Cristen kingis roiaumes.
570 A courageous   O, then, ye most noble and Cristen prince, for not-
     recomfortyng. withestanding gret conquestis and batailes had in the said roiaume be the famous knight King Edwarde the Thrid, he neuer atteyned to that souuerain honoure, but by valiauntnes of Englisshe-men, whiche haue in prowes auaunced hem and gouerned so nobly,
f. 10^r as is before briefly historied | and specified be youre saide noble puis-
576 saunt and vailaunt progenitours in diuers regions and in especialle in Fraunce and Normandie and in the duchie of Gascoigne and Guyen, that this sodenly wern put oute of by vsurpacion ayenst alle trouthe and knyghthode!
580   Now, therfore, in repairing ʼtʼhis vndew intrusion vppon yow, mantelle, fortifie and make yow strong ayenst the power of youre said aduersaries of Fraunce. For now it is tyme to clothe you in armoure of defenʼsʼe ayenst youre ennemies withe the cotes of armes of youre auncien feernesse, haueng in remembraunce the victorious
585 conquestis of youre noble predecessours; the whiche clothing many histories, cronicles and writinges witnessithe, moo than myn simple entendement cannot suffice to reherse in this brief epistle.

---

556 How] *reader 1 in marg.* nota bene pro titulo Regis henrici vij^i; *reader 2 crosses out* vij^i *and interl.* sexti   558 And] *illegible marg. n.*   559 crouned] *reader 2 in marg.* Coronatio Regis henrici sexti   563 bysshop of Wynchester] *WW interl.*
565 thʼeʼir] *scr. interl.* e   566 For] *reader 1 in marg.* de magna fame regni anglie tempore Regis henrici vj^{ti} 580 Now] *reader 1 in marg.* Exortacio militaris   ʼtʼhis] *WW* t *in space before*   583 defenʼsʼe] s *over uneras.* c   585 predecessours] *preceded by long letter, perhaps* s *or* p (*with abbrev.?*), *eras.*

Of the noblesse of Ectour and other mighty kinges of Grece.

And also let be brought to mynde to folow the steppis in conceitis of
noble courage of the mighty dedis in armes of the vaillaunt knight   590
Hector. Hector of Troy, whiche bene enacted in *The Siege of Troy* for a
perpetuell remembraunce of cheualrie 'that your noblesse ys decended
Agamenon. of'. Also of the dedis in armes of Agamenon the puissaunt
king of Grece that thoroughe cruell and egre werre ayenst the Troiens bethin .x. yere day conquerid the gret cite of Troie. In like wise   595
Vlixes. of the famous knight Vlixes that alle his daies despendid in
marciall causis. And of the xij puissaunt entreprinses and auenturous
Hercules. dedis that Hercules (as it is figured and made mencion in 'the'
vij.'the' metre of the .v. booke of Boecius) toke vppon hym, putting hymsilf frome voluptuouse delites and lustis, being subget to grete laboure,   600
wynnyng renomme and worship; whiche .xij. entreprinses of Hercules,
albeit it be thought 'but a poesye', impossible to any mortall man to doo
1, j. or take vppon hym—'a's for to bereffe the skyn of the rampant lion,
2, ij. wrestlid withe Anthen and Poliphemus, the gret giauntes, and hym
3, iij. ouerthrew; he slow the serpent clepid | Ydra; made tame the proude   f. 10ᵛ
beestis clepid centaurus that be of halfe man and halfe best; and many   606
soche wonderfulle entreprises as is wreten that Hercules did—whiche is
writen in figure of a poesy for to courage and comfort alle othre noble
men of birthe to be victorious in entreprinses of armes. And how in
conclusion that there is no power, puissaunce ne strenght, whoso lust   610
manly 'wyth prudens' put forthe hymsilf, may resist and withestande
ayenst such gret entreprises.

How a conquerour shulde vse in especialle thre thingis.

And as Vegecius in his *Booke of Cheualrie* counceilithe that a conquer-
nota .3ᵃ our shulde vse thre thinges in especialle whiche the Romains   615
vsed, and alle that tyme they had the victorie of here ennemies. That
j. is to wete: the first was science, that is for to vndrestonde prudence
ij. to seene before the remedies of bonchief or the contrarie; the second

588 Of] *reader 2 in marg.* Nota de exemplis aliorum nobilium   591SN Hec-
tor] *red siden. duplic. black*   592–3 that...of] *WW interl.*   593SN Agamenon]
red siden. duplic. black   596SN Vlixes] *red siden. duplic. black*   598SN Hercules]
red siden. duplic. black   598 the] *WW interl.*   599 vij.'the'] *WW interl.* the
602 but a poesye] *WW interl.*   603SN 1, j] *black numeral by scr. duplic. by WW in
red roman numeral*   603 'a's] *one-compartment* a *changed to two-compartment* a
611 wyth prudens] *WW interl.*   613 How] *reader 2 in marg.* A Conqueroure
shuld vse iij thinges

was exercitacion and vsage in dedis of armes, that they might be apte
620 iij. and redie 'to bataille' whan necessite fille; the thrid was naturalle
loue that a prince shulde haue to his peple, as doing his trew diligence
to doo that may be to the comon wele of his peple, whiche is to be vndrestonde in executing of iustice egallie, and for to kepe them in tranquillite
and pece within hemsilfe.

625 **How men of noblesse ought lefe sensualitees and delites.**

Lete it no lenger be suffred to abide r[i]ote no for to vse the pouder and
semblaunce of sensualite and idill delites. For Water Malexander seiethe
that voluptuous delitis, led be sensualite, be contrarie to the exercising
and haunting of armes.
630 Wherfor li`k'e and after the example of the boore whiche knowethe
not his power but foryetithe his strenght tille he be chafed and see his
owne bloode, in like wise put forthe youresilf, auaunsing youre cora-
geous hertis to werre. And late youre strenght be reuyued and waked
ayen, furious, egre and rampanyng as liouns ayenst alle tho nacions |
f. 11ʳ that soo without title of right wolde put you frome youre said rightfulle
636 enheritaunce.
And where is a more holier, parfiter or a iuster thing than, in youre
aduersary is offence and wrongdoing, to make hym werre in youre
rightfull title, whereas none other moenys of pease can be hadde? And
640 therfor considering be this brief declaracion, that youre right and title
in all this royaumes and contrees is so opyn.

**Here is briefly made mencion of the first title of Normandie, and
how frely it holdithe.**

For as youre first auncien right and title in youre duchie of Normandie,
645 it is knowen thoroughe alle Cristen landes and also of highe recorde by
many credible bookis of olde cronicles and histories, that William Conqueroure descendid frome Duc Rollo, after cristned and called Roberd,

620 to bataille] *WW over eras.*   622 the] the his *with* his *subpuncted and crossed
out*   625 How] *reader 2 in marg.* Men of noblenesse shuld lefe sensualites
and delites   626 riote] rote *marked with a cross*   630 li`k'e] liche, *with* che
crossed out; ke *interl.*   639 whereas] *reader 2 in marg.* nota   And] *WW symbol
at fore-edge*   642 Here] *reader 2 in marg.* Mentio brevis de titulo ducatus
de (*corrected from* do) Normandie   644 For] *unidentified reader annot.* nota
646 William] *reader 1 in marg.* nota pro titulo Ducatus Nomanie (*sic*)

that came out of Dennemarke, aboute the yere of Crist .ix^C xij., was
right duke of Normandie by yeft of `Charlys le Symple´, king of Fraunce,
[who] maried his doughter to Rollo and gaue hym the saide ducdome.   650

And after, Richarde, duc of Normandie, in the yere of Crist ix^C xlv.
in plaine batell before the cite of Rone toke Lowes, king of Fraunce,
prisoner. And the said Lowes relesid the seide dukedom to the saide
Richarde and to alle his successours to holde frely in souuereinte and
resort of none creature but of God (as in *Act* therof is made mencion,   655
that was sene and rad vppon this writing).

And after, the said William Conquerour, being king of Englond, of
whome ye and youre noble progenitours bene descendid and entitled
535 anni. this .v^C xxxv. yere and beere in armes by the saide duchie of
Normandie in a feelde of gulis ij. libardis of golde.   660

Mayn. **How long the king is entitled to the right enheritaunce of
Angew and Mayne.**

And that as for youre next enheritaunce, that fille to youre seide |
Angeu. progenitoures and to you in the duchie of Aniou `and´ countee f. 11^V
of Mayne and Tourayne, it is also notorily knowen among alle Cristen 665
princes and be parfit writing, how that Dame Maude, whiche was
doughter and soule heire to that puissaunt King Henry the First, that,
after she weddid was to the emperour of Almayne, after his decese the
1127. saide Maude, emperesse, was maried the yere of Crist M^l. Cxxvij.
to Geffrey Plantagenest, son to Fouke, king of Iherusalem, that was erle 670
of Aniou, of Mayne and Toreyne, by whome the saide Maude had issue:
that most famous king in renomme, Henry the Seconde, whiche be
right of his moder Maude was right king and enheritoure of Englonde,
also duke of Normandie seisid; and be right of his foresaide father

649 Charlys le Symple] WW Charl *over eras. and interl.* ys le Symple   650 who
maried] maried (*see n.*)   651 And] *WW symbol at fore-edge*   653 dukedom]
Richarde dukedom *with* Richarde *subpuncted*   654 Richarde] *reader 2 in marg.*
Richardus dux Normandie cepit in bello lodovicum regem francie qui resingnauit [*sic*]
totum titulum Ricardo de ducatu predicto   655 Act] `act´ act; WW *duplic.* act *at
l. end*   657 And] *WW symbol at fore-edge*   659 .v^C xxxv.] *reader 2 in marg.*
CCCCCth xxxv^{te} armes] *reader 2 in marg.* Arma ducatus illius   663 And]
reader 2 in marg. Nota de tempore quo Rex anglie intitulatur ducatui (*corrected from*
comitatui) de Angew et `comitatui´ Mayne   664SN Angeu] *red siden. duplic. black*
664 progenitoures] *reader 2 at top of p.* Mautilda filia et heres henrici primi (*with* p *written over* s) copulata fuit imperatori eoque mortuo copulata fuit (*followed by* s *crossed out*)
galfrido plantagenet et ex ea henricus ij^{us} natus est   Aniou] *reader 2 in marg.* Angew.
and] *WW interl.*   countee] *followed by eras. letter*   667 heire] *reader 1 in marg.*
nota pro Titulo Ducatus andegeuie

675 Geffrey Plantagenet was, bethout any clayme or interupcion, right
enheritour and seised of the said countee of Aniou, Mayne, Toreyne,
continued this .iij^C. xlvij. yere.

'And the noble actys of the seyd erles of Angew wyth her lynealle
dessentys ben wryten yn the cronicles called *Ymago historiarum* that
680 Maister Raff de Duceto, dene of Poulys, yn Seynt Thomas of Canter-
bery days wrote notablye. And therfor the armys of tho noble erlys,
that for her prowesse were chosen kyng of Iherusalem, wold be wor-
shypped, because your hyghnes ys decended of the eyr masle, that ys to
wete, of Geffrey Plantagenest, erle of Angew, and the countee of Mayn
685 by maryage was vnyoned to the erledom of Angew to long to wryte.'

Gyen. **Here is made mencion of the title of Gascoigne and Guien,
and how long agoo passed possessid.**

And than for to be put in remembraunce of youre auncien enheritaunce,
verray right and title in youre duchie's' of Gascoigne and Guien withe
690 the countrees, baronnyes and seigniouries therto belonging.

It is in like fourme knowen of highe recorde enacted in diuers
cronicles, as amongis many other historiall bookis of auctorite, that
aboute the yere of Crist M^l. Cxxxvij William, the duke of Guien, died
bethout heire masle vppon his voiage he made to Seint Iames, hauyng
695 .ij. doughters, [an] heire called Alienore, the second Alice. And King
Lowes of Fraunce in his yong age, by the agrement of Lowys le Gros,
his father, spoused the said Alienor, to whome the said duchie was hole
enheriter. And after the said King Lowes came to yeris of discrecion,
the archebisshoppis of Sens, of Rayns, of Rone and of Burdeux, withe
f. 12^r others barouns, made relacion to the said King | Lowes that the seide
701 Alienor was so nere of his blode that he might not laufullie be the
chirche kepe her to wiffe; so be theire counceile they bothe were departed laufully. And the said King Lowes maried after that Constance,
the king of Spayne doughter.

705   And the said Alienor, the duches of Gascoigne and Guien, went to

676 countee] *followed by eras. letter*   678–85 And the noble . . . to wryte] *WW in
marg.*   685 by] *after* by *with after crossed out*   686sn Gyen] *red siden. duplic.*
black   686 Guien] *reader 2 in marg.* Gyon   689 title] *reader 1 in marg.* nota
pro titulo vasconie   duchie's'] s *over uneras.* r   693 M^l. Cxxxvij] *reader 2 in marg.*
M^l Cxxxvij^te   695 an] and   Alienore] *reader 2 in marg.* Alienora et Alicia filie
et heredes willelmi ducis Guien   703 laufully] *reader 2 in marg.* Nota de diuortio
facto inter Regem Francie et Alienoram

Burdeux. Than came the forsaid King Harry the Seconde of Englande, that was the erle of Aniou is sonne and heire, and wedded the said Alie-
1146. nor aboute the yere of Crist M^l. Cxlvj., by whome he was duke of Gascoigne and Guien, and his heires after hym, of whome ye bene descendid and come right downe. And the said King Henry the Seconde 710 bare in armes frome that day forthe the said libarde of golde withe the other two libardis of the same that is borne for duke of Normandie.

So in conclusion he was be right of his moder, Dame Maude the empresse, king of Englonde and duke of Normandie; and be right of his father, Geffrey Plantagenest, erle of Aniou and of Mayne and Torayne; 715 be right of his wiffe, Dame Alienor, duke of Guien. Of whiche duchie of Gascoigne and Guien youre noble progenitours haue continuelly be possessid and seased of this .iij^C xxviij yere complete; tille that by intrusion of youre said aduersarie, Charlis the .VIJ^{the}. of Fraunce haue disseasid yow in 'or about' the monithe of Iune the yere of Crist .M^l. 720 iiij^C. lj., as he hathe late done, of youre enheritaunce of Fraunce and Normandie and of the counte of Mayne, thoroughe vmbre of the said fenied colour of trewes ayenst alle honoure and trouthe of knighthode.

How the historier procedithe in his matier of exortacion.

And for to think to alle Cristen nacions for to fight in bataile, if the 725 cas require it, soo that youre said enheritaunce cannot be recuuerid by none other due meane of pease, bothe for youre defens for the recuuerey of youre roiaume of Fraunce, duchie of Normandie | and sithen sone f. 12^v after the duchie of Gascoigne, that alle Cristen princes opynly may know it is youre verray true enheritaunce and for sa'l'uacion of youre 730 enheritaunce by vndew menys lost.

For th'at' 'yt ys wryten by Maister Aleyn Chareter, *id est de Auriga*, in hys boke of *Quadrilogue*, secretaire to Charlys le Bien Amee, the yere

706 Harry] *reader 2 in marg.* Henricus ij^{us} Anglie Rex superduxit alienoram filiam (duci *crossed out*) et heredem willelmi ducis de Guien circa annum M^l Cxlvj^m 713 So] *reader 2 in marg.* Nota pro titulo henrici ij^i 715 Mayne] *followed by eras. word, with line-filler over eras.*   717 Guien] Gascoigne Guien *with* Gascoigne *subpuncted*   718 seased] *reader 1 in marg.* nota bene   iij^C] iij *over uneras. letter(s)* 719 Charlis] *reader 2 in marg.* karolus vij^{us} Rex francie primo intrusionem fecit in ducatui Norman gasco Guien et cetera circa annum M^l iiij^C lj   720 or about] *WW interl.*   726 soo] *reader 1 in marg.* nota bonum concilium   728 and] *reader 1 at top of p.* nota concilium; *at top of p., 16th-c. note on Lat. verb* esse   730 sa'l'uacion] *scr. interl.* l   732 th'at'] *WW at over uneras.* e   732–6 yt ys wryten . . . how the famous clerk of eloquence] *WW in marg. with signes-de-renvoi either side of* famous Clerk of Eloquence *in main text, which WW's marg. addn duplic.*

of Crist .1422., yn thys termys ayenst Herry the .Vte, named kyng, yn
735 provokyng the aduerse partye to werre ayenst the seyd Kyng Herry, how
the' famous clerk of eloquence, Tullius, seithe in his *Booke of Rethorique*
that, li`k'e as a man receiuethe his lyuing in a region or in a countree,
so is he of naturall reason bounde to defende it; and law of nature as
welle as law imperiall, whiche is auctorised by popis and emperours,
740 wol condescende and agre to the same. Also Caton affermithe withe the
said Tullie.

Therfor late not this gret and importune losses now, by infortune
and of ouer-grete fauoure and trust put to youre aduersaries, fallen
ayenst this lande vndre the vmbre and coloure of trewes and abstinence
745 of werre late hadde and taken at Towris atwixen Charlis the VIJ^{the},
youre aduersaire of Fraunce, and youre predecessour Harry the Sext,
and now, vppon the exercise and vsaige of bataile disused and left by so
litille a tyme, for to discomfort or fere to a new recouere. Not so: God
defende that!

750 Magister Alanus
de Auriga dicit. For the famous poet Ouide seiethe that whoso leuithe
the pursute and foloweng of good fortune for one mysauen-
ture, it shall neuer come to hym. And namely the said Water Malexander
agreithe hym to the same, saieng and affermyng that good courages of
hertis be not mynussed, broken ne lessid for disusage and leuyng armes
755 for a litill season, nether for sodeyn recountres and hasty comyng on be
force, of whiche one mysaduenture may folow.

How, for the defaute of exercise of armes, the gret nombre of Romains were scomfited by men of Cartage.

Magister Alanus
de Auriga. A, mercifull God! What was the losses of the Romayns,
760 whiche in defaute and by negligence lost, by a litill tyme
left the exercise of armes, was full gret ayenst the doughty men of
Cartage, whan alle the puissaunce of the Romains were assembled in
f. 13^r bataile, where | that were so many noble men and coragious peple,
Notandum est. the whiche were innumerable, assembled and ioyned in
765 bataile, that, men say, was betwene Camos and Hanibal, prince of
Cartage; the whiche discomfit before Duke Camos in Puylle be suche

737 li`k'e] liche; *scr. interl.* k *without deleting* ch   750SN de] dicit (*crossed
out*) de   757 How] *reader 2 in marg.* Nota quod pro defectu excerccij
armorum mala sequuntur   759 What] *reader 2 in marg.* Exemplum Romanorum
763 that] *reader 1 at top of p.* nota concilium   766 discomfit] *reader 2 in marg.*
Nota de cede Romanorum   Camos] *WW symbol at fore-edge*

power that the ringis of golde take frome the fingers of ded bodies
of the said Romains, whiche were men of price and renomme, and
(Titus Liuius seiethe in his *Booke of Romayne Batailes*) were extendid
and mesured to the quantite of, mesure of, .xij. quarters or more, 770
whiche Hanibal brought withe hym to his countre of Cartage in signe
of victorie.

How after the seide gret descomfiture that a few nombre of Romains expert in werre.

But the worthy Romains, for alle that, left not the hope and trust of 775
recouering on another day, whan God lust ounere and fortune theyme;
so exercised daily armes after, accustumyng hem ayene to werre, were
by experience lerned and enhardid, that, as by the exorting and com-
forting of one of theire princes, he assembled another time in bataile
ayenst the litill residue that were left of the said Romayns, and by sub- 780
tile craft of wise policie and good conduyt in actis of werre they fille and
tooke vppon theyme and charged theym, so moche that, by vnware of
theire purueiaunce met withe, the said Haniball at certein streightes and
narow places fille into the handis of Romains to the gret discomfiture
and destruccion of Haniballe his gret oost of Cartage.   785

Excercicio
armorum ex-
cedit omnes
diuicias.

How men of armes welle lerned and excercised is of a grettir tresoure then any precious stones or riche tresour.

Dame Cristen saiethe in the first booke of *The Tree of Batailes* that there
Nota ⟨——⟩. is none erthely thing more for to be allowed than a countre 790
or region whiche be furnisshed and stored withe good men of armes,
wele lerned and | exercited. For golde, siluer ne precious stones sur- f. 13ᵛ
mountethe not ne conquerithe not ennemies, nother in time of pease
wardithe the peple to be in rest, the whiche thing a puissaunt man in
armes dothe.   795

    767 ringis] *reader 2 in marg.* Nota de annulis inventis super digitos Romanorum
occisorum   772 victorie] *unidentified reader annot.* nota   773 How] *reader 2
in marg.* Nota de Experiencia armorum ex parte Romanorum   778 experience]
WW symbol at fore-edge   781 policie] *WW symbol at fore-edge*   786 How]
reader 2 in marg. Exercitium armorum excedit omnes diuicias   790SN Nota]
followed by word obliterated

How a few nombre of the Romains that were expert and connyng in the werre descomfited Ciiij^{xx}. M^l. of Frenshemen, that the prince of hem tolde and set right litille by.

Magister Alanus de Auriga: id est, compilaui de libro suo.

800 Also ye may considre by example of King Bituitus of the countre of Gaule, clepid Fraunce, the whiche went ayenst the Romains withe an hondred and foure score thousande men of armes. And he saw so few a companie of the Romains comyng that he despraised hem and seid of gret pride that there were not inoughe of the Romains for to fede the doggis of his oost. Neuerthe-
805 lesse, that few company were so welle excersised and lerned in armes that there were ynoughe, whiche ouercome and destroied the said king of Gaule and alle his gret oost.

Whiche storie may be verified in euery bataile or iournay atwix youre aduersarie of Fraunce and youre predecessoures entreprises this .xxxv.
810 yeris, that continued in possession frome King Henry 'named' the .V. is conquest till it was lost.

For at the bataile of Agincourt descomfited 'by seyd' King Henry the .V^{the} 'wyth a few nomber'.

And at the bataile of the see ayenst the carrakes descomfited by
815 Iohn, duke of Bedforde, and the erle of the Marche being principalle cheueteins, also in that bataile 'wyth a few nombre yn comparyson of the grete Frensh navye'.

Also at the iournay of Ke-de-Cause descomfited be Thomas Beauforde, Erle Dorset, after was duke of Eccestre, 'the erle off
820 Armonak, conestable of Fraunce, beyng aboute x. M^l. fyghtyng men ayenst aboute ix^C. accompanyed wyth the Erle Dorset'.

Also at the bataile of Crauant descomfited by 'Iohn, duc of Bedford, as by hys lieutenaunt' Thomas Montague, the erle of Salisbury, and Roberd, 'Lord' Willugheby, chief teyns'.

825 And at the bataile of Vernelle fought and decomfited by Iohn, regent, duke of Bedforde, the said erle of Salisbury and the erle of Suffolk, 'Lord Wyllughby, Lord Pownyngys, Ser Iohn Fastolf and many othyr noblemen yn armys'.

Also at the 'bataylle of Roveraye' foughte 'ayenst the Bastard of Bur-

810 named] *WW interl.*   812 For] *reader 1 in marg.* In multitudine gencium non consistit victoria . vt infra . nota bene   by seyd] *WW over eras*   813 wyth . . . nomber] *WW interl.*   816–17 wyth . . . navye] *WW interl.*   819–21 the erle . . . Dorset] *WW interl. and continues in marg.*   822–3 Iohn, duc . . . lieutenaunt] *WW interl.*   824 Lord] *WW interl.*   chief teyns'] *WW interl.* teyns 827–8 Lord Wyllughby . . . armys] *WW interl.*   829 bataylle of Roveraye] *WW over eras.*   829–30 ayenst . . . Orlyance] *WW below last l. on p.*

bon, the Bastard of Orlyance', | be Ser Iohn Fastolfe, Ser Thomas Remp-   f. 14ʳ
stone, chiefteins vpon the vitailing the siege of Orliaunce.   831

Aueraunces: Domi-   Also at the rescue of the cite Aueraunces fought by
nus Talbot; Dominus
Fauconberge.   Edmonde, duke of Somerset, and the erle of Shrewisburie and Lorde Faucomberge, chiefteins.

Harflete: Iohannes,   'And' '"a"t' the second wynnyng of Hareflete, fought,   835
dux Somerset;
Edmundus Dorset.   'beseged', by Iohn, duke of Somerset, by Edmond, erle
of Dorset, and the erle of Shrewisbury.

Cane: Fastolf;   'A't the rescue of Cane fought by Ser Iohn Fastolf and Ser
Harynton.   Richarde Harington and his felouship 'ayenst .xxx. Mˡ. men'.

And so in many other 'sodeyn iorneys and' sharpe recountres   840
sodenly met and foughten, to long to write here. And also for the gret
part at any maner bataile, iourney, entreprise'z', 'seges' and rescue of
place'z', it hathe bene alway seen that the power of Fraunce haue be
in nombre of peple assembled ayenst youre power by double so many,
or by the thrid part; yet youre right and title haue bene so goode and   845
fortunat, and men so welle lernid and exercised in armes that withe
few peple haue descomfited the gret multitude of youre aduerse partie.

How Vegesse in his *Booke of Cheualrie* also gretly recomendithe exercise in men of armes.

Vegesius, *De re*   'O then', seith Vegecius in his *Booke of Cheualrie*, 'ther   850
militari.   be none that knowethe the grete merueilles and straunge
auentures of armes and knighthode, the whiche be comprehendid and
nombred in dedis of armes, to tho that be exercised in suche labouris
of armes, that withe wise condu'y't prudently can auenture and hardely
take vppon theym suche sodein entreprinses on hande.'   855

Animacio.   O then, ye noble Englisshe cheualrie, late it no merueile
be to yow, in lessing youre courage ne abating of youre hardiesse, they
that ye renew youre coragious hertis to take armes and entreprinses,
seeing so many good examples | before yow of so many victorius dedis   f. 14ᵛ
in armes done by youre noble progenitoures. And that it hathe be a thing   860
to moche left, discorage you not. For thoughe that ye were in renomme

835 And] *WW over* uneras. *at* at the end of l.   '"a"t] *WW at* added before start of l.
with a paraph; then minuscule *a changed to majuscule* A   836 beseged] *WW interl.*
838 'A't] *minuscule* a *changed to majuscule* A   839 ayenst . . . men] *WW interl.*
840 sodeyn iorneys and] *WW at* l. end   842 entreprise'z'] *WW adds* z *at end*
seges] *WW interl.*   843 place'z'] *WW adds* z *at end*   845 yet] *reader 1 in*
marg. nota bene et optima   854 condu'y't] y *over eras.*   856SN Animacio] *red*
siden. duplic. black Anima.

accepted alleway withe the most worthi as in dede of armes, 'but' now at
this time ye ben take and accepted, in suche marcialle causes that concernithe werre, on the left hande as withe the simplest of price and of
865 Concideracio. reputacion. And it is to suppose that it is rather in defaute of
exercising of armes, left this .xxiiij. yere day, that the londes were lost;
thoroughe the said coloure of trewes; and for lak of good prouisions,
bothe of artillery and ordenaunce for the werre and soudeyng to be
made in dew season; and for singuler couetice reignyng among som
870 peple endowed with worldly goodes that cannot depart but easily withe
finaunce, 'wagyngys', and soulde theim in tyme of nede; then for defaut
of good corage and manhode, whiche, is to deme, werre neuer feerser ne
corageouser to dedis of armes, so they may be cherissed and auaunced
therafter as ben at this day.

875 **How Dame Cristen counceilithe to make true paimentis to
sowdieris.**

Nota optime
pro solucione   For ye shalle rede in the first part of *The Arbre of Batailes*
soldariorum.   where Dame Cristen exhortithe and counceilithe that
euery chieftein and capiteyne of men of armes ought haue goode
880 paimentis and sewre for assignacion of paiment for his sowdieris for
so long tyme that he trustithe to endure and be souded in that voiage
and armes. For to that singulerly, before alle thing, alle chieueteyns
shulde haue regarde, by as moche as it is the principalle and chief cause
of the good spede and conduit of here entreprise, and the vndoing and
885 mischief of it 'the contrarye', if the paimentis be not duely made to the
soudeours. For late it be put in certein that no cheueteyn cannot haue
f. 15ʳ ne kepe long tyme good men of | armes euille paied or long delaied;
but discoragethe them, as sone as paiment failethe, and takethe theire
congie and licence of theire prince, if they can haue licence, or ellis
890 they departethe bethout licence.

   And also of ouermoche trust and auauntage gyuen to youre aduersaries be this dissimiled trewes as otherwise. And also when that the
cheueteins take more kepe to good than to worship vsing iustice, and
as welle as in defaute of largesse to youre obeissauntes, not reward-
895 ing ne cherisshing youre obeissauntes subgettis, yolden and sworne

---

862 but] *WW interl.*   871 wagyngys] *WW at l. end*   872 whiche] *WW symbol at fore-edge*   877 For] *WW symbol at fore-edge before his siden.*   882 For]
reader 1 in marg. nota concilium   885 the contrarye] *WW interl.*   887 armes]
reader 1 at top of p. nota bene ne forte   891 And] *WW symbol at fore-edge*

stedfastly abiding vnder youre obeissaunce, but suffring them to be
oppressid and charged vndeuly in diuers wises as well by ouer-gret
taskis and tailis rered vppon them; and therto they, finding bothe
hors-mete and mannys mete to youre soudeours riding be the contre,
without contenting or agreing hem becaus of nom-power of youre said   900
men, ben not paide of here wages and soude by lak of simple payment;
`[which] caused the rather the ducdom of Normandy to be lost'.

And the saide Dame Cristin in the xiiij chapiter seiethe that a noble,
good cheueteyn whiche wol be a leder of a felouship in werre, he must
vse `i'ustice to Goddis pleasure; and, that he may stande in the grace   905
and fauoure of the worlde and of his retenu and of other peple vndre
hym, that the said chieftein must pay his men of soude so iustly and
truly bethout any defalking, abbregging of here wagis, that they haue
no nede to lyue by pillage, extorcion and rapyn vppon the countreis of
here frendis that be yolden vndre obeisaunce of here prince.   910

And be this way the ost may neuer faut, for then the ost shal be furnisshed of alle costis, oostis commyng withe vitailes inoughe, so that it be
prouided that marchauntes `a'nd vitailers may surely passe and come;
and that a payne resonable be made that, vppon forfeting that payne, no
man take vitaile be force without payment made in hande (as the pro-   915
clamacions made by Henry the V^{the}, that victorious prince, in his host,
`and also the statutes made by Iohn, regent of Fraunce, "duc of Bed-
ford", by a parlement at Cane yn the .ij^{de}. yeere of Herry VJ^{te}, named
kyng, vppon the conduyt of the werre, that I delyuered to your hyghnes
enseled the day before your departyng owt of London, that remayned   920
yn the kepyng of Ser Iohn Fastolf for grate autoritee'); and that | no   f. 15^v
damage or offence be done to the marchauntes.

It is fulle gret iupardie and perille to an oost, whereas couetise of
pillage and rappyne reignithe among men of armes, more than theire
entencion is to kepe and meinteine the right of theire princes partie, and 925
the worship of cheualrie and knighthode `ys' that they shulde peine hem
to wynne. And suche as ben of that `i'nordynat condicion of couetise

901 not paide] *WW symbol at fore-edge*   902 which caused . . . lost] *WW
interl.* caused . . . lost   903 And] *reader 1 in marg.* nota peroptime concilium
istud   905 `i'ustice] *minuscule* i *changed to majuscule* I   912 oostis] coostis
913 `a'nd] *one-compartment* a *changed to two-compartment* a   917–21 and also the
statutes . . . grate autoritee] *WW adds after* and that *below last l. on the page and continues
in marg.* statutes] *reader 1 in marg.* Inquire pro libro illo . bonum est   duc of Bedford]
WW interl. into his addn   918 Herry] *reader 1 interl.* blessed   921 and that]
WW duplic. at top of next p. no] *reader 1 at top of p.* nota bene ne forte   926 ys]
WW interl.   927 `i'nordynat] *minuscule* i *changed to majuscule* I

and rapyne ought rather be clepid pilleris, robberis, extorcioneris, than
men of armes cheualerous.

930   In example the said Dame Cristen puttithe that the men of armes
of the countre of Gaule, whiche now is Fraunce, that had in a tyme a
discomfiture and the ouerhande vppon the Romains, being assembled
withe a grete oost embatailed vpon the riuer of Rosne in Burgoyne, and
the men of Gaule had wonne gret praies and goode'z', as hors, harneis,
935   vessell of gold and of siluer gret plente; but as to the worldly goodes they
set no count ne prise of it but cast it into the riuer. And in semblable wise
Dux Bedfordie.   it was saide of Iohn, duke of Bedforde, then regent, that the
day he had the victorie at the bataile of Vernaile he exhorted, making
Notandum.   an oracion to his peple, that they attende not to couetise
940   for no sight of iuelx and riches, of cheynes of golde or nouches, ringis,
cast before hem or lost in the feelde to take them vp, whiche might be
the losse of the feelde, tille God had shewed his power and fortune, but
onely to worship and to doo that that they come for. And so, be the
iugement of God, had the victorie withe gret worship and riches be the
945   raunsonyng of prisoneris and be rewardis of the said regent in londis
and goodis to euery man for theire welle-doing that day, rewarded in
lifelode of londis and tenementis youen in the counte of Mayne to the
yerely valeu of .x. M^l. marc yerely, whiche was lx. M^l. 'liures' turneis, as
it is of record to shew. The whiche 'was don aftyr' the Romayns 'con-
f. 16^r dicion', seeing that thei set so litill by goodis dispising but | onely by
951   worship, [at] the whiche the saide Romains were gretly astonied and
dred her power, for thei saw it neuer done before.
Exhortacio.   And wolde Ihesus for his highe grace, that euery prince,
chieftein or captein wolde be of so noble condicions, as is before made
955   mencion of. I haue be credibly enfourmed by tho as were present in
bataile withe the 'fulle' noble and victorius prince of renomme, King
Henry the Vte, youre cousin and antecessour, vsed the saide counceile
among his ostes. And also at the bataile of Agincourt, be the exortacion
of that 'forseyd' noble prince, Henry the .V^{the} counceiled to set not be
960   no tresure, praies ne iuelx and vesselle of golde and of siluer, as welle
of tho that were his there lost ne of the iuelx that he wonne, but only to
his right and to wonne worship.

930 In] *WW symbol at fore-edge*   934 goode'z'] *WW adds* z *at end*
936 And] *reader 1 in marg.* nota bene   943 And] *reader 1 in marg.* nota
bene   945 prisoneris] *WW symbol at fore-edge*   948 liures] *WW interl.*
949 was don aftyr] *WW interl.*   condicion] *WW interl.*   951 at the] the (*see n.*)
956 fulle] *WW over eras.*   King] *WW symbol at fore-edge*   958 And] *reader 1 in*
marg. nota bene   959 forseyd] *WW interl.*

And that also fulle noble prince, youre cousin, Iohn, duke of Bedforde, another victorius prince, folowed his stappis tho daies that he
was regent of the roiaume of Fraunce. And whan his chariottes of his   965
tresoure and vesselle at the bataile of Vernelle-in-Perche was bereued
frome hym by Lombardis and other sowdieris holding youre aduerse

Exhortacio ad   partie, he comaunded the oost embatailed not for to
obseruandam
ordinacionem   breke ne remeue 'theyr aray' for wynnyng or keping
principis in bello.   worldly goodis but only to wynne worship in the right   970
of Englonde that day, whiche he hadde the victorie to his grettist
renomme.

But yet it most be suffred paciently, the fortune that is geuyn to youre
ennemies at this tyme. And late the case be taken for a new lerning and
to the sharping of goode corages, to the refourmyng and amendement   975

Verba Magistri   of theire wittis. For the saide Ouide, the lawreat poet,
Alani de Auriga.   saiethe that it happithe oftentimes that mysauentures
lernithe tho that bene conquerid to be wise, and so at other times in
actis and dedis of armes that for lak of prouidence or mysfortune were
ouerthrow, enforcethe hem to be conquerours 'another seson'. Here is   980
yet noone so | gret inconuenient of auenture ne mysfortune falle at this   f. 16ᵛ
tyme but that it hathe be seene fallen er now 'yn Kyng Iohn dayes and
in Kyng Edward .IIJᵈ. dayes, yn hys gret age put owt of Normandye and
off many castells and townes yn Gyen by Kyng Charlys the .Vᵗᵉ.'

Defectus pe-   **How the duchie of Normandie for lak of a sufficient**   985
cunie ad
soluendos solda-   **arme waged in due time, that King Iohn 'of**
rios fuit causa   **England' had not sufficiently wherof to wage**
vna perdicio-
nis ducatus   **'hys peple', he lost the duchie of Normandie.**
Normanie.

For a like mysfortune and ouerthrow fille vnto vs for defaute of proui-

Infinita mala   dence and helpe in dew tyme, and sensualite of lustis of   990
ex sensualitate   the bodie idely misspendid, and for lak of finaunce and
corporis.
goode'z' to soude and wage goode mennys bodies ouer into Normandie
and other contrees. Ande thoroughe the vmbre of trewes the hole priuacion of your duchie of Normandie and of Angew, Mayne and Torayn
and a gret part of Gascoigne and Gu'y'en was in King Iohn daies by   995

969 theyr aray] WW interl.   973 But] WW symbol at fore-edge   980 another
seson] WW interl.   982–4 yn Kyng Iohn ... Charlys the .Vᵗᵉ.] WW adds yn over eras.,
then interl. from Kyng and continues in marg.   985SN perdicionis] perdicicionis
986–7 of England] WW interl.   988 hys peple] WW interl.   989 For] WW
symbol at fore-edge   992 goode'z'] WW adds z at end   995 Gu'y'en] WW y
over uneras. i

1203. King Philip Dieudonne of Fraunce the yere of Crist M^l. ij^C. iij^o. in the monithe of Maij began.

How many diuers times trewes that were taken betwene King Richarde the First, King Iohn and King Edward the Thrid at the
1000 **finalle peas generalle betwene tho kinges and the Frenshe kinges were afterwarde be the Frenshe partie first broken.**

Treuge plures   And thus vndre the coloure of trewes at diuers tymes taken
infracte.   atwixt youre noble progenitoures King Henry the Seconde, and also diuers treties taken betwene the said King Iohn and King
1005 Phelip, and also sondry tymes trewes taken betwene King Richarde the First and the Frenshe King Philip Dieudonne, and notwithestanding so oft tymes trewes and alliaunces taken and made betwene the forsaide kinges of Englonde and of Fraunce, alleway whan the Frenshe partie coude haue and fynde any auauntage or coloure to breke here trewes,
f. 17^r they did | make new werre ayenst this lande.
1011 *Treuga pessima,*   Also there was another trewes made at Paris the monithe
anno Christi
1259.   of Octobre the yere of Crist M^l. CClix betwene King Henry the Thrid and Lowes, king of Fraunce, the whiche King Lowes, haueng grete conscience that he heelde bethout title of right the duchie of Nor-
1015 mandie, the counte of Angew, Mayne and Toureyne out of the handis of the kinges of Englonde, therfore toke a trewes withe King Henry the Thridde. And the saide King Lowes graunted and confermed to the saide King Henry and to his heires foreuer alle the right that he hadde or myght haue in the duchie of Gascoigne, withe thre *eueschies,*
1020 clepid *diocesis,* and citees in the saide duchie, that is to wete, *Limo-gensis, Caourcensis* 'and' Pieregourt, also at Agenois and Peito. And
De infinitis   a peas to be made atwix bothe kinges vndre the condi-
dampnis ex illa
treuga sine pace.   cion that the saide King Henry Thrid shulde relese vnto King Lowes alle his right in Normandie and in the countre of Aniou, of
1025 Mayne and Toreyne, your verray auncient enheritaunce tailed.
    Whiche albeit if the said King Henry Thrid had done made any suche relese, it was of none strenght ne effect, for it was neuer graunted be the auctorite of the parlement of thre astatis of his roiaume. For it is to

1002 And] *WW symbol at fore-edge*   1010 make] *reader 1 at top of p.* nota fallacias Francorum in rupcione trugarum . vide et attende bene   1011 Also] *WW symbol at fore-edge*   1021 and] *WW interl.*   1024 King] seint king *with* seint crossed out   1026 Whiche] *WW symbol at fore-edge*   1028 For] *WW symbol at fore-edge*

be vndrestande that be no law imperialle ne by no dew reason can be
founded that a prince may not gyue away his duchees or countees ne   1030
his demaynes that is his propre enheritaunces to a straunge parsone of
what astate or degre he is, bethout the agrement and consenting of a
parlement of his Lordis Spirituelle and Temporelle and of his Comyns
assembled, and a sufficient nombre of euery of hem, as it hathe bene
accustumed. So in conclusion the relese of King Henry Thrid to King   1035
Lowes was and is voide. And if any relese of King Lowes to the said
King Henry in the said duchie of Gascoine had be made, it standithe of
full litille effect becaus it was the said King Henry propre enheritaunce
by his aiel, King | Henry the Second, that weddid Dame Alienor, duch- f. 17ᵛ
De pluribus treu- esse and heriter of Guien, as is before expressid. And so   1040
gis sine effectu
dura[nte].   the said King Lowes relese was a confirmacion of the said
duchie of Guien into King Henry Thrid is possession and a disclayme
frome the kinges of Fraunce foreuer.

　　Also ther was another trux and pease made the yere of Crist Mˡ.
CC. lxxix. at Amyeus betwen King Edwarde First and King Philip of   1045
Fraunce, that the said King Edwarde shulde holde peasibly a`ll' the saide
londes in Gascoigne.

　　Another trewes and peas made at Paris the yere of Crist Mˡ. ijᶜ. lxxxvj.
betwene the said King Edwarde First and King Philip of Fraunce for the
saide duchie of Guien.   1050

　　Another trews made at Paris the yere of Crist .Mˡ. iijᶜ. iijᵒ. the
monithe of Maij betwene King Edwarde First and King Philip of
Fraunce, that marchauntes and alle maner men might passe to bothe
roiaumes of Englond and Fraunce bethout empeshement, and heelde
not long.   1055

　　Another trux made in the yere of Crist Mˡ. CC. xiij. in a towne clept
in Latyn *Pissaicus* betwene King Edwarde Second and King Phelip, king
of Fraunce, for the said duchie of Guien.

　　And in the yere of Crist Mˡ. iijᶜ. xxiiij. King Charles of Fraunce and
of Nauarre seased certein townes and forteresses in Guien, for defaut 1060
of homage of the King Edwarde Second for the said duchie of Guien;
whiche townes and forteresses after was deliuerid ayen to King Edwarde
by the moyen of Edmonde, erle of Kent, his lieftenaunt.

　　Also another pease made in the yere of Crist Mˡ. iijᶜ. xxv. betwene

　　1039 Henry] *reader 1 at top of p.* Titulum Regis . vt infra; *and reader 2 in marg. either
side* Edwarde furst *and* Edwarde ijᵈ   1040ꜱɴ durante] durauit   1046 a`ll'] ll
over uneras. s   1054 empeshement] empeshemement   1057 King] *reader 2
in marg.* Edwarde ijᵈ   1064 Also] *reader 1 in marg.* nota pro titulo Regis

1065 King Edwarde Second and King Charles de Valoys of Fraunce, be reason

Effectus ma- and meane that the saide King Edwarde weddid Dam Isa-

ritagij Isabelle bel, King Charlis 'of Fraunce' doughter, 'soule' enheriter
Regine, heredis

regni Fr[a]ncie. of Fraunce. And at that tyme King Edward made Edmond,

his brother, erle of Kent, his lieftenaunt for the duchie of Guyen, whiche

f. 18ʳ fulle nobly gouerned and kept | that contre.

1071 1340. Also in semblable wise in the yere of Crist .Mˡ iij Cxl., the .xiij.

yere of King Edwarde the Thrid, after the saide king had wonne the

Bellum Scluse. gret bataile of Scluse ayenst Philip de Valois, his aduersarie,

and besieged Tourenay in Picardie, whan the saide Philip de Valois

1075 and the 'kyng "[y]s"' Frenshe lordis were gretly rebuked and put abak,

they desired a trux of King Edwarde, frome the monithe of Septembre

tille the Feest of Saint Iohn next sueng, to the gret damage of the King

Edwarde conquest, and the Bretons making vnder that colour mortalle

werre to this land; but they were kept in subgeccion, and a gret bataile

1080 of descomfiture ayenst theim had by the erle of Northampton, then the

kingis lieutenaunt in that parties.

Also the yere of Crist Mˡ. iij C xliijᵒ, the xix day of Ianuarij, another

gret trux for the yere, take withe Philip de Valois, calling hym king,

youre saide aduersarie and his allies; and the saide trux broken be the

1085 saide Philip bethin thre yeris after comaunding the Bretons to make

werre ayenst youre progenitours. And the noble King Edwarde the

Thrid seeing that, in the monithe of Iuile the yere of Crist Mˡ. CCC

Obcidio Cane. xlvijᵒ., the xx yere of his reigne, disposed hym ayen to

werre withe the saide Philip and wanne vpon hym the strong towne

1090 Bellum Cressye. of Cane 'and had' the sore-fought bataile of Cressy, the

castelle of Calix by a harde siege bethin few daies after leide.

1066sn Francie] Frncie   1067 of Fraunce] WW at l. end   soule] WW interl.
1070 kept] reader 2 at foot of p. Edwardus ijᵘˢ duxit Isabellam filiam et heredem karoli
regis francie anno christi Mˡ CCC xxvᵗᶜ   that] reader 1 at top of p. Titulum Regis vt
infra   1071 Also] WW symbol at fore-edge   1075 kyng "ys"] WW adds kyng
and abbrev. for and at l. end; the abbrev. for and was later overwritten as kidney-shaped
s   1078 and] WW symbol at fore-edge   1089 withe] ayen withe with ayen
lightly crossed out   1088sn Obcidio Cane] red siden. partly duplic. black Cane
1090 and had] WW interl.   1091 leide] leide and with and lightly crossed out

De pace finali,
quamuis non
sortiebatur diu
efectum.

How, notwithestonding a finalle peas was made solempnely be the fulle assent of King Iohn of Fraunce, prisoner, as it is the chief auctorite and comprehendid in many articles most sufficiauntly grounded, by auctorite of the pope confermed, that for alle that it helde not passe vij. or viij yere after.

1095

And so contynued | by xiij. yeris fro the saide tyme mortal werre, con- f. 18ᵛ
tinued tille a final generalle peas was made after by agrement of King
Iohn of Fraunce, that was take betwene the said noble King Edwarde the 1100
Thrid and the saide King Iohn the monithe of Maij the yere of Crist M¹.
iij ᶜ lx. at Bretigny, the pope `assentyng´, and be mediacion of cardinalx,
archebisshoppis, bisshoppis, abbotis, dukes, erles, barons and lordis;
and by the assent of bothe parties of Englande as of Fraunce, and con-
ferme`d´ by the saide pope and the sacramentis of bothe Cristen kinges, 1105
made bothe by hemsilfe and by here commissaries in suche solempne
wise that alle Cristen princes wolde haue thought it shulde stande ferme
and haue bene stable foreuer. Ande whiche finalle peas dured not scant
viijᵗʰᵉ yere after but that it was broke fraudulentlie be feyned causes and
colourable quarellis of the Frenshe partie, as of the erle of Armenak and 1110
other lordis of Guien.

And after King Charles the Vᵗʰᵉ of Fraunce, son to King Iohn, vnder
colour of the seid trux and fynal peas made be his father, put King
Edwarde the Thrid and his sonnes and other his lieutenauntes out of
alle his conquest, as welle of alle the londis that King Edwarde con- 1115
querid in Fraunce, Normandie, Burgoyne and Flaundres, and out of
many other counteez, baronies and lordshippes, and of a gret part of
the duchie of Guien. Whiche counteez and lordshippes in Gascoigne
and Guien were gi`v´en vtterly and plenerlie to doo none homage, ne
souereinte to holde but of the saide noble King Edwarde and of alle his 1120
enheriteris, neuer to resort ayen in homage ne feute to youre aduersaries of Fraunce, as it is expresly enacted and recorded in the registres of
alle the homagieris of Guien and Gascoigne. That was made by the erle
of Armenak, the lorde | de la Brette, vicecountes, barons, cheualers and f. 19ʳ
escuiers and alle other nobles of the saide duchie[z], made to the saide 1125
King Edwarde and to Prince Edwarde, the duke of Guien, the kingis
lieutenaunt, that is to wete in the cathedralle chirche of Saint Andrieu at

1098 by] *reader 1 at top of p.* Titulum Regis   1102 assentyng] *WW at l. end*
1104-5 conferme`d´] d *over uneras.* th   1112 And] *WW symbol at fore-edge*
1119 gi`v´en] v *over uneras.* u   1124 de] *reader 1 at top of p.* Titulum Regis vt infra
1125 duchiez] duchier   1127 Andrieu] Andrieu chirche

1363. Burdeux the xix day of Iuilly the yere of Crist M^l. iij^C lxiij.; present there Ser Thomas Beauchamp, erle of Warewik, that auenturous 'and' most fortunat knighte in his daies, and Ser Iohn Chaundos of Herfordshire, vicount de Saint-Saueoure 'in Norman-dye', whiche had bene in many batailes and had the gouernaunce of M^l. speris and was comissarie for King Edwarde withe a fulle grete ost of multitude of peple wele-defensid in Guien.

1130 De magnificen-cia Iohannis Chundos.

And so after that Prince Edwarde had receiued alle the homages aboute Bourdeux, Bordelois and Bassedois within the seneschalcie of Gascoigne, than he and the saide comissaries went to alle the countees foloweng and receiued theire homages and feutees bothe in the name of King Edwarde 'IIJ^d.', and than in like fourme did homage to the prince as duc of Guien. And was no differens betwene the bothe homages doing to the king and to the duc of Guien, except that homager at his othe-making to the saide duke, he reserued the souereinte and the ressort dew to his highe souerein seigniour king.

1135 Princeps Edwardus.

Edwarde toke the homages of alle the vassallis and subgettis in the seneschalcie of Agenois, after in the seneschalcie of L'a'ndis, after in the counte of Bigorre, then in the seneschalcie of Pierregort, in the seneschalcie of Caoursyn and Roerge'v' and Lymosyn, also in the counte of Engwillom, also in the seneschalcie of Xantonge, than in the counte of Poitou and Poytiers.

De pluribus comitatibus in Vasconia sub obediencia *1145* regis Anglie.

By whiche it may be considerid be the said countees and | countrees before specified, it was of a wide space and many a thousand peple that were at that tyme and yet ought be vnder youre obeisaunce. And the saide Prince Edwarde and the kingis comissaries made here iourneis by .viij. monithes day, as tille the iiij^{the} day of Aprille the yere of Crist 1364. M^l. iij^C lxiiij. or thei coude receiue alle tho saide homagiers.

f. 19^v
1151

1155

Whiche now in the yere of Crist M^l. iiij^C. lj., after that hole Nor-maundie was lost, and also Gascoigne and Guien youen vp in defaute of socoure 'of an armee made' in season, many of youre saide trew liege-peple be ouercome by youre aduersaries of Fraunce, and many a thousand peple of nobles and others coherted and be force ayenst theire hertis wille and entent to become homagiers to youre saide aduersarie by the hole priuacion of the saide duchie of Guien as of Normandie,

1160

1129 and] WW interl.   1130SN De . . . Chundos] red siden. partly duplic. black Chaundos cheualier   1131–2 in Normandye] WW interl.   1139 IIJ^d.] WW over eras.   1146 L'a'ndis] a over uneras. o   1148 Roerge'v'] v over uneras. n 1150 and] at foot of f. 19', a 16th-c. hand doodles an alphabet   countrees] reader 1 at top of p. Titulum Regis   1157 and] WW symbol at fore-edge   1158 of an armee made] WW interl.   1162 priuacion] WW symbol at fore-edge

whiche withe the helpe of almightie God and Saint George, chief
defendoure and protectoure of these youre londis, withe the comfort
of youre true subgectis, shal not abide long in theire possession ne   1165
gouernaunce.

De pace finali.   And now of late tyme a peas finalle was made and
take withe King Charlis the Sext. And the whiche finalle peas, made
solempnelie at Trois in Champayne the .xxj. day of Maij the yere of
1420. Crist M^l. CCCC xx. and registred in the court of parlement,   1170
confermed that alle diuisions and debates betwene the roiaume of
Englande and the roiaume of Fraunce shulde foreuer cease. And the
saide finalle peas heelde not fullie .ij. yeris but brake sone after the
decese of that victorioux prince, King Harry the V^{the}, vpon his mariage
withe Quene Katerin. And now last of alle the gret trewes taken and   1175
made at Towris betwene Henry the Sext, the `innocent' prince, and
Charlis the .VIJ^{the}., youre aduersarie of Fraunce, in the said .xxiiij. yere
of his reigne solempnely sworne and sealed | and sone after broken be   f. 20^r
De infraccione   the Frenshe partie. And none of alle these trewes hathe
treugarum: nota §. ben obserued ne kept, notwithstanding any sacrement,   1180
othes, promisses, made by youre aduersarie and be his dukes, erlis and
barones of the seide Frenshe partie; but alway brake the saide trewes
whan they coude take any auauntage ayenst vs, as it shewethe openly
and may be a mirroure foreuer to alle Cristen princes to mystrust any
trewes-taking by youre saide aduersarie or his allies and subgeitis, be   1185
it the duke of Breteyne, the duke of Orliens or any suche other his
complisses.

De continuacione hereditatis   For whereas youre noble progenitours were
ducatus Normandie.   seased and possessid of the said duchie of Nor-
912 §.   mandie, sithe that Duke Rollo of the nacion of   1190
Rollo, dux vocatus
Robertus, filius magnifici   Denmarke the yere of Crist .ix^C xij. conquerid
domini in regno Dacie
vocati Byercoteferre.   it vpon Charlis le Simple, to whome he gaue his
doughter in mariage withe the seide duchie, and so hathe continued
Nota bene. fro heire to heire .CC iiij^{xx} xj. yere, but after, as it may be cast,
it was .CC iiij^{xx} xj. yere that it was neuer in no king of Fraunce is hande   1195
tille it was lost in King Iohn is daies of Englande. And than for suche
inconuenientis as was vsed now be mysfortune vnder `the vmbre of
trewes and for puttyng down Arthur of Breteyn' it was lost and youen

1173 peas] WW symbol at fore-edge   1174 mariage] reader 1 in marg. pro Titulo Regis . nota   1175 And] WW symbol at fore-edge   1176 innocent]
WW over. eras.   1178 and] reader 1 at top of p. vt infra   1191 the] WW
symbol at fore-edge after his siden.   1196 And] reader 1 in marg. nota causam etc
1197 the vmbre . . . Breteyn] WW interl.

1203. vp to the seide King Phelip Dieudonne in the yere of Crist M^l.
1200 CCiij., about the first 'and second' yere of the seide King Iohn. And
frome the saide first yere of King Iohn the possession of the saide
duchie of Normandie discontynued .Cxxxvj yere, that was to the yere
§ Nota optime.   of Crist M^l. CCCxxxix., that youre right and possession
was refourmed by youre noble progenitoure King Edwarde the Thrid,
1205 whiche by many yeris leide segis and had batailes withe Philip de Valois
and Iohn of Fraunce, occupieris of that kingdom.

f. 20^v **How King Edwarde | the Thrid made first grete alliaunces withe
gret astatis or he began to make werre in Fraunce.**

And therto King Edwarde allied hym withe fulle mighty princes to
1210 socour and relief hym in his werres, or he began to set on hem: first
withe Lowes, emperoure of Allemayne, to whome he rewarded fifty
thousande sak wolle for purueaunce and soulde men of werre that he
shulde make to helpe King Edwarde the Thrid in his conquest; and
after allied hym to the erle of Heynew and to the erle of Flaundres and
1215 also withe the duke of Bretein, the whiche alliaunces was a fulle gret
Conciderandum.   socoure and helpe to his conquest in Fraunce and Normandie. For he wanne at the first raise that he made ouer the see .M^l.
M^l. v^C. townes and castellis and so forthe reigned and continued in
armes xxxiiij yeris, by putting the Frenshe king and his allies in gret
1220 subgeccion for the right of his enheritaunces, like as whoso lust rede
In *Cronicis*   the book [of] his actis clepid '*Mayster'* Froddesarde more
Frodssard.   plainly may perceyue.
And so alle his daies contynued tille vnto the tyme that be dissimila-
Pax finalis   cion of the gret peas taken atwix hym and his prisoner King
sperata fuit.
1225 1360.   Iohn of Fraunce, made at Bretigny the yere of Crist .M^l.
iij^{C}lx, that vndre vmbre of the seid trewes Charles le Sage, his sonne,
after the decese of King Iohn did put King Edwarde Thrid out of alle his
said conquest in Fraunce and Normandie and partie of Guyen.
And sithen more effectuelle laboures and dedis of armes hathe be
1230 done by that victorioux prince, Henry the V^{the}, he being parsonelly
bothe at many sieges leyng, at assautes, at batailes and iourneis frome

1200 and second] *WW interl.*   1202 .Cxxxvj] *WW symbol at fore-edge*
1207 the] *reader 1 at top of p.* Titulum Regis   1212 soulde] *WW symbol
at fore-edge*   1213 and] *reader 1 in marg.* nota de auxilio Regis Edwardi
1219 xxxiiij] *WW symbol at fore-edge*   1221 of his] his   Mayster] *WW
interl. in red*   1230 victorioux] *unidentified reader annot.* nota

the second yere of his reigne 'exclusyfe' into the day of his trespasse-
ment the space of .vij. yere, | whiche labouris parcellis of them briefly   f. 21ʳ
bene specified before.

  And there youre obeisaunt subgeitis and trew liege-peple be put   1235
'owt' of theire londis and tenementis youen to hem by youre predecessoures, as wel as be that highe and mighty prince, Richarde,
duke of Yorke, youre father, being at two voiages lieutenaunt and
gouuernaunt in Fraunce, for seruice done vnto hem in theire conquest
not recompensid ayen to theire vndoing.   1240

Exclamacio. 'He'h', allas!', thei did crie, and 'Woo be the tyme!', they
saide, 'that euer we shulde put affiaunce and trust to the Frenshe partie
or theire alliez in any trewes-keping, considering so manyfolde tymes
we haue ben deceiued and myscheuid thoroughe suche dissimiled
trewes', as is late before specified.   1245

Concideracio. And yet not for alle these inconuenientis that haue falle to
vs be conspiring of deceitis vndre vmbre of suche dissimiled trewes,
late it be out of doubte that thoughe they holde theym neuer so proude,
puissaunt and strong, ne so sotill and crafty in suche deceitis conspiring, they by Goddis might shal be ouercome and brought to the right   1250
astate that it ought be, whereas the title and clayme of th'enheritaunce
of Fraunce is verray trew, whan dew diligence haue be shewed by vs in
executing the saide right, as it is verefied briefly by examples herebefore.

Divina concide-   **How be it that at som tymes that God suffrithe the**
racio enodanda
per theologos.   **partie that hathe a true title and right to be**   1255
ouercome, yet for alle that a man shulde not be discouraged
alway to sew his right.

And albeit that at som tymes God suffrethe the partie that hathe right
and a trew title and that liueth after his lawes to be gretly parsecuted
and to be put to ouer-gret auenture, laboure and peyne, sometyme to   1260
be | ouerthrow, sometyme to be prisoner or slaine in bataile be diuine   f. 21ᵛ
prouidence, whan hym lust to be iuge, thoughe the peple be neuer so
goode ne the querelle, title and right neuer so trew.

1450.   And yet not for no suche aduersite, and 'as' haue fallen the yere
of Crist Mˡ. iiijᶜ. l. be the last ouerthrow of a notable arme at Fremyny,   1265

1232 exclusyfe] *WW at l. end*   1233 whiche] *reader 1 at top of p.* vt
infra   1236 owt] *WW interl.*   1241 He'h'] *WW* h *over uneras.* 2nd e
1261 ouerthrow] *reader 1 at top of p.* nota ne forte vt infra   sometyme] *WW symbol at*
fore-edge   1264 as] *WW interl.*

where Ser Thomas Kiriell, knight lieftenaunt in that voiage, ʼwas take
prysoner wyth many othyrs to the nombre about .ix$^{C/}$. A grete caus was
that the pety capteins wolde not obbey at the day of that

Infortunium belli apud Fermenye vltima vice.

iournay at that sodeyne recountre to her chieftein and
1270 taried lengir in his voiage, after he was londed or he came to any strong-
holde was present. Also another gret armee and voiage fordone for
defaut and lak of spedy payment this yere of Crist M^{l}. CCCClj., whiche

Gyen.

were at last redy to goo to Gyen: the armee taried vpon the
see-coostis in Englande almost a quarter of a yere, or theire pay-
1275 *Burdeux.* ment was redie, and the cite of Burdeux lost in the meanetyme
for lak of rescue.

Yet God defende that thoroughe suche aduersitees we shulde be
vtterly discoraged! Late vs take example in according to this. It is
wretin in the Booke of Machabeus in the viij. chapitre, how the wor-
1280 shipfull Iudas Machabeus, seeyng Goddis peple gretly febled and
abasshed be diuers discomfitures of theym, seide to his knightis, ʻA, a!
It is bettir to vs to auaunce vs forthe and rather to die in bataile then
lengir to suffre the gret passions and troubles of oure infortune.ʼ And
fro thensforthe by the wille of God, good corage and comfort taken
1285 to theyme, they were made conquerours and had the victorie in alle
theire batailes.

De Sancto Lo- dowico, rege Frʼaʼncie.

Also another example by Seint Lowes, king of Fraunce,
whiche in encresing the Cristyn feithe made gret armees
f. 22^{r} into the Holy Land | in ʻaboutʼ the yere of Crist ʻM^{l}. ij^{C}lxxʼ ʻaʼnd suff-
1290 rethe gret aduersiteis among the Sarrasyns, he and his knightis ouerthrow and take prisoneris to the soudan of Babilon, and the king put
to gret raunsom paide, his peple died vp by gret mortalite of pestilence,
suffred famyne, hungur and thurst; yet God at the last releuid hym; and
came into Fraunce withe gret worship.

1295 **Annother exhortacion of the historier.**

Animacio. O ye highe and myghtifulle prince, king of Englande and of
Fraunce, and alle ye other noble princes and other puissaunt lordes
and nobles of diuers astates, olde or yong, of so auncien a stok and of
so worthy a lineage as of the noble Troian is blode descendid (as it is

---

1266–7 was take . . . about .ix^{C}] *WW interl.*   1287SN Frʼaʼncie] *red abbrev. for* a
interl. into black siden.   1289 about] *WW interl. directly above* in *at the top of the*
p. M^{l}. ij^{C}lxx] *WW over eras.* ʻaʼnd] *one-compartment* a *changed to two-compartment*
a   1295 Annother] *WW symbol at fore-edge*

auctorised and may appere by many croniclers ande histories of noble 1300
doctours enacted and registred), that ye alonly haue euer ben halden
without note of errour or deformite of the law, withe the most puissaunt
and of power thoroughe alle regions Cristen or hethen, haueng alway
vnder youre regencie and gouernaunce the habondaunce of noble men
of cheualrie passing alle othir landes, after the quantite and afferaunt of 1305
youre roiaume. Lete then be as a mirrour noted and had before youre
eyen by contynuell remembraunce, to th'entent that the excersising of
theire noble actis in conquestis may the more vigorously endeuce you
to succede the prowesse and vaillauntnesse of youre highe predecessoures in armes. Like as it shewethe welle at this tyme, of what worship 1310
they haue bene by here victorious dedis for they in difference of other
nacions haue euer ewred and shewed the renomme | and excellence f. 22ᵛ
of youre highe and mighty antecessours corages, as well in straunge
regions as among the Sarrasyns in the region of Sirie and Turkie as in the
saide neere regions of Fraunce, Spayne, Lumbardie, Spruce and other 1315
countrees. And therfor ye shulde yeue laude and praisingis alway to
God, for sithe the trespassement of Prince Edwarde and good Henry,
duc of Lancastre, that was, 'ther were but few lyke to hem in armys'.

Here is brieflie made mencion of the recomendacion of acyn worship of Henry the Vᵗʰᵉ and his bretheryn Thomas, Iohn and Humfrey, .iiij. noble princes. 1320

Where was he of late daies descendid of noble bloode that was so cora-
geous in dedis of armes 'as was that' mightifull prince of renommee of
youre noble lynage Henry .Vᵗᵉ. and his said thre full mighty and noble
princes, his brethern, and next .ij. cosyns-germayns of youre kynne, 1325
that in here daies were as the pilours and chief postis of the holders-vp
of the 'last' conquest and of the possession of youre rightfull enheritaunce bothe of youre roiaumes of Fraunce as of iustice-keping, tranquillite and pease in youre roiaume of Englond, also of the duchies of
Normandie, Gascoigne, Guyen and of the counte of Mayne. 1330

For as for a brief aduertisement and remembraunce how Thomas,
Dux Clarence. the duc of Clarence, in his yong age the yere of Crist Mˡ.
CCCCiij. lieutenaunt of alle Irelonde and after that lieutenaunt and
gouernoure of youre duchees of Gascoyne and Guien, defending the
true subgettis frome theire aduersaries, holding vp youre right and 1335

1318 ther were . . . armys] WW interl.   1323 as was that] WW adds as over eras.,
was at l. end, and that over eras. on next l.   1327 last] WW interl.

keping youre peple and subgettis vnder youre lawes; and after that 'the
Concideran- seyd duc' in company of the victorioux prince Henry the
dum est.   .Vte labourid in armes vpon that noble conquest in Fraunce
and the duchie of Normandie, there being lieutenaunt for that marchis;
f. 23^r whereas he in bataile among youre aduersa|ries in the duchie of Aniou
1341 at Bowgee most worshiplie at a sodeyn recountre, fighting withe a few
felouship of lordis and nobles, leuyng his hoste behynde, not abiding
1421. theire comyng ayenst a gret multitude of fighters, the yere of Crist
M^l CCCCxxj among the Frenshemen and Scottis was slayn. Whiche
1345 not long after, God thoroughe power suffred the seid capteyns of Scottis to be ouerthrow bothe at the batailes of Crauant, also at the bataile
of Vernell and 'also' at the bataile of Rouuerey.

Iohannes, dux   Also youre second cousyn Iohn, duc of Bedforde, that
Bedfordie, regens
regni Fr[a]ncie.   in his grene age was lieutenaunt of the Marchis, werrid
1350 ayenst the Scottis, keping them in subgeccion, hauyng gret iourneis
and batailes ayenst them; after that made admirall and kepar of the
see, hauyng a gret mortal bataile and victorie ayenst the carrakes,
galeis and othir gret shippis; beyng also a certayn tyme lieutenaunt and
protectoure in this lande; and sethe yeede vpon youre said conquest
1355 into Fraunce and Normandie, therof being regent and gouuernoure in
the daies of the deuout prince, Henry the Sext, ouer all the subgeitis
Conquestus   of Fraunce and Normandie xiij. yeris; and conquerid the
comitatus de
Mayn.   counte of Mayne, defending, keping and gouuernyng the
said countreis in gret tranquillite and peace to the gret worship of
1360 bothe roiaumes; and there made his faire ende at Rone, where he
1435. liethe tombid, the yere of Crist M^l. CCCCxxxv. the xiiij day of
Septembre.

Dux Gloucestrie.   And how the thrid brother Humfrey, duc of Gloucestre,
withe a notabill power was vpon youre conquest in Normandie withe
1365 his said brother and at the bataile of Agyncourt was sore woundid. And
Comes de   after, he wanne 'wyth help of the noble erle of March and
Marche.
Comes   the erle of Suffolk acompanyed', brought in subgeccion be
Suffolchie.   force of siegis lieng among youre aduersaries, Base Normandie: the castell of Chierbourgh, the cite of Bayeux, Costances withe
1370 all the Close of Costantyne and Auerances, Seynt-Lowe, Carenten and
f. 23^v Valoignez withe all othir forteressis and villages in that marcher. | And

1336-7 the seyd duc] WW interl.   1341 worshiplie] at top of p., 5 manicules
pointing away from text   1347 also] WW interl.   1348SN Fr[a]ncie] Frncie
1366-7 wyth help of the noble . . . acompanyed] WW adds wyth help over eras. and adds
of the afterwards at l. end; interl. noble . . . acompanyed in next l. after brought (see n.)
1371 in that marcher] imitated in pen-trials in marg.

ouer that, sithe he was protectoure and defendoure of youre roiaume
of Englond in the tyme of the said Henry the Sext of grene age, keping
gret iustice, tranquillite and peace withyn youre saide roiaume. And
Calix. after, whan youre nobill castell and towne of Calix was besiegid in   1375
the yere of Crist .M^l CCCCxxxvj. without long respit or tarieng he puissauntly rescued it. And many other souuereyne and princely condicions
he vsed in this youre roiaume of Englond, as in `bokys yovyng, as yt ys
seyd, to the value of M^l. mark of all the vij. sciences and of dyvinite, as of
lawe spirituell and cyvyle, to the Vniuersite of Oxford; and' cherisshing   1380
the noble clergie of youre said roiaume; and also hauyng gret charge and
cost aboute the gret tendirnesse and fauoure shewed and done to alle
straungiers, were they ambassatours, messangiers and other noblesse
that sought worship of armes, that of diuers regions visited this lande.
For whiche fauoure and bounteuous chier withe gret rewardes done to   1385
theym, the renome of his noble astate and name sprad thoroughe alle
Cristyn roiaumes and in hethynesse. And after he had by many wyntris
1447. lyued in worship, he making his ende at the towne of Bury the yere
of Crist M^l. CCCCxlvij. the xxv. day of Februarie.

　　And ouer all these puissaunt dedis done and meynteyned by the fore-   1390
seid .iiij. noble princes in theire daies, and now sithen many of youre
noble bloode as cosins-germayns and other alliez of youre nere kyn, as
dukis, erlis, barons, bene deceasid, sithe the tyme of the last conquest
of Fraunce and Normandie.

For what cause the knightys of the Order and Felouship of Saint   1395
George was ordeigned.

And also of the vaillaunt, chosen knightis of the noble and worshipfull
Ordre of the Garter, founded by the right noble prince King Edward
Thrid; and to bere aboute his legge a tokyn of the Garter in the castell of Wynsore the xxii`j'. yere of his reigne, and, `as yt ys seyd', in   1400
token of worship that he being in bataile, what fortune fill, shuld not
voide the feeld but abide the fortune that God lust sende; whiche, for
gret prowesse and | here manlynesse approued in armes, was founded.   f. 24^r
For here gret labouris in werre and vaillaunt dedis of armes be `now'

1376 .M^l CCCCxxxvj.] *unidentified reader annot.* 1436   1378–80 bokys . . .
Oxford; and] *WW at l. end and continuing in marg.*   1395 For] *reader 1 in marg.*
nota de ordine Militum de la gartere   1400 xxii`j'] *final i changed to* j   as yt ys
seyd] *WW at l. end*   1404 now] *WW at l. end*

1405 Non sunt obliuioni passid to God and ought be put in memoriall, that in
tradendi. what distresse of bataile or siege that they haue ben yn
for the right title in the crowne of Fraunce, they alway auaunsid hem
forthe withe the formost, in example of good corage gyuyng to all theire
feloushbip, to opteyne the ouerhande of here entreprise.

1410 He, allas! Sethe that none suche were neuer sene withdrawers or
fleers frome batailes or dedis of worship, but rathir vigorouslie foryet-
Nobilitas Iohannis ing theymsilf, as did the full noble knight, a Felow of
Chaundos de comitatu the Garter, Ser Iohn Chaundos as a lion fighting in the
Herefordie, senescalli
de Peytou. feelde 'at the bataylle of Nazar yn Spayn wyth Prince
1415 Edward' of the lion condicion; 'and' defendid youre roiaume of Fraunce
frome youre aduersaries, preseruyng theire princes right and theire subgettis; auaunced youre conquest of Fraunce and Normandie, Angew and
Mayne and the noble duchie of Gascoigne and Gyen; and maynteyned
theire honoure and astate to the well of youre bothe roiaumes and relief
1420 of youre true subgettis of this lande. And therto they haue ben of the
condicions of lyons fighting withe gret strenght, puissauntlie and stifly,
sett to withestande youre ennemies, notwithestanding gret part of the
said aduerse partie haue voided, fledd and forsake the feeld and theire
feloushbip at suche tyme as they ought to abide.

1425 Senlys. In example of the full noble iorney late had in the yere of Crist
1431. M¹. CCCCxxxj. at Senlys, where youre lieutenaunt and youre
power being present, and Charlis the VIJ^the, youre gret aduersarie of
Fraunce withe all his power to the nombre of .l^ti. M¹. fighters on his side,
and embatilled by thre daies in the feeld fled and voided vnfoughten at
1430 the said iourney of Senlis, youre saide kynnesman Iohn, duc of Bedford,
being then lieutenaunt and present in the feeld before hym thre daies.
f. 24^v And also | sone after the saide worshipfull iourney of Senlis, youre saide
aduersarie of Fraunce after that made his entreprise, comyng before
Parys. the noble cite of Paris withe all his roiall power, to haue entred
1435 the said cite and to put out youre saide cosyn duke of Bedford; whiche,
hauyng knoulege therof, incontinent disposed hym, albeit he had vpon
so soden warnyng but a few feloushbip to mete ayen withe youre saide
aduersarie, and put hym in gret auenture and entred in youre saide cite
of Paris to relief and defende theym as he promised; and sent worde
1440 vnto hem late before to theire grettist 'y'oie and comfort; and youre
said aduersarie that ententid to gete the saide cite, besieging theym

1414–15 at the bataylle . . . Edward] *WW interl.* 1415 and] *WW interl.*
1425SN Senlys] *red siden. duplic. black* 1434SN Parys] *red siden. duplic. black*
1438 entred] *WW symbol at fore-edge* 1440 'y'oie] *WW y over uneras.* i

withe a grete nombre, mightilie resisted withe men and ordenaunce so greuously hurt, being fayne to voide incontinent.

And as in this maner it shewithe euidently that youre true obeisaunt lordis and noble chieueteins, also true subgettis, haue abandonned 1445 theire bodies, putting them in gret iupardie vnto the parell of dethe or to be taking prisoneris; and yet God hathe eured hem soo that, thoroughe his grace and theire manhod withe wise gouernaunce, haue had the ouerhand of youre aduersaries and kept bothe the said citee and the feeld withe other good men that aboode, whan theire partie contrarie 1450 haue ben nombred double or treble moo than youris (as is before expressid). And at whiche tyme the saide citee was so mightly besegid, Ser Iohn Radclif, knight, withe his felouship had gret worship.

Exclamacio.   O, ye right noble martirs, whiche that for youre verray righte of the coroune of Fraunce and for the welfare of the kingis 1455 highenesse and for the worship of his bothe roiaumes of Englond and Fraunce! Ye for to susteyne righte and for to wynne worship haue ben often put in gret auenture, as was oftentymes of the worshipfull Romayns. And therfore of you may be saide, that ye were alway stedfast and obeieng youre souuereyn vnto the iupardie and perill of dethe.   1460

So wold Ihesus that in the brief seson | of this sodeyne and wrec- f. 25ʳ chid intrusion late had by the vnmanly disseising and putting oute of Fraunce, Normandie, Angew and Mayne withe the duchees of Gasquien and Guyen, whiche is done bethin the space of i. yere and xiiij. wekis Nota.   (that is to wete, frome the xv. day of Maij in the yere of Crist 1465 1449.   Mˡ. CCCC. xlix. vnto the xv. day of the monithe of August the 1450.   yere of Crist Mˡ. CCCCl.), that euery castell, forteresse and towne defensable of the saide duchiees 'were delyuered vp by force or composicion to the aduerse partye'. And if they had be alway furnisshed and stuffed withe suche suffisaunt nombre of men of armes with orde- 1470 naunce, vitaile and wages duely kept, and be paied that they myght [haue] couraged and enforced hem to haue kept stille the possession; and they so being of the lyouns kynde, as to haue bene of soo egir courage and so manly and stedfast as they were before this tyme in that parties of Normandie, conquering, keping and defending it as they did 1475 Tempus vltimi   by the space of xxxv. yeris complete and vij. daies frome conquestus.   the begynnyng of the last conquest, the thrid yere of King

---

1444 And] WW symbol at fore-edge   1450 whan] WW symbol at fore-edge
1468–9 were . . . partye] WW interl.   1469 to] to to   And] WW symbol at
fore-edge   1472 haue couraged] couraged   kept] bene kept   1475 as] WW
symbol at fore-edge

Henry the .V^the.; and not the whele of fortune turned ayenst this lande
as it hathe.

1480   Notwithestanding, King Edwarde the Thrid occupied not in his conquest of Fraunce and Normandie passe `x'xx `iiij' yere. Whiche that
after vndre certayne condicions vpon apoyntement of a finall pease
made atwix hym and King Iohn of Fraunce was graunted that the saide
King Iohn shulde be seased and possessid ayen of a part of the said
1485   roiaume and duchie for certeyne counteez, baronnyes and seigniouries that we shulde in chief halde in Guien and other contrees; whiche

De pace finali   is more amplie declared in the saide finall trety of pease
apud Bretygnye.   made at Bretygny. Yet for alle tho othes, sacrementis, seles
of bothe kingis and here lordis made, the said trety of pease was sone
1490   broken by the aduerse partie, when they couthe take theire auauntage,
1371.   about the yere of Crist M^l. CCC. lxxj.

Exclamacio alia.   He, allas! We dolorous parsones suffring intollerabill
persecucions and miserie, as well in honoure lost as in youre lyuelode
f. 25^v   there vnrecompensid as in oure meueable goodes | bereued! What
1495   shalle we doo or say? Shalle we in this doloure, anguisshe and heuynesse contynew long thus? Nay, nay! God defend that suche intrusions,
grete wrongis and tiranye shuld be left vnpunisshed, and so gret a losse
vnpunysshed and not repared!

De amicicia per   For one good moyen (vndre correccion) may be this:
maritagia et al[i]as
1500   alligancias fienda.   and if youre lordis wolde enforce hem to renew theire
olde alliez of straunge regions and countrees, as the Romayns did whan
they werred in Auffrik ayenst the Cartages. And of late daies King
Edwarde the Thrid gafe example, and sithe King Harry the Vte in oure
daies, and also his noble brothir Iohn, duke of Bedford, after hym.
1505   Whiche allie`s' be almost werid out and foryete, to oure grete deso-
lacion. Whiche, and they were renewed by meane of mariages of gret
birthe; by cherisshing of lordis, nobles and marchauntes of tho regions

Nota et concidera   that we haue bene allied vnto or desire to be; gyuyng
ad honorandum
extraneos.   renomme and honoure in armes to tho princes that we
1510   desire alliaunce of; sending, at suche tymes as the cas shalle require, to
tho princes ambassiatours that be halden worshipfull men of astate and
degree, that haue sene worship in diuers contreis, whiche prudently can
purpose and declare the vrgent cause and necessite of this royaume: it
wolde be to think verralie than, that they, oure people, true subgettis

---

1481 `x'xx] WW adds x in space before   iiij] WW interl.   1494 oure] pre-
ceded by eras. y   1499SN alias] allas   1499 For] WW symbol at fore-edge
1505 Whiche] reader 1 in marg. nota bene   allie`s'] s over uneras. z

of Fraunce, were mynusshed or abated, as it is, but oure saide allie`s´ 1515
wolde enforce hem withe alle hir power and might to the reformacion
of the saide intrusions, and vnder colour of trewes wrought ayenst vs.
In example of this matier, it hathe bene specified herebefore.

And how it hathe be rad among the Romayne stories, that whan
Haniballe, prince of Cartage, had so gret a descomfiture ayenst Camos, 1520
gouernoure of the Romayne ooste, that the men of Cartage gaderid
of the fingers of the ded Romayns thre muys fulle of golde ringis, so
it shewed that the power of Rome was gretly mynusshed and febled.
Than, whan this tidingis come to Cartage, one Hamon, a wise man, a
senatoure, demaunded if it so were that, for all so gret a discomfiture, 1525
is | [. . .]

[*A leaf is lost between f. 25ᵛ and f. 26ʳ.*]

Tullius Cicero.   [. . .] whiche may noie vs. For Cicero seiethe in the booke f. 26ʳ
                   that he made *Of Diuinacion*, and the famous doctour Seint
Boecius.   Austyn in the booke *Of Fre Will* and also Boecius in his
booke *Of Consolacion of Comfort ayenst Mysfortune* accorden to the 1530
same: that we shuld not only trust that tho thinges whiche sounethe
to aduersite or infortune, and the whiche comethe to vs aduersarily or
on the lift side for oure offenses not keping the lawes of God, that oft
tymes comythe, they dyuynyng that they fallithe be casuelte of fortune,
Constellacio non   by prophesies or ellis thoroughe influence and con- 1535
necessit`a´t sed forte
disponit mores hominum   stellacions of sterris of heuyn; whiche iugementis
altorum bene vel econtra; `be´ not necessarilie true. For, and if it were like to
ac impressiones aieris
et ea mere naturalia   trouthe, it were but as contingent and of no neces-
conceruencia. §   site, that is to sey, as likely to be not as to be. And if
a constellacion or prophesie signified that suche a yere or bethin suche a 1540
tyme there shulde falle werre, pestilence or deerthe of vitaile to a contree
or region, or priuacion of a contre, it is said but dispositiflie and not of
necessite or certente. For than it shulde folow that the prophesies, constellacions and influence of sterris were maistris ouer Goddis power,
and that wolde soune to an herisie or ellis to a gret erroure. And if suche 1545
Contra fiduciam adhi- prophesies and influence of the seide constellacions
bendam in prophesijs,
nisi fuerit sanctissimis might be trew, yet God hathe gyue that souuereynte in
viris.
Nota conclusionem.   mannys soule that he, hauyng a clene soule, may turne

    1515 allie`s´] s *over uneras. letter*   1519 And] *WW symbol at fore-edge*
1527 For] *WW symbol at fore-edge overlapping his siden.*   1535SN necessit`a´t]
WW writes a *over uneras. letter*   1537 be] *over uneras. word, perhaps* is

the contrarie disposicion that iugement of constellacion or prophesies
1550 signified, as it is verified by the famous astrologien Ptolome in his booke
called *Centilogie*, the capitall seieng 'Quod homo sapiens dominatur
astris', that a man is souereyn abofe suche domes of constellacions. And
therfor ye oughte not deme ne conceyue the gret aduersite that fallithe
to vs is not falle to vs by prophesie or by influence of constellacion of
1555 sterris but only for synne and wrecchidnes and for lak of prudence and
politique gouernaunce in dew tyme prouided, and hauyng no consideracion to the comen wele but rathir to magnifie and enriche ouresilfe
by singuler couetise, vsing to take gret rewardis and suffring extorcions
f. 26ᵛ ouer the pore peple. For whiche inconuenientis, by the iugementis | and
1560 suffraunce of God and of his diuine prouidence, the whiche, by diuers
and of his secretis and as misteries vnknowen to vs, he hathe suffred
this mysfortune among vs here and priuacion of the saide roiaume of
Fraunce and contreis ther to falle vpon vs.

And whoso wolle considre welle the histories of olde croniclers as of
1565 Iosephus.   Iosephas, *Libro antiquitatum*, Orosius, *De Ormesta mundi*,
Orosius.
Titus Liuius. Titus Liuius, *Of the Romayn Batellis* and suche othirs, how
that gret chaunge of roiaumes and countreis frome one nacion to
another straunge tong hathe be for synne and wrecchidnesse and
mysgouernaunce reignyng in the roiaume so conquerid.
1570 Gyldas: de expulsione   And as it is made mencion in the olde historier
Britonum in Walliam et
Cor'n'ewaylle propter called Gildas, that for pride, couetice and flesshely
peccata.   lustis vsed amongis the olde Breton bloode, lordis
of this roiaume, God suffred the Saxons of Duche 'ys' tung, a straunge
nacion, 'to' dryue them out of this land in Angle, in Cornewale
1575 and Walis.

Destruccio regnorum: And where is Nynnyue, the gret cite of thre daies,
Nynyve, Babylon, Troye,
Thebes, Athenes, Rome, and Babilon, the gret toure, inhabited now withe
Ierusalem.   wilde bestis? The citeis of Troy, Thebes, .ij. grete
magnified citeis? Also Athenes, that was the welle of connyng and of
1580 wisdam, and Cartage, the victorioux cite of gret renomme, most doubtable, by the Romayns was brent to asshes. And also Rome, so gloriously
magnified thoroughe alle the world: ouerthrow the gret part of it, as
well as was Iherusalem.

1549 disposicion] *16th-c. pen-trial* Thomas Claspam *in marg.*   1559 and]
WW *symbol at fore-edge*   1570SN Gyldas] *in black; rest of siden. in red after it*
Cor'n'ewaylle] WW *writes* n *over uneras. letter*   1573 Duche'ys'] WW *interl.* ys
1574 to] WW *interl.*   1576SN Destruccio regnorum] *in red, added before and*
overlapping rest of siden. in black   Athenes] *written to the right between* Babylon *and*
Troye   Ierusalem] *written to the right between* Thebes *and* Rome

And to take an example of the many ouerthrowes and conquestis
of this lande by straunge nacions sithen the Breton bloode first inha-   1585
Picti gentes. bited, as withe peple callid Picteis commyng out of ferre
              northe partie of the worlde; then after the Saxones droue
Saxones, Dany, out the olde Breton bloode; than after the Danys peple con-
Normanni,
Andegauenses. querid the Saxons; and than the Normans conquerid the
              Danys; and sone after the Angeuyns of Highe Fraunce, full   1590
Galfridus   noble knightis of renomme, Geffrey, Erle Plantagenet, erle
Plantegenest.
of Angew, maried withe Dame 'Maud, doughter of the' duke of Nor-
mandie 'and' king of Englande, Harry the Second, 'whych' doughter
[was] called Dame Maude, emperesse; and so haldyn stille the Normandie bloode and the Angeuyns into this tyme.   1595

    And Iob in his booke seiethe that | nothing fallithe or risithe on the   f. 27ʳ
erthe without a cause, as who saiethe that none aduersite fallithe not
to vs but only for wikkidnesse of lyuyng and synne that reignithe on
vs; as pride, enuye, singuler couetice and sensualite of the bodie nowa-
daies hathe most reigned ouer vs to oure destruccion, we not hauyng   1600
consideracion to the generall profit and vniuersall wele of a comynalte.
    And to bring to mynde how the worshipfull senatours Romayns did
gife vs many examples, as Lucius Valerius, and also the noble iuge, cenatoure of Rome, Boecius 'of the grete lofe' had alway to the cite of Rome.
Lucius Valerius. For the saide Lucus Valerius despendid so gret good vpon   1605
the comyn profit of the said cite, to kepe and maynteyne the honoure
of the citee, defending the cite and contreis about from here ennemies,
that he died in gret pouertee; but by the cenatours releuyng and for his
worshipfull dedis they buried hym in the most solempne wise according
Boicius.   to his worship. And the said iuge Boecius loued rightwis-   1610
nesse to be kept and the pore comyns of Rome in that susteyned and
maynteyned, that he spared nothir lord ne none astate but suffred hym
to stande in the daunger of the hethyn king of Rome and to be in
exile rathir than he wolde offende iustice, notwithestanding the saide
De re publica aduersite and tribulacions felle vnto hem for auaunsing and   1615
custodienda.   tendring the comyn wele. And alle men of worship may
put hem in worshipfull remembraunce among worthy princes to here
gret renomme and laude. Also it is to be noted that was one of the gret
causis that the princes Romayns were so gret conquerours and helde the

1586 peple] bretey peple *with* bretey *crossed out*   1588SN Normanni] *with extra*
abbrev. for third n   1592 Maud, doughter of the] *WW interl.*   1593 and] *WW*
interl.   whych] *WW interl.*   1594 was called] called   1596 And] *WW symbol*
at fore-edge   1599 as] *WW symbol at fore-edge*   1604 of the grete lofe] *WW*
interl.   1608 but] *WW symbol at fore-edge*

1620   De iusticia.   straunge roiaumes so long in subieccion, but only vsing of
trouthe and iustice-keping in here conquestis.

De iusticia Camilli **A fulle noble historie how that Cauillus, the duke**
in obcidionibus
historia gloriosa.   **of Rome, wolde vse iustice in his conquest.**

Quod princeps debet vincere In example, I rede in the Romayns stories of Titus
1625   cicius per iusticiam quam per
tradicionem.   Liuius, in the booke of the first Decade, that a
Titus Liuius, Decado primo. prince Romayn clepid Cauillus, whiche did so
many victorioux dedis and loued so welle the comyn profit of the cite
f. 27ᵛ   of Rome that he was called the second Romulus, whiche | founded first
Florens cytee.   Rome, besiegid a gret cite of Falistes, whiche is now, as it
1630   is saide, called Florence, to haue hem vndre the gouernaunce of the
Romayne lawes. And as he had leyne long at the siege, and after gret
batailes and scarmysshes, it fortuned that a maister of sciencis of Falliste, called now Florence, the whiche had all the enfauntes and childryn
of the gouuernours and worshipfull men of the saide citee in his reule
1635   to lerne hem vertuous sciencis, thought to wynne a gret rewarde and
thank of the noble prince Cauillus; and, by the vmbre of treson ayenst
iustice that the said maistre wolde wirke to cause the senatours of Fal-
iste 'the rather' to deliuer vp the cite to the prince, the said maister by
flatering and blandisshing wordis meoued his clerkis to desport bethout
1640   the cite in the feeldis and so fedde hem forthe withe sportis and plaies
tille he had brought hem withyn the siege and power of Cauillus and
came to his presence saiyng to hym that he had brought to hym the
sonnes of the chief lordes and gouernours of the cite of Falliste, whiche
and he wolde kepe the said childryn in seruage, the faderis of hem woll
1645   deliuer hym the cite bethout any more werre-making. Than saide that
Cam'i'llus.   iust prince Cauillus that it was not the Romayns condicions
to werre and punisshe suche innocentis as neuer offendid in werre ne
knew not what werre meo'u'ed; and wolde not suffre that the Falistes
be defrauded of here contre and cite by vniust menes of treason or fals
1650   co'v'yn or vndew alliaunce but, as naturall werre wol fortune, by manhod and iust dede of armes to take the cite. And there the saide prince
comaunded the scolemaister for his gret deceite to be dispoilid and to be
betyn nakid withe baleese and sharpe roddis withe his owne clerkis into
the cite ayen. Than the gouernours and maistres of the cite, hauyng con-
1655   Conciderandum. sideracion of the gret iustice and manhod that he vsed in

---

1638 the rather] *WW interl.*   1646sn Cam'i'llus] *WW interl.* i   1648 meo'u'ed] u
over uneras. letter   1650 co'v'yn] v *over uneras.* u

his conquest, sent to Cauillus ambassatours withe the keies of the cite

Proposicio ad Romanos gentes. and purposid vnto hym, saieng, 'O ye fathir and prince of iustice, wheras the well, honoure and renommee of iustice and of | victorioux dedis reignithe among you Romayns by vsing of iustice.' And that for as moche they perceyued that princes Romayns vsed feithe and iustice and peyned theym to kepe theire peple, con-querid hem to be subgettis to Rome by iustice, they were full ioifull and glad to lyue vndre theire lawes and so deliuerid hym the 'keys and the' citee, to the gret renomme of the saide prince and to all the Romayns gretly to be magnified.

f. 28^r

1660

1665

Dame C[r]isten. Notandum est quod Cristina Domina, preclara natu et moribus, et manebat in domo religiosarum dominarum apud Passye, prope Parys; et ita virtuosa fuit, quod ipsa exhibuit clericos studentes in Vniuersitate Parisiensi; et compilare fecit plures libros virtuosos vtpote Librum arborum bellorum. *Et doctores racione eorum exhibicionis attribuerunt nomen auctoris Cristine. Sed aliquando nomen autoris clerici studentis imponitur in diuersis libris. Et vixit circa annum Christi 1430 sed floruit ab anno Christi 1400.*

Historie of Dame Cristyn, declaring how a prince and a ledar of peple shulde vse prudence and iustice, by example of the noble cenatoure called Fabricius.

And also as Dame Cristyn in the xv. chapitre of the first partie of hir seid booke of *The Tree of Bataises* leiethe a noble example that among alle vertues that shulde long to a prince, a duke, a chieueteyne or to a gouernoure of a contre, citee or towne or a leder of peple, rehersithe how it is necessarie that he shulde be a prudent man and a wise and of gret trouthe. As by example it is write of the noble and trew sena-toure Fabricius, leder of the Romayn oostis, the which, for his gret trouthe, vailliaunce and manhod and wise gouernaunce, King Pirrus, his aduersarie, offred to gyue hym the iiij^{the} part of his roiaume and of his tresoure and goodis, so that the saide Fabricius wolde yelden and turne to his partie and become his felow in armes. To whiche Pirrus, the said Fabricius answerd that a trew man might not to ouermoche hate and dispreise tresoure and ricchesse by treason and falshed euyll-geten, whereas by possibilite and alle liklinesse may be honourablie and truly vinquisshid and wonne bye armes, and not in noo maner wise by vntrouthe and falshed.

1670

1675

1680

1685

In whiche matier verifieng saiethe Vigecius in his *Booke of Cheualrie* to a chiefteyne to whome is commytted so gret a thing, as is deliuerid

1659 victorioux] *reader 1 at top of p.* nota concilium vt infra   1663 keys and the] *WW at l. end*   1666SN Dame . . . quod] *in red, added before rest of siden. in black*   C[r]isten] Cisten   vtpote] vt (*crossed out*) vtpote   libris. Et] *over eras.* 1674 how] *WW symbol at fore-edge, overlapped by lengthy siden.*

hym the charge and gouernaunce of noblesse of cheualrie, the dedis
and entreprises of a prince is office is principally comytted hym for the
1690 Res publica.   gouernaunce of comon publique of a roiaume, dukedom,
f. 28ᵛ erledom, | barnage or seigniourie, castelle, forteresse, cite and towne,
that is clepid vulgarilie the comon profite, the suerte and saufegarde of
alle tho saide contreis. And if by the fortune of batailes he might not
only haue a generall consideracion and cure of all his ooste or ouer all
1695 the peple, contree or cite that he hathe take the charge of, but he must
entende to euery particuler charge and thing that nedithe remedie or
relief for his charge. And any thing mysfortune to a comon vniuersall
damage in defaut of ouersight of remedie of a particuler and singuler
thing or charge, thoroughe whiche might grow to an vniuersall damage,
1700 than it is to be wited his defaute.

And therfor in conclusion of this late it take example to folow the
noble and fructufull examples of the noble cenatours.

And we ought so to kepe vs frome the offending and greuyng of oure
souereyne maker, not to vsurpe ayenst iustice, as hathe be doo in suche
1705 wise, that thoroughe oure synfull and wrecchid lyuyng ayenst his lawes
he be not lengir contrarie to vs, suffring vs this greuouslie for oure offensis to be ouerthrow, rebukid and punisshed, as we bee; but lyue and
endure in suche clene life obseruyng his .x. preceptis, that he haue no
cause to shew on vs the rod of his chastising, as he dothe.

1710 **Another exhortacion to kepe the lawes of God, for in doubte
that ellis God wull suffre oure aduersaries punisshe vs withe his
rodde.**

Deploracio contra iniquos   O mightifull God! If it be soo, as holy scripture sei-
malefactor`e´s prevalentes.   ethe, the whiche is not to mystrust, haue not we
1715 deserued cause this to be punisshed, seeyng so many wrecchid synnes as
among vs dailie vncorrectid hathe reigned? For whiche we ought know:
we be right worthy of moche more chastising and grettir punisshement
of God, he being iust and not chaungeable. For it is wretyn in the booke
of Paralipomenon that, for the gret synnes vsed be theym of Israell, God
1720 of his rightwisnesse suffred the Phillistyns, that were they neuer so euill
ne in so euill a quarell, to be persecutours and destroiers of the lande of
Iudee and of Goddis peple; and the rathir that the saide Israelites had a
law gyuen hem by Moises and kept it not.

How euery officer spirituell | and temporelle shulde put hym in   f. 29ʳ
his deuoire to the auaunsing of the comon profite.   1725

De re publica   And it is for to remembre among alle other thingis that
augmentanda.   is made mencion in this epistill, that euery man after his
power and degre shuld principallie put hym in deuoire and laboure for
the auaunsment of the comon profit of a region, contre, cite, towne or
householde.   1730

For as alle the famous clerkis writen, and in especiall that wise
cenatoure of Rome, Tullius, in his booke *De officijs*, ʼ*De republica* (that
Novius Marcellus makyth mencion of yn dyuers chapters)ʼ, and in
other bookis of his, *De amicicia*, *Paradoxis* and *Tusculanis questionibus*,
that *res publica* well-attendid and obserued, it is the grounde of welfare   1735
and prosperite of alle maner peple. And first to wete the verray declaracion of these .ij. termys *res publica*: as Seint Austyn seiethe in the .v.
booke and .xviij. chapitre of *The Cite of God*, and the saide Tullius, the
famous rethoricien, accordithe withe the same, saieng in Latyn termes:
ʼRes publica est res populi, res patrie, res communis. Sic patet quod   1740
omnes qui intendit bonum commune et vtilitatem populi vel patrie vel
ciuitatis augere, conseruare, protegere, salua iusticia intendit et rem
publicam augere et conseruare.ʼ

And it is for to lerne and considre to what vertues *res publica* strecchithe, as I rede in a tretie that Wallensis, a noble clerk, wrote in his book   1745
clepid *Communeloquium, capitulo .3ᵒ prime partis*; seithe quod, ʼRes
publiqua ordinatur hijs virtutibus: scilicet, legum rectitudine, iusticie
soliditatis equitate, concordie vnanimitate, fidelitate mutua adiuuante,
concilio salubri dirigentʼerʼ, morum honestate decorante, ordinata in-
tensione consumpnante.ʼ   1750

Tullius in Noua   As for the first partie, it is verified by Tullie in his *Retho-*
rethorica.   *rik*, the first booke: ʼOmnes leges ad comodum rei publice
iudices referre oportet. Et lex nichil aliud est quam recta racio, et anime
iusta imperans honesta, prohibens contraria.ʼ

And it is right expedient that alle tho that be ʼiusticesʼ, gouernours   1755
or rulers of contreis, citees or townes to a comon profit must doo it
by prudent counceile and good auise of auncien approued men. For
a gouernoure of a comon profit were in olde tyme named amongis
the Romayns, hauyng the astate that at this daies bene vsed [by] | alle   f. 29ᵛ

1724 and] *reader 1 at top of p.* nota peroptime   1732–3 *De republica . . .*
chapters] *WW at l. end and in marg.*   1749 dirigentʼerʼ] *scr.* er *over uneras.* vi
1751SN Tullius . . . rethorica] *15th-c. pen-trial duplic. the siden.*   1755 iustices]
WW at l. end   1759 vsed by] vsed   alle] *WW symbol at fore-edge; reader 1 at top*
of p. nota

1760 tho that bene callid to highe digniteis: the emperoure, kingis, princes, dukis, marques, erlis, vicountes, barons, baronettis, consules, cheualiers, esquiers and aldermannes, iustices, baillifis, prouostis, maires and suche othirs officers. And Tullius in the first booke *Of Offices* seiethe: 'Parua sunt foris arma, vbi consilium non est domi.'

1765 **How auncient men growen in yeris be more acceptable to be elect for a counceilour or for to gouuerne a cite `for a comyn proffyt´ than yong men.**

Tullius, De senectute. Tullius in his book *De senectute* saiethe that auncient men that bene growen in age bene more profitable in gyuyng counceile 1770 for the auaunsing and gouernyng a comon profit o`f´ a citee, town or village, as to bere offices, than othirs that bene yong of age, althoughe he be [of] mighty power of bodie.

Exemplum amplum. For an example he puttithe as there be men in a ship, som that be yong of mighty power halithe vp the ankirs; othirs 1775 goithe feersly aboute the ropis fastenyng; and some goithe to set vp the saile and take it downe, as the gouernoure, the maister, auisithe hem. Yet the eldist man that is halde wisist among hem sittithe and kepithe the rothir or sterne [of] the ship and seethe to the nedill for to gide the ship to alle costis behofefull to the sauyng of the ship frome dangers and 1780 rokkis; whiche dothe more profit and grettir auauntage to the vessell than alle tho yong lusty men that rennen, halithe or clymethe. Wher-Experiencia, etc. for it may be concluded that the auncien, approued men, by long experience made gouernours and counceilours of roiaumes, contrees, citees and townes done grettir dedis by theire wise counceile 1785 than tho that labouren in the feelde, cite or towne by mighty power of her hand.

Iob. And it is saide by Iob .12°. that Rob`o´am whiche forsooke the counceile of olde men and drew after the counceile of yong men lost the`r´ kingdom [of] whiche he had the gouuernaunce. And whiche 1790 example is right necessarie to be had in remembraunce in euery wise gouernoure is hert. And so wolde the mightifull God that euery |
f. 30ʳ gouernoure wolde haue a verray parfit loue to the gouernaunce of a comon wele by wise and goode counceile; and to folow the pathis and

1766–7 for a comyn proffyt] *WW interl.*   1770 o`f´] f *over uneras.* r
1772 of mighty] mighty   1778 of the] the   1787 Rob`o´am] o *interl.*
1789 the`r´] *WW* r *at end*   of whiche] whiche   1792 gouernoure] *reader 1 at top*
of p. concilium   1793 comon] *WW symbol at fore-edge*

weies and examples of the noble senatours of Rome, how they were
attending to the commyn profit, setting aside singuler auaile, so tho 1795
famous region and citeis aboute vndre theire obeissaunce reigned alle
that tyme by many reuolucion of yeris in gret worship and prosperite,
as I shall in example put here in remembraunce and is founden writen
in diuers stories, as of one among othir ʼysʼ:

De prefer-
ramento rei
publice.

How Fabius, the noble cenatoure, set by no worship of 1800 vayneglorie but only laboured for the comon profit of Rome.

Tullius, *De senectute*, the first partie, makith mencion of a noble prince
Fabius, cenator, dexspexit Romayne clepid Fabius, whiche had gret batailes
vanam gloriam. and iourneis withe Hanibal, prince of Cartage, to 1805
kepe the conquest of Romayne contreis and to see theire libertees and
fraunchises obserued and kept for the wele of alle maner peple, whiche
Fabius despraised renommee and vayneglorie but onlie gafe his solicitude, thought and his bisy cure about the comon profit of Rome; for
whiche cause the saide Fabius after his dethe was put in gret renomme 1810
and more magnified among the Romayns than he was in his liffetyme.
Quomodo Romani gentes And the saide Fabius, after the right and
fuerant diuinatores et auguriste vsage was in tho daies, did gret diligence to
pro conseruacione rei publice. lerne and know by angures and diuinacions
of briddis and by other causes naturell, after the ceasons of the yeris 1815
and in what tymes prosperite, welthe and plente, derthe or scarsite, of
cornes, wynes, oilis shulde falle to the contre of Romayns, to his grettist
comfort for the auauncement of the comon wele.

And he delited gretly to rede actis and dedis of armes of straunge
nacions to haue a parfiter remembraunce and experience to rule a 1820
comon wele that was moche bettir than before his daies; ne sithe was
no consull like to his gouernaunce, except the worthy Scipions.

And it were full necessarie that princes and lordis shuld know by
naturall | cause of philosophie the seasons and yeris of prosperite or f. 30ᵛ
aduersite falling to the region that he is of, to thʼentent he might make 1825
his prouision thereafter. But more pite is: few profound clerkis in this
lande ben parfitelie grounded in suche workis; or they fauten her principales in scolis, so they haue no sufficient bookis; or ellis they taken

1795–6 tho famous] tho famous that famous, *with only* that *crossed out*   1799 ys]
WW at l. end   1823 And] *WW symbol at fore-edge*

vpon them the connyng of iudiciell matieris, to know the impressions
1830 of the heire, and be not expertid. And be this maner the noble science
of suche iudiciell mater in causis naturell concernyng the influence of
the bodies of heuyn ben defamed and rebukid.

How Lucius Paulus, Fabricius and Curius Cornicanus, cenatours,
in her grete age onlie studied and concellid for the proferring of
1835 **the comon wele.**

Also to bring to mynde for to folow the steppis of the full noble consull
of Rome Lucius Paul'us' (whiche the wise Caton is sonne maried the
doughter of the saide Lucius Paule), also the senatours clepid Fabricius
and Curiois Cornicanois, that they as well as the forsaide Fabius in her
1840 grete age did none othir bisinesse but only by theire counceile and by
theire auctorite counceiled, auised and comaundid that that shulde bee
to the comon profit of the saide cite of Rome.

How Appius, the highe preest of the tempill of Myner'f'e, albeit
he was blinde, of good corage purposid tofore the Romains
1845 **to make werre withe King Pirrus then to becom subget to her**
auncient ennemy, King Pirrus.

In like wise 'the hygh' preest of the tempill of Mynerue of Rome, clepid
Tullius, *De*   Appius, after he was for gret age blinde and feble, whan
senectute.   King Pirrus, king of Epirotes, werrid so ayenst Rome that
1850 he had 'febled and' weried them so sore and wan vpon hem so gret
contreis, that the Romains ayenst theire worship wolde haue made
pease and alliaunces withe hym to her vttermost deshonoure. But
f. 31ʳ the said Appius | purposed tofore the noble senatours Romayn and
Ennius, poeta.   required hem to doo after the counceile of Ennius, the wise
1855 consul: that the Romains shulde take good hert to hem and not to abate
here noble courages to become subget to theire auncient aduersarie
Pirrus; and that they shulde take new entreprinses vpon Pirrus and
destroie his gret armees. Whiche the saide senatours were reuiued in
theire courages thoroughe the wise exhortacions of Appius and had
1860 the victorie of Pirrus.

1837 Paul'us'] *abbrev. for* us *over uneras.* e   1843 Myner'f'e] f *over uneras.* s
1847 the hygh] WW *at l. end*   preest] the preest *with the* crossed out   1850 febled
and] WW *interl.*   1855 consul] WW *symbol at fore-edge*

De officijs **This chapitre declarithe how many gret offices of highe**
Catonis. **dignite Caton was called and auctorised for his gret**
manhode and wisdom, and how he in his age couraged the yong
knightis to goo to feelde to venquisshe Cartage or he died.

Also the noble senatoure of Rome, Caton, that was so manlie, prudent   1865
and of holsom counceile, whiche in his yong daies occupied the office of
a knight in excersising armes, anothir season he occupied the office of
tribune as a chief iuge among the Romains, another season was a legat as
an ambassatoure into ferre contreis, yet anothir tyme in his gret auncien
age, that he might not gretlie laboure, was made consul of Rome to sit   1870
stille and auise the weies and meenys how the Romayns might alway be
puissaunt to resist ayenst Cartage; whiche he hopid verralie or he died
to see the saide cite destroied.

    And the said Caton in presence of yong Scipio and Lelius, .ij. noblest
yong knightis of Rome that visited Caton to here of his wise conduit   1875
and counceile, he being than of full gret age, tendred so feruentlie the
well of comon profit of Rome that he required and besought the inmor-
tall goodis of licence that he might not die till he might know Cartage
destroied by victorie of bataile, and to be auengid of the seruage and
miserie | of the noble Romayns whiche were prisoneris withe Quintus   f. 31ᵛ
Fabius in Cartage xxxiij yere passed.   1881

Of a semblable noble condicion of Quintus Fabius, according to Caton.

And Quintus Fabius, albeit he might not in his gret age laboure, le'f't
Doctor militum   the vsage that he in his youthe taught yong knightis, as to   1885
in armis.   renne, lepe, iust withe speris, fight afoote withe axes; yet
he had in his olde age alway gret solicitude and thought for the auauncement of the comon profit of the citee by counceile, by reason and by
mure deliberacion of hymsilf and of the wise senatoure.

The diffinicion of the office that belongithe to the senate.   1890

And whiche terme *senat* is as moche for to say 'a companie of aged men
assembled togither'.

Tullius, `D'e senectute. **How Caton writithe that citeis and contreis that were gouerned by men of yong age were destroied, and they**

1895 **lost also theire lifelode wastefullie.**

And Caton saide that whoso wolde rede in auncien histories, he shulde

Contra officia danda iuuenibus. finde that citeis whiche were conduit and gouerned by men of yong age were destroied and brought to desert, as well Rome as othirs; and it was not reuiued ne encresid ayen but onlie

1900 be the counceile of auncien men.

And the saide Cato makith a question to tho saide yong ioly knightis Scipion and Lilius, demaunding them why they and suche othir yong counceilours had wasted and brought to nought theire inheritaunce, callid patrim`o'nie, and the comon profit of theire cite and countre

1905 destroied.

And Nemnius the poet made answere for hem and saide: tho that were made counceilours for the comon profit of the towne, also suche that were of Scipion and Lelius counceile, were but new, `not expert' drawen maistris, ignoraunt aduocatz and pledours, yong men not roted

1910 ne expert in the law ne in policie gouernaunce; whiche by theire fole-hardiesse and be the proprete and nature of grene age caused the patri-

f. 32ʳ monie of L`e'lius and | Scipion to be lost, and also the contreis that they hadde to gouernaunce.

And he that woll haue prudent avise and sure counceile must doo by

1915 counceile of men of gret age, as well in counceile of ciuile causes as in conduit of armees and oostis of men of armes in werre for the defence of the comon publique.

Agamenon. **Of the answere and reson of Agamenon, duke and leder of the Greekis hoost ayenst the Troiens.**

1920 For Agamenon, the noble knight that was leder and gouernoure of the Grekis batailis ayenst the noble Troiens,

Nestor. **Of the wisdom of King Nestor, a Troian.**

De concilijs antiquorum militum in experiencia preferrendorum. whan he herde of King Nestor how he was holden the wisist lyuyng of counceile-yeuyng and of gret

1925 eloquence in his auncien age;

1893SN `D'e] WW D over uneras. letter          1904 patrim`o'nie] o over uneras. letter   1906 And] WW symbol at fore-edge   1908 not expert] WW at l. end
1912 L`e'lius] e over uneras. i

Ayax. **Of the recomendacion of the prowesse of Ayax, a knight of Grece.**

and in like wise one Ayax, a knight of Grece, was halden the best fighter amongis the Grekis ayenst the Troiens, in so moche that the Grekis desired of the inmortell goddis to haue only but .xl. suche batellous 1930 knightis as Ayax is to fight withe the Grekis ayenst the Troyens:

How Duke Agamenon trusted so gretlie in the counceile of agid men that he required the inmortell goddis to haue suche vj. olde kingis as Nestor is; doubted not to wynne Troie in short tyme.

but that noble Duke Agamenon required of the goddis six suche wise 1935 viellars as was Nestor, that then he doubted not within short tyme that Troie shulde be take and destroied.

Publius Decius. **How that most noble cenatoure ˋPublius Deciusʹ, so hardie an entreprennoure, in the bataile whan the Romains were almost ouerthrow, he auaunsid hymsilfe so ferre in the** 1940 **bataile to die, to thʼentent to make the Romains more gret and fell for his dethe in fighting, till they had the victory. |**

In semblable wise Tullius writithe of that vaillaunt citezin Romayne f. 32ᵛ
Publius Decius non est Publius Decius: at a tyme he was chosen consull and
recomendandus in hoc
negocio. as a chiefteyne among the Romayne ostes, he saw how 1945 the Romayne oost was almost bete downe to grounde. He thought in his soule that he wolde put his bodie in iubardie frely to die for to make the Romains more egir and fellir in that bataile to reuiue hemsilfe thoroughe cruelte of his dethe. He tooke his hors withe the sporis and, auaunsing hymsilfe among his aduersaries, and at the last was so sore 1950 charged withe hem that he was fellid to grounde deede. The Romayns, hauyng consideracion in theire couragious hertis how knyghtˋlyʹ he auaunsid hym in bataile fighting, and suffred dethe for here sake, tooke courage and hert to hem and recomforting hem foughten so vigorouslie ayenst theire aduersaries that they hadde the victorie. 1955

1938 Publius Decius] *WW interl.*   1943 In] *reader 1 at top of p.* nota bene diuersitatem Militum   1949 He] *WW symbol at fore-edge*   1952 knyghtˋlyʹ] *WW* ly *over uneras.* e

How the son of the saide Publius died in the same case.

And the sonne of the said Publius that was foure tyme electe and chose
consul among the Romains put hym in so gret iupardie of bataile for
the helthe, prosperite and welfare of the Romains that he died in bataile
1960 in like wise.

'Hyt ys to remembre that I hafe herd myne autor Fastolf sey, whan
he had yong knyghtys and nobles at hys solasse, how that there be twey
maner condicions of manly men, and one ys a manlye man called,
another ys an hardye man. But he seyd the manly man ys more to
1965 be commended, more then the hardy man. For the hardy man that
sodenly bethout discrecion of gode avysement auauncyth hym yn the
felde, to be halde courageouse and wyth grete auentur he scapyth,
voydith the felde allone but he levyth hys felyshyp destrussed. And
the manly man ys policie ys that, or he auaunce hym and hys fely-
1970 shyp at skermyssh or sodeyn racountre, he wille so discretely auaunce
hym that he wille entend to hafe the ovyrhand of hys aduersarye and
safe hymsylf and hys felyshyp. And therfor the auenture of Publius
Decius ys not aftyr Cristen lawes comended by hys willfull deth, nother
hys son.'

1975 **Here folowithe the historie of the most noble recomendacion**
in parpetuite of Marcus Actilius, a chief duke of the Romayne
hostes, of his gret prouidence vsing in hostes ayenst derthes
and scar[se]tees of cornes, wines, oilis; and how he, of fortune
of werre being prisoner in Cartage amongis his dedlie aduer-
1980 **saries, albeit he was put to raunson, suffred wilfullie for to die in**
prison, because he was so gretly aged and wered in bataile, then
to the Romains to pay so infenite a somme for his finaunce and
raunson.

Hit is historied also of worshipfull remembraunce how that verray trew
1985 louer of the comon wele of the Romayns, Marcus Actilius, that first
f. 33ʳ Autor rei publice. yaue | hym to labouragis and approwementis of londes
and pastures to furnisshe and store the saide countre withe plente of
corne and vitaile, after for his gret policie, wisdom and manhod was
made consull and conestable of the Romayne batailes and full often-
1990 sithis discomfited theire aduersaries of Cartage.

And he at a tyme by chaunge of fortune in bataile was take prisoner into Cartage, being of gret age than. And for deliueraunce of which
Actilius, the gouernours of Cartage desired hym that he shulde laboure
and sende to Rome for to deliuer out of prison a gret nombre of yong
§ men of werre of Cartage that were prisoneris in Rome, and he shulde 1995
goo frank and quite.

And the saide Actilius denyed and refused it vtterly, but that he wolde
rathir die in prison than to suffre the werrours of Cartage to be dely-
uerid for his sake, for he loued the comon wele and proffit of Rome. And
becaus that noble Actilius wolde not condescende to deliuer the priso- 2000
neris of Cartage, they turmentid hym in prison in the most cruell wise
to dethe that, and it were expressid here, it wolde make an harde-hert
man to falle the teris of his yen.

The voluntarie dethe of whiche Marcus Actilius for the welfare,
prosperite and comon profit of Rome causithe hym to be an example 2005
to alle othir and to be put perpetuelly in remembraunce for worship.

**How the noble duke Scipion Affrican put hym in so gret auen-
ture in his gret age ayens the Cartages that he died vpon, rathir
than to life in seruage.**

Also to haue in remembraunce to folow the steppis of the full noble 2010
Scypio and glorious champions, two bretherin, Scipion Affricanus
Africanus.
Scipio Asyanus. and Scipion Asian, whiche all theire lyue-daies emploied
and besied hem in diuers entreprises of armees and batailes ayenst the
Affricans for the saufegarde and defense of the comon wele of theire |
Scipio contre. And the saide Scipion Affrican wilfully died in f. 33ᵛ
Africanus.
armes of cheualrie rathir than to lyue in seruage and distresse among 2016
his aduersaries in Cartage.

**How Scipion Asian, a noble conqueroure for the Romains, yet in
his age he was enuyed, accused to King Antiochus, died pitouslie
in prison for his rewarde.** 2020

And notwithstanding after many triumphes and victories done by
Scipion Asian, that put in subieccion the contre of Asie and enriched
gretlie the tresoure of Rome thoroughe his conquestis, he was by

1995 he] *WW symbol at fore-edge*

enuious peple accused falsely to King Antiochus that he hadde with-
2025 halde the tresoure of Rome and was condempned to prison where he
endid his daies.

Lucius Paulus. **How Lucius Paulus, a cenatoure, in defaute that his
hoste wolde not doo by counceile, he was slayne in bataile.**

Quod capitanei non
debent renunciare Also Lucius Paulus, a noble consul Romayne, that
2030 concilia peritorum. spared not hymsilf to die in bataile in Puylle withe
CCC noble Romains that were assemblid: vnwiting the saide Lucius
Paulus, and alle for lak of counceile, that the saide .iij^C. nobles Romayns
wolde not be gouerned by hym, he, seeng anothir consul Romayn toke
the entreprise, was so ouerthrowen withe his felouship, the saide Lucius
2035 Paulus auaunced hym wilfully among his aduersaries withe the residew
of the Romains that lefte and there died withe them, to th'entent that it
shulde be noted and know that the saide entreprise was not lost in his
defaute.

Marcus **How Marcus Marcellus, a consul, for the welfare of**
Marcellus.
2040 **Rome bethout avise went hastilie to bataile ayenst**
Hanyballe. **Haniball of Cartage; and he being so sorie for the**
dethe of so manlie a duke did hym to be buried in the most
worshipfull wise.

Also it is remembrid of Marcus Marcellus, a consull Romayne that set
2045 nought of dethe, for he vpon a tyme bethout gret deliberacion or aduisement desired to fight ayenst Haniball, prince of Cartage, assemblid
withe a gret power ayenst the Romains, whiche were feerse | [. . .]

[Two leaves are lost between f. 33^v and f. 34^r.]

f. 34^r [. . .] of man, his beeis for hony, his medewis purueied for sustenaunce
of his grete bestis; and euery man after his degree to store hymsilfe
2050 that, whan ther falle by fortune of straunge wethirs, as thoroughe
excessife moist, colde, heet, mildewis, or by fortune of bataile and
werre, the saide countre, cite, towne, village or menage so prouided
and stuffid before shall mow withe gret ease endure the persecucion
of a scarsete or derthe, fallen [by] suche straunge menys. And as well

2035 auaunced] *WW symbol at fore-edge*   2039 for] that for   2054 by
suche] suche

Res publica.   the terme of *res publica*, whiche is in Englisshe tong clepid   2055
'a comyn profit', it ought as well be referred to the prouision and wise
gouuernaunce of a mesuage or a householde as to the conduit and wise
gouernaunce of a village, towne, citee, countree or region.

'**Hyt ys to remembre thys caase of rebellyon of Parys, felle in**
abcence of Herry .Vte**., "kyng", beyng in England wyth hys**   2060
queene.

And bethoute noote of vaynglory yff I do wryte of myne autor, I fynde
by hys bokes of hys purveours, how yn euery castell, forteresse and cyte
or towne he wold hafe grete providence of vitaille of cornys, of larde and
beoffes, of stokphysh and saltfysh owt of England commyng by shyppes.   2065
And that policie was one of the grete causes that the regent of Fraunce
and the lordes of the kyng ys grete councell lefft hym "to" hafe so many
castells to kepe, that he ledd yerly .iij^c. sperys and the bowes, and also yn
semblable wyse purveyed yeerly for lyuerey, whyte and rede, for hubes
for hys soudeours, and for armurs, wepyns, "re"dye to a naked man that   2070
was hable to do the kyng and the seyd regent service.

  And yt fille yn the .viij^te. yere of Herry the V^the, named kyng, when
he was capteyn of the Bastyle of Seynt Antonye off Parys, and Thomas
Beauford, dux of Excestyr, beyng then capteyn of the cytee, hyt fortuned
that for the arrestyng of the Lord L'Ysel-Adam, "and" was yn so grete   2075
fauour of the cyte, that "a"ll the comyns of the seyd cyte "stode" sodenly
to harneys and rebelled ayenst the duc of Exetyre and ayenst hys armee
and felyshyp. So the duc for more suerte wyth hys felyshyp were coherted to take the Bastyle for her deffence. And at hys commyng the chieff
questyon he demaunded of the seyd Fastolf: how well he was stored of   2080
greynes of whete, of benys, pesyn and aueyn for hors-me"t" and of othyr
vitaille. He seyd, 'For half yere and more suffisaunt.' And hyt comforted
gretely the prince. Then the "duc" made redy the ordenaunce, wyth shot
of grete gonnys amongys the rebells and shot of arowes myghtlye, that
they kept her loggeyns. And the F"r"ensh kyng and the quene beyng yn   2085

2059–87 Hyt ys ... grace] *WW in marg. without signalling position in text*   2060 kyng]
WW interl.   2066 the] the the   that] *WW symbol at fore-edge; revision skirts*
round it   2067 to] *WW interl.*   2070 "re"dye] *WW crosses out* re *with*
long r *and interl.* re *with short* r   2075 and] "stode" "and", *with* stode *over eras.*
and and *interl. by WW (see n.)*   2076 "a"ll] *WW changes one-compartment* a
to two-compartment a   "stode" sodenly] sodenly, *with* stode *over eras. on l. above*
(see n.)   2081 hors-me"t"] *WW interl.* t   2083 duc] *WW over uneras.* princ
2085 F"r"ensh] *WW crosses out long* r *and interl. short* r

the cytee helde ayenst the rebellys, so yn short tyme the burgeyses were constreyned to submytt hem and put hem yn the duc ys grace.'

De magnificen- **Caton magnifiethe that prince that cherisshith and**
cia felicitatis **fauourithe erthe-tiliers.**
cultoribus
terrarum adhibenda, specialiter Cyro Regi.

2090 And as Caton writithe that it is one of the principalle dedis of a prince to maynteyne, kepe and auaunce labourage of the londe and of all tho that bee laboureris of the londe, whiche men soo cherisshed most of verray necessite cause a roiaume, countree or cite to be plenteuous, riche and well at ease.

2095 Socrates. And the philosophur Socrates writithe that Cirus, king of Perse, was excellent in wit, glorious in seigniourie terrien. In the daies
De quodam Lysander, of whiche Cirus, one Lisander of the cite of Lace-
philosopho. demone in Grece, a man halden of gret vertue and noblesse, came out of ferre contrees to see the saide King Cirus being in
2100 the cite of Sardes and presented hym withe clothis of golde, iuellis and
§ othir ricchesses sent by the citezeins of Lacedemonois; the whiche King Cirus receiued the saide Lizander fulle worshiplie in his palais. And for the grettist ricchesse roiall and pleasure that the said King Cirus had, to doo hym worship and pleasure and chier, he brought
2105 the saide Lisander to see his gardins and herbers, which gardins were so proporcionallie in a conuenient distaunce 'sett and' planted withe treis of verdure of diuers fructis, the gardyns so well ale`y'ed to walke
f. 34ᵛ vpon and rengid withe beddis, | bering full many straunge and diuers herbis, and the herbers of so soote smyllis of flouris and herbis of diuers
2110 colours, that it was the ioieust and plesaunt sight that euer the saide citesyn Lisander had see beforne.
De Ciro, rege And the saide Cirus saide vnto Lisandere that he had
Persarum. deuised and ordeined the herbers to be compassid, rengid and made, and many of tho treis planted withe his owne hande. And
2115 the saide Lisander behelding the gret beaute, semlinesse of his parson, the riche clothis he ware of tissue and precious stones, he saide that
§ fortune and felicite mondeyn was ioyned and knyt withe his vertue and noblesse roiall, for as moche as the saide Cirus emploied [an] intentif besynesse in tymes oportune in tilieng, ering and labourage
2120 of his londis to bere corne and fruit, whiche is the principall partie of

2106 sett and] WW *at l. end*   2107 ale`y'ed] WW y *over* uneras. i
2114 withe] it withe   2118 an] and

beneurte and felicite mondeyne, that is to wete the naturell ricchesse
of worldlie ioie.

Tullius.   Also Tullius writithe that Valerius Corninus, an auncien citesyn
Romayne, did his gret peyne and diligence to laboure londes and make
it riche withe labourage and tilieng vpon the londe for the comon wele   2125
of the cite of Rome, that in tyme and yeris of scarsete the garners in
Rome shulde be alway furnisshed and stuffid withe greyn, that a meane
price of corne shulde be alway hadde.

How the noble cenatours of Rome auaunced here parsones in gret perill and iubardie ayenst theire aduersaries for the comon welfare of the Romains.

2130

De re publica.   And the saide famous clerk Tullius in the .`5´. distinctio of the
saide booke puttithe in remembraunce whiche of the noble and famous
dukis, princes and cenatours of Romains abandonned here bodies and
goodis, only putting them to the vttermost iubardy in the feelde ayenst   2135
theire aduersaries for the auauncement and keping in prosperite, worship and welfare of Rome.

Lucius Brutus.   Among whiche, one of the saide Romains was Lucius
Brutus that, whan Aruus, a leder of peple, assemblid a gret oost ayenst
the Romains to haue descomfit hem and put hem in seruage out of | here   f. 35ʳ
Lucius Romanus.   fraunchise, the saide noble Lucius being then gouernoure   2141
of the ooste of Romains thought rathir to die vpon the said Aruus, so
§   that he might subdew hym, rathir than the saide citee shulde stande
in seruage. He mounted vpon his hors and leide his spere in the rest and
Non est laudendum   withe a mightie courage renne feerslie vpon the saide   2145
secundum legem
Christianorum.   Aruus, being in the myddill of his oost; and fortuned
by chaunce that bothe of hem wound[ed] othir to dethe. And whan it
was vndrestonde in the hooste that the saide Aruus, capitall aduersarie
to Romains, was dede, his gret oost departed out of theire feelde, whiche
had not soo done had not bene by mightie auenture the wilfull dethe of   2150
the saide Lucius Brutus.

How a prince, be he made regent, gouernoure or ˋduke,ʹ chieueteyne, lieutenaunt, capetaine, conestable or marchalle make alwaie iust paiment to here soudeours for escheweng of
2155 **gret inconuenientis might falle.**

Autor. Notandum est super omnia effectus istius articuli, quo ad execucionem iusticij. And ouermore, most highe and excellent prince, of youre benigne grace and prouidence, if it please youre highnesse to haue consideracion in way of iustice-keping to remedie one singuler offence and dammage to youre
2160 liege-people, the whiche by Goddis law and by law of reason and nature is the contrarie of it, right dampnable; and which greuous offence, as it is voised, accustumablie rennythe and hathe be more vsid vnder ˋtho that ought be [vnder]ʹ youre obeisaunce in Fraunce and Normandie than in othir straunge regions; and to euery well-aduised man it is
2165 easie to vndrestande that it is a thing that may well bene amendid and correctid, and to be a gret mene to the recuuere of youre londes in the saide aduerse partie.

Notandum est de ordinaria solucione Iohannis, ducis Bedfordie. That is to say: that ˋshall beʹ men of soude and of armes, as well tho that ˋshallʹ be vndre youre
2170 lieutenauntis, as the chiefteins and capetains, may be duely paide of here wages by the monithe ˋlyke as Iohn, regent of Fraunce, paydʹ or by quartere, bethout any rewarde ˋof curtesyie, oˋfʺ colourʹ gyuen,
Concidera. bribe, defalcacion or abreggement, or vndew assignacion
f. 35ᵛ not leuable assigned | or made vnto them, as welle in this londe as
2175 in Normandie, to deceyue hem or cause hem be empouerisshed in straunge contreis, as it hathe be accustumed late in the saide contreis; and that such paymentis be made content bethout delaie or nede of long and grete pursute, vpon suche a resonable peyne as the cause
§ shall require it; and that none of youre officers roiall, nethire hire
2180 debitees or comissioneris, shall darre doo the contrarie to take no bribe, rewarde, or defalke the kingis wagis. Wherbie youre souldeours shalle not haue cause to oppresse and charge youre obeissauntis and youre peple in taking theire vitaile bethout paieng therfor, whiche gret part of theym in defaut of due payment hathe ben accustumed by .x. or
2185 .xij. yere day contynued, or the saide londes were lost; vncorrectid ne

2152 duke] *WW over eras.* a *and at l. end*　　　2153 conestable] conestable constabb *with* constabb *crossed out*　　　2159 iustice-keping] iustice and keping 2162–3 tho that ought be vnder] *WW interl.* tho that ought be (*see n.*)　　2168 shall be] *WW at l. end*　　2169 shall be] *WW interl.* shall be, *duplic.* be *by scr.* 2171 lyke . . . payd] *WW interl., along with* hy⟨m⟩ *later eras.*　　　2172 of . . . colour] *WW over eras.*　oˋfʺ] *WW* f *over uneras.* r　　2174 assigned] *at foot of p.,* *16th-c. pen-trial* Robert Savylle　　2177 of] or of

punisshid, [it] turned to the gret vndoing of youre saide obeisauntes, and one othir of gret causis that they haue turned theire hertis frome vs, breking theire alligeaunce by manere of cohercion for suche rapyn, oppressions and extorcions.

Nota multi-
plicacionem
officiariorum.   And also the officers than being nedithe not to haue so 2190 many lieutenauntis or vndre-officers as they haue hadde, whiche wastithe and destroiethe youre saide peple by vndew charges § to enriche hemsilfe. And many of tho officers haue be but esy vaile-able to the defense of youre countre thoroughe negligence of excersising of armes for theire defense and proteccion in tyme of necessite. For it 2195 was neuer sene that any countre, cite or towne did encrece well wher ouermany nedeles officers and gouernours, that onlie wolde haue a renomme and vnder that colour ʻbʼe a extorcioner, piller or briboure, was reignyng and ruling ouer theym.

Exclamacio.   O mightie king and ye noble lordes of this roiaume, if ye 2200 were wele aduertised and enfourmed of the gret persecucions by way of suche oppressions and tirannyes, rauynes and crueltees that many of suche officers haue suffred to be done vnponisshed to the pore comons, laborers, paissauntes of the saide duchie of Normandie, it is verailie to deme that certez ye of noble condicions naturally pitous wold not haue 2205 suffred suche | greuous inconuenientis, to be redressid and amendid f. 36ʳ long or the said intrusion fille, and the regalite of iustice had be in tho daies in youre possession!

De lamentabili oppressione
subditorum nostrorum in
Francia.   For oftentymes suche as haue pretendid theym officers wastid of youre ʻpredecessoursʼ liuelode 2210 more than nedithe and oftentymes suffred them to be manassed, beten, and mischieued theire bestis withe theire wepins that they were nighe out of theire wittis for sorow ʻaʼnd so enforced for duresse to forsake youre title and youre lawes, and but esilie releuyd and socoured.

And therto they haue ben so often surcharged greuouslie withe 2215 paieng of tasques, tailis, subsides and imposicions beside theire rentis-paieng to the somme right importable, sommes paide to youre predecessours for youre demains and to theire landlordis that halden of you. And many of theym duelling vpon the marches patised to youre aduerse partie also to dwell in rest. And this innumerable charges 2220 and diuers tormentis haue ben done to theym to theire vttermost vndoing.

    2186 it turned] turned   2198 ʻbʼe] scr. b over uneras. h   2209 For]
WW symbol at fore-edge   2210 predecessours] WW adds predece over eras.
and interl. ssours before uneras. is   2213 ʻaʼnd] one-compartment a changed to
two-compartment a

Alia exclamacio soldariorum vltimo in Normannia commorancium. He, allas! And yet seeing they bene Cristen men and lyuyng vnder youre obeissaunce, 'lawes',

2225 youyng and yelding to youre lawes a`s´ trew Englisshemen done, by whome also we lyue and be susteyned and youre werre the bettir born out and mainteyned, why shulde it hereafter be suffred that suche

Deploracio miserie. tormentrie and cruelte shulde be shewed vnto theym? O God, whiche art most mercifull and highest iuge, souerein

2230 and iust, how maist thow long suffre this regnyng without the stroke of vengeaunce and ponisshement c`o´mm`yng´ vpon the depryuyng or yelding-vp of that dukedom?

Late it be noted and construed what gret inconuenientis haue folow

Nota tria. herof. There may be vndrestonde to folow .iij. thingis in espe-

2235 Prima. ciall of gret hurtis. One is the ire of God and his rod of ven- geaunce fallen now vpon vs by his dyuyne punisshement 'of God', as well in suffring oure saide aduersaries to haue the ouerhand vpon vs as in destroieng of oure lordis by sodeyn fortunes 'of dyvysyons' in this lande the saide yere and season the yere of Crist M[l]. iiij[Cl]., that `y´oure

2240 `grete´ aduersarie made his intrusion in the saide Normandy for pite of his peple so oppressid, hiring theire clamours and cries and theire

f. 36[v] ij[da]. curses. The second is theire rebellion, as | thoroughe theire wan-

§ hope hauyng no trust of hastie socoure and relief of an armee to come in tyme couenable, be turned awaie frome here ligeaunce and obe-

2245 dience to youre aduerse partie, seeing theym thus vngoodelie entretid vnder tho whiche were commytted to kepe, defende and maynteyn

iij[a] causa. them. The .iij[de]. is famyn of vitaile and penurie of money

Conciderandum est super omnia. and lak of prouision of artillerie and stuffe of ordenaunce, whiche youre saide obeissauntis for faute of these 'were' constreined to

2250 flee to youre aduerse partie and to leue rathir theire natif contree or ellis to die for famyn and pouertee.

2224 lawes] WW at l. end   2225 a`s´] s over uneras. n; followed by one eras. let-
ter   2231 c`o´mm`yng´] WW o over uneras. a and yng over uneras. e   2236 of
God] WW at l. end   2237 haue the ouerhand] 3 or 4 words interl. above this,
but then eras.   2238 destroieng] WW symbol at fore-edge   of dyvysyons] WW
interl.   2239 `y´oure] WW adds y in space, partly obscuring o, and interl. duplic. of
o   2240 grete] WW interl.   2249 were] WW over eras.   constreined] WW
symbol at fore-edge

Ecclesia
honoranda.

An exortacion how princes, lordes and officers roiall shulde worship and meynteyne the chirche and defende hem from oppression.

And moreouer in way of gret pitee and in the worship of God, suffre 2255
ye not the prelates of the chirche of that lande, as archebisshoppis, bisshoppis, abbatis, priours, denes, archedenes and theire ministrours to
be oppressid, revaled ne vileyned as they haue bene in youre predecessoure daies, accepted in full litill reuerence or obedience. For how that
men vsurpen in tho daies in surchargeyng them vnduelie, it is by experi- 2260
ence knowen well ynoughe. As they, by manere of a priue cohercion to
lyue in more rest withe theire lyuelode, be dryue too for to gyue out to
rulers, gouuernours and maistris of the marchis and contrees that they
dwellin vpon, or haue her lyuelode, gret fees and wages and rewardis
nedelese. And the peple 'that' were well set, and oftentymes they ben 2265
visited withe straungiers of gret astatis as well spirituell as temporell,
and namelie withe tho that haue the lawes to mynistre and to kepe,

Hospitalitas in ecclesia
est preferranda.

and withe other nedeles peple that waste and surcharge theym. For they were founded to that entent
but to kepe theire nombre of fundacion, praieng for theire foundours, 2270
and 'kepe hospitalitee for' to feede the pore and the nedie in case of
necessite.

Lamentacio.

A, mercifull Ihesu! Many auctours rehersithe in here
cronicles that Pompeus, whiche that was so cheualrous a p'a'ynym
knight amongis the Romains, the cause of his wofull dethe and mor- 2275
tall ende was alonlie that he on a tyme di's'deyned to reuerence and
worship holy places as chirches and seyntuaries, stabled his hors in |
Salamon is temple, the whiche the saide Salamon had edified to be the   f. 37^r
most souereyn chirche or temple of the erthe to serue and praise God.

And in example of late daies 'yn' King Iohn of Fraunce 'tyme', suche 2280
chieueteins as was in his armee before he was take at the bataile of
Peitiers, as it is saide, auaunted h'e'msilfe to stabill her hors in the
cathedrall chirche of Salisbury. And after he was take and had sight of
the saide chirche, 'they' had gret repentaunce of.

And therfor full noble king and ye puissaunt lordis of renomme, let 2285
a couenable and a necessarie medecyn be counceiled and youen to vs

---

2252 An] *WW in marg.* capitulum   2265 that] *WW interl.*   and] *reader 1 in*
marg. nota bene   2271 kepe hospitalitee for] *WW adds* kepe hospitalitee for to *in*
marg., with a caret in text, duplic. to *by scr.*   2274 p'a'ynym] *WW* a *over uneras.* e
2276 di's'deyned] s *over uneras.* d   2280 yn] *WW interl.*   tyme] *WW over eras.*
2282 h'e'msilfe] e *over uneras.* y   2284 they] *WW interl.*   of] *followed by eras.* of
1–2 letters

for prouision and reformacion of this infirmite; and that it may be purueied for by so dew meene`z´ that it may be to God is plesaunce; and
that we may withedraw and leue oure wrecchid gouernaunce that tem-
2290 porell men wolde so inordinatlie rule and oppresse the chirche; so that
now this begon mischief and stroke of pestilence in youre predecessour daies be not set as a iugement in oure arbitracion as to be decreed,
iuged or determyned for oure wele and auaile, but as a chastising of oure
mysdoeng, so to be take for oure sauacion.

2295   What saiethe Saint Ieroyme amongis his dolorous lamentacions
Cogita. vpon the prophesie of Iooell? 'If we haue not', seiethe he, 'know
God in welthe and prosperite, then at the leest let vs know hym in oure
aduersite.' In suche wise there we haue erred and fauted by ouere-gret
haboundaunce of suche chargeable crimes and synnes of delites of
2300 suche oppression, couetice, in especiall pride and enuy, etc., let vs
withedraw vs frome hem withe goode corage, and to that ende that
we be not chastised ne punisshed by the stroke of vengeaunce and
pestilence nor of none suche affliccions as we `hafe´ ben dailie by youre
predecessours daies by youre saide aduersaries.

2305 Quod officium   **How lordis sonnes and noble men of birthe for the**
       deffencionis
       aduersario-   **defense of here londe shulde excersise hem in armes**
       rum patrie est
       preferrandum   **lernyng.**
       qu`a´mcumque singularem facultatem siue practicam.

And also moreouer for the grettir defens of youre roiaumes and
f. 37ᵛ saufegarde of `y´oure contreis in tyme of necessite, also | to the auaunce-
2310 ment and encrece of cheualrie and worship in armes, comaunde and
Introduccio iuuenum   doo founde, establisshe and ordeyn that the sonnes of
nobilium natu.   princes, of lordis and for the most part of all tho that
bene comen and descendid of noble bloode, as of auncien knightis,
esquiers and other auncient gentillmen, that while they ben of grene
2315 age, ben drawen forthe, norisshed and excersised in disciplines, doctrine and vsage of scole of armes: as vsing iustis to can renne withe
speer-handle, withe ax, sworde, dagger and all othir defensible wepyn;
to wrestling, to skeping, leping and rennyng; to make hem hardie,
deliuer and wele-brethed; so as when ye and youre roiaume, in suche
2320 tyme of nede, [nede] to haue theire seruice in entreprises of dedis

    2288 meene`z´] WW adds z at end     2303 hafe] WW interl.     2305SN qu`a´m-
cumque] WW writes a over uneras. letter   2309 `y´oure] WW interl. y
2310 encrece] encrecece   2320 nede, nede] nede

of armes, they may of experience be apt and more enabled to doo
you seruice honourable, in what region they become; and not to be
'vnkonnyng,' abasshed ne astonied for to take entreprises, to answere
or deliuer 'a' gentilman that desire in worship to doo armes in liestis
to the vtteraunce or to certein pointis, or in a quarell rightfull to fight;   2325
and in cas of necessite [you] and youre roiaume for to warde, kepe and
defende frome youre aduersaries in tyme of werre.

And this was the custom in the daies of youre noble auncestries
bothe of kingis of Fraunce as of Englonde. In example wherof, of King
Edward .IIJ^{de} that excersised his noble son Edwarde, the prince, in right   2330
grene age and all his noble sonnes in such maistries wherby they were
Ser Iohn Fastolf.   more apt in haunting of armes. And, 'as myne autor seyd
me,' the cheualrous knight, 'fyrst' Henry, duke of Lancastre, which is
named a chief auctour and foundoure in law of armes, had sent to hym
frome princes and lordis of straunge regions, as out of Spayne, Aragon,   2335
Portingale, Nauerre and out of Fraunce, here children, yong knightis,
to be doctrined, lerned and brought vp in his noble court in scole of
armes and for to see noblesse, curtesie and worship, | wherthoroughe   f. 38^{r}
here honoure spradde and encresid in renomme in all londis they came
vntoo. And after hym in youre antecessour daies other noble princes   2340
and lordis of gret birthe accustomed to excersise maistries apropred to
defense of armes and gentiles to them longing.

But now of late daies, the grettir pite is, many one that ben descendid of noble bloode and borne to armes, as knightis sonnes, esquiers
and of othir gentille bloode, set hemsilfe to singuler practik, 'faculteez'   2345
straunge frome that fet, 'a's to lerne the practique of law or custom of
lande or of ciuile matiere, and so wastyn gretlie theire tyme in suche
nedelese besinesse as to occupie courtis-halding, to kepe and bere out
a proude countenaunce at sessions and shiris-halding, also there to
embrace and rule among youre pore and simple comyns of bestiall con-   2350
tenaunce that lust to lyue in rest. And who can be a reuler and put
hym forth in suche matieris, he is, as the worlde goithe now, among
alle astatis more set of than he that hathe despendid .xxx. or xl yeris of
his daies in gret iubardies in youre 'antecessourys' conquestis and wer-
Optatiuus modus.   ris. So wolde Ihesus they so welle lerned theym to be as   2355

2323 vnkonnyng] *WW over eras. and at l. end*   2324 a] *one-compartment* a
changed to two-compartment a   2326 you] youre   2332-3 as myne autor
seyd me] *WW interl.*   2333 fyrst] *WW interl.*   2345 faculteez] *WW at
l. end, after* straunge   2346 'a's] *one-compartment* a *changed to two-compartment* a
2349 there] theire *with i eras.*   2354 antecessourys] *WW interl.*   2355 welle]
woll welle

good men of armes, chieueteyns or capetains in the feelde that befallithe
for hem, where worship and manhod shulde be shewed moche bettir,
rathir then as they haue lerned and can be a captaine or a ruler at a
sessions or a shire-day to endite or amercie youre pore bestiall peple
2360 to theire ʼenpouerysshyngʼ and to enriche hemsilfe or to be magnified
the more.

But only they shulde maynteyn ʼyourʼ iustices and ʼyourʼ officers
wʼsyngʼ the goode custom of youre lawes. And than ye shuld haue right
litill nede to haue thought, anguisshe or besinesse for to conquere and
2365 wyn ayen youre rightfull enheritaunce or to defende youre roiaume
from youre ennemies. ʼAndʼ that suche singuler practik shulde ʼnotʼ be
accustumed and occupied ʼvndewlyʼ withe suche men that be come of
noble birthe, ʼbut he be the yongere brother havyng not whereof to lyve
f. 38ᵛ honestlyʼ. And if the vaillaunt Romayns had suffred | theire sonnes to
2370 mysspende theire tyme in suche siʼnguʼleʼreʼ practik vsing, oppressing
by colours ʼof custom of the law, they had not conquered twyesʼ Cartage
ayenst alle the Affricans.

**How officers of the law shulde be chosen, welle-disposid and
temperʼatʼ men vertuous in condicion, and they to be protectid
2375 by lordis and noble men of birthe.**

Hit was in auncient tyme vsed that suche practik and lernyng of the custumes and law of a lande shulde onlie be comytted to suche parsones
of demure contenaunce that were holden vertuous and well-disposid,
thoughe he were descendid but of esie birthe, to occupie in suche facul-
2380 tees and to mynistre duelie and egallie the statutis and custumes of the
law to youre peple, bethout meintenaunce ayenst iustice; and the saide
officers and ministrours of the law to be protectid and meyntened by
the princes, lordis and men of worship, when the case shalle require;
namelie tho that ought defende yow and youre roiaume, that halden
2385 theire londis of you by that seruice onlie, and gyuen to that entent by
youre noble auncestries; and ouer this, that they be lerned and intro-
ducid in the drede of God and not presumptuously take vpon hem to
offende theire law.

2360 enpouerysshyng] *WW over eras.*   2362 your¹] *WW over eras.*   your²]
WW over eras.   2363 wʼsyngʼ] *WW* syng *over eras.*   2366 And] *WW over
eras.*   not] *WW at l. end*   2367 vndewly] *WW interl.*   2368-9 but he
be . . . honestly] *WW interl.*   2370 siʼnguʼleʼreʼ] *WW over uneras. simple, rewriting*
mp *as* ngu *and adding* r *and abbrev. for* e   2371 of custom . . . twyes] *WW interl.*
2374 temperʼatʼ] at *over uneras. letter*

For the whiche and in example to this purpose, it is wretin in the .36.
chapitre of the prophete Ieremye: because that Ioachym, king of Iuda, 2390
despraised the admonestementis, aduertisementis and the doctrines of
God that Ieremie had doo set yn certein bookes and quaiers, the whiche
he made to be cast in the fire and disdeyned to hire theym, but vsid after
his owne wilfulnesse and hedinesse and without counceile; therfor God
seiethe by the mouthe of the prophete that of hym shuld issew ne come, 2395
none heire to succede ligneallie that after hym shulde enioie and holde
his roiaume; and ouermore that he shulde visit hym by punisshement,
and that as well his kynne as hym, that had suffred and caused to be so
euill inducid. And so it fille after the prophesie.

Exclamacio.   O ye, than, in the same wise puttithe away the delites of sen- 2400
sualitees of suche inconuenient occupacion | as before is specified frome f. 39^r
the children of noble men; and late theym be inducid and lerned of
youthe, that in thingis 'of noblesse' that apparteynithe and belongithe
to theym to lerne, as in excer[si]sing of armes and to suche occupacions
of worship. These thingis prouyded and ordeined ought not be long 2405
delaied but incontinent stedfastlie to be perseuered; that then doubte
not but that God, whiche is most mercifull and alway in euery necessite
to relief vs, despraisithe not the humble and contrite hertis, but that he
of his infinite goodenesse wolle accept and take in gree and his grace
oure good entent and shal be withe vs in all oure 'gode' actis and dedis. 2410

How ouer-gret cost and pomp in clothing shulde be eschewed.

And therfore in witnesse herof, eschew and leue the superfluite and
excesse of arraie and clothing, and late euerie astate vse as the worthie
Romains did, the whiche in tyme of affliccions and turmentis or anguisshes by occasion of werres and batailes vsed one manere clothing, 2415
and anothir maner clothing in tyme of prosperite and felicitee reignyng.

  And the same maner, 'the ryte' and custom youre aduerse partie
of Fraunce hathe vsed, escheweng all costius arraiementis of clothing,
garmentis and bobauncees; and the vsaige of pellure and furres they
haue expresselie put away; which costues arraymentis and disgising 2420
of clothing of so many diuers facion vsed in this youre roiaume, in
Nota. especiall amongis youre pore comyners, hathe be one of the gret

   2403 of noblesse] WW interl.   2404 excersising] excersing   2406 doubte]
WW symbol at fore-edge   2410 gode] WW at l. end   2417 the ryte] WW over
eras. custom] followed by of interl. by WW   2420 which] WW symbol at fore-edge

inconuenientis of the empouerisshing of youre lande, and enforced gret
pride, enuy and wrathe amongis hem, whiche hathe holpe brought them
2425 to gret indigence and pouertee.

**How that gret hurt and inconuenientis haue fallen to the roi-
aume, because the creditours haue not be duelie paide of here
lonys and prestis made to highe souereins.**

Moreouer, youre pore comyns 'yn your ante[ce]ssour dayes', not
f. 39ᵛ paied holy theire duteis for theire lones, | prestis of vitailis and othir
2431 marchaundise, as by opyn example was oftentymes lent and taken to
the behofe of youre predecessoure Henry Sext, named king, but in
sondrie wises be delaied and despende gret part of here goode, or they
can nighe here deutees and paiementis; and fayn to suffre to defalke
2435 and relese partie of here dutee to receyue the othir part, which is the
Nota optime.   cause of gret charge and hinderaunce of youre peple.
And therfor to voide this inconuenient, right noble king, withe the
discrete avise of youre noble lordis, let youre riche tresours be spradde
and put abrode, bothe iuellis, vessell of golde and siluer, among youre
2440 true subgettis, and in especiall to the helpe and auauncement of youre
conquest and to the relief of youre indigent and nedie peple, and in
especiall to tho that haue lost theire londis, liuelode and goode in the
werres, so that the saide tresoure may be put forthe; and late it be set in
money, to the remedie and socoure of this gret importunyte and neces-
2445 site and to the defens of youre roiaume from youre aduersaries before
specified. For it is saide that 'an empyre or' roiaume is bettir without
tresoure of golde than without worship. And also bettir it is to lyue a
pore life in a riche roiaume in tranquillite and pease than to be riche in
a pore roiaume, where debate and strife reignithe. And if ye woll doo
2450 thus, euery man than in his degree wolle doo the same, and to example
of vs alle, ye, 'soo' puissaunt and mightie men of good counceile, and
stere euery man helpe after his degree.

2429 Moreouer] WW symbol at fore-edge   yn your antecessour dayes] WW interl.
antecessour] antessour   2435 which] WW symbol at fore-edge   2439 golde]
WW symbol at fore-edge   2446 an empyre or] WW changes one-compartment **a** to
two-compartment **a**, adds n em over eras., and continues at l. end   2447 And] WW
symbols at fore-edge and close to text   2451 soo] WW interl.

How Saint Lowis, king of Fraunce, in his testament writen of his owne hande counceiled his sonne after hym reigned to cherisshe and fauoure the good citeis and townes of his lande and vse   2455 iustice and peas.

And to doo and werke after the blissid counceile of Saint Lowes, king of Fraunce, declared among othir exhortacions and counceile in his | testament, the chapiter where he exorted and comaundid his sonne f. 40ᵣ Phelip, that reigned king after hym, that he shulde put and doo alle 2460 his diligence that he shulde kepe his peple in pease and iustice; and in especiall to fauoure and cherisshe the good citeis and townes of his roiaume, and to kepe theym in fraunchise and fredoms, soo as they may encrese and lyue puissauntlie. For if they be tendred, that they be of power and mightie of goode, the ennemies of youre roiaume or 2465 of youre aduerse partie wol doubt and be ware to take any entreprise ayenst youre noble mageste. And if the aduersaries wolle wirke ayen the honoure of youre parsone and the welfare of youre roiaume, youre saide citesins and burgeis and good comyns shal be of power and of goode courage and wille withe here bodies and goodes largelie depart 2470 to be youen for to resist them. And therfor fauoure and forbere the pore peple, and namelie the nedie, in signe that ye in youre hertis may bring to mynde and remembre the vengeaunce of hard offensis to this roiaume shewed, and to the recuuere of the worship of the roiaume late lost.

And whoso hathe not a bodie habill herto or vsage to emploie hym 2475 in dedis of armes, or think it long not to hym, as men of religiouste and spirituell, temporell men wolde sey, 'Yet com forthe withe a goode courage, and not by constreint ne in manere of tasque ne of thraldom in tyme to come but of fre will withe a bounteuous hert at this tyme, that is so expedient and necessarie, as trew Englisshemen shulde doo, 2480 euery man bring and put forthe of his goodes after that his power is!' Now in the worship of God, let this be tymelie don. It shall now shew, or it may be shewed, who that shal be founde goode and profitable to the comon wele or set hymsilf to the employ and fortheraunce of this dede of gret necessite. And whoso hathe no power to ley out finaunce, 2485 good or tresoure, yet put his goode will therto.

A, noble roiaume of gret | price and of noble renomme, as thow hast f. 40ᵛ be! Whan God lust to shew thy power and to be victorious, who may noy the? Shall thou than suffre the to bee confunded withe simpler people of reputacion then thow art? Withe tho whiche ye and youre 2490

noble progenitours haue conquerid and ouercom diuerse tymes before
this? It is well to vndrestonde that ye haue no protectoure, kepar ne
defendour but it come of God, of the whiche he is witnesse and the
leder. Som say that the floode of Temmys rennythe beting hier than
2495 the londe in stormye seasons; yet for alle that, withe Goddis might and
grace thow art not in the extremitee of tho stormes, ne neuer mote it
come there in suche indigence and necessite.

**How that when the Romains were yn that vttermost necessite
that bothe mete and money failed hem, and here cheualrie**
2500 **destroied, yet tho that left toke goode hert to hem, bothe
widowes and othirs, that releued ayen the frauncheis and
libertees of Rome.**

And whereas the Romains fonde theym yn that most vrgent necessite, whan that bothe mete and monney failed theym to susteyne and
2505 support theire manhode, neuerthelesse noble courage ne goode hope
failed not among hem; so that what tyme the auncien gentill bloode
was wastid in bataile, than they made knightis of theire boundemen to
auaunce theire conquest, for to encrese withe theire hoost; and that the
goode worshipfull ladies of Rome, and namely the soroufull widowes
2510 whiche at that tyme were not vsid of custom nothing to pay ne yelde
to the souding of men of armes, yet at that tyme whan suche necessite
fille, they offred and brought right liberallie of theire iuellis and goodis,
for the whiche they were right gretly thanked and praised and, after the
victorie had, well recompensid and contentid.

f. 41ʳ Titus Liuius. A noble   Also I rede of a noble | example in Titus Liuius,
2516 historye of the largesse of the .5 booke of the seconde Decade of *Punica*
       Romaynys: how amplye
       they departed ther godes yn *bella*, that whan the noble Romains, in the tyme
       a tym of vrgent necessite, of werris long continued ayen theire aduersaries
       to make an armee ynto the
       contree of Auffrique.   of Aufrik, what by tasques, tailes and imposicions
2520 had for the defens of theire countree habandonned and youen largelie
of theire goodis meueable, that the saide Romains had no more in
substaunce to lyue by except theire londes. And it fille soo that the
countree of Cisiliens and Champenois hadde doo puruoie for a gret
armee and an oost of peple, as well of men for to defende and kepe the
2525 see as the lond. And so the comons of Rome had borne so many gret
chargis before that they might no more, but if the lordis, senatours and
counceilours of Rome wolde put too theire hande.

And in so moche that the comons of Rome complained and grugged
in open marketplaces ayenst the saide gret astatis and gouernours
of Rome, seieng but they wolde sill theire bodies and goodis of the   2530
comons, they might pay no more tasque ne taile, the saide gouernours
of Rome to appaise the peple saiden they wolde counceile togither and
aduise a day to puruey for the comon wele and seiden in conclusion
that 'Where it right or wrong, we senatours, astatis and gouernours
must put out largelie of oure goodis and so yeue example to the comons   2535
for the defens of the contree of Cesille and keping of the lande and see
frome ennemies.'

Lenius.   And one Lenius, a noble senatoure, pronounced and saide that,
'Forasmoche the senatours haue power of goode and rule of the cite in
preferraunce of worship and dignite, in like wise it is reason that they   2540
bere a charge to defende the comons and yeue example to doo, as thow
woldist comaunde hem to doo. Therfor late vs, in yeuyng the comons
example, tomorne yn opyn marketplace before hem bring forthe the
gret part of the golde and siluer of coyne and print money that euery of
vs senatours | and statis hauen; so that none of vs reserue and kepe to   f. 41ᵛ
his propre vse but ringis and nouches for to worship his wiffe and chil-   2546
dren withall; so that euery officer shulde haue noo more siluer vessell
but for a chapell and a cupbourde; and euery senatoure to kepe but a
pounde of coyned siluer; and euery weddid man hauyng wiffe and children to kepe for euery of hem an ounce of siluer or suche a litill weight;   2550
and euery citesyn of hauyoure and degre to reserue only but .vᴹˡ. pens
of brasse money: and soo that alle othir golde, siluer and brasse money
coyned to be brought to the tresorers of the citee.'

And after than, the comons of Rome hauyng consideracion that the
senatours and gouernours of Rome of here owne fre voulente haboun-   2555
donned and put out so habundantlie and largelie of here golde and
tresour for the comon wele, to the defense and keping of the see withe
shippis and maryneris, to the defens and rebutting of here aduersaries, that euery of the comons of Rome after here power and hauyoure
of gret courage brought frelie of gold, siluer and othir coyne-money to   2560
the tresorers and chaungers that were comytted to receyue the money.
The prese was so grete that they had no tyme to write the names of the
noble citesins ne for to nombre and telle the quantite and porcion of
euerie man is part that they brought. And by this accord and moien the
comon profit was soo augmentid that the knightis and men of werre   2565
had suffisaunt and more than nedid to defende and kepe the countre

2545 and] 15th-c. pen-trial eras. in marg.

of Cecilians and Champenois and also to be maistris of the see. And all
thingis and ordenaunces that longid to werre was purueied for and put
forthe in onure and worke, that all the senatours, counceilours, had no
2570 nede to tarie lenger for counseiling, but euery of hem went forth into
here countre to dispose for hemsilfe. And in so gret discomfort stode
neuer the Romayns as they did in this vrgent necessitee; and was | by   f. 4
this moien of largesse repared and brought ayen to worship, prosperite
and welfare.

2575   And wolde the mightifull God that euery harde, couetouse hert were
of suche largesse and distributif of here meueable good and tresoure to
the comon wele, as for defending vs frome oure aduersaries and keping
the see as well as the londe, that we may alway be lordis and maistris
`there'of, as noble gouernours were before this tyme.

2580 `Here endyth thys epistle vndre correccion the xv. day of Iune the yeere
of Crist M^l iiij^C lxxv. and of the noble regne of Kyng Edward the .IIIJ^{the}.
the xv^{ne}.'

2579 `there'of] *WW interl.* there   2580–2 Here endyth . . . the xv^{ne}.] *WW in
blank space;* Here . . . correccion *imitated, with variants in spelling, in 15th-c. pen-trial
below*

ENGLISH TEXTS FROM THE CODICIL

PROLOGUE BY WILLIAM WORCESTER'S SON

Moste hyghe, myghty and excelente Cristen prince, [Rich]arde by the   f. 2ʳ
dyvyne prudence of God the Thred, kyng of Englande and of Fraunce,
lorde of the grette famouse isle of Irlonde and of many othir isles
and contrees habitable, environed and belongyng to the seide bothe
reaulmes.   5
    Worshipp and laude be to almyghty God, dred and obedience with all
due reuerence and legeaunce by youre true lovyng sogettes obserued for
the auauncyng and preferring the comon publique, for the deffence and
conseruacion yn tranquilite of youre seide bothe roymes, by executyng
of the .iiij. cardinall vertuse named iustice, prudence, force and tem- 10
peraunce, euery of them in their order and as the case shall require.
And, moste exellent redoubted prince, forasmoche as youre full mighty
and mooste noble courage ys dayly dysposed and moved to accom-
plyshe th'offices of the forsaide cardinall vertuse, and in especiall for
to execute the cardinall vertue of force, as to vaynquische thorow the 15
myghte of God, fyrst callyng to hym dayly for his grace and helpe, as
Seint Poule councellithe in hys epistill, 'Gracia in me non vacua fuit', to
subdew youre gret aduersarye of Fraunce and to make vpon hym a new
conqueste or, by the meane of a fynall pease, for the recuuere of youre
rightfull title of enheritaunce and possession in youre seide realme of 20
Fraunce and ducdom of Normandy, and which ducdom, as yt ys sayde
by auncyent wrytyng, holdeth of noon higher souuereyn in chief but
of God.
    And sith that youre most couragiouse princely disposicion sheweth
noterily ye be sett | dayly more feruientlier purposing the rather to f. 2ᵛ
obteyne youre most worshipfull enterpryse, to atteyn youre seide 26
enheritaunce. And inasmoche as yn token of due possession of the
same by long tymes contynewid, hyt is of highe recorde by youre righte
noble auncestres, kynges of this lande, how they haue contynewid by
many yeres in possession, as yt is well knowen to all Crysten princes. 30
And I as moost symple of reason, youre righte humble lege-man,

---

1 Richarde] Rich *eras. and overwritten with* Edw *in 15th- or 16th-c. hand*
2 dyvyne] dyvynce   Thred] *marked with cross in different, dark brown ink; late*
16th- or early 17th-c. hand adds fourth *in the marg.*

cannot atteyne to vndyrstond the reasons and bokes that many wyse
philosophurs of gret auctorite haue writen vpon this vertue of force;
but that my pore fadyr William Worcestre, somtyme seruaunte and
35   sogett withe his reuerent master Iohn Fastolff, cheualier, he exercised
in the werres contynuelly aboute .xliiij^{ti} yeris, toke vpon hym to write
in this mater and compiled this boke to the moste highe and gretly
redoubted kyng, your most nobill brodyr and predecessoure, shewyng
after his symple connyng aftir the seyng of the masters of philosophie
40   as Renatus Vegesius in his *Boke of Batayles*, also Iulius Frontinus in
his *Boke of Knygh`t'ly Laboures* callid in Greke *Stratagematon*, a new
a`u'ctoure callid *The Tree of Batayles*. But for all the deciplyne of the
seide auctours, the experiense of men in cheualrouse dedes exercised
in armys with the conduyte by goode polecye, as wele vpon the see
45   foughten as vpon the lande, preuaylethe moste.

      And vndre youre graciouse pardon and noble correccion [I] submytt
me vnto, in all humble wyse, that I take vpon me to put in remem-
f. 3^r braunce onely by way of example in this litill Codicelle the | ordre and
the conduyte of the righte nobill cheualrie of the prynce of gret renoune
50   in his dayes Iohn, duc of Bedford, regent of the realme of Fraunce, that
was of nere bloode to youre progenitours. And he, beyng electe as well
by th'assent of the lordes of Fraunce of your partie obidience as by the
lordes agrement of Englonde, agreed to be regent of the seid reaulme
of Fraunce and ducdom of Normandie and there conty[n]ewid in gret
55   renoune of cheualrie, as heraftir is made a lytill mencion, .xiij. yeres
in the seide office of regencye till his decease; by his example in the
conduyte of dedes of armys, batayles, iurneyse, segys and rescues of
places doon in his tyme of regencye; and also as by the moost noble and
prudent examples in fette of werre by the experience of mony viages,
60   seges, bataylis by see and by lande don and sped by the righte victorioux prince of noble memorie Kyng Edward .IIJ^d., of his conqueste in the
seide reaulme of Fraunce aboute .xxxiiij^{ti} yeres contynewelly laboured;
and also sethyn by the example of many gret enterprises and many noble
dedes of armys doon by the cheualry of gret prowesse in the conqueste
65   of that excellent and famouse prince Herry the Vte., named kyng, as wele
in the seide ducdom of Normandie as ynne the seide reaulme of Fraunce
in his owne parson by .vij hole yeres complete and .xv. days. And incon-

      34 William] *late 16th- or early 17th-c. hand in marg. The author*   41 *Knygh`t'ly*]
scr. t *interl.*   42 auctoure] *scr.* u *over uneras.* c   46 I submytt] submytt
50 Iohn] *late 16th- or early 17th-c. hand in marg. adds trefoil and* the subiecte of this
Booke   54 contynewid] contyewid   56 by] for by

tynent aftir his trespasemente the seid Iohn, duc of Bedforde, aftir that,
he was made regente of the seide reaulm in the | kynges grene age, beyng   f. 3ᵛ
.ix. monethis of age whiche oughte be by the statutes of Fraunce of .xiiij.   70
yere age or he shulde take vpon hym to rule his realme. In which seid
.xiiij. yere of hys regne the seide 'Iohn', regente, deceased as regente,
and for a memoriall of perpetuall recorde [of] that office and dignite
so long contynewid, for the gret auctorite and p[re]hemynens in that
office, desired to leue his body to be buried withyn that realme in the   75
cathedrall chirche of Roon, whereas Kyng Richarde Cueur de Lion his
herte ys tombed.

    And yf the seide duc of Bedforde had refused to take vpon hym at the
decease of Herry Vᵗʰᵉ., named kyng, that office of regencye, a lorde of
astate, a pere of Fraunce, by the eleccion of the Parlement of .III. Astates 80
of Fraunce, shuld haue be regente, whiche myghte haue ben a grete
reuaylyng to the noblesse of thys youre realme. And yn the yntrest of
the title of youre highe enheritaunce and in concernyng and auauncyng
the blode in the ryall parsones that oughte of youre most noble [line]
succede in the coroune of Fraunce, the seyde duc toke vpon hym to   85
gouerne the comyn publique and kepe and defende the seide royaume
and ducdom and sone after assemble a myghty power of cheualrye, lyke
as in this boke to youre moste royall parsone now compyled ys particu-
lerly made mencion of theyr names, of ther charges and of there offices
to hym commytted, to that intent that his grete renoune of cheualrie,   90
nother her actis yn dedes of worshipp, shuld remayne as a perpetuell
memoriall and not be foryete; concyderyng also his nerenesse of youre
most noble blode and | also anothir concideracion in especiall that so   f. 4ʳ
neere of aliaunce was knytt vnto the moste highe souuereyn princesse,
the quene ys modyr, Dame Iaques, ducesse of Bedforde, and was fyrste   95
maried vntoo.

    And so in this writyng is particulerly declared how euery astate in
her degre for her berthe and manhode were named and assigned to
offices of gret worshipp: as certeyn of them to be lyeutenauntis and
chiefteynes of werre for the feelde and certeyne to be capteynes of cas-   100
tels, forteresis, citese and townes; and also othir certeyne nombre of
lordes and nobles, for her long experience in the werre and for the gret
wysdom and polesye, assigned and deputed to be of the grete councell
of Fraunce for to advice the forseid cardinall vertue of iustice withe the

    72 Iohn] *scr. interl.*   73 of that] that   74 prehemynens] phemynens
84 noble line] noble (*see n.*)   88 boke] *over eras., preceded by red line-filler*
88–90 ys . . . of] *late 16th- or early 17th-c. hand underlines and in the marg. adds trefoil;
the same or a different hand adds* fol: 1 (*see n.*)

105 vertu of temperaunce, withe moderacion to be admynestred; and also
to ordeyne and provide for all maner of ordinaunces, the fortificacions,
for the ablementes of werre, as of arterie, for the auauncemente for the
werre in youre seide conqueste. And also to exercise the seid .iiij.^{the} cardinall vertue called prudence most be pondred, that the seide cardinall
110 vertue of force may the surere take effecte and be conduyted as wele for
the conqueste of the felde as of castellys, forteresis, cyteis and townes
besegyng and hesteyng.

Also here ys made mencyon what pencyon, fees and wages at that
tyme was deputed and assigned vnto euery of the officers and councel-
115 loures. And ys declared the astate of officers royall, as chauncelere, tre-
f. 4ᵛ sorere, precedent of parlement, iustices, maysters | of requestes, maystre
of the chambre of accomptis, receyuoures, procu[rat]ours, vocatis and
all suche othir officers royall and mynystroures belongyng aftir the custom of Fraunce, withe the pencions, wages and fees to euery of tho
120 offices accustomed. And also ys made mencyon of the substaunce of
the reuenues and profites ordinarie, with the emolumentes of the seid
realme and ducdom yerly for certeyn yeris, comyng of the demaynes
and of othir particuler countes belongyng by yefte in the regentes owne
hand as his propre enheritaunce, of his counte of Mayne by hym onely
125 conquered, of the counte of Harecourte, of the counte of Dreux and of
the vecounte of Ellebeff, of the vicounte of Lyslebone, of the vecount
of Beamount, as wele as of the baronyes de La Ryuere-de-Tybovyle
and of the baronye and lordshipp of Dauvers, and also of the barony
and lordshipp of Newborough, as wele as of othir lordshippis; of grete
130 comodytes growyng of the tasques, taylles, inposicion of the comyns,
gabelle comyng of salt yerly, quaterismes comyng of beuerages; and also
of the wynnyngis of werre of the tʼhʼreddis for prysoners than takyn in
werre; and with the declaracion of the ordenarie paymentes, costis and
chargis made for the tuycion and sauegard of the seid realme, ducdo[m]
135 and countes bethyn the tyme of the seid regencye.

Also in this boke ys made mencyon of a parte of the worshipfull
cheualrye with a declaracion of the costis and chargis for one yere in
f. 5ʳ the tyme that the righte highe and | myghty prynce Richard, duc of
Yorke, youre moste noble fadyr, when he was made gouuernaunte in
140 his secunde viage, makyng his armye into Fraunce and Normandye;
and in especiall for the conseruacion of the ducdom of Normandye

111 felde] fer felde, *with* fer *crossed out*   117 procuratours] procubours (*see n.*)
121 emolumentes] emolumientes   132 tʼhʼreddis] h *interl.*   134 ducdom]
ducdon   136 parte] prt parte, *with* prt *crossed out in red*

withyn the tyme that the last truxe was take betwene Herre the VJ. kyng
and his aduersarie of Fra[un]ce, Charlys the VIJ^{the}.—how many sperys
on horsebac and on fote, and the nombre of archers, were assigned
and deputed to eueri castell, forteresse, cite and towne—whiche was   145
afore righte nakedly provided for, as the dede shewed aftir, before
that the seide 'gouuernau'nte terme was expired; and after hys terme
exspired, the seide charge commytted from his hignesse to Edmond,
duc of Somersett, takyng the charge of gouuernaunte aftir the seid duc
of Yorke.   150

   Also ys made abrygement of the substaunce in articles at the conu-
encyon at Calix, of the vndew petycions that the councell in the name
of Charlis, the forseid gret aduersarie, demaundyd at the conuencion
at Calyx, present the cardynall of Englonde, bysshopp of Wynchestre,
accompayned withe othir ambassatours for this lande, and the duc of   155
Orlyaunce, beyng long tyme here prysonere .xxiiij. yere, accompanyed
with othir ambassatours of the Frenshe partie the xviij yere of Herry the
VJ. kyng. Whiche petycions and demaundes were in substaunce accordyng to the moost vnresonable petycions that the Frenshe partye purposed in the conuencion of the mooste solempne anbassiat assembled   160
at the cite of | Arras duryng by .x. wekes and more, the seide car- f. 5ᵛ
dinall of Englande and dyuerse othir astates of noble degre for þis
lande assembled; also then present ij. cardinallys of Seint Crosse, of
Cypres, from the pope sent with many othir gret astates of the Frenshe partye, in the tyme of the seid regent of Fraunce, duc of Bedforde,   165
lyued and deceasid, and in the dissoluyng of the forsaide conuencion.
Which bothe conuencions wolde be effectuelly studyed, the originals of
them with the ripe ansuers that were then made in writyng by the seid
councelloures of the kynges councell for the partye of this lande beyng
then at Roon, that aduysed the ansuers of the contynua[un]ce in the   170
righte of the corowne of Fraunce. And in case the seid peticions and
demaundes be put heraftir by youre aduerse partye vnto youre highnesse for to ansuere, when the case shall require, ayenst theyre erroures
and demaundes youre noble and prudent councell may be the rypare in
tho highe maters to ansuere.   175

   Also in the laste partye of this Codycelle ys put in writyng the
oppynyons and reasons of the gret stiward of the howsolde of the seid

   143 and] preceded by eras. of 5–6 letters and 3 letters ⟨-d⟩ crossed out in red and black
Fraunce] Framce   147 'gouuernau'nte] gouuernau over eras.   158 kyng]
preceded by eras. of 5–6 letters   161 of] duplic. at foot of f. 5ʳ and top of f. 5ᵛ
167 originals] 15th-c. hand adds nota in marg.   170 contynuaunce] contynuamce

regente, devised at Roon cyte, sent to the seid councell of Arras in
reualyng and adnullyng the seide grete aduersaries demaundes.

180   And also ys shewid the reasons and the grounde maters for the iuste
tytle of enheritaunce and for the auauncemente and maytenyng of the
werre ayenste the seid grete aduersaries of Fraunce, after the case and
the chaunce of werre was then tho'uȝ'te beste to be conduyte.

f. 6ʳ   And albeyt that the | case ys now gretly chaunged from the fortune
185 and chaunce of the worlde as was at tho days at the decease of the seide
regente, yit for all that the reasons and causes shewid and moved then,
albeyt that in the oppynyon of som parsones yt myghte be takyn and
seid they wil be but of litle effecte at this daye, yit for all that they wold
not be sett aside ne foryetyn, neyther theyre good purpose loste. For by
190 som article made then, a man may fynde and fortyfe a better mater and a
more effectuall reason vaylable, and as the cas shall require at this tyme.

Also there is declared in the latter partie of this writyng certeyne
avertisementis and instruccions concernyng the auauncement of the
werre, made and aduysed by the gret deliberacion of the chief coun-
195 cell for the werre to the forseid highe and myghty prynce, youre moost
noble fadere, in his secund vyage beyng electe gouuernaunte of the
reyaume of Fraunce, that weren taken and wretyn oute of the writyng of
many othir grete articles and auertisementis at the seide tyme devised
and councellyd. Whiche þat albeyt these artichles of auertisementis be
200 at this tyme but of easye wighte, and the case chaunged, yit be the
articles men of gret discresion, experte in the werre, may the more
rypliere delyuer and avise moche the surere the thynges whiche shal be
moost behofull and expedient for the auauncement of the werre and,
f. 6ᵛ as yt shal be thoughte, | mooste expedyente as the werre ys conduyt by
205 youre gret aduerse partye at this daye.

Also ys here specyfied a gret parte of an inuentorie of the gret
ordynaunce of the seid duc of Bedforde and artillerie for the werre that
remayned but in one of his chief castels of Normandye, at the castell
of Roone, besyde his ordenaunce and artillery in othir chieff castels
210 of Fraunce and at the castels of Maunce, Mayn, Sent-Zusan, as in
othir castels, cites, towns and forteressis in the ducdom of Normandye,
as within his castels, fortes, cites and townes withyn the ducdom of
Gasquyn and Gyen, as in the isles of Gersie and Guernesey.

Also yn this Codycelle ys made mencyon of certeyn articles brefly
215 drawen, the oppynyons of certeyn instruccions for the werre to the

noble prynce Edmonde, duc of Somersett, when he toke the charge to be
the kynges lyeutenaunte for to protecte the realme of Fraunce and ducdom of Normandy. Whiche, and the seide articles had ben provided
fore and obserued by the seid duc, the contreys, castelles, forteresses
and cites had not by lyklynesse be loste so sone as they were, nother in   220
the ducdom of Gasq`u´yn and Gyen as yt was, neyther the ducdom of
Normandye, lyke as the seid articles more playnly chauntithe.

TEXT 2

SIR JOHN FASTOLF'S ARTICLES RELATING
TO THE CONGRESS OF ARRAS, 1435

'Here folowen certeyn articles and instruccions made and avysed by   f. 38ʳ
wey of auertisment by Iohn Fastolf, knyght, baron of Cyllyguyllem and
graunt maister of the famouse and grete housold of the regent of the
royaume of Fraunce, Iohn, duc of Bedford, for to be admynestred to
the lordys of the grete councelle beyng yn Fraunce for Kyng Herry the   5
.VJᵗᵉ., kyng of England and of Fraunce, and of the seyd regent ayenst the
vnryghtfull demaundes and peticions purposed by the greete ambassyade assembled at ⸢the convencion of⸣ Arras on the behalf of Charlys the
.VIJ.ᵗʰ, grete aduersarye to the seyd Kyng Herry that desyred to make
a perpetuelle peas or a trux generalle wyth the seyd Kyng Herry vppon   10
the condicion that he shuld ⸢renounce and disclayme⸣ hys title and
name yn the corowne and royaume of Fraunce entierlye forevyr; and
for the second poynt desyred that, as for such ⸢cuntrees⸣, lordshyppys
and dignitees as shuld vppon accord betwene hem be delyuered and
lefft to the kyng of England by the moyen of a peas, that he shuld hald   15
yt of ⸢hys seyd aduersarye o⸣"f the corowne of Fraunce, yn feyth and
yn homage lyege, ressort and souuereynte, as paree one of the pares
of Fraunce. To whych peas fynall and demandes the ambassyatours of
the seyd regent of Fraunce, Iohn, duc of Bedford, yn kyng ys behalf of
Englond yn no wyse wold graunt or condecend; vppon whych the seyd   20
Ser Iohn Fastolf ys auertismentys ⸢were⸣ wryt ⸢and sent to⸣ the kyng

221 Gasq`u´yn] *scr.* u *interl.*   1–24 Here folowen . . . Herry VJᵗʰ.] *WW adds in
blank space above, continuing in left marg.*   8 the convencion of] *WW in marg. of
own addn*   11 renounce and disclayme] *WW interl. in own addn*   13 cuntrees]
WW interl. in own addn   16 hys seyd aduersarye o] *WW* hys seyd *and* o *over eras.
in own addn;* aduersarye *interl. in own addn*   21 were] *WW in marg. of own addn*
wryt] *preceded by* were by hym made *and crossed out*   and sent to] *WW interl. in own
addn; duplic. to in orig. addn*

ys ambassatours of England at Arras, by agreement of the seyd regent
and hys grete councelle, wyth "the othyr oppinions and avi"ses of the
regent and lordys of the seyd grete concelle of Kyng Herry VJth."

25   First, in cas that the king shulde take appointement offred now late
vnto hym at Arras be his ennemis and aduersaries at the conuencion
assembled there for the trete of pees etc., hit semyth that longeth nere
sitteth to the saide persones to touche ner speke of so high and so grete
matiers, sauyng only be the comaundement of my 'lordys of the kyngys
30   concelle' on the kingis behalue, obbeiyng vnto. It is thought them in
f. 38ᵛ there trouthis (vndere the beniuolence and goode | correccion of my
lordis of the kingis bloode and of his noble counseile), that if the king
shulde take the said offre in the manere and wise as it is offred hym
be his said aduersaries, that it myght be said, noised and demed in all
35   Cristen londis, where it shuld be spoken of, that nothere the king nor
his noble progenitours had ner haue no right in the corone of Fraunce,
and that all there werres and conquest hath be but vsurpacion and ti-
rannie, howbeit that God, the souereine iuge in the pursuyng of theire
right, hath euer gretely eured them herebefore and yeuen them many
40   worthy victories. Or ellis it shulde be said and demed, that the king had
no powere nor puissaunce to susteyn his right with. And so it semyth
vndere theire acquitaile (vndere the noble correccion abouesaide), that
the said taking offre and appointement were none honorabil to the king
but gretely to the worship and auauntage of his enemies and aduersaries.
45   Item. And in cas that the kyng be counseiled for the good of pees to
take any tretie or allie hym be mariage with his aduersaries of Fraunce,
hit semyth (vndere the noble correccion abouesaid), that he aught to be
aduertised and haue right gret aduis and take grete exsample of diuers
treties that haue be made in tyme passed in Fraunce with his worthy
50   progenitours, as with King Richard Cuere de Lion, with King Edward
the last, and now late with noble King Harry, his fadere, of the tretie of
pees finall. And also sieth now, in the kingis owne daies, of the tretie and
appoyntement made at Amyenx betwixt his vncle, my lord of Bedford,
and the dukis of 'Burgoyn and' of Bretaigne, and also the treties made |
f. 39ʳ semblabely with the king of Nauarre in Fraunce herebefore. Which all
56   treties, notwithstonding any lettres, seales, othes, sacramentes or promises, were euer sone aftirwarde brokin by colourid dissimilacions and
disseitis of the aduerse party, at all tymes whan thei cowd take or auise

23 the othyr . . . avi] *WW over eras. in own addn;* gode *uneras. adjacent*
29–30 lordys . . . concelle] *WW mostly over eras., with* elle *interl.*   54 Burgoyn
and] *WW at the end of the l.*

thaire auauntage; and the kingis men and also the kingis of Nauarre
put oute of Fraunce and Normandie and thaire placis taken opon them 60
bothe, be sieges, bi puissaunce and bi tresons; and no[r] neuere no
tretie nere appointement kepte bi the party aduersarie, whereas was to
supp'ose' more faith, stabilnes and trouth in them that tyme than can
be demed in them this day for many causes, as shewith openly, etc.

Item. And therfore it semyth (vndere the noble correccion aboue- 65
saide), that the king with all his myght and powere and with all his helpe
and allies shulde susteyne his right and title that he hath in the corone
of Fraunce, which he standith this day possessid of; not hauyng nor
taking rewarde vnto the clamour of the peple, which of nature loue his
aduersarie more than hym, nor for wasting of the contrey, for bettir is a 70
contrey to be wasted for a tyme than lost; ner to departe frome his right
be tretie and wilfully disherite hymsilf, his heiris and all his successours
aftere hym, and bi assignacion and limitacion of his aduersaries to take
a parte of his enheritaunce as Normandie alonly and yet to holde it as
suget to his said aduersarie and to stond in auenture daily to lese it be 75
subtill mene of his ennemies, as hath be done vnto his worthy and noble
predecessours aforetyme; but rathere to abide the aduenture that God
shulde like to sende in the defence and pur| suing of his right; which, f. 39ᵛ
though it be turned contrarie—that God defende—his name, his right
and his title wolde abide; than be the said offre and tretie agre to his 80
disheriting wilfully, for any distruccions of contreis that myght befall;
for parauenture God of his grace and rightwisnes myght send the king
soche on goode day among many, that all his right shulde be recouered
be iugement of God.

Item. And in case that the king conclude not to the werre, be his high 85
wisdome, noble and discrete counseile, yt is thought (vndere the good
correccion abouesaide), than that his right myght be put in iugement
of certeyn nombre of men of Holy Chirch and of Cristen kingis and
princes, and to abide thaire ordynaunce and iugement, rathere to leve
and departe frome his right and coroune of Fraunce bi the offre and 90
request of his ennemies and aduersaries; notwithstanding that he hath
no souuerayn in erth that may be his iuge ner knoueth none erthely man
that hym aught to put his right in iugement nere in determynacion of,
sauyng at his owne pleasure and will.

Item. In cas that the king leue the said appoyntment and tretie 95
and take hym to the werre, oolesse than the werre were and myght
be puissantly susteined and borne oute and contenued, and therby

61 nor] non   63 supp'ose'] scr. ose over eras.   82 king] kingis

his ennemyes myghtly oppressid and rebuked, yt is thought (vndere
the noble correccion abouesaide), that there myght fall and come
100 therof right grete inconuenient both in England and in Fraunce specially, yef fortune turned with th'ennemyes ayens the kinge—which
f. 40ʳ God defende—or | ellis, of lak of a grete and myghty puissaunce,
th'ennemyes gate any auauntage or distrusse opon the kingis peple.

Item. And in cas the king conclude to the werre, yt is thought expedi-
105 ent (vndere the noble correccion abouesaide), that, aftere that the case
stondith now, that the werre shulde be demened and con[d]ui[t]e[d]
in the manere that foloueth for the auauncement of his conquest and
distruccion of his ennemies.

First, it semyth (vndere the noble correccion abouesaid), that the
110 king shuld doo ley no sieges nere make no conquest oute of Normandie,
or to conquest be way of siege as yet. For the sieges hath gretely hindred
his conquest in tyme passed and distruyd his peple, as well lordis, capetaines and chieftaines as his othere peple, and wasted and consumed
inumerable good of his finaunces bothe in England and in Fraunce
115 and of Normandie. For there may no king conquere a grete reaume be
continuell siegis, and specially seing the habillementis and ordinaunces
that beth this day vsed for the werre and the knoulege and experience
that the ennemyes haue theryn, both in keping of there placis and otherwise; and also the fauoure that thei fynde in many that shulde be the
120 kingis true sugettis. Wherefor (vnder the noble correccion abouesaide)
it is thought right expedient, for the spede and the auauncement of the
kingis conquest and distruyng of his ennemies, to ordeyn two notable
chieftains, discrete and of one accorde, hauyng eithere of them .vijᶜ. l.
speris of well-chosen men; and thei to holde the felde contynuelly and
125 oostay and goo vi., viij. or x. lekis asondre in brede, or more or lesse
f. 40ᵛ aftere there discre| cion. And iche of hem may answere to othere and
ioigne togithers in cas of necessite. And that thei begyn to oostay frome
the first day of Iuyne contynuelly vnto the first day of Nouembre, landing for the first tyme at Cales or at Crotay or the tone at Caleis and the
130 tothere at Crotay, as shal be thought expedient, and so holding forth
there way thorough Artois and Picardie and so thorough Vermandoys,
Lannoys, Champaigne and Bourgoyne, brennyng and distruyng all the
lande as thei pas, both hous, corne, viegnes and all treis that beren
fruyte for mannys sustenaunce; and all bestaile that may not be dry-
135 uen to be distroied, and that that may be well dryuen and spared euer

the sustenaunce and aduitailling of the ostis, to be dryuen into Normandie, to Paris and to othere placis of the kingis obeissaunce, and if
goodely them thinke it to be doone. For it is thought that the traitours
and rebellis must nedis haue anothere manere of werre and more sharpe
and more cruell werre than a naturell and an[c]ien ennemye; or els be   140
liklines in proces of tyme no manere of man ner tounes ner countreis
shall reke nere shame to be traitours nere to rebell causeles ayens theire
souuereyn lorde and ligeaunce at all tymes aftere theire owne wilfull
[h]edi[ne]s.

Item. It is thought that it is nedefull to send into Normandie .v^C.   145
speris, to be set vppon the borders and to make werre opon Anyou and
Mayne and Chartraine, and also for to holde Britayne in suggestion, and
to releue and ioing with the garnisons of Normandie, there it shulde be
nedefull.

Item. It is thought (vndere the noble correccion abouesaide), that   f. 41^r
none of the chieftains shuld in no wise raunsone, appatise ner fauour   151
no contre nor place that thei passe thorough, for no singuler lucre nor
profite of themsilfe; but that thei doo and execute duely that that thei
come fore. And it semeth veraly that be these weies and gouernaunce
the king shall conquere his reaume of Fraunce and greue and distruye   155
his ennemyes and saue his peple and his soldiours and yeue them grete
courage to the werre; and shall cause the citeis, tounes and contreis that
be rebellid causeles fayne to seche vnto his grace; and shall yeue also
grete exsample to all thayme that bith this day in his obeissaunce to
kepe allweies of theire trouthis.   160

Item. It is thought (vndere the noble correccion abouesaide), that
the king may and aught resonablye make all this cruell werre without
any noote of tirannye, seing that he hath offered vnto his aduersaries,
as a goode Cristen prince, that all men of Holy Chirche and also the
comyns and labourers of the reaume of Fraunce duelling or being oute   165
of forteresse shuld duell in seuerte pesible without werre or prince;
but that the werre in eithere partie shuld be rest alonly betwixt men
of werre and men of werre; the which offre the said aduersaries haue
vtterly refused and be concluded to make theire werre cruell and sharpe
without sparing of any parsone.   170

Item. It is thought (vndere the noble correccion abouesaide), that
the saide chieftains shuld haue with them all manere ordinaunces | for   f. 41^v
the felde as ribaudekyns, culueryns, artillerye; wode-axes, hachettis and

140 ancien] anoien (see n.)   142 reke nere] rekenere (see n.)   144 hedines]
ediens (see n.)   146 borders] borderers

billis to cutte viegnes and trees with; gonners, carpinters and othere
175 men of necessarie for the conduyt of the saide ordinaunces; without
that the said chieftains shulde lay any siege or make any assautis but if
the placis were right prenable; and yet than to kepe no maner of place,
if it happenid any to be won, but it were a notable passage opon som
of the grete ryuers of Fraunce or ellis a notable key of the lande, which
180 myght be puissantly kept bi the werre without charge to the king.

Item. If any man wolde ymagine that th'ennemies wolde make the
same werre vnto the contreis of the kingis obeissaunce, (vnder the noble
correccion abouesaide) yt is thoughte, nay, but that thei shulde be kepte
right well therefrome, so that the garisons be well stuffed and purueied
185 of paymentis, and that the lieftenauntis and gouuernours of the lande be
lose frome sieges and may ride frome place to place and assemble both
garnesons and the peple of the contreys at all tymes of necessite; which
hauyng comfort of the garnisons wolde gladly defende themsilfe rather
than to suffre thaym to be brente. Notwithstanding that th'ennemyes
190 haue fully determyned amongis them, as it is said, that if the king accept
not there offre at the day to entre into the contreis of his obeissaunce
and to bren and to distroie, and the vttermost and the worst that thei
can or may, as thei haue late begonne in Normandie, and so, be that
mene, to put oute the king and his men of werre oute of this lande, and
f. 42ʳ that thei shuld haue no vitaile theryn nere aide of his peple | to pay and
196 sustene them with.

Item. It is thought (vndere the noble correccion abouesaide), that
this werre shulde be continued fourth still puissantly iij. yere day at the
leste, to th'entent to driue th'ennemies therbie to an extreyme famyn;
200 and to begyn yerelie at the sesons in the manere abouesaide; to be
emploied in soche contreis as shal be thought most expedient, and speciallie whereas there most sustenaunce, both of theire vitaile and of
theire finaunces; and as shal be aduised be the king and his counseile.
And in this wise, it is thought that the king may make and sustene this
205 said werre iij. yere day fully, in the sesons aforsaide, with the wagis of
one yere and a quarter to pay for euery yere .v. monthis wagis only.

Item, that seing that the king hath his portis and hauen tounes and
his lordis on eithere side of the see, that it may be ordeined (vnder the
noble correccion abouesaide), that the see may be kepte myghtelie, as
210 well for the kingis worship and the reaumes, as for the saluacion of
the marchaundise and of the nauy of Englonde and of Normandie; and
that euerie towne of Englonde and of Normandie set therto hand and

helpe forth, now considering how thei haue be faren with foule and
distroied long tyme herebefore be th'ennemies vppon the see; and that
the said nauye make sharpe warre and kepe the cours of marchaun-   215
dice, as moche as thei can or may, fro Scluse, vndere soche prouision of
admiralles of bothe landis, that thei be not suffred to take nere robbe the
king[is] verray trew frendis and auncien allies instede of th'ennemies. |

Item. (Vnder the noble correccion abouesaide) yt is thought expedi-   f. 42ᵛ
ent, that the king ordeyne that frome hensforth al manere of traitours   220
attaint of treson be ponysshed rigereuslie, and that no priuelage of clergie saue thayme, as hath be vsed herebefore, but that the baillies doo
vnto thaym vppon iustice after there cas and demeritis, and liche as ye
vsed in Englonde.

Item. It is thought (vnder the noble correccion abouesaide), that if   225
the forsaide chieftains doo well there deuoire and duelie execute theire
charge the first yere, that than the king shuld can them thanke, with
grete worship and cherisshing and rewarde of hym and of the reame,
and so to sende them agayne the next yere aftere; and if thei execute
not there charge, to change them and sende othere.   230

Item. It is thought (vndere the noble correccion abouesaide), that the
king shulde make alliaunces with Venise and with Iene speciallie for
vttering of the wullis of Englande, wherin the reaume shall euer haue
redie outeraunce of there wullis; and also the keping of the see well-
helpen and strenghted be the saide alliaunce. And Flaundres shal be   235
pouresshid and lie the lesse in there powere to helpe the Duke Burgoyne
with goode and finaunce to susteyne his werre. And also that England
shuld feith for the king and the reaume othere alliaunces with all soche
othere landis, both of old frenship and othere, as shal be thought expedient, and mo than thei haue vsed to doo in tyme passed. For ellis   240
it wolde be thought that the leuyng of soche alliaunces is done of grete
pride and outrecuidaunce, and setting noo store be none othere mannes
frenship; or ellis it is done of to grete slouthe and | negligence of the wise   f. 43ʳ
men of the lande. And which thing hath done grete harme herebefore
and yet doith day[li]e grete damage bothe in the helpyng forthe of the   245
kingis werris and in furthering of his rightfull title.

Item. In cas that it be aduised to lay any siege to any place, it is
thought (vnder the noble correccion abouesaide), that in the meane-
while it be purueied for a puissaunce redy that myght, if nede were,
releve and socoure the siege and also the kingis placis, in cas that   250

---

213 foule] fou | led *over the l. break* (*see n.*)   218 kingis] king   234 wullis]
late 16th- or early 17th-c. hand in marg. woolles   245 daylie] day be (*see n.*)

th'ennemyes wolde lay any othere siege to any of them or that thei
gate be treson or be scaling any place of the kingis, whereas there were
a castel or a donion or toure kept, that myght be hastelie rescowed
ayen[e] be the said puissaunce, and th'ennemies put frome there
255 entirprise, and the kingis siege not raised.

Item. It is thought (vnder the noble correccion abouesaide), that
be this manere, and hauyng the saide ordinaunces for the felde, if
th'ennemys wolde yeve bataile, it shulde 'not' lie in there powere to
fight on horsebak but as the chois of the saide chieftains; and also that
260 all tounes and castels shall [be] famyn be fayne to seche the kingis
grace or ellis to yeue bataile on foote, as thei were wont to done.

Item. It is thought right nedefull (vndere the noble correccion abouesaide), that with all diligence in the grete tounes of this lande that haue
no castellis be made a strenght and a forte for to rescow them bie, as hath
265 bene Vernueile, Mans, Diepe, Eu, Hareflew, Mante, Pontoise, Monster-
uylers, Eureux, Coustances and othere. Or ellis thei woll euermore rebel
with the biggist of the felde; the which streynghtis and fortificacions in
f. 43ᵛ euery of these | placis abouesaide woll be made and done with right
resonable coste.

270 Item, that the king ordeine in this lande sufficient counseiles of Englisshemen expert and knouyng them in the werre; and that the werre
may be counseiled and gouuerned bi [them] speciallie, and not it to
be demened so moche be the Frenshe counseile, as hath be done herebefore.

TEXT 3

ARTICLES OF THE COUNCIL OF
RICHARD, DUKE OF YORK, 1440

f. 44ʳ 'Here folowen othyr aduertys'men''tys and instruccions concernyng
the werre made and avysed by the grete deliberacion of the chieff
councelle of the ''ryght'' hygh and myghty prince, Rychard, duc of
York, beyng made gouuernaunt of the royaume of Fraunce: that ys to
5 weete, ''Ser'' Iohn Fastolf, Ser William Oldhall, Ser William ap Thomas,

---

254 ayene] ayens   258 not] scr. over eras.   260 be famyn] famyn (see
n.)   272 them speciallie] speciallie (see n.)   273 hath] he hath   1–7 Here
folowen ... Hery the .VJ.] WW in the top marg.   aduertys'men''tys] men WW over eras.
in own addn   3 ryght] WW interl. into own addn   5 Ser] WW interl.

knyghtys, and othyrs of hys "discrete" councelle, at hys second voyage
goyng ynto Fraunce wyth a greete armee the .x"viij" yere of Kyng Hery
the .VJ.;' 'toke the charge from "the ij. day of Iulle the xviij yere of
Herry the .VJ^{te}. vnto the yere of" Crist at the Fest of Myghell the yere
of Crist M^l. iiij^C. xlv.'   10

Articles of the declaracion of my lorde of Yorkis entent, vppon certain suche articles as ye haue now late, vnto my lordis of the king, oure
souueraine lordis, counseile; with other which my said lorde desireth
to haue grauntid hym and to be parfourmed for his going into Fraunce.
The names of soche lordis and knightis as my said lorde desireth shulde 15
be entretid on oure said souueraine lordis behalue, or iiij. or iij. [of]
them, that is to say, of euereche astate one to attende and assiste in
the kingis counceile in Fraunce and in Normandie for the goode publique of the same: the bisshop of Lincoln, the bisshop of Norwiche, the
bisshop of Salisbury, the vicount of Beaumont, the Lord Hungerford,   20
the Lord Faunhop, Sire Rauffe Bouteller, Sire Iohn Stourton, Sire Iohn
Popham.

First, as touching my said lordis powere of Yorke. He desireth, if it
please the kingis good grace, to haue like and semblable power as my
lord of Bedforde had by comission at the kingis last departing oute of 25
Fraunce, or as my lord of Gloucestre had or shulde haue had now late.
And for the declaracion of more ample powere, yf the cas required yt,
conteyned in othere of my said lordes articles, my said lord vnderstode
it but only for the duke of Bretaigne, in cas that he made any new alliaunce with the king, that my said lorde myght call hym and his sugettis 30
to his helpe and ayde in cas of necessite, like as he wolde desire ayde
and helpe of my said lorde, as for the king in his necessite and generally
for all othere that stande or be like to stande with the king in like case. |

Item, as touching continuacion forth of my said lorde being in f. 44^V
Fraunce and in Normandie for the terme of .v. yere after his endenting. 35
As he hath be answerde in his other articles, yt hath liked the king,
be the aduis of my lordis of his noble counseile, to apoint my saide
lorde for the second yere and so forthe yerelie during the saide terme
the somme of xx. M^1. liures of the kingis finaunce and reuenue out
of Englond for th'entretenement and seuerte, defence and sauuegarde 40
of that lande of Fraunce and of Normandie to be treuly deliuered and
paid yerelie vnto my saide lorde of Yorke, or to his officers comytted

6 discrete] WW adds before the l. in marg. of own addn, partly over eras. word
7 .x"viij"] viij WW over eras. in own addn   8–10 toke . . . M^l. iiij^C. xlv.] WW adds
to his prev. addn, in a different ink, continuing in the marg.   8–9 the . . . yere of]
WW over eras. in own addn   16 of them] them

and ordeined thervnto in his name. Of the which somme my said lord
desireth to haue so the seuerteis and assignacions of payment as may
45   be truly kepte and holden hym; and the saide good in no wise to be
emploied to none othere wise, so that for defaute therof he may haue
no cause to leue the kingis seruice there. And in cas that during the
said terme there fall a pees or a sure abstinence of werre in Normandie,
than that the king may rebate yerely of the said som as shal be thought
50   resonable for the well of hymsilff and seuerte of his lande; and in
that cas my saide lord of Yorke to haue resonable warnyng and to be
entretide with in the matiere on the kingis behalue, as he can accorde
therto; and in cas also of grete werre or laieng of grete sieges, for the
which grettire prouision aught to be desired, my saide lorde of Yorke
55   to haue also of the king gretter aide, helpe and socours after, as the cas
may or shall require.

Item, as touching my saide lordis estate for his housolde. Notwithstanding the grete repaire of peple and countrees that dailie shall resorte
vnto hym, for the grete desire that he hath to do the kingis seruice [he]
60   holdeth hym content, if it plese the king, with the somme of xxxvj. M^l. |
f. 45^r frankis, which is xij M^l frankis lesse than my lord of Bedforde toke
laste there for his estate, and but vj. M^l frankis more than my lorde of
Warwike toke.

Item, as touching ordonaunce, artillerie and abillementis of werre.
65   My saide lorde desireth that it like the king of his goode grace to doo
puruey hym of .vj. grete gonnes of diuers sortis; and for euery gonne
.iiij. douzaines of stones of Maideston stone, with xij. grete foulers
fournysshe semblably with like stones; and also xij last of saltpetire
with the brimstone according therto; seyng and considering that in all
70   Normandie is none or right litill nethere for stuffe of the garnisons ner
for the felde; and also xij. gonners, .ij. maistre gonners and xij yemen
gonners.

Item, that my saide lorde be purueied semblabelie of .M^l. speres-
shaftes, .iiij. M^l bowes, .xij M^l sheuys of arowes, .CC. groos of stringis,
75   .CC. of long paueis of ordonnaunce and .ij. M^l. of lede, with cartis and
cariage competent bothe for the cariage herof and also for the gonnes,
stones and poudres aboue-rehersid.

Item. My saide lorde desireth, that it like the king of his goode
grace for the grete well of bothe his royau[m]es to ordeyn, charge and
80   comaunde specially the capptaines which, as it is saide, be appointed to
goo this yere to kepe the see, that thei entende diligently to the keping

59–60 he holdeth] holdeth   79 royaumes] roy *and abbrev.* nes

of the mouth of Sayne, as well for letting and empeschement of the
vitailing of Hareflewe as for the seure going of vesselx and vitaillers
vnto Rouen; and also that thei woll lette and distourbe vppon the same
coost all the hering-fisshing of Diepe, which is the grettist comforte   85
and riches that the same towne hath and the grettist aduitailing of all
the tounes and contreis of the aduerse partie. And in cas that my said
lorde be aduised to lay siege before Hareflew, Diepe | or any othere   f. 45ᵛ
place vppon the coste of that side of the see, that it like the king to
doo ordeyne and pourueie an arme of .ij. Mˡ. men vppon the see to   90
kepe any of the saide sieges be the see, vnder a notable captaine or
two which in cas of necessite, as for rescous and bataile, myght be the
comaundement of my saide lord lande and acompaignie and strenght
hym, as the necessite shulde or myght require.

Item. My saide lorde of Yorke desireth to haue fre licence to tarie   95
whete and othere vitailles, paieng therfore as the parties and his officers
may accord, as often as the necessite shall require, as well for the vitailing of tounes of sieges as otherewise; and to haue for the said vitaile
fre shipping and passage without any letting of oure souuerain lord the
king or of any of his officers during the tyme of my saide lordis abiding 100
in the kingis saide seruice, notwithstanding any act or statute made of
the contrarie.

Item. If it fortune my saide lord to die in the kingis, oure said souueraine lordis, seruice on that side of the see or to be empeschid or lettid be
sekenes or other caus ayenst his will, so that he may not fully parfourme 105
the kingis entent touching the said seruice during the terme that he shal
be witholden fore, that neithere my saide lorde ner his heiris nor execu-
tours be not compellid to restore the money, the which he shall receiue
of the king for hym and his retenue [b]ecause of his saide seruice, nor
none acompt to make therof in any wise.   110

Item. My saide lorde desireth, if it like the kingis goode grace, that
he may haue to goo with hym into the saide parties a notable nombre
of knyghtis, squiers, yemen and othere parsones of the kingis housolde,
soche as may be forborn | and entretid; and that at there comyng ayene   f. 46ʳ
they may be receiued to there seruices and offices and better recomaun-   115
ded vnto oure said souuereine lorde good grace, because of thaire grete
labours and goingis.

Item, if any of th'appointementis aboue-rehersed and all othere
which at this tyme haue be made betwix the king, be th'aduis of his
counceile, and my said lord of Yorke touching his going into Fraunce,   120

109 because] se cause   119 king] king lord (see n.)

be brokyn and not fulfilled nor parfourmed in any point, and the
king and the lordis of his counseile certiffied and notiffied therof, that
than in soche cas my saide lorde of Yorke may be at his fredome and
liberte for to departe thens and to retourne ayene into this reaume
125 of Englond with the king, oure souuereine lorde, goode lordship, and
without that any empeschement, charge or blame may be laied opon
hym therfore or his heiris hereafter in any wise be the king or his heiris,
what inconuenient that euer fall to that lande aftere and opon his saide
departing frome thens—which God defende.

130   Item, that it please vnto the king, oure souuerayne lorde, to be
aduertised and take tendre consideracion that, the first halue-yere of
the seruice of my lorde of Yorke and of his retenue doone and expired,
yt is thing vncertaine and doubtefull how and in what wise and what
placis he shall lay all soche lordis and notabill capitaines, which of
135 his saide retenue he shall holde togithers and kepe with hym in that
lande for the seuerte and sauffgard therof and the recouueraunce of
the kingis inheritaunce and grounde of the same; seing that the grettist
partie of the capitaineries of the most notable tounes and placis in
that lande, which the said halue-yere done shuld be retrait for the
f. 46ᵛ said captaines and | there feleshippes, be yeuen, some for terme of
141 lyfe and some of thayme for terme of certain yeris; which thing well
peised, withouten that the more conuenient remedie be had theropon,
is gretely ayenst the kingis conquest of that land, like as is supposed
that bi cours of laps of tyme it shall openly be parceiued and knouen.
145 For it hath be sene herebefore that soche parsones that haue hadde like
chargis and capitaineries for terme of yeres haue for theire singuler
and particuler lucre laten them to ferme and haue not bene resident
vppon them but contynuelly be here in Englande, not labouring nor
emploieng theire parsones in the kingis seruices, ner nothing doone
150 for the well of his conquest. Wherefore my said lord desireth that 'it'
like to oure said souuerain lord highnes that, for the well of hymsilffe
and of the goode publique of that reaume, in cas that any soche lordis,
knightis, squiers, whatsoeuer thei be, haue any soche graunt of the said
capitaneries or of any othere charge within that reaume for terme of
155 liffe or for certaine yeres, be not continuellie resident vppon thaire said
chargis, or ellis that thei be not surelie kept for the sauffgarde of them
and the well of oure said souueraine lorde and his trew suggettis and
his liege-peple within thayme, and also that the termes and graunte of
the saide capitaneries or of any other of the saide chargis within that

150 it] scr. interl.

reaume expired and ended, my said lord of York may prouide, comitte 160
and ordonne notable capetaines vnto the keping of the same placis and
chargis, soche as be his discrecion he shall think most expedient for
the seuirte and sauffegarde of thaime; considering that, if for defaute
of politique | gouuernaunce any inconuenient behapped to fall to any f. 47ʳ
of the saide placis or charges, whiles my saide lorde shulde stonde 165
the kingis lieuten[aunt] there—which God defende—grete noise and
charge shulde be laied therfore in grete partie ayenst hym.

Item, that it please the kingis goode grace to graunte that, in cas
that any inconuenient fall to the saide reaume and duchie—which God
defende—during the tyme of my saide lord, the duke, charge and abid- 170
ing there, bee it be bataile, rebellion of the peuple or otherewise—God
forbede—my saide lorde the duke putting hym and doing alway his deuoure, the said inconuenient be not laied vpon hym in no wise; but that
he and his heiris stande and be vtterly discharged therof ayens the king
and his heiris for euermore.   175

Item, that my said lorde may haue as many lettris vnder the kingis
Grete and Priue Seales as shal be thought to hym and his counseile in
any wise necessarie or behouefull, vppon euereche of th'articles aboue-
reherced, withouten any difficulte to be made in any wise.

TEXT 4

SIR JOHN FASTOLF'S INSTRUCTIONS TO EDMUND
BEAUFORT, DUKE OF SOMERSET, MARCH 1448

These bene the aduertismentis and instruccions youen and made vnto f. 47ᵛ
the noble prince Edmond Beauford, duke of Somerset, lieuetenaunt
and gouuernour generall of Fraunce and Normandie vnder the king,
declared before his going ouer into Fraunce and Normandie, aduised be
Sire Iohn Fastolffe in the month of Marche the xxvj. yere of the reigne 5
of King Harry the Sexte, ʿwhych instruccions, and they ʿʿmyght hafe be
parformed" had ben the safegard of the seyd lond.'

First, it is thought right necessarie (sauyng the goode correccion
of you, my lorde, and of youre counsaile), that ye make you seure of
youre trew and stedfast alliaunce of youre kynne and stedfast frendis in 10

166 lieutenaunt] lieu | tene *over the l. break (see n.)*   6–7 whych . . . lond] *WW*
adds after 1st parag. and in marg.   myght . . . parformed] *WW interl. into own addn,*
above had be well kept *deleted by underlining*

stedfast feith and loue to the kingis wele and the welfare of his royaume,
that thei may in youre absence laboure and quyte hem truly vnto you,
as nature, reason and trouth wolle, in supportacion of the kingis right
and of youre trouth, yff any charge in tyme comyng myght be ymagined
15 ayenst you; and that ye purueie you of wise and sadde counseile in this
royalme of soche as may, can or dare done for you in youre absence.

Item. It is thought (sauyng the correccion beforesaide), vppon the
wise and sewre conueieng of the appointement to be made with the kingis counceill in what fourme ye shall be paid without any appointement
20 breking, and the termes truly holden, and to considre what inconuenientis myght fall for the defaute of payment.

Item. It is to be thought, vppon that there be ordeined a wise and a
f. 48ʳ discrete chaunceller, a man of astate, assigned and ioined vnto | hym
sadde and wise counseile, nought couetous ne parciall but egall, right-
25 wiselie to obserue and kepe iustice that may be to the kingis worship,
relefe, increce of the goode comons; that there may, be soche menes as
ye and thei may accord, confourme them to all soche reason and ordinaunces as may be to the kingis worship, auauncement and welfare of the
lande; and that the kingis counseile there be sworne that thei shall not
30 fauoure no persone there, of what degre he ben, more one then othere,
but that the trouthe may bene inquired and knowen of the demenyng
and gouuernaunce of euery man, and after as thei haue demened hem
in here offices, soo to be sene too, as the case shall require.

Item, that ye be purueied or youre departing oute of this lande to
35 haue goode and notable captains, discrete and konnyng in the werre,
nought couetous oppressours ner extorcioners and soche as can and
dare reule there peple vnderneth hem in iustice-keping, good reule and
gouernaunce on the felde; and that thei bee soche men as woll not
enriche hemsilffe but vppon the kingis ennemies, if it fortune so that
40 it fall to werre, not lieng nor charging opon the contre but dailie paieng
for theire vitaile, in no wise abbregging her souldeours wages.

Item, that it be purueied fore here in England of ordinaunce for the
felde, al maner thing that longith to the werre as speres, bowes, arowes,
axes, malles, ridbawdkyns and all other stuffe necessarie, so that noth-
45 ing be to seke in that parties, if the case shall require; and that all youre
principall places be stuffed of all manere of artillerie, furnysshid with
vitaile for all manere doubtes, so that thei may be the more abillere to
f. 48ᵛ contynew and resiste youre | ennemies in caas of necessite, etc., and as
well for the felde as for the forteresses.

50 Item, that all soche places as bene frontures vppon the marches, as

Pounthorson, Aueraunshes and other places which may be goode frontures, be fortiffied and repaired sufficeauntlie that thei may be strong
and abill to resiste the kingis ennemies; and that to all the saide places,
which bene goode frontures vppon the see coost in especiall as well
as vppon the londe, be chosen suche notabill captains as can and woll 55
vndertake to leefe and purueie there liuelode vppon the frountours
and vppon the marches, which shal be assigned vnto them, finding
you a certeine noumbre of men of armes to the felde, when ye woll
require hem, after the [a]fer[r]aunt of his fronture and the auaile of his
apatismentis.   60

   Item, that there be assigned and chosen a notable knyght to be lieutenaunt vnder you for the gouuernaunce of Gaskyn and Gyenne; and
that the king hable the said knight to th'entent, that ye shall not be
charged therwith, whatsoeuer fall to that parties inasmoche as neithere
of you may not lightlie relefe and socoure other, if the case require it. 65

   Item, that of the poortes of the see there, as Hareflew, Hunflew, Crotey, Chirborgh and other being in oure obeissaunce, be purueied a nauie
of shippes to helpe resiste ayenst youre ennemies, when it shall nede,
forsean alway that be the admiralle of Englonde and Normandie the see
be well kepte becaus of conveieng of vitaile and for comyng ouersee of 70
souldeours, when it shal be necessarie.

TEXT 5

SIR JOHN FASTOLF'S ADVICE ON
RELIEVING THE DUKE OF SOMERSET, 1450

'Here folowen othyr articles of aduertissmentys and instruccions for the f. 49^r
werre and for the deffence and saf‵e″gard of the royaume of Fraunce
and ducdom off Normandye, the tyme that the ‵seyd noble″ prince
Emond, duc of Somerset, was made the kyng ys lieutenaunt generalle
‵for Fraunce and Normandye″ and was yn grete iubardye of hys per- 5
son and ‵yn doubt of″ losyng of all that contree. Whych articles were
made by the seyd Ser Iohn Fastolf, knyght, ‵(vnder correccion)″ beyng

   59 aferraunt] feruaunt (see n.)   1–21 Here folowen . . . Herry VJ^{tc}.] WW adds,
in blank space above, continuing in right marg.   1 Here] WW in marg. abbrev. for
capitulum   2 saf‵e″gard] WW e over uneras. letter   3 seyd noble] WW in
different ink over eras. in own addn   5 for . . . Normandye] WW interl. in different
ink into own addn after and   6 yn doubt of] WW interl. in different ink into own
addn   7 vnder correccion] WW interl. in different ink into own addn

then of the kyng ys grete councelle "yn England": whate provysyon and
ordenaunce were moste necessarye to be conduyt and had for such a
10 cheveteyn, as most be deputed and assigned yn alle goodely haste to goo
wyth a new armee ynto Normandie for to relyeff and socour the forseyd
kyng ys lieutenaunt gener"a"lle, beyng beseged at Caen by Charlys the
.VIJ., the kyng ys grete aduersarye. And yt semyth that yn deffaut of
the sa"y"d auertisment "were" not kept, Ser Thomas Kyriell, kny3t, the
15 kyng ys lieutenaunt made for the feelde, was destrussed at the infortune
iorn"e"y of Fermynye in Normandie or he came to the kyng ys lieutenaunt generall, "as yt was seyd th[en]", by dyvyson and contrauersye
of hys pety capteyns negligently tary[ng] yn Normandie at her landyng
and sped hem not "w"yth hys armee to goo spedlye to the seyd Emond
20 Duc, the kyng ys lieutenaunt generalle. And so was the losse off all
Normandye the xxviij yere of Ky"ng" Herry VJ^te.'

In aduertisyng yow, my lordis, obeieng your comaundement, yt
is thought (vnder youre noble correccion), that it is first necessarie
that this armie, which is first now appointed, be in alle haste possible
25 ordeyned to goo forthe with the nombre of peple thei haue endentid
for, and with as many moo thei haue be ordeined to goo after, to the
nombre of .iij. M^l fighters at the leest; in the menetyme that the grete
armie and puissaunce may be made redie for the felde, and this in
all haste possible without any delaie. The captaynes that thus shall
30 first goo to haue in comaundement that, after here landing there to
be gouuerned, as shall be thought most necessary by the kingis lieu-
f. 49^v tenaunt and gouuernour there, | thei to obbeie his ordinaunce, as he
woll reule or assigne hem, to be demened as may be moost aduaileable
be the saide lieutenauntes grete wisdome, as the avice of the kingis
35 grete counceile there.

Item. In cas it fortuned—as God defend—the saide captaines were
lettid be the grete puissaunce of th'ennemies or otherwise that thei
myght not come to the saide lieutenaunt as thei wolde, that then thei to
see to the purueaunce for the sauffegarde of Cane, Harflew, Hounflue
40 and other placis, which as may abide the comyng of the saide grete puissaunce, thei in the menetyme to emploie hem and doo there power for

8 yn England] WW interl. in different ink into own addn   12 gener"a"lle]
one-compartment a changed to two-compartment a   by] by the, with the crossed out
14 sa"y"d] a unclear; WW squeezes y between other letters in different ink   were] WW
interl. into own addn, after ys crossed out   16 iorn"e"y] WW e over uneras. letter
17 as yt was seyd then] WW interl. into own addn; th incomplete   18 tary[ng]
tary, with ng perhaps faded and trimmed at the page edge   19 "w"yth] WW w over
uneras. letter   21 Ky"ng"] WW ng over uneras. letters   22 In] WW in marg.
abbrev. for capitulum

the saufgarde of thoo placis and contreis, there where it shal be thought most nedefull.

Item. As for the grete puissaunce that shall come after and kepe the felde to the socoure and saufgarde of the londe, yt is thought that for the said grete puissaunce must be intretid be the kingis highnes a chevetaine of noble and grete astate, hauyng knoulege and experience of the werres; with hym to be ordeined in companye notable lordis and captaines, with soche a noble puissaunce as may be abill to kepe the felde and to resiste the myght and power of the kingis aduersaries; the said chevetaine chargyng his lordis and captaines to see that here souldeours be trulie paide of here wagis soo that they haue no caus to compleine, robbe nor pille the kingis liege-peple there.

Item, that the said chieveteyne haue two lordis for to be his constable and marchal of his hooste—well-ensured knyghtis that afore this tyme haue had grete knoulege and experience in the werris—to gouuerne his hooste in executing of the lawes of armes and soche ordenaunces as shal be thought most necessarie be the saide | chieveteine.

Item, that the saide chieveteyne ordene before his departing oute of Englande to be stuffed of ordynaunces for the felde, as in all maner thingis that longith to the werre: that is to say, speres, bowes, arowes, axes, malles, gonnes, ridbaudekins and all other stuffe necessarie, so that nothing that may long to hym or his ooste be to seke when he is comyn into parties.

Item, that the admiralles of Englonde and Fraunce gyffe in comaundement and streitlie see, that the see be kepte and the portes in especiall bi a sufficient navie of shippes, in soche wise as the soudeours may haue sure conueieng at all tymes, as well for passage and comyng ouer as for conueiaunce of vitaile; the saide nauie to be ordeined as well at the portis on the other side the see, as Hounflue, Harflue, Crotay, Chirborough and soche other, as at any portis on this side the see, bothe as for the resseyuyng of the capteins that now be ordeined to goo and for the nombre that shall goo after, as for the saide chieveteine and his hooste, when thei be redie.

Item. And in especiall be the kingis highnes it be prouided, sene and ordeined, that atwixt the forsaide chevetaine and the saide lieutenaunt bee none debate ner enuy but in vnite and one accorde, not holding any oppinions that one myght contrarie anothere, as in making any appointement, ordinaunce or prouision other enterprises, otherwise

68 comyng] comiyng

80 then of one will and assent; thei to haue this in comaundement and
    streitlie charged be the king vppon theire ligeaunce.
        'Explicit ad presens hoc opusculum.'

    82 Explicit . . . opusculum] *WW in marg.*

APPENDIX

UNPRINTED MATERIAL
FROM THE CODICIL

Most of the Latin and macaronic documents in the Codicil (London, Lambeth Palace Library, MS 506) were printed by Joseph Stevenson in 1864, but he omitted three sections.[1] They are printed here for completeness of record.

The texts are lightly edited transcriptions (following policies set out in the Introduction). Where the documents are lists, the line breaks follow the manuscript, with a few silent corrections; a hanging indent is introduced for clarity. No emendations are made to correct the Latin, facts, figures, or names; the Index clarifies the identity of some names of people or places confusingly spelled. Where the scribe deliberately leaves a gap, it is recorded as (*gap*).

The frequent French words and the French title to Appendix 1 are italicized; most place names are not. While macaronic usage is often unmarked in documents of this period, here scribe B does remark on the difference of language (App. 2/36, App. 2/96). While it is debatable whether abbreviated forms can or even should be expanded as one language or another (e.g. *lanc'*, which could be Latin *lancea* or French *lance*),[2] in most cases here an expanded form somewhere suggests a preference. Scribe B's abbreviation *li t* for a unit of currency is expanded by him always as *liures turneys* but only in passages not printed here.[3]

---

[1] See *Wars in France*, ii. 529–607, as itemized on pp. xxxvi–xxxviii above.

[2] As argued by Laura Wright, 'Bills, Accounts, Inventories: Everyday Trilingual Activities in the Business World of Later Medieval England', in D. A. Trotter (ed.), *Multilingualism in Later Medieval Britain* (Cambridge, 2000), 149–56 at 149–51.

[3] Six times in various spellings: Codicil, ff. 19ʳ–20ᵛ, 24ᵛ. Also, Worcester twice expands as *liures turneys* (App. 3/17–18, App. 3/26), though once as *librarum turonencium* (App. 3/24).

London, Lambeth Palace Library, MS 506, ff. 8ʳ–11ʳ: the household and retinue of John, duke of Bedford, in France, 1422–35, and the knights and men-at-arms in Aquitaine, 1422–37.

These lists were copied by scribe B of the Codicil but were heavily revised with additions in the handwriting of William Worcester; the crossing out is also probably by him. Worcester added an additional title and further biographical facts and deleted some other comments. In places, scribe B or Worcester left a gap for names of people or places, something Worcester does frequently in his notebooks. Scribe C made a few alterations.

Stevenson omitted these lists from the documents he printed from the Codicil.[1] He instead printed, elsewhere in his anthology, an English translation of this list found in a sixteenth-century manuscript, London, British Library, Harley MS 782, ff. 52ᵛ–53ᵛ (here collated as H1); he also printed variants from a seventeenth-century copy of H1 into London, British Library, Harley MS 6166, ff. 69ᵛ–70ᵛ (here collated as H2).[2] As these later MSS offer only a translation, the collation in the textual apparatus here is selective: only from H1, except where the copyist of H2 reverts to the Codicil's text or makes a clarifying correction; and only of the omission, alteration, or rarely addition (see e.g. App. 1/31, App. 1/54) of substantive details. Variants are recorded from the seventeenth-century transcription in London, Society of Antiquaries, MS 41 (here collated as SA), in substantives only where they diverge from the text as corrected and altered in the Codicil. Where the text of the Codicil has been obliterated by a stain, we supply it from that transcription in SA.

In addition, in 1844 F. Dubosc printed a transcription of part of this text from a sixteenth-century quire of similar texts, which he saw in the archives at the Maison de Matignon at Torigni-sur-Vire, *département* of La Manche, Normandy (and now in a private collection).[3] Dubosc's source abbreviated the content only a little in early entries and then included after the mention of Richard Curson (App. 1/108) only two entries, out of order, Ralph Buxhale (App. 1/134) and John Clifton (App. 1/123). Dubosc's text does, however, include seven passages which in the Codicil were added by Worcester, including an abbreviated version of the French heading (in Dubosc's text: 'La declaration de la chevalerye de Jehan Regent de France duc de Bedford par l'espace de

---

[1] In *Wars in France* they would appear in the sequence from the Codicil on ii. 529.

[2] *Wars in France*, ii. 433–8, as noted in McFarlane, 'Worcester', 216 n. 107. For a brief description of BL, Harley MS 782, see Introduction, pp. xliv–xlv.

[3] F. Dubosc, 'Manuscrit inédit tiré des archives de la maison de Matignon', *Journal des Savants de Normandie* (Rouen, 1844), 52–61, 209–18 at 52–5. On the provenance, see Anne Curry, 'The Garrison Establishment in Lancastrian Normandy in 1436 according to Surviving Lists in Bibliothèque Nationale de France manuscrit français 25773', in Gary P. Baker, Craig L. Lambert, and David Simpkin (eds.), *Military Communities in Late Medieval England: Essays in Honour of Andrew Ayton* (Cambridge, 2018), 237–69 at 239.

treize ans': cf. App. 1/1–3 below) and biographical details about six figures.[4]
Either Worcester added them to the Codicil to correct omissions in scribe
B's copy of a prior exemplar, from which Dubosc's text independently descended, or Dubosc's source descended, at whatever remove, from the Codicil
with Worcester's alterations. Interestingly, among the entries that Dubosc's text
omits earlier in the document are four which are damaged badly on the page
of the Codicil (App. 1/65–8), just as some such are omitted in H1 (as noted in
the Introduction, pp. xliv–xlv). Dubosc's manuscript also contained App. 2 of
the Codicil (as noted below). But as the original manuscript of his transcription
could not be traced, and as it omits a lot, it has not been collated here.

f. 8ʳ `Le declaracion de la cheualry du Iohan, regent du royaume de Fraunce,
duc de Bedforde, demurrant en Fraunce par le espace du .xiij. ans, comme
icye ensuiuent.'

Nomina principum, ducum, comitum, baronum, banerettorum et mi-
5 litum baculariorum `ac aliorum nobilium virorum de hospicio' et re-
tinencia in feodo, vadijs at pensionibus sub prepotentissimo principe
Iohanne, regente regni Francie, xiij. annis continuis; `ac' duce de Bed-
ford `in regno Anglie'; duce de `Angew', `duce de Allaunson', comite
Cenomanie, de Harecourt et de `Dreux', vicecomite de Beaumond in
10 Francia; necnon capitanei magnifici et regalissimi turris de Falloyse in
ducatu Normannie.

Ricardus Beauchamp, comes Warwici, capitaneus ciuitatis de Meaulx-
in-Brye, locumtenens pro campo in absencia domini regentis supradicti pro dicto regente tempore Regis Henrici Sexti.

15 Thomas Mountague, comes de Salisbury, locumtenens sub dicto rege
pro campo.

1 Le . . . ensuiuent] WW in blank space at top of p.; om. H1   5 ac . . . hospicio]
WW over eras.   7 xiij. . . . continuis] crossed out but marked 'stet' perhaps by WW;
om. H1   ac] WW interl.   8 in . . . Anglie] WW interl., followed by perhaps three
letters eras.; overwritten in darker ink; om. H1   Angew] scr. or WW over eras.   duce
de Allaunson] WW interl.; overwritten in darker ink   9 Harecourt] followed by de
Richemond crossed out; restored SA   Dreux] WW over eras.; preceded by dreu crossed out before l. break   Beaumond] followed by interl. de Elb⟨– – –⟩e (?) by WW, then
eras.   9–11 in Francia . . . Normannie] etc. H1   13–14 supradicti . . . Sexti]
om. H1   15 rege] regent H1

4 F. Dubosc, 'Manuscrit inédit', 52–5: the descriptions of Henry Bourchier as 'capi-
taneus castri de Ewe' (cf. App. 1/22), John Beauchamp as 'capitaneus de Ponte Arche'
(cf. App. 1/28), Fastolf as 'capitaneus' (but not 'annis intermedijs') before 'de Cane' (cf.
App. 1/47), Nicholas Burdet, whom Dubosc's transcriber calls 'Ricardus', as 'ballivus de
Constentin' (cf. App. 1/99), Robert Conyers as 'locum tenens castri de Cherebourg' (cf.
App. 1/104), and John Clifton as 'capitaneus castri de Vire' (cf. App. 1/123).

Iohannes Mauteruers, comes de Arundell, tunc capitaneus castri et ville de Vernoile-in-Perche.

Willelmus Pole, comes Suffolchie, capitaneus castelli et ciuitatis de Averances et aliorum castrorum et fortaliciorum in dicto regno Francie 20 ac ducatu Normanie.

Henricus Bourcere, comes de Ewe, `necnon *capitane* castri de Ewe,´ `et modo comes de Essex´. |

Iohannes, dominus de Talbote et de Furnyvale, capitaneus de Cowntan- f. 8ᵛ ces, nobilis in armis et postea comes de Shrewisbury, ac locumtenens 25 regis pro ducatu de Gyen.

`Iohannes Beauchamp myles, postea´ dominus de Beau`champ´, conciliarius regentis, `et capitaneus de Pount-l'Arge´.

Thomas Beaumond, dominus de Basquevile, miles, frater domini (*gap*) de Beaumonde, capitaneus de Gailarde. 30

Thomas, dominus de Scalis, capitaneus de Domfroit.

Robertus, dominus de Willugbie, capitaneus de Bayux.

Radulphus Botillere, dominus de Sudeley, capitaneus de Crotey, primus camerarius dicti domini regentis, et de suo principali concilio in armorum actibus. 35

Andreas Ogarde, miles, de regno Dacie natus, secundus camerarius, capitaneus de Vyre.

Thomas Rempston, miles, tercius camerarius, capitaneus de Saynt-Iaques de Beverton.

Bernardus de Monferaunt, miles de Vasconia, quartus camerarius dicti 40 principis, capitaneus de Charmesnylle.

Iohannes Fastolffe, miles banerettus, baro de Gylliguillem, magnus senescallus (aliter dictus magnus magister hospicij) dicti regentis in ducatu Normanie, ac postea gubernator de Angewe et Mayne pluribus annis, et capitaneus de ciuitate de Mauns ac castrorum et vil- 45 larum de Allaunson, de Mayn et de Fresney-le-Vicount .xiiij annis,

---

17 tunc] *om. H1*   19 Averances] Aberances *SA*   20 et aliorum . . . Normanie] *om. H1*   22 necnon . . . Ewe] *WW interl.; om. H1*   et modo . . . Essex] *scribe C adds*   24 capitaneus . . . Gyen] *after Erle of Shrewsbury Capitayn of Costences H1*   27 Iohannes Beauchamp . . . postea] *WW Iohannes over eras. and interl. Beauchamp . . . postea; WW in marg. Iohannes* `dominus´ *Beauchamp postea capitaneus de pountlarge then incompletely crossed out*   Beau`champ´] *WW champ over eras.*   28 et capitaneus . . . Pount-l'Arge] *WW at the end of the l., duplic.* capitaneus   31 Domfroit] Domfroir *H1*; Domfront *H2*   32 Bayux] Baion *H1*   34–5 et de . . . actibus] *om. H1*   36 camerarius] haberlayn (*sic*) to the Regent *H1 adds* to the Regent   38 camerarius] *H1 adds* to the Regent   41 principis] Regent *H1*   43 regentis] *followed by* et pro vno anno fuit locumtenens regis *crossed out; WW also interl.* stet *and then crossed it out; restored SA*   in . . . Normanie] *om. H1*   45 et capitaneus . . . annis] *om. H1*

et similiter ʼannis intermedijs capitaneusʼ de Cane, de Vernolle et
Hounflue certis annis.

f. 9ʳ Iohannes Popham, miles ʼbanerettusʼ, cancellarius de le | *counte* de An-
50   gew et de Mayne et conciliarius dicti domini regentis, et capitaneus
de Seyn-Suzan in *le counte* de Mayne.

Iohannes Mongomerie, miles banerettus, capitaneus castri fortissimi de
Arques et balliuus de Caux et conciliarius domini regentis.

Iohannes Salveyne, miles banerettus, balliuus, vt capitalis iusticiarius
55   ciuitatis de Rone et conciliarius domini regentis; ʼcapitaneusʼ.

Willelmus Oldhale, miles ʼbanerettusʼ, capitaneus de Argenten et de
Esse ac fortalicij de Laurens-Martire in *le counte* de Angew.

Robertus Harlyng, miles, capitaneus de Pount Melank et de Esse et
balliuus de Allaunson.

60   Willelmus Breton, miles, balliuus de Caen.

Iacobus Botillere, filius comitis de Ormond, ʼin curia domini regentisʼ,
postea comes de Wilteshire et ʼcomesʼ de Ormonde.

N. (*gap*), filius et heres domini de Clifforde, iuuenis ʼin curia dicti
regentisʼ; postea fuit dominus de Clifford.

65   ʼIohannesʼ Bourcere, ʼiuuenis etatisʼ, filius domini de Bourcere, [miles,
postea dominus de Berners in curia domini regentis].

Wi[lliam Mauteruers], frater comitis Arun[dellie, ⟨?⟩] postea comes
Arundellie ac dominus de Mauteruers ʼ[18 annorum in curia] domini
regentisʼ.

70   N (*gap*) , dominus de Powes, miles, iuuenis ʼin curia domini regentisʼ.

Iohannes Robsarde, miles banerettus, de Henaudia prima natus, et de

---

47 annis . . . capitaneus] *WW interl.*   49 banerettus] *WW interl.*   de . . . *counte*]
om. H1   50 et . . . regentis] *om. H1*   51 in . . . Mayne] *om. H1*   52 castri
fortissimi] *om. H1*   53 et . . . regentis] *om. H1*   54 balliuus] Capitayn *H1*;
Bayliffe *H2*   55 ciuitatis] *om. H1*   et . . . capitaneus] *om. H1*   capitaneus] *WW
in space at the end of l.*   56 banerettus] *WW interl.*   56-7 et de Esse . . .
Angew] *om. H1*   58 Esse] *followed by eras., with line-filler over eras.; om. H1*
61 Ormond] *followed by* iuuenis *crossed out; restored SA*   in . . . regentis] *WW over
eras.; om. H1*   62 comes] *WW interl.; om. H1*   Ormonde] *WW adds* in curia
Regentis, *then crossed out; restored SA*   63 N] *H1 joins this entry to the end of the
previous*   63-4 iuuenis . . . regentis] *om. H1*   in . . . regentis] *WW interl. above
lengthy eras.*   65 Iohannes] *WW interl. above* Henricus *crossed out;* Henricus *SA*
iuuenis etatis] *WW interl.; om. H1*   65-6 miles . . . regentis] *obliterated; supplied
from SA*   66 in . . . regentis] *om. H1*   67 Wi[lliam Mauteruers] *obliterated;
supplied from SA*   Arundellie] *followed by obliterated word; om. H1, SA*   postea . . .
regentis] *om. H1*   68 18 . . . regentis] *WW interl.*   18 annorum in curia] *obliterated; supplied from SA*   70 iuuenis . . . regentis] *om. H1*   in . . . regentis] *WW over
eras.*   regentis] *followed by* dicti domini regentis *by scribe C, then crossed out; om. H1*
71 prima natus] *om. H1*

consorcio ordinis militaris Sancti Georgij, capitanei castri 'de Caud-
beke et postea capitaneus' de Seynt-|Savire de Ive in Normania.   f. 9ᵛ

Tirry Robsarde, frater eius, capitaneus de Hombye, 'similiter capitaneus de Seynt-Sauour-Vicount'.   75

Bertyne Entwesill, *cheualier*, dominus de Hambie, natus (vt dicitur) de
Lancasshire.

Franciscus le Arrogonoys, dictus Syrene, de Arrogonia natus, capitaneus nominatissimus de Mount-Targis et aliorum nobilium castello-
rum, ordinis militaris Sancti Georgij.   80

Thomas Blount, miles, capitaneus de (*gap*).

Iohannes Hankforde, miles, capitaneus pontis de Roone.

Willelmus Chambirleyn, miles, capitaneus de 'Meaulx et postea' Gurnay et aliorum fortaliciorum.

Willelmus Bysshopston, miles, capitaneus et tercius senescallus dicti 85
domini regentis 'et capitaneus de Gayllard'.

Thomas Kyryell, miles, capitaneus de 'Gurnay'.

Ricardus Harington, miles banerettus, balliuus de Cane, capitaneus
diuersorum fortaliciorum in Normannia, 'locumtenens sub Andrea
Ogard apud Seynt-Suzan'.   90

Here Iohn, miles, capitaneus de Pounto-d'Oo.

Ricardus Merbery, miles, capitaneus de Ponteys

Willelmus Heron, miles bacularius.

Iohannes Dedham, miles, 'capitaneus de Nogent-le-Roy'.

Willelmus Burton, miles bacularius.   95

Thomas Kingeston, miles, locumtenens castri de Falleyse, 'postea capitaneus de Bayoux, decens miles'.

72–3 capitanei . . . Normania] *om. H1*   de Caudbeke . . . capitaneus] *WW interl., con-*
tinuing in marg.   74–5 similiter . . . Vicount] *WW in space at the end of the l.; om. H1,*
SA   76 vt dicitur] *om. H1*   78 le] de *SA;* lord *H1*   78–80 capitaneus . . .
castellorum] *om. H1*   81 capitaneus de] *om. H1*   de] *followed by* Argen *by WW at*
the end of the l., then eras., leaving gap   82 pontis de Roone] of the Bridge at Rone
. Pontis de Rone *H1;* of þe bridge att Roane *H2*   83 Meaulx et postea] *WW interl.*
84 et . . . fortaliciorum] *om. H1*   85–6 capitaneus et . . . Gayllard] *om. H1*   86 et
capitaneus de Gayllard] *WW at the end of the l.*   87 capitaneus de 'Gurnay'] *om.*
H1   Gurnay] Gysors *crossed out; WW adds* Gurnay *at the end of the l.;* Gysores (*underl.*)
Gurney *SA*   88–90 balliuus . . . Seynt-Suzan] *om. H1*   89 locumtenens . . .
Seynt-Suzan] *WW at the end of the l.*   sub . . . Seynt-Suzan] *om. SA*   93 bacularius]
followed by in armis fortunatus *then crossed out; restored SA*   94 Iohannes . . . No-
gent-le-Roy] *om. H1*   capitaneus . . . Nogent-le-Roy] *scribe C interl., above* in fortitudine
nominatissimus *crossed out, and restored SA*   Nogent-le-Roy] *WW duplic. in marg.*
95 Willelmus . . . bacularius] *om. H1*   bacularius] *followed by* et semper ad pugna pro
iure regni paratus *crossed out; restored SA*   96–7 locumtenens . . . miles] *om. H1*
postea . . . miles] *WW at the end of the l.*   97 decens miles] *om. SA*

Nicholaus Burdeyt, miles, locumtenens ciuitatis de Rone et capitaneus de Carrantan, ʽballiuus de Constantynʼ.

100 Iohannes Harpeley, miles, capitaneus de Chirburgh. |

f. 10ʳ Ricardus Gethyn, miles *North* Wallie, capitaneus fortaliciorum in *le counte* de Mayne.

Thomas Flemyng, miles, locumtenens castri de Cane.

Robertus Conyers, miles, ʽlocumtenens castri de Chyrburghʼ.

105 Iohannes Bernarde, miles, locumtenens insularum de Gersye et Guernesye.

Iohannes Gray, miles, capitaneus de Yemmys.

Ricardus Curson, miles, locumtenens portarum, murorum ciuitatis de Rothomagensis.

110 Nicholaus Conwey, miles bacularius.

Iohannes Gresley, miles bacularius.

Rogerus Chamberleyne, miles.

Iohannes Marcelle, miles bacularius.

Philipus Braunche, miles bacularius, ʽlocumtenens fortaliciorum Iohanne Fastolf in Mayn comiteʼ.

115

Robertus Hungerforde, miles banerettus, postea dominus Hungerforde.

Ricardus Wydevile, miles, ʽiuuenis in curia domini regentisʼ, postea comes de Ryuers.

Iohannes Shardlow, miles bacularius.

120 Thomas Gargrafe, *cheualier*, ʽcapitaneus de (*gap*)ʼ.

Willelmus Plompton, *cheualier*, ʽcapitaneus de (*gap*)ʼ.

Henricus Hosey, *cheualier*.

Iohannes Clifton, miles, ʽcapitaneus de Vyreʼ.

Thomas Griffyn, miles bacularius.

98–9 locumtenens . . . Constantyn] *om. H1*   99 balliuus de Constantyn] *WW at the end of the l.*   100 Chirburgh] *followed by* pro certo tempore *crossed out; restored SA*   101–2 capitaneus . . . Mayne] *om. H1*   103–4 Thomas Flemyng . . . Robertus Conyers . . .] *order of 2 entries reversed in H1*   103 locumtenens . . . Cane] *om. H1*   104 locumtenens . . . Chyrburgh] *WW interl.; om. H1*   Chyrburgh] *followed by* postea marescallus in excercitu sub locotenente in Francia tempore Regis Henrici Sexti *crossed out; restored SA*   110 bacularius] *followed by* ad arma deditus *crossed out; restored SA; om. H1*   112 miles] *followed by* inter pugna probatus *crossed out; restored SA*   114 bacularius] *followed by* equestre approbatus *crossed out; restored SA*   114–15 locumtenens . . . comite] *WW at the end of the l.*   114 fortaliciorum] *om. H1*   114–15 Iohanne] *preceded by* sub *crossed out;* Sir *SA*   115 Mayn] Angiow and Maine *H1*   comite] *om. H1, SA*   117 miles] *followed by* famosus *crossed out; restored SA;* knight bachelour *H1*   iuuenis . . . regentis] *WW interl.*   iuuenis] *om. H1*   120 capitaneus de] *WW at the end of the l.; om. H1*   121 capitaneus de] *WW at the end of the l.; om. H1*   123 capitaneus de Vyre] *WW interl.; om. H1*   Vyre] *followed by* et captus prisonarius *by WW, then crossed out*

Sampson Meyvervyle, miles bacularius.   125
Willelmus Wawdesbury, miles bacularius.
Thomas Lounde, miles bacularius.
Thomas Barkeley, miles, 'filius domini de Barkley'. |
Robertus Iamys de Hangmere, miles bacularius de *North* Wallia.   f. 10ᵛ
Walterus Hungerford, miles banerettus, filius et heres domini de Hun- 130
    gerforde, 'armiger pro corpore ducis Bedfordie'.
Willelmus Drurie, miles bacularius.
Iohannes Clerk, miles.
Radulphus Buxhale, miles, capitaneus de Clynchampe.
Robertus Markham, miles.   135
Iohannes Fitzsymond, miles.
Willelmus Fulford, miles.
Ricardus Tunstale, miles.
Willelmus Plompton, miles.
Dauid Howelle de Wallia.   140
Willelmus Wolffe de Wallia, miles.
Thomas Griffitz, miles.
Thomas Kirkebie, miles.
Thomas Lounde, miles.
(*gap*) Turnebeff, *cheualier*, de Perche.   145
Lancelet de Lisle, marescallus comitis de Salisbury, bonus iusticer, ca-
    pitaneus de B'e'llham.
'Robert Iamys, milles.'

Ista sunt nomina militum et hominum armorum tempore Iohannis, ducis Bedford, regentis regni Francie, in ducatu de Gyen, qui militauerunt 150
ibidem pro salua custodia dicti ducatus ab anno primo regni Henrici
Sexti vsque xv. annum regis predicti.

Iohannes Radcliff, miles banerettus, senescallus de Gyen, .xvj. annis de
    'ducatu Lencastrye natus'. |
Baro qui dicitur Dominus Duras.   f. 11ʳ

128 filius … Barkley] *WW at the end of the l.*; Lord of Barkley *H1*   131 armiger …
Bedfordie] *WW at the end of the l.; om. H1, SA*   137 Fulford] *scr. in marg.* Anglici
139 Plompton] *WW in marg.* bis+   140 Wallia] *followed by* capitaneus *by WW
at the end of the l., then crossed out;* of Walles Capitayn *H1*   142 Griffitz] *WW in
marg.* bis+   144 Lounde] *WW in marg.* bis+   146 Lancelet] *scr. in marg.* Anglici; *om. H1*   146-7 marescallus … B'e'llham] *om. H1*   147 B'e'llham]
e *over uneras. letter*   148 Robert … milles] *scribe C adds; WW in marg.* bis+
149 Ista] *WW capitulum in marg.*   151 pro … ducatus] *om. H1*   153-4 de
Gyen … natus] of Aquytayn *H1*   .xvj. … natus] *om. H1*   154 ducatu … natus]
scribe C adds, partly over eras.   155 Baro qui dicitur] *om. H1*

156 Dominus Bernardus Mountferand, miles banerettus magnificus.
Dominus capitaneus de Bouche.
Galfridus Radcliff, miles.
Iohannes Radcliff de Chateron, miles.
160 Galfridus Werberton, miles.
Edmondus Langledes, miles.
Dominus de la Bade.
Gadyuer Shorthose, anglicus, miles.
Iohannes Strangweys, miles, capitaneus de Rewlie.
165 'N. (*gap*) Beauchamp, armiger nominatissimus, capitaneus inter armigeros.'

APPENDIX TEXT 2

London, Lambeth Palace Library, MS 506, ff. 28^r–31^r: list of garrisons and retinues in Normandy under Richard, duke of York, after the Truce of Tours (28 May 1444), and probably over 1444-6.

This list is also in the handwriting of scribe B of the Codicil, but Worcester adds a title (and two further alternative titles, later crossed out: see textual notes) and further revisions. (These extensive passages marked for deletion, given in the textual notes, have been given editorial capitalization and punctuation, like the main text.).

Stevenson omitted this list from the documents he printed from the Codicil.[1] A sixteenth-century transcription of this list was printed by F. Dubosc.[2] In Dubosc's text, Appendix 2 is part of a longer transcription of military documents in the same quire as a version of Appendix 1 (as noted above). Worcester's first title, which was later crossed out (and appears here in the textual notes), is the only title for this section in Dubosc's text,[3] but otherwise that text seems less close to the Codicil than his text of Appendix 1. There are no substantive variants in the seventeenth-century transcription in London, Society of Antiquaries, MS 41.[4]

156 magnificus] *om. H1*   160 Galfridus...miles] *om. H1*   161 Langledes]
Langleuers *H1*   163–4 Gadyuer Shorthose ... Iohannes Strangweys ...] *order of 2 entries reversed in H1*   163 anglicus] *om. H1*   164 capitaneus ... Rewlie] *om. H1*   165–6 N ... armigeros] *WW in space below the list*   capitaneus ... armigeros] *om. H1*   armigeros] *preceded by duplic.* a *before l. break*

[1] In *Wars in France* it would appear in the sequence from the Codicil on ii. 565.

[2] Dubosc, 'Manuscrit inédit', 212–17.

[3] See Anne Curry, 'John, Duke of Bedford's Arrangements for the Defence of Normandy in October 1434: College of Arms MS Arundel 48, folios 274r–276v', *Annales de Normandie*, 62 (2012), 235–51 at 236–7.

[4] C&A, 39, 68, suggest that Appendix Text 2 and also Codicil, ff. 16^v–20^r, were originally in French but translated into Latin as a language more appropriate for the English royal dedicatee of the Codicil.

'Pro tempore illustri principis ducis de York quando fuit locumtenens   f. 28^r
generalis et gubernator in Francia in vltimo viagio suo tempore treugarum.'

Declaracio gencium armorum 'et' architenencium tam equestrium
quam pedestrium, existencium in vadijs recentis in *lez garnisons*, ca-   5
stris et fortalicijs ducatus Normandie pro salua custodia eorum quam
villarum et locorum infra dictum ducatum, et ad seruiendum in campis
cum necesse fuerit. Et fuit ordinatum sub tempo're inclitis principis'
domini gubernantis regni Francie Ricardi, ducis de York, tempore
et anno quo treuga velut pax tracta'ta' et appunctuata fuit int'er'   10
Henricum VJ^{tum}, regem Anglie et Francie, et Carolum Septi'mum',
nominantem se Francorum regem.

In primis pro municione, defensione ac salua custodia ciuitatis de Rone
ordinate et assignate per 'Ricardum' Dominum, 'gubernantem', et
concilium regis: .v. lancee | equestres, .xj lancee pedestres et .iiij^{xx}viij.   f. 28^v
archiers.   16

Item, pro defensione *de le palais* de Rone: .ij. lancee equestres, .xvij
lancee pedestres et lx. *archiers.*

Item, pro tuicione in castro de Rone: .i. lancea equestris, viij lancee
pedestres et xxvij *archiers.*   20

Item, pro salua custodia *de le ponte* de Rone: i. lancea equestris, .ix
lancee pedestres et xxx *archiers.*

Item, apud monasterium Sancte Katerine prope Rone: i. lancea equestris, .ix. *archiers.*

1–3 Pro . . . treugarum] *WW adds in blank space, beneath* capitulum *in marg., then an
alternative title in WW's hand, later crossed out:* Declaracio onerum, solucionum et ex-
pensarum proueniencium ducatus Normandie pro (*eras.:* guerra) defencione et salu'a'
custodi'a' (*each* a *over* uneras. o *or one-compartment* a) dicti ducatus per inclitum prin-
cipem Ricardum, gubernantem regni Francie, ducis Eboraci, tempore treugarum habi-
tarum inter Henricum Sextum, regem Anglie et Francie, ac Carolum .VIJ. nominantem
se Francorum regem, aduersarium domini Henrici Regis predicti, in anno Christi (*gap*)
tempore secundi viagij   2–3 treugarum] *followed by another alternative title in
WW's hand, crossed out:* Status gubernacionis ducatus Normandie, tempore quo illustris
princeps Ricardus, dux de York, gerebat officium gubernantis ac locumtenens (*sic*) generalis pro regno Francie in vltimo anno (*crossed out:* sue) sui oneris, tempore treugarum
capte, (*crossed out:* vt) videlicet in anno Christi .M^l. iiij^{C}xliiij^{to}.   4 Declaracio]
WW adds in marg.: totam (?) valoris normandie tempore ducis Eboraci   et] *interl.*
8 tempo're inclitis principis'] *WW* re inclitis principis *at the end of the l.;* re *duplic. by
scr. at the start of the next l., then eras.*   9 York] *followed by* ibidem gubernantis *eras.*   10 tracta'ta'] *WW* ta *interl.*   int'er'] *WW* er *over scr's abbrev. for* er
11 Septi'mum'] Sept *and minim followed by eras.;* m *interl.*   14 Ricardum] *WW
interl.*   gubernantem] *WW over eras.*

25 Pount-l'Arge et *le Isle* de Ellebeff: .ij. lancee equestres, .xij. lancee pedestres et xlij *archiers*.

Gisors: .ij. lancee pedestres, .viij. lancee pedestres et xxx. *archiers*.

Gournay et Gerbray: .ij. lancee pedestres, .viij. lancee pedestres et xxx
archiers, et pro campis custodiendis: .x. lancee equestres et xxx *ar-*
30 *chiers.*

Newchastell: .x. lancee equestres, .x. lancee pedestres et lx *archiers*.

Arques: ij. lancee equestres, .viij lancee pedestres et xxx *archiers*.

Vernon et Vernonel: .ij. lancee equestres, .x. lancee pedestres et xxxvj
archiers.

35 Gaillarde: .ij. lancee equestres, .viij lancee pedestres et xxx *archiers*. Et
de *crew* (id est, cum augmentacione): .i. lancea equestris, .i lancea
pedestris et vj *archiers*.

Roche-Gyon: .i. lancea equestris et xx *archiers*. Et dictum fortalicium
de Roche-Gyon erit custoditum pro summa viij^C. *liures turneys* per
40 annum, incipiendo primo die Maij, anno Christi M^l. iiij^C .xlvj. |

f. 29^r Mant: .v. lancee equestres, .xxv. lancee pedestres et iiij^{xx}. v. *archiers*. Et
pro campo: x. lancee equestres et .xxx. *archiers*.

Tankervile: .i. lancea equestris, .v. lancee pedestres et xviij *archiers*. Et
dicta duo fortalicia erunt custodita per annum pro xj^C. *liures turneys*,
45 incipiendo primo die Aprilis, anno Christi .M^l. iiij^C. xlv.

Hareflete: .ij lancee equestres, xlvij pedestres et Cxlvij *archiers*.

Monsterdevillers: i. lancea equestris, .vj. lancee pedestres, xx. *archiers*.
Et dictum fortalicium erit munitum pro M^l. lx. *liures turneys* per annum istum, qui facit pro ij. quarterijs anni finientibus in Septembri,
50 anno Christi .M^l. iiij^C. xlvj. videlicet.

Hunflue: .ij. lancee equestres, .viij pedestres, xxx *archiers*. Et dictum fortalicium erit custoditum pro .v^C. *liures turneys* pro omnibus rebus
pro tempore incipiente xxx. die Marcij, anno Christi M^l. iiij^C. xlv. et
finiente xxvij die Septembri proximo sequente.

55 Pont-l'Evesque: .ij. lancee equestres et .x. *archiers*.

Ponte-Audemer: .x. lancee equestres, .xxx. *archiers*.

Liseux.

Bernay.

Conches.

60 Orbek.

Vernoile et Loignye: x. lancee equestres, .xv. lancee, lxxv *archiers*.

Donfront: xv. lancee equestres, .xv. lancee pedestres, .iiij^{xx}x *archiers*.

Argenton: .ij. lancee equestres, ix. lancee pedestres, xxxvj *archiers*. |

⁹^v Exmes, id est Yemmys: .i. lancea equestris, .vj. lancee pedestres, .xxj
    archiers.   65

Essay: i. lancea equestris, .v. lancee pedestres et xviij *archiers.*

Allaunson, pro tempore incipiente primo die Aprilis, anno Christi M^l.
    iiij^C xlv: xviij lancee equestres, vj. lancee pedestres et lxxij *archiers.*

Fresnay-le-Viscount, pro dicto incipiente primo die Aprilis: .ij. lancee
    equestres, vij. lancee pedestres et xxvij. *archiers.* Et pro campis: .v. 70
    lancee equestres et xv. *archiers.*

Caen: .iij. lancee equestres, xxv lancee pedestes et iiij^{xx}x *archiers.* Et de
    crew (id est, in augmentacione): .i. lancea equestris, ix lancee pede-
    stres et xxx *archiers.*

Baioux: .i. lancea equestris, .v. pedestres, .xviij *archiers.*   75

Fallois: .ij. lancee equestres, .xv. pedestres, .lj. *archiers.* Et pro campo:
    xiij lancee equestres, .xlj *archiers.*

Vire: v. lancee pedestres et .xv. lancee pedestres, .lx. *archiers.*

Aueraunces: .iij. lancee equestres, .x. lancee pedestres, .xxxix. *archiers.*
    Et pro campo: .xvij. lancee equestres, .lj. *archiers.*   80

Tombeleyn: v. lancee equestres, .x. pedestres, .xlv *archiers.*

Chirebourgh: .ij. lancee equestres, .xxviij pedestres et iiij^{xx}x *archiers.*

Coutances: .i. lancea equestris, .vij lancee pedestres et xxvij *archiers.*

Rennevile: .i. lancea equestris, .iiij. lancee pedestres, xv *archiers.* |

Gaverey: .i. lancea equestris, .vij lancee pedestres, .xxiiij. *archiers.*   f. 30^r

Seint-Lo: .ij. lancee *a cheuale*, .iiij lancee pedestres, xxiiij *archiers.*   86

Carentan: .ij. lancee equestres, vij pedestres, .xxvij *archiers.*

Ponto-d'Oue: .i. lancea equestris et ix *archiers.*

Valoignes: .i. lancea pedestris et .x. *archiers.*

Summa totalis: Ciiij^{xx} xvj. lancearum *a cheuale* (id est, equestrium).   90

Summa: iiij^C xxvj lancearum *a pie* (id est, pedestrium).

Summa: M^l. viij^C. iiij^{xx}x. *archiers.*

Et inter ista loca Bernay, Liseux, Conches et Orbek non est de numero,
nec inter istas lanceas computatur.

Item, dominus Thomas Scalis habet pro salua custodia ducatus de 95
    Normandy, dicto tempore treugarum (gallice, *treues*) captarum inter
    dictos duos principes, Ricardo gubernante, duce de York, in dicto
    ducatu, tempore Regis Henrici Sexti anno xxij. regni sui: .xx. lanceas
    a cheuale et lx. *archiers.*

Andreas Ogarde, *cheualier baneret*: iij. lanceas *a cheuale*, .xiiij. *archiers.* 100

Simon Morchier, *prouost* de Paris, *cheualier baneret*: iij. lanceas *a che-*
    uale, .xiiij *archiers.*

Willelmus Oldhall, *cheualier baneret*: .iij. lanceas *a cheuale*, .xiiij *archiers.* |

f. 30ᵛ Ricardus Harington, balliuus de Caen, *cheualier baneret*, ij lanceas *a*
106   *cheuale*, xxx. *archiers.*

Hugo Spencer, armiger Anglie, *le baillie* de Constantyne: .ij. lanceas *a cheuale*, .xxiiij *archiers.*

Iohannes Stanlow, thesaurarius Normandie, armiger: ij. lanceas *a che-*
110   *uale*, xiiij *archiers.*

Item, receptor generalis Normandie: i. lanceam *a cheuale*, .ix. *archiers.*

Item, *le countroller* super receptorem generalem: ij. *archiers.*

Summa: xxxviij lancearum *a cheuale* et ij^C. *archiers.*

Summa gencium armorum sub retinencia domini Ricardi, gubernantis,
115   et locitenentis pro Rege Henrico VJ. Anglie et Francie, ducis de Yorke,
et conducte in vadijs de domino et conciliario: CCxxxiiij lancearum
a cheuale.

Summa: iiij^C xxvj. lancearum *a pie.*

Summa: ij. M^l. iiij^{xx}x. *archiers.*

120 Summa de gentibus armorum pro campo qui sunt vltra numerum armorum, vt superius specificatorum, et sunt positi sub pluribus capitaneis et vltra eorum retinencia et sunt hospitati in diuersis villis et locis in Normania pro salua tuicione patrie, quod si aliqua sedicio per tradicionem aut cautelam gencium armorum aduersario-
125 rum ex parte Dolphini, nominantis se Francorum regem, infringeret predictas treugas colore seu vmbre alicuius rei pretense inuaderent in aliqua fortalicia sub obediencia domini Ricardi, gubernantis, ducis de York, aut sui locitenentis, quod tunc dicti gentes armorum
f. 31ʳ pro campo assignati essent patrie parati vel eque cito | sicut et alij
130   capitanei fortaliciorum ad iuuandum et resistendum contra dictos infractores treugarum.

Summa gencium armorum pro campis: Cxlj. lancearum *a cheuale.*

Summa de *archiers* pro campis: iiij^C. iiij^{xx} vij *archiers.*

Summa totalis gencium armorum pro presenti anno qui vadijs sub pre-
135   fato Ricardo, *gouuernour de Normandie*, non compriso siue incluso sub isto numero Liseux, Bernarum, Conches et Orbek, vt dictum est superius: iij^C lxxv. lancearum *a cheuale.*

Summa: iiij^C xxvj. lancearum pedestrium.

Summa: ij. M^l. v^C lxxvij *archiers.*

140 Memorandum quod vadia ac regarda gencium armorum predictorum pro vno anno compriso siue incluso, .x. milites baneretti et ij milites

bacularij, ascendunt ij^C. lxij M^l. iij^C. iiij^{xx} xviij. libras, .i. s., viij. d., que faciunt in moneta regni Anglie vocata sterlingis.

Et sciendum est quod pro solucione vadiorum et stipendiariorum necnon pensionum dictorum gencium armorum, gentes dominorum   145 tam spiritualium quam temporalium necnon plebum congregatorum vice parliamenti in ducatu predicto (gallice dicti, gentes Trium Statuum) sic insimul congregati ad duas conuenciones per ipsos tentas in villa Rotomagi non concesserunt pro defensione et conseruacione dicti ducatus in tranquillitate et pace nisi summam monete dicte patrie   150 Ciiij^{xx}. x. M^l. *liures turneys*, que faciunt in moneta regni Anglie vocata sterlingis.

APPENDIX TEXT 3

London, Lambeth Palace Library, MS 506, ff. 59^v, 60^v: notes on the duke of Bedford and men serving under him, notably at the battle of Verneuil, and notes on various other figures.

These notes are on blank pages at the end of the Codicil. The preceding text, a letter in French from the English council at Rouen to Henry VI reporting on   5 affairs in 1441, ends, as currently misbound, at the foot of f. 58^v. The rectos of the next two leaves, ff. 59^r and 60^r, are blank; this text is on the versos.

The text is in Worcester's handwriting. It is written without ruling, cramped and untidy in presentation, with frequent interlineation and crossing out. The text frequently extends into the gutter, and is not always easily read or parsed.

The status of these notes is unclear. They were not part of the neatly copied Codicil. The first lines are very close to the start of Appendix 1 (above). They might be Worcester's further notes for preparing a revised version. Notes by Worcester of a similar rough kind about the French wars appear at the end of *Basset's Chronicle* in London, College of Arms, MS M.9, f. 120^r + an unfoliated slip.[1]

Stevenson omitted these notes from the documents he printed from the Codicil.[2] These notes are not included in the seventeenth-century transcription of the Codicil in London, Society of Antiquaries, MS 41.

Further notes in the outer margin of f. 59^v are completely obliterated by a stain.

Nomina principum ducum, comitum, vicecomitum, baronum, 'mili-   f. 59^v tum' banerettorum, militum baculariorum ac aliorum nobilium virorum 'armatorum', tam de hospicio quam retinencia in feodo, vadijs et

1–2 militum] *interl.*   3 armatorum] *interl.*   feodo] feodo feodo *either side of l. break; 1st* feodo *crossed out*

[1] Printed in C&A, 375–6.
[2] In *Wars in France* they would appear in the sequence from the Codicil on ii. 607.

pencionibus sub illustre principe Iohanne, regente et gubernante re-
5 gnum Francie in absencia Henrici Sexti, regis Anglie et Francie, sed
non de iure, tresdecim annis continuis; duce de Bedford, comite de
Rychemond et de Kendale ac aliorum plurimorum dominiorum in regno Anglie, anni valorum iiij. M^l viij^C marcarum sterlingorum; necnon
duce de Angew, duce de Allaunson ex dono supradicti regis ac comite
10 de Mayn ex proprio conquestu prefati regentis, ʼetʼ comite de Harecourt, comite de Dreux, ʼac vicomite de Charuelle, de Quatermarsʼ, de
Ellebeff et de Lyslebon; ac dominus de la Ryver, de Dauvers, de New-
burgh, de Combon, Bryncourt, de Hamby, de Hay-de-Puys, de Torcy, de
Charmenysle, tam ʼin ⟨Francia⟩ quam inʼ ducatu Normandie, ac eciam
15 habens officium magni admirallitatis tam Francie quam Anglie; ac capitaneus castrorum regalium de ʼMaunsʼ, de Allaunson, de Cane et de
Falloys, annui valoris cum supradictis dominijs ʼxij. M. vij^C lxxiij *liu-*
res turneysʼ ʼque faciuntʼ ij. M Cxxij. marcarum, ij. s. ij. d. librarum
sterlingorum.
20   Et prefatus regens habuit annuatim pro statu dignitatis officij regencie pro ʼofficio guerre contra Carolum Septimum aduersarium suum ac
proʼ salua custodia ac deffencione regni Francie et iusticia ʼplebeisʼ sub
obediencia regni Anglie viuenʼtesʼ administranda annuatum xxxiij. mi-
lia librarum turonencium, que faciunt .V. M^l. V^C . marcarum monete
25 Anglie; et pro annuo valore comitatus de Mayn omnibus annis perce-
pit lvj M^l ij^C *liures turneys*, que faciunt ix ʼMʼ iij^C lxvj. marcarum vj in
monete Anglie, que fac⟨iunt⟩ xxj. M^l vij^C iiij^{xx} viij. marcas sterlingorum.
    Apud bellum de Vernelle.
    Memorandum quod dux Bedfordie fuit ʼinʼ die Iovis belli de Ver-
30 noylle apud castrum de Damvyle ʼprope Vernelleʼ et .30. haraldorum
ʼet prosecutorumʼ ex parte Francorum veniebant duci Bedfordie ad-

5 Sexti] *preceded by* Regis *crossed out*   8 iiij.] *preceded by another incomplete*
letter crossed out   marcarum] m *over uneras. letter, perhaps* x   10 et] *in-*
terl.   11 ac vicomite . . . Quatermars] *interl. after* vicecomite de Beaumond *crossed*
out   14 tam] *preceded by* ac Admiralli, *crossed out*   tam . . . in] in *and word*
obscured by the gutter added at the end of one l.; quam in *added before the start of the*
next l.   eciam] *followed by* ad, *crossed out*   15 Anglie] *followed by* annui valoris *crossed out*   16 regalium] Ciuitatis et castri de Mayn *interl. then crossed out*
Mauns] *interl. above* Cane *crossed out*   17–18 xij. . . . turneys] *interl. above* ij. M
Cxxj *crossed out*   18 que faciunt] *interl.*   20 statu] *followed by* prenominati
crossed out   21–2 officio . . . pro] *interl., above* deffencione regni Francie et *crossed*
out   21 Carolum] *preceded by* aduersarium *crossed out*   suum] *followed by* et pro
crossed out   22 plebeis] *interl., above* subditis *crossed out*   23 viuen'tes'] tes
over two letters, perhaps ns, *incompletely crossed out*   26 lvj] *followed by* lij *crossed*
out   M] *interl.*   27 fac⟨iunt⟩] *partly obscured in gutter*   28 de] *followed by*
Bedford *crossed out*   29 in] *interl.*   30 Damvyle] *preceded by* Dom *crossed out*
prope Vernelle] *interl.*   31 et prosecutorum] *interl.*

nunciantes sibi bellare cum duce, sed *le herode* ducis Allauncon dicit
primo messagium duci Bedfordie. |

Willelmus Stafford, armiger, filius Humfry Stafford.   f. 60^v

Andreas Ogard fuit baro de D'Ennabale in Caux ʿet dominus castri de   35
    Auuillersʹ.

Radulphus Sage fuit baro de Runcyvale, vbi Humflete est; saluauit du-
    catum Normandie.

Iohannes Tybetot de Normania.

Comes Salysbery.   40

Comes Suffolchie.

Dominus Wyllughby.

Dominus Scalys.

Iohannes Beauchamp, postea Dominus Beauchamp, capitaneus Pount-
    l'Arge.   45

Dominus Pownynges apud bellum Vernelle.

Raff Botiller.

A. Ogard, iuuenis, apud Vernell factus miles.

(*gap*) Rempston, validus.

Iohannes Clyffton, miles.   50

I. Fastolf.

Willelmus Chambyrleyn.

Dominus Cromewell, capitaneus Boys Vyncent.

Iohannes *of the pantrye* fuit valettus.

Swerdberer apud Coventree ʿcorduanarius fuitʹ.   55

Thomas Maunsell, armiger.

Matheus Gough de hospicio mynoris.

W. Albon de hospicio, valettus corone.

Henricus Seyn-Low, armiger de.

Partrych, clericus capelle.   60

Iohannes Barton.

Iankyn Randolf.

Selby, valettus de *le Scurelery*.

Apud *le brakefast* officiariorum festi Aleyn Byrton exspensiti fuerunt x.
    pipas vini.   65

Iohannes Iare, coquinarius, habuit 1500 sue allocacionis ad salatham
    Domine Anne, ducisse Bedfordie.

35–6 et . . . Auuillers] *WW interl.*   54 valettus] *followed by* d *crossed out*
55 corduanarius fuit] *interl.*   59 de] *followed by mark, perhaps* s   66 habuit]
preceded by habitis *partly crossed out*   67 Domine] *preceded by* regine *crossed out*

EXPLANATORY NOTES TO
THE BOKE OF NOBLESSE

Historical figures are identified by birth and death dates, where known (and not, for monarchs, by regnal years). Essential information (dates, titles, posts) for figures from England follows *ODNB* unless otherwise noted; *ODNB* is only cited if there is need to distinguish between it and other sources, or if it might be uncertain which name to look up in *ODNB*. In general, the notes refer to people and places by the form of their name in their own language (e.g. *Foulques, count of Anjou* not *Fulk*), unless it would be confusing to do so (e.g. *Eleanor of Aquitaine*). References to the *OED* and *MED*, each undergoing revision, were checked in June 2022. References to English texts from the Codicil are to our edition of them, C1 to C5, with text and line numbers, e.g. C1/1–2. Other references to 'Codicil' are to the MS, LPL, MS 506, with parenthetical cross-references to printed versions in *Wars in France*, e.g. Codicil, f. 12^r (*Wars in France*, ii. 531), or, where hitherto unprinted, to our transcriptions in Appendices 1 to 3 below, e.g. Codicil, f. 30^v (Appendix 2/126).

2 *Kyng Edward the IIIJ^{the}*. WW's red heading recording the dedication to Edward IV (1442–83) was unequivocal, but (see textual note) reader 1 altered it to Henry VII (1457–1509), then another later reader restored the original number. Cf. C1/1–2.

3 *preferryng* = 'promotion'. Antedates 1st citation in *OED, prefer, v.*, I.2 = 'to promote', and antedates any citation of the n. in this sense in *OED, preferring, n.*; no such sense or context occurs in *MED, preferring, ger.*

3 *comyn publique*. The least common of *BkNob.*'s translations of Lat. *res publica*, occurring only at 1690, 1917, as *comon publique* in passages based on Fr. sources or Fr. translations of Lat. sources. Cf. *comon wele* (15 times) or *comon profit* (21 times), in variant sp. Cf. 1599–1600n. 1606n., 1690–2n., 2055–6n. and Glossary, s.v. **comon publique**.

7 *sithe* = 'then, afterwards', completing the temporal sequence from *First* 5; see also *sithen* 40.

7 *epistle*. Recurs at 587, 1727, 2580. Perhaps literally = 'letter', as *BkNob.* purports to be addressed to Edward IV (see 42n.); the word is used to refer to Aristotle's letter to Alexander in Earl Rivers's translation of *The Dicts and Sayings of the Philosophers* (cited in *OED, epistle, n.*, 1.a); but Eng. *epistle* usually describes a literary or biblical text merely imitating a letter (*MED, epistel, n.*, 1).

10–16 *Kayus son . . . genuere*. *Kayus* underlined in red in MS. Quotation from Buonaccorso da Montemagno, *De nobilitate tractatus* [*Controversia de nobi-*

litate], in *Prose e rime de' due Buonaccorsi da Montemagno, con annotazioni, ed alcune rime di Niccolò Tinucci*, ed. Giovambattista Casotti (Florence, 1718), 2–97 at 22 (this section not printed in *Prosatori latini del Quattrocento*, ed. Eugenio Garin (Milan, 1952), 139–65); see also Albert Rabil Jr (ed. and trans.), *Knowledge, Goodness, Power: The Debate over Nobility among Quattrocento Italian Humanists*, MRTS, 88 (Binghampton, NY, 1991), 36. WW quotes just one of two interlocutors in the debate, Cornelius Scipio, the defender of inherited nobility; but the description of him as *Kayus son* recalls his opponent Gaius Flaminius, the defender of nobility earned by virtuous deeds; Cornelius' father is not named. No MS of the Lat. has yet been identified in England in the 15th c., but there is other evidence of its accessibility. William Caxton printed an Eng. translation as *The Declamacion of Noblesse* ascribed to John Tiptoft, identified only as 'therle of worcestre', in 1481 alongside a translation of Cicero's *De amicitia* also ascribed to Tiptoft and WW's translation of *De sen.*: see Cicero, *Tullius de senectute* (Westminster: William Caxton, 1481; *ISTC* ico0627000). Wakelin, *Humanism*, 153–4, 162, 168–70, notes (170 n. 32) that Tiptoft's translation (in R. J. Mitchell, *John Tiptoft (1427–1470)* (London, 1938), 215–41 at 221, l. 1) omits to translate one line of Lat. ('Dein ii, qui litterarum eruditi . . . nobilitas sit'), which would immediately follow but is not included in the quotation in *BkNob*. In addition, the Lat. was quoted by an English merchant and clerk: 'Grants of Arms, etc. from the Reign of Edward IV', ed. W. H. St John Hope, *Proceedings of the Society of Antiquaries*, 2nd ser., 16 (1897), 340–56 at 347, quoted in Maurice Keen, *Origins of the English Gentleman: Heraldry, Chivalry and Gentility in Medieval England c.1300–c.1500* (Stroud, 2002), 108.

17 *De remedio . . . publice.* Picks out and loosely translates the Eng. words *reformacion* of the *losse* 19–21. WW adds this in the only space left blank in the MS, a layout that differs from other chapter titles (on which see Introduction, p. xxviii).

21–2 *Gascoyne and Guyen.* WW treats these both as pl. *duchies* (689, 1334, 1463–4), and together as a sg. *duchie* (577, 716–17, 1418). C1/212–13, C1/221, refer to the sg. *ducdom of Gasquyn and Gyen*.

22–3 *Pontif.* (In the MS, a red paraph follows, which could obscure a final **e**.) The county of Ponthieu in Picardy. Spelling with ⟨f⟩ for the voiced labiodental spirant /v/ follows the Latinization *Pontivus*. Cf. *Pontyue* 284, with medial ⟨u⟩ instead of ⟨f⟩, and the Fr. sp. *Pontieu* 376. Eng. *erledom* commonly refers to territory, as well as the title to it: *OED*, *earldom*, *n.*, 2; *MED*, *erldom*, *n.*, 1(a).

23 *reaume, dukedoms.* On such apposition, see Introduction, pp. lxxx–lxxxiii.

23–4 *vndre correccion of amendement.* Common formula in 15th-c. Eng. literature (see also 1499, 2580n.); C1/46, C2/31 and n., C5/23, etc.), evoking submission to a superior, especially an ecclesiastical one: e.g. the start and end of WW's 1470 plea to Bishop William Waynflete (*PL*, no. 1046, ll. 125–33 and address); Daniel Wakelin, *Scribal Correction and Literary Craft: English Manuscripts 1475–1510* (Cambridge, 2014), 33–6. It was also a common courtesy in letters: e.g. by Fastolf, in WW's handwriting, 'savyng the correc*c*ion of my frendz there' (*PL*, no. 983, l. 13).

25 *auctorite . . . experience.* A commonplace contrast; see e.g. The Wife of Bath's Prologue (*Canterbury Tales*, III. 1). Picked up in WW's son's prologue to the Codicil contrasting *auctours* and *experiense* C1/43.

27–9 *first originall . . . Crist.* Claims that Britain was founded by Brutus, greatgrandson of Aeneas, and that English kings descended from him were widespread. A list of kings originally from Brutus to Henry VI (extended by a later reader), is in Arundel, ff. 22^r–30^r; that list (at f. 22^r) and another list in Arundel, f. 71^r, date Brutus's arrival in 'Ingelond' to 1135 BCE, which would explain *more than .M^l. yere before.* WW also recorded the Trojan ancestry of English kings in Titus, f. 68^r, in his notes taken from Brunetto Latini, *Li Livres dou tresor*, I. 35 (e.g. ed. Francis J. Carmody (Berkeley and Los Angeles, 1948), 43–4), and ff. 73^v–74^r from *GCF*, Origines, ch. 1 (Viard, i. 11), where WW's copy includes a sentence not found in other copies (to our knowledge): 'Et einsi Il est certaine chose que lez Roys de Angleterre et de Fraunce furent descendu de la ligne et et [*sic*] noble sanc de Troye . comme les aunciens croniques Orosius et lez graunt croniques de Fraunce tesmoignet' (f. 74^r). On WW's (pseudo-)Orosius, see 1565n. Trojan ancestry is invoked further at 591–3, 1298–9.

30–3 *langage . . . corrupt Greke.* Based on Geoffrey of Monmouth, *Historia regum Britannie*, I. 21 (*The History of the Kings of Britain*, ed. Michael D. Reeve, trans. Neil Wright (Cambridge, 2007), 29), 'Vnde postmodum . . . Britannica'. Excerpts about Brutus taken from the *Historia*, including this sentence at f. 109^v, are in Arundel, ff. 108^v–109^v. The odd formulation *langage of the Brutes bloode* < Lat. 'loquela gentis'. WW read from Geoffrey's *Historia* more than once: see also 246–8n. Reader 1 alters the text here, by interlineation above the top l. of f. 1^v (see textual note), misinterpreting the *langage of the Brutes bloode* which *remayne`th'* spoken in Wales and Cornwall as a reference to *bloode* of Celtic rulers, i.e. remaining in the addressee's body (*yn your most noble persone*), which would make sense for Henry VII, of Welsh descent, in whose reign reader 1 was annotating: see Introduction, pp. xxviii–xxix.

34–5 *Cerdicius.* Cerdic, king of Wessex. WW might follow Ranulph Higden, *Polychronicon*, V. 5 (ed. Churchill Babington and J. Rawson Lumby, 9 vols., RS 41 (London, 1865–6), v. 330–3), who reports that Cerdic often fought Arthur, and that after 26 years Arthur gave him Hampshire and Somerset and called that area Wessex. The end of book VI, starting mid-text, and all of book VII of the *Polychronicon* are bound into WW's miscellany, Royal, ff. 1^r–37^v; extracts from the *Polychronicon* and its continuation, covering 1327–69, are copied into Arundel, ff. 119^r–121^v. Cerdic is listed as 1st king of Wessex in Arundel, f. 26^r (see 27–9n., 37–8n.), and mentioned in notes datable to 1480 in *Itineraries*, 318–

20, 326, neither describing conflict with Arthur. Or WW might follow *Flores historiarum*, ed. Henry Luard, 3 vols., RS 95 (London, 1890), i. 259–60, which mentions the arrival of 'Cheldricus' and 'Saxones' from 'Germannia', and their pact with Arthur. Extracts from *Flores historiarum* are in Arundel, ff. 76ʳ–79ʳ, 112ʳ–119ʳ (see 250–3n.), but they do not include this passage. WW does not follow Geoffrey of Monmouth, *Historia*, VI. 101 (ed. Reeve, trans. Wright, 131), who says that Vortigern invited 'Cherdich'.

35 *whiche whan* = 'at which time', a construction not identified in *MED*, *whanne*, *adv.* and *conj.*, or *OED*, *when*, *adv.* (*conj.* and *n.*), though echoing standard use of *when* as a rel. pron. (and as a n., 1st cited in *OED*, III.11, from 1616).

37–8 *Berthilmew . . . nacion of Grekis*. As WW says, borrowing from Bartholomew the Englishman, *De proprietatibus rerum*, XV. 138. WW's phrasing could come from Bartholomew's Lat., from Trevisa's Eng. (*On the Properties of Things: John Trevisa's Translation of Bartholomaeus Anglicus, De Proprietatibus Rerum: A Critical Text*, ed. M. C. Seymour, 3 vols. (Oxford, 1975–87), ii. 805), or Jean de Corbechon's Fr. trans. *Lez propretes dez choses* (e.g. BL, Add. MS 11612, f. 233ʳ), which WW's employer Fastolf owned (Beadle, 'Fastolf's French Books', 102–3). The list of kings in Arundel (see 27–9n.), includes a note on the arrival of the Saxons (f. 25ʳ). In 1480 WW again took notes on the Danish defeat of Saxons due to their 'desidia et neglicgencia' (*Itineraries*, 318–19).

38–9 *feers manly Danys . . . Grekis*. Bartholomew the Englishman, *De proprietatibus rerum*, XV. 47. Corbechon's Fr. trans. (e.g. BL, Add. MS 11612, f. 218ʳ) calls the Danes 'fiers', and Trevisa's translation (ed. Seymour, ii. 750–1), 'fers', either of which might prompt WW's *feers*.

39–40 *the gret iusticer, King Knowt*. Cnut (d. 1035). *MED*, *justicer*, *n.* records this rare word twice in works by Stephen Scrope, a member of Fastolf's household.

42 *ye*. Edward IV, directly addressed. Cf. 72n. and see Introduction, p. liii. Many verses and genealogical rolls emphasized this inheritance in the mid- to late 1400s: Alison Allan, 'Yorkist Propaganda: Pedigree, Prophecy and the "British History" in the Reign of Edward IV', in Charles Ross (ed.), *Patronage, Pedigree and Power in Later Medieval England* (Gloucester, 1979), 171–92.

44 *Erle Geffrey Plantagenet*. Geoffrey Plantagenet (1113–51), count of Anjou and duke of Normandy. Eng. commonly uses *earl* to render Lat. *comes* or Fr. *comte*: see *OED*, *earl*, *n.*, 3, and *MED*, *erl*, *n.*, 1c.

44–5 *Fouke, king of Iherusalem*. Foulques (d. 1143), count of Anjou. King of Jerusalem from 1131.

45 *Dame Maude, emperes*. Matilda (1102–67), daughter of Henry I of England, married to Emperor Heinrich V, and then to Geoffrey Plantagenet.

49 *vppon . . . hadde* = 'whenever a new conquest is called for'.

52–3 $M^l iiij^C. l. \dots xv. monithes.$ At 1464–7 WW states that the loss of Normandy took place between 15 May 1449 and 15 August 1450, dates that correspond roughly to the fall of Pont-de-l'Arche (dated by WW to 15 May 1449: see 132–5n.) and that of Cherbourg (12 August 1450). The list of places lost 'durant la charge et gouvernance du duc de Somerset', copied in Arundel, ff. 286^r–288^r (*Wars in France*, ii. 619–34) and annotated by WW, begins and ends with these losses. Jean Chartier famously stated that Normandy fell 'en l'espace seulement d'ung an et six jours, qui est grant miracle et moult grant merveille': *Chronique de Charles VII, roi de France*, ed. Vallet de Viriville, 3 vols. (Paris, 1858), ii. 234.

52 *lost*. A pa. p. in a parenthetical absolute clause modifying the *duchie* 51.

52 *bethyn* = 'within'. See Introduction, p. xciii, and also 176n., 223n.

54–5 *vndre the vmbre and coloure of trewis*. The Truce of Tours, 28 May 1444 (see 109–11 and n., 744–6). For similar phrasing see 109, 131–2, 722–3, 744, 993, 1002, 1197–8, 1226, 1247. The Lat. cognate 'colore seu vmbre' occurs in Codicil, f. 30^v (Appendix 2/126), to characterize truce-breaking.

55 *youre antecessoure King Harry the Sext*. Henry VI (1421–71), predecessor to the addressee of 1475, Edward IV: on the date, see Introduction, pp. liv–lix. *MED*, *antecessour*, *n.*, 1, and *OED*, *antecessor*, *n.*, 1 = 'predecessor' rather than 'ancestor', is little attested but recurs at 436 (see n.), 957.

56 *then named king*. In this work addressed to Edward IV, a Yorkist king, WW often describes Henry V and Henry VI, Lancastrian monarchs, as *named* king, i.e. implicitly not rightfully king. See 734, 810, 918–19, etc.

56–7 *Charles the VIJ^{the}*. Charles VII (1403–61), king of France, frequently termed *youre aduersarie* or *youre grete aduersarie*, as here, in *BkNob*. (e.g. 719, 746, 1177, 1427–8).

57 *And whereas* = 'and even though': *MED*, *wher-as*, *adv. and conj.*, 3.

57–9 *complaintes . . . haue had*. Two n. *complaintes* and *lamentacions* are in grammatical apposition (on which see Introduction, pp. lxxx–lxxxiii); so are two v. phrases *may not be* and *haue had*, which both take *complaintes* and *lamentacions* as grammatical subject. The effect of the asyndeton is emphatic.

61 *bataile[z]*. The final **r** in MS *Batailer* is perhaps misreading WW's pl. marker ⟨z⟩ in an exemplar (see Introduction, pp. xciii–xciv) as the 'round' or zetoid shape of **r**, so we emend to **z**. See also *bataile[z]* 113n. and compare alterations to allographs of **r** at 204 (see n.), etc.

64 *reualed*. *MED*, *revalen*, *v.*, and *OED*, *revale*, *v.*, cite only this text (see also 230, 292, 2258). For the n. *reuaylyng*, see C1/82. From Fr. *ravaler*, widely attested (*DMF*).

70–1 *Boicius . . . querele*. Boethius, *De consolatione philosophiae* (*De consolatione philosophiae; Opuscula theologica*, ed. Claudio Moreschini (Munich,

2000)), I. pr. 2). Quotation underlined in red in MS. Somebody, perhaps the scribe, restores *quam* in margin before the l. begins with *querele*; *quam* is in the original Lat. and could have been missed by eyeskip with ⟨qu⟩ of *querele* at the l. break. WW annotated Chaucer's *Boece* in Cambridge, Pembroke College, MS 215, where this incipit for I. pr. 2 is given in Lat. with one substantive variant ('Set magis medicine inquit tempus est quam querele', f. 3ʳ): see Daniel Wakelin, 'William Worcester Reads Chaucer's *Boece*', *Journal of the Early Book Society*, 5 (2002), 177–80). WW also summarized or extracted Lat. passages of Boethius in *Itineraries*, 391, and Julius, f. 115ᵛ; and in May 1449 he received a letter about accessing a copy of 'verse vp-on Boicius' (*PL*, no. 969, ll. 20–9). See also 593–606, 1529, 1606, 1610–16 and nn.

72 *alle ye louyng liege-men*. While some passages address the king (cf. 42n., 570, 658, etc.), here and elsewhere (e.g. 228–42, 856–65, etc.) WW imagines a wider readership.

82–3 *King Edwarde . . . Fraunce*. Edward III (1312–77), king of England, assumed the title of king of France on 26 Jan. 1340. His claim was through his mother, Isabella, daughter of Philippe IV.

83–4 *Prince Edwarde . . . bretherin*. Edward of Woodstock (1330–76), known as the Black Prince; Lionel of Antwerp (1338–68), duke of Clarence; John of Gaunt (1340–99), duke of Lancaster; Thomas of Woodstock (1355–97), duke of Gloucester; and Edmund of Langley (1341–1402), duke of York.

85 *Mˡ. iiijᶜxv*. Henry V's invasion of Normandy.

88 *tho thre noble prynces, his bretherne*. Contrasting *bretherin* 84 of the Black Prince and those of Henry V: Thomas (1387–1421), duke of Clarence; John (1389–1435), duke of Bedford; Humphrey (1390–1447), duke of Gloucester. See also 1319–89 and nn.

89–90 *that parties*. A common use of the pl. in this sense (= 'region'), as at 1081, 1474–5, C4/45. See Glossary, s.v. **partie**, and *OED, party, n.*, I.2.b, and *MED, parti(e, n.*, 3(c). For *that* with a pl. n. (as at 1339), see *OED, that, pron.*¹, *adj.*¹ *adv.* and *n.*, B.1.c.

90 *notorily*. 1st citation in *OED, notorily, adv.*, and *MED, notorili, adv.*, is from Gairdner, no. 309, a document in WW's handwriting (BL, Add. MS 27444, f. 38ᵛ); WW also uses it in *PL*, no. 1046, l. 52. His idiolectal coinage is perhaps calqued on Fr. *notoirement*, which *DMF* cites repeatedly from Froissart, from whose work WW borrowed (see 400–22n. and *passim*). Recurs, sometimes pejorative, sometimes positive, at 218–19, 665, C1/25.

95 '*bys'nes*. Nichols reads *vyfnes*, then cited in *MED, vivenes, n.*; *OED* does not record such a word. The initial has a more elaborate approach-stroke than **v** and is **b** with a hooked ascender; the distinction between **f** and long **s** is not clear here, where these letters are written over others; and either pair of letters could be misread by scribes. *OED*, *business*, *n.*, Forms, β lists 15th- and 16th-c. sp. without the medial syllable; sense I.4 = 'eagerness' fits.

95–6 *of egre courages.* 2nd n. phrase in apposition with *of here spiritis* (see Introduction, pp. lxxx–lxxxiii), so that *bysnes* arises *of* = 'from' both their *spiritis* and their *courages* (= 'passions'). See also 230n.

97–8 *as ire . . . lion.* See similarly 1413–14, 1473. WW's *egrenesse* and *feersnesse* were proverbial qualities of lions: Bartlett Jere Whiting and Helen Wescott Whiting, *Proverbs, Sentences and Proverbial Phrases: From English Writings Mainly before 1500* (Cambridge, MA, 1968), L306–L363, especially L309, L311. See e.g. Chaucer, *Canterbury Tales*, I. 1598, and John Lydgate, *Troy Book*, ed. Henry Bergen, 4 vols., EETS ES 97, 103, 106, 126 (1906–35), II. 1752, III. 1252–3. A lion was a common symbol or simile for anger but often implied criticism of anger in Christian and classical thought (Prov. 20: 2; Seneca, *De ira*, I. 16; *De officiis*, I. 41). But Brunetto Latini, *Li Livres dou tresor*, I. 179 (ed. Carmody, 154), praises lions' 'mervilleuse fierté'; and Aristotle, *Nicomachean Ethics*, VII. vi. 1 (1149a31–3), trans. H. Rackham (Cambridge, MA, 1934), 407, defends anger as a rational response to a slight (like WW's *a wrong shewed vnto theym* 101): Christopher Tilmouth, *Passion's Triumph over Reason: A History of the Moral Imagination from Spenser to Rochester* (Oxford, 2007), 44–8. WW knew Latini (see 27–9n.) and Aristotle's *Ethics*: he lent a copy of *Ethics* to Thomas Yong (*Itineraries*, 262), took notes from books VIII and IX (Julius, ff. 74^r–75^v) and made casual reference to it in a letter (*PL*, 604, ll. 1–2); his employer Fastolf owned the Fr. trans. by Nicole Oresme (Beadle, 'Fastolf's French Books', 104).

104–5 *vapour, sprede out.* *MED*, *vapouren*, *v.*, 1(a) cites only this text for this metaphorical sense; *DMLBS*, *vaporare*, records no similar metaphorical sense; and *OED*, *vapour* | *vapor*, *v.*, 1.a, lists metaphorical senses from e.g. Lydgate. After this rare usage, the synonym *sprede out*, in grammatical apposition, could serve as a gloss: see Introduction, pp. lxxx–lxxxiii.

105 *floure-de-lice.* The fleur-de-lis, the French royal arms. Edward III quartered the leopards of England with the fleur-de-lis of France to underscore his claim to the French throne: W. M. Ormrod, 'A Problem of Precedence: Edward III, the Double Monarchy, and the Royal Style', in J. S. Bothwell (ed.), *The Age of Edward III* (York, 2001), 133–53 at 134. WW uses its splayed shape to imagine how troops will *sprede out*, a distinct use of the v. recorded in *MED*, *spreden*, *v.*, 3.(a).

109 *vmbre and coloure.* See 54–5n.

109–11 *trewis . . . M^l. iiij^C xliiij^{to}.* The Truce of Tours, correctly dated to 28 May 1444, which WW copied into Arundel, ff. 278^r–281^v.

113 *duchee[z].* MS *ducheer* recurs at 283, 314, and, as *duchier*, 1125. With only two syllables, it is unlikely a variant sp. for *MED*, *ducherie*, *n.* (*OED*, *duchery*, *n*.), and is more likely *MED, duche, n.* (*OED, duchy, n.*). Each instance refers to a pl. list of duchies (though see 21–2n.), but final ⟨r⟩ fails to mark the pl. By contrast, at *ducheez* 21 the pl. is marked with the inflection ⟨z⟩, often used by WW (Davis, 'Epistolary', 270; and see Introduction, pp. xciii–xciv), including on other words with a final syllable sound /i/ (e.g. *PL*, no. 960, l. 6 'feffeez', and no. 982, l. 21 'dewteez', in letters composed by Fastolf but in WW's handwriting); and in 689, *duchier* is corrected to *duchies* by overwriting. So here the final **r** in MS *ducheer* probably misreads that pl. marker ⟨z⟩ as the zetoid shape of **r**, as in *bataile*[z] 61 (see n.). The 1st *ducheez* 21 might have been copied more carefully on f. 1ʳ as part of an early stage of 'working in' by the scribe. See also 61n.

116 *it approuethe*. Neither *OED, approve, v.*¹, nor *MED, ap(p)reven, v.*, records this impersonal construction, = 'is proven'.

121–2 *men . . . vndre youre predecessoure obedience* = 'men under obedience to your predecessor', equivalent to the *lieges-men* 122 (see n.). Neither *MED, predecessour, n.*, nor *OED, predecessor, n.*, has any citation with the uninflected possessive, but it is common in WW's usage on *predecessor* and *antecessor*, e.g. 2258–9, 2291–2, 2340, but cf. inflections on 145, 809, 1313, 2304, as well as 2210 and 2354 interlineated by WW. See Introduction, p. xcv.

122 *lieges-men*. On inflected adjectival elements, as in the 1st half of this compound, see Introduction, p. xci. Neither *MED, lege, adj.*, nor *OED, liege, adj.* and *n.*, cites the adj. thus inflected, nor do *OED, liegeman, n.*, nor *MED, lege-man, n.*, record a sp. with medial ⟨s⟩.

123–5 *Ser Gilis . . . prison*. Gilles de Bretagne (d. 1450), son of Jean V (d. 1442), duke of Brittany. By the time WW was writing, the dukedom had passed to Jean's eldest son, François. Gilles was arrested in 1446 for conspiring with the English, was allegedly poisoned, and died in prison: M. H. Keen and M. J. Daniel, 'English Diplomacy and the Sack of Fougères in 1449', *History*, 59 (1974), 375–91.

126 *Fugiers*. The capture of Fougères by the Aragonese mercenary François de Surienne on 24 Mar. 1449. WW interlineated 'Miles Franciscus Arragoneys' and 'vocata Fugiers' in the account in Royal, f. 85ᵛ (*Giles' Chronicle*, 'Henrici VI', 36), and noted the capture of Fougères ('Fugyers') in a memorandum in Arundel, f. 285ᵛ, there dating it to 24 Mar. 1448 (just, by Lady Day dating) as a 'causa infraccionis treugarum inter Reges Anglie et Francorum Rex'. In this section (120–38), WW emphasizes French infractions of the truce before the taking of Fougères. The point that Simon Morhier and others were imprisoned without cause beforehand was repeatedly made by English ambassadors in the negotiations of June 1449. The taking of Pont-de-l'Arche (see 132–5 and n.) was also a bone of contention: 'Conferences between the Ambassadors of France and England', in *Narratives of the Expulsion of the English from*

Normandy: MCCCCXLIX–MCCCCL, ed. Joseph Stevenson, RS 32 (London, 1863), 379–514 at 429, 479–80.

126–8 *Ser Simon Morhier . . . deliuerid.* Mentioned in Codicil, f. 12ʳ (*Wars in France*, ii. 531), in similar wording ('Simon Morchier Miles Banerettus prouost de Paris . et de Concilio domini Regentis'). His capture in late Feb. 1449 near Dieppe (*Deepe*) is recorded in letters of 28 Feb. ('Mardi derrierement passe') and Apr. 1449 from the duke of Somerset to the king of France (*Wars in France*, i. 228–9, 236–7).

129 *Mauncell.* We have not found a reference to this specific event, but violations of the truce and attacks on the king's subjects were reported when parliament reconvened in May 1449: *PROME*, xii. 54–5. WW specifies that Mauncell's capture occurred in Jan., and *after* the taking of Simon Morhier, which occurred in late Feb. 1449 (see 126–8n.). WW has confused dates slightly. 'Thomas Maunsell, armiger' appears in Codicil, f. 60ᵛ (Appendix 3/56).

132–5 *Lord Faucomberge . . . day.* Pont-de-l'Arche was taken in the early hours of 16 May 1449. William Neville, Lord Fauconberg (d. 1463), was captured. WW interlineated 'die 15 Maij' into the account of its capture in Royal, f. 85ᵛ (*Giles' Chronicle*, 'Henrici VI', 36).

133 *cautel.* This deception is reported by Berry Herald: Jean de Brézé, Robert de Flocques, and others captured Pont-de-l'Arche by persuading a merchant from Louviers, who frequently travelled to Rouen via Pont-de-l'Arche, to pretend to be taking his merchandise to Rouen and to ask the porter to open the castle gates the following morning; this allowed the attackers to enter the castle, take it, and then take the town: 'Le Recouvrement de Normendie par Berry, Herault du Roy', in *Narratives of the Expulsion*, ed. Stevenson, 239–376 at 246–50.

139 *this paast.* OED, *past, adj.* and *n.*, B.1.b, only records the sense=‘That which has happened in the past’ from 1589, but B.1.a records a different sense from Blayney, 120, l. 30; *MED, passed, ppl. adj.*, 1(a) does record the nominal usage. *DMF, passé*, records the usage in Fr., citing e.g. Chartier, *Le Livre de l'espérance*, Pr. XV. 282, a text WW knew (see 750–2n.).

141 *allie`s'.* The scribe wrote pl. *alliez* with ⟨z⟩, a common inflection for WW (see Introduction, pp. xciii–xciv), but somebody wrote ⟨s⟩ over the top of ⟨z⟩, suggesting confusion at **z**, which resembled zetoid or round **r**. See also 1505, 1515, and cf. 1371n.

141 *irnesse*=‘irons’ burning hot in the fire. The unusual sp. is attested in *MED, iren, n.*, but it might (unconsciously?) recall *ire*. The comparison of readiness to act with irons ready to be struck is proverbial: e.g. collocated with *courage* by Thomas Hoccleve, *The Regement of Princes*, ed. Frederick J. Furnivall, EETS ES 72 (1897), ll. 2015–16. See Whiting and Whiting, *Proverbs*, I60.

146–7 *Iob . . . bloode.* Rather than a quotation, this perhaps paraphrases Job's

repeated appeals to three friends (e.g. Job 2: 13 to 3: 26, 6: 1 to 7: 21, 13: 1–13).
Job once directly asks his *frendis* to *Criethe and bewailethe* (e.g. Job 19: 21, 'Miseremini mei, miseremini mei, saltem vos, amici mei'), after a lament that his
family has abandoned him (Job 19: 13–14, 'Fratres', 'propinqui', 'uxor', and 'fi-
lios'), but there is no direct address there to *kyn* nor mention of pity for *bloode*,
unless WW has misunderstood 'carnibus meis saturamini' in Job 19: 22 as referring to family (as in 'flesh and *bloode*'). WW cites Job later from John of Wales
(see 1596–9n., 1787–9n.), so he might not have known the Book of Job directly.

151–63 *But first . . . God.* Loosely trans. from Christine de Pizan, *Livre des faits
d'armes*, I. 2 (BL, Royal MS 15 E. vi, f. 405ᵛ; Laennec, ii. 23–4), 'Cest premiere-
ment asauoir . . . permises de droit et de Dieu'. After *werres and batailes*, WW
omits Christine's grammatical apposition 'cheualerie et faiz darmes de la quelle
chose nous esperons parler'; after *answerde* he omits her 'magnifestement'; he
adds *And the oppinion . . . ne iust thing* 154–6; and WW's litany of crimes omits
Christine's mention of rape ('efforcemens de femmes') found in other MSS (but
not in Laennec, ii. 24). WW must have consulted a Group A MS, as he knows
that Christine is the author; Group B MSS remove references to her: Christine
Reno, 'The Manuscripts of the *Livre des fais d'armes et de chevalerie*', *Digital
Philology: A Journal of Medieval Cultures*, 6/1 (2017), 137–62 at 137–40. Of the
Group A copies made in 15th-c. England (e.g. also BL, Harley MS 4605 and BL,
Royal MS 19 B. xviii), we quote from BL, Royal MS 15 E. vi, a MS made for John
Talbot, an associate of Fastolf. In WW's milieu, John Paston II had a 'tretys of
werre in iiij book*es*' copied by William Ebesham in or before 1469 (*PL*, no. 755,
l. 25), which Summit, *Lost Property*, 72, suggests could be Christine's.

152 *Tree of Batailles.* Despite knowing that Christine was author of *Le Livre des
faits d'armes*, WW here and at 789, 1671 refers to the text as *The Tree of Batailles*, and at 163–4, 877 as *The Arbre of Batailes*, recalling *L'Arbre des batailles*
by Honoré Bouvet, one of Christine's sources for parts III and IV of her work
but not for part I, cited here. WW's MS of Christine's *Livre*, which we have not
identified, might have misled him. Two Group A MSS also contain Bouvet's
work: BL, Royal MS 15 E. vi, ff. 293ʳ–326ᵛ (see 151–63n.), and Brussels, KBR,
MS 9009–11, ff. 1ʳ–115ʳ (Reno, 'Manuscripts', 143–4). One Group B MS has a
deleted colophon 'Explicit larbre des batailles': BnF, MS fr. 1243, f. 130ʳ (Reno,
'Manuscripts', 151). Summit, *Lost Property*, 75–8, observes that Lord Lumley,
who owned *BkNob.* (see Introduction, p. xxxiii), noted the error, citing *BkNob.*,
in his copy of Bouvet.

156 *infinite.* We emend MS *infinitee* by comparison with the repetition *infinite
damages* 159, and because an adj. fits between *many*+n.

159 *to*='too', adv., followed by 'zero' subordination (i.e. omission of *that*). Nichols deletes *to*, supplies *that*.

164 `A'rbre*. The MS correction might suggest confusion with the Fr. article, as in 'larbre' (see 152n.).

165–76 *maynteyne werre . . . straunge countrees*. Translated from Christine, *Livre des faits d'armes*, I. 4 (BL, Royal MS 15 E. vi, f. 406^r; Laennec, ii. 26), 'dempendre guerres et batailles . . . conquerir seignouries estranges'. WW has skipped the rest of I. 2 and I. 3 since the previous translation at 151–63 (see n.). He takes much Fr.-derived vocabulary from Christine's Fr.: see Introduction, pp. lxxxix–xc. In the MS, f. 4^r, the enumerated causes are marked with red paraphs, added in spaces between words, after WW had corrected the text by adding *of* 170, which requires the subsequent paraph to be between the lines.

167 *vallente*. The only citation in *MED*, vallente, n., and *OED*, vallente, n. = 'might', but more likely a variant sp. of *OED*, volunty, n., or *MED*, volunte, n. = 'will'; see also *voulente* 2555. The source, Christine, *Livre des faits d'armes*, I. 4 (BL, Royal MS 15 E. vi, f. 406^r; Laennec, ii. 26), has 'volente', which William Caxton (trans.), *The Book of Fayttes of Armes and of Chyualrye*, 11, l. 23, renders as 'wyll'. It echoes the classical Greek and proverbial contrast (Whiting and Whiting, *Proverbs*, M534) between *right*, here war motivated by justice, and *might*, here the wilfulness of the prince. But cf. *violen`c'e*, originally written as *violente*, 174, in place of *vallente*, which suggests some confusion by WW about Christine's word or the scribe about WW's spelling.

173 *to whome* = 'to which', viz. which seignoury or other land; *whom* often had inanimate or pl. referents: *OED*, whom, pron., III.9.a; *MED*, whom, pron., 4a, 4b.

173–4 *apparteine, be meinteined vnder*. On such apposition, see Introduction, pp. lxxx–lxxxiii, here glossing *apparteine*, closely calqued from Fr. 'appartenir' (Christine, *Livre des faits d'armes*, I. 4; BL, Royal MS 15 E. vi, f. 406^r; Laennec, ii. 26). *MED*, ap(p)ertenen, v., 1, records that the sense = 'to belong to' was not rare by 1475.

176–9 *bethat any title . . . vse them*. Based on Christine, *Livre des faits d'armes*, I. 4 (BL, Royal MS 15 E. vi, f. 406^r; Laennec, ii. 27), 'sans y auoir aucun tiltre . . . guerre ne bataille'. Christine uses Alexander and the Romans as examples of those who conquered lands without right. WW mistranslates, with the result that Alexander conquers the Romans.

176 *bethat*. A variant sp. for *bythout* (= 'without'), perhaps a scribal error (as at 223, see n.) misunderstanding WW's *bethout* as = 'by that'. Like *bethyn* (see 52n.), *bethout* is common in *BkNob*. and letters composed or copied by WW (e.g. *PL*, no. 1005, l. 9) but rare outside of south-west England; in transcribing one of WW's letters, Richard Calle of Norfolk confuses it as 'be thut', with uncertain corrections (*PL*, no. 604, l. 33). See *MED*, bithoute, prep.; *OED*, bythout | bythinne, prep., and *LALME*, dot map 295, cited in Introduction, p. xciii.

180–3 *before a prince . . . prince is of*. An elaboration of Christine, *Livre des faits d'armes*, I. 4 (BL, Royal MS 15 E. vi, f. 406^r; Laennec, ii. 28), 'afin quil oeuure iustement . . . sil est subget'. WW's addition *to* makes the syntax more awkward than it already was.

183–5 *in a iust quarell . . . vertues.* Close to a phrase in an earlier chapter of Christine, *Livre des faits d'armes*, I. 2 (BL, Royal MS 15 E. vi, f. 405ᵛ; Laennec, ii. 24), 'Et nest aultre chose guerre ou bataille . . . de iustice'. WW's addition that *iustice* is *one of the principall .iiij. cardinall vertues* may reflect his reading of other works but was known widely enough not to require a source. The emphasis on *execucion of iustice* recalls Fastolf's ownership of a tapestry 'of ymagery work of Justice adminystryng' (*PL*, no. 1049, l. 25). Cf. C1/9–16 with an emphasis on *fortitudo*.

184 *of iustice, [as iustice] requirithe.* The text is hard to parse without emending. Nichols deletes *it is* 183–4. MS *of iustice requirithe* is perhaps eyeskip on an Eng. rendering of the Fr. source's repetition of *droit(te)* in 'la droitte execucion de iustice pour rendre le droit la ou il appartient' (Christine, *Livre des faits d'armes*, I. 2; BL, Royal MS 15 E. vi, f. 405ᵛ; Laennec, ii. 24). For a similar repetition, by Fastolf in WW's handwriting, see *PL*, 996, ll. 29–30: judge 'Ʒeluerton, justice . . . wolle as fer as justice, reson, *and* concience do that justice may [be] egallie mynistred'.

188 *Viue le plus fort.* This phrase sounds like a common idiom (e.g. a battle cry), but it is difficult to find contemporary evidence that it was well known: Philippe Contamine, 'L'Idée de guerre à la fin du Moyen Age; aspects juridiques et éthiques', *Comptes rendus des séances de l'Academie des Inscriptions et Belles-Lettres*, 123/1 (1979), 70–86 at 85, cites only *BkNob*. It might be that WW has invented it to characterize the French negatively. It is the only phrase in Fr. in *BkNob*.

189–206 *lyke as when . . . the seyd yere.* WW adds in the right margin and at the foot of the page. The *signe de renvoi* mark for insertion clearly appears after *feelde* 189. The examples interrupt the implied *if X, in such X* syntax with a subclause of over 200 words, but the effect is typical of WW's style, and the added examples illustrate the argument of 185–9, 206–7.

189–200 *duc off Burgoyn . . . Seynt-Clowe.* Details from the Armagnac-Burgundian civil war. The duke of Burgundy, Jean sans Peur (d. 1419), expelled Charles (d. 1465), duke of Orléans and his supporters from Paris, following the battle of Saint-Cloud (*Seynt-Clow*, 196) because of the *synguler querel* between them due to the assassination of Louis (1372–1407), duke of Orléans (*duc off Orlyance*) by Raoulet d'Anquetonville (*Raulyn Actovyle*, 195), on the orders of Jean sans Peur, on 23 Nov. 1407. (WW's *vigille of Seynt Clement* would usually mean the evening before 23 Nov.) The battle of Saint-Cloud, a victory for Anglo-Burgundian forces, took place on 9 Nov. 1411 or, according to some sources, 10 Nov. at night. The English soldiers were not *waged* by the duke of Burgundy (contrary to 197) but by Prince Henry, the future Henry V, although he perhaps expected to be reimbursed by the duke. The following year, however, on 18 May 1412, an Anglo-Armagnac alliance was agreed. An English army was raised against the duke of Burgundy, and the Armagnacs were to pay its wages for three months. See Chris Given-Wilson, *Henry IV* (New Haven, 2016), 493–5, 497–9. Some of this information is in *Giles' Chronicle* ('Henrici IV', 60–1), which WW read in Royal, f. 129^v, which correctly dates the events to the 13th year of Henry IV's reign. As Henry IV acceded 30 Sept. 1399, the year should be 1411, not WW's M^l. *iiii^C. xij* (191–2).

190 *maisterdom.* 1st citation in this sense in *OED, masterdom, n.*, 2.a, and *MED, maisterdom, n.*, 1(a).

193 *be venge.* This passive construction (*OED, venge, v.*, 1.c; *MED, vengen*, 1[c]) usually requires a prep. before any accompanying n. (as at 175).

198 *myghtly.* For consistency (see Introduction, p. cv), here and at C2/98 we do not expand a crossbar on **ght** by supplying ⟨e⟩ (e.g. *myghtely*): see *mightly* without any crossbar on **ght** 1452, but cf. *mightilie* 1442, *myghtelie* C2/209. The two-syllable form is widely attested: see *OED, mightly, adv.*, and *MED, mightli, adv.*

202–4 *the yeere of . . . Motreaw.* The assassination of Jean sans Peur, not *Phelip* (Philippe le Bon, 1396–1467), at Montereau (for which *Motreaw* may reflect the oversight of an abbreviated ⟨n⟩ or a nasalized pronunciation of Fr.), occurred on 10 Sept. 1419, not 1418: Sumption, iv. 651–4. *Chronique de Normandie*, copied in Arundel, ff. 257^v–258^r (Williams, 195–6), contains an account of this, with events of 1419 erroneously dated to 1418, which WW corrects to 1419 (f. 256^r), but the error may have misled him at the point of composition of this section. The sense of *yeer day* here and at 595, 866, is less specific than defined in *MED, yer-dai, n.* (='year to the day'), and is not registered in *OED, year-day, n.*

204–6 *cyte of Pa`r"ys . . . seyd yere.* The retaking of Paris for the Burgundians on 29 May 1418, under the leadership of Jean de Villiers, lord of L'Isle-Adam (*Lord L'Ysel-Adam pryncipall capteyn*). During the riots and massacre that followed, Bernard VII, count of Armagnac, constable of France (*erle of Armonak, conestable*), was killed by the mob (Sumption, iv. 564–71). WW had access to these details in the *Chronique de Normandie* in Arundel, ff. 248^v–250^v (Williams, 184–6).

204 *Pa`r"ys.* WW wrote the short **r** of secretary script but then wrote over it the long **r** from anglicana script. See other alterations of allographs of **r** at 355, 2070, and 2085, and in a letter by Fastolf in WW's handwriting, where zetoid 'round' **r** is overwritten with long **r** (BL, Add. MS 34888, f. 109^r, l. 9; *PL*, no. 509/20). Compare problems with understanding forms of **r** at 61 (see n.), etc., and changes to **a** at 264 (see n.), etc.

211 *Seint Lowes.* Louis IX (1214–70), king of France, known as St Louis.

211–14 *Seint Lowes . . . sonne Philip. Les Enseignements de Saint Louis à son fils*, the letter from St Louis to his son, Philippe III, circulated in various forms in medieval England and was incorporated into *GCF*, St Louis, ch. 115 (Viard, vii. 277–80): see Frédérique Lachaud, 'The Knowledge and Use of the "Teachings of Saint Louis" in Fourteenth-Century England', in Hannah Skoda, Patrick Lantschner, and R. L. J. Shaw (eds.) *Contact and Exchange in Later Medieval Europe: Essays in Honour of Malcolm Vale* (Woodbridge, 2012), 189–209. On WW's access to *GCF*, see Introduction, pp. lxxii, lxxiv–lxxv. The date of 1270 for St Louis's death is accurate; see 290–5n.

214–18 *he shulde kepe . . . pleasid*. Translated from *GCF*, St Louis, ch. 115, 'Garde toi de mouvoir guerre . . . Diex t'en sache gré' (Viard, vii. 279). WW translates from it again at 2457–64 (see n.).

215 *meoue no werre*. *OED, move, v.*, I.11, records this idiom before WW (see also *MED, meven, v.*, 2b), but notes its calquing on Fr., as here < 'mouvoir guerre' (Viard, vii. 279). Cf. 1648n.

216, 222 *waies of pece*. Collocation not in *MED*, but cf. similar idioms, with sg. *weie*, in *MED, wei, n.* (1), 7b(a), 'weie of love', etc.

219 '*y'oure*. The hand of interlineated **y** cannot be determined with certainty but is probably WW revising, addressing Edward IV more directly, as at 42 and in a longer addition at 234 (see nn.), and in other additions of *your* or changes of *oure* to '*y'oure* at 2239–40 (see n.), 2309, 2362.

220 *meoued, excited*. On such apposition, see Introduction, pp. lxxx–lxxxiii. On the sp. ⟨meo⟩, see Introduction, p. xcii.

221 *iustice, title*. On such apposition, see Introduction, pp. lxxx–lxxxiii.

223 *note of tiranye*. Echoes C2/163.

223 *be 'be'thout*. Scribal haplography, which WW corrects, might reflect not only eyeskip but a mistaken parsing of *be thout* as = 'be thought', reflecting the lesser familiarity of *bethout* for the scribe than for WW, as at 176 (see n.).

225 *m'o'y'e'ne*. The ⟨o⟩ over another letter and interlineated ⟨e⟩ bring the spelling of PDE *mean* ('method') closer to its etymology in Fr. *moyen* (see *DMF, moyen*[1], where all recorded forms are disyllabic) than AN *mene* (although *AND, mene*[1], records variant sp. with ⟨o⟩). *MED, mene, n.* (3), records spellings with ⟨o⟩ but disyllabic forms with double ⟨e⟩ 'meyen', including Blayney, 176/29 (and see *MED*'s form *moien*, for which no quotation is given). The sp. *moyen* recurs at 1063, 1499, *moien* at 2564, 2573; cf. *moenys* 639. *OED, moyen, n.*[1], I.2.a, identifies a separate Fr. borrowing of *moyen*. It appears in e.g. a 1440 letter by Humphrey, duke of Gloucester (*Wars in France*, ii. 444), Fastolf's 1435 articles on the congress of Arras (C2/15), letters by Fastolf in Worcester's handwriting (e.g. *PL*, nos. 509/15; 579/62), and Cicero,

De Amicitia, supposedly translated by Tiptoft (printed in Caxton, *Tullius de senectute*, sig. b1^v, alongside WW's *Tulle*).

229 *Brutis bloode of Troy.* See 27–9n.

230 *couragis* = 'valour', widely attested in *MED*, *corage, n.*, 3(a), *OED*, *courage, n.*, 4.

230 *reualid.* See 64n.

230 *desteined* = 'dishonoured' or = 'outshone'. See *OED*, *distain, v.*, 2 = 'to dishonour', or 3 = 'to outshine', and *MED*, *disteinen, v.*, 3(b).

233–4 *that it may be in goodely hast remedied.* This subclause and the interlineation in 234 (see n.) awkwardly separate the n. phrase *straunge nacions* from its dependent rel. clause *whiche ye haue be conquerours of* (234–5).

234 *as youre hyghnesse now entendyth.* Interlineated by WW when he revised the text in 1475. See Introduction, pp. lv–lvii.

235–8 *deffaute of goode . . . relief them.* See also 865–71.

239–40 *manlinesse and of strenght.* The syntax with *of* concludes the list awkwardly, but the sense is clear.

246–8 *King Arthur . . . Rome.* Arthur's various conquests and the Roman campaign, in which the emperor, Lucius, is killed. In Geoffrey of Monmouth, *Historia*, X. 175 (ed. Reeve, trans. Wright, 247), Lucius is 'cuiusdam lancea confossus' ('struck down [*strictly* 'pierced': *DMLBS*, *confodere*, 1] by an unknown lance'), hence WW's point that that Lucius was not killed by Arthur but 'vndre his banere'. WW later took notes from Geoffrey in *Itineraries*, 210–12, 280, 284–6, 326, including in 1480 from a book owned by John Murylynch of Muchelney Abbey, noting that Lucius was not emperor (260).

246–7 *whiche . . . vndre his banere* = 'under whose banner'. See 246–8n. For the genitive rel. pron. *whiche* alongside a pleonastic personal pron. in the genitive form (*his* in 247), see *OED*, *which, adj.* and *pron.*, B.II.8.a.(b), and *MED*, *which, pron.*, 6(a), 'rel. pron. with ellipsis of preceding prep.'

248 *conquerid.* Arthur resumes as subject; a rel. pron is perhaps understood (as at e.g. 650n.).

250–3 *Brenus . . . Capitoile of Rome.* Two lists of ancient kings in WW's miscellany, Arundel, ff. 76^r, 112^v, say that Brennius's army 'vrbem ceperunt usque ad capitolium', and 'usque' could imply that he did *not* capture that part of Rome. The 1st list cites 'historia britonum aliisque cronicis' (f. 76^r), i.e. perhaps Geoffrey of Monmouth, *Historia*, III. 43 (ed. Reeve, trans. Wright, 57–9); but Geoffrey does not mention the failure to conquer the capitol. That is mentioned in *Flores historiarum*, ed. Luard, i. 63; and a later part of the 1st list cites information 'secundum floris historiarum' (f. 79^r), while the 2nd list's colophon states that it was compiled from 'libro vocato flores historiarum' (f. 119ʳ); this therefore is the likely source. WW also had access to a brief account in Nicholas Trevet, *Cronicles*, in OMC, MS Lat. 45, f. 15ᵛ, a MS WW annotated on other leaves (ff. iiᵛ, 86ʳ; identified by Rundle, 'Worcestre'), and in Julius, f. 59ᵛ, he copied a reference to *Belynus* in a list from Trevet's chronicle in a MS in the library of Michaelhouse, Cambridge, on 9 Jan. 1468.

251 *chosen duke.* Brennius being *chosen* perhaps='noble', a common use of the pa. p. (see also 2373 and *MED*, *chesen*, *v.*, 5[a];), or alternatively because Seginus, duke of the Allobroges, selects him to marry his only daughter and succeed him (Geoffrey of Monmouth, *Historia*, III. 40; ed. Reeve, trans. Wright, 53).

254-5 *Edmonde Irensede . . . to safe Englond.* Edmund II (d. 1016). WW had notes on his battles against the Danes in Arundel, ff. 84ᵛ–85ʳ.

257 ‵*in*″ *conquestys.* WW interlineated *many conquestys*, but **ma** and the tail of **y** were rubbed off, leaving *in*.

257-60 ‵*Kyng*′ *Harry . . . Frenshe partie.* Henry I (d. 1035) spent a lot on castle building on the Norman frontier: David Bates, *The Normans and Empire* (Oxford, 2013), 104.

261-5 *his brother Roberd . . . victorie after.* Robert Curthose (d. 1134), eldest son of William the Conqueror, who took part in the First Crusade (1096–1100). The tradition that Robert was punished by God for refusing the crown of Jerusalem was well established (e.g. William of Malmesbury and Henry of Huntingdon). WW may draw on Trevet, *Cronicles*, in OMC, MS Lat. 45, f. 80ᵛ (on which MS, see 250–3n.), or more likely Higden, *Polychronicon*, VII. 12 (ed. Babington and Lumby, vii. 424), in Royal, f. 9ʳ. Both state that Curthose refused the crown because he coveted England, not Normandy as here, but Higden adds, as WW says, 'Qua de causa nunquam postmodum in bello fortunatus fuit'.

262 *that*='who', introducing four rel. clauses that expand on Robert Curthose (see previous n.) but rather diminish his exemplarity.

264 ‵*a*′*nd.* Somebody adds a stroke to one-compartment **a**, typical of secretary script, to create two-compartment **a** typical of anglicana, and also found in secretary script as a word-initial positional variant in the 3rd quarter of the 15th c. This happens often in the MS: see also 603, 913, 1289, 2076, 2213, 2324, 2346, and, with a possibly different cause, 835, 838 (see n.), and cf. changes to **r** at 204 (see n.), etc.

265-70 *Fouke . . . .Mˡ. Cxxxj.* The date, 1131, is correct but straddles the page break, so WW duplicates the missing half of the date at the end of the last l. of f. 5ʳ and the start of the 1st l. of f. 5ᵛ. For Foulques, count of Anjou, see 44–5n.

270-1 *King Richarde . . . croiserie.* Richard I (1157–99), one of the leaders of the Third Crusade. Last citation in both *OED*, *croiserie*, *n.*, and *MED*, *croiserie*, *n.*

272 *Baldewyn, archebisshop of Caunterburie.* Baldwin of Forde (c.1125–90), archbishop of Canterbury; he went on crusade and died at Acre in 1190.

272–3 *Hubert, bisshop of Salisburie.* Hubert Walter (d. 1205), justiciar, bishop of Salisbury and later archbishop of Canterbury. He did go on crusade.

272 *Randolf, the erle of Chestre.* Ranulf (III) (1170–1232), sixth earl of Chester, did not in fact accompany Richard I on crusade, although the Dieulacres chronicle asserts that he did. See Philip Morgan, 'Historical Writing in the North-West Midlands and the Chester Annals of 1385–88', in James Bothwell and Gwilym Dodd (eds.), *Fourteenth Century England IX* (Woodbridge, 2016), 109–29 at 116. WW's red sidenotes 273SN and 274SN misplace the reference to the earl of Chester after the earl of Gloucester; we reorder.

273–4 *Roberd Clare, erle of Gloucestre.* No such person accompanied Richard I on crusade. According to Roger of Hoveden, *Chronica*, ed. William Stubbs, 4 vols., RS 51 (London, 1868–71), iii. 89, one 'Ricardus de Clare' died on the crusade; WW may have been thinking of him.

275 *King Phelip Dieudonne.* Philippe II (1165–1223), king of France, known as Philip Augustus or Dieudonné.

277–8 M^l. *C. iiij^{xx} vij^o.* Incorrect date. Richard I went on crusade in the summer of 1190. WW may have confused the date of the commitment to crusade (Jan. 1187, by Lady Day dating), as related in *GCF*, Philippe II, bk. I, ch. 23 (Viard, vi. 167–8), with the crusade itself.

278–81 *toke the king . . . Ferranus.* Richard I did conquer Cyprus and capture its ruler and others (John Gillingham, *Richard I* (New Haven, 1999), 145–54), but he did not conquer Damascus (*Damask*) or defeat a Spanish king *Ferranus*. That name suggests Catalan *Ferran* or Castilian *Fernando*, a common name for monarchs of Spanish kingdoms, but the only one whose reign overlapped Richard I, Fernando II of León, died on pilgrimage. Events in Cyprus are related in *GCF*, Philippe II, bk. II, ch. 5 (Viard, vi. 201). *Damask* may be an error for Darum, which was taken by Richard and his men (Gillingham, *Richard I*, 203), as related in e.g. Ralph of Diceto's *Ymagines Historiarum* (*The Historical Works of Master Ralph de Diceto, Dean of London*, ed. William Stubbs, 2 vols., RS 68 (London, 1876), ii. 104), a work named by WW at 679.

283 *duchee[z].* See 113n.

286–307 *King Edward First . . . Sarasines.* All the details (time in Acre, the assassination attempt, news of the death of Henry III) are in *GCF*, Philippe III, ch. 9 (Viard, viii. 24–7). At 305–6 WW cites the *Actis* of *Prince Edwarde*; while *Actis* might evoke a separate text of *Gesta* or *Fais* of Edward I (< Lat. *Gesta* [?], as at 655–6: see n.), at 347 (see 338–48n.) WW refers to his source, which is certainly *GCF*, as the *Actis of . . . King Philip*, and in MSS of *GCF* this chapter is often separately titled 'Incidence de edouart filz au roy dangleterre' (e.g. BnF,

MSS fr. 2813, f. 353ʳ; fr. 20350, f. 339ᵛ). Prince Edward (1239–1307), future Edward I of England, went on crusade in the summer of 1270 and did reach Tunis (*gret cite of the roiaume of Thunes*) in Nov. 1270, but Tunis was not conquered by the crusaders. If WW's *gret cite* is Carthage, described in his probable source as 'la real cité et la mestresse de toute Aufrique' (*GCF*, St Louis, ch. 111; Viard, vii. 273), then Edward was not at its capture in July 1270. Edward and his army arrived at Acre in May 1271. The attempted assassination took place in June 1272. See Michael Prestwich, *Edward I* (New Haven, 1997), 73–9.

290–5 (*yn whych cuntree . . . off England*). WW interlineates and continues in the margin. He evidently added this after he had already added a doublet *hys armee and* 297 in the margin, as that shorter addition got in the way of this longer one, and WW had to bracket it off. See Introduction, pp. lxiii–lxiv. Information and vocabulary in the interlineation are shared with, and perhaps taken from, *GCF*, St Louis, ch. 106 (Viard, vii. 280–2). St Louis died at Tunis on 25 Aug. 1270: Prestwich, *Edward I*, 73. His death is recorded in the notes WW took from *GCF* in Titus, f. 76ʳ. As WW's red sidenote 291sɴ refers to the death of St Louis, only mentioned in this revision, it was probably written at the same time or later.

292 *trespassement*. *MED* and *OED* cite only *BkNob.* 1232–3 and C1/68 (but see also *BkNob.* 1317); perhaps < Fr. 'trespassement' describing the death of St Louis in *GCF*, St Louis, ch. 106 (Viard, vii. 281). Nichols reads the abbreviation as giving *trespasseinte*, the only citation in *MED*, *trespasseinte n.*

294 *Iherusalem*. WW abbreviates to *Irlm*; elsewhere in *BkNob.* 44–5, 263, 269, 670, and in Fr. in *GCF* the sp. begins ⟨Iher⟩, as therefore expanded here.

297 *hys armee and*. See 290–5n.

300–1 *he was . . . hym*. Pleonastic use of the object pron. *hym*, typical of the over-explicit syntax of WW's subordinate clauses.

304 *doubte*. Etymological sp. with medial ⟨b⟩. Obsolescent sense = 'apprehension, fear' (*OED*, *doubt, n.*¹, 3.a; *MED*, *dout(e, n.*, 3.[a]), perhaps calqued on Fr. *doubte*, which appears, as v. rather than n. and in a different context, in the source here: *GCF*, Philippe III, ch. 9 (Viard, viii. 25).

308–11 *Richard, emperoure of Almaine . . . Mˡ. ijᶜ. xl*. Richard (1209–72), earl of Cornwall, and king, not emperor, of Germany. Son of King John and brother of Henry III. Richard arrived in Acre on 8 Oct. 1240. Richard's actions in the Holy Land are referred to in *GCF*, St Louis, ch. 23 (Viard, vii. 79), and his coronation as king is in *GCF*, St Louis, ch. 71 (Viard, vii. 182). WW's red sidenote 308sɴ correctly identifies him also as earl of Cornwall, as the text does not; this title occurs in *GCF* (e.g. Viard, vii. 79, 182). WW wrote notes on Richard in BL, Cotton MS Domitian A. ii, f. 4ʳ, on which see Introduction, p. lxxiii n. 194 above, and in *Itineraries*, 86, 90, 98.

313 *rebellis and wilde peple*. National stereotypes, widely attested, e.g. by WW (later, in 1478), in *Itineraries*, 120, citing Gerald of Wales that both the Welsh and the Irish are 'precipites in ira et ad vindictam in vita proni'. For other anti-Welsh prejudice by WW, see *PL*, no. 572, ll. 55–6.

314 *duchee*[*z*]. See 113n.

316–18 *King Edward . . . 'wanne Calix by sege'*. Battle of Sluys, naval battle fought 24 June 1340; the siege of Caen (July 1346); battle of Crécy (26 Aug. 1346); and siege of Calais (Sept. 1346 to Aug. 1347).

319–25 *And sithen . . . barges*. The naval battle of Sluys (i.e. Sluis, now in the Netherlands) is related in *GCF*, Philippe VI, ch. 19 (Viard, ix. 181–4), but there the number of dead is 'près de' 30,000 (Viard, ix. 184), and that source does not include the number of destroyed ships and mistakenly dates the battle to 23, not 24, June ('la veille de la Nativité monseigneur saint Jehan Baptiste'). But the Feast of St John Baptist (i.e. 24 June) 1340 is given as the date for Sluys in WW's notebook, Arundel, f. 122^r (*Wars in France*, ii. 747), and WW's claim that there were 25,000 French dead echoes other English chroniclers: e.g. *Chronicon Galfridi le Baker de Swynbroke*, ed. Edward Maunde Thompson (Oxford, 1889), 69; *Knighton's Chronicle 1337–1396*, ed. and trans. G. H. Martin (Oxford, 1995), 30); *Adæ Murimuth Continuatio chronicarum Robertus de Avesbury de Gestis Mirabilibus Regis Edwardi Tertii*, ed. Edward Maunde Thompson, RS 93 (Oxford, 1889), 109. The figure of *CCxxx*^{ti} destroyed French ships is not far wrong: Sumption, i. 327, says that there were 213 French ships, of which 190 were captured.

321 *the day . . . Baptiste*. WW adds the date after the v. *wanne* at the l. end, but as other dates are added directly adjacent to the year (e.g. 365, 368, 387, 392), we move the addition there; the position seems dictated by available space.

322–3 *Philip de Valoys, calling hym*. Philippe VI (1293–1350), king of France. With normal use of *hym* as the unemphatic refl. pron. (='himself'). Philippe VI is 'calling himself' king of France, wrongly in WW's view. See also 369, 402, 521, 547 (see nn.), 548, 1083, and in Lat. in the Codicil, Appendix 2/12.

325–37 .*M*^{l}. *iij*^{C} *xlvj*. . . . *'by segyng yt'*. Follows *GCF*, Philippe VI, ch. 37 (Viard, ix. 270–4), closely for details of Philippe VI's intention to invade England; the use of Genoese ships; the number of ships (1200) assembled by Edward; Edward's landing at Saint-Vaast-la-Hougue, *département* of Manche (= *The Hagge*); the capture of castles and towns of the Cotentin; taking the constable and the chamberlain prisoner; retreat of the bishop of Bayeux to the castle, and Edward's refusal to lay siege to it *for he wolde not lese his peple* 337 < 'car il ne vouloit mie perdre ses gens' (Viard, ix. 274).

333 *erle of Eu, connestable*. Raoul II de Brienne (d. 1350), count of Eu, and constable of France, taken prisoner at Caen: Clifford J. Rogers, *War Cruel and*

Sharp: *English Strategy under Edward III, 1327–1360* (Woodbridge, 2000), 250; Guy Perry, *The Briennes: The Rise and Fall of a Champenois Dynasty in the Age of the Crusades, c. 950–1356* (Cambridge, 2018), 175. Viard, ix. 272, has the sp. with ⟨nn⟩, and the commonest form recorded in *DMF*, connétable has ⟨nn⟩; *AND*, conestable, records ⟨conn⟩ but not ⟨coun⟩; we read the MS's minims as ⟨conn⟩.

334 *erle of Tancaruille.* Jean II de Melun (d. 1382), count of Tancarville, chamberlain of Normandy. Captured at Caen in 1346 and at Poitiers in 1356 (see 377–8n.): W. M. Ormrod, *Edward III* (New Haven, 2011), 273–5, 352.

336 *bisshop of Baieux.* Guillaume Bertrand (d. 1356), bishop of Bayeux: Sumption, i. 507–9.

338–48 .*M^l. iij^C. xlvj. . . . historied.* As noted at 347 (.39. chapitre . . . Philip), the source is *GCF*, Philippe VI, ch. 39 (Viard, ix. 282–4). Subsections of *GCF* are often titled as being about 'des faiz et du temps' or 'la vie et les fais' (e.g. BnF, MS fr. 2813, ff. 353^v, 389^r), or 'faitz et gestes' (*GCF-1476-7*, ii. ff. 209^v, 264^v) of each king (>WW *Actis* 347; see also 286–307n.). Cf. WW's notes in Titus, which he describes as taken from 'le premiere chapitre du Roy Philipe de Valoys' (f. 77^r). One different detail is the reference to *l. knightis sleyne*, which is a low estimate of the French dead. English newsletters reported the deaths of over 1,500 French noblemen, knights, and esquires, and chronicles give much higher numbers than WW: e.g. Jean le Bel reported the deaths of 12,000 knights (Andrew Ayton and Philip Preston, *The Battle of Crécy, 1346* (Woodbridge, 2005), 19–20, 151). WW has perhaps misunderstood or conflated a reference to 50 knights who died with the king of Bohemia at Crécy later in the same ch. of *GCF* (Viard, ix. 287: 'L chevaliers esleus qui aveques li moururent').

339–40 *dolorous . . . bataile of Cressy.* Echoes the title in some MS copies of *GCF*, Philippe VI, ch. 39 (Viard, ix. 282): 'De la dolente bataille de Créci' or 'La douloureuse bataille contre les francoys'. (A different title is in *GCF-1476-7*, ii, f. 254^v.)

340 *the .xxvj. day of August.* WW has added the correct date, not given in his source in *GCF*, but available to WW elsewhere (e.g. extracts from *Polychronicon* in Arundel, f. 119^v, and *Annales* in Arundel, f. 122^r; *Wars in France*, ii. 747).

341–5 *king of Beame . . . Fennes.* The list of those killed at Crécy follows the order in *GCF*, Philippe VI, ch. 39 (Viard, ix. 283; *GCF-1476-7*, ii, f. 255^r).

341 *king of Beame . . . emperoure.* Jean de Luxembourg (d. 1346), king of Bohemia, killed at Crécy: Sumption, i. 529. The detail that he was the son of Emperor Heinrich VII is in *GCF* (see 338–48n.).

343 *erle of Alaunson . . . brother.* Charles II (d. 1346), count of Alençon, brother of King Philippe VI, killed at Crécy: Sumption, i. 531.

344 *duke of Lorraine.* Raoul (d. 1346), duke of Lorraine, killed at Crécy: Sumption, i. 531.

344 *erle of Bloys.* Louis de Châtillon (d. 1346), count of Blois, killed at Crécy: Sumption, i. 531.

344 *erle of Flaundres.* Louis de Nevers (d. 1346), count of Flanders, killed at Crécy: Sumption, i. 531.

344–5 *erle of Harecourt.* Jean (d. 1346), count of Harcourt, killed at Crécy: Sumption, i. 531.

345 *erle of Sancerre.* Louis II (*c.*1305–46), count of Sancerre, killed at Crécy: Ayton and Preston, *Crécy*, 20.

345 *erle of Fennes.* The correct reading in *GCF* is 'conte de Samues' (Viard, ix. 283)=Simon, count of Salm, who died at Crécy: Ayton and Preston, *Crécy*, 20. But WW's error is present in many witnesses, e.g. 'fiennes' (BnF, MS fr. 2606, f. 409ᵛ, and BnF, MS fr. 2619, f. 403ᵛ) and 'vienne' (*GCF-1476–7*, ii, f. 255ʳ).

347 *.39. chapitre . . . Philip.* See 338–48n.

348 *historied.* 1st citation in *MED*, *historien*, *v.*, and *OED*, *history*, *v.* Perhaps calqued on the rare Fr. *historier* (*DMF*, *historier*, recording examples only from Froissart).

348–52 *erle of Darby . . . entreprises.* Summarizes events in *GCF*, Philippe VI, ch. 39 (Viard, ix. 287).

348–51 *erle of Darby . . . Peyters.* Henry of Grosmont (*c.*1310–61), 1st duke of Lancaster and earl of Derby; made lieutenant of Aquitaine on 13 Mar. 1345; his 1346 campaign in the Agenais, Saintonge, and Poitou included the capture of Saint-Jean-d'Angély (*Saint-Iohn-Euangelist*) in late Sept., and Poitiers (*Peyters*), taken 4 Oct. 1346.

351 *he wanne also. he*=Edward III, referred to at 349. WW changes grammatical subject.

354–6 *King Edward tyme . . . Scotlond.* Mentioned briefly at the end of *GCF*, Philippe VI, ch. 39 (Viard, ix. 291), 'En ce temps, David le roy d'Escoce fu pris des Anglois'. WW elaborates, and *as I haue vndrestond* 355 suggests that he takes detail from another source. In *Annales* in Arundel, f. 122ʳ (*Wars in France*, ii. 747), under 1346 is a note 'xvij° die 'octobris' erat bellum atrox apud durham et Rex scocie dauid captus est'.

354–6 *Dauid . . . of Scotlond.* David II (1324–71), king of Scotland, taken prisoner at the Battle of Neville's Cross on 17 Oct. 1346.

355 *De'r'am.* Durham, the city closest to the Battle of Neville's Cross. WW or the scribe changed the short **r** of secretary script: see 204n.

357–61 *Bretaine . . . King Edward.* Summarizes English involvement in the Breton war of succession. Of two claimants to the duchy following the death of Jean III in Apr. 1341, Edward III supported Jean de Montfort (1295–1345) and then his heir, also Jean (d. 1399), while Philippe VI supported Charles de Blois (c.1319–64): Ormrod, *Edward III*, 249.

358–9 *leid a siege . . . true subgectis*=Edward III's initial siege and capture of La Roche-Derrien (*département* of Côtes d'Armor) in 1345; the reference to it being *kept by his* [i.e. Edward's] *true subgectis* (under Sir Thomas Dagworth) refers to Charles de Blois's failed attempts to retake it (see 359–61n), which are prominent in WW's likely source, *GCF*, Philippe VI, ch. 41 (Viard, ix. 297), e.g. the chapter title 'Comment messire Charles de Bloyes, duc de Bretaigne, fist siege sus les Anglois de la Roche Deryan'. WW's *and kept* would be clearer as *which was*.

359–61 *assautes . . . King Edward.* Charles de Blois laid siege to La Roche-Derrien in 1346, and again in 1347, the latter ending in battle (20 June 1347), at which Charles was captured. Edward paid 25,000 écus for him the following year: Sumption, i. 473, 495, 573–5. *GCF*, Philippe VI, ch. 41 (Viard, ix. 304), includes the *.vij. woundes.*

359–60 *escarmisshes.* Only citation in *MED, escarmish, n.*; 1st citation in *OED, escarmouche, n.* Although *OED, skirmish, n.*, and *MED, scarmuch(e, n.*, had long been in use in Eng., WW might calque afresh from Fr. *escarmouche*, which is not in the relevant passage of *GCF* (see 358–9n.) but is elsewhere in the *GCF* tradition (e.g. *Chron-Jean-Charles*, ii. 189).

361 *he*=Edward III.

361–5 *he also wanne Calix . . . M^l. CCCxlvij.* All details present in *GCF*, Philippe VI, ch. 42 (Viard, ix. 310–11). *GCF* give the date of surrender as 4 Aug. 1347, but modern historians give 3 or 4 Aug. In the account from *Polychronicon* in Arundel, f. 120^r, and in the *Annales* in Arundel, f. 122^v, its fall is dated to 'circa festum sancti bartholomei', i.e. around 24 Aug.

362 *sieges keping.* On this construction, see Introduction, pp. lxxxvii–lxxxviii.

365–6 *also put . . . in subgeccion.* As recounted at 329–31.

367–86 *his eldist sonne . . . bataile.* Closely follows *GCF*, Jean II, ch. 'De la bataille . . .' (*Chron-Jean-Charles*, i. 71–5).

368 *xix day . . . M^l. iij^Clvj.* The battle of Poitiers, correctly dated to 19 Sept. 1356, as in *GCF* (*Chron-Jean-Charles*, i. 71).

368–9 *discomfiture . . . vppon*='victory . . . over'. *OED, discomfiture, n.*, does not distinguish this sense of 'victory' from 'defeat by' (but cf. its quotation from *Mandeville's Travels*); *MED, discomfiture, n.*, sense 1(b), does distinguish them and has earlier citations. Davis, 'Epistolary', 264, notes that this sense, also in *PL*, no. 883, l. 38, a letter by WW, is rare. See Glossary, s.v. **descomfiture**.

369–70 *Iohn, calling hym king of Fraunce.* Jean II (1319–64), who calls himself king of France, wrongly in WW's view (see 322–3n.). Captured at Poitiers: Sumption, ii. 245.

369–72 *in whiche bataile . . . the oriflamble.* The list of French dead follows the names and order of *GCF* (*Chron-Jean-Charles*, i. 72–3), but omits the details that Lord Clermont was marshal and that the duke of Athens was constable.

371 *the duke of Bourbon.* Pierre (1311–56), duke of Bourbon, killed at Poitiers: Sumption, ii. 247.

371 *the duke of Athenes.* Gautier de Brienne (1304–56), constable of France, titular duke of Athens, killed at Poitiers: Sumption, ii. 247.

371–2 *the Lord Clermont.* Jean de Clermont (d. 1356), marshal of France, killed at Poitiers: Sumption, ii. 247.

372 *Ser Geffrey Chauny.* Geoffroi de Charny (d. 1356), carrier of the oriflamme, killed at Poitiers: Sumption, ii. 247.

372 *baner of the oriflamble.* The oriflamme, a standard from St Denis, borne by the kings of France. The only citation in *MED*, *oriflamble, n.*; 1st citation in *OED*, *oriflamme, n.* WW calques the term from the Fr. 'qui portoit l'oriflemble' in *GCF* (*Chron-Jean-Charles*, i. 73), but in effect glosses it with *baner of*.

373 *Ser Philip 'le Hardye', duc of Bourgoine.* WW interlineated the epithet. He places the caret for insertion after *duc* but the convention is to place the epithet after *Philip*, so we emend. Philippe le Hardi (1342–1404), duke of Burgundy, was, as said, following *GCF*, youngest son of King Jean II. At the point of his capture at Poitiers, however, he was not duke of Burgundy, not becoming so until 1363: Richard Vaughan, *Philip the Bold: The Formation of the Burgundian State* (London, 1962), 3.

374–5 *raunson . . . sterlinges.* Not in WW's source *GCF* (*Chron-Jean-Charles*, i. 73), but correct. Edward III promised to give Prince Edward £20,000 for three prisoners—the count of Sancerre, Lord Craon, and Philippe: Chris Given-Wilson and Françoise Bériac, 'Edward III's Prisoners of War: The Battle of Poitiers and its Context', *EHR* 116 (2001), 802–33 at 815.

374 *othres . . . lordes.* For the pl. inflection on the adj., see Introduction, p. xci.

376–7 *Ser Iaques . . . cosins-germains.* Charles is not the brother of Jacques de Bourbon but of Jean d'Artois, omitted in WW's version. WW's confusion was perhaps caused by eyeskip between two instances of 'frere' in *GCF* (*Chron-Jean-Charles*, i. 73): 'monseigneur Jacques de Bourbon, conte de Pontieu et frere du dit duc de Bourbon, monseigneur Jehan d'Artois, conte d'Eu, monseigneur Charles, son frere, conte de Longueville-la-Giffart, cousins germains du dit roy de France'.

376 *Ser Iaques . . . Pontieu.* Jacques de Bourbon (d. 1362), count of La Marche and of Ponthieu, captured at Poitiers: Sumption, ii. 247.

376-7 *Charles his brothir, erle of Longville.* Charles d'Artois (d. 1385), count of Longueville, captured at Poitiers: Ormrod, *Edward III*, 352; Sumption, ii. 462. See 376–7n. Jean d'Artois and Charles d'Artois were cousins of the king, because their mother, Jeanne de Valois, was the aunt of King Jean II.

377 *cosins-germains.* The compound follows *cousins germains* from *GCF* (*Chron-Jean-Charles*, i. 73) but is conventional in Eng. (see *OED*, *cousin-german, n.*). For the pl. inflection and postposed adj., see Introduction, pp. xc–xci.

377-8 *Ser Iohn . . . Sens.* The brothers Jean de Melun, count of Tancarville (see 334n.), and Guillaume de Melun (d. 1376), archbishop of Sens, both captured at Poitiers: Rogers, *War Cruel and Sharp*, 384, 398. Various sp. of their toponymic surname *Melun* are attested in other sources. In particular, the 2nd sp. *Meleum* with final ⟨m⟩ is found in *GCF-1476-7*, ii, f. 276ᵛ.

378-9 *the Erle Dampmartyn.* Charles de Trie, count of Dammartin, captured at Poitiers: Sumption, ii. 244–5.

379 *the Erle Vendosme.* Jean VI (d. 1365), son of Bouchard, count of Vendôme. Captured at Poitiers: Ormrod, *Edward III*, 352.

379 *the Erle Vaudemont.* Henri de Joinville, count of Vaudémont, captured at Poitiers: *Chronicon anonymi Cantuariensis: The Chronicle of Anonymous of Canterbury 1346–1365*, ed. and trans. Charity Scott-Stokes and Chris Given-Wilson (Oxford, 2008), 23.

379 *the Erle Salebruce.* Jean II, count of Saarbrücken, captured at Poitiers: *Chronicon anonymi Cantuariensis*, 23.

380 *the Erle Nauson.* The scribe's clear use of final **n** produces an error (see Introduction, p. xcix) for Jean, count of Nassau, captured at Poitiers: *Chronicon anonymi Cantuariensis*, 23.

380 *Ser Arnolde . . . Fraunce.* Arnoul d'Audrehem, marshal of France, captured at Poitiers: Émile Molinier, *Étude sur la vie d'Arnoul d'Audrehem, maréchal de France (130.–1370)* (Paris, 1883), 69–70; Ormrod, *Edward III*, 352. See also 420.

381-2 *many other . . . knightis banerettis.* Close translation of *GCF*, Jean II, ch. 'De la bataille . . .' (*Chron-Jean-Charles*, i. 74), 'pluseurs autres, tant chevaliers . . . chevaliers bannerez'.

382 *knightis banerettis.* Knights of a rank above knights bachelors. *OED*, *banneret, n.*, 1.c, and *MED*, *baneret, n.* (1), 1(b), give this as the 1st citation of *banneret* in a compound, unhyphenated, after *knight*; < Fr. 'chevaliers bannerez' (*GCF*, in *Chron-Jean-Charles*, i. 74). For the pl. inflection and postposed adj., see Introduction, pp. xc–xci.

382–6 *the kingis eldist . . . bataile.* Based on *GCF* (*Chron-Jean-Charles*, i. 74), but WW changes the order of the names, adds detail about the count of Poitiers, and adds, incorrectly, that the count of Flanders was with them.

383 *Charlis, calling hym duc of Normandie.* Charles (1338–80), duke of Normandy and future King Charles V of France, correctly identified as Jean II's eldest son here, following *GCF* (*Chron-Jean-Charles*, i. 74). As elsewhere (see 322–3n.), WW prefaces his title with 'calling hym'. Referred to as *Charles le Sage* 1226. For his retreat at Poitiers, see Sumption, ii. 241.

383–4 *the duc of Orliauns . . . brother.* Philippe (d. 1375), duke of Orléans, correctly identified as the brother of Jean II, following *GCF* (*Chron-Jean-Charles*, i. 74). For his retreat at Poitiers, see Sumption, ii. 241–2.

384 *the duc of Aniou.* Louis I (d. 1384), duke of Anjou, son of Jean II and brother of future Charles V. For his retreat at Poitiers, see Sumption, ii. 241–2.

384–5 *the erle . . . duc of Berrie.* Jean (d. 1416), count of Poitiers, son of Jean II, and brother of future Charles V. WW adds his first name and detail that he *after was clepid* duke of Berry, not in *GCF* (*Chron-Jean-Charles*, i. 74). Jean became duke of Berry in 1360: Ormrod, *Edward III*, 415. For his retreat at Poitiers, see Sumption, ii. 241–2.

385 *the erle of Flaundris.* The count of Flanders at the time of the battle of Poitiers was Louis de Mâle (1330–84), but he was not at the battle. WW adds this incorrect detail.

387–90 *And sone after . . . reuerence.* Closely follows *GCF*, Jean II, ch. 'En quel temps le roy . . .' (*Chron-Jean-Charles*, i. 110), with the exception of two dates: *Chron-Jean-Charles*, i. 110 says that King Jean and the Black Prince set sail for England on 11 Apr., and King Jean entered London on 23 May; WW and the textual tradition represented in e.g. *GCF-1476–7*, ii, f. 284ʳ, and BnF, MS fr. 20350, f. 434ᵛ, give 16 Apr. and 24 May respectively. Reader 2's marginal note (see textual note) adds the detail, not given by WW or his source *GCF* (*Chron-Jean-Charles*, i. 110), that Prince Edward and King Jean landed near Dover.

392 .*Mˡ. iijᶜ lxvij, the 'month' of Maij.* The year should be 1360, as WW correctly states at 1101–2. Relevant chapters of *GCF* (*Chron-Jean-Charles*, i. 259–97), including the Treaty of Brétigny clearly dated to 8 May 1360, are copied in Arundel, ff. 159ʳ–164ᵛ, with a title in WW's hand (f. 159ʳ), and are followed, ff. 164ᵛ–166ᵛ, by the additions incorporated in the Treaty of Calais, ratified 24 Oct. 1360, but included in *GCF* in its account of the events of 1368 (*Chron-Jean-Charles*, ii. 47–58). WW may have been misled by the statement there that the 'final paix' occurred 'le viijᵉ iour de may derrain passe' (Arundel, ff. 164ᵛ–165ʳ; *Chron-Jean-Charles*, ii. 48) to date Brétigny here to 1367. WW's *month* is written over erasure and differs from the usual spelling of the MS *monithe* (e.g.

720, 997, 1011). The correction might betray some disagreement over the sp., as in Fastolf's will of 1459, where WW writes *month* in a draft (OMA, FP 64), but the scribe of the fair copy writes *moneth* (OMA, FP 65).

392–9 *King Iohn . . . fullie paied.* Closely based on Article XIV of the Treaty of Brétigny, given in full in *GCF*, ch. 'Ci commence toute l'ordenance . . .' (*Chron-Jean-Charles*, i. 280–1), 'le roy de France . . . seront parpaiez'. Copied into Arundel, f. 161ᵛ, but there numbered XV ('le Roy de france . . . seront payez').

393 *put to finaunce.* OED, *finance*, n.¹, 1.a, derives this idiom from Fr. *mettre à finance.* That Fr. idiom does not appear in *GCF* here (see 392–9n.).

394 *scutis.* Coins, the Fr. *ecu.* MED, *scute*, n. (1), notes that two *ecu* are equivalent to one English noble, as WW and his source in *GCF* here (see 392–9n.) explain.

397 *pease finall.* The postposed adj. recurs in this set phrase in 1167, C2/18, C2/52 and in one of WW's letters (*PL*, no. 884, l. 10); see also Introduction, pp. xc–xci. It is calqued on Lat. *pax finalis*, found in sidenotes by WW later (1167SN, 1224SN), and often used for peace treaties. A similar Fr. phrase occurs with reference to the Treaty of Brétigny elsewhere in *GCF*, Jean II, ch. 'Une lettre comment monseigneur le regent . . .' (*Chron-Jean-Charles*, i. 300), 'bonne paix et accort final'. But cf. the inverted word-order in 68, 1000, 1092, 1099, 1108, 1113, 1168, 1173, 1482, C1/19.

398 *millions.* The scribe writes the usual abbreviation, the majuscule roman numeral *Mˡ*, for *mill* followed by *ions.* Unusually, we here expand the abbreviated number. See Introduction, p. ci.

399 *whiche . . . was not parfourmed.* WW adds to Article XIV of the Treaty of Brétigny (see 392–9n.). For problems with payment of the ransom, see G. L. Harriss, *King, Parliament, and Public Finance in Medieval England to 1369* (Oxford, 1975), 466–508.

400–22 *Prince Edwarde . . . of Aprill.* WW's source here changes from *GCF* to Jean Froissart's *Chroniques.* WW follows closely the numbers and order of names in Froissart's bk. I, ch. 562, vii. 7, l. 18—8, l. 6 ('Jehans Chandos, qui bien . . . dix mils chevaus'), adding further names from later in Froissart's account: ch. 567, vii. 13, ll. 9–14: Felton, Knolles, and Ralph Hastings; ch. 570, vii. 19, ll. 6–8: Hugh and Philip Courtenay, John Trivet; ch. 581, vii. 38, ll. 30–1: Matthew Gournay; ch. 583, vii. 43, ll. 17–22: the list of those captured in the battle (on whom see nn. below); and ch. 584, vii. 46, ll. 24–5: the (incorrect) date 'en l'an de incarnation Nostre Signeur mil trois cens soissante et six, le tierch jour dou mois d'avril'. WW refers to *Mayster Froddesarde* at 1221. Fastolf owned various chronicles in Fr. but in the inventory of his books only a confused and brief reference to 'Cronicles Danglele' (OMA, FP 43, f. 10ʳ; Gairdner, no. 389) might be Froissart, as proposed by Beadle, 'Fastolf's French Books', 103, 111 n. 44.

400–1 *Harry, that noble duke of Lancastre.* WW misidentifies the duke of Lancaster at the time of the battle of Nájera as Henry of Grosmont (d. 1361: see 348–51n.), rather than John of Gaunt (1340–99).

401 *bataile of Nazar.* The battle of Nájera, 3 Apr. 1367.

401–2 *King Petir.* Pedro (1334–69), king of Castile.

402 *Bastarde Henry . . . Spaine.* Enrique de Trastámara (1334–79), king of Castile, and half-brother of Pedro. Enrique became king following his murder of his half-brother in 1369. As elsewhere (see 322–3n.), WW implies that the royal title is illegitimately claimed (*calling hym*).

403 *.lxiij. M^l. fighting men.* Figures vary in Froissart (e.g. chs. 565, 572, 577, vii. 10, l. 25; 26, ll. 25–32; 33, ll. 4–14) and across MS variants. Enrique reckons his own forces to number 99,000 (ch. 575, vii. 30, ll. 20–6). Other chronicles give wildly divergent figures.

403 *hym descomfit.* Pa. p. used akin to a Lat. ablative absolute, describing Enrique de Trastámara:='with him having been defeated'. See similar constructions at 1275–6n., etc., and Introduction, pp. lxxxvi–lxxxvii.

407–10 *Ser Iohn Chandos . . . and x. M^l. horsmen.* The vanguard was commanded by Sir John Chandos (d. 1370) and John of Gaunt: Anthony Goodman, *John of Gaunt: The Exercise of Princely Power in Fourteenth-Century Europe* (Harlow, 1992), 228. Froissart, ch. 562, vii. 7, ll. 19–20 states that Chandos had 1200 'pennons desous lui'. *DMF, pennon* [1], only records the metonymic sense= 'Chevalier portant un pennon' from the Chandos Herald; this sense is recorded more widely in Eng.: *OED, pennon, n.*, 2; *MED, penoun, n.*, 1.(c.).

408 *auauntgard.* Only one prior citation in *OED, avant-garde, n.*, and *MED, avaunt-gard, n.*, from Malory, *c.*1469/1470. WW perhaps borrows afresh from Froissart, ch. 562, vii. 7, l. 25, 'Là estoient en l'avantgarde', but this is an interlineation by WW and so probably made in 1475.

410–11 *Ser William . . . sonne.* William Beauchamp (*c.*1343–1411), fourth son of Thomas Beauchamp, earl of Warwick. WW translates Froissart's 'filz au conte de Warvich' (ch. 562, vii. 7, ll. 26–7).

411 *Lorde Hue Hastinges.* One of John of Gaunt's retainers: Simon Walker, *The Lancastrian Affinity, 1361–1399* (Oxford, 1990), 271, 294–5.

412 *Lord Neuyle.* John Neville (*c.*1330–88), 5th Baron Neville.

412 *Lorde Rais, a Breton.* Girard Chabot, lord of Rays: *Letters, Orders and Musters of Bertrand du Guesclin, 1357–1380*, ed. Michael Jones (Woodbridge, 2004), 37. Froissart, ch. 562, vii. 7, l. 28, notes that he was a Breton.

412 *lorde 'of Aubterre.* Gourderon de Raymont, lord of Aubeterre: *Letters, Orders and Musters of Bertrand du Guesclin*, 44, 60. WW's sidenote 406SN, which repeats this list of combatants, omits this name.

412–13 *many Gascoignes.* For Gascons in the army, see Sumption, ii. 552.

413 *Ser Raufe Hastingis.* Sir Ralph Hastings (c.1322–97), *ODNB*, s.n. Hastings family.

413 *Ser Thomas Felton.* Sir Thomas Felton (d. 1381), seneschal of Aquitaine.

413–14 *Ser Roberd Knolles.* Sir Robert Knollys (d. 1407).

415–16 *streit highe 'monteyns'. . . into Spaine.* An accurate account of the route (Sumption, ii. 550), echoing Froissart, bk. I, ch. 562, vii. 7, where the mountains are repeatedly described as 'destroit' (vii. 7, l. 7; 8, l. 7) on the way to Roncesvalles (vii. 11, l. 2). See 400–22n.

416–17 *Ser Hughe Courtney.* Sir Hugh Courtenay (d. 1374), knighted at Nájera: David S. Green, 'The Household and Military Retinue of Edward the Black Prince', 2 vols. (PhD thesis, Nottingham, 1998), ii. 45; *Calendar of Inquisitions Post Mortem*, xiv: *Edward III*, ed. A. E. Stamp, J. B. W. Chapman, Cyril Flower, M. C. B. Dawes, and L. C. Hector (London, 1952), 305–6, 325.

417 *Ser Philip Courtnay.* Sir Philip Courtenay (d. 1406): Green, 'Household and Military Retinue', ii. 46.

417 *Ser Iohn Tryuet.* Sir John Trivet (d. 1386): Green, 'Household and Military Retinue', i. 167; ii. 183.

417–18 *Matheu . . . Somerset.* WW's interlineated wording, unusually in Latin, is similar to a Lat. memorandum in *Itineraries*, 248, 'Matheus de Gornay miles comitatus Somersetie obijt die .28. Augusti', which the editor dates to 1479. While that similarity might date this particular interlineation to 1479, after the date of other revisions completed in 1475, Gournay's name also occurs in WW's red sidenote 406SN listing combatants, and these sidenotes might have been made alongside his revisions in 1475 (see Introduction, pp. lxiv–lxvi). The use of Lat. in this revision could echo the sidenote. The Lat. note in *Itineraries* perhaps follows *BkNob.*, or perhaps coincidentally shares its conventional phrasing. Catherine Nall and Daniel Wakelin, 'Le Déclin du multilinguisme dans *The Boke of Noblesse* et son Codicille de William Worcester', *Médiévales*, 68 (2015), 73–91 at 85, note the shift to Lat. WW also recorded Matthew Gournay's death (d. 1406: see *ODNB*) at two other points in *Itineraries*, 80, 320.

418–19 *Ser Barthilmew Clekyn.* Bertrand du Guesclin (d. 1380), military commander, and constable of France from 1370, captured at Nájera: Richard Vernier, *The Flower of Chivalry: Bertrand du Guesclin and the Hundred Years War* (Woodbridge, 2003), 115–18. WW's rendering of his surname is common: e.g. 'bertrandus cleykyn' in a note on this event in *Annales* in Arundel, f. 123ʳ; 'Bertran Claiekin' in Froissart, ch. 565, vii. 10, ll. 12–13; or 'Bartrem de Claikyn' in

La Vie du Prince Noir by Chandos Herald, ed. Diana B. Tyson (Tübingen, 1975), l. 1813).

420 *mareshall of Fraunce*. Arnoul d'Audrehem, captured at Nájera: Molinier, *Étude*, 179. See 380n. The detail that he was marshal of France is not given at this point in Froissart, ch. 583, vii. 43, ll. 20–1, but is earlier in the account, e.g. ch. 581, vii. 40, l. 10.

420 *the Besque*. Pierre de Villaines, known as 'le Bègue de Villaines', captured at Nájera.

421–2 *M^l. iij^{C}lxvj., the thrid day of Aprill*. WW follows Froissart, ch. 584, vii. 46, l. 24, and gives 1366, rather than 1367, for the date of the battle. 1366 is also given in *GCF* ('De la prise . . .', *Chron-Jean-Charles*, ii. 30). The *Annales* in Arundel, f. 123^r, correctly date it to 1367.

425 *.vij. yere and .xv. daies*. The number might be WW's invention, part of his widespread fascination with enumerating and dating; it is echoed in C1/67.

426–56 *wan the . . . Herry . V^{the}*. WW adds a long passage describing the capture of Harfleur and the defence of it from French attempts to retake it by siege. It interrupts a doublet listing Henry V's two methods for conquering Normandy (*thoroughe sieges lieng, | albeit that it consumed gretlie his peple, and also by batailes yeueng* 425, 456–7). The doublet was already delayed by a parenthesis (*albeit . . . peple*); the addition breaks it entirely, so that *and also* 457 now contrasts the v. phrase *batailes yeueng* with no other method of conquest. It seems that WW began with a short interlineation but later extended it down the right margin (with the transition from interlineation to margin at the erroneous repetition of *yt* 428: see textual note) and then across the bottom margin. This left no room for the sidenote 426SN, which is written unusually at the head of the page (f. 8^r). Also, WW's sp. of *Harflete* (426) in the interlineation and in another short addition later (457) differs from the sp. *Har(e)flue* in the right and bottom margins (432, 438, 439, 444, 446, 450). The main scribe uses both *Harflete* 462 and *Hareflue* 467, and sp. with final ⟨t⟩ recurs elsewhere: (e.g. *PL*, no. 439, ll. 7–10: 'Arfleet' and 'Arflet').

426 *wan the . . . xl. days*. WW is correct. The siege began on or shortly after 17 Aug. 1415 and Harfleur surrendered on 22 Sept. 1415. *Chronique de Normandie* in Arundel, f. 236^v (Williams, 168) states that the siege lasted 30 days; *Annales* in Arundel, f. 124^v (*Wars in France*, ii. 759), note Harfleur's surrender on 22 Sept. In an abbreviated version of Pseudo-Elmham, *Vita et gesta Henrici Quinti*, in Royal, ff. 62^r–71^v, which now begins imperfectly in the middle of the English attack on Harfleur (Hearne, 41), WW adds a heading for the 1st page, or perhaps the whole text, if the MS was already imperfect, 'de obsidione ville de hareflu' (f. 62^r), but WW takes no details thence.

427–8 *Thomas Beauford . . . yt*. Thomas Beaufort (d. 1426), duke of Exeter, half-brother of Henry IV, and so Henry V's uncle. WW correctly states that, at the time of the siege of Harfleur, Beaufort was earl of Dorset, as he did not become duke of Exeter until 8 Nov. 1416. WW makes the same distinction at 819. *Gesta Henrici Quinti*, a text WW annotated in BL, Cotton MS Julius E. iv, notes that Beaufort was made captain of Harfleur (f. 117ʳ; Taylor and Roskell, 54), as does *Basset's Chronicle*, f. 31ʳ (C&A, 181), which also notes his titles and his relation to Henry V. WW later recorded Beaufort's creation as duke of Exeter after the battle of 'Kedecaux' (see 818–21n.) in *Itineraries*, 358.

428–9 *the seyd erle . . . sudeours*. The same point is made in *Basset's Chronicle*, f. 31ᵛ (C&A, 181) where WW adds the number of the retinue (1500) and the number of knights (there 35, not *.xxxiij.* as here).

429–30 *baron of Carew wyth .xxxiij. knyghtys*. Sir Thomas Carew (d. 1431). WW adds him to the list of those defending Harfleur in the account in *Basset's Chronicle*, f. 31ᵛ (C&A, 182), which makes it clear that Carew is one of the knights under Fastolf and not himself the commander of 33 knights.

430–2 *defended . . . Hareflue*. For French attempts to retake Harfleur, see Anne Curry, 'Henry V's Harfleur: A Study in Military Administration, 1415–1422', in L. J. Andrew Villalon and Donald J. Kagay (eds.), *The Hundred Years War (Part III): Further Considerations* (Leiden, 2013), 259–84.

433–42 *And the seyd towne . . . sustenaunce*. WW owned three accounts of this naval battle, known as the battle of the Seine: in the *Gesta Henrici Quinti*, read by WW in BL, Cotton MS Julius E. iv, f. 124ʳ⁻ᵛ (Taylor and Roskell, 144–8); the abbreviated text of Pseudo-Elmham, *Vita et gesta Henrici Quinti*, read by WW in Royal, f. 64ʳ⁻ᵛ (Hearne, 78); and *Chronique de Normandie*, in Arundel, f. 241ᵛ (Williams, 175), which WW annotated with his symbol. Some of WW's factual details (*Spayn* 434, *erle of Marche* 435, the price of food) do not appear there, but all three accounts mention the French use of Genoese 'Carrykes', 'Carrerkes', or 'carraques', which might suggest *carekys* (434, 437). WW's sidenote 466SN shifts from Lat. to Fr. *lez carrikes*, suggesting the term's unfamiliarity.

434 *off Spayn*. The French used ships provided by their Genoese and Castilian allies: Christopher Allmand, *Henry V* (New Haven, 1997), 104.

435 *Iohn, duc of Bedfor[d]*. John, duke of Bedford, was given command of the expedition to relieve Harfleur: Allmand, *Henry V*, 107. This point is made in *Gesta Henrici Quinti*, read by WW in BL, Cotton MS Julius E. iv, f. 124ʳ (Taylor and Roskell, 144); *Chronique de Normandie*, annotated by WW in Arundel, f. 241ᵛ (Williams, 175); Pseudo-Elmham, *Vita et gesta Henrici Quinti*, read by WW in Royal, f. 64ᵛ.

435 *erle of Marche*. Edmund Mortimer (1391–1425), fifth earl of March, did participate in the relief of Harfleur in 1416, but he is not listed in WW's usual sources.

436 *antecessour*. Cf. 55n. As this is one of WW's additions of 1474/75 addressed to Edward IV, *antecessour* must='predecessor', as it is applied to Edmund Mor-timer, Edward IV's great-uncle but not direct ancestor, after whose death without issue the title passed to his nephew, Richard (d. 1460), duke of York and then to Edward IV himself.

437 *shyppis.* MS has *shypp* and a macron, unusually. We expand for pl. gram-mar and sense, following WW's *shyppis* 434 (cf. *shyppys* 444, *shyppes* 2065), but it is possible that WW intended a zero pl. marker such as *armee of shypp* (cf. the idiom *army of foot*).

437–9 *fought wyth . . . drowned.* Battle of the Seine, fought off Harfleur on 15 Aug. 1416. The high death toll drew comment from chroniclers: *Gesta Henrici Quinti*, read by WW in BL, Cotton MS Julius E. iv, f. 124ᵛ (Taylor and Roskell, 146); the abbreviated text of Pseudo-Elmham, *Vita et gesta Henrici Quinti*, read by WW in Royal, f. 64ᵛ (Hearne, 81); John Hardyng, *The Chronicle of John Hardyng, together with the Continuation by Richard Grafton*, ed. Henry Ellis (London, 1812), 377. See Allmand, *Henry V*, 108. *Seyn-Hede* was a common term for Cap d'Antifer, *département* of Seine-Maritime, north of the mouth of the Seine: see e.g. 'The Earliest English Sailing Directions', ed. Geoffrey A. Lester, in Lister M. Matheson (ed.), *Popular and Practical Science of Medieval England* (East Lansing, MI, 1994), 331–67 at 365, and e.g. ll. 81, 86, 88, 105.

439–42 *and so vytailled . . . of sustenaunce.* The French blockade prevented the supply of provisions to the town. The 'Aduertirimentes' (*sic*: see 2391n.) in Arundel, f. 324ᵛ, refer to the price of a cow as 10 marks (not the *cow ys hede . . . and the tong*, as here) as an indication of the famine in Harfleur and give the number of dead through famine as 400. But in the margin adjacent to the men-tion of the famine in *Gesta Henrici Quinti* in BL, Cotton MS Julius E. iv, f. 124ʳ (Taylor and Roskell, 144), WW wrote 'Memorandum Vᶜ homines'. As the num-ber is not found in other sources, it perhaps derives from an eyewitness's guess. *Chronique de Normandie* in Arundel, f. 241ᵛ (Williams, 175), refers to the threat of famine because Genoese ships blockaded the town.

443–6 *Iohn . . . Hareflue.* John Holland (1395–1447), earl of Huntingdon, com-manded the fleet which defeated the flotilla of mostly Genoese ships and cap-tured their French commander, son of the duke of Bourbon, on 29 June 1417: Allmand, *Henry V*, 113. WW owned accounts in the *Chronique de Normandie* in Arundel, f. 242ʳ (Williams, 176), there dated incorrectly to 6 Oct., and in a text of Pseudo-Elmham, *Vita et gesta Henrici Quinti*, in Royal, f. 65ʳ⁻ᵛ, which though it abbreviates some details from Pseudo-Elmham adds an additional reference to Huntingdon (f. 65ʳ). There are no close echoes of either text in *BkNob.*, but the *Chronique* mentions the 1st and 2nd relief of Harfleur in quick succession, as WW does, even though a year separated them.

444, 446 *of the new.* This phrase is less common than *of new*, in citations in *MED*, *neue*, *n.*, 1.(c), and *OED*, *new*, *adj.* and *n.*, phrases P1 and P2. *OED* cites

PL, no. 996, l. 19, in a letter by Fastolf but drafted in WW's hand, so the construction with *the* is perhaps an idiolectal preference by WW. WW also uses the phrase in the colophon he adds to Scrope, *The Dicts and Sayings of the Philosophers*, 292, 'this booke was of the new correctid'.

445–6 *were foughten . . . fyghtyng*. Rel. clause describing the defeat of the French *partye* (see 443–6n.), with zero rel. marker. WW might lose his thread by omitting *which* or might intend to use the pa. p. *foughten wyth* adjectivally, not needing *were*.

447–8 *Sygemendus*. Sigismund (1368–1437), king of the Romans and emperor-elect, arrived in England on 1 May 1416 and left on 25 Aug. 1416 (Taylor and Roskell, 128 n. 2, 156 n. 1). WW's phrasing implies that Sigismund was in England during the 2nd relief of Harfleur, which is incorrect.

452 *wach and ward*. WW has *and* (abbreviated) here, following a common idiomatic doublet='guard duty' (*OED*, *watch*, *n.*, II.7.a). However, the context might suggest the compound (*OED*, *watchword*, *n.*, 4.a, in the obsolete sense= 'premonitory sign, a warning event') which could describe a dog's warning bark; its 1st citation in *MED*, *wacche-word*, *n.*, (b), is by Geoffrey Spirleng, another of Fastolf's servants, in 1460 (*PL*, no. 603, l. 11).

456–81 *And the seyd prince . . . in gret subieccion*. The subject continues as *the seyd prince, Herry. V^{the}* for ten verbs, supplemented by three subclauses. *Because of whiche* 472 is technically another relative subclause, but the subject shifts to *gret part of the roiaume of Fraunce* 473, so we add a full stop for ease of reading.

456–7 *albeit . . . gretlie his peple*. Fastolf's 1435 articles advise the king not to wage war by siege: C2/109–15.

457 *the towne of Harflete*. WW adds a 2nd, shorter interlineation to emphasize the role of Harfleur in Henry V's campaigns. See 426–56n. on the sp. *Harflete*.

462 *his first viage at Harflete*. See 426n.

462–3 *in the second viage he made*. Henry V and his army landed near Touques (*département* of Calvados) on 1 Aug. 1417: Wylie and Waugh, iii. 53.

463–4 *Cane . . . Meulx-en-Brie*. WW read of the conquest of all these towns in an abbreviated text of Pseudo-Elmham, *Vita et gesta Henrici Quinti*, in Royal, ff. 66^r–67^v, 70^v (Williams 112–16, 118, 123–9, 131–2, 154), and in the margin he picked out the names, like a list, of all apart from Melun (sp. 'Mulant', f. 67^v) or Meaux.

463 *Cane*. Caen, *département* of Calvados. The town was taken on 4 Sept. 1417; the castle surrendered on 20 Sept.: Wylie and Waugh, iii. 59–62.

463 *Rone*. Rouen, *département* of Seine-Maritime, surrendered 19 Jan. 1419, following a siege lasting more than 5 months: Wylie and Waugh, iii. 140.

463 *Falleise.* Falaise, *département* of Calvados, surrendered 2 Jan. 1418, the castle on 16 Feb.: Wylie and Waugh, iii. 71.

464 *Argenten.* Argentan (Orne), surrendered 9 Oct. 1417: Wylie and Waugh, iii. 65.

464 *Maunt.* Mantes, *département* of Yvelines, surrendered in early Feb. 1419: *Annual Report of the Deputy Keeper of the Public Records*, 41 (London, 1880), 723.

464 *Vernon-sur-Seyne.* Vernon, *département* of Eure, is not always expanded thus in modern Fr. It surrendered on 3 Feb. 1419: *Foedera*, IV. iii. 88.

464 *Melun.* Melun, *département* of Seine-et-Marne, surrendered on 18 Nov. 1420: Wylie and Waugh, iii. 214. *Itineraries*, 358, records that the siege of Melun lasted 31 weeks and 3 days.

464 *Meulx-en-Brie.* Meaux, *département* of Seine-et-Marne, is in the region known informally as Brie; other place names in the region have the suffix *en-Brie* in modern Fr., but Meaux tends not to. Surrendered mid-Mar. 1422, but 'Marché', where the defenders held out, only surrendered on 10 May 1422: Allmand, *Henry V*, 164–9.

466–7 *gret batailes . . . was Englisshe.* See 433–52 (and nn.).

468 *bataile of Agincourt.* 25 Oct. 1415. Here and at 812–13, 958–62 WW says little about Agincourt; this might reflect the fact that his employer, Fastolf, was not there: see Anne Curry, *The Battle of Agincourt: Sources and Interpretations* (Woodbridge, 2000), 86, *pace ODNB, s.n.* Fastolf, Sir John.

471–3 *after allied . . . his obeisaunce.* WW presents the submission of the *gret part* of France as resulting from the marriage (*alliaunce*) between Henry V and Catherine de Valois, Charles VI's daughter, one of the terms of the Treaty of Troyes, ratified 21 May 1420. A copy of the Treaty is in Arundel, ff. 174^r–179^r.

477–8 *Iohn, duke . . . .xiij. yeris.* Echoed at 1357, C1/55–6.

482–4 *[he], be his lieutenaunt . . . Crauant.* The v. *had* needs a subject, and eye-skip over *he*, for the duke of Bedford, seems possible in the sequence of short syllables *he, be his* (='he, by his'). Bedford did not win the battle of Cravant himself; it was fought by Thomas Montagu, earl of Salisbury. At 822–3, WW adds similarly that Bedford won at Cravant *as by hys lieutenaunt.* Cf. Bedford's victory *yn his owne parsone* at Verneuil 514–15.

483 *erle of Salisburie.* Thomas Montagu (1388–1428), earl of Salisbury, com-manded the left flank of the Anglo-Burgundian army at Cravant. Listed as present in *Basset's Chronicle*, f. 48^r (C&A, 205), as 'lieutenant general' of John, duke of Bedford. See Codicil, f. 8^r (Appendix 1/15).

483–4 *batell of Crauant.* On 31 July 1423 an Anglo-Burgundian force defeated a

Franco-Scottish force at Cravant (*département* of Yonne). WW adds the month to the account in *Basset's Chronicle*, f. 48ʳ (C&A, 205).

485 *first yere of the reigne.* Correct, but see 517–18n. for WW's confusion about Henry VI's regnal dates.

490 *erle of Suffolk.* William de la Pole (1396–1450), duke of Suffolk (from 2 June 1448), earl at the time of Cravant. Not listed as present in *Basset's Chronicle*, f. 48ʳ (C&A, 205), but cf. Jean de Waurin, vol. 5, bk. 3, chs. 16 and 17 (*Recueil des croniques et anchiennes istories de la Grant Bretaigne, a present nomme Engleterre, 1422–1431*, ed. William Hardy and Edward L. C. P. Hardy, 5 vols., RS 39 (London, 1864–91), iii. 62, 70). WW's red sidenote 490SN adds the duke's name *Willelmus Pole*; it was presumably common memory to somebody of WW's generation.

490 *marchall of Bourgoine.* Jean de Toulongeon (d. 1427), marshal of Burgundy: J. Louis Bazin, *Brancion: Les seigneurs, la paroisse, la ville* (Paris, 1908), 103, 105. The marshal of Burgundy is listed as present at Cravant in *Basset's Chronicle*, f. 48ᵛ (C&A, 205, 319) but is there named as the 'Sire de chasteluz' (=Claude de Beauvoir, lord of Chastellux), who was marshal of France, not of Burgundy.

490–1 *Lord Willoughebie.* Robert Willoughby (1385–1452), 6th Baron Willoughby. Listed as present in *Basset's Chronicle*, f. 48ʳ (C&A, 205).

490–1 *Phelip, the duke of Bourgoine.* Philippe le Bon (1396–1467), duke of Burgundy.

495 *.j̄'x. Mˡ Frenshemen and Scottis.* *Basset's Chronicle*, f. 48ʳ (C&A, 205), gives the number of the Franco-Scottish army as 20,000. Perhaps *.j̄'x.*, originally *.ix.*, could be miscopied from **xx**.

496–8 *There were slayne . . . Scottis.* *Basset's Chronicle*, f. 49ʳ (C&A, 206), states that almost 8,000 men of arms were killed or taken prisoner; Waurin, vol. 5, bk. 3, ch. 17 (ed. Hardy and Hardy, 69) that about 4,000 Scots were killed, that there were around 1,200 French dead and 300–400 French captured. The *Journal d'un bourgeois de Paris*, ed. Alexandre Tuetey (Paris, 1881), 187–8, states that 3,000 or more died, 2,000 were captured and 1,500 drowned.

498–9 *Erle Bougham . . . ouerthrow.* John Stewart (*c*.1380–1424), earl of Buchan. Buchan was not, in fact, at Cravant: WW has mistaken Sir John Stewart of Darnley (*c*.1380–1429), who was captured at Cravant and was constable of Scotland, for John Stewart, earl of Buchan. The letters addressed to the former by Charles VII (e.g. Lady Elizabeth Cust, *Some Account of the Stuarts of Aubigny, in France, 1422–1672* (London, 1891), 7), make clear that Darnley was constable of the Scottish army. Mistakenly identified as 'Willam Styward connestable descoce' in *Basset's Chronicle*, f. 48ʳ (C&A, 205); William was the brother of Sir John Stewart of Darnley: *Journal du siège d'Orléans, 1428–1429*, ed. Paul Charpentier and Charles Cuissard (Orléans, 1896), 43.

499–513 *cause of the . . . knightis.* WW turns from the battle of Cravant to the earlier battle of Baugé. The relevance is that *God* sent the defeat of the Scots at Cravant and Verneuil as *chastisement* for their cruel victory at Baugé. WW's long sentence (this whole chapter) has a rough conceptual symmetry. He makes the same point at 1344–7.

499 *whiche* = The Scottish.

499 *male-infortuned.* Antedates 1st citation of *OED, mal-, prefix,* and sole citation in *MED, male infortuned, phr.* The rare *infortuned* is attested by Chaucer, *Troilus and Criseyde*, IV. 744, and in Lydgate's work (*MED, infortunen, v.*).

500 *iourney at Bougee.* Battle of Baugé, 22 Mar. 1421, a victory for the Franco-Scottish forces against the English, at which Thomas, duke of Clarence, was killed. See also 1340–4.

501 *youre nere cousyn.* Addressed to Edward IV. Thomas, duke of Clarence's grandfather (John of Gaunt), was the brother of Edward IV's great grandfather (Edmund of Langley, duke of York).

502–3 *withe a smale . . . grete nombre.* The numerical inferiority of the English side at Baugé was commented on by chroniclers, with varying degrees of exaggeration, e.g. Waurin, vol. 5, bk. 2, ch. 10 (ed. Hardy and Hardy, ii. 358–9). Works owned or annotated by WW emphasize the size of the Franco-Scottish army: *Basset's Chronicle*, f. 43^r (C&A, 198), a 'grant puissance'; *Chronique de Normandie*, in Arundel, f. 265^v (Williams, 205), a 'grant compaignie'; Pseudo-Elmham, *Vita et gesta Henrici Quinti*, in Royal, f. 70^r (Williams, 150), 'innumerosus et pomposus'. Wylie and Waugh, iii. 304 n. 3, state that there 'seems no doubt' that the English were outnumbered.

504–6 *withe many . . . take prisoneris.* English casualties were high (Wylie and Waugh, iii. 305), as many accounts, including those known by WW, state: *Basset's Chronicle*, f. 43^v (C&A, 199); *Chronique de Normandie*, in Arundel, f. 265^v (Williams, 205); the abbreviated text of Pseudo-Elmham, *Vita et gesta Henrici Quinti*, in Royal, f. 70^r (Williams, 151).

506 *cote-armes.* Soldiers entitled to bear coats of arms. WW's use of this form antedates *OED, coat, n.,* sense C3, dating from 1623, and only with reference to coat-armour itself; *MED* does not list this form, though *MED, cote, n.* (2), has one citation for the more accurately Fr. form *cote darmes*. The metonymically transferred sense 'one who bears coat-armour' is attested, though, for *OED, coat-armour | coat-armor, n.,* 3, and *MED, cote-armure, n.,* 1(b), from 1415 on.

507 *as yt was seyd.* With this interlineation, WW perhaps acknowledges that his source is oral report by witnesses, unlike the written sources elsewhere. See also 452–3, 955, 1378–9, 1400, 1961, 2332–3.

508–10 *Whiche God . . . was sent a chastisement vpon the saide Scottis.* The sense is clear (=God punishes the Scots for Baugé with Cravant and Verneuil), but the syntax is muddled. The rel. pron. *whiche* functions like a conj., as often in 15th-c. Eng. (*OED*, *which*, *adj.* and *pron.*, sense B.II.8.a); see similarly e.g. 1481, 1858. But *God* seems the subject, until the passive v. *was sent* seems to have *a chastisement* as subject. Perhaps an authorial error, as though WW, with the heavy adverbial phrase between subject and v., had forgotten his structure.

509–10 *bateile of Vernell.* See 517–18n.

517–18 M^l. *iiij*^{C}. *xxiii . . . August.* This gives the correct day and month (17 August) but wrong year (*recte* 1424) for the battle of Verneuil. The year initially read M^l. *iiij*^{C}. *xxiiij* and was altered by erasure, either by the scribe for some reason, or by WW or a reader perhaps in response to the first red sidenote hereabouts, 517sn, which picked out the brief mention of the battle of Cravant, dating it to 1423. The second red sidenote 520sn clarifies the correct year 1424 for the battle of Verneuil, as does 554 below (see n.). By coincidence, the date 17 Aug. 1423 is given in *Annales* in Arundel, f. 124^v (*Wars in France*, ii. 759), and an account in Royal, f. 72^v, has 1423 in the margin (*Giles' Chronicle*, 'Henrici VI', 5). WW also misassigns Verneuil to the 3rd year of Henry VI's reign; Henry acceded 1 Sept. 1422, so Verneuil took place in the 2nd regnal year. At 560, WW describes 1429 as the 9th year of Henry VI's reign; and at 1177, the Truce of Tours (1444) as the 24th; likewise, a letter of 14 Sept. 1450, by Fastolf but in WW's handwriting, was misdated 'the xxx yeere of Kyng Herry vj^{te}' but then altered by a hand, not definitely WW's, slotting in 'j' to give the 29th year 'xxjx' (*PL*, no. 457, l. 20): WW seems to believe that Henry VI acceded in 1420. WW also accessed an account of the battle of Verneuil in *Basset's Chronicle*, ff. 53^v–55^r (C&A, 212–15); and on 1 Dec. 1477, after his revisions to *BkNob.*, Walter Bellengier, Ireland King of Arms (d. 3 May 1487), informed WW which captains and men-at-arms were at Verneuil (*Itineraries*, 2–4, on which see C&A, 125–7, and below 917–21n.).

520 *Vernell-en-Perche.* Verneuil, site of the battle of 1424, was formally known in Fr. as Verneuil-au-Perche until the Revolution, when the county of Perche was absorbed into the *département* of Eure.

521–2 *Iohn . . . that day.* Jean II (1409–76), duke of Alençon, captured at Verneuil. Fastolf claimed him as his prisoner, and the money he was owed for the ransom formed part of his complaints against the Crown (e.g. in *PL*, nos 541, ll. 10–11, 1027, l. 20, in WW's hand). WW implies that Alençon claims the title illegitimately (*cleping hym*) as at 547 (and see also 322–3n.). WW's list of Fastolf's complaints in BL, Add. MS 27444, f. 38^r, refers to the capture of 'Iohn `callyng hym´ Duc of Allauncon at the bataille of Vernell', with the same claim ('callyng hym') interlineated by WW. *Basset's Chronicle*, f. 51^v (C&A, 210) describes him as 'chief et lieutenant general'. See also 547–52.

522–5 *Erle Bougham . . . sleyne.* See 498–9n. John Stewart, earl of Buchan, was made constable (not *marchall*) of France following Baugé and was killed at

Verneuil. The charge that he *was cause* of Clarence's death presumably means that he was commander of the enemy forces, rather than that Clarence died by Buchan's own hand. Of the different accounts discussed by Wylie and Waugh, iii. 305 n. 4, only the *Scotichronicon* claims Buchan as literally responsible for Clarence's death.

525–9 *Erle Douglas... batell.* Archibald Douglas (*c.*1369–1424), earl of Douglas and duke of Touraine, killed at Verneuil. Douglas had, as WW claims here, fought at Shrewsbury (21 July 1403) and Homildon Hill (14 Sept. 1402), at which John, duke of Bedford, then aged 13, was not present. WW owned accounts of these in *Giles' Chronicle* ('Henrici IV', 28–9, 33–4, 'Henrici VI', 5–6) in Royal, f. 121ᵛ (Homildon Hill), f. 123ʳ (Shrewsbury), f. 72ᵛ (Verneuil), and in *Annales* in Arundel, f. 124ʳ (*Wars in France*, ii. 758). *Basset's Chronicle*, f. 55ʳ (C&A, 215), gives Douglas in its list of dead. Douglas was rewarded for his service to the Dauphin with the duchy of Touraine on 19 Apr. 1424. After Douglas's death, the duchy passed to his eldest son, the earl of Wigtown. Père Anselme, *Histoire généalogique et chronologique de la maison royale de France*, 3rd edn. (Paris, 1712–33), iii. 322.

529–30 *withe many other... bataile.* Among sources WW knew, *Basset's Chronicle*, f. 54ᵛ (C&A, 214–15), names the French captured or killed; the *Annales* in Arundel, f. 124ᵛ, mention 15,000 captured and many Scots killed (*Wars in France*, ii. 759); the account in Royal, f. 72ᵛ (*Giles' Chronicle*, 'Henrici VI', 5), has 11,000 French and Scots dead.

531–2 *grettir part . . . Mauns.* Both the county of Maine and Le Mans, its principal city, in grammatical apposition (as often: see Introduction, pp. lxxx–lxxxiii). The pairing recurs at C1/210.

533–8 *And ouermore . . . men of worshyp.* Le Mans (*Maunce*) was taken on 10 Aug. 1425, and by 1427 almost all of Maine had fallen: A. J. Pollard, *John Talbot and the War in France, 1427–53* (London, 1983), 12; Bertram Wolffe, *Henry VI* (New Haven , 2001), 53.

533–4 *counte... Maunce.* See 531–2n.

534–6 *conquerid and brought . . . in subgeccion.* The auxiliary v. *was* is understood in rhetorical ellipsis. Given the rhetorical effect, we have not emended to supply the v.

536–8 *by the erle . . . worshyp.* WW's addition identifies a core of men central to the campaigns and conquests of the 1420s under John, duke of Bedford. The names, including the omission of the forename of Montgomery, recur in a list of those involved in the conquest of Maine, in a marginal addition by WW to Codicil, f. 23ʳ (*Wars in France*, ii. 553). Fastolf, Popham, and Montgomery (see next nn.) recur in this order in the Codicil, ff. 8ᵛ–9ʳ (Appendix 1/42–53).

536 *erle of Salysbery.* See 483n.

536 *Lord Scalys.* Thomas Scales (d. 1460), Baron Scales.

536–7 *Ser Iohn Popham.* Sir John Popham (*c.*1395–1463).

537 *Ser N. Montgomery.* Sir John Montgomery (d. 1449). Gilbert Bogner, 'Military Knighthood in the Lancastrian Era: The Case of Sir John Montgomery', *Journal of Medieval Military History*, 7 (2009), 104–26. WW uses the conventional abbreviation *N.* for Lat. *nomen* when a name is unknown. Montgomery is named *Iohannes* in Appendix 1/52.

537 *Ser William Oldhall.* Sir William Oldhall (d. 1460). See C3/5.

539–42 *Mayne . . . x. M^l liures sterlinges.* The figure broadly corresponds to the 'Lvj. M^l ij^C liures turneys' added by WW to Codicil, f. 21^v (*Wars in France*, ii. 550), as a total of the annual value of Maine, dated 1433–4; as roughly 6 *livres tournois* equalled one *livre sterling* in this period (according to Rémy Ambühl, *Prisoners of War in the Hundred Years War: Ransom Culture in the Late Middle Ages* (Cambridge, 2013), p. xii), 56,200=9,366.

541 *subgettis obeisauntes.* Final inflectional ⟨s⟩ on the adj. *obeisauntes* as at 895 (but cf. 1235), and in two other texts in *MED, obeisaunt, adj.*, in echo of the Fr. set phrase and its postposed, inflected adj.: see Introduction, pp. xc–xci.

542–6 *Also the . . . Frenshe partie.* WW returns to the battle of Verneuil, adding that there were 40,000 on the French side. *Basset's Chronicle*, f. 53^v (C&A, 212), also gives the number as around 40,000 on the French side, 10,000 on the English. M. K. Jones, 'The Battle of Verneuil (17 August 1424): Towards a History of Courage', *War in History*, 9 (2002), 375–411 at 387, estimates 14,000–16,000 on the French side, 8,000 on the English.

544–5 *Vernell-in-Perche.* See 520n.

547–52 *Iohn . . . charges.* The ransom was 200,000 écus. Bedford received half of it partly in jewels, plate, and vestments: Jenny Stratford, *The Bedford Inventories: The Worldly Goods of John, Duke of Bedford, Regent of France, 1389–1435* (London, 1993), 61.

552 *salux.* The gold coin of Lancastrian France, the *salut*, with an image of Gabriel's salutation to Mary. See *OED, salute, n.*²; *MED, salu, n.,* 1(b).

554 *M^l. iiij^C xxii̇ij′, the 'seyd .iij^d.' yere.* The date in the MS has been twice altered (see textual notes) and as a result is correct for Verneuil. Cf. an alteration and error at 517–18 (see n.). But writing over erasure, WW incorrectly attributes this to the *seyd .iij^d.* (3rd) year of Henry VI's reign, not the 2nd, with *seyd* perhaps referring to the previous mention of the regnal year at 517.

558 *for a gret . . . in writing.* This seems to ascribe a solely propagandistic intention to Henry VI's coronation, to serve in later written record. An account of Henry VI's entry into Paris is in Arundel, ff. 270^r–272^r. Edited from another

MS in *Collection générale des documents français en Angleterre*, ed. J. Delpit (Paris, 1847), 239–44.

558–66 *was crouned . . . Dolphin.* Henry VI was crowned king of France in Paris on 16 Dec. 1431, not in 1429. Neither would 1429 be the *ix yere of his reigne*. See 517–18n. Cardinal Beaufort made the largest contribution of £8,333 towards the expedition (*ODNB*). For this expedition, see Anne Curry, 'The Coronation Expedition and Henry VI's Court in France 1430–32', in Jenny Stratford (ed.), *The Lancastrian Court* (Donington, 2003), 29–52.

562–3 *graunt-oncle . . . Wynchester'.* Henry Beaufort (d. 1447), bishop of Winchester and cardinal; half-brother of Henry IV and so Henry VI's great-uncle. 1st citation in *OED*, *grand-uncle, n.*; only citation under *MED*, *graunt, adj.*, 2.

566 *calling hym Dolphin.* The agent is not Bedford, as for *being* 565, but the *aduersarie*, Charles, who was wrongly declaring himself Dauphin (*calling hym*: see also 322–3n., etc.). Cf. Codicil, f. 30ᵛ (Appendix 2/125). WW is not correct, as Charles VII had already been crowned king on 17 July 1429 at Reims.

567 *was neuer* = 'there was never'. Omission of the anticipatory adv. *there* was possible but becoming rarer in 15th-c. Eng.: Fischer, 'Syntax', 235, 345.

570 *O, then, ye most noble.* Underlined in MS as though a chapter title but not in display script like other chapter titles, and not syntactically separate from the following words.

578 *this* = 'thus', i.e. describing how Englishmen lost their land.

581 *mantelle . . . yow. OED*, *mantle, v.*, 3.a, cites only *MED*, *mantelen, v.*, 1(c), in turn citing only *BkNob.*, defining it as 'protect', whereas this seems a figurative use = 'clothe yourself' (i.e. *OED*, sense 1.a); cf. *clothe you in armoure* 582–3.

591–3 *Hector . . . decended of.* Mythical Trojan warrior, widely known from many classical and medieval sources. See e.g. comparisons to him in WW's notebook Julius, f. 168ʳ. The pr. tense in *bene enacted* seems to refer to a particular text, so we capitalize and italicize *The Siege of Troy* as a title. John Lydgate's *Troy Book* is titled thus in some MSS (e.g. Manchester, John Rylands Library, MS Eng. 1, f. 1ʳ; BodL, MS Douce 148, f. 336ᵛ) and implicitly in the poem itself (e.g. prol. 106–7, V. 3464, V. 3606). On Trojan genealogy, see also 27–9, 1298–9 (and Lydgate, *Troy Book*, prol. 103–4, V. 3376–7).

593–606 *Agamenon . . . halfe best.* This list of classical heroes comes from Boethius, *De consolatione philosophiae*, IV. m. 7 (and not *the .v. booke* as WW claims), perhaps read in Chaucer's *Boece*. The copy of *Boece* annotated by WW in Cambridge, Pembroke College, MS 215, has lost the relevant leaves (lacking all after f. 72ᵛ, IV. m. 5. 13, except one fragment f. 73ʳ⁻ᵛ, V. pr. 6. 197–222, V. pr. 6. 235–61). See 70–1n. and 1610–16n. for WW's reading of Boethius. The pertinence might have been suggested by Boethius' preceding passage (Chaucer,

Boece, IV. pr. 7. 76–106), which argues that strong men are not daunted by adversity but fight 'a ful egre bataile in thy corage ayeins every fortune', finding strength in inner 'vertu' (Chaucer, *Boece*, IV. pr. 7. 87, 93–4).

593 *Agamenon*. A macron on the final minims might suggest a spelling *Agamenoun*, attested by rhyme in some other Eng. texts; but this macron is here treated as disambiguating **n** from **u**. See Introduction, p. cv. The sp. recurs at 1935 ff. (see n.).

595 *.x. yere day*. Boethius, IV. m. 7, and Chaucer, *Boece*, IV. m. 7.3, mention the ten-year duration of the Trojan War. The phrase *yere day* is used of this topic in Lydgate, *Troy Book*, II. 5959 ('At ten ȝere day, þei wynne schal þe toun'). See 202, 866.

600 *voluptuouse delites and lustis*. Detail not in the description of Hercules in Boethius, IV. m. 7, but *voluptuouse delites* is perhaps suggested by Chaucer's use of same collocation in *Boece*, III. pr. 2. 43; WW repeats it at 628. And the collocation of *lustis* perhaps echoes the previous prose section of Chaucer, *Boece*, IV. pr. 7. 91–2, in which Lady Philosophy suggests that Boethius has inner virtue as he refuses 'to fleten with delices, and to welken in bodily lust'.

601–8 *whiche .xij. entreprinses . . . whiche is writen*. Syntax is interrupted by a list of labours of Hercules, and when the syntax resumes, *whiche* is recapitulative. WW treats *.xij. entreprinses* as a unit, with a sg. pron. *it* and v. *is writen*.

602 *but a poesye*. The reference to classical myth reflects the wider sense of *poesye*:= 'fiction' rather than verse (*MED*, *poesie, n.*, 1); it perhaps also acknowledges that these details come from one of Boethius' metrical sections. WW took notes from Boethius' Lat. verse in *Itineraries*, 391.

603 `a's`. See 264n.

603 *bereffe . . . rampant lion*. Echoes text and gloss from Chaucer, *Boece*, IV. m. 7. 30–2, 'byrafte . . . rafte hym his skynne'.

604 *Anthen*. Antaeus, a Libyan giant (Chaucer, *Boece*, IV. m. 7. 51, 'geaunt') slain by Hercules. Nichols reads 'Antheus', but final **n** is clear (see Introduction, p. xcix). For the macron over final **n**, see 593n. and Introduction, p. cv.

604 *Poliphemus*. Boethius, IV. m. 7, and Chaucer, *Boece*, IV. m. 7. 18–27, report that Polyphemus is killed by Ulysses, not Hercules; WW has misread or misrecalled the passage.

604 *hym*. Possibly the 3 pl. pron. *hem*=PDE 'them', but more likely a lapse in concord from pl. referents *Anthen and Poliphemus* to sg.; =PDE 'him'.

605 *slow the serpent clepid Ydra*. Hydra, a many-headed monster killed by Hercules. Closely echoes Chaucer, *Boece*, IV. m. 7. 42, 'slowh Idra the serpent'.

606 *centaurus . . . halfe best*. Echoes a gloss supplied by Chaucer in *Boece*, IV. m. 7. 29–30, 'the proude Centauris (*half hors, half man*)'.

609 *And how.* Resumes the injunction *let be brought to mynde* 589.

610–11 *strenght . . . may.* The rel. pron. is understood, after the interruption of the adverbial clause *whoso . . . hymsilf.*

614–24 *Vegecius . . . within hemsilfe.* Expanding the Fr. translation of John of Wales, *Breviloquium*, citing 'vng acteur apelle vegesse' on three qualities—science, exercise, and fidelity to the public good—which a prince needs and which gave the Romans victory. WW annotated this passage in CUL, MS Add. 7870, f. 5ʳ, with 'Vegesius', the comment 'causa quare Romani habuerunt potestatem' and numbering of the three qualities. The Fr. text, entitled *Des Quatres Vertus Cardinaulx*, is identified by Gianni Mombello, 'Notizia su due manoscritti contenenti "l'Epistre Othea" di Christine de Pizan ed altre opere non identificate', *Studi francesi*, 31 (1967), 1–23 at 13–21, and Jenny Swanson, *John of Wales: A Study of the Works and Ideas of a Thirteenth-Century Friar* (Cambridge, 1989), 205–6.

618 *remedies of bonchief or the contrarie.* The doublet of *bonchief* and its opposite was common, e.g. 'myschef' or 'Inconvenientz': see *MED, bon-chef, n.*, e.g. citation from *Foedera*. It may also recall Petrarch's *De remediis utriusque fortune*, which circulated in several MSS in England: see Nicholas Mann, *Petrarch Manuscripts in the British Isles*, Italia medioevale e umanistica, 18 (Padua, 1975), nos. 6, 20–1, 82, 128, 152, 235, and maybe 266.

619 *exercitacion . . . armes.* Expanding the Fr. translation of John of Wales, *Breviloquium*, 'excercitacion en armes', which WW read in CUL, MS Add. 7870, f. 5ʳ. WW's *exercitacion* was not entirely new to Eng. (see *MED, exercitacioun, n.*), but his doublet *vsage* suggests that it felt like a new calque from Fr.

622 *comon wele.* <Fr. translation of John of Wales, *Breviloquium*, which WW read in CUL, MS Add. 7870, f. 5ʳ⁻ᵛ, 'la chose publique'. Cf. comparable terms at 3n., 1599–600n., 1606n., 1690–2n., 2055–6n. and Glossary, s.v. **comen wele**.

626 *abide r[i]ote.* In the MS a cross above *rote* and another in the margin suggest a scribe or reader's uncertainty about the word. The context, discussing moral dissipation, suggests *MED, riot(e, n.*, 1.(a).

626 *pouder. MED, poudre, n.*, 5b='culinary spice', used figuratively, for='false appearance' in the doublet with *semblaunce*, disparaging the *idill delites*.

627–9 *Water Malexander . . . armes.* The sentiment is commonplace. The source named (as at 752–6: see n.) remains unidentified but recalls Walter of Châtillon, *Alexandreis*, which was widely known. A scribe might misread *in* in, e.g. 'Walter in Alexandreide' as *m* giving *Water Malexander*. Authors regularly cite the *Alexandreis* thus: e.g. Christine de Pizan, *The Book of Peace*, ed. and trans. Karen Green, Constant J. Mews, Janice Pinder, and Tania van Hemelryck (University Park, PA, 2008), 246, 271, 'Galterus in *Alexandreide*'; William Caxton, *The Game and Playe of Chesse*, ed. Jenny Adams (Kalamazoo, MI, 2008), II.

3. 370, 'Galeren . . . in *Alexandrye*'. But WW in Julius, f. 22ʳ (perhaps in a sequence dated 1462: f. 20ʳ), transcribed the opening 8 lines of the *Alexandreis* as
'primi versus libri poetrie de Actibus Alexandri Regis Macedon⟨ie⟩', suggesting
that he did recognize *Alexander* as subject of the text, named in the title, and
not as the author. Walter's *Alexandreis* does warn that sensuality harms military power but not in terms close enough to be a definite source: see Walter
of Châtillon (Galteri de Castellione), *Alexandreis*, ed. Marvin L. Colker (Padua,
1978), e.g. I. 164–70; II. 2–10; VI. 17–21; and Walter of Châtillon, *Alexandreis*,
trans. David Townend (Philadelphia, 1996), I. 191–9; II. 5–11; VI. 22–35. It is
possible that WW misrecalls another source. In Royal, f. 136ʳ, WW wrote 'contra luxuriam inter exercitus' in the margin of notes from Chartier, *Quadrilogue*
(Bouchet, 20, l. 5), noting that Scipio Africanus banned anything 'prouocans
a volupte' in his army, as did Alexander. It is possible but unlikely that **Al** on
'Alixandre' in the Fr. handwriting of Royal, f. 136ʳ could be misread as **M**, giving 'Malixandre'. The same sentiment is in Chaucer's gloss which ends *Boece*,
IV. m. 7. 70–2, a passage that was the source for the previous lines (see 593–
606n.). And WW read a Fr. translation of the section of the *Alexandreis* that
purported to be Aristotle's letter to Alexander circulating in England (see Lisa
Jefferson, 'Fragments of a French Prose Version of Gautier de Châtillon's *Alexandreis*', *Romania*, 115 (1997), 90–117), but not till 1478 after revising *BkNob.*,
and his wording then ('alium librum de papiro in gallico vocatum Aristotelis
ad Alexandrum': *Itineraries*, 94) suggests that this Fr. work was not previously
familiar to him.

628 *voluptuous delitis.* See 600n.

630 *li`k′e.* Somebody, perhaps not WW, corrects ⟨liche⟩ to ⟨like⟩ by interlineat-
ing ⟨ke⟩ over ⟨che⟩, but without deleting ⟨che⟩. See similarly 737. *MED*, *like*,
adv., and *OED*, *like*, *adj.*, *adv.*, *conj.*, and *prep.*, record both sp.

630-2 *boore . . . bloode.* Whiting and Whiting, *Proverbs*, B387–91, notes boars'
proverbial enraged state and bravery. Nichols reads *chafed* as 'chased', but **f** is
unmistakable; *chafed*='enraged', 'vexed': *MED*, *chaufen*, *v.*, 4(d), with citations
referring both to boars and warriors, and *OED*, *chafe*, *v.*, I.5.

639 *moenys.* Perhaps simply='means', but likelier *OED*, *moyen*, *n.*¹, as identified
at 225n.

644-723 *For as youre first . . . knighthode.* WW sets out English claims to lands
in France. None of the other examples listed in *Debating the Hundred Years War:
Pour ce que plusieurs (La Loy Salique) and A declaration of the trew and dewe
title of Henrie VIII*, ed. Craig Taylor, Camden Society, 5th ser., 29 (Cambridge,
2008), 33, seems to be WW's source.

644-50 *duchie of Normandie . . . ducdome.* Points repeated at 1188–93. The
Treaty of Saint-Clair-sur-Epte between Charles le Simple (879–929) and Rollo
(d. *c.*928) in autumn 911 granted Rouen and its surrounding area to Rollo

and, according to some accounts, arranged for the marriage between Rollo and Gisla, the daughter of Charles. Rollo was baptized in 912 and adopted the name Robert. Dudo of Saint-Quentin claimed that Rollo was Danish: David Bates, *Normandy before 1066* (London and New York, 1982), 2, 8; David Crouch, *The Normans: The History of a Dynasty* (London, 2002), 4–8, 25, 292–3; Mark S. Hagger, *Norman Rule in Normandy, 911–1144* (Woodbridge, 2017), 45–50. WW had access to at least four accounts, of which two could be the source. WW saw a copy of Trevet, *Cronicles*, in OMC, MS Lat. 45, ff. 68ᵛ, 69ᵛ (see 250–3n.), which has similar wording (Rollo came from 'denemarche' and Charles 'dona a Rollo sa fille en mariage oue tote la terre') and gives the date 912. WW copied, or compiled, summaries of passages from *GCF* in Titus, f. 78ʳ⁻ᵛ (summarizing Viard, iv. 314–16, vi. 274), with similar wording ('vng dane au quel lemperour donna sa fille a femme'), but without the date 912 for the baptism, though 912 is present in the full text of *GCF*, Charles le Simple, ch. 2 (Viard, iv. 316), and *GCF*, Philippe II, bk. 1, ch. 12 (Viard, vi. 143). WW also owned Lat. notes on the topic, including the date 912, in Royal, f. 56ᵛ, but these do not mention that Rollo was Danish. There are also notes in Latin on Rollo and his descendants, not mentioning 912, in WW's notebook Arundel, ff. 86ʳ⁻ᵛ, 95ʳ⁻ᵛ; and to a list of the dukes of Normandy in French in Arundel, f. 209ʳ⁻ᵛ, WW added a note that it was 'trouue escript de vng 'veile' liure fraunceys de vng tresauncien escripture et icie escript le moys de nouember lan de grace .1451.' (Arundel, f. 209ʳ), which title and interlinear addition might prompt *BkNob.*'s reference to *olde* sources, though *olde* could also apply to Trevet or *GCF*.

644 *as*. Introduces the n. phrase *youre first . . . Normandie* as the complement of *it is knowen* 645 (*OED, as, adv.* and *conj.*, B.I.11.b).

649 *Charlys le Symple*. Charles III (879–929), king of the Franks, added by WW over erasure and by interlineation. The epithet *le Simple* recurs at 1192.

650 [*who*] *maried*. We supply *who*, to clarify the shift of subject in this sequence of clauses. Given the apparent initial omission of the name *Charlys* 649, another erroneous omission hereabouts seems possible. WW does lose control of long strings of subordinate clauses (see e.g. 601–8n.) and omit a rel. pron. elsewhere, but here the change of subject makes the rel. clause factually erroneous, in a way that WW could have recognized.

651–5 *Richarde . . . God*. WW offers a simplified account of events from *GCF*, Louis IV, ch. 5 (Viard, iv. 343–6), in which Harold, king of Denmark, in alliance with Richard (932–96), duke of Normandy, defeats Louis IV (920–54) in battle and takes him prisoner. The treaty which follows confirms Richard's rights in Normandy ('De illuec en avant, tint li dux Richarz paisiblement Normandie . . .'; Viard, iv. 346).

653 *in plaine batell* = 'in pitched, formal battle', an idiom widely attested (*MED*, *plein(e, adj.*, 1(d)), calqued from Fr. 'a plene bataille' (*OED, plain, adj.*¹) in the ethical sense of *plaine* = 'just, formally complete'.

653–6 *relesid . . . writing.* The terms *relesid, resort* and perhaps *Act* (but see next n.) have specific legal senses, as WW defends the title to Normandy: see *MED, relesen, v.* (1), 5(b); *resort(e, n.*, 5; and *BkNob.* 666n., 691–4n., and 1118–23.

655–6 *as in Act . . . writing. Act* (duplicated by WW at the l. break) = not 'law or ordinance' (< Lat. *acta*) in a technical, legal sense (cf. *enacted* 672) but an historical source, e.g. Lat. *Gesta* (see 286–307n.), like that mentioned as a source for Norman history in Arundel, f. 209ʳ (see 644–5on.). Such was consulted *vppon this writing* = 'for the purpose [of composing] *BkNob.*'.

657 *And after . . . Englond.* Unlike the parallel 651, *And after* introduces not a clause with a main v. but only a n. phrase; perhaps dummy subject and v. 'there was' are understood.

659–60 .*vᶜ xxxv. yere . . . golde.* The count of years (535) is approximately the time elapsed since either the accession of Rollo or Richard's defeat of Louis (1475 minus 535 = 940), but the phrasing implies that it is the time elapsed since the accession of William the Conqueror; that implication would be wildly inaccurate. These arms were commonly ascribed to William the Conqueror by later writers: see e.g. Nicholas Upton, *De studio militari, c.*1446 (e.g. New Haven, Beinecke Library, MS Takamiya 86, f. 39ᵛ) or Sir Thomas Holme's Book of Arms, *c.*1445–50 (BL, Harley MS 4205, f. 3ʳ).

663–77 *next enheritaunce . . . yere.* WW had access to notes on the descent of Henry II from Empress Matilda and Geoffrey Plantagenet in Arundel, f. 95ᵛ.

666 *parfit writing.* Specific legal sense of *parfit* (see *OED, perfect, adj., n.*, and *adv.*, A.I.3.d, and *MED, parfit, adj.*, 3(d)). WW again (see 653–6n., 691–4n.) stresses the legal basis and documentary evidence for the title to French territories.

666–71 *Dame Maude . . . had issue.* See 42–7 and nn. WW's details are correct, apart from the date of the marriage between Matilda and Geoffrey Plantagenet, which took place in June 1128, not 1127.

667 *that.* Pleonastic, repeated from *how that* 666, after the parenthetical epithet describing the subject *Maude*.

677 *continued this .iijᶜ. xlvij. yere.* If this refers back to the date WW gives for Geoffrey and Matilda's marriage, then this section was written in 1474 or early 1475; *continued* refers to the legal right, despite the de facto loss. See similarly 718 (and n.).

678–85 *And the noble . . . wryte.* WW adds in the margin starting at the end of the l. which concludes with *yere* (677) and before the next chapter title (686).

679–81 *Ymago . . . wrote notablye.* Ralph of Diceto (d. 1202), *Ymagines*

Historiarum, covering the reigns of Henry II, Richard I, and King John (to 1202) and with notes on the counts of Anjou (*Historical Works of Master Ralph de Diceto*, ed. Stubbs, i. 291, 293, 295–6, ii. 15–16). Ralph of Diceto's MSS were made by him or at his command at St Paul's Cathedral, and some remained there in the 15th c.: Diana E. Greenway, 'Historical Writing at St Paul's', in Derek Keene, Arthur Burns, and Andrew Saint (eds.), *St Paul's: The Cathedral Church of London, 604–2004* (New Haven, 2004), 151–6. In Julius, f. 43ʳ, WW took notes from an 'ancient book of chronicles' at St Paul's Cathedral, London ('in fine antiqui libri cronicorum in librario 'Ecclesie' sancti pauli'), but they are on classical and biblical history, similar but not identical to those in Ralph's MS, BL, Cotton MS Claudius E. iii, ff. 10ʳ–15ʳ. MSS of Ralph's *Ymagines historiarum* do contain details of the Plantagenet dynasty: e.g. BL, Cotton MS Claudius E. iii, ff. 154ʳ–157ᵛ (which remained in St Paul's: Diana E. Greenway, 'The Succession to Ralph de Diceto, Dean of St Paul's', *Historical Research*, 39 (1966), 86–95 at 86–7), or BL, Add. MS 40007, f. 39ʳ⁻ᵛ, which also contains a marginal annotation in a 15th-c. hand noting a reference to Ralph of Diceto that 'Iste 'est' Radulphu de Diceto qui hunc librum compilauit' (f. 35ᵛ; this remained at St Mary's Abbey, York: see *Medieval Libraries of Great Britain*, mlgb.3.bodleian.ox.ac.uk, *s.n.* Diceto).

682 *chosen kyng of Iherusalem.* Foulques, father of Geoffrey Plantagenet (on whom see 43–5 and nn.), and so ancestor of the addressee Edward IV (*your hyghnes*). For the sp. *Iherusalem*, see 294n.

685 *vnyoned.* 1st, by date of MS, of only 2 citations in *MED*, *unionen*, *v.*, and 1st in *OED*, *union*, *v.*

687 *passed possessid.* After the temporal adj. *passed* (for which sp., see *MED*, *passed*, *ppl. adj.*), the subject and v., e.g. 'it was', are elided before the pa. p. *possessid*.

691–4 *recorde enacted . . . heire masle.* The terms again (see 653–6n., 666n.; cf. 655–6n.), including *MED*, *male, adj.* (2), 1(b), have legal connotations.

693–5 *aboute the yere . . . Alice.* WW correctly states that Guillaume (1099–1137), duke of Aquitaine, died in 1137 on pilgrimage to Santiago de Compostela (*Seint Iames*), without a male heir; his daughters were Eleanor of Aquitaine (*c.*1122–1204) and Petronilla, also known as Alix (*Alice*). As the elder daughter, Eleanor was his heir. These details are in *GCF*, Louis VI, ch. 25 (Viard, v. 279–82), and *GCF*, Louis VII, ch. 2 (Viard, vi. 7). WW's *vppon his voiage he made to Seint Iames* perhaps suggested by a variant in some MSS, 'ou voyage monseigneur saint iaque' (e.g. BnF, MS fr. 20350, f. 258ᵛ).

695–8 *King Lowes . . . enheriter.* Eleanor married Louis VII (1120–80), king of France, in July 1137. Aged only 17, Louis was *in his yong age*. See *ODNB*, *s.n.* 'Eleanor [Eleanor of Aquitaine]'; Elizabeth A. R. Brown, 'Eleanor of Aquitaine Reconsidered: The Woman and Her Seasons', in Bonnie Wheeler and John

Carmi Parsons (eds.), *Eleanor of Aquitaine: Lord and Lady* (New York, 2002), 1–54 at 5–6. That the marriage was *by the agrement of Lowys le Gros* (Louis VI (1081–1137), king of France, known as Louis the Fat), is either because Louis VII had not reached his majority or because Louis VI arranged the marriage.

697–8 *hole enheriter* = 'sole heir', an obsolete sense of PDE *whole*, common in collocations with *heir* and other terms referring to inheritance: *OED, whole, adj.* (and *int.*), *n.* and *adv.*, A.II.9.a; *MED, hole, adj.* (2), 8b(a).

698–704 *the said King Lowes . . . doughter.* Their divorce was pronounced on 21 Mar. 1152 on the grounds of consanguinity. Louis then married Constance, daughter of Alfonso VII, king of Castile-León, in 1154: James A. Brundage 'The Canon Law of Divorce in the Mid-Twelfth Century: Louis VII c. Eleanor of Aquitaine', in Wheeler and Parsons (eds.), *Eleanor of Aquitaine: Lord and Lady*, 213–21. Perhaps based on *GCF*, Louis VII, ch. 23 (Viard, vi. 67–9), which lists the same archbishops of Sens, Reims, Rouen, and Bordeaux in the same order; points out the involvement of barons; gives consanguinity as grounds; and states that Louis married Constance, described as the daughter of the king of Spain in some MSS (e.g. BnF, MS fr. 20350, f. 266^r).

698 *yeris of discrecion.* Legal sense: *MED, discrecioun, n.*, 1(e).

699 *archebisshoppis . . . Burdeux.* Hugues de Toucy (d. 1168), archbishop of Sens; Samson de Mauvoisin (d. 1161), archbishop of Reims; Hugues de Boves (d. 1164) archbishop of Rouen; Geoffroi du Loroux (d. 1158), archbishop of Bordeaux.

700 *others barouns.* Adj. inflected for the pl., as in Fr. See Introduction, p. xci.

705–10 *Alienor . . . downe.* Henry and Eleanor were married in May 1152, not 1146, and Henry was not yet *King Harry the Seconde*, which he became only in 1154.

710–12 *King Henry . . . Normandie.* These arms were commonly ascribed to Henry II by later writers: e.g. Nicholas Upton, *De studio militari, c.*1446 (e.g. Beinecke Library, MS Takamiya 86, f. 40^r) or Sir Thomas Holme's *Book of Arms, c.*1445–50 (BL, Harley MS 4205, f. 3^r).

718 *.iij^C xxviij yere complete.* Given that WW dates the marriage of Henry and Eleanor to 1146, 328 years would make the date of WW's writing of this section 1474 or early 1475; as with *continued* 677 (see n.), *complete* describes the continuing legal right, not the de facto loss.

718–21 *by intrusion . . . .M^l. iiij^C. lj.* Charles VII recovered Aquitaine in June 1451: M. G. A. Vale, 'The Last Years of English Gascony, 1451–1453', *Transactions of the Royal Historical Society*, 5th ser., 19 (1969), 119–38. Although English campaigns to regain territory saw some success over the following two years, WW does not refer to them. See also 1156n., 1272n. and Introduction, pp. liv–lix, on dating.

718–23 *by intrusion . . . trewes.* Syntax is uneasy: the *said aduersarie* is referred to thus in an adverbial phrase, before he is named, *Charlis*, as subject of the clause; the v. *haue disseasid* is separated from the indirect object *of youre enheritaunce* by a recapitulative subclause *as he hathe late done.*

722–3 *vmbre . . . colour of trewes.* See 54–5n.

723 *fenied.* The 3rd minim mid-word suggests uncertainy over the sp.; *MED, feinen, v.*, has other citations with the 1st syllable sp. ⟨fen⟩.

724 *historier.* Here and at 1295, a chapter title refers to WW as *historier* when describing him exhorting the listener. Classical historical writing was understood to have a hortatory function.

725 *for to think to . . . bataile* = 'so that it seems fit to all Christian nations to fight in battle'. Usually *for to*+infin. v. indicates the result of an action (*OED, for, prep.* and *conj.*, A.IV.11a; *MED, forto, adv.* and *particle*, 1, as at 748: see n.), this result perhaps arising from the arguments of Cicero quoted afterwards (736–40). *think to* = 'seem fitting to', a sense perhaps obsolescent in the 15th c. (*MED, thinken, v.* (1), 5; *OED, think, v.*[1], 4).

732–8 *Maister Aleyn Chareter . . . defende it.* Follows the thinking of Alain Chartier, *Le Quadrilogue invectif* (Bouchet, 15, ll. 5–8): 'Nature vous a devant toute autre chose . . . naistre et avoir vie.' With this marginal addition, WW might wrongly imply that Chartier cites the passage from Cicero at 736–40 (as though Chartier has *wryten . . . how*), but *how* introduces a rel. clause, *how* (= 'in the way that'), stating that Chartier says something like Cicero (*MED, hou, conjunctive adv.*, 5; *OED, how, adv.* and *n.*[3], A.IV.13). WW annotated excerpts from Chartier, *Quadrilogue*, in Royal, ff. 136ʳ–138ᵛ: see Introduction, p. lxxix. For other uses of Chartier, see 762–72n., 972–80n., 1576–83n., 2273–9n., 2413–16n., 2417 –20n., 2503–8n, 2509–14n., and cf. 775–85n.

732–3 *Aleyn Chareter . . . Bien Amee.* WW notes Alain Chartier's Lat. name *de Auriga* ('of the chariot'), used in several MSS in England. To the title of 'Extraict du quadrilogue maistre Alain' in Royal, f. 136ʳ, WW adds a reference to him as 'secretaire' to Charles VI (1368–1422), king of France, widely known as *Le Bien Aimé*. Chartier is similarly described as 'secretarie' in one Eng. translation (Blayney, 135, ll. 2–3). Nall, 'William Worcester Reads Alain Chartier', describes Chartier's influence on political thought in England.

734 *named kyng.* Cf. 56n., 810n.

736–40 *Tullius . . . to the same.* Similar sentiments occur in *Rhetorica ad Herennium*, then ascribed to Cicero, e.g. IV. xlii. 54–IV. xliii. 55, and especially IV. xliv. 57 (trans. Harry Caplan (Cambridge, MA, 1954), 364–9, 370–5). WW took quotations from it, entitled, as often, 'Rhetorica noua', in Julius, f. 48ᵛ, f. 97ᵛ, and wrote a note on the flyleaf of OMC, MS Lat. 82, f. iiᵛ, identifying that MS as 'Tullius in noua Rethorica cum commento' by Magister Alanus. (On the title, see

1751–4n., and Rundle, 'Worcestre'.) WW's wording in *BkNob.* is closer to Brunetto Latini, *Li Livres dou tresor*, II. 99 (ed. Carmody, 284–5), who cites Cato, mentioned at 740: 'Catons dit, fius, combat toi pour ton païs, on doit faire tot son pooir por le commun profit de son païs et de sa vile. A ces choses faire nous amaine force de nature, non pas force de loi.' This could be the *Disticha* ascribed to Cato or an allusion to Cato's imagined words in *De senectute*. For WW's access to Latini, see 27–9n.

737 *li`k′e.* See 630n.

737 *lyuing.* < Fr. 'vie' (Bouchet, 15, l. 8) = 'life'. This rendering recurs in an Eng. translation of Chartier, *Quadrilogue* (Blayney, 151, l. 12) at the point with echoes in 732–8 (see n.).

739 *law imperiall.* Presumably = 'civil (Roman) law', extending from the Rome of Cicero to the Holy Roman Empire. *MED, imperial, adj.,* and *OED, imperial, adj.* and *n.,* A.I.2.a, have many citations with reference to Rome, albeit none collocated with *law* before ?1556.

740 *Caton.* See 736–40n.

740 *affermithe withe* = 'agrees with' (i.e. Cicero): the sense is close to examples in *MED, affermen, v.,* and *OED, affirm, v.,* but the collocation with *with* and a person is not recorded there.

744–8 *vndre the vmbre . . . recouere.* WW repeats the claim that the lands were lost under cover (*vmbre*) of the Truce of Tours (*Towris*), and adds that the lack of practice of arms should not discourage them.

746 *aduersaire.* Despite the sp. *aduersaries* nearby (743), this sp. with medial ⟨ai⟩ and only ⟨e⟩ in final position is well attested in *MED, adversaire, n.* and *adj.,* where 3 of 5 citations refer to the 15th-c. French wars. Both forms are attested in Anglo-Norman (*AND, adverser*[1]) but only ⟨aire⟩ in Continental Fr. (*DMF, adversaire*), which might influence the form in this context referring to French wars.

747 *disused.* Antedates 1st citation in *OED, disuse. v.,* 2 = 'discontinued'; this sense not in *MED, disusen, v.* See 754n.

748 *for to discomfort or fere to a new recouere* = 'leading to discouragement or fear of any new recovery', where *for to* is resultative (as at 725: see n.). Neither *MED, discomforten, v.,* 1, or *fere, v.,* 1, nor *OED, discomfort, v.,* 1, or *fear, v.,* 2.b, record the collocation with *to,* rather than *fro/from.*

750–2 *Ouide seiethe . . . to hym.* Close in sentiment but not in wording to Ovid, *De arte amandi,* I. 471, I. 473–6, which urges persistence when faced with misfortune. WW transcribed those lines in 1462 in Julius, f. 20ᵛ, among 'excerpcio certorum versuum prouerbialium et fa`ce′cie siue moralium' (Julius, ff. 20ʳ–21ᵛ). In May 1449 John Crop obtained copies of Ovid's *De arte amandi* and *De* *remedio amoris* (*PL*, no. 969, ll. 20–9) for WW, and a copy of *De arte amandi* was promised to WW's associate John Paston II in 1467 (*PL*, no. 745, ll. 18–20). WW copied or annotated extracts from most of Ovid's works in Lat. (Julius, ff. 22^r–23^v, 158^v) and annotated verses and illustrations from a Fr. translation of *Metamorphoses* (Julius, ff. 6^r–13^r). Ovid often expresses resistance to fortune, though in less close wording elsewhere (e.g. *Amores*, II. xix. 7; *Ex Ponto*, II. iii. 51–3, IV. ix. 90; *Metamorphoses*, VI. 195, VII. 518, X. 585, XIII. 90; *Tristia*, IV. iii. 79–80, V. xi. 3–4, V. xiv. 29–30), and was understood in general to offer advice in adversity (e.g. in the aforementioned letter of 1467 to John Paston II: *PL*, no. 745, ll. 18–20). See also 976–80n. As at 976SN (discussed at 972–80n.), WW's sidenote 750SN, in black and boxed, remarks that Alain Chartier 'dicit' this, but Chartier is perhaps implied to support the general sentiment rather than to supply the quotation from Ovid, whom Chartier does not mention in a relevant context. The extracts which WW annotated from Chartier, *Quadrilogue* (see Introduction, p. lxxix), are labelled repeatedly by their scribe as 'pour prendre couraige en aduersite' (Royal, ff. 136^v, 137^r), and those from Chartier, *Le Livre de l'espérance*, labelled twice by the scribe as 'Examples pour esperer prosperite et victoire non obstant que on soit en aduersite' (f. 134^r), and 'Comme on ne doit point laissier esperaunce pour les aduersitez etc' (f. 140^v).

752–6 *Water Malexander . . . may folow.* As at 627–9, perhaps referring to Walter of Châtillon, *Alexandreis*: for the sentiment, see e.g. ed. Colker, V. 385–9, V. 394–7, V. 417–21 (ed. Townend, V. 448–52, V. 458–62, V. 487–91). WW's copy of Walter's opening lines in Julius, f. 22^r (see 627–9n.), followed opening lines from Ovid, the author just cited here (see 750–2n.). Chartier, named in the sidenote 750SN, does not cite Walter's *Alexandreis* in a relevant context (as he does not Ovid: see 750–2n.). In Royal, f. 138^r, WW annotated excerpts from Chartier, *Quadrilogue*, 62, l. 6–63. l. 9, citing Aristotle teaching Alexander that he could overcome anything by his knighthood ('firent toutes choses subgectes et surmontables a la cheuallerie de Alixandre'), but that seems only loosely relevant, unless 'Alixandre' were misread (as discussed 627–9n.).

754 *disusage* = 'lack of practice in using'. The only citation in *MED*, *disusage*, *n.*, and the 1st in *OED*, *disusage*, *n.* WW perhaps calques Fr. *desusage*. See 747n.

755 *for a litill season. OED*, *season*, *n.*, II.12.b = 'for a while'.

755 *recountres* = 'hostile attacks'. Would antedate 1st citation in *MED*, *recountre*, *n.*, and *OED*, *rencounter*, *n.*, by date of possible composition for parts of *BkNob.* (see Introduction, pp. liv–lix) but not by date of MS. Perhaps a calque from Fr. *rencontre*. Recurs at 840, 1269, 1341.

759–61 *What was . . . was full gret. What* = 'How!' or 'How great!' as an interj. rather than question (*MED*, *what*, *adv.* and *conj.*, 2); the sg. v. follows pl. subject *losses*; the 2nd *was* seems recapitulative after the subclause describing the *Romayns*.

762–72 *whan alle . . . signe of victorie.* The Battle of Cannae in Apulia (*Puylle*), 216 BCE, between Hannibal's Carthaginians and the Romans. WW uses the story to make the same point as Christine de Pizan, *Livre des faits d'armes*, I. 8 (BL, Royal MS 15 E. vi, f. 407ᵛ; Laennec, ii. 41), 'les Rommains meismement . . . et de victoire'. Though not translating closely, WW occasionally echoes Christine's wording: *lost, by a litill tyme left the exercise of armes* < 'delaisserent tellement ou temps de excercite des armes'; *brought withe hym to his countre* < 'fit porter en son pais'; *in signe of victorie* < 'en signe de Ioye et de victoire'. But cf. the error at 766–7 (see n.). In addition (as at 732–8: see n.), WW's sidenote 759SN implies that this story is told by Alain Chartier, and it is in his *Quadrilogue* (Bouchet, 46), excerpted in Royal, f. 136ᵛ, which WW annotated, but Chartier is not the source; WW uses the story to make a different point from Chartier. See Nall, *Reading and War*, 71. WW repeats the story from a different source at 1519–25 (see n.), and the story recurs in Giovanni Boccaccio, *De casibus virorum illustrium*, in OMC, MS Lat. 198, f. 92ʳ⁻ᵛ, which WW acquired in 1461 and then donated to Waynflete (f. iiᵛ).

766–7 *the whiche discomfit before Duke Camos . . . be suche power* = 'the which [Hannibal] defeated Duke Camos . . . by such an extent'. From Christine de Pizan, *Livre des faits d'armes*, I. 8 (BL, Royal MS 15 E. vi, f. 407ᵛ; Laennec, ii. 41) WW mistranslates 'deuant cannes', a reference to Cannae outside which the battle occurred, into a defeated person *Duke Camos*, but preserves 'deuant', separating him from the transitive v. *discomfit*. The pa. tense of *discomfit* was often marked only by ⟨t⟩ by analogy with the Fr. root (see *OED*, *discomfit, v.*, Forms; and e.g. *descomfit* pa. 3 sg. 338, and the pa. p. *discomfit* 246–7, *descomfit* 2140; but cf. other past tenses with -*ed* e.g. 797, 1990); by contrast, for the n. WW uses *des-* or *discomfiture(s)* (e.g. 369, 932, etc., and *descomfiture ayenst Camos* 1520).

769 *Titus Liuius . . . Batailes.* WW adds to Christine de Pizan (see 762–72n.) a reference to Livy, *Ab urbe condita*, ed. and trans. B. O. Foster and others, 14 vols. (Cambridge, MA, 1919–59), bk. XXII and bk. XXIII, as another source for this story, which Christine and Chartier do not mention. WW might have known Livy in Lat.: Julius, f. 205ʳ includes a letter by William Selling, prior of Christ Church, Canterbury (*c.*1430–94: A. B. Emden, *A Biographical Register of the University of Cambridge* (London, 1963), 15–16; for another mention of Selling, see Julius, f. 118ʳ), asking 'vmfrido Gentyll lucano', a merchant from Lucca, to show WW a copy of Livy (Wakelin, *Humanism*, 97–8, 121, 125; and *England's Immigrants 1330–1550*, www.englandsimmigrants.com, *s.n.* Humphrey Gentill [24089]). But WW's employer Fastolf owned Pierre Bersuire's 14th-c. Fr. translation of Livy, *Ab urbe condita* (Beadle, 'Fastolf's French Books', 102), and other citations from Livy (see 1566, 1622–65, 2515–71 and nn.) seem close to the Fr. translation, so this reference might be to Bersuire, II. iii. 5 (e.g. Paris, Bibliothèque Sainte-Geneviève, MS fr. 777, f. 208ʳ). (Chapter numbers vary between MSS of Bersuire: cf. e.g. BodL, MS Canon. misc. 438,

f. 53^{r-v}, where this is ch. II. iii. 8.) We cite Bersuire from Paris, Bibliothèque Sainte-Geneviève, MS fr. 777, as a MS from the French royal library which was acquired by John, duke of Bedford, who later gave it to Humphrey, duke of Gloucester (Alfonso Sammut, *Unfredo duca di Gloucester e gli umanisti italiani* (Padua, 1980), 122, no. 35). Fastolf's copy of Bersuire's Fr. translation, 'the Cronicles of Titus leuius' (OMA, FP 43, f. 10^r; Gairdner, no. 389; Beadle, 'Fastolf's French Books', 102) was presumably a different one.

770 *quantite of, mesure of.* On such apposition, see Introduction, pp. lxxx–lxxxiii. Although *quantite* (< Fr. 'quantite': Laennec, ii. 41; BL, Royal MS 15 E. vi, f. 407^v) was widely attested (*OED, quantity, n.; MED, quantite, n.*), it might have felt Latinate enough to need glossing with *mesure.*

770 *.xij. quarters.* Cf. Christine, 'troys muys' (BL, Royal MS 15 E. vi, f. 407^v; Laennec, ii. 41); Bersuire, II. iii. 5 (Paris, Bibliothèque Sainte-Geneviève, MS fr. 777, f. 208^r), '.iij. muis' (< Livy's Lat. 'tres modios'); and WW's later *thre muys* 1522 (see n.). WW might misread roman numerals *.iij.* as *.xij.* or might calculate 'troys muys'/'tres modios' as *.xij.* bushels, because a *muy* could often be four bushels (*AND, mui, 1; MED, mui, n.*, citing only *BkNob.* 1522 and one other text; *OED, muid, n.*^{1}), 3×4 giving 12. But in practice Fr. *mui* and Eng. cognates were highly variable in denotation: Fr. *mui* could also mean a single bushell (*DMF, muid; AND, mui, 2*), and some Eng. translators rendered it or Lat. *modios* thus: e.g. *1408 Vegetius*, 75, ll. 11–13, 'iii busshelles of gold rynges'; Caxton, *The Book of Fayttes of Armes*, 26, l. 5, translating Christine, 'mues or busshelis'. Either way, *quarters* seems the wrong unit, as this was 8 bushels (*MED, quarter(e, n.,* 3(e); *OED, quarter, n.,* I.1.a). But one Eng. translation of *Le Quadrilogue invectif* translates 'muys' as '.iij. quarters' in telling the same story (Blayney, 193, l. 16), which suggests that this was an acceptable rendering. Cf. WW's preservation of *muys* 1522.

773–4 *How after . . . in werre.* Nichols suggests that the chapter title is incomplete, but *expert* is perhaps the pa. tense of the v. = 'trained in' or 'knew by experience' (*MED, experten, v.,* 3b or 4; *OED, expert, v.*^{1}), formed with elision of final ⟨ted⟩ to ⟨t⟩.

775–85 *But the worthy Romains . . . Cartage.* Based either on one sentence in Christine de Pizan, *Livre des faits d'armes,* I. 8 (BL, Royal MS 15 E. vi, f. 407^v; Laennec, ii. 41), 'mais aprez Reprinse la ditte exercitacion orent les dessus-dis Rommains tousiours victoire', or on a fuller version later, I. 28 (BL, Royal MS 15 E. vi, f. 415^r; Laennec, ii. 101). WW also knew the account in Chartier, *Quadrilogue* (Bouchet, 46–7), summarized in extracts in Royal, f. 136^v, though Chartier focuses on different elements of the story.

779–80 *he assembled . . . ayenst . . . the said Romayns, and.* A parenthetical absolute clause, = 'he [i.e. Hannibal] being assembled . . . against the Romans', sets the occasion of fighting; *and* introduces the Romans' new manner of fighting.

782 *tooke vppon theyme*. The phrasal v. *to take on* somebody in a fight, etc., is only attested from the 1800s (under *OED, take, v.: to take on*, 6.c), but the sense of attack is evident in context.

782 *charged theym*. Possibly literally = 'attacked' (*MED, chargen, v.*, 12) but more likely figuratively = 'pressed hard, burdened', recorded in *OED, charge, v.*, II.10, but not in this specific sense or context in *MED, chargen, v.*, 3(a). See also 897n.

782–3 *by vnware of theire purueiaunce met withe* = 'due to lack of knowledge of their [the Romans'] preparations he encountered'. *MED, unware, n.*, and *OED, unware, adj., n.* and *adv.*, cite only this passage for this sense and construction.

789–95 *Dame Cristen . . . dothe*. Close translation of Christine de Pizan, *Livre des faits d'armes*, I. 8 (BL, Royal MS 15 E. vi, f. 407ᵛ; Laennec, ii. 41), 'nulle rien . . . de puissant cheualerie'.

792 *exercited*. *MED, exercited, ppl.* = 'trained', cites only this passage with medial ⟨t⟩, closer to Lat. *exercitatus*, and another text with medial ⟨d⟩; 1st citation in *OED, exercite, v.*

799–807 *King Bituitus . . . gret oost*. Close translation of Christine de Pizan, *Livre des faits d'armes*, I. 8 (BL, Royal MS 15 E. vi, f. 407ᵛ; Laennec, ii. 42), 'roy bituitus de gaule . . . tout son ost'. WW's *were so welle excersised and lerned in armes* has no equivalent in the Group A MS of Christine cited here. *King Bituitus* led the Arverni who fought the Romans (*OCD, s.n.* Arverni). WW's sidenote 799SN claims to compile this from Alain Chartier, yet Bituitus does not appear in *Quadrilogue* or *Le Livre de l'espérance*.

800 *Gaule, clepid Fraunce*. The gloss is not in texts of Christine de Pizan, *Livre des faits d'armes*, I. 8 (BL, Royal MS 15 E. vi, f. 407ᵛ; Laennec, ii. 42). See also 931n.

808–9 *atwix . . . predecessoures entreprises*. The prep. *atwix* awkwardly contrasts one human combatant (*youre aduersarie*) and the inanimate *entreprises*, rather than *predecessoures*.

810 *named*. See 56n., 734n., etc.

812–39 *For at the bataile . . . .xxx. Mˡ. men*. A list, separated by paraphs, of instances when a larger French force was defeated by a smaller English force. The first five instances (812–828) are treated like passive constructions with 'The French force was' to be understood before the pa. p. *descomfited* and the victor in a prepositional phrase with *by/be*. The last four instances (829–39) are merely n. phrases naming events. (Paragraph breaks are editorial.) WW's frequent interlineations clarify facts or emphasize the disparity in the size of the armies.

812–13 *Agincourt . . . number*. See 468–71. The point was commonly made (see

Nall, *Reading and War*, 99–100), and WW encountered it in e.g. *Gesta Henrici Quinti*, read in BL, Cotton MS Julius E. iv, f. 117ᵛ (Taylor and Roskell, 78).

814–17 *bataile of the see . . . navye*. Battle of the Seine, 15 Aug. 1416: see 433–9 and nn. Chronicles tend not to present this battle as one where the English were outnumbered. Wylie and Waugh, ii. 360, suggest that the English outnumbered the French.

818–21 *Ke-de-Cause . . . Dorset*. The chronology of this sequence of battles is broken, as this encounter between Thomas Beaufort, earl of Dorset, and Bernard VII, count of Armagnac and constable of France, took place in Mar. 1416 (Allmand, *Henry V*, 102–3), before the naval battle mentioned at 814–17. *Ke-de-Cause* is the Chef-de-Caux, *département* of Seine-Maritime. In his copy of *Gesta Henrici Quinti* (Taylor and Roskell, 114–16), in BL, Cotton MS Julius E. iv, f. 122ʳ, WW added the marginal note 'quod vocatur De Kedecause' to *Gesta*'s point that Dorset led an expedition into 'interiores partes Normannie'. The numerical disadvantage of the English forces and miraculous victory are emphasized in other accounts: *Gesta Henrici Quinti* (Taylor and Roskell, 116, 120; BL, Cotton MS Julius E. iv, f. 122ʳ), like WW, has 900 men with Dorset, but 5,000, not 10,000, with Armagnac; Thomas Walsingham has 1,500 English troops, 15,000 French (Thomas Walsingham, *The St. Albans Chronicle. The Chronica Maiora of Thomas Walsingham, ii: 1394–1422*, ed. and trans. John Taylor, Wendy R. Childs, and Leslie Watkiss (Oxford, 2011), 688). See also 427–8n.

818–19 *Thomas Beauforde . . . duke of Eccestre*. See 427–8n.

819–20 *the erle off Armonak, conestable of Fraunce*. See 204–6n.

822–4 *Crauant . . . chief teyns'*. See 485–99 and nn.

822–3 *Iohn, duc of Bedford, as by hys lieutenaunt*. See 482–4n.

823 *Thomas Montague, the erle of Salisbury*. See 483n, 826.

824 *Roberd, 'Lord' Willugheby*. See 490–1n., 827n.

825–8 *Vernelle . . . armys*. See 517–18n., etc., and, for the size of both armies, 542–6n. WW read in *Giles' Chronicle*, 'Henrici VI', 5, in Royal, f. 72ᵛ, that Bedford's men were fewer than the opposing side.

826 *erle of Salisbury*. See 483n. At Verneuil.

826 *erle of Suffolk*. See 490n. At Verneuil.

827 *Lord Wyllughby*. See 490–1n. At Verneuil.

827 *Lord Pownyngys*. Robert Poynings (1382–1446), fourth Baron Poynings (under *ODNB, s.n.* Michael, first Lord Poynings). At Verneuil.

827 *Ser Iohn Fastolf*. At Verneuil.

829–31 *Roveraye . . . Orliaunce.* Battle of Rouvray, 12 Feb. 1429. According to the account in *Basset's Chronicle*, f. 64ʳ⁻ᵛ (C&A, 227), Fastolf and Sir Thomas Rempston (d. 1458) were sent, with 1,500 men, to relieve those besieging Orléans (WW's *vitailing the siege of Orliaunce*, 831), but were intercepted close to Rouvray by a Franco-Scottish force of 9,000–10,000. On this, known as the 'battle of the Herrings', see Kelly DeVries, *Joan of Arc: A Military Leader* (Stroud, 2003), 61–2.

829–30 *Bastard of Burbon.* A mistake. WW perhaps means Charles de Bourbon, eldest (and legitimate) son of the duke of Bourbon, who led the French contingent: see De Vries, *Joan of Arc*, 61. He is listed in *Basset's Chronicle*, f. 64ᵛ (C&A, 227).

830 *the Bastard of Orlyance.* Jean de Dunois (1402–68), illegitimate son of Louis (1372–1407), duke of Orléans: DeVries, *Joan of Arc*, 3, 61. He is listed in *Basset's Chronicle*, f. 64ᵛ (C&A, 227).

832–4 *Aueraunces . . . chiefteins.* The relief of Avranches took place on 22/23 Dec. 1439: Pollard, *John Talbot*, 52. The *Journal d'un bourgeois de Paris*, ed. Tuetey, 351, gives 40,000 French against 8,000 English; Michael K. Jones, 'The Relief of Avranches (1439): An English Feat of Arms at the End of the Hundred Years War', in Nicholas Rogers (ed.), *England in the Fifteenth Century* (Stamford, UK, 1994), 42–55 at 49, suggests that the English army was just over 1,200 and the 'French army five times its size'.

833 *Edmonde, duke of Somerset.* Edmund Beaufort (*c.*1406–55), earl of Dorset and later duke of Somerset, who led the army sent to the rescue of Avranches: Pollard, *John Talbot*, 52. He was not, at this point, duke of Somerset, not becoming so until 31 Mar. 1448. Below (836) WW ascribes the title to his brother, John.

833–4 *erle of Shrewisburie.* John Talbot (*c.*1387–1453), not in fact created earl of Shrewsbury until 1442. At the relief of Avranches: Pollard, *John Talbot*, 52. WW's sidenote 832SN names him as Lord Talbot, presumably from common knowledge.

834 *Lord Faucomberge.* See 132–5n. Lord Fauconberg seems not to have been at the relief of Avranches. Perhaps a mistake for Lord Scales, who was.

835–7 *Hareflete . . . Shrewisbury.* Harfleur had been taken by the French in 1435. It was retaken by the English at the end of Oct. 1440: Curry, 'Henry V's Harfleur', 260. A letter from Robert Repps to John Paston I, dating from 1440, describes how 'our Lordes wyth here smal pusaunce' defeated 'Freynchemen and Pykardes a gret nowmbre': *PL*, no. 439, ll. 7–10.

835, 838 "*a"t*, '*A't*. As the list is broken into separate units by paraphs, somebody changes minuscule **a** into majuscule **A** for new sentences (despite the majuscule on *And* 835). Compare changes of one-compartment **a**

to two-compartment **a**, where no majuscule would be expected, at 264 (see n.), etc.

835–6 *fought,* `beseged`. On such apposition, see Introduction, pp. lxxx–lxxxiii.

836 *Iohn, duke of Somerset.* John Beaufort (1404–44), at this point earl, not duke, of Somerset, involved in the recapture of Harfleur: M. K. Jones, 'The Beaufort Family and the War in France, 1421–1450' (PhD thesis, Bristol, 1982), 138–48.

836–7 *Edmond, erle of Dorset.* See 833n. Confirmed as earl of Dorset in Aug. 1442, but styled as such from 1438 onwards; involved in the recapture of Harfleur: Jones, 'The Beaufort Family', 102–3, 138–48.

837 *erle of Shrewisbury.* See 833–4n. For his role in the recapture of Harfleur, see Pollard, *John Talbot*, 52–3.

838–9 *Cane . . . men.* The attempted siege of Caen by local inhabitants in Jan. 1435, successfully resisted by Sir Richard Harington (d. 1462) and Fastolf, from whom WW's interlineation *.xxx. M^l. men* may derive. A request for payment dated 15 Jan. refers to a message sent from Fastolf to Thomas, Lord Scales, asking for reinforcements to resist the 'très grant nombre' of attackers: *Chronique de Mont-Saint-Michel (1343–1468)*, ed. Siméon Luce, 2 vols. (Paris, 1879–83), ii. 50. *Chronicles of London*, ed. Charles Lethbridge Kingsford (Oxford, 1905), 137, notes that Fastolf took 120 men to fight the besieging force of 10,000 peasants and gentry. WW's sidenote 838SN was interrupted by a revision of *sodeyn iorneys and* 840 which extends into the margin, f. 14^r.

838–9 *Ser Richarde Harington.* Named as bailiff of Caen in the request for payment (see previous n.), and in *Itineraries*, 352, under the heading 'De le rescus de Cane'; as captain of the castle of Argentan and *bailli* of Caen in the list of places lost 'durant la charge et gouuernance du duc de Somerset', in Arundel, ff. 286^v, 288^r, annotated by WW; and in Codicil, ff. 9^v, 30^v (Appendix 1/88–90, Appendix 2/105–6). For his career, see Linda Clark (ed.), *The House of Commons 1422–1461*, 7 vols. (Cambridge, 2020), iv. 787–93.

845 *by the thrid part* = 'three times as many', in the obsolete sense of *part* as a multiplier: *MED, part, n.,* 1c(d); *OED, part, n.*^{1}, I.2.b.

850–5 'O then', seith Vegecius . . . hande'. Not directly from Vegetius. Equally, no direct source is evident in Christine de Pizan, *Livre des faits d'armes*, but close in sentiment are 3 statements: I. 8 (BL, Royal MS 15 E. vi, f. 407^v; Laennec, ii. 43), 'O quesce de gens de guerre . . . non acoustumee', with *straunge auentures* perhaps < Fr. 'aduenture estrange'; or I. 10 (BL, Royal MS 15 E. vi, f. 408^v; Laennec, ii. 48), the brief 'lusaige est necessaire'; or I. 12 (BL, Royal MS 15 E. vi, f. 409^r; Laennec, ii. 53), praise for 'Les anciens qui . . . auoient aprins par experiences'. All three statements follow other passages ascribed by Christine to Vegetius.

853 *to tho* = 'compared to those'. WW contrasts people who know of military deeds merely described (*comprehendid and nombred*) in books (*dedis* < Lat. *res gestae* = 'deeds reported') with people who have *exercised* (= 'trained') in them.

855 *take vppon theym . . . on hande.* By zeugma the v. *take* both introduces the prep. *vppon* with refl. pron. *theym* (= 'take upon themselves') and is part of the phrasal v. *take . . . on hande.* Cf. zeugma with *tooke vppon theyme* 782.

861 *discorage you.* Neither *MED*, *discoragen*, v., nor *OED*, *discourage*, v., includes the refl. construction; the sense is close to that of the intransitive usage = 'dishearten', in *OED*, *discourage*, v., 1.b. See 888.

861 *For thoughe* = 'even though, nothwithstanding', a collocation not in, but close in sense and construction to, *OED*, *for*, prep. and conj., VII.23.a or 23.b.

864 *on the left hande* = 'adversely'. See *MED*, *lift*, adj., 2.

866 *this .xxiiij. yere day* = 'these 24 years'. See Introduction, pp. liv–lix, on dating.

868 *soudeyng* = 'paying wages (to soldiers)'. *OED*, *sold*, v.¹, only cites *BkNob.* for this participial n.; *MED*, *souden*, v. (2), does not list this form, but does cite the v. from *soulde* 871.

870 *but easily.* 1st citation in this sense = 'only meagrely', in *OED*, *easily*, adv., 6, but antedated by one citation in *MED*, *esili*, adv., 5.

871 *wagyngys.* A terminal flourish on final **g** suggests a pl. inflection, for a count-noun (i.e. = 'wages'), added by WW as a more precise alternative to *finaunce*. (On such apposition, see Introduction, pp. lxxx–lxxxiii.) A pl. is not attested in *OED*, *waging*, n., 1. Antedates 1st citation in *OED*; *MED*, *waginge*, ger., gives a different sense and only one citation.

871 *soulde theim.* An infin. dependent on *cannot* 870. The object *theim* may be *wagyngys* 871 (see n.) or may be soldiers, as tentatively glossed by *MED*, *souden*, v. (2).

872 *whiche . . . werre* = 'which, [it] is to be judged, were'.

877–89 *The Arbre of Batailes . . . theire prince.* As WW says, translated from book I of Christine de Pizan, *Livre des faits d'armes*, viz. I. 12 (BL, Royal MS 15 E. vi, f. 409ʳ; Laennec, ii. 54), 'quil aura bonne assignacion . . . congie au prince'. For *Livre des faits d'armes* as *The Arbre of Batailes* see 152n.

886 *late it be put in certein* = 'be certain of it'; see *MED*, *putten*, v., 23b(a); *OED*, *certain*, adj., n. and adv., B.III.8.

888 *discoragethe them.* As at 861, the refl. use = 'are disheartened'; the subject = *good men of armes* 887, is here understood. For 3 pl. pr. inflection ⟨th⟩, see Introduction, p. xcvi.

889–90 *if they . . . licence.* WW elaborates on his source.

891–902 *And also of ouermoche trust . . . to be lost'.* WW's interlinear addition *caused . . . to be lost* (902) roughly completes the sense, explaining the result of the aforementioned financial mismanagement; but it is not integrated with the syntax, so we add a rel. pron. Frequent use of the pa. p. (*yolden and sworne* 895, *rered* 898, *ben* 901) is perhaps modelled on Lat. constructions.

892–902 *And also when . . . to be lost'*. These connections are made elsewhere: e.g. C4/34–41, C5/50–3; and also in a set of accusatory questions drawn up to be put to the duke of Somerset about his actions in Normandy, in Arundel, ff. 323^{r-v}, 328^r (*Wars in France*, ii. 718–22); and York's articles against Somerset (printed in Gairdner, i. 104–5). WW returns to the point at 2168–89.

895 *obeissauntes subgettis*. See 541n.

897 *charged*. Alongside *taskis and tailis* 898, likely the technical sense = 'taxed', common in *PROME* (*MED, chargen, v.*, 8).

900 *contenting or agreing hem* = 'compensating them': a common collocation (*MED, contenten, v.*, 2a), e.g. in *PROME*.

901 *men, ben* = 'men who are': a zero marker of the rel. clause, as possible in 15th-c. Eng. most often with a stative v.: see Fischer, 'Syntax', 306.

902 *caused . . . to be lost*. Antedates 1st citation of the construction with infin. passive in *OED, cause, v.*^{1}, 1.c, but *MED, causen, v.* (1), 2(a), has an earlier citation.

903–4 *And the saide Dame Cristin . . . cheueteyn*. As at 570 (see n.), the 1st l. and a half of this sentence are underlined in MS as though a chapter title, but only *And the saide Dame* is in display script like chapter titles, and the clause is syntactically integrated into the paragraph.

903–22 *Dame Cristin . . . marchauntes*. As WW says, based on Christine de Pizan, *Livre des faits d'armes*, from the start of I. 14 (BL, Royal MS 15 E. vi, f. 409^v; Laennec, ii. 57), 'le bon cheuetain . . . aux marchans meffait', with the exception of (*as the proclamacions . . . grate autoritee*), where WW adds examples of the good practice that Christine recommends.

903–7 *Cristin . . . seiethe that . . .; and, that he may . . ., that the said chieftein*. 1st and 3rd *that* (903, 907) introduce parallel subclauses after *seiethe*; 2nd *that* (905) = 'so that', giving the result of the following subclause before it begins.

907 *men of soude* = 'paid soldiers'. This l. is cited in *OED, sold, n.*^{1}, but this collocation is not distinguished; *MED, soud(e, n.* (2), 1(b), cites this collocation.

908 *defalking, abbregging*. On such apposition, see Introduction, pp. lxxx–lxxxiii. This pairing recurs in a triplet at 2173. The only citation in *MED, defalking, ger.* (= 'deducting from wage') and the earliest of *defalking* in *OED, defalk, v.*; the finite v. recurs below at 2181 (see n.), 2434. < Lat. *defalcatus*, used in bureaucratic records of wars in France, e.g. Codicil, f. 21^r (*Wars in France*, ii. 548). See Fastolf's warning against *abbregging* soldiers' wages in C4/41.

913 `a'nd. See 264n.

914 *payne resonable.* For postposing of the adj., see Introduction, pp. xc–xci. It is perhaps a borrowing from a set phrase in legal Fr.

915–16 *proclamacions . . . in his host.* For Henry V's proclamations and ordinances prohibiting pillage, see Anne Curry, 'The Military Ordinances of Henry V: Texts and Contexts', in Chris Given-Wilson, Ann Kettle, and Len Scales (eds.), *War, Government and Aristocracy in the British Isles, c.1150–1500: Essays in Honour of Michael Prestwich* (Woodbridge, 2008), 214–49.

917–21 `and also . . . autoritee'); and that.* WW's addition (see textual note) follows *and that* by the scribe at the foot of f. 15^r, where there is more space, but the sense requires the addition to follow *host*; and WW then duplicates *and that* overleaf on f. 15^v to begin the next unit of sense afresh.

917–21 *statutes . . . grate autoritee.* The *statutes* are the ordinances of John, duke of Bedford, issued at Caen on 10 Dec. 1423, which survive in BL, Add. MS 4101, ff. 65^r–69^v, printed in Rowe, 'Discipline in the Norman Garrisons under Bedford 1422–35', 201–6. That manuscript is a collection of documents, dated by one of its scribes to 13 Dec. 1477, made for Walter Bellengier, Ireland King of Arms from 1467 to 1484. (On this MS, see Introduction, pp. xxxix–xl.) The ordinances' survival in Bellengier's MS suggests that he might have been the intermediary for WW to provide a copy of them to Edward IV. (Bellengier certainly knew WW by 1 Dec. 1477, when he provided WW with the names of captains and men-at-arms at the battle of Verneuil: *Itineraries*, 2; and above 517–18n.) Bellengier accompanied Edward IV on the French campaign (C&A, 125–7). If WW handed Bedford's ordinances to Edward IV *the day before your departyng owt of London*, that was 29 May 1475, as Edward left London on 30 May 1475 (Ross, *Edward IV*, 222). (See Introduction, pp. lvi–lvii.) In the MS, reader 1 comments that he should seek out this book (see textual note). People did collect statutes of war in MS and print: e.g. William Paston II, in the reign of Henry VII, when reader 1 was annotating. See Beadle and Hellinga, 'William Paston II and Pynson's *Statutes of War* (1492)'.

918–19 *Herry VJ^{the}, named kyng.* As at 56, WW describes Henry VI as only *named* and not rightfully king. Reader 1 interlineates *blessed*. For Henry's posthumous reputation, see John W. McKenna, 'Piety and Propaganda: The Cult of King Henry VI', in Beryl Rowland (ed.), *Chaucer and Middle English Studies: In Honour of Rossell Hope Robbins* (London, 1974), 145–62. See also 1141, 1313.

923–9 *It is fulle gret . . . cheualerous.* Translated closely from Christine de Pizan, *Livre des faits d'armes*, from the start of I. 14 (BL, Royal MS 15 E. vi, f. 409^v; Laennec, ii. 57), 'peril est en fait . . . hommes darmes et cheualereux'.

928 *pilleris, robberis, extorcioneris.* On this grammatical apposition, a stylish tricolon, see Introduction, pp. lxxx–lxxxiii. It expands Christine de Pizan, *Livre* *des faits d'armes*, I. 14 (BL, Royal MS 15 E. vi, f. 409ᵛ; Laennec, ii. 57), 'Robeurs et pillars'.

929 *cheualerous*. On the adj. after the n., see Introduction, pp. xc–xci; here it echoes Christine's Fr. (BL, Royal MS 15 E. vi, f. 409ᵛ; Laennec, ii. 57).

930–6 *In example the said Dame Cristen . . . riuer*. Translated, intermittently closely (but cf. 931n., 933n.), from Christine de Pizan, *Livre des faits d'armes*, I. 14 (BL, Royal MS 15 E. vi, f. 409ᵛ; Laennec, ii. 57–8) : 'Et de ce monstrerent bien exemple . . . en la Riuiere'. WW delays the lesson which Christine draws from the story (that this terrified the Romans) until 949–52.

931 *Gaule . . . Fraunce*. Gloss not in Christine de Pizan, *Livre des faits d'armes*, I. 14 (BL, Royal MS 15 E. vi, f. 409ᵛ; Laennec, ii. 57). See also 800n.

933 *Rosne in Burgoyne*. Location of the River Rhône not in Christine de Pizan, *Livre des faits d'armes*, I. 14 (BL, Royal MS 15 E. vi, f. 409ᵛ; Laennec, ii. 57).

933–4 *and the men of Gaule*. Recapitulates the subject (formerly *men of armes of the countre of Gaule* 930–1) after two long postmodifying subclauses, before the main v. *had wonne*.

936 *set no count*.<Christine de Pizan, *Livre des faits d'armes*, I. 14 (BL, Royal MS 15 E. vi, f. 409ᵛ; Laennec, ii. 57), 'faisoient nul compte'. Only citation in *MED*, *counte, n.* (1), 2, for the sense='regard as valuable', but *OED*, *account, n.*, IV.9, has an earlier use of the similar *set of no account*.

937–43 *Iohn, duke of Bedforde . . . come for*. Detail of Bedford's speech prohibiting pillage is not included in the main chronicles nor in *Basset's Chronicle*, ff. 53ᵛ–55ʳ (C&A, 212–15), but Waurin, present at the battle, refers to the many 'belles exhortacions et remoustrances' made by Bedford the day beforehand (vol. 5, bk. 3, ch. 29, ed. Hardy and Hardy, iii. 108). The phrase *it was saide* suggests an oral source for this information, perhaps Fastolf, who fought at Verneuil.

939 *oracion*. Antedates 1st citation of this sense (='a formal speech') in *OED*, *oration, n.*, 2; no such sense given in *MED*, *oracioun, n.*

940 *nouches, ringis*. On such apposition, see Introduction, pp. lxxx–lxxxiii. WW later pairs *ringis and nouches* 2546 as separate items, as do two citations in *MED*, *nouche, n.*

943–4 *And so . . . had*. The implied grammatical subject of the v. *had* shifts from *Iohn* 937 to the *peple* 939 rewarded *of* (='by') *the said regent* 945.

946–9 *rewarded . . . record to shew*. Codicil, f. 22ʳ (*Wars in France*, ii. 550–1), lists lands and tenements in Maine given to combatants at Verneuil, with the same *yerely valeu* as in *BkNob*. The Codicil's heading 'Declaracio dominiorum terrarum et tenementorum . . . Mˡ. iiijᶜ. xxiiijᵗᵒ', is added in WW's hand.

948 *marc.* A slight curl on **c** might denote an abbreviated pl. inflection (as added by Nichols), but *marc* was often uninflected: see *OED, mark, n.*[2], headnote.

948 'liures' turneis. Antedates the 1st citation in *OED, livre tournois, n.*, and the only citation of this exact phrase under *OED, Tournois, adj.* and *n.*, and *MED, tourneis, n.* (2).

949-52 *The whiche* 'was don aftyr' *the Romayns* 'condicion' . . . *done before.* The sentence bears traces of two stages of flawed revision. The latter part of the sentence *the whiche the saide Romains were . . . done before* resumes the translation from Christine de Pizan, *Livre des faits d'armes*, from the start of I. 14 (BL, Royal MS 15 E. vi, f. 409ᵛ; Laennec, ii. 58), 'la quelle chose espouenta moult les Rommains qui oncques ce nauoient veu faire', and syntax and sense continue from *cast it into the riuer* 936. That suggests that the comparison to Bedford 936-49 was an interpolation at an earlier stage (i.e. before this MS was made). Then the former part of the sentence *The whiche the Romayns, seeing . . . worship* restated the context, after that interpolation, but thereby made *the whiche the saide Romains* redundant. WW's two interlinear additions remove the redundancy by forming an additional clause *The whiche* 'was don aftyr' *the Romayns* 'condicion', but that disrupts the sense of the comparison: Bedford's behaviour was not like the Romans' but like the Gauls', which made the Romans *astonied*. We preserve his erroneous revision but supply *at* 951 to complete it.

955-62 *I haue be credibly enfourmed . . . wonne worship.* Many accounts of Agincourt give Henry V's words before the battle (Anne Curry, 'The Battle Speeches of Henry V', *Reading Medieval Studies*, 34 (2008), 77-97) and comment on his enforcement of discipline, particularly around pillage (Nall, *Reading and War*, 111-13). However, no other account (as far as we are aware) includes this particular exhortation. *I haue be credibly enfourmed by tho as were present* suggests eyewitness report.

957 *cousin and antecessour.* See 55n.

959 *that* 'forseyd' *noble prince*=Henry V.

960-1 *as welle of tho that were his there lost.* Perhaps a reference to the loss of items because of pillaging of the king's baggage, reported in *Gesta Henrici Quinti*, a text WW annotated in BL, Cotton MS Julius E. iv (f. 119ᵛ; Taylor and Roskell, 84).

965-72 *whan his chariottes . . . renomme*=the plundering of the baggage train by Lombard horsemen. As far as we are aware, no account mentions Bedford's prohibition, which perhaps points to Fastolf, present at this battle, as WW's source.

971 *whiche.* As elsewhere, a loose connective particle in an anacoluthic sentence;='when' or 'on which'.

972-80 *But yet it most be suffred . . .* 'another seson'. As at 750SN (see 750-2n.),

WW's sidenote 976SN registers a general likeness with works of consolation in adversity by Alain Chartier (*de Auriga*), although this passage is not translated from Chartier.

976–80 *Ouide . . . 'another seson'*. Closest in sentiment to, but more expansive in expression than, Ovid, *De Arte amandi*, II. 43, 'Ingenium mala saepe movent'. That was a widely cited maxim (Hans Walther, *Proverbia sententiaeque latinitatis medii aevi*, 6 vols. (Göttingen, 1963–9), no. 12371), but WW had access to this poem from 1449 (see 750–2n.) and in 1462 transcribed passages from book I (only) of *De Arte amandi* in Julius, ff. 20^r–21^v. Ovid is *saide* because he was cited at 750–2.

980 *enforcethe*. Antedates 1st citation in this sense = 'obliges', in *OED*, *enforce*, *v.*, II.10, but widely attested in *MED*, *enforcen*, *v.*, 1. For this sense, see also 2213, and for other senses see Glossary, s.v. **enforce**.

981 *inconuenient* = 'difficult situation' or 'disaster'. Although this use as n. is 1st attested in *OED*, *inconvenient*, *adj.* and *n.*, B.3, contemporary with *BkNob.*, *MED*, *inconvenient*, *n.*, records it frequently earlier in *PROME*. The Lat. cognate *inconueniens* occurs in documents handled by WW (e.g. Arundel, f. 333^r); compare *DMLBS*, *inconveniens*.

982–4 *Kyng Iohn dayes . . . Charlys the .Vte*. WW's interlineation refers to territorial losses under King John and Edward III, elaborated on below (993–7, 1112–18, 1196–1200).

989–97 *For a like . . . began*. Refers to the loss of lands in France between 1202 and 1205, here presented as a parallel to the losses of the mid-15th c. WW summarizes information on the campaign in Normandy from *GCF*, Philippe II, bk. II, ch. 23 in Titus, f. 78^r (cf. Viard, vi. 272–4). *GCF*, Philippe II, bk. II, chs. 22–5 (Viard, vi. 269–85), recounts the campaigns in Normandy, Aquitaine, and Anjou. The detail that Philippe II and his army entered Normandy in May 1203 is in *GCF*, Philippe II, bk. II, ch. 23 (Viard, vi. 272).

993 *vmbre of trewes*. See 109, 131–2, 722–3, 744, 1002, 1197–8, 1226, 1247.

994 *Torayn*. For consistency in handling ambiguous strokes (see Introduction, p. cv), we ignore a long stroke above final **n**, but final ⟨e⟩ is common in the Fr. name; cf. *Tourayne* 284, 525, 665; *Toureyne* 1015.

1011–25 *another trewes . . . tailed*. The Treaty of Paris, 13 Oct. 1259. Henry III surrendered his claims to Normandy, Anjou, Touraine, Maine, and Poitou. In return, Louis IX (see 211n.) relinquished his rights to the bishoprics and cities of Limoges, Cahors, and Périgueux (*Limogensis, Caourcensis 'and' Pieregourt*) and promised to return parts of the Agenais, Quercy, and Saintonge, lands then held by Alphonse of Poitiers, should Alphonse and his wife die childless (*Foedera*, I. ii. 50–1). Henry agreed to do liege homage for these lands and others held as duke of Aquitaine. WW's account is accurate, with the exception of his claim that Louis confirmed Henry's right in Poitou (*Peito*). The point that Louis had *grete conscience* that he held lands *bethout title of right* is also made by Matthew Paris in his *Chronica majora*: see F. M. Powicke, *The Loss of Normandy, 1189–1204: Studies in the History of the Angevin Empire*, 2nd edn. (Manchester, 1960), 270.

1019 *eueschies*. Nichols gives *eveschies* (= 'bishoprics'), the only citation in *OED*, *eveschie, n.*, and *MED, eveschie n.*, but the text glosses it as though a foreign word, and so we italicize. Cf. *AND, evescherie*, and *DMF, évêché*.

1026–43 *Whiche albeit if . . . foreuer*. Careful legal argument, with much legal vocabulary, e.g. *relese, effect, auctorite, parlement, astatis, law imperialle*, etc. The point is that English kings could not surrender their titles to lands in France, without parliamentary approval (and with *sufficient* members present). The coda, that Louis IX could not grant that title to English kings, as English kings had acquired it independently by the marriage of Henry II to Eleanor of Aquitaine, cleverly avoids any similar argument being made about French kings' release of French territory.

1026 *had done made* = 'caused [others] to make'. Mustanoja, *Syntax*, 605–6, and Norman Davis, 'Margaret Paston's Uses of *Do*', *Neuphilologische Mitteilungen*, 73 (1972), 55–62 (59–60, 62), suggest that the construction, found in Chaucer, etc., was declining.

1029 *law imperialle*. See 739n.

1040 *as is before expressid*. See 691–712 (and nn.).

1044–91 *Also ther was . . . leide*. A list of truces, many not complete sentences, separated in MS by paraphs. *Also* here functions like Lat. *Item* in lists. Cf. 812–39 (and n.).

1044–7 *Also ther was . . . Gascoigne*. The Treaty of Amiens, 23 May 1279, between Philippe III (1245–85), king of France, and Edward I (1239–1307), king of England. Philippe agreed to surrender the Agenais, which he had taken following the death of Alphonse of Poitiers's widow, Jeanne, despite the terms of the Treaty of Paris (see 1011–25n.): Prestwich, *Edward I*, 316: *Foedera*, I. ii. 179. The minims in the MS sp. *Amyeus* are clearly **u**, but the error for Amiens is surprising: see Introduction, p. xcix.

1048–50 *Another trewes . . . Guien*. Concluded in Paris in Aug. 1286 between Edward I and the new king of France, Philippe IV (1268–1314): *Foedera*, I. iii. 14–15.

1051–5 *Another trews . . . not long*. The Treaty of Paris, 20 May 1303 (Prestwich, *Edward I*, 397). WW alludes closely to and borrows some phrases directly from its article stipulating freedom of trade: *marchauntes and alle maner men* < 'les gentz & les Marchanz' and *bethout empeshement* < 'sanz empeschement';

perhaps *bothe roiaumes* < 'ou Reaume de l'autre' and *alle maner* [*men*] < 'toutes manieres [des biens]' (*Foedera*, I. iv. 24–6 at 26).

1056-8 *Another trux . . . Guien.* Agreed between Philippe IV and Edward II (1284–1327), king of England, on 2 July 1313, at Poissy (*Pissaicus*): *Foedera*, II. i. 43–4; Seymour Phillips, *Edward II* (New Haven, 2010), 212. Mistakenly dated by WW to 1213, rather than 1313.

1059-63 *in the yere . . . lieftenaunt.* Edward II's delay in performing homage to Charles IV (1294–1328; acceded 1322), king of France and of Navarre, and the attack on the French *bastide* of Saint-Sardos in the Agenais, led to the confiscation of Aquitaine in June 1324: Sumption i. 91–7. Edmund (1301–30), earl of Kent, half-brother of Edward II, was appointed lieutenant in Aquitaine on 20 July 1324: *Foedera*, II. ii. 105.

1064-8 *Also another . . . Fraunce.* The treaty, ending the war of Saint-Sardos (see 1059–63), was agreed on 31 May 1325: *Foedera*, II. ii. 137–8; Phillips, *Edward II*, 474–5. WW makes several errors. King Charles IV was not *de Valoys* (1065): WW has conflated Charles IV and his uncle Charles de Valois, who commanded French forces in Aquitaine in 1324. *Dam Isabel* (Isabella of France, 1295–1358) was daughter of King Philippe IV, not of Charles IV, who was her brother. WW's wording might imply that Isabella and Edward II married in 1325, but they were betrothed in 1303, married in 1308. These confusions perhaps come from WW's summary taken from *GCF*, Philippe VI, ch. 1 (cf. Viard, ix. 71–5) in Titus, f. 76ᵛ, where he left a gap for the name of which French king was Isabella's father and for the date of her marriage to Edward II. WW also misrepresents the English position, as Isabella was not considered '*soule' enheriter of Fraunce*, but able rather to pass on the claim to her son: Craig Taylor, 'Edward III and the Plantagenet Claim to the French Throne', in James Bothwell (ed.), *The Age of Edward III* (Woodbridge, 2001), 155–69 at 159. In Arundel, ff. 155ʳ–156ᵛ (printed by Hearne, ii. 534–41), is a copy of the document sent to Pope Benedict XII in 1340 that makes clear that Isabella was Charles's sister, and the grounds of the English claim to the French throne.

1068-70 *King Edward . . . contre.* See 1059–63n.

1071-8 *Also in semblable . . . conquest.* For the battle of Sluys (*Scluse*), see 319–25 (and nn.). Edward III laid siege to Tournai (*Tourenay*) on 1 Aug. 1340; a truce was negotiated at Esplechin on 25 Sept. 1340 to last until 24 June 1341, the *Feest of Saint Iohn next sueng* (1077): *Foedera*, II. iv. 83–4; Ormrod, *Edward III*, 227. WW's claim that, had it not been for this truce, Edward might have capitalized on his conquests is the interpretation of Sumption (i. 359) and of some chroniclers, e.g. Geoffrey le Baker (*Chronicon Galfridi le Baker*, ed. Thompson, 71) and Adam Murimuth (*Adæ Murimuth Continuatio*, ed. Thompson, 116).

1075 *kyng* "[y]s". WW's first addition with *and* oddly implied an additional *kyng* other than Philippe VI; he later corrected *and* to a separated genitive *s*. As he usually spells this *ys*, we emend.

1078–81 *Bretons . . . that parties*. For context, see 357–61n., and Sumption, i. 370–402. The claim that the Bretons made war *to this land* suggests that WW, or his source, imagines a Breton component to the French attack on Portsmouth of 1342. WW might pick up mention of Breton mariners among those who 'avoient moult dommagié le royaume d'Angleterre' in 1339 in *GCF*, Philippe VI, ch. 17 (Viard, ix. 171). The *gret bataile of descomfiture*=battle of Morlaix, 30 Sept. 1342, at which the forces of William de Bohun (*c*.1312–60), earl of Northampton, who had been appointed *kingis lieutenant* in Brittany on 20 July 1342, defeated the army of Charles de Blois. Northampton was reappointed 24 Apr. 1345.

1082–91 *Also the yere . . . after leide*. The truce agreed at Malestroit, 19 Jan. 1343, included in the chronicle of Adam Murimuth (*Adæ Murimuth Continuatio*, ed. Thompson, 129–35); its terms outlined in *GCF*, Philippe VI, ch. 30 (Viard, ix. 231–4). The more common charge, used as justification for reopening the war, was that Philippe VI and the French violated the truce by imprisoning and executing Breton supporters of Edward III: *PROME*, iv. 362; *Foedera*, II. iv. 193–4. At 325–8, WW presents Edward III's preparation for war as due to Philippe's mobilization of the navy.

1087–8 *Iuile . . . M^l. CCC xlvij^o*. The year should be 1346, as WW correctly states at 325, 338. For the siege of Caen, battle of Crécy, and siege of Calais, see 331–47, 361–5 (and nn.). Edward did lay siege to Calais *bethin few daies after* Crécy.

1091 *leide*. The MS follows *leide* with *and*, lightly crossed out; the scribe perhaps erroneously started the next chapter, after the chapter title, *And so contynued* 1098. Such an erroneous continuation might suggest that the chapter titles were situated in the margin of the exemplar.

1097 *passe*. Variant of the adv. *past*. *OED*, *pass*, *prep*. and *adv*., records this only from the 1800s onwards. Neither *OED*, *past*, *adj*. and *n*. or *past*, *prep*. and *adv*., or *MED*, *passed*, *ppl. adj*., or *passed*, *prep*., record forms without final consonant ⟨t⟩ or ⟨d⟩.

1098–1108 *And so contynued . . . foreuer*. For the Treaty of Brétigny, see 391–9, correctly dated here (cf. 392n.). Because he has just dated Crécy, etc., to 1347, the Treaty of Brétigny is indeed 13 years later.

1098, 1099 *contynued . . . continued*. The 2nd *continued* either (i) helpfully recapitulates the main v. after the lengthy subject or (ii) is a pa. p. modifying the n. *werre*.

1102, 1104–5 *the pope 'assentyng' . . . conferme'd' by the saide pope*. The adj. *saide* confirms that the repeated *pope* is not an error (despite the omission, necessitating an interlineation, of *assentyng*) but distinguishes two stages of the peace treaty: the pope's *assentyng* to the formation of it and his later confirming of it.

1108–11 *Ande whiche . . . lordis of Guien.* The secret alliance made between Charles V, king of France, and Jean, count of Armagnac; Archambaud, count of Périgord; and Arnaud-Amanieu, lord of Albret, on 30 June 1368. The issue once more was the right to hear appeals: Ormrod, *Edward III*, 498–9; Sumption, ii. 575. Among accounts WW may have read were *GCF*, Charles V, ch. 'De la solempnité . . .' and 'De la confirmacion . . .' (*Chron-Jean-Charles*, ii. 67–8; 70–2).

1112–18 *And after King Charles . . . Guien.* War resumed in 1369. For this phase of the war, see Sumption, iii. 1–170.

1118–55 *Whiche counteez . . . saide homagiers.* According to the terms of the Treaty of Brétigny, Edward III was given sovereignty over an enlarged duchy of Aquitaine, hence WW's point at 1118–22. Edward III created the principality of Aquitaine, and on 19 July 1362 Prince Edward did homage to Edward III and was invested as prince of Aquitaine. WW's source here, as he claims, is a register (*registres* 1122) of those who paid homage to Edward III and Prince Edward between 9 July 1363 and 4 Apr. 1364, which survives in copies in e.g. TNA, E 36/188, one of the base texts for *Le Livre des hommages d'Aquitaine: Restitution du second livre noir de la connétable de Bordeaux*, ed. Jean-Paul Trabut-Cussac (Bordeaux, n.d.), 70–117, and, TNA, E 36/189, printed in *Collection générale*, i. 86–121. An error in a date here at 1128 (see next n.) is also found in TNA, E 36/189 but not TNA E 36/188, which suggests that WW saw either TNA, E 36/189, or a MS closely related to it. We quote from TNA, E 36/189.

1123–34 *That was made . . . in Guien.* That=homage, performed at the cathedral of Saint André, Bordeaux, on 9 (not 19) July 1363. The date of 19 July is given in TNA E 36/189, p. 3.

1123–4 *erle of Armenak.* Jean (1319–73), count of Armagnac (see 1108–11n.). This homage is recorded in the register as being performed at Agen on 20 Jan. 1364: TNA, E 36/189, p. 12; *Collection générale*, 119.

1124 *lorde de la Brette.* Arnaud-Amanieu (1338–1401), lord of Albret (see 1108–11n.). The first to perform homage in the cathedral of Saint André, Bordeaux, on 9 July 1363: TNA, E 36/189, p. 3; *Collection générale*, 88.

1125 *duchie[z].* See 113n.

1126 *Prince Edwarde, the duke of Guien.* Prince Edward was prince of Aquitaine, not duke (see 1118–55n.); WW's source repeatedly refers to Edward as 'prince daquitayne': e.g. TNA, E 36/189, p. 3; *Collection générale*, 86.

1129 *Ser Thomas Beauchamp, erle of Warewik.* Thomas Beauchamp (1313/14–69), earl of Warwick. TNA, E 36/189, p. 3 (*Collection générale*, 87), describes him and Chandos as 'commissaries' of Edward III.

1130 *Ser Iohn Chaundos.* See 407–10n. WW gives the detail, present in his source (TNA, E 36/189, p. 3; *Collection générale*, 87), that Chandos was *vicount de Saint-Saueoure*. Chandos was granted Saint-Sauveur-le-Vicomte in Normandy (*département* of Manche) on 12 May 1360: *Calendar of the Patent Rolls: Edward III*, xi: *1358–61* (London, 1911), 329. This John Chandos was from the Derbyshire branch of the family, but WW mistakenly refers to him here and in a later red sidenote (1412SN) as from Herefordshire, a detail not in his source, confusing him with Sir John Chandos (d. 1421) from that branch of the family. Chandos was appointed as the king's lieutenant to oversee the transfer of lands in Aquitaine following Brétigny. The source for Chandos's 1,000 spearmen is perhaps a misreading of *GCF*, Charles V, 'Comment le duc' (*Chron-Jean-Charles*, ii. 134), which says that Chandos held Saint-Sauveur-le-Vicomte and that 1,000 combatants retreated there.

1134 *wele-defensid.* Antedates 1st citation in *OED*, *well-defenced, adj.*, from 1535 (and *defenced, adj„* and *well-defended, adj.*); this construction not recorded in *MED*, *defensen, v.*

1136–7 *Bordelois . . . Gascoigne.* Translated from his source ('Bourdeloys et Bazadoys en la seneschalcie de Gascoigne'; TNA, E 36/189, p. 4; *Collection générale*, 88). The Bordelais is the hinterland of Bordeaux; *Bassedois* is Bazadais, the hinterland of Bazas, *département* of Gironde, south-east of Bordeaux.

1137–40 *he . . . receiued theire homages . . . bothe in the name . . . and than in like fourme did homage.* The *bothe . . . and* construction confusingly switches the grammatical subject from Prince Edward who *receiued* homage to those who *did homage*.

1140 *And was no differens.* Omitting dummy subject *there*.

1142–3 *reserued the souereinte . . . seigniour king.* Translated directly from the source 'reseruez la souereinete et le resort deue a nostre dit tres souerein seignour roi dengleterre' (e.g. TNA, E 36/189, p. 3; *Collection générale*, 87 : for 'dengleterre' see 1144n.). Sovereignty and ressort—the right to hear appeals—belonged to the king, not the prince.

1143 *seigniour.* The sp. consists of the abbreviations used elsewhere in the MS for the title *Ser* and for *ur*, a standard rendering in Fr. for *seigneur*, but *OED*, *seigneur, n.* = 'French feudal lord', has no citations before 1592; see instead *OED*, *seignior, n.*, and *MED*, *seignour, n.* Perhaps a fresh borrowing by WW from his source (e.g. TNA, E 36/189, p. 3; *Collection générale*, 87, 'seignour'). For medial ⟨i⟩, see the full sp. of cognate *seignio(u)rie(s)* at 173, 690 and 1691 (but cf. 170–1 without ⟨i⟩). See also 1485–6n.

1144 *Edwarde toke*=Prince Edward, the Black Prince, who was in France and *toke* homage in person. He is nowhere else named without his title (twice postmodified: *Edward, prince of Walis* 366; *his noble son Edwarde, the prince* 2330), and *Edwarde* without his title risks misreading as the king, Edward III. We hypothesize that the exemplar read . . . *souerein seigniour king of England. Prince Edwarde toke* . . . (< 'roi dengleterre', TNA, E 36/189, p. 3; *Collection générale*, 87) or . . . *King Edwarde. Prince Edwarde toke*, and that the copyist of the present MS made eyeskip between majuscules *E* and *E*.

1145 *seneschalcie.* 1st citation in *OED*, *seneschalsy, n.*; *MED*, *seneshalcie, n.*, has antedatings from documents concerning French territories. Perhaps understood as a Fr. word borrowed from WW's source < 'seneschalcie' (TNA, E 36/189, p. 13; *Collection générale*, 100).

1145–9 *Agenois . . . Poitou.* These place names appear in TNA, E 36/189, in the same order (though in a different order in the printed edition): Agenais (p. 8); Landes (p. 13); the county of Bigorre (p. 16), corresponding roughly to the *département* of Hautes-Pyrénées; the regions round Périgueux (p. 19); Cahors and Rouergue (p. 21), the latter corresponding roughly to the *département* of Aveyron; Limousin (p. 23); the county of Angoulême (p. 24); Saintonge (p. 27); and Poitou (p. 30).

1154 *iiij^{the} day of Aprille.* The final date given in TNA, E 36/189 on p. 37.

1156 *M^l. iiij^C. lj.* For implications for dating *BkNob.*, see 1272n. and Introduction, p. lviii.

1157–8 *Gascoigne . . . in season.* For consequences of *defaute of socoure*, see 1271–6 (and nn.).

1159 *liege-peple. MED*, *lege, adj.*, 2, records the collocation but only lists among forms the sg. *lege-man* and *lege-woman*; likewise *OED*, *liege, adj.* and *n.*, and *liegeman, n.*

1160 *coherted.* 1st citation in *OED*, *cohert, v.*; not in *MED*. See 2078–9n., 2188n.

1167–75 *And now of late tyme . . . Katerin.* The Treaty of Troyes, correctly dated to 21 May 1420. A copy of the Treaty is in Arundel, ff. 174^r–179^r. Henry V's death (31 Aug. 1422) is only loosely *vpon* [= 'following'] *his mariage* to Catherine de Valois (see 471–3n.); they married 2 June 1420.

1175–9 *And now last . . . be the Frenshe partie.* See 54–5n. On the claim that the Truce of Tours of 1444 was the *.xxiiij. yere* of Henry VI's reign, see 517–18n.

1176 *innocent.* For contemporary allusions to Henry VI's innocence or simplicity, see e.g. Waurin, vol. 5, bk. 6, ch. 13 (ed. Hardy and Hardy, iv. 350), and John Watts, *Henry VI and the Politics of Kingship* (Cambridge, 1996), 103. Cf. 918–19n., 1356.

1179–83 *alle these trewes . . . auauntage.* Closely echoes C2/55–9.

1182 *brake the saide trewes.* The v. *brake* is transitive with *trewes* as object and an elided subject, understood to be the *aduersarie* and his *dukes, erlis and barones* (1180–1), and not stated explicitly until *they* in the next subclause.

1187 *complisses.* 1st citation in this sense in *OED, complice, n.,* 1; recorded in other senses earlier in *MED, complice, n.*

1188–96 *For whereas . . . Englande.* Repeats points from 644–50 (see nn.) but adds that Normandy passed *fro heire to heire* for 291 years, during which time the kings of France were not dukes of Normandy. Given that WW dates Duke Rollo's conquest to 912 and the loss of Normandy under King John to 1203, the number makes sense. Summarizes the excerpts and digests of the history of Normandy from *GCF*, Philippe II, bk. II, ch. 23 (Viard, vi. 274), which WW made in Titus, f. 78ᵛ, though the length of time that the kings of France were not dukes of Normandy is there counted as 316 years. WW's sidenote 1190SN calls Denmark *Dacia*, a common term found in e.g. Bartholomew the Englishman, *De Proprietatibus rerum*, XV. 47, or as 'Dace' in the Fr. translation by Jean Corbechon (e.g. BL, Add. MS 11612, f. 218ʳ), a copy of which WW's employer Fastolf owned (see 37–8n.). WW's sidenote 1190SN also describes Rollo as son to a Danish lord called *Byercoteferre,* i.e. Björn Ironside (i.e. Fr. *côte de fer*). This name 'Bier Costae Ferree' is used by William of Jumièges's widely copied *Gesta Normannorum ducum* (*The Gesta Normannorum ducum of William of Jumièges, Orderic Vitalis, and Robert of Torigni,* ed. Elisabeth M. C. Van Houts, 2 vols. (Oxford, 1992), ii. 18). Neither term occurs in the accounts of the Norman dynasty which WW took down or to which he had access in OMC, MS Lat. 45, ff. 68ᵛ, 69ᵛ (see 250–3n.); Arundel, ff. 86ʳ⁻ᵛ, 95ʳ⁻ᵛ, 209ʳ⁻ᵛ; Royal, f. 56ᵛ; Titus, f. 78ʳ.

1196–200 *And than for . . . King Iohn.* WW returns to the loss of Normandy during King John's reign (see 989–97 and nn.), but includes the detail that the loss was partly due to King John's murder (*puttyng down*) of his nephew, Arthur (1187–1203), duke of Brittany. The short addition was perhaps suggested by Higden, *Polychronicon*, VII. 33, which WW read in Royal, f. 25ᵛ; this describes how John captured and killed Arthur, for which reason the king of France occupied Normandy, Brittany, Poitou, Anjou, and Maine (ed. Babington and Lumby, viii. 184). As at 989, WW draws a parallel (*as was vsed now*) between that loss and the recent loss of Normandy.

1201–6 *frome the saide . . . that kingdom.* Edward III's 1st campaign against Philippe VI, into the Cambrésis and the Thiérarche, was in 1339, as WW might have known from *GCF*, Philippe VI, ch. 17 (Viard, ix. 170–2).

1209–17 *And therto King Edwarde . . . Normandie.* Edward III made alliances with the emperor, Ludwig of Bavaria, who was promised £45,000 in return for providing 2,000 men-at-arms, in Aug. 1337 (*Treaty Rolls Preserved in the Public Record Office,* ii: *1337–1339,* ed. John Ferguson (London, 1972), 1; Sumption, i. 198); and with Willem II, count of Hainault, in July 1337 (*Foedera,* II. iii. 179). Merchants from the Low Countries were offered privileges for buying wool in England (*Treaty Rolls,* ed. Ferguson, 16–17). An embargo on its export had been in place since Aug. 1336. In 1337 Edward III gave a syndicate of merchants the right to purvey 30,000 sacks of wool (not precisely *fifty thousande sak wolle*) and a monopoly of export, thus guaranteeing high profits when the wool was sold in the Low Countries. In return, they loaned the king £200,000: E. B. Fryde, 'Edward III's Wool Monopoly of 1337: A Fourteenth-Century Royal Trading Venture', *History*, NS 37 (1952), 8–24; Ormrod, *Edward III*, 194. The transport of sacks of wool to Brabant in 1337 is mentioned in the chronicles of e.g. Adam Murimuth (*Adæ Murimuth Continuatio*, ed. Thompson, 80) and Henry Knighton (ed. Martin, 2). It is not clear which particular alliances with Flanders and Brittany WW is thinking of, but Edward did make alliances with Louis de Mâle, count of Flanders, in Oct. 1364 and in May 1367 (*Foedera*, III. ii. 90–1, III. ii. 134; Sumption, ii. 576–7); and with Jean IV, duke of Brittany, in July 1362 (*Foedera*, III. ii. 65–6; Ormrod, *Edward III*, 431).

1211–13 *he rewarded . . . and soulde men of werre that he shulde make.* Edward III (1st *he*) awards the wool to Ludwig; Ludwig (2nd *he*) *shulde make* the *men of werre* (=‘soldiers’). It is unclear whether WW thinks that the grammatical subject of the v. *soulde* (i.e. the person paying the men of war) is Edward or Ludwig.

1212 *sak wolle.* MED, *sak, n.*, 2a, and *OED, sack, n.*[1], I.2, cite the construction *sak*+n. without *of* only collocated with *lime*, but *sak wolle* is attested elsewhere (e.g. in quotations under *MED, subsidi(e, n.*, 2[a]); and *sack* is the regular measurement for wool (*MED, sak, n.*, 2b; and cf. *MED, wol, n.*[1], 2b, *wol sak*).

1217–22 *For he wanne . . . perceyue.* WW claims, as at 1480–1 (see n.), that Edward III fought for 34 years.

1221 *the book . . . Froddesarde.* For WW's knowledge of Froissart, see 400–22n.

1223–8 *And so alle . . . partie of Guyen.* Restates points made at 1099–1111.

1229–34 *And sithen . . . specified before.* See 424–71.

1232 *exclusyfe.* MED, *exclusive, adj.*, has only one citation; *OED, exclusive, adj. and n.*, gives its earliest citation from 1515: the word seems rare. The sense= ‘completely’+*into* is close to *OED*'s numerical senses A.I.4.a and 4.b with *to*.

1232–3 *trespassement.* See 292n.

1233 *them.* Recapitulative pron.;=*labouris*.

1235–40 *And there . . . vndoing.* Richard (1411–60), duke of York, was confirmed as *lieutenaunt and gouuernaunt* in France for one year on 8 May 1436, and again, until Michaelmas 1445, on 2 July 1440, as correctly stated in C3/8–10: see Griffiths, *The Reign of King Henry VI*, 455, 459. See also Codicil, ff. 28ʳ–31ʳ (Appendix 2 below). For the Lancastrian land settlement and Richard's distribution of lands, see C. T. Allmand, 'The Lancastrian Land Settlement in Normandy, 1417–50', *Economic History Review*, NS 21 (1968), 461–79, and *Lancastrian Normandy, 1415–1450: The History of a Medieval Occupation* (Oxford, 1983), 60; R. Massey, 'The Lancastrian Land Settlement in Normandy and

Northern France, 1417–1450' (PhD thesis, Liverpool, 1987). The petition from the inhabitants of Maine requesting compensation, dated 1452, is copied into Codicil, ff. 55ʳ–56ᵛ (*Wars in France*, ii. 598–603), to which WW added a note that it was not granted and that various harms resulted (f. 56ᵛ). One of the 'Aduertirimentes' (*sic*: see 2391n.) in Arundel, f. 325ᵛ, claims that the king's 'verray true sugettes' did not receive compensation.

1235 *obeisaunt subgeitis*. Cf. 541, 895.

1238 *youre father*. Richard, duke of York (see 1235–40n.), so the intended addressee is Edward IV.

1241–5 *He`h', allas . . . before specified*. WW dramatizes laments of English landholders in France, betrayed by the broken truce. On his exclamations, see Introduction, pp. lxxxv–lxxxvi.

1241 *He`h', allas*. WW's interlineated **h** (see textual note) avoids ambiguity between the interj. and the male pron., which might be taken, inopportunely, to refer to Richard, duke of York, with a rueful *allas*.

1258–63 *And albeit that . . . trew*. The subclause introduced by *albeit that* 1258 seems dependent on the 2nd half of the preceding chapter title *a man shulde not be discouraged*.

1264 *and `as'*. The *and* has its rare function as adv. = 'even' as in Lat. *et* (*MED, and, conj.* (and *adv.*), 7; *OED, and, conj.*¹, *adv.* and *n.*¹).

1264–71 *`as' haue fallen . . . present*. The battle of Formigny (*Fremyny*), 15 Apr. 1450, at which Sir Thomas Kyriell (1396–1461) was captured. See C5/14–20. A list of losses under the charge of the duke of Somerset, copied into Arundel, ff. 286ʳ–288ʳ, and annotated by WW, includes a note on Formigny (f. 287ᵛ; *Wars in France*, ii. 630), which, as here (1267), states that Kyriell and 900 others were taken prisoner. Other sources give different numbers of captives, often between 1,400 or 1,500, or casualties: e.g. Robert Blondel, 'De Reductione Normanniæ' in *Narratives of the Expulsion*, ed. Stevenson, 1–238 at 175; Berry Herald, 'Recouvrement de Normendie', ibid., 336. See also *PL*, no. 450, ll. 39–43 (on Kyriell's capture); and Gairdner, no. 309 (Fastolf's claim for reimbursement for loans for Kyriell's 'voyage').

1268 *pety capteins*. See C5/18n.

1270 *or he came to*. Perhaps = 'until he came to where', but the conj. *to* usually has a temporal rather than spatial sense: *OED, to, prep., conj.* and *adv.*, C.1.a, and *MED, to, conj.*, 1(a). The account is clearer in C5/15–20.

1271–6 *Also another . . . rescue*. Preparations for an expedition to Aquitaine were under way from Aug. 1450 (e.g. commission for the arrest of ships, 30 Aug. 1450: *Calendar of the Patent Rolls: Henry VI*, vi: *1446–1452* (London, 1909), 389), but there were delays, and the expedition had been cancelled by mid-Aug. 1451. Bordeaux surrendered at the end of June 1451: Griffiths, *The Reign* *of Henry VI*, 529–30; M. G. A. Vale, *English Gascony, 1399–1453* (Oxford, 1970), 131–41; Vale, 'Last Years of English Gascony'. Chroniclers noted that the army was delayed because of non-payment of wages: 'Bale's Chronicle', in *Six Town Chronicles of England*, ed. Ralph Flenley (Oxford, 1911), 114–53 at 136–7; 'John Benet's Chronicle', ed. Harriss and Harriss, 205.

1272 *this yere of Crist M^l. CCCClj.* Deictic *this* could suggest a passage written in 1451. See also 718–21n., 1156n., and Introduction, p. lviii.

1275–6 *the cite of Burdeux lost.* See Introduction, p. lviii.

1278 *in according to this* = 'in proof of this', a sense not recorded in, though close to, 'agreement' between dissenting views, in *MED, according(e, ger.*, and *OED, according, n.*

1279–86 *Booke of Machabeus . . . batailes.* Apparently echoing 1 Macc. 9: 7–10, misremembered as the *viij. chapitre* or from a copy with different chapter divisions: there Judas, rather than his army, is *abasshed* ('confractus est corde'), though this follows closely a reference to his 'exercitus', and Judas exhorts the army to *auaunce* ('Surgamus et ascendamus') and *die* ('moriamur'). WW knew the story in other sources, e.g. Nicholas Trevet, *Cronicles*, in OMC, MS Lat. 45, f. 22^r (on which MS, see 250–3n.); some of Trevet's terms are similar to *BkNob.* (*discomfitures* ≅ 'desconfist'; Judas comforts his *peple* or 'genz'). Judas Maccabeus's and his father Mattathias's triumph over defeat, at risk of death, is mentioned in excerpts from Chartier, *Le Livre de l'espérance*, Pr. XIV. 19–71, in Royal, ff. 134^r, 135^r, and from *Le Quadrilogue invectif* (Bouchet, 62, ll. 9–17), in Royal, f. 137^r, but the quoted speech is nowhere given. Judas Maccabeus was widely praised as one of the Nine Worthies, of whom WW's employer Fastolf had a tapestry ('ix. Conquerours' from OMA, FP 43, f. 4^v; Gairdner, no. 389: see Alasdair Hawkyard, 'Sir John Fastolf's "Gret Mansion by me late edified": Caister Castle, Norfolk', in Linda Clark (ed.), *Of Mice and Men: Image, Belief and Regulation in Late Medieval England*, The Fifteenth Century, 5 (Woodbridge, 2005), 39–67 at 60), and his actions were recounted by Josephus, whose work WW knew (see 1565n.).

1284–5 *good corage and comfort taken to theyme.* An absolute construction: see Introduction, pp. lxxxvi–lxxxvii.

1287–94 *Also another example . . . worship.* Refers to events that took place not in 1270, when Louis IX died on crusade, but during the Seventh Crusade (1248–54). The crusaders were defeated at the battle of Fariskur on 6 Apr. 1250, where Louis IX was captured. The *soudan of Babilon* = al-Muazzam Turanshah (d. 1250), sultan of Egypt: see Jean Richard, *Saint Louis: Crusader King of France*, ed. Simon Lloyd, trans. Jean Birrell (Cambridge, 1983), 113–41. All details are in *GCF*, St Louis, chs. 42–59 (Viard, vii. 117–58), including the payment of 8,000 'besanz sarrazinois' (Viard, vii. 154), though if this is WW's source, he condenses greatly.

1289 `a'nd*. See 264n.

1290–2 *ouerthrow and take . . . put to*. An absolute construction: see Introduction, pp. lxxxvi–lxxxvii.

1293–4 *and came*. Grammatical subject shifts back to *Seint Lowes*.

1295 *historier*. See 724n.

1299–1301 *of the noble Troian is blode . . . registred*. For similar wording about descent from *noble . . . blode* of Troy *enacted* in texts, see 27–9n., 591–3n. The terms for textual evidence of this descent sound legal (*enacted, registred*: see 653–6n., 691–4n., 1170); the vague *doctours* could refer to any learned authority.

1302 *deformite of the law*. Only citation in *MED*, *deformite, n.*, 1(e), in a sense (=‘defectiveness [in law]’) not captured in *OED*, *deformity, n.*

1306 *Lete . . . be*. The dir. object for *Lete* is *the prowesse and vaillauntnesse* of predecessors (1309), which will inspire the reader to *succede* or follow in their footsteps (see Glossary, s.v. **succede**; *OED*, *succeed, v.*, 1.a; *MED*, *succeden, v.*, 2 or 3).

1309 *vaillauntnesse*. Depending on date of composition of this section, this might antedate the 1st citations in *OED*, *valiantness, n.*, and *MED*, *vaillauntnesse, n.*, from Malory.

1312 *ewred*. *MED*, *euren, v.*, does not record the intransitive use of the v. (presumably=‘have good fortune’), and *OED*, *ure, v.*², cites it (as a variant of *eure, v.*) only once *c*.1440. The (also rare) transitive v. appears in C2/39.

1313–16 *straunge regions . . . countrees*. For English involvement in crusades in Prussia (*Spruce*) and Turkey, see Maurice Keen, ‘Chaucer’s Knight, the English Aristocracy and the Crusade’, in V. J. Scattergood and J. W. Sherborne (eds.), *English Court Culture in the Later Middle Ages* (London, 1983), 45–61, and Timothy Guard, *Chivalry, Kingship and Crusade: The English Experience in the Fourteenth Century* (Woodbridge, 2013). For English mercenaries in Lombardy, see Kenneth Fowler, ‘Sir John Hawkwood and the English Condottieri in Trecento Italy’, *Renaissance Studies*, 12 (1998), 131–48.

1317–18 *for sithe . . . in armys'*. Edward of Woodstock, the Black Prince (see 83–4n.), who died in 1376, and Henry of Grosmont, duke of Lancaster (see 348–51n.), who died in 1361, and is here referred to as *good* Henry, as in other texts (e.g. *A Chronicle of London from 1089–1483*, ed. N. H. Nicolas and E. Tyrell (London, 1827), 65).

1317 *trespassement*. See 292n.

1319 *acyn*=‘similar’ (i.e. to the Black Prince and Henry of Grosmont). Scribe splits over the l. break, perhaps uncertain of the word. Antedates by *c*.40 years the 1st citation of the grammaticalization in *OED*, *akin*, *adj.*, in either sense (here sense 2), which is also seldom recorded in attributive constructions. Also antedates the source phrase *of kin* (*OED*, *kin*, *n.*[1], P1, dated 1486). But see similar constructions in *MED*, *kin*, *n.*, 5(b).

1325 *.ij. cosyns-germayns*=ʻ2nd cousins', i.e. of Edward IV, as at 1348.

1331–44 *Thomas . . . slayn.* Thomas of Lancaster, duke of Clarence (see 88n.), appointed lieutenant of Ireland on 18 July 1401 (*ODNB*), of Aquitaine on 11 July 1412 (*Foedera*, IV. ii. 20–1), and of Normandy in his brother's absence on 18 Jan. 1421 (*Foedera*, IV. iii. 200). WW's erroneous date of 1403 (*M*[1]. *CCCC iij.*) for the lieutenancy of Ireland in 1401 seems to reflect his confusion over the date of accession of Henry IV (see 189–200n.), for from his miscellany Arundel, f. 218[v] (printed, out of sequence, in *Wars in France*, ii. 758), WW knew that Thomas, duke of Clarence, was appointed lieutenant of Ireland in the 2nd year of Henry IV's reign; the error seems to concern the date of the start of that reign. On the battle of Baugé, see 499–508 and nn. As in these lines, there is implied criticism of Clarence's rashness in *Chronique de Normandie*, which WW read in Arundel, f. 265[v] (Williams, 205), and Pseudo-Elmham, *Vita et gesta Henrici Quinti*, read in Royal, f. 70[r] (Williams, 150) and several other chronicle accounts of Baugé. On such accounts, see John D. Milner, ʻThe Battle of Baugé, March 1421: Impact and Memory', *History*, 91 (2006), 484–507.

1331–8 *Thomas . . . and after that ʻthe seyd duc' . . . labourid.* The subject of *labourid* (1338) had been *Thomas* (1331), and the pr. p. in 1334–6 postmodified that subject. But WW's interlineation makes *the seyd duc* the subject of *labourid* and leaves *Thomas* without a finite v. Though ungrammatical, our punctuation follows that revision (and the MS's punctuation with a paraph).

1339 *marchis.* Despite sg. *that*, here, as usually, in pl.;=ʻterritory'. See *OED*, *march*, *n.*[3], and *MED*, *march(e, n.* (2). See similarly 89–90n.

1344–7 *Whiche not . . . Rouuerey.* Repeats argument of 508–13 but adds Rouvray (see 829–31n.) to the defeats of the Scots.

1345 *thoroughe power.* The *power* is presumably God's, despite the omission of *his*.

1348 *second cousyn*=ʻsecond cousin' to the addressee, Edward IV: see 1325n.

1348–62 *Iohn . . . Septembre.* John, duke of Bedford (see 88n. and *passim*), was appointed warden of the East March aged 14 (*in his grene age*) and held that office until 1414, and in that capacity *werrid ayenst the Scottis*. For his command of the fleet sent to relieve Harfleur and the victory at the battle of the Seine, see 435–9 (and nn.). He was lieutenant of England during the Agincourt campaign, the 1417–19 campaign, and between June 1421 and May 1422. He was regent of France between 1422 and 1435. For conquests in Maine, see 533–8 (and nn.). Bedford died at Rouen castle on 14 Sept. 1435 and was buried in

Rouen cathedral, as WW correctly states, as recorded twice in Arundel, f. 125^{r} (*Wars in France*, ii. 760, 761).

1355–7 *regent . . . xiij. yeris.* As in 478, C1/55–6.

1356 *deuout.* See 918–19n., 1176n.

1363–77 *Humfrey . . . rescued it.* Humphrey (1390–1447), duke of Gloucester, was *sore woundid* at Agincourt, as stated in the *Gesta Henrici Quinti*, read by WW in BL, Cotton MS Julius E. iv, f. 120^{v} (Taylor and Roskell, 98). For Edmund Mortimer, earl of March, see 435n., etc., and for William de la Pole, earl of Suffolk at this point, 490n. The places listed (see 1368–71n.) surrendered during 1418, with the exception of Bayeux, which fell in Sept. 1417 (Wylie and Waugh, iii. 64, 73). *Chronique de Normandie*, annotated by WW in Arundel, refers to the surrender of Bayeux (f. 244^{v}; Williams, 179), Cherbourg (f. 254^{r}; Williams, 190–1), and all other places (f. 247^{r}; Williams, 182; see 1368–71n.), and to the assistance of the earls of March and Suffolk (f. 247$^{r–v}$; Williams, 182–3). WW writes the names of Gloucester, March, and Suffolk in the margin of its account of the surrender of Cherbourg (f. 254^{r}), and lists the places taken by Duke Humphrey as given in Pseudo-Elmham, *Vita et Gesta Henrici Quinti* (Williams, 120–1) in the margin of his copy in Royal, f. 66^{v}. *Basset's Chronicle*, ff. 37^{v}–38^{r} (C&A, 190–1), also lists the 1418 conquests.

1366–7 *wyth help of the noble . . . acompanyed.* WW's revision is muddled: on the 1st l. he adds *wyth help* over erasure and *of the* afterwards at the l. end; on the next l. he interlineates *noble . . . acompanyed* but after *brought*, which makes no sense, so we combine WW's additions. The erasure under *wyth help* was perhaps *and* joining *wanne and brought*. As incompletely revised, two v. phrases *wanne . . ., brought in subgeccion* are in apposition: on deliberate apposition, see Introduction, pp. lxxx–lxxxiii.

1368–71 *Base Normandie . . . Valoignez.* The French region of Basse-Normandie, the modern *départements* of Calvados, Manche and Orne, and places within it: Cherbourg, Bayeux, Coutances, Avranches, Saint-Lô, Carentan, and Valognes. *Close of Costantyne* is the area within the peninsula of the *département* of Manche known still as Clos du Cotentin, which might be considered to include some of the latter four listed towns, but which WW names separately. Humphrey is praised for winning 'Of Constantyn . . . the cloos and yle' in Thomas Hoccleve, *Complaint and Dialogue*, ed. J. A. Burrow, EETS 313 (1999), *Dialogue*, l. 576.

1371 *marcher.* 1st citation in this sense (='territory') in *OED*, *marcher, n.*^{1}, 3; only citation in this sense in *MED*, *marcher(e, n.*, 1(c). The final letter is uncertain in the MS: unlike other instances of zetoid or round **r**, it has an otiose flourish bottom left. (By contrast, **z**, e.g. on *Valoignez* 1371, has a flourish that descends bottom right.) The scribe is perhaps miscopying WW's common pl. marker ⟨z⟩ (see Introduction, pp. xciii–xciv) from *marchez* or is perhaps adding an otiose flourish to round **r**, as in textualis. Cf. 141n.

1372 *protectoure and defendoure.* Humphrey was protector and defender of England for the first years of Henry VI's minority (until 15 Nov. 1429): Griffiths, *The Reign of Henry VI*, 38.

1373 *of grene age.* The prep. *of* relates this description to *Henry the Sext* in his age of minority, and not to the relative youth of Humphrey. See also 1349.

1375–7 *Calix... rescued it.* Philippe le Bon, duke of Burgundy, laid siege to Calais on 9 July 1436, but by the time Humphrey and his army arrived on 2 Aug., the siege had already been raised. Many accounts, however, credit Humphrey with lifting the siege, usually stating that the news of his imminent arrival was enough to break it (e.g. *Annales* in Arundel, f. 126^r; *Wars in France*, ii. 761). Another account of this siege owned by WW (*Giles' Chronicle*, 'Henrici VI', 15–16; Royal, f. 75$^{r–v}$) credits Edmund Beaufort instead (on whom see 833n.): David Grummitt, 'The Burgundian Siege of 1436', in *The Calais Garrison: War and Military Service in England, 1436–1558* (Woodbridge, 2008), 20–43.

1378–80 *bokys yovyng . . . Oxford.* Between 1439 and 1444 Duke Humphrey gave 274 books to the University of Oxford; his donation was widely acclaimed: Sammut, *Unfredo duca di Gloucester*, 60–84; Rodney M. Thomson and James G. Clark (eds.), *The University and College Libraries of Oxford*, 2 vols., Corpus of British Medieval Library Catalogues, 16 (London, 2015), i. 8–54, UO1-UO3. A note in a humanist-influenced hand added to *Annales* in Arundel, f. 126^v (*Wars in France*, ii. 764), describes him as 'amator virtutis et rei publice sed precipue clericorum promotor singularis'. Cf. 1823–32n.

1382–7 *gret tendirnesse . . . hethynesse.* Perhaps a reference to Duke Humphrey's patronage of foreign scholars, which was widely praised (Wakelin, *Humanism*, 25–32).

1388–9 *his ende . . . Februarie.* Humphrey, at Bury St Edmunds for a parliament there, died on 23 (not 25) Feb. 1447, following his arrest on 18 Feb. (*ODNB*). The correct date is in *Annales* in Arundel, f. 125^v (*Wars in France*, ii. 765), but a separate note in a humanist-influenced hand, f. 126^v (see 1378–80n.), dates this to 1446, which it would be by Lady Day dating.

1390 *ouer all these.* The prep. *ouer* has the obsolete sense = 'after' (*OED, over, prep.* and *conj.,* V.18; *MED, over, prep.,* 5b(f)).

1392 *cosins-germayns.* See 377n., 1325, and Introduction, pp. xc–xci.

1397–1405 *And also of . . . be 'now' passid.* Continues the syntax of the last sentence of the previous chapter: *many of youre noble bloode . . . bene deceasid* (1391–3) . . . *And also* [many] *of the . . . knightys.*

1398–1400 *Ordre . . . reigne.* The foundation of the Order of the Garter is given as the 23rd year of Edward III's reign (25 Jan. 1349–24 Jan. 1350) in the copy of the Order's statutes in Arundel, f. 185^r, printed by Lisa Jefferson, 'MS Arundel 48 and the Earliest Statutes of the Order of the Garter', *EHR* 109 (1994), 356–85 at 376, ll. 3–5: 'l'an de son regne xxiij^e ordonné, estably et fondé . . . en son chastel de Wyndesore'. On the date of the foundation, see Hugh Collins, *The Order of the Garter, 1348–1461: Chivalry and Politics in Late Medieval England* (Oxford, 2000), 13–14.

1400–2 *in token . . . sende.* Not in the statutes of the Order of the Garter, and WW's addition *as yt ys seyd* 1400 implies that this is oral report or folklore.

1402–3 *whiche . . . was founded.* The subject reverts to the *Ordre* (1398).

1410–12 *none suche . . . foryeting theymsilf.* Fastolf was temporarily expelled from the Order of the Garter for leaving the field at the Battle of Patay in 1431: Hugh Collins, 'Sir John Fastolf, John Lord Talbot and the Dispute over Patay: Ambition and Chivalry in the Fifteenth Century', in Diana Dunn (ed.), *War and Society in Medieval and Early Modern Britain* (Liverpool, 2000), 114–40.

1410 *withdrawers.* 1st citation in *OED, withdrawer, n.,* but *MED, withdrawer(e, n.,* cites *1408 Vegetius,* 150, l. 25, a copy of which was owned by WW's associate, John Paston II, in BL, Lansdowne MS 285, ff. 84^r–138^r: see Lester, *Sir John Paston's 'Grete Boke'*, 159–63.

1411 *fleers.* Antedates 1st citation in *OED, fleer, n.*^{1}, but *MED, fleer, n.* (1), has earlier citations, including again *1408 Vegetius,* 156, l. 15 (not *MED*'s 92a, i.e. f. 92^r of the edition's base MS).

1413 *Ser Iohn Chaundos.* For Sir John Chandos and the battle of Nájera, see 407–10n. WW correctly identifies him as a member of the Order of the Garter. He is listed as such in the copy of the Order's statutes in Arundel, f. 185^r (see 1398–1400n.). Chandos was one of the Order's founding members. WW's red sidenote 1412SN incorrectly states that Chandos was from Herefordshire (see also 1130n.) but correctly states that he was seneschal of Poitou, as WW would know from Froissart's *Chroniques* (e.g. vii. 167, ll. 26–7; 196, ll. 11–12).

1413–15 *as a lion . . . of the lion condicion.* WW might repeat the point in error, but he more likely compares both Chandos and Prince Edward to lions, as he later also compares other members of the Order, in a tricolon (1420–2). On the lion as a positive symbol, see 97–8 and n.; 1473.

1415, 1417, 1418 *defendid . . . auaunced . . . and maynteyned.* After the parenthesis on Chandos, the string of verbs resumes with the subject = 'they' implicit from *none suche were* 1410, and *theymsilf* 1412. WW's interlineation *and* is otiose, after parenthetical *as did . . . condicion.*

1416–17 *theire princes right and theire subgettis* = 'the rights of the members' princes and of the princes' subjects'; the referent of repeated *theire* must shift.

1425–31 *In example . . . daies.* The meeting of English and French armies at Montépilloy, outside Senlis, on 15 Aug. 1429 (not 1431). While there was some skirmishing, there was no general engagement, and the French treated it as a victory. WW's *.l^{ti}. M^{l}. fighters* on the French side is very high. Details and emphases are not in WW's usual sources or Waurin, vol. 5, bk. 4, ch. 18 (ed. Hardy and Hardy, iii. 324–9), or the three accounts printed in *Procès de condamnation et de réhabilitation de Jeanne d'Arc dite la Pucelle*, ed. Jules Quicherat, 5 vols. (Paris, 1841–9), iv. 21–3, 82–4, and 192–6. *Hall's Chronicle*, ed. H. Ellis (London, 1809), 153, does mention Charles VII's cowardly flight, and that the size of his army was double that of Bedford's, which could be based on some unidentified 15th-c. source, perhaps even the now lost *Acta Domini Iohannis Fastolf*. For events, see DeVries, *Joan of Arc*, 137–40.

1429 *vnfoughten*. 1st citation in *OED*, *unfoughten*, *adj.*, but *MED*, *unfoughten*, *ppl.*, has a citation *c*.1437.

1432–43 *youre saide aduersarie . . . incontinent*. The successful defence of Paris in Sept. 1429. See *Joan of Arc: La Pucelle*, ed. and trans. Craig Taylor (Manchester, 2006), 124–5; Guy Llewelyn Thompson, *Paris and its People under English Rule: The Anglo-Burgundian Regime 1420–1436* (Oxford, 1991), 106–10. Bedford ordered the sending of 'al the felashipe that ye may raise or gete in any wise' (*Wars in France*, ii. 118–19), in anticipation of the attack. Other accounts, e.g. Waurin, vol. 5, bk. 4, ch. 21 (ed. Hardy and Hardy, iii. 338–41), focus on the contribution of Jeanne d'Arc to the attack on Paris and mention Bedford's role barely or not at all. *Hall's Chronicle*, 155, describes Bedford's response and the 'gentle exhortacion' he delivered to the citizens. It also details the 'no small nombre' of wounded and Charles VII's retreat 'seyng the greate losse'.

1435–6 *whiche . . . disposed hym*. With this rel. clause, the subject shifts to Bedford.

1440–3 *youre said aduersarie . . . incontinent* = 'Charles VII (*aduersarie*) . . . was resisted by men and artillery'; *withe* = 'by'.

1448 *haue had*. The implied subject remains the *lordis*, *chieueteins* and other *subgettis*, as it is for *haue abandonned* 1445.

1451–2 *as is before expressid*. See 812–839.

1453 *Ser Iohn Radclif . . . worship*. WW returns to the defence of Paris. Sir John Radcliffe (d. 1441) arrived in France with reinforcements in July 1429: *Proceedings and Ordinances of the Privy Council*, ed. N. H. Nicolas, 7 vols. (London, 1834–7), iii. 295, 326; Thompson, *Paris and its People*, 106–7. *Journal du siège d'Orléans* states that an English knight 'Jean Ratelet' was left to defend Paris with a force of 2,000 men: *Procès de condamnation*, ed. Quicherat, iv. 197. *Hall's Chronicle*, 155, emphasizes how 'thenglishe capitaines . . . manfully and fiersly' defended the city against a large French force. WW might have focused on Radcliffe's contribution because he was Fastolf's brother-in-law and fellow member of the Order of the Garter: see Gairdner, no. 385; J. S. Roskell, Linda Clark, and Carole Rawcliffe (eds.), *The House of Commons, 1386–1421*, 4 vols. (Stroud, 1993), iii. 7. Of the two men of this name in Codicil, f. 10ᵛ and f. 11ʳ, the relevant one is Appendix 1/153–4.

1454 *martirs.* The deceased warriors mentioned at 1390–4, 1444–5.

1462 *vnmanly.* In 15th-c. Eng., the opposite of the virtue befitting a human being, from a folk etymology of Lat. *virtus < vir.* Cf. 1963 (and n.) and see e.g. Blayney, 202, l. 26, 'vnmanly tiranny' (also 203, l. 25).

1464–7 *i. yere . . . Mˡ. CCCCl.* See 52–3n. Despite the implication, the dates refer to the loss of Normandy only and roughly correspond to the fall of Pont-de-l'Arche (16, not 15, May 1449) and the fall of Cherbourg (12, not 15 Aug. 1450). The list of places lost under Somerset in Arundel, annotated by WW (see 52–3n.), dates the fall of Pont-de-l'Arche to 9 May (f. 286ʳ; *Wars in France*, ii. 619) and that of Cherbourg to Aug. 1450, where WW, annotating, leaves a gap for the specific day in Aug. (f. 288ʳ; *Wars in France*, ii. 634).

1468–9 *were delyuered . . . partye.* Without WW's interlineation, the sense was incomplete.

1469–79 *And if they had . . . as it hathe.* Although we punctuate as a complete sentence, the syntax is incomplete, like a rueful exclamation. It is made less clear by what seem like scribal errors (see textual note).

1473 *lyouns kynde.* See 97–8n., 1413–15n.

1474–5 *that parties.* See 89–90n.

1476–8 *xxxv. yeris . . . Henry the .Vᵗʰᵉ.* The claim that Normandy was held for 35 years and 7 days is not far wrong. Henry V landed 13 Aug. 1415 and Harfleur surrendered on 22 Sept. WW's calculation places the first conquest on 8 Aug. 1415.

1480–1 *King Edwarde . . . yere.* WW corrected the duration of Edward III's conquests from 20 to 34 years. See also 1219.

1481 *Whiche that.* Unclear referent; the rel. pron. functions loosely like a co-ordinating conj. (see 508–10 and n., and similarly 1858) or in place of the impers. pron. *it.*

1485–6 *seigniouries.* For the expansion of abbreviations, see *seigniour* 1143n.

1488–91 *Yet for alle . . . Mˡ. CCC. lxxj.* Cf. 1108–11.

1499–1517 *For one good . . . ayenst vs.* Fastolf's 1435 articles relating to the congress of Arras urged the importance of alliances for the furthering of the conquest: C2/231–46. The government emphasized the existence of alliances with Burgundy, Brittany, and Aragon in its attempts to secure finance for Edward IV's French campaign: *Literae Cantuarienses*, ed. Sheppard, iii. 280–1.

1499 *vndre correccion.* See 23–4n.

1505, 1515 *allie˚s'.* See 141n.

1506–16 *Whiche, and they were renewed . . . but oure said allie˚s' wolde.* A controlled periodic sentence, of multiple delaying subclauses: if (=*and*: OED, *and, conj.*¹, *adv.* and *n.*¹, A.II.13.a) allies were renewed by this long list of means, then *it wolde be* expected that, when (=*than*) our subjects were attacked, as they are (*as it is*), that undoubtedly (*but,* i.e. *but that*='Introducing an inevitable . . . result': OED, *but, prep., adv., conj.* and *n.*², C.II.10.b) then the *allie˚s' wolde* assist.

1508–9 *gyuyng renomme . . . in armes.* The English court regularly welcomed foreign noblemen for chivalric tournaments. Such visits are recounted in, among other MSS, a collection owned by WW's associate John Paston II in BL, Lansdowne MS 285, ff. 15ʳ–25ᵛ, 29ᵛ–43ʳ (Lester, *Sir John Paston's 'Grete Boke'*, 98–117, 123–33).

1517 *and vnder colour of trewes.* The *and* is emphatic, introducing an explanatory detail (OED, *and, conj.*¹, *adv.* and *n.*¹, A.I.9.a) of the *intrusions.*

1519–25 *among the Romayne . . . discomfiture.* From an anecdote ascribed to Valerius Maximus, V. i., in Jean Courtecuisse, *Sénèque des III vertus: La Formula Honestae Vitae de Martin de Braga (pseudo-Sénèque),* ed. Hans Haselbach (Bern, 1975), 393, ll. 275–92, which WW read in CUL, MS Add. 7870, ff. 42ᵛ–43ʳ; at this point, he wrote his only annotation in that MS in Fr., 'pro le courage dez Anglez', and one in Lat., 'Exemplum capientis cenatoris de Cartage voce Hanon contra obuersionem exercitus Romanorum' (f. 42ᵛ; Courtecuisse, *Sénèque,* 393, l. 275). Courtecuisse's Fr. 'muys', 'demanda', and 'desconfiture' are recalled in *BkNob.* in *muys, demaunded,* and *descomfiture,* but Courtecuisse's 'Hanon' becomes *Hamon* and the site of the battle of Cannae becomes a person, *Camos* (as at 765–6: see 766–7n.). Here, the MS of *BkNob.* lacks a leaf; in the remaining story told in CUL, MS Add. 7870, Hanon asks whether the Romans' allies had defected to the Carthaginians; when told no, he correctly foretells that the Romans will revive to victory, as in time they did in the Second Punic War.

1522 *thre muys.* From Courtecuisse's Fr. *muys* (see previous n.). See 770n. on WW's use of the alternative *quarters.*

1527 The leaf preceding f. 26 is lost here. The passage might have reported that some blame England's misfortunes on chance, to which this citation of authorities is a riposte.

1527–8 *Cicero . . . Of Diuinacion.* Cicero, *De Divinatione,* perhaps II. viii. 2, either cited second-hand from Boethius, *De consolatione philosophiae,* V. pr. 4 (see 1529n.), or recalled directly, as WW wrote the title into a copy of *De Divinatione* in OMC, MS Lat. 62, f. iiiᵛ (identified by Rundle, 'Worcestre'), and added the incipit to the title in a list of Cicero's works in Julius, f. 97^r. WW's point generally accords with Cicero's wariness of divination.

1528–9 *Seint Austyn.* St Augustine (often sp. *Austyn*), *De libero arbitrio.* It is not clear whether, and in which copy, WW knew this work. In his notebook Julius, f. 115^r, in 1468 he copied a decontextualized saying on God's knowledge of human life ascribed to St Augustine in a collection of sayings from William Plombe of Gonville Hall, Cambridge. See also 1603–10n., 1737n.

1529 *Boecius.* Boethius, *De consolatione philosophiae*, V. pr. 4, makes a similar argument, that God's foreknowledge does not bring about necessity or erode free will. Henry Chadwick, *Boethius: The Consolations of Music, Logic, Theology and Philosophy* (Oxford, 1990), 250, notes that Boethius follows St Augustine, *De civitate Dei*, V. 9, in mis-citing Cicero (but see 1527–8n.). In Julius, f. 115^{r-v}, WW copied a quotation with a slightly different lesson ('Impaciencia sortem exacerbat quam mutare non possis') from Boethius, *De consolatione*, II. pr. 1, in a list of proverbs and authoritative sayings from a book of Roger 'Marchale' written in London, perhaps the well-known physician: see the list of Marchall's books by Linda Ehrsam Voigts, 'A Doctor and his Books:The Manuscripts of Roger Marchall (d. 1477)', in Richard Beadle and A. J. Piper (eds.), *New Science out of Old Books: Studies in Manuscripts and Early Printed Books in Honour of A. I. Doyle* (Aldershot, 1995), 249–301.

1532 *aduersarily.* A nonce usage. 1st citation in *OED, adversarily, adv.*, with the next in 1715 and in a different sense, and the only citation in *MED, adversarili, adv.* No obvious cognate in Lat. or Fr. (where *adversairement* was rare, according to *DMF*).

1542 *dispositiflie.* 1st citation in *OED, dispositively, adv.*, and the only citation in *MED, dispositifli.* Also earlier than any in *OED, dispositive, adj.* and *n.*, cited from Caxton in 1483, though *MED, dispositif, adj.*, cites an earlier translation of Guy de Chauliac. WW perhaps draws on scholastic vocabulary for fate and freewill: *DMLBS, dispositivus*, cites e.g. Bradwardine.

1550–2 *Ptoleme . . . constellacions.* (The Lat. is in display script and underlined, as also, in error, are the rest of the words on that line.) A maxim commonly but wrongly ascribed to Ptolemy, *Centiloquium*, instead summarizing his work, and frequently cited to assert free will against astrology, e.g. by Thomas Aquinas and Albert the Great (Thomas Litt, *Les Corps célestes dans l'univers de saint Thomas d'Aquin* (Louvain, 1963), 207 n. 3), and in Eng. ('A Treatise on the Elections of Times', ed. Lister M. Matheson and Ann Shannon, in Matheson (ed.), *Popular and Practical Science in Medieval England*, 23–59 at 25, 46). See also G. W. Coopland, *Nicole Oresme and the Astrologers: A Study of his Livre de Divinacions* (Liverpool, 1952), 175–7; S. J. Tester, *A History of Western Astrology* (Woodbridge, 1987), 177; Richard Kieckhefer, *Magic in the Middle Ages* (Cambridge, 1989), 129. Ptolemy is called 'astrologien' by Chaucer, *The*

Canterbury Tales, III. 324. WW noted Ptolemy's works, including *Centiloquium*, in Julius, ff. 35^v, 100^v, and Fastolf had Ptolemy's *Almagest* on a list of books purportedly in Fr. ('liber Almagesti', OMA, FP 43, f. 10^r; Gairdner, no. 389), though no Fr. translation is known (Beadle, 'Fastolf's French Books', 103).

1551 *capitall.* This variant sp. is not listed in *MED, capitle, n.*, nor is this sense = 'chapter of a book' recorded in *MED, capital, n.* (1), *MED, capital, n.* (2) or collocations in *MED, capital, adj.* By contrast, *OED, capital, n.*^{1}, 3, gives this as a separate lemma, albeit obsolete and rare, citing only John Lydgate before WW.

1553-6 *ye oughte not . . . prouided.* WW's putative addressee, Edward IV, sought advice from astrology and used prophecy as a tool for propaganda: see Jonathan Hughes, *Arthurian Myths and Alchemy: The Kingship of Edward IV* (Stroud, 2002). In the light of such practice by the monarch, this rebuke of fatalism (and the 2 sg. pron. *ye*) might be pointed or inept. The interest instead in the *lak of prudence and politique gouernaunce in dew tyme* echoes Ciceronian terms, *prudentia* and *temperantia*, two of the cardinal virtues, and political reason, increasingly invoked in this period in rejection of fatalism: see Paul Strohm, *Politique: Languages of Statecraft between Chaucer and Shakespeare* (Notre Dame, IN, 2005), 3. WW also annotated 'prudencia' in Walter Burley's commentary on Aristotle's *Problemata*, in OMC, MS Lat. 65, f. 18^r, which noted that 'prudentes' eschewed riches and set an example to their subjects.

1557-8 *comen wele . . . singuler couetise.* A common contrast in *BkNob.*: see also 1599-1601. The MS sp. *singler* with crossbar on single *l* probably reflects the usual Eng. sp. with a medial ⟨u⟩, as in WW's letters (e.g. *PL*, no. 529, l. 12).

1559-63 *For whiche inconuenientis . . . falle vpon vs.* The sense is clearer when *inconuenientis* = 'immoral acts' (i.e. taking *rewardis* and allowing *extorcions*), rather than = 'disasters' (cf. 1197, 1246). The balance of *mysfortune . . . here* and *priuacion . . . ther* is neat.

1560 *diuers* = 'diverse means'. Use of the adj. as n. is attested in *OED, divers, adj.*, 3.c, only in an uncertain citation from *c*.1450 and then from 1526 on. The use as n. is not captured in *MED, divers(e, adj.*

1565 *Iosephas.* A copy of Josephus, probably in Fr. translation, is recorded in an inventory of WW's employer Fastolf's castle (OMA, FP 43, f. 10^r: 'liber de Sentence Ioseph'; Gairdner, no. 389; Beadle, 'Fastolf's French Books', 104-5), and is recorded as a gift to Sir William Yelverton after Fastolf's death in a document probably copied by the scribe of *BkNob.*, to which WW added a valuation of the book at £5 (OMA, FP 70/1, on which see Introduction, pp. xxiii, xxv). Also, WW took notes from a Lat. translation of Josephus, *De Iudeorum antiquitatum*, VIII. ii. 9–VIII. iii. 1, about the building of the temple, in Titus, f. 65^{r-v}, and copied a second-hand reference in *Itineraries*, 316-17.

1565 *Orosius.* Orosius, *Historia adversum paganos*. WW gives a title *De Ormesta mundi* found in many Lat. MSS and many of WW's other sources, e.g.

Ralph de Diceto, Nicholas Trevet (on which see Cameron Wachowich, 'On *Ormesta*', *Quaestio insularis*, 22 (2021), 107–62 at 117–20). But WW probably drew on Fr. intermediaries. WW made notes *c*.1444 in Titus, ff. 73^v–74^r, on the Trojan ancestry of English kings 'comme lez aunciens croniques Orosius et lez graunt croniques de Fraunce tesmoignet', but this was only from *GCF* (see 27–9n.). In Paris in Dec. 1453, from a book belonging to Fastolf, WW copied 'extractus siue compilacio certorum actuum armorum gentis Romanorum contra Cartaginenses extra ~~librum orosij~~ cronicis Orosij' (Royal, ff. 135$^{r–v}$); these were transcriptions from and summaries of sections on Roman history from the universal history often ascribed to Wauchier de Denain (*The Histoire ancienne jusqu'à César: A Digital Edition*, ed. Morcos and others, chs. 905–1055), which drew on Orosius and was sometimes titled as Orosius's work in MSS and early prints: see *Les Archives de littérature du Moyen Âge* (*ARLIMA*) *s.n.* Wauchier de Denain, https://www.arlima.net/uz/wauchier_de_denain.html#hac, and Louis-Fernand Flutre, *Les Manuscrits des Faits des Romains* (Paris, 1932), 52, 56, 83. Equally, copies of *Li Fet des Romains*, also read by WW (see 1670–85n., 2273–9n.), sometimes add Orosius to the commoner colophon (cf. 1670–85n.) listing Sallust, Suetonius, and Lucan as its sources (e.g. with Eng. provenance in BL, Royal MS 17 F. ii, f. 353^v, or BL, Royal MS 20 C. i, f. 295^v). Either the *Histoire ancienne* or *Li Fet* could be the volume in the inventory of Fastolf's books entitled 'a booke of Iullius Cesar' (Beadle, 'Fastolf's French Books', 102), as MSS of the *Histoire ancienne* note that it ends with Caesar, while incipits to *Li Fet* sometimes mention Caesar (e.g. BL, Royal MS 20 C. i, f. 1^r). *Histoire ancienne* and *Li Fet* circulated together in at least 14 extant copies (see Flutre, *Manuscrits*, 27–87) and could be treated as books I and II of one work (e.g. BL, Royal MS 16 G. vii, f. 215^r).

1566 *Titus Liuius.* See 769n.

1571–5 *Gildas . . . Walis.* The story was widely known, as was Gildas's diagnosis that the Britons' sins were cause of their downfall (e.g. Geoffrey of Monmouth, *Historia*, XI. 195, ed. Reeve, trans. Wright, 269); Gildas's *De excidio Britannie* itself was not widely circulated. WW cites Gildas in *Itineraries*, 42–6, for different details which in fact come from Nennius, *Historia Brittonum*.

1572 *Breton.* See 27–9, 30–3 (and nn.) on Celtic origins.

1573 *Duche `ys' tung.* The initial reading *Duche* would be the customary adj.= 'German' (antedating the 1st citation in *OED*, *Dutch, adj., n.*[1] and *adv.*, A.1, as adj.; there are earlier citations in *MED*, *Duch, adj.* and *n.*, 1), but WW's separated genitive *ys* turns the adj. into a n. in the pl. genitive='the Germans' tongue' (and so is written separate from the n., as are his other genitives of this type: see Introduction, pp. xciv–xcv). That use is unattested in *MED* or *OED*. There was general recognition that the pre-Conquest English spoke a language like German: see e.g. William Caxton, 'Eneydos: Prologue', in *The Prologues and*

Epilogues of William Caxton, ed. W. J. B. Crotch, EETS 176 (1928), 107–10 at 108.

1574 *in Angle. in* = 'into Anglesey', treated as separate from Wales.

1576–83 *where is . . . Iherusalem*. Translated selectively, with the addition of *Iherusalem*, from a full text of Chartier, *Quadrilogue* (Bouchet, 5, l. 8—6, l. 3), rather than from the excerpts (which do not include all these details) of the same passage by another scribe in WW's notebook Royal, f. 136^r. Nineveh is *the cite of thre daies* because it took three days to walk its circumference, as Chartier reports. The wording *where is* casts the passage as set-piece *ubi sunt* lament, as in Chartier's Fr.

1584–95 *ouerthrowes . . . this tyme*. As at 1573–5, returning to events recounted more fully at 30–47. WW mistakenly refers to Matilda's father as Henry II, her son, rather than Henry I.

1590 *Highe Fraunce* = 'inland France', i.e. in contrast with the coast of Normandy. See *OED, high, adj.* and *n.*^{2}, I.2.c, antedated only by one uncertain citation; *MED, heigh, adj.*, 1.(c), with more citations; and cf. the modern Fr. idiom *la France profonde*.

1591 *Erle Plantagenet*. See 44n.

1592–4 *maried withe . . . emperesse*. Scribe wrote *Dame* (1592) in error before *duke*. WW's 1st interlineation *Maud, doughter of the* corrected the incomplete *Dame* but introduced repetition; his 2nd interlineation *whych* made that repetition into a separate clause but was itself incomplete without a v. *was* (which we supply).

1596–9 *Iob . . . reignithe on vs*. Perhaps related to Job 38: 33, misquoted in *Communiloquium*, I. ii (f. 10^r), 'Iob .xxxvii. Nunquid nosti ordinem celi / et rationem eius pones in terram', amid John's argument that peace in earthly realms will come from emulating the kingdom of heaven. WW knew John of Wales's *Communiloquium*: in May 1449 John Crop reported seeking to obtain for WW a copy of 'Wallens *De vita* et *doctrina philosoforum*', presumably this work (*PL*, no. 969, ll. 20–9); and in Julius, ff. 141^r–142^v, WW annotated a list of 120 chapter titles from *Communiloquium*, entitling it 'Multiloquium' and saying that it 'primo de Re publica tractanda loquitur'. See also 1738–43n. V. Scholderer, 'The Early Editions of Johannes Vallensis', *National Library of Wales Journal*, 3 (1944), 76–9 at 76, notes interest in John of Wales's work in the 1470s by printers both for its use for preachers and as a political tract.

1599–1600 *pride . . . comynalte*. Contrasting *singuler* (= 'self-interested') behaviour with service of the common good, as at 1556–7. The rendering of the common good as *generall profit and vniuersall wele* is unusual: *OED, weal, n.*^{1}, cites the collocation 'vniuersall weale' only from Thomas Elyot (dated 1531), and *MED*, *wele*, *n.* (1), does not cite it. Cf. comparable terms at 3n., 622n., 1606n., 1690–2n., 2055–6n.

1602 *senatours Romayns*. This adj. is frequently placed after the n., when the n. is human, and inflected as pl. See Introduction, pp. xc–xci.

1603–10 *Lucius Valerius . . . worship*. An error for Publius (not *Lucius* or *Lucus* [*sic*]) Valerius Poplicola (d. 503 BCE), a dedicated public servant (*OCD*, *s.n.* Valerius Poplicola, Publius). The story recurs, with the same misnaming as 'L. Valerium', in St Augustine, *De civitate Dei*, V. 18, immediately after examples of the Decii and Marcus Attilius Regulus (ed. Bernhard Dombart and Alfons Kalb, 5th edn., 2 vols. (Turnhout, 1981, repr. 1993), i. 223–8 at 227), which are also re-told in *BkNob.* 1938–60, 1975–2006, albeit from another source (see nn.). WW took notes from other parts of book V of *De civitate Dei*, on different topics, in BL, Sloane MS 4, ff. 50ʳ, 57ʳ. He could also have found the story in John of Wales, *Communiloquium*, IV. ii (which he knew: see 1596–9n.), but told more briefly without *Lucius*: 'Quod Valerius post tres consulatus populo Romano ac-ceptissimus.' sic mortuus est: quod patrimonium ad exequiarum expensam non sufficiebat' (f. 50ʳ).

1606 *comyn profit*. WW has previously used *comyn wele* (on which see 3n., 622n.) but here he echoes Chaucer's 'commune profite' (*Boece*, I. pr. 4. 89; Cambridge, Pembroke College, MS 215, f. 7ʳ). He annotates the start of this passage in *Boece* (f. 6ʳ; I. pr. 4. 25), with a manicule and 'nota nobilitatem ad exercendum officium rei publice'. He continues with this phrase a further 20 times alongside *comon wele*. Cf. 3n., 622n., 1599–600n., 1690–2n., 2055–6n., and Glossary, s.v. **commyn profit**. He uses both in quick succession, apparently interchangeably, in *PL*, 888/39.

1608 *by the cenatours releuyng* = 'with (financial) relief from the other sena-tours'.

1610–16 *Boecius . . . comyn wele*. Summarizing Boethius, *De consolatione philo-sophiae*, I. pr. 4, perhaps from Chaucer's translation *Boece* (see 1606n.), though the only close echo is *loued rightwisnesse* perhaps < 'loue of ry3twysnesse' (f. 7ʳ; Chaucer, *Boece*, I. pr. 4. 105). See also Boethius as source at 70–1, 593–606 (see nn.).

1615 *hem* = 'him', i.e. Boethius, afflicted by *tribulacions*.

1616–17 *men of worship . . . worshipfull*. Repetition, in the rhetorical figure of *traductio*, playing on two senses of *worship* = 'social rank' *v.* 'reputation for vir-tue', evoking the debate about true nobility raised at the start from Buonaccorso da Montemagno (11–16, see n.).

1619 *princes Romayns*. For the word-order, see Introduction, pp. xc–xci.

1622–65 *A fulle noble historie . . . magnified*. The siege of Falerii from Livy, *Ab urbe condita*, 1st Decade (*first Decade* 1625), V. 27, trans. Bersuire, I. v.

12 (Harvard, Houghton Library, MS Richardson 32, vol. 1, f. 143^{r-v}, without chapter numbers; chapter number from BodL, MS Rawl. C. 447, f. 90^v). (Paris, Bibliothèque Sainte-Geneviève, MS fr. 777, has lost the relevant four leaves between f. 93^v and f. 94^r; we cite for this episode MS Richardson 32, vol. 1, illuminated by the 'Bedford Master', who also worked in Fastolf's milieu.) For WW's knowledge of Livy, see 769n., etc. WW's employer Fastolf had in the nether hall at Caister Castle a tapestry, recorded as 'the sege of Faleys' in a 1448 inventory annotated by WW (OMA, FP 43, f. 4^v; Gairdner, no. 389) and in an inventory for the Pastons in 1462 clarified as 'sege of Phalist' (*PL*, no. 64, l. 54), a similar misspelling with final ⟨st⟩ to *BkNob.*'s *Falistes* (1629, etc.). Discussed by Hawkyard, 'Sir John Fastolf's "Gret Mansion by me late edified"', 60; Wakelin, 'England', 271–2. The anecdote of Camillus and the Faliscan schoolmaster was frequently retold in antiquity and later as a symbol of Roman civic virtue: R. M. Ogilvie, *A Commentary on Livy Books 1–5* (Oxford, 1965), 685–9. The story was used for decoration on Tuscan *cassoni* of 1472 and *c.*1480–1500 respectively now in the Courtauld Gallery, London, F.1947.LF.5, and the National Gallery, London, NG 3826.

1622, 1626 *Cauillus*=Camillus. The scribe apparently misreads four minims *mi* in his exemplar as three or does not notice *i* abbreviated by a crossbar on *ll*. (The scribe clearly differentiates **ui** from **m** by a more rounded stroke curving upwards from the 1st minim to the 2nd.) WW also seems uncertain: he does not correct it in the text, but in one sidenote he has the name correct (*Camilli* 1622SN) and in another sidenote makes the same error, then corrects himself by adding a minim (*Cam`i'llus* 1646SN).

1624 *Romayns*. For the adj. inflected as pl., see Introduction, p. xci.

1627 *prince Romayn*. For postmodification, see Introduction, pp. xc–xci.

1632 *maister of sciencis.*< Livy, *Ab urbe condita*, V. 27, trans. Bersuire, I. v (e.g. Harvard, Houghton Library, MS Richardson 32, vol. 1, f. 143^r), 'maistre . . . excellent en science'. A schoolteacher, distinguished by his MA degree (rendering *magister artium* as *sciencis*). *OED*, *master*, *n.*^{1} and *adj.*, A.II.11; *MED*, *maister*, *n.*, 3, have similar but not identical phrases.

1637 *that.* Subordinating conj., for a second subclause dependent on *it fortuned* 1632.

1639 *desport*. *OED*, *disport*, *v.*, does not record the intransitive construction, without a refl. pron., before 1480; *MED*, *desporten*, *v.*, 1(a), does. Perhaps *meoued his clerkis to desport* mistranslates Livy, *Ab urbe condita*, V. 27, trans. Bersuire, I. v (e.g. Harvard, Houghton Library, MS Richardson 32, vol. 1, f. 143^r), 'Il les esloingna des portes'.

1640 *fedde hem forthe*='deceived': *MED*, *feden*, *v.*, 7.

1646 *Romayns*. See 1624n.

1648 *meo`u´ed*. Antedates the 1st citation, from Caxton in 1485, of *OED, move, v.*, II.27.b, with an intransitive construction with war, etc., as subject. Not in *MED, meven, v.*, in this construction, but cf. 2(b) with war as dir. object. Cf. 220n.

1650-1 *by manhod and iust dede of armes*.<Livy, *Ab urbe condita*, V. 27, trans. Bersuire, I. v (Harvard, Houghton Library, MS Richardson 32, vol. 1, f. 143ʳ), 'par vertu par oenures et par armes'.

1652 *dispoilid*.<Livy, *Ab urbe condita*, V. 27, trans. Bersuire, I. v (Harvard, Houghton Library, MS Richardson 32, vol. 1, f. 143ʳ), 'despouillier'.

1657-8 *O ye fathir and prince of iustice*.<Livy, *Ab urbe condita*, V. 27, trans. Bersuire, I. v (Harvard, Houghton Library, MS Richardson 32, vol. 1, f. 143ᵛ), 'O vous peres conscrips'. WW telescopes the Faliscan ambassadors' trip to address the senators in Rome into their submission to Camillus.

1660 *princes Romayns*. See 1627n., etc.

1666 *Historie of Dame Cristyn*. WW's sidenote 1666SN here recalls Stephen Scrope's preface to his translation of Christine de Pizan's *Epître d'Othéa à Hector* (*c*.1440-59): 'And this seyde boke, at the instavnce & praer off a fulle wyse gentyl-woman of Frawnce called Dame Cristine, was compiled & grounded by the famous doctours of the most excellent in clerge the nobyl Vniuersyte off Paris'; Scrope, *The Epistle of Othea*, ed. Bühler, 122, ll. 34-7. On this, see Summit, *Lost Property*, 72-8; Everett L. Wheeler, 'Christine de Pizan's *Livre des fais d'armes et de chevalerie*: Gender and the Prefaces', *Nottingham Medieval Studies*, 46 (2002), 119-61 at 134-5.

1670-85 *Dame Cristyn . . . falshed*. Translated expansively from Christine de Pizan, *Livre des faits d'armes*, I. 15 (BL, Royal MS 15 E. vi, f. 410ʳ; Laennec, ii. 60), 'Entre les aultres vertus . . . desloyaulte non'. WW adds *a prince* 1672; he mistranslates 'preudomme' as *a prudent man and a wise* 1674; he expands 'tresgrant vaillance et bonte' as *gret trouthe, vailliaunce and manhod and wise gouernaunce*. See 1843-60 for more on Pyrrhus. In Nov. and Dec. 1453, in Paris, WW transcribed another version of the story from what he refers to as 'folio .94. parte dextra' of a (now unidentified) copy owned by Fastolf of *Li Fet des Romains*, ed. L.-F. Flutre and K. Sneyders de Vogel, 2 vols. (Paris, 1937-8), i. 394, ll. 28-33 (III, 3, § 9), in Royal, f. 143ᵛ. See also 2273-9n. WW titled those extracts 'compilacio et extractus actuum armorum gentis Romanorum Inter Iullium Cesarem et Pompeium et aliorum secundum lucanum et Suetonium historiografos scripta' (f. 143ʳ). Twenty-nine extant copies of *Li Fet des Romains* have titles or colophons claiming it as compiled from Sallust, Lucan, and Suetonius (Flutre, *Manuscrits*, 27-87: e.g. with English provenance, BL, Royal MS 16 G. vii, f. 219ʳ, and BL, Royal MS 20 C. i, f. 1ʳ); and at least three of those twenty-nine and one other had titles which focused on the strife of Pompey and Caesar (see Flutre, *Manuscrits*, 35 (Chantilly, Musée Condé, MS 769, f. 1ʳ),

54–5 (BnF, MS fr. 246, f. 158ʳ), 58 (BnF, MS fr. 251, f. 1ʳ), as well as BL, Royal MS 16 G. vii, f. 215ʳ), as opposed to only naming Caesar (cf. 1565n.).

1671 *The Tree of Batailes.* See 152n.

1673 *rehersithe.* Otiose, in apposition to *leiethe* (1671), and repeating its sense and lacking a subject; reiterating for clarity after the subclause *that among . . . peple* (1671–3). On other apposition, see Introduction, pp. lxxx–lxxxiii.

1675–6 *noble and trew senatoure Fabricius.* < Fr. 'bon fabricius' (Christine de Pizan, *Livre des faits d'armes*, I. 15 (BL, Royal MS 15 E. vi, f. 410ʳ; Laennec, ii. 60), adding a reference to a *senatoure* as at 1838.

1682–3 *euyll-geten.* Antedates 1st citation in *OED*, *evil-gotten*, under *OED*, *evil, adv.*, but *MED*, *ivel(e, adv.*, 1(a), cites the N-Town Cycle, which text, if not MS, might antedate *BkNob*.

1686–700 *Vigecius . . . defaute.* Translated expansively from Christine de Pizan, *Livre des faits d'armes*, I. 15 (BL, Royal MS 15 E. vi, f. 410ʳ; Laennec, ii. 60), 'Auecque ce dit vegece . . . sa coulpe'.

1690–2 *comon publique . . . comon profite.* The idiom *comon publique* < Fr. 'chose publique' (Christine de Pizan, *Livre des faits d'armes*, I. 15: BL, Royal MS 15 E. vi, f. 410ʳ; Laennec, ii. 60). WW adds to the Fr. the gloss *comon profite*, suggesting that this phrase is common (*clepid vulgarilie*), while *comon publique* is rare (though it recurs at 3 (see n.), 1917). See 3n., 622n., 1599–600n., 1606n., 2055–6n.

1691 *barnage* = 'barony': 1st citation in this sense in *OED*, *baronage, n.*, 2; antedated by citations in *MED*, *barnage, n.* (1), 2.

1692 *vulgarilie.* Far pre-dates 1st and only citation in *OED*, *vulgarily, adv.*; not in *MED*. *MED*, *vulgarli, adv.*, is also rare; this word may be misremembered by WW here.

1692 *suerte and saufegarde.* < Fr. 'seurte' (Christine de Pizan, *Livre des faits d'armes*, I. 15: BL, Royal MS 15 E. vi, f. 410ʳ; Laennec, ii. 60). The doublet suggests that WW thinks *suerte* (PDE *surety*) is little known, but it and *saufegarde* were widely attested (*OED*, *surety, n.*, II.4; *MED*, *seurte, n.*, 2; *OED*, *safeguard, n.*, 2; *MED*, *sauf-gard(e, n.*, 1.

1698 *defaut of ouersight of remedie.* The 1st *of* could be an error for *or*, by attraction to the 2nd *of*, so that *ouersight* = 'omission' in a doublet with *defaut*.

1702 *fructufull.* Etymological sp. with medial ⟨c⟩, as at *fructis* 2107. See Introduction, p. xcii.

1707–8 *lyue and endure.* The infinitives, in parallel to *kepe*, depend on the main clause *we ought* 1703.

1713–23 *O mightifull God . . . kept it not.* 1 Chr. (in the Vulgate *Paralipomenon*, as WW calls it), 10 (e.g. 10: 13), recounts how God allows the Israelites' enemies victory over them as chastisement for the Israelites' sins. Apparently recalled directly (but cf. 1787–9n.). Use of this analogy for Britons' or England's defeats was common in historical writing, e.g. Gildas (see 1571–5n.).

1722 *the rathir that.* Sense close to *OED, rather, adv.*, II.4.a = 'the more readily (for this reason)', and *MED, rather(e, adv.*, 3(b) = 'the more especially, the more so', with *that* (= 'because') introducing a cause.

1727 *epistill.* See 7n., 587, 2580.

1732–6 *Tullius . . . peple.* Based on John of Wales, *Communiloquium*, I. i (see 1596–9n.), who invokes Cicero by name alone as the source for St Augustine, cited next (1737: see n.). WW adds titles of Cicero's works which he knew of independently. In a letter he cited *De amicitia* (*PL*, no. 604, l. 3). In Julius he transcribed lists of Cicero's works (ff. 67^v–68^r, by Leonardo Bruni, and f. 97$^{r–v}$) and extracts from *De amicitia* (ff. 71$^{r–v}$, 75^v), *Paradoxa* (ff. 73^r, 81^v, 115^v), *Tusculanae quaestiones* (f. 77^v), and *De officiis* (f. 115^r). He also marked with his symbol excerpts of Cicero's *De officiis* and *De republica* in Nonius Marcellus, *De conpendiosa doctrina*, in OMC, MS Lat. 206, ff. 113^r–273^v, and then transcribed them into Julius, ff. 124^r–128^r, especially f. 125^r for the *res publica* from Nonius Marcellus, IV. 244. 22–7. Cicero's *De republica* was otherwise lost. On his reading of Nonius Marcellus, see Wakelin, *Humanism*, 101–2.

1735 *well-attendid.* As compound, far antedates 1st citation in *OED*, *well-attended, adj.*

1737 *Seint Austyn.* St Augustine, *De civitate Dei*, V. 18 (which WW also knew first-hand: see 1603–10n.), cited, with the following quotation ascribed to Cicero (1738–43: see n.), from John of Wales, *Communiloquium*, I. i (f. 9^r); *pace* McFarlane, 'Preliminary Survey', 212 n. 7, who links this passage to WW's own notes from *De civitate Dei*, V (see 1603–10n.).

1738–43 *Tullius . . . conseruare.* Verbatim from John of Wales, *Communiloquium*, I. i, where these words are ascribed not to Cicero (*Tullius*) but to St Augustine (*Seint Austyn* 1737), who is said to pick up the ideas from Cicero. Of the many early printed editions, WW's text is closest (apart from *omnes* for 'omnis') to the 1475 edition of Anton Sorg at Augsburg (*Communiloquium*, f. 9^r, from which we therefore cite *passim*), and differs in details of wording from e.g. John of Wales (Iohannes Gallensis), *Summa collationum, sive Communiloquium* (Cologne: Ulrich Zel, *c.*1472; *ISTC* ij00328000), 13. See 1596–9n. on WW's interest in this text.

1745–50 *Wallensis . . . consumpnante.* Taken, with variants, from John of Wales, *Communiloquium*, I. iii (f. 10^v). WW reorders the opening ('quibus virtutibus ordinatur res publica. Et sciendum quod ordinatur scilicet . . .') to fit the context and omits John's 'connectente' after *vnanimitate* and 'quasi omnia' before *consumpnante*.

1751–4 *Tullie . . . contraria.* The 1st half of the quotation *Omnes . . . oportet* is from Cicero, *De inventione*, I. xxxviii. 68, taken verbatim from John of Wales, *Communiloquium*, I. iii (f. 10ᵛ). In *De inventione*, the words are quoted from an exemplary legal speech, and *iudices* is a vocative address to the judges listening; out of context in *Communiloquium* and here, *iudices* are the dir. object of *oportet* and agent of *referre* (= 'it befits judges to refer . . .'). The 2nd half of the quotation *Et lex . . . contraria* is also verbatim from John of Wales (f. 10ᵛ), with the error *anime iusta* for 'a nemine tracta', difficult to parse (with the next words, perhaps = 'commanding honest, just deeds of the soul'?). It comes later in John's chapter, and John ascribes this phrase to Cicero, *Philippics*, 9, but WW splices the quotations together as though from *De inventione*. WW's sidenote 1751SN calls *De inventione* by the title *Noua rethorica*, which is more commonly used in the 15th c. for *Rhetorica ad Herennium* (see 736–40n.); John of Wales calls it 'prima rethorica'.

1761 *consules.* At this point in the list of contemporary ranks or offices comparable to Roman ones, but not identical, *consul* = 'counts, earls' (antedating the 1st citation in English as opposed to Roman contexts, in *OED, consul, n.*, II.3), or = 'councillor or official of a guild, etc.' (antedating senses II.4 or III.7). *MED, consul, n.*, records only the Roman historical sense (1[a]) or the vague sense = 'governor' (1[b]).

1763 *othirs officers.* On pl. inflections on adj., see Introduction, p. xci.

1763–4 *Tullius . . . domi.* Originally Cicero, *De officiis*, I. xxii. 76, but taken from John of Wales, *Communiloquium*, I. vii (f. 13ʳ), inverting John's word-order 'arma foris' and giving *non est* for John's 'deest'. WW twice copied variant forms of this saying ('parua sunt arma foris . nisi est concilium domi') from a collection of proverbs gathered from John Halle, rector of Garboldisham, Suffolk (Julius, f. 47ᵛ; *Itineraries*, 364–6).

1768–72 *Tullius . . . bodie.* General summary of *De sen.* (e.g. X. 32, XI. 38), which WW did know independently (see 1803–11 to 2138–51nn.), but here probably prompted by a brief *précis* in John of Wales, *Communiloquium*, I. vii (f. 13ᵛ), 'Quorum dantes consilium in republica plus agunt quam alij'.

1771–2 *othirs . . . he be.* The subject pron. switches from pl. to sg. *he*; switches from pl. to sg. occur mid-sentence elsewhere (e.g. 1823–5).

1773–86 *For an example . . . hand.* Prompted by the brief *précis* of *De sen.*, VI. 17, ascribed to Cicero, *De sen.*, 'cap. iij', in John of Wales, *Communiloquium*, I. vii (f. 13ᵛ), which supplies sources for the previous and following passages, but expanded with details not given there. Some details recall John's source, *De sen.*, VI. 17, and the doublet *rothir or sterne* recalls WW's separate Eng. translation (*Tulle*, 17) from the Fr. version of de Premierfait, 71, ll. 23–30 (< 'la poupe'). But in sequence between other passages from *Communiloquium* (1732–89: see nn.), John is the likelier source. The metaphor, ultimately from Plato, *Repub-*

lic, VI. 488b–e, recurs in other works known to WW: e.g. de Courtescuisse's Fr. translation of John of Wales, *Breviloquium*, in CUL, MS Add. 7870, f. 15ᵛ ('Car ceulx qui doiuent bon conseil sont plus que les aultres et sont semblenz a ceulx qui gouuerent la nef'), by which WW annotates 'Exemplum de consilio adhibendo . et sunt similes ipsis qui gubernant nauem'.

1787–9 *Iob . . . gouuernaunce.* Translated closely from John of Wales, *Communiloquium*, I. vii (f. 13ᵛ), 'Unde et Roboam . . . iuuenam amisit regnum'. WW (as at 1751–4: see n.) misreads John of Wales's previous citation of Job 12 ('In antiquis est enim sapientia', from Job 12: 12) as referring to the subsequent narrative of Rehoboam, which John instead cites from 2 Kgs 12. Rehoboam also occurs in 2 Chr. (Paralipomenon), 10: 8 (see 1713–23n.), and in WW's miscellany Royal in Lat. (f. 53ʳ) and excerpted from Chartier, *Quadrilogue* (f. 136ʳ; Bouchet, 31, ll. 9–13). He appears frequently in 15th-c. political writing as an analogy for ill-advised monarchs: e.g. John Fortescue, *The Governance of England*, ed. Charles Plummer (Oxford, 1885), 133 (with useful analogues in nn. on 269, 323); and *Four English Political Tracts of the Later Middle Ages*, ed. Genet, 206.

1797 *many reuolucion.* For *many* with sg. n. and no determiner, see *OED, many*, *adj.*, *pron.*, and *n.*, and *adv.*, A.1.a.

1800 *Fabius* = Quintus Fabius Maximus Verrucosus (d. 203 BCE: *OCD, s.n.*).

1803–11 *Tullius . . . liffetyme.* Translated from *De sen.*, IV. 10, trans. de Premierfait, 61, ll. 15–21 (cf. *Tulle*, 10): 'ung homme romain . . . lors que il vesqui'. This is in *the first partie* as de Premierfait's Fr. translation is divided ('le preambule', 51, l. 28, 67, l. 21). Sometimes *BkNob.*'s wording echoes de Premierfait's Fr. (*renommee and vayneglorie* < 'renommee ne d'aultres vaines gloires'; *for whiche cause* < 'pour ceste cause'). Sometimes it is similar to WW's separate Eng. translation therefrom: e.g. *libertees and fraunchises* < 'oure fraunchises & oure libertees' (*Tulle*, 10, expanding de Premierfait, 61, l. 16, 'nostre liberté'). We have not identified WW's MS of de Premierfait, so for convenience all quotations are taken from the printed edition of Marzano.

1803–4 *prince Romayne.* See 1602n. Perhaps echoing the Fr. word-order 'homme romain' (de Premierfait, 61, l. 15), while changing the noun. See Introduction, p. xci, on placement of this adj.

1808–9 *solicitude, thought.* See 1887.

1812–18 *the saide Fabius . . . comon wele.* Summarizes and adapts two statements of Fabius's skill in divination: *De sen.*, IV. 11 and IV. 12, trans. de Premierfait, 63, ll. 1–7, 63, ll. 19–21 (cf. *Tulle*, 11, 12), 'Fabius feust augure . . . par les oiseaulx' and 'il savoit de l'art . . . les Rommains'. WW might conflate Fabius's knowledge of Roman customs to explain augury as a Roman custom (*vsage was in tho daies* < 'la maniere que lors avoient les Rommains' ?). WW adds the provision of food supplies. WW had access to Cicero's sceptical account of Roman divination in *De divinatione* in OMC, MS Lat. 62 (on which MS, see 1527–8n.).

1812 *after* = 'as'. See *OED*, *after*, *adv.*, *prep.* and *conj.*, C.2.b., and C1/182.

1814 *angures*. < De Premierfait, 63, l. 1, 'augure'. The scribe's clear but erroneous spelling with ⟨n⟩ recurs in a sing. n. in a cognate word at this point in *Tullius de senectute*, sig. b6v, 'Angure' (which Susebach, editing *Tulle*, 11, emends to 'Augure'; i.e. *OED*, *augur*, *n.*[1], and *MED*, *augur*, *n.* = 'augur, soothsayer'). The error suggests the unfamiliarity of this word borrowed from Lat. In WW's Lat. sidenote 1812SN, **u** and **n** are less distinct, so it is possible that it also reads *anguriste*. In *BkNob.* in a doublet with *diuinacions*, this is the 1st citation in *OED*, *augur*, *n.*[2] = 'auguries, divinations'. *MED* cites this line as a variant sp. of *augurie*, *n.*, but *BkNob*'s sp. without final ⟨i⟩ or ⟨y⟩ suggests that it is not that word.

1815 *causes naturell* = 'nature as source of causation', defended here as a source of rational predictions by *ceasons*, etc. Antedates the 1st citation of *OED*, *natural causes*, *n.*, 1. WW clarifies the point at 1823–32 (see n.). The postposed adj. evokes Lat. *causae naturales*. No obvious lexical cognate in de Premierfait, 63, ll. 1–7, 63, ll. 19–21.

1819–22 *he delited gretly . . . Scipions*. Summarizes *De sen.*, V. 13, trans. de Premierfait, 63, ll. 22–65, l. 6 (cf. *Tulle*, 12), 'Fabius retenoit en sa memoire . . . furent les Scipions'.

1819 *actis and dedis*. Synonyms, as in Lat. *acta* and *gesta* (see 286–307n., 655–6n.); *dedis* = 'narratives of actions' (*MED*, *dede*, *n.*, 5[a]).

1823–32 *And it were full necessarie . . . rebukid*. WW, clarifying approval of Fabius's *diuinacions*, now criticizes scholars' attention to *iudiciell matieris*, i.e. = 'astrology' (a term used in a condemnation by Chaucer in *Treatise of the Astrolabe*: see *MED*, *judicial*, *adj. and n.*, 1.(c)), and instead defends it as the study of *causis naturell*, i.e. environmental and meteorological science (see 1815n. and 2050n.). He tangentially complains of a lack of *bookis* in *scolis* or universities for that. He frequently consulted books in the universities' libraries and noted the donation of books by Humphrey, duke of Gloucester, to Oxford (above, 1378–80), so perhaps spoke from knowledge. *De sen.*, V. 13, trans. de Premierfait, 65, l. 11–28, following the source for 1803–22 (see nn.), praises the old age of philosophers, which might prompt praise for philosopher-kings here.

1825 *he*. The exemplary figure switches from pl. to sg.

1827–8 *principales*. Antedating both *OED*, *principal*, *adj.*, *n.* and *adv.*, B.II.4.c = 'primary or fundamental point of a subject', and *OED*, *principle*, *n.*, III.8 = 'elementary aspects of a field of study', two forms frequently conflated in sp.

1836 *consull*. A classicizing detail added to *De sen.*, VI. 15, trans. de Premierfait, 69, ll. 29–30 (and not in *Tulle*, 15).

1837–8 *Lucius Paul'us' . . . Paule*. Extrapolated from Cato's dialogue in *De sen.*, VI. 15, trans. de Premierfait, 69, ll. 29–30 (cf. *Tulle*, 15), 'Lucius Paule . . . espousé la fille'. The original MS sp. *Paule* echoes the Fr., but WW or the scribe corrects to Lat. *Paulus*, which recurs in *Tulle*, 15, 'Paulus'. De Premierfait and therefore WW err: the daughter of Lucius Aemilius Paullus (see *OCD*, *s.n.*), i.e. Aemilia Paulla Tertia, married not Cato's son but Cornelius Scipio Aemilianus Africanus, the speaker being addressed by Cato in *De sen.* here.

1838–42 *senatours clepid Fabricius . . . Rome*. Translated slightly expansively from *De sen.*, VI. 15, trans. de Premierfait, 69, ll. 30–2 (cf. *Tulle*, 15–16), 'vieillars appellez les Fabriciois . . . de nostre cité'. WW also took notes from this passage of *De sen.* in Lat. in Julius, f. 72ʳ, but with fewer details than here. WW's *senatours*<Fr. 'vieillars' gives more classical colouring, as at 1675–6 (see n.). De Premierfait turns two senators, Tiberius Coruncanius and Manius Curius Dentatus (see *OCD*, *s.n.*), into two families, 'les Curiois et les Cornicanois'; WW conflates the two families into one person *Curiois Cornicanois*. The minims of medial **ni** (not Lat. **un**) are ambiguous but the spelling, erroneous in Lat., recurs in de Premiefait, 69, l. 31, 'Cornicanois', and *Tullius de senectute*, sig. c1r, 'Cornycanoys' (which Susebach, editing *Tulle*, 15, emends to 'Coruncanoys'). See also 2123–8n.

1841 *that that* = 'that (course of action) which'.

1847–60 '*the hygh' preest . . . Pirrus*. Summarizes *De sen.*, VI. 16, trans. de Premierfait, 71, ll. 1–20 (cf. *Tulle*, 16), 'A Romme fut Appius . . . par eulx fut desconfit'. De Premierfait has fuller detail than Cicero of Appius Claudius' career and has a different sequence of actions. WW's doublet *pease and alliaunces*<Fr. 'paix et alliences' recurs in *Tulle*, 16. *Pirrus, king of Epirotes* is Pyrrhus, king of Epirus (see *OCD*, *s.n.*). WW's sidenote 1848SN identifies the source.

1853 *senatours Romayn*. For the word-order, see Introduction, p. xci.

1854–5 *Ennius . . . consul*. Ennius was not a consul but a poet, as 1854SN correctly identifies; WW adds this error to de Premierfait, 71, l. 12.

1858 *Whiche*. Functions loosely as a general co-ordinating conj. (*OED, which, adj.* and *pron.*, sense B.II.8.a); see similarly 508–10 and 1481 (see nn.).

1865–73 *Caton . . . destroied*. Adapting Cato's speech from the 1st person to 3rd person, from *De sen.*, VI. 18, trans. de Premierfait, 73, ll. 3–10 (cf. *Tulle*, 18), 'je qui souloie . . . victoire de bataille'. The mistranslation *puissaunt to resist* 1872 (< Fr. subjunctive 'puisse resister', 73, l. 7) does not recur in *Tulle*, but the phrase *the office of a knight* 1866–7 (< 'chevalier') does.

1877–81 *he required . . . passed*. Based, with errors, on de Premierfait, 73, ll. 11–14, 'je desire que . . . trente trois ans passez', which itself mistranslates *De sen.*, VI. 19. WW inherits and extends errors here. Cicero referred to the death, 33 years before the imagined date of the dialogue in *De sen.* (i.e. 150 BCE), of Publius Cornelius Scipio Africanus (236/235–183 BCE), grandfather by adoption of WW's *yong Scipio* 1874 or Publius Cornelius Scipio Africanus Aemilianus, one of the speakers in *De sen*. But de Premierfait confused that grandfather with Quintus Fabius Maximus Verrucosus (d. 203 BCE: *OCD, s.n.*), who adopted younger Scipio's brother, Quintus Fabius Maximus Aemilianus (*OCD, s.n.*). WW repeats de Premierfait's erroneous identification of *Quintus Fabius*. WW then misunderstands de Premierfait's account of how the supposed grandfather Quintus Fabius left ('laisse') the remnants ('remenens') of the Carthaginian forces unharmed as a reference to prisoners left in Carthage; and he treats *xxxiij* not as the date of the grandfather's death but as the duration of imprisonment. By contrast, *Tulle*, 18, translates de Premierfait (and his erroneous identification) closely.

1884–9 *Quintus Fabius . . . deliberacion.* Translated from *De sen.*, VI. 19, trans. de Premierfait, 73, ll. 19–24 (cf. *Tulle*, 18–19), 'qu'il eust lessié . . . par meure deliberacion'. WW mistranslates a reference to young knights proving themselves (cf. *Tulle*, 18, 'preuen and assaye themsilf'; < Fr. 's'esprouvent', 73, l. 20) as an account of how Fabius *taught yong knightis*, as he later will claim that Fastolf did (1961–72).

1887 *solicitude and thought.* See 1808–9.

1889 *of hymsilf and of the wise senatoure* = 'by his own and the wise senator's [i.e. Cato's]' deliberation.

1891–2 *senat . . . togither.* Translated from a gloss added to *De sen.*, VI. 19, by de Premierfait, 73, ll. 25–6 (cf. *Tulle*, 19), 'conseil . . . appellé "senat", qui signifie compaignie de vieillars'.

1896–900 *Caton . . . auncien men.* Translated from *De sen.*, VI. 20, trans. de Premierfait, 75, ll. 5–9 (cf. *Tulle*, 19), 'se vous voulez . . . gouvernement des vieillars'.

1897 *conduit* = 'guided', in figurative sense. Antedating slightly the 1st citation in *OED, conduct, v.*, I.2.a, and figurative citations in *MED, conduiten, v.*, 1. No Fr. cognate in de Premierfait, 75, ll. 6–7, which uses 'admoindries'.

1898 *desert* = 'desolation'. Antedates 1st citation of this sense in *OED, desert, n.²*, 3, and *MED, desert, n.* (2), 2(c). Mistranslates Fr. v. phrase ('ont esté . . . desertés', de Premierfait, 75, ll. 6–7).

1899 *it.* Shifts from pl. subject (*citeis*) to sg., perhaps referring specifically to *Rome*.

1901–11 *Cato makith . . . grene age.* Based on *De sen.*, VI. 20, trans. de Premierfait, 75, ll. 9–16 (cf. *Tulle*, 19–20), 'Or, dites moy . . . du juene eage'. WW invents *yong men not roted . . . policie gouernaunce.*

1902 *Lilius* = Lelius. Cf. correction of the name at 1912 (textual note).

1904–5 *and the comon profit . . . destroied. and* = 'so that', followed by an absolute clause with *destroied* in a passive sense; i.e. it is not claimed that Scipio and

Lelius had actively themselves *destroied* their inheritance, but that they had let it be so.

1906 *Nemnius.* Underlined in MS. The MS's sp. with 8 indistinct minims, here rendered ⟨mniu⟩, is probably an error by this scribe, overlooked by WW; < de Premierfait, 75, l. 14, 'Nevius' (< Lat. 'Naevius', the poet quoted in *De sen.*, VI. 20); *Tulle*, 19, has 'Nevyus'.

1908–9 *new, ʽnot expert' drawen* = 'newly, not expertly educated' (?). No sense in *MED, drauen, v.*, or *OED, draw, v.*, or *drawn, adj.*, fits. In context the men are newly educated (< de Premierfait, 75, l. 15, 'nouveaulx maistres'), so *drawen* may be a calque on the etymology of Lat. *educo, -are*, as in *drawen forthe* 2315. If *drawen* is positive in sense, then in context WW's addition *not expert* must negate it, as *new* originally had, and so must function as an adv. = 'not expertly'. No adverbial function is included in *MED, expert, ppl., adj.* (and *n.*), or *OED, expert, adj.*[1]; *MED, expertli, adv.*, is little attested.

1910 *policie gouernaunce.* Perhaps two nouns in apposition, on which see Introduction, pp. lxxx–lxxxiii; but we parse *policie* as the adj. = 'politic', cited in *MED, policie, n.*, 1(e), from Scrope, *Othea*, ed. Bühler, 122, l. 11, in the preface dedicated to Fastolf. Perhaps an idiosyncratic, local usage in this milieu.

1910–11 *folehardiesse.* 1st citation in *OED, foolhardice, n.*, and only citation in *MED, fol-hardiess(e, n.*; < Fr. 'folle hardiesse' (de Premierfait, 75, ll. 16–17).

1918–37 *Of the answere . . . destroied.* Based on *De sen.*, X. 31, trans. de Premierfait, 89, ll. 22–8 (cf. *Tulle*, 30), 'le roy Agamenon . . . prinse et destruicte'. The last phrase *he doubted . . . destroied* is almost verbatim in *Tulle*. The four chapter titles interrupt a sentence which flows across 1920–37. They might have been in the margin, more like this MS's sidenotes, in an exemplar (and compare the error discussed at 1091n.), copied into the main text in error, but WW let them stand. Nichols removes them, but we preserve the unusual arrangement; however, to capture the sentence's continuity we omit capital letters and full stops on each chapter.

1918 etc. *Agamenon.* This sp. for Agamemnon, without a 2nd ⟨m⟩, is in de Premierfait, 89, ll. 22, 24, 26 (which Susebach, editing *Tulle*, 30, emends to 'Agamemnon'). The sp. recurs at 593 (see n.) and is widely attested in 15th-c. Eng. MSS on classical topics, e.g. Lydgate, *Troy Book*, III. 539, 563, 622, 712, and in Fr., as e.g. in WW's notes in Fr. from various texts in Titus, ff. 69[r], 71[v].

1922, 1923 *King Nestor.* Not a Trojan king but a Greek one: cf. de Premierfait, 89, l. 14, 'ung des rois de Grece'.

1930 *.xl.* De Premierfait, 89, l. 24 (cf. *Tulle*, 30), mentions ten Ajaxes. This *.xl.* might be a misreading of *x* in a MS for Fr. 'dix'. Lat. recommendations of 1449 on conduct of the wars, in WW's miscellany Arundel, f. 329[v] (*Wars in France*, ii.

726), make a parallel point but with one Antenor worth more than ten Hectors: 'prouidencia vnius Anthenor quam strenuitas aut fortitudo decem Ector'.

1933, 1935 *.vj. . . . six.* De Premierfait, 89, l. 26 (cf. *Tulle*, 30), 'six'. Susebach, editing *Tulle*, emends to ten Nestors, as in modern critical editions of Cicero, although some MSS of *De sen.* mention six, according to Powell's apparatus criticus.

1936 *viellars.* 1st citation in *OED*, *vieillard*, *n.*, and one of only three citations of uncertain date or usage in *MED*, *viellar*, *n.*; < de Premierfait, 89, l. 27, 'vieillars'.

1939 *entreprennoure.* 1st citation in *MED*, *enterprenour*, *n.*, and *OED*, *entreprenour*, *n.*, and far antedating the reborrowing from Fr. in *OED*, *entrepreneur*, *n.* Despite the apparent calquing from Fr., the cognate term is not in de Premierfait here (147, ll. 19–32) or elsewhere.

1943–55 *Tullius writithe . . . victorie.* Based on *De sen.*, XX. 75, trans. de Premierfait, 147, ll. 20–32 (cf. *Tulle*, 78), 'je racompte l'istoire . . . eurent la victorie'. Cicero writes a short list of selfless heroes; de Premierfait expands each hero's story; WW expands slightly more. There is a one-line reference to Publius Decius among people who served 'le bien publicque' in excerpts from Chartier, *Quadrilogue* (Bouchet, 68, ll. 16–17), annotated by WW in Royal, f. 137ʳ. The narrative of the Decii is expanded by Augustine, *De civitate Dei*, V. xviii (ed. Dombart and Kalb, i. 225–6), adjacent to a possible source for 1603–10 (see n.).

1943 *citezin Romayne.* For the word-order, see Introduction, p. xci.

1951 *charged withe hem* = 'attacked by them'. Antedating 1st citation of *OED*, *charge*, *v.*, I.1.b, 'To load with blows', and a sense not recorded in *MED*, *chargen*, *v.*, though close to 12, 'To assault (sth.), charge against' (recorded only in Lydgate, *Troy Book*). Not paralleled in de Premierfait, 147, ll. 20–32.

1957–60 *And the sonne . . . like wise.* Based on *De sen.*, XX. 75, trans. de Premierfait, 147, ll. 32–5 (cf. *Tulle*, 79), 'Le filz aussi . . . la chose publique'. The *sonne* is Publius Decius Mus II (see *OCD*, *s.n.*).

1961–74 *Hyt ys to remembre . . . hys son.* WW's marginal addition reports Fastolf's household's conversation *at hys solasse.* Cf. 1884–9n. For other comments on Fastolf's conversation, see *PL*, no. 559, ll. 14–21 and no. 514, ll. 1–14. For *Hyt ys to remembre*, see 2059.

1961 *myne autor Fastolf.* Here *autor* = 'informant' (*OED*, *author*, *n.*, II.5), but the connotation = 'literary writer' contrasts Fastolf's practical experience with Cicero and other *auctores* just invoked. See 2332–40.

1963 *manly men . . . manlye man.* Evokes Lat. *vir virtutis* = 'man of virtue', a common term in humanist writing for somebody who serves the *res publica*: cf. *vnmanly* 1462n. and see Quentin Skinner, *The Foundations of Modern Political Thought*, 2 vols. (Cambridge, 1978), i. 87–91.

1968 *destrussed.* Antedates 1st citation in sense='defeated in battle' in *OED*, *distress, v.,* 2.a; many earlier citations, often from *PL*, in *MED, distrussen, v.*

1969–74 *manly man ys policie . . . hys son.* Criticizes the preceding defence of suicidal self-sacrifice by Roman heroes as a sin in *Cristen lawes* and recommends instead cautious preservation of oneself and one's followers. Wakelin, *Humanism*, 112–14, notes precedents, e.g. Aristotle, *Nicomachean Ethics*, V. xi. 1–3 (1138a4–16) (trans. Rackham, 317–19), which Fastolf owned in a Fr. translation (Beadle, 'Fastolf's French Books', 104). Collins, 'Sir John Fastolf', 132, suggests relevance to Fastolf's alleged cowardice at the Battle of Patay. WW's sidenote 1944SN appears near the start of the chapter, but echoes not the initial praise for Publius Decius but the later addition's retraction of it.

1981 *wered*='worn out', antedating this sense in *OED, wear, v.*[1], II.10, but with earlier citations, if not with reference to *bataile*, in *MED, weren, v.* (2), 5a(a). The regular pa. p. with ⟨ed⟩ is well attested in 15th-c. Eng.

1984–2003 *Hit is historied . . . his yen.* Translated from *De sen.,* XX. 75, trans. expansively by de Premierfait, 147, l. 37–149, l. 12 (cf. *Tulle,* 79–80), 'je racompte comment . . . sanz larmes recorder'. *Tulle,* 80, adds further gory detail. For other Eng. retellings, see e.g. Hoccleve, *Regement of Princes,* ll. 2248–96. De Premierfait alternates between the sp. 'Attilius' and 'Actilius' with ⟨c⟩ for Marcus Atilius Regulus.

1986 *labouragis.* 1st citation in *MED, labourage, n.,* and *OED, labourage | laborage, n.,* 2, in this sense='cultivation (of land)'; <Fr. 'laboureur' (de Premierfait, 147, l. 38).

1986 *approwementis.* 1st citation in *OED, approvement | approwment, n.*[2]= 'efficient management (of land)', but *MED, approu(e)ment, n.,* has earlier citations, including *PL,* no. 982, l. 42, a letter by Fastolf written in WW's hand. Not paralleled in de Premierfait, 147, l. 38.

1996 *frank and quite*='free from captivity'. 1st citation in this sense in *MED, frank, adj.,* 1(b), and *OED, frank, adj.*[2], 1.b, which describes it as calqued on Fr. *franc et quitte*; but de Premierfait does not use this phrase here (147, l. 37–149, l. 12) or elsewhere.

1998 *werrours.* Perhaps PDE *warrior*, omitting in error a medial ⟨i⟩ (cf. *werriour* 265 and all forms recorded in *OED, warrior, n.,* and *MED, werreiour, n.*); but we leave it unemended as an instance of *MED, werrour, n.,* derived from Fr. (see *OED, warrer, n.*), though there is no Fr. cognate in de Premierfait, 147, l. 37–149, l. 12.

2002–3 *make an harde-hert man to falle the teris of his yen.* Perhaps calqued on Fr. constructions which state the person and the afflicted body part separately. 1st citation in *OED, fall, v.,* I.1.c, the transitive usage 'To cause or allow (something) to drop'.

2010–17 *the full noble . . . Cartage.* Summarizes, with confusion, *De sen.*, XX. 75, trans. expansively by de Premierfait, 149, ll. 13–25 (cf. WW, *Tulle*, 80–1), 'deux tresnobles . . . eschaper la servitute'. This is Quintus Caecilius Metellus Pius (Cornelianus) Scipio (*c*.100/98–46 BCE), an enemy of Caesar, but WW removes de Premierfait's accurate biography and conflates this Scipio with his more famous ancestor, Publius Cornelius Scipio Africanus Maior (236–183 BCE), who fought the Carthaginians, and suggests that he dies in battle, as did neither man, rather than by suicide. See Ronald Syme, *The Augustan Aristocracy* (Oxford, 1986), 244–54; *OCD*, s.n. Caecilius Metellus Pius Scipio, Quintus. Perhaps misplaced hypercorrection, as Scipio Africanus was more famous from other sources (e.g. in Seneca, *Epistulae*, letter 86, to which WW had access at some point, in OMC, MS Lat. 22, ff. 114^v–116^v; on which see Rundle, 'Worcestre'); or perhaps an attempt to create a story focused on fighting external foes.

2019 *he.* Recapitulative pron. (= *Scipion Asian*).

2021–6 *many triumphes . . . his daies.* Summarizes *De sen.*, XX. 75, trans. expansively by de Premierfait, 149, ll. 28–35 (cf. *Tulle*, 81), 'par batailles subjuga . . . sans impacience'. De Premierfait expands, from Cicero's passing mention of the 'duos Scipiones', the exploits of one, Scipio Asianus, against the Seleucid King Antiochus III (*OCD*, s.n. Cornelius Scipio Asiagenes, Lucius).

2027 *in defaute that* = 'because of the failure in which'. Construction not recorded in *MED*, *defaut(e, n.*, or *OED*, *default, n.* (but similar to phrase P3.a. *in default of*).

2028 *he.* Recapitulative pron. referring to Lucius Paulus, after interruption of *in defaute that*.

2029–38 *Lucius Paulus . . . defaute.* Summarizes *De sen.*, XX. 75, trans. expansively by de Premierfait, 149, l. 36–151, l. 12 (cf. *Tulle*, 82), 'Lucius Paulus, consul . . . entreprist la besoingne'. Lucius Aemilius Paullus (d. 216 BCE) shared leadership at the Battle of Cannae in *Puylle* or Apulia (cf. 762–72n.) with *anothir consul* Gaius Terentius Varro, who led troops into the battle against the advice (*counceile*) of Lucius Paulus. *OCD*, s.n. Aemilius Paullus, Lucius (1).

2029–34 *Lucius Paulus . . . ouerthrowen.* The syntax is serpentine. The grammatical subject *Lucius Paulus* is first reiterated (*the saide L. P.*) and premodified as *vnwiting* (= 'unknowing'), where the object of *vnwiting* is the subclause *that the saide .iij^c. nobles . . .*; then the subject is reiterated (*he*) and postmodified as *seeng*, where the object of *seeng* is the subclause with zero-subordination, implying 'that', *anothir . . . toke the entreprise*. After that comes the main v. *was . . . ouerthrowen*, where *so* leads to more zero-subordination, implying 'that', Lucius Paulus, again reiterated (*the saide L. P.*), *auaunced hym* on a reckless mission.

2029 *consul Romayne.* For the word-order, see Introduction, p. xci. < Fr. 'consul rommain' (de Premierfait, 149, l. 36).

2032 *nobles Romayns.* For the word-order and pl. inflection, see Introduction, p. xci. < Fr. 'nobles jouvenceaulx romains' (de Premierfait, 151, l. 5).

2041 *and he.* The subject shifts to *Haniball*, who gave Marcus Marcellus an honourable burial. See *OCD, s.n.* Claudius Marcellus, Marcus (1). MS *that* 2039 (which we delete: see textual note) is misleading, as it implies that *he* is still Marcus Marcellus.

2044-7 *Marcus Marcellus . . . feerse.* Summarizes *De sen.*, XX. 75, trans. expansively by de Premierfait, 151, ll. 13–16 (cf. *Tulle*, 82), 'je racompte comment Marcellus . . . en leur courage'. *BkNob.* and *Tulle* both name the hero *Marcus Marcellus*; de Premierfait, 151, ll. 13–25, only names him 'Marcellus'. Either WW or his exemplar expanded the detail (cf. 1837–8, 1838–42), perhaps from another source, e.g. Livy, *Ab urbe condita*, XXVIII. xxvi–xxvii), which WW knew (see 769n.).

2044 *consull Romayne.* See 1602n. < Fr. 'consul rommain' (de Premierfait, 151, l. 13). On the word-order, see Introduction, p. xci.

2048-58 *. . . of man . . . region.* After two leaves lost preceding 2048, WW is in the midst of a periodic sentence listing elements of agricultural management, presumably in times of prosperity, in readiness for times of hardship. The loss makes it hard to identify the source. This could be an original observation, born of WW's experience running Fastolf's estates (recorded in his notebook, BL, Add. MS 28208, and in documents at OMA). It loosely shares the praise for agriculture in a long passage of *De sen.*, XVI. 56–XVII. 60, trans. de Premierfait, 123, l. 5–127, l. 27 (cf. *Tulle*, 60), 'cultivement des terres . . . labouraige de champ', immediately preceding the source of 2090–2128, which followed this passage directly (before WW's added ll. 2059–87). WW also praises agriculture, in terms generally evoking *De sen.*, in his revisions of Scrope, *Dicts* (ed. Bühler, 28–30), dated Mar. 1473 (by the Julian calendar).

2050 *falle* = 'befall' (as in *fallen* 2054), but lacking a subject; the implied subject is some equivalent to the *scarsete or derthe* 2054 that is the object of the main clause.

2050 *wethirs.* Compare WW's defence of the need to study meteorological and environmental science at 1823–32.

2051 *mildewis.* Antedates 1st citation as a count-noun = 'attacks of crop blight', in *OED*, mildew, *n.*, 2.a; no such construction is cited in *MED*, mil-deu, *n.*

2054 *fallen.* Postmodifying *scarsete or derthe*, reiterating the point of *ther falle by* 2050; so the prep. *by* is needed.

2055-6 *res publica . . . comyn profit.* WW's clearest statement of his preferred translation of this key Lat. term, though other renderings appear elsewhere (see 3n., 622n., 1599–600n., 1606n., 1690–2n.).

2059–87 *Hyt ys to remembre . . . grace.* WW makes a large marginal addition, in effect a whole chapter, as the 1st sentence is underlined like the chapter titles by the main scribe (so we set it in bold type).

2059 *Hyt ys to remembre.* See 1961 (and 1961–74n.).

2062 *autor.* See 1961n.

2062–71 *I fynde by hys bokes . . . service.* Fastolf stressed the importance of guarding ports and keeping the seas in policy recommendations of 1435, 1440, 1448, and 1450: C2/207–18, C3/78–94, C4/66–71, C5/65–74. The *bokes of* Fastolf's *purveours* 2063 are records of his stewards for provisions. Fastolf's bureaucratic rigour is attested by letters to, from or about him, which often mention his 'bok*es* of accompt*es*', etc. (*PL*, no. 589, ll. 6–7; nos. 996, l. 93, and 1009, ll. 103–4, both in WW's handwriting; no. 571, l. 21, by WW about Fastolf), a 'book' for a 'stiward' (*PL*, no. 985, l. 38), and many other records in books (*PL*, nos. 589, ll. 6–7; 981, ll. 23–9; 983, ll. 17–31; 1009, ll. 39–43).

2068 *.iijᶜ. sperys and the bowes.* Fastolf's retinue is described identically in the prologue to Caxton, *Tullius de senectute*, sig. i2v: 'thre honderd speres and the bowes' (not printed by Susebach in *Tulle*). The shared phrase and recurrence in the prologue of other words common in *BkNob.* suggest that Caxton's preface borrows in part from some preface by WW.

2068 *bowes.* Antedates 1st citation in *OED*, bow, *n.*, II.4.b.='bowmen'; *MED*, boue, *n.* (1), 5, has earlier citations.

2069 *hubes. MED*, houve, *n.*, under supplementary material to be incorporated, glosses this citation as='caps', but notes that it is also cited, perhaps in error, under *MED*, hobi, *n.* (2)='small horses', which is possible (if the horses are caparisoned). Neither *MED* nor *OED*, houve | hoove, *n.*, records a form with medial ⟨b⟩, but WW's **b** cannot be mistaken for **v** with an approach-stroke, as often in 15th-c. hands.

2070 *armurs, wepyns.* On such apposition, see Introduction, pp. lxxx–lxxxiii.

2070 ⟨re″dye.* See 204n.

2072–87 *And yt fille . . . grace.* Reports the successful suppression of an uprising in Paris in June 1421, provoked by the arrest of the Burgundian Jean de Villiers, lord of L'Isle-Adam (see 204–6n.) on 8 June 1421 by the duke of Exeter (see 427–8n.), governor of Paris. Exeter was forced to retreat to the Bastille of St Antoine. See Wylie and Waugh, iii. 323; Sumption, iv. 727; Thompson, *Paris and its People*, 92. Fastolf had been appointed its captain in Jan. 1421 (John Gough Nichols, 'An Original Appointment of Sir John Fastolfe to be Keeper of the Bastille of St Anthony at Paris in 1421', *Archaeologia*, 44 (1873), 113–22), and was given permission on 20 Feb. 1421 to transport 'ducentas minas frumenti, ac ducentas minas ordei, avenæ et pisarum' from Rouen to the Bastille:

Lettres de rois, reines et autres personnages des cours de France et d'Angleterre, ed. J. J. Champollion-Figeac, 2 vols. (Paris, 1839–47), ii. 343–4. Fastolf's complaints against the Crown (in WW's hand) refer to unpaid expenses incurred 'for the kepyng and vitaylyng of the Bastyle of seint Anthonye in Parys' (BL, Add. MS 27444, f. 40ʳ; Gairdner, no. 310). Codicil, f. 16ʳ (*Wars in France,* ii. 538), records that the cost of guarding the Bastille and rest of Paris in the year 1427–8 was 1,800 francs. An inventory of 1428 refers to handguns and cannon in the armoury and to cannon on the terraces of the Bastille: L. Douët d'Arcq, 'Inventaire de la Bastille de l'an 1428', *Revue archéologique,* 12 (1855–6), 321–49; Thompson, *Paris and its People,* 83–4. The main accounts (e.g. *Journal de Clément de Fauquembergue, greffier du Parlement de Paris, 1417–1435,* ed. Alexandre Tuetey and Henri Lacaille, 3 vols. (Paris, 1903–15), ii. 17–18; Waurin, vol. 5, bk. 2, ch. 9 (ed. Hardy and Hardy, ii. 357); *Chroniques des cordeliers,* in *La Chronique d'Enguerran de Monstrelet en deux livres avec pièces justificatives 1400–1444,* ed. L. Douët-d'Arcq, 6 vols. (Paris, 1857–62), vi. 191–327 at 296) refer to the use of archers but not guns and give different details, so the source is probably Fastolf's oral report. The praise for Fastolf's supplying of a garrison might indirectly counteract accusations by Jack Cade's rebels, still reported in a letter of 1465 after Fastolf's death, that Fastolf had 'mynnysshyd all the garrisons of Normaundy *and* Mauns *and* Mayn, the whech was the cause of the lesyng of all the Kyng*es* tytyll *and* ryght of an herytaunce' (*PL,* no. 692, ll. 26–30).

2072 *named kyng.* See 56n., etc.

2073 *he=*Fastolf.

2074 *hyt fortuned.* Syntax recommences, repeating sense of *yt fille* 2072 after the long subclause *when . . . cytee* 2072–4.

2075–6 ``*and*'' *was yn . . . the cyte.* WW began an explanatory subclause describing the Parisian commoners' favour for the lord of L'Isle-Adam who *was yn so grete fauour of the cyte;* then he erased a word before that subclause and wrote *stode* over it, too early in error (see *stode to harneys* 2076–7n.); then he realized that the explanatory subclause lacked a conjunction, perhaps the word erased under *stode,* and interlineated *and,* in its emphatic subordinating function,=*'*who indeed' (*OED, and, conj.*¹, *adv.* and *n.*¹, I.9.b; *MED, and, conj.* [and *adv.*], 3[a]).

2076 ``*a*''*ll.* See 264n.

2076–7 ``*stode*'' *. . . to harneys=*'took up arms'; 1st citation in this construction in *OED, harness, n.,* 2.b, but *MED, harneis, n.,* 1(a), cites it from Malory. WW supplied *stode* over erasure, but mistakenly on the l. immediately above *sodenly* in the MS before the previous subclause (*was yn . . . the cyte:* see 2075–6n.) and the grammatical subject *all the . . . cyte.*

2078–9 *coherted.* See 1160 (and n.). Nichols printed *coherced,* which is the 1st citation in *OED*, *coerce*, *v.* (but antedated in *MED*, *cohercen*, *v.*). But the etymological note in *OED* asks whether Nichols's *coherced* is a misprint for *cohert*, 'the ordinary word at that time'. Similarly, Davis, 'Epistolary', 263–4, suggests that in a letter by WW which *PL*, no. 1050, l. 29, prints as 'coherced', the same word should be 'coherted'. See *cohercion* 2188, 2261 (and nn.).

2081 *aueyn*. *MED*, *aveine*, *n.*, has two earlier citations, but this is the 1st and only citation in *OED*, *aueyn*, *n.* = 'oats', perhaps borrowed afresh by WW from Fr. *aveine*, given the context.

2085 *loggeyns* = 'defensive positions': *MED*, *logging(e, n.*, 1(c).

2085 F`r"ensh. See 204n.

2090–4 *principalle dedis . . . at ease*. Loosely echoes *De sen.*, XVII. 59, trans. de Premierfait, 125, ll. 21–8.

2095–122 *the philosophur Socrates . . . ioie*. Translated closely from *De sen.*, XVII. 59, trans. and expanded by de Premierfait, 125, l. 28–127, l. 21 (cf. *Tulle*, 61–2), 'Le philosophe Socrates . . . bieneurté mondaine'. WW ascribes the passage directly to Socrates, whereas de Premierfait, following Cicero, clarifies that it comes from Xenophon's *Oeconomicus*, a dialogue with Socrates as one speaker.

2095 *Cirus, king*. < de Premierfait, 125, l. 30, 'roy'. In fact, Cyrus the Younger, the ally of Lysander the Spartan, was only the younger son of a king and mounted a failed coup: see *OCD*, s.n. Cyrus (2), the Younger.

2096 *seigniourie terrien* = 'worldly power'. Antedates 1st citation in *OED*, *terrien*, *adj.*, and MS dating of 1st citation in *MED*, *terrien*, *adj.* < Fr. 'seignorie terrienne' (de Premierfait, 125, l. 30). For the postposed adj., see Introduction, pp. xc–xci.

2103 *ricchesse roiall*. For the postposed adj., see Introduction, pp. xc–xci. It might here echo a different Fr. collocation 'hostel roial' in de Premierfait, 127, l. 2 (cf. *Tulle*, 61, 'rialle palais').

2104 *hym* = Lysander.

2107 *fructis*. On the Latinate sp. with medial ⟨c⟩, see *fructufull* 1702 (and n.) and Introduction, p. xcii. No cognate in de Premierfait, 127, ll. 4–8 (and cf. *Tulle*, 61, 'fruytes').

2107 *ale`y'ed*. 1st citation in *OED*, *alleyed*, *adj.*, and *MED*, *aleied*, *adj.* No Fr. cognate in de Premierfait, 127, ll. 4–8.

2110 *ioieust*. 1st citation in this sense in *OED*, *joyous*, 2 = 'productive of joy'; earlier citations in *MED*, *joious*, *adj.*, 1(b), 'causing joy'.

2115 *behelding*. Sp. with ⟨e⟩ in the 2nd syllable is unusual but recorded by *MED*, *biholding*, *ger.*, from Margery Kempe who, as WW did later in his life, lived in

Norfolk. *LALME*, dot-map 174–60, records sp. ⟨he(a)ld(e)⟩ mostly in Norfolk, Suffolk, and London.

2117 *felicite mondeyn*. 1st citation in *OED*, *mundane, adj.*, or *MED*, *mondeine, adj.*, here = 'earthly'. See also 2121n. Cf. *Tulle*, 62, 'worldly felicitee'. Adj. postposed after n. < Fr. 'félicité mondaine' (de Premierfait, 127, l. 19): see Introduction, pp. xc–xci.

2118 *noblesse roiall*. For the word-order, see Introduction, pp. xc–xci.

2119 *tymes oportune*. For the word-order, see Introduction, pp. xc–xci. Here it helps to introduce the prepositional phrase *in* . . .

2121 *beneurte and felicite mondeyne*. Expanding < Fr. 'bieneurté mondaine' (de Premierfait, 127, ll. 20–1; cf. *Tulle*, 62, 'worldly blessidnesse') to resemble 2117 (see n.). 1st and only citation in *MED, beneurte. n.*, and antedating the 1st and only citation for *beneurte* listed as a derivative under *OED, beneurous, adj.*, and for *beneurous* itself and cognate terms. < Fr. 'bieneurté' (de Premierfait, 127, l. 20).

2123–8 *Valerius Corninus . . . hadde*. As claimed, based on *De sen.*, XVII. 60, trans. de Premierfait, 127, ll. 28–31 (cf. *Tulle*, 62–3), 'ung noble vieillart . . . labouroit les terres'. WW adds the claim that Valerius Corvinus' motive was to prepare for times of *scarsete* and stabilize crop prices. The minims give the erroneous **nin** in the name of Valerius Corvinus (or Corvus), Marcus (fl. 348–302 BCE) (*OCD*); the error recurs in *Tullius de senectute*, sig. f6ᵛ, 'Carninus' (which Susebach, editing *Tulle*, 62, emends to 'Corvinus'). See similarly 1838–42n., 2139n.

2123–4 *citesyn Romayne*. For the word-order, see Introduction, p. xci. Perhaps echoing the Fr. word-order 'vieillart rommain' (de Premierfait, 127, l. 29), while changing the noun.

2132–7 *Tullius . . . Rome*. The subsequent section 2138–51 comes from the 5th section of *De sen.*, as divided by de Premierfait, 137, l. 1 (cf. *Tulle*, 69, 'the fyfthe part'). The correction to '5'. *distinctio* suggests that section-marking was unclear either in the Fr. MS consulted by WW or in the exemplar for this MS of *BkNob*.

2138–51 *Lucius . . . Brutus*. Based on *De sen.*, XX. 75, trans. de Premierfait, 147, ll. 10–18 (cf. *Tulle*, 77–8), 'Lucius Brutus . . . du dict Brutus'. WW here incorporates the only other example, the 1st, from de Premierfait's expanded catalogue of exemplary lives, at 1943–2047. WW also encountered Lucius Junius Brutus in Cicero, *De oratore*, I. ix. 37, in OMC, MS Lat. 206, e.g. f. 4ʳ, where he was highlighted in red in the margin.

2139 *Aruus*. Four medial minims in the MS are the scribe's usual form of **uu**, misreading 'Aruns' from de Premierfait, 147, ll. 10–18, perhaps expecting a Lat. masculine n. ending -*us*. *Tullius de senectute*, sig. g7ᵛ–g8ʳ, has 'Arnus' and 'Appius' (which Susebach, editing *Tulle*, 77, emends to 'Aruns'). This is Ar(r)uns, son of Lucius Tarquinius Superbus. See similarly 2123–8n.

2142 *to die vpon*. MED, *dien, v.*, 1c.(e), records little use of *vpon* in the figurative sense = 'due to'; OED, *die, v.* [1], does not record this collocation.

2146 *fortuned*. Technically, the clause *that . . . dethe* 2147 is the grammatical subject, though other impers. uses have a dummy pron. *it/hyt* (1632, 2074) or adv. *there*, as do citations in *MED, fortunen, v.*, 3(c). *OED, fortune, v.*, 3.b and 3.c, has instances without a dummy pron., albeit both late 16th-c. See also 2150n.

2147 *wound[ed]*. As the impers. v. *fortuned* requires a finite clause, MS *woun|ding* is perhaps an error, caused by the l. break.

2150 *had not bene*. Omits impers. dummy adv. *there*. See 2146n.

2155 *might falle*. Zero subordination understood, = 'that might befall'.

2159 *iustice-keping*. MS *and* seems an error, caused by the l. break after it or by WW's idiolectal preference for a gerund following its direct object, especially for this exact phr. (at 1328, 1621): see Introduction, pp. lxxxvii–lxxxviii.

2161 *it, right dampnable*. *it = iustice-keping* 2159; *right dampnable* refers to the *offence and dammage* 2159.

2162 *accustumablie*. 1st citation in OED, *accustomably, adv.*, and MED, *accustomabli, adv.*

2162 *rennythe* = 'is prevalent'. Only 1 citation in this sense in *MED, rennen, v.* (1), 16(d), from Scrope, *Dicts* (ed. Bühler, 48, l. 3).

2162–3 *tho that ought be [vnder]*. WW's interlineation interrupts and adapts the set phrase *vnder youre obeisaunce* and forgets to restore *vnder*.

2168–251 *That is to . . . pouertee*. WW returns to the importance of paying soldiers' wages: see 877–910. He adds that the mistreatment of non-combatants by unpaid soldiers and oppressive officers caused their defection. Similar arguments are made in accusatory questions to be put to the duke of Somerset, in Arundel, f. 323[v] (*Wars in France*, ii. 721; see 892–902n.).

2168–9 *that 'shall be' men . . . as well tho that 'shall' be vndre*. On WW's repeated interlineation *shall be* (duplicating the scribe's *be*), see Introduction, p. lxxxv. The use of *that* = 'those who', as subject of a rel. clause without any antecedent n. or pron., was a widely attested elliptical construction (see OED, *that, pron.* [2], I.3.b.), but the presence of *tho* obscures the parallel.

2172 *of curtesyie* = 'by favour (as opposed to legal entitlement)', antedating this sense in OED, *courtesy, n.*, 3.a; earlier citations in MED, *courteisie, n.*, 5.(a).

2173 *defalcacion*. Antedates, by one year, 1st citation in OED, *defalcation, n.*; sole citation in MED, *defalcacion, n.* See 908n., 2181n.

2177 *content*. 1st citation of this form of the pa. p. in *OED*, *content*, *adj.*[2] and *n.*[4], II.4, but several such sp. from documentary sources with financial senses (='paid' or 'compensated') in *MED*, *contenten*, *v.*, 2b(a). Cf. 2514.

2177-8 *of . . . pursute* = 'with . . . pursuit', i.e. nor with need to chase up one's entitled payments, as often in the 15th c.: e.g. Gairdner, no. 309, 'after long pursewt*ys*', a document in WW's handwriting, in BL, Add. MS 27444, f. 38ᵣ, or Hoccleve, *Male Regle*, 426, which *OED*, *pursuit*, *n.*, I.1.b, and *MED*, *pursuit*(*e*, 4.(a) and 5.(b), cite under less specific senses.

2179 *officers roiall*. For the word-order, see Introduction, pp. xc–xci.

2181 *defalke*. 1st citation in *MED*, *defalken*, *v.*, and in *OED*, *defalk*, *v.*, 1, though 2.b. has earlier citations in a different, specific sense in Scots. The v. like the n. *defalcacion* (see 2173n.) had a strict administrative usage (< Fr.: see *DMF*, *defalquer*, and *DMLBS*, *defalcare*). See also *defalking* 908n. On this construction, see Introduction, p. lxxxxii.

2186 *punisshid*, [*it*] *turned*. The emendation repairs a break in the syntax, where there is l. break in the MS and possible auditory confusion at the word breaks *-id it t-*.

2188 *cohercion* = 'feeling of compulsion' due to others' use of force (*rapyn* . . .): cf. 2261 (and n.). Antedates 1st citation in *OED*, *coercion*, *n.*; *MED*, *cohercioun*, *n.*, has earlier citations. Compare *coherted* 1160, 2078–9 (and see nn.).

2193 *esy*. Only citation in this sense in *OED*, *easy*, *adj.*, *adv.* and *n.*, B.2, but *MED*, *esi*, *adv.*, has two earlier citations in related senses.

2204 *paissauntes*. Relatively rare word, with only one prior citation shared by *OED*, *peasant*, *n.*, and *MED*, *paisaunt*, *n.* WW might have thought he was borrowing it directly from Fr., given the context, or denoting French people in particular.

2206-7 *inconuenientis, to be redressid . . . fille, and*. 'crimes (*inconuenientis*) which would have been *redressid* long before (*or*) the French incursions occurred (*intrusion fille*), if (*and*)' the king had been in charge.

2211 *to be manassed, beten*. On such grammatical apposition, see Introduction, pp. lxxx–lxxxiii; they are both actions *suffred* (='allowed'); *mischieued* is then the finite v. in a new clause.

2213 `*a'nd*. See 264n.

2213 *enforced*. See 980n.

2217 *rentis-paieng*. *OED*, *rent*, *n.*, C1.b, *rent-paying*, *n.* and *adj.*, and *MED*, *rent*(*e*, *n.*, 4.(b), treat the compound as a set phrase but do not record the pl. inflection ⟨s⟩.

2219 *patised*. The payment of *appatis* (protection money). 1st citation in this sense in *OED*, *patise*, *v.*, 2.a; only citation in this sense in *MED*, *patisen*, *v.*, 1(b).

See also the sp. *appatise* in C2/151n. and the n. *apatismentis* in C5/60n. Compare *DMF, apatis*. For context, see M. H. Keen, *The Laws of War in the Late Middle Ages* (London, 1965), 251–3; Clifford J. Rogers, 'By Fire and Sword: *Bellum Hostile* and "Civilians" in the Hundred Years War', in Mark Grimsely and Clifford J. Rogers (eds.), *Civilians in the Path of War* (Lincoln, NE, 2002), 33–78; Nicholas Wright, 'Ransoms of Non-combatants during the Hundred Years War', *Journal of Medieval History*, 17 (1991), 323–32.

2224 *obeissaunce,* `*lawes*'. On this instance of grammatical apposition, here created by interlineation, see Introduction, p. lxxxiii. Nichols, cited in *MED, laue, n.,* 6a(a), parses this with the following word as 'lawes-yovyng'.

2236 *his dyuyne . . .* `*of God*'. WW's interlineation duplicates the referent of *his*.

2239–40 `*y'oure* `*grete' aduersarie*. See 219 (and n.), etc. WW only describes 'aduersaries' as *oure* when the address is to a wider audience or the referent is to enemies in general (107, 1711, 2237, 2577).

2244 *be turned*. Subject='they', the residents of territories in France, understood from *theire* 2242.

2244–5 *frome . . . to*. They turn *frome* their *obedience* to the English king and *to* his enemy.

2249 *whiche . . . for faute of these*. Pron. *these* recapitulates the referent of *whiche*.

2252 *officers roiall*. For the word-order, see Introduction, pp. xc–xci.

2254 *hem*. The pl. people implied by *the chirche* 2253.

2255–72 *And moreouer . . . necessite*. WW claims to write *by experience knowen* (2260–1), presumably the reports of veterans of the wars in France. He contrasts *nedeles(e)* impositions on clergy (2261–9) with their charity to those *in case of necessite* (2269–72). Cf. 2477–81n. For harm to the Church, see H. Denifle, *La Désolation des églises, monastères et hopitaux en France pendant la Guerre de cent ans*, 2 vols. (Paris, 1897–9).

2257 *archedenes*. Antedates *OED, archdean, n.*, which records the term as Scots only; *MED* has no entry. *AND, arcedekene*, lists variants *erchedene* and *arcediaen*, so WW might borrow the term from (Norman) Fr., given that he describes abuses in France.

2257 *ministrours*. *OED, minister, n.*, and *MED, ministre, n.*, record other sp. with medial ⟨r⟩ but not ⟨rour⟩. Sp. with metathesized ⟨r⟩ might reflect Fr. *ministre*, given the context; sp. with ⟨rour⟩ recurs at 2382 and in the Codicil, C1/118.

2258 *revaled*. See 64n.

2258 *vileyned*. 1st and only citation in *MED, vileinen, v.*, but *OED, villain, v.*, cites Lydgate, *Troy Book*, I. 2491.

2258–9 *predecessoure daies.* See 121–2n.

2261 *priue cohercion* = 'secret force', a slightly different sense from 2188 (see n.), the phenomenon known as *appatis* (on which see 2219n.).

2264 *or haue her lyuelode* = 'or whence [the clergy] draw their income'.

2265–72 *And the peple . . . necessite.* A surprisingly specific complaint, which sounds more like anticlerical critique, about enclosed religious being overly engaged in hospitality for wealthy and powerful guests and neglecting their charitable mission and intercessionary duties. Fastolf's will expressed concerns about the monks of his own chantry foundation neglecting their duties. See Richmond, *The Paston Family . . . Fastolf's Will,* 56–61.

2265 *peple* = members of religious houses, especially the wealthy (*well set* 2265) institutions.

2269 *they* = religious foundations, established only to support their stipulated number of members (*fundacion*).

2273–9 *Many auctours . . . God.* WW knew this story from three sources (hence *Many auctours*). Perhaps *stabled his hors in Salamon is temple* < Chartier, *Livre de l'espérance,* Pr. VIII. 310–20, 'establa ses cheuaulx ou temple Salomon', in Royal, f. 139ᵛ, annotated by WW. In addition, in Paris in Nov. and Dec. 1453 WW copied extracts from folio 138 of a copy owned by Fastolf (see 1670–85n.) from *Li Fet des Romains,* ed. Flutre and Sneyders de Vogel, i. 571 (III, 13, §26), into Royal, f. 144ʳ, which he annotated as 'pro Ecclesia honoranda', which recount the story but lack the name of Solomon. WW also owned (see 762–72n.) Giovanni Boccaccio, *De casibus virorum illustrium,* in OMC, MS Lat. 198, in which another 15th-c. reader annotated Pompey's biography with the story about the temple, but not mentioning Solomon (f. 112ᵛ).

2280–4 *King Iohn . . . repentaunce of.* The men of King Jean II only *auaunted h'e'msilfe* (= 'boasted of themselves [that they could]') stable their horses in Salisbury cathedral. See *MED, avaunten, v.,* 1, and *OED, avaunt, v.*ˡ, 2.b (perhaps merging in sense with *MED, auntren, v.,* 3[a]). WW's *as it is saide* perhaps implies an oral source.

2291 *begon* = 'past': *OED, bygone, adj.* and *n.; MED, bi-gon, ppl.*

2291–2 *predecessour daies.* See 121–2n.

2295–8 *Saint Ieroyme . . . aduersite.* Close paraphrase of St Jerome, *In Ioelem,* ch. 1 (*Libri commentariorum,* ed. J. Migne, Patrologia Latina, 25 (Paris, 1845), col. 954, paragraph 174; Hieronymus, *Commentarii in prophetas minores,* ed. M. Adriaen, 2 vols., Corpus Christianorum Series Latina, 76 and 76A (Turnhout, 1969 and 1970), 166): 'ut qui non cognoverunt Deum in prosperis, cognoscant in adversis'. Jerome describes this as the frequent providence of God, which supports WW's rebuke in 2290–4. The l. is a memorable one, likely to be quoted, but

it is not in WW's other usual sources. Jerome's commentary on the minor pro-
phets did circulate in England: see e.g. Cambridge, Trinity College, MS B.3.28,
ff. 64^r-83^r, then at Christ Church, Canterbury (*Medieval Libraries of Great
Britain*, mlgb3.bodleian.ox.ac.uk); Eton College, MS 21, then at Peterborough
Abbey (Ker, Piper, and Watson, *Medieval Manuscripts in British Libraries*, ii.
647-8; *Medieval Libraries of Great Britain*); and Eton College, MSS 22 and 23,
at Eton by *c*.1465 and *c*.1500 respectively (Ker, Piper, and Watson, *Medieval
Manuscripts in British Libraries*, ii. 648-50). In Julius, f. 115^r, WW in 1471
copied a quotation from Jerome on a different topic in a collection of sayings
from William Plombe of Gonville Hall, Cambridge.

2298-303 *In suche wise . . . affliccions.* Might summarize the idea that people
are afflicted by troubles related to their sins ('poetic justice') that follows the
previous quotation from St Jerome, *In Ioelem*, ch. 1 (*Libri commentariorum*,
ed. Migne, col. 954, paragraph 174; Hieronymus, *Commentarii in prophetas
minores*, ed. Adriaen, 166): 'et qui divitiis male abusi sunt, ad virtutes penuria
corrigantur . . . vesanum'. Jerome's 'luxuria' might suggest *delites* 2299, which
otherwise does not fit the kinds of crimes specified by *BkNob.*, and 'abundan-
tiam', albeit there of drink ('ebrium'), might suggest *ouere-gret haboundaunce*,
here of *crimes* 2298-9. Thereafter *BkNob.* diverts into the 7 Deadly Sins (*couetice, . . . pride and enuy*).

2299 *chargeable.* Antedates 1st citation in *OED*, *chargeable, adj.*; many earlier
citations in this sense (='grave') and other senses in *MED*, *chargeable, adj.*

2304 *predecessours daies.* See 2210, but cf. 121-2n, 2258-9, 2291-2, and similarly 2340.

2309 'y'oure. See 219 (and n.), etc.

2311-18 *the sonnes . . . rennyng.* These proposals might come from experience
or from Fastolf (as at 2332-40), but they can be found also in WW's reading: e.g.
the Fr. translation of John of Wales, *Breviloquium*, in CUL, MS Add. 7870, ff. 7^v,
4^r (pages misbound before WW read them and noted the misbinding), says that
noble-born youths must be 'exarcites' in chivalric arts: 'on les doit aprendre a
courre a faillir a Ruer a getter la pierre a lancier glauellos et dars / et traire
dabalestre et darc' (f. 4^r), which pages WW annotated 'disciplina filiorum mag-
natorum' (f. 7^v) and 'nota de sciencijs practicandi pro armis exercendis' (f. 4^r).
The list of activities differs, but the process of listing is similar. Also close to
Vegetius, *Epitoma rei militaris*, I. iv, cited by John of Wales, *Breviloquium*, in
CUL, MS Add. 7870, f. 7^v, where WW annotated the reference to Vegetius; and
by Christine de Pizan, *Livre des faits d'armes*, I. 9 and I. 10 (BL, Royal MS 15
E. vi, f. 408^{r-v}; Laennec, ii. 43-50). Caxton in the epilogue to his translation of
Ramon Lull's *Order of Chivalry* (*c*.1484) makes the same point about practice:
see William Caxton, 'Order of Chyualry: Epilogue', in *Prologues and Epilogues*,
ed. Crotch, 82-4 at 84.

2315 *drawen forthe.* See 1908–9n.

2316 *to can renne* = 'to know how to ride on horseback': see *MED, rennen, v.* (2); *OED, run, v.,* I.3.a.

2317 *speer-handle.* Collocation unrecorded in *OED, spear, n.*¹, or *MED, spere, n* (1).

2322 *seruice honourable.* For the word-order, see Introduction, pp. xc–xci.

2324 *a.* See 264n.

2332–40 *as myne autor . . . vntoo.* About Henry of Grosmont (see 348–51n.), 1st duke of Lancaster. WW interlineated *fyrst* before Henry, distinguishing him from his grandson, Henry IV, from the opposing dynasty to WW's Yorkist addressee. This is apparently reported by Fastolf, named in WW's sidenote 2332SN, and called *myne autor* 2332 (see 1961n.), who is said at 1961–2 himself to have advised younger knights. WW's fellow Norfolk author John Capgrave, *Liber de illustribus Henricis*, ed. Francis Charles Hingeston, RS 1 (London, 1858), 161, confirms Henry of Grosmont's reputation for military instruction. There might be a literary model: the Fr. translation of John of Wales, *Breviloquium*, in CUL, MS Add. 7870, f. 5ᵛ (adjacent before misbinding to passages close to 2311–18: see n.), lists ancient rulers who had their sons educated.

2337 *doctrined.* 1st citation in *OED, doctrine, v.*; in *MED, doctrinen, v.,* antedated by WW's associate Scrope, *Dicts,* ed. Bühler, 16, l. 13.

2340 *antecessour daies.* See 121–2n.

2342 *gentiles.* Unclear sp. with single ⟨s⟩, but in context likely = 'noble behaviour', viz. *OED, gentilesse, n.,* 1.a, and *MED, gentilesse, n.,* 2(b). *MED* cites forms with single ⟨s⟩ from Lydgate, *Troy Book,* I. 155, II. 6811.

2343–51 *But now . . . lyue in rest.* Complaints about lawyers harming the commonweal are a commonplace of 15th-c. moralists (e.g. William Caxton, 'The Game and Playe of the Chesse: Prologue', in *Prologues and Epilogues,* ed. Crotch, 10–16 at 14), but also have classical precedents in works known to WW and his milieu (e.g. Vegetius, *Epitoma rei militaris*; known to the Pastons in the Eng. translation, *1408 Vegetius,* 74); but this extended complaint could have been occasioned by specific incidents in WW's Norfolk milieu, lamented in a petition to parliament in 1455 about lawyers in Norfolk and neighbouring Suffolk going to public gatherings to stir up needless cases for themselves (*PROME,* xii. 441–2).

2345–6 *'faculteez' straunge frome that fet* = 'skills unrelated to that business': see *OED, strange, adj.* and *n.,* A.6; *MED, straunge, adj.,* 3(b). WW added *faculteez* after *straunge,* i.e. one word too late, in space at the l. end. This sense of *fet* antedates the 1st citation of the more general sense *MED, fet, n.,* 5, 'kind of action'; earlier citations in *MED, fet, n.,* 3, do not exactly capture that sense.

2346 `a's. See 264n.

2348 *courtis-halding.* Combination not in *OED, court, n.* [1], though the v. phrase *to hold court* is (IV.13.a); *MED, court, n.* (1), 9(c), has an earlier citation of sg. *court-holding.* Editorial hyphenation by analogy with *OED*'s *court-holder.* See also 2349n.

2348 *bere out.* Antedates 1st citation under *OED, bear, v.* [1], phrasal verbs; only citation in *MED, beren, v.* (1), 13(e), 'put on a front', from BodL, MS Tanner 407, also from Norfolk and in a similar context 'beryt owte as riche men goo'.

2349 *shiris-halding.* Combination not in *OED, shire, n.,* or *MED, shire, n.* Editorial hyphenation by analogy with 2348 (see n.).

2350 *embrace.* Cited under *MED, embracen, v.,* 3b.(b)='to prejudice a jury'; and 1st citation in *OED, embrace v.* [3]. Jonathan Rose, *Maintenance in Medieval England* (Cambridge, 2017), 104–6, explains embracery and, at 188, attempts to control it under Edward IV.

2353–5 *.xxx. or xl yeris . . . werris.* WW's comparison evokes Fastolf, who was said to have served in the wars in France for 'fourty yeres' in Caxton's preface to *Tullius de senectute,* sig. i2ʳ (not ed. by Susebach in *Tulle*), and 44 years in WW's son's preface to the Codicil, C1/35–6.

2354 `antecessourys' conquestis. Cf. uninflected possessive at 2340n., etc.

2362 `your' *iustices and* `your' *officers.* See 219 (and n.), etc.

2363 *w`syng'.* The sp. of *use* with initial ⟨w⟩ is well attested in *OED, use, v.,* and *MED, usen, v.,* but its use here might be a remnant of a different word which WW's erasure and overwriting replace.

2369–72 *And if the vaillaunt Romayns . . . Affricans.* While the Romans did twice defeat the Carthaginians, they also allowed their sons to study law, as WW might have known from the works of Cicero.

2379 *he.* A change from pl. *suche parsones* to a sg. example of such a person, *he.*

2384 *tho*=the *princes, . . . of worship* 2383.

2385 *gyuen to.* Glossing *theire londis* 2385.

2386–8 *they be . . . take vpon hem to offende theire law. they* and *hem*=the *princes, . . . of worship* 2383; *theire*=the *ministrours of the law* 2382. May echo Ps. 110: 10 'Initium sapientiae timor domini'.

2389–99 *.36. chapitre . . . prophesie.* Jer. 36: 22–31, in which Jehoiakim, king of Judah, destroys the scroll containing God's rebukes, which Jeremiah had transcribed by Baruch. The biblical passage is not closely relevant to *BkNob.*'s account of former habits of protecting legal officers. Quoting it might obliquely suggest that *BkNob.* itself, as unwelcome vatic speech, should not suffer the displeasure of its addressee, Edward IV. The book of Jeremiah is often cited by

WW's associate Friar Brackley: *PL*, nos. 606, l. 21 (Jer. 7: 4); 609, ll. 23–4 (Jer. 8: 8); 655, ll. 28–30 (Jer. 17: 18).

2391 *aduertisementis.* 1st citation in this sense = 'warnings', in *OED*, *advertisement, n.*, 1.b; *MED*, *advertis(e)ment, n.*, does not distinguish this sense. In Arundel, f. 324ʳ, a set of such warnings is titled 'Aduertirimentes', perhaps from a scribe misreading z, rendering the medial sound /z/, as a round or zetoid r in an unfamiliar usage of this word.

2392 *bookes and quaiers.* Perhaps mistranslating genitive sg. *libri* in Lat. 'volumen libri' in Jer. 36: 2 ('the roll of a book', with reference to ancient scrolls constituting one book) as nominative pl. *libri*; or perhaps = the three or four 'pagellas' read to Jehoiakim in Jer. 36: 23.

2399 *And so . . . prophesie.* Jer. 37: 1–2. Jehoiakim's son did not inherit Judah.

2413–16 *the worthie Romains . . . reignyng.* Recounted by Christine de Pizan, *Livre des faits d'armes* (a source earlier in *BkNob.*: see 151–63, etc.), I. 10 (BL, Royal MS 15 E. vi, f. 408ᵛ; Laennec, ii. 50), 'Et encore en continuant . . . habit de Ioye', though WW's phrasing does not suggest close translation here. WW also read in Royal, f. 136ʳ, an extract from Chartier, *Quadrilogue* (Bouchet, 21, ll. 18–20), about the women of Rome who renounced fine clothing following defeat at the battle of Cannae.

2417–20 *the same maner . . . away.* Perhaps suggested by Chartier, *Quadrilogue* (Bouchet, 21, ll. 20–4), 'Le pays de Languedoc . . . leesce et festivité', or the fuller account of the same in *GCF*, Jean II, ch. 'De l'ordenance . . .' (*Chron-Jean-Charles*, i. 86–7).

2417–18 *the same maner, 'the ryte' and custom youre aduerse partie . . . hathe vsed.* We omit WW's interlineation *of*, which made the abstract nouns rather than the animate *aduerse partie* the subject of *hathe vsed*, a usage of *MED*, *usen*, *v.*, 5.(b), in a passive sense not otherwise attested; the *maner*, *ryte* and *custom* are the object of the v.

2419 *bobauncees.* 1st and only citation in this concrete sense = 'fine trappings', in *OED*, *bobance, n.*, b; *MED*, *bobaunce, n.*, does not distinguish this sense.

2420–5 *costues arraymentis . . . pouertee.* Moralists and political commentators frequently lamented costly clothing as causing the *empouerisshing of youre lande*. E.g. the petition in parliament in 1463 claiming that the wearing of 'excessive and inordynat arayes' has led to the 'enpoverysshing of this youre seid reame' (*PROME*, xiii. 108).

2424 *holpe brought.* The use of the v. *help* with a tense in concord with the accompanying v., rather than infin. or a *that* subclause, is not recorded in *OED*, *help, v.*, 5, or *MED*, *helpen, v.*, 1(b). Davis, 'Epistolary', 260–1, notes that WW often uses *help*+infin. without *to*.

2429-36 *youre pore . . . peple*='people are not wholly repaid (*paied holy*) the money due to them (*duteis*) for various loans in the reign of Henry VI, but are *delaied* in repayment; therefore they *despende* their wealth before (*or*) they can recover their debts and would rather (are *fayn*) endure withholding one part of what is owed them and *relese* the crown from repayment, in order to receive the *othir part*; and this causes hardship'. The complaint about Henry VI's debts was made widely, e.g. in *Giles' Chronicle*, 'Henrici VI', 38, in WW's miscellany Royal, f. 86ʳ. For bad tallies, see Anthony Steel, 'Mutua per talliam, 1399-1413', *Historical Research*, 13 (1935), 73-84, and G. L. Harriss, 'Fictitious Loans', *Economic History Review*, NS 8 (1955), 187-99; and for the wider economic context, see G. L. Harriss, 'Marmaduke Lumley and the Exchequer Crisis of 1446-9', in J. G. Rowe (ed.), *Aspects of Late Medieval Government and Society* (Toronto, 1986), 143-78. After a passage translated below (see 2446-7n., 2447-9n.) from the Fr. trans of John of Wales, *Breviloquium*, the subsequent passage in CUL, MS Add. 7870, f. 16ᵛ, criticizes prodigious generosity by kings, and in 1450 WW added a manicule and annotated 'Nota bene pro Regno Anglie verificato tempore Regis nunc' (i.e. Henry VI).

2434 *nighe*='collect', a sense not recorded in *OED*, *nigh*, *v.*, *OED*, *nighing*, *n.* or *MED*, *neighen*, *v.* (1), but captured in a similar context in *MED*, *neighing(e, ger.* (1). A 1455 common petition, cited in Harriss, 'Marmaduke Lumley', 170, refers to the 'leuee, gadring and neighyng of the kinges reuenues'.

2442 *tho that haue lost . . . goode.* On compensation for those who lost their lands in France, see 1235-40n.

2444 *importunyte.* 1st citation in this sense='difficulty', in *OED*, *importunity*, *n.*, 3; only citation in *MED*, *importunyte*, *n.*, 1(b).

2446-7 *it is saide . . . worship.* Loose rendering of an idea from John of Wales, *Breviloquium*, in Fr. translation in CUL, MS Add. 7870, f. 16ᵛ, 'la fin de nostre Ciuille et politique vie nest pas de grans Ricesses et assembler et ne conqueillier ains est de honneur et gloire acquerir', there ascribed to Aristotle, *Ethics*, bk. I ('comme dist le philosophe' > *it is saide*), and annotated by WW. In *BkNob.* WW's interlineation *an empyre or* (including altering the allograph for **a**: see 264n.) before *roiaume* might echo a doublet in the preceding Fr. sentence, which mentions 'dominacion ne seigneurie' (f. 16ʳ) as things not to be sought over honour.

2447-9 *bettir it is . . . roiaume.* Translated from John of Wales, *Breviloquium*, in Fr. translation in CUL, MS Add. 7870, f. 16ᵛ, of a saying ascribed there to Valerius Maximus, annotated by WW as 'Valerius de re publica Exemplum notabile': 'Car vng chascun amoit mieulx viure et conuerser comme poure homme en vng Rice ~~homme~~ Roiaume que estre riche et viure en vng poure ~~homme~~ roiaume'.

2454 *after hym reigned*='who . . . reigned': zero rel. clause without rel. pron.

2457–64 *Saint Lowes . . . puissauntlie.* Translated loosely from St Louis's *Enseignements* as it was incorporated into *GCF*, St Louis, ch. 115: 'A ce doiz tu metre t'entente comment tes genz et ton pueple puissent vivre en pais et en droiture; meesmement les bonnes villes et les bonnes citez de ton reamme, et les garde en l'estat et en la franchise où tez devanciers les ont gardez; quar par la force de tes bonnes citez et de tes bonnes villes douteront li puissant homme à mesprendre envers toi' (Viard, vii. 279). See 211–14n. on the circulation of this text.

2470 *wille withe . . . depart* = 'will part with'. See *MED*, *departen*, *v.*, 4(d), and *OED*, *part*, *v.*, I.5.a.

2472–4 *in signe that . . . and to the recuuere.* The parallel results are obscured by different prepositional phrases. See Introduction, p. lxxxv.

2477–81 *Yet com forthe . . . power is.* Imperative construction, urging all, even religious and secular clergy (cf. 2255–72: see n.), who paid under duress in the past, to pay voluntarily in the future (*tyme to come*).

2484 *employ.* Far antedates 1st citation in *OED*, *employ*, *n.*; not in *MED*. Probably = 'task' (*OED*, *employ*, *n.*, 2.a). By contrast, *OED*, *employ*, *v.*, is attested from 1429.

2494–7 *floode of Temmys . . . necessite.* For references to flooding of the Thames, see 'John Benet's Chronicle', ed. Harriss and Harriss, 192, and 'A Short English Chronicle', in *Three Fifteenth-Century Chronicles with Historical Memoranda by John Stowe*, ed. James Gairdner (London, 1880), 1–80 at 66.

2503–8 *the Romains . . . hoost.* Summarizing Chartier, *Quadrilogue* (Bouchet, 40, ll. 12–23), as excerpted in WW's miscellany, Royal, f. 136ᵛ, marked there by the scribe as an example 'pour prendre couraige en aduersite et pour habandonner tout pour sauuer le bien publique'.

2508 *and that.* Continuing *so that* 2506 with a parallel result.

2509–14 *goode worshipfull . . . contentid.* Summarizing Chartier, *Quadrilogue* (Bouchet, 40, l. 23– 41, l. 6), as excerpted in WW's miscellany, Royal, f. 136ᵛ, where WW annotates it as an example, 'quod ciues 'et mulieres' exponerent bona libente animo pro re publica'.

2515–71 *Also I rede . . . hemsilfe.* Long summary with occasional close translation (see subsequent nn.) of Livy, *Ab urbe condita*, XXVI. xxxv–xxxvi, in the Fr. translation of Bersuire, II. vi. 19 (Paris, Bibliothèque Sainte-Geneviève, MS fr. 777, f. 254ʳ⁻ᵛ). (Chapter numbers vary between MSS: cf. e.g. Harvard, Houghton Library, MS Richardson 32, vol. 2, f. 103ᵛ, where this is ch. II. vi. 25, and BodL, MS Canon. misc. 438, ff. 126ᵛ–128ʳ, where this is ch. II. vi. 18.) This is not *the .5 booke of the seconde Decade* but the 6th book of the 3rd Decade; the 2nd Decade was lost until fragments surfaced in 1986 (*OCD*, *s.n.* Livy), and although 14th-c. Italian scholars behind the reconstructed Livy, on whose work Bersuire drew, recognized the loss of the 2nd Decade, Bersuire and others did not (G. Billanovich, 'Petrarch and the Textual Tradition of Livy', *Journal of the Warburg and Courtauld Institutes*, 14 (1951), 137–208 at 162, 168–9). MSS of Bersuire's translation call the 3rd Decade 'la seconde decade de Titus Liuius', including using the Lat. form of his name as does WW (e.g. Paris, Bibliothèque Sainte-Geneviève, MS fr. 777, ff. 172ʳ, 274ᵛ). MSS of Bersuire's translation keep the 'book' numbers within each Decade, e.g. as running titles, so WW's *.5 booke* is his error or might reveal a slip in the layout of his exemplar. On WW's access to Livy, see 769n.

2521 *goodis meueable. MED, mevable, adj.*, 5(a), records the adj. frequently postposed in legal contexts, perhaps from uses in legal Fr. For other postposed adj., see Introduction, pp. xc–xci.

2523 *Cisiliens and Champenois* = 'Sicilians and people of Campagna', < Livy, *Ab urbe condita*, XXVI. xxxv, trans. Bersuire, II. vi. 19 (Paris, Bibliothèque Sainte-Geneviève, MS fr. 777, f. 254ʳ), 'des siciliens et des campenois'.

2529 *open marketplaces.* < Livy, *Ab urbe condita*, XXVI. xxxv, trans. Bersuire, II. vi. 19 (Paris, Bibliothèque Sainte-Geneviève, MS fr. 777, f. 254ʳ), 'publiquement en marchie'.

2530 *they wolde sill theire bodies and goodis.* < Livy, *Ab urbe condita*, XXVI. xxxv, trans. Bersuire, II. vi. 19 (Paris, Bibliothèque Sainte-Geneviève, MS fr. 777, f. 254ʳ), 'il pueent bien uendre noz biens et forsener en noz corps'. WW changes the crowd's direct speech (with 1st pl. pron.) to free indirect style and removes reference to punishing their bodies.

2533–4 *seiden in conclusion that 'Where it right or wrong.* < Livy, *Ab urbe condita*, XXVI. xxxv, trans. Bersuire, II. vi. 19 (Paris, Bibliothèque Sainte-Geneviève, MS fr. 777, f. 254ʳ), 'la final oroison et la conclusion a este ceste Cest assauoir que il conuenoit fust tort fust droit'.

2538 *Lenius.* Marcus Valerius Laevinus (*OCD, s.n.* Valerius Laevinus, Marcus) < Livy, *Ab urbe condita*, XXVI. xxxv, trans. Bersuire, II. vi. 19. The set hand in Paris, Bibliothèque Sainte-Geneviève, MS fr. 777, f. 254ʳ, and the calligraphic secretary hand in Harvard, Houghton Library, MS Richardson 32, vol. 2, f. 104ʳ, both carefully form this as 'leuinus', dotting **i**; but minim confusion and haplology were easy errors. WW's sidenote 2538SN clearly repeats the error *Lenius*.

2540 *in like wise it is reason.* < Livy, *Ab urbe condita*, XXVI. xxxv, trans. Bersuire, II. vi. 19 (Paris, Bibliothèque Sainte-Geneviève, MS fr. 777, f. 254ʳ), 'aussi est il raisons'.

2543 *tomorne yn opyn marketplace.* < Livy, *Ab urbe condita*, XXVI. xxxvi, trans. Bersuire, II. vi. 19 (Paris, Bibliothèque Sainte-Geneviève, MS fr. 777, f. 254ʳ⁻ᵛ), 'en publique ou iour de demain'.

2543–53 *the gret part of the golde and siluer of coyne . . . to be brought to the tresorers of the citee.* Details come, in a different order, from Livy, *Ab urbe condita*, XXVI. xxxvi, trans. Bersuire, II. vi. 19 (Paris, Bibliothèque Sainte-Geneviève, MS fr. 777, f. 254ᵛ), 'tout lor et argent signe . . . soient portez aus tresoriers'.

2544 *print money* = 'printed money'. 1st citation in *OED*, *print*, *adj.*¹, where the gloss and other citations imply that this = 'paper money'; but *MED*, *prenten*, *v.*, 1(a), records reference to stamped coins as 'printed', and *print* seems a variant of that pa. p. (cf. *content* 2177: see n.). < Livy, *Ab urbe condita*, XXVI. xxxvi, trans. Bersuire (II. vi. 19; Paris, Bibliothèque Sainte-Geneviève, MS fr. 777, f. 254ᵛ), 'largent signe'. See also *coyned siluer* 2549 and *brasse money* 2552.

2555 *of here owne fre voulente.* < Livy, *Ab urbe condita*, XXVI. xxxvi, trans. Bersuire, II. vi. 19 (Paris, Bibliothèque Sainte-Geneviève, MS fr. 777, f. 254ᵛ), 'de si grant volente'.

2560 *coyne-money.* Collocation not recorded in *OED*, *coin*, *n.*; the only citation of this collocation in *MED*, *coin*, *n.*, 2a(b).

2564 *this accord.* < Livy, *Ab urbe condita*, XXVI. xxxvi, trans. Bersuire, II. vi. 19 (Paris, Bibliothèque Sainte-Geneviève, MS fr. 777, f. 254ᵛ), 'Cest accort'. The remainder of the sentence extrapolates narrative from the context.

2568 *was.* Subject = pl. *thingis and ordenaunces.*

2569 *senatours, counceilours.* On such apposition, see Introduction, pp. lxxx–lxxxiii. < Livy, *Ab urbe condita*, XXVI. xxxvi, trans. Bersuire, II. vi. 19 (Paris, Bibliothèque Sainte-Geneviève, MS fr. 777, f. 254ᵛ), 'li consul sen alerent chascuns en sa prouince'. WW is perhaps glossing 'consul' or misreading 'sen' (= modern Fr. *s'en* = 'from there') as an abbreviation for *senatours.*

2576 *distributif.* Follows subject and v. *euery . . . hert were* 2575. 1st citation in *OED*, *distributive*, *adj* and *n.*, and only citation in this sense = 'freely giving', in *MED*, *distributif, adj.*, 1.

2580–2 *Here endyth . . . the .xvⁿᵉ.* On *epistle*, see 7n., 1661. On the date 15 June 1475, see Introduction, pp. lvi–lvii.

2580 *vndre correccion.* See 23–4n. for literary models and other uses of this phrase. The sense in this colophon might more literally evoke WW's autograph corrections of the text, as in many references in Fastolf's letters in WW's handwriting to 'correccion *and* amendement' of documents (e.g. *PL*, nos. 983, ll. 24–30; 986, ll. 1–7; 988, l. 6; 989, l. 10, 42–5, 115).

EXPLANATORY NOTES TO ENGLISH
TEXTS FROM THE CODICIL

In cross-references, line numbers or note numbers without prefix refer to the text or notes for *The Boke of Noblesse* itself. Line numbers or note numbers prefixed by C1, C2, etc., refer to the five numbered texts from the Codicil.

TEXT 1: PROLOGUE BY WILLIAM WORCESTER'S SON

C1/1–2 [*Rich*]*arde . . . the Thred*. A later 15th- or early 16th-c. reader altered *Richarde* to *Edwarde*; a late 16th- or early 17th-c. reader, perhaps that of the contents list on f. 7ʳ⁻ᵛ (see Introduction, p. xli, and C1/88–90n.), marked *Thred* with a cross for correction and wrote 'fourth' in the margin. The alteration to Edward IV, WW's dedicatee of *BkNob*. (see 2n., etc. and Introduction, pp. lv–lvi), might suggest some knowledge of the accompanying *BkNob*. *Wars in France*, ii. 521, prints *Edwarde*, suggesting that 'The first three letters . . . have been altered, and are written upon an erasure', but Sutton and Visser-Fuchs, *Richard III's Books*, 85–8, 291–2, argue that this prologue rededicated *BkNob*. and the Codicil to Richard III.

C1/8 *auauncyng . . . publique*. Precisely echoes *BkNob*. 3.

C1/10–11 *.iiij. cardinall vertuse . . . temperaunce*. The *.iiij. cardinall vertues* are mentioned in *BkNob*. 185, as are individual virtues (e.g. *prudence and iustice* 1668), but WW emphasized *iustice* (184–5); this prologue emphasizes fortitude or *force* (here and at C1/33). See also C1/97–112.

C1/17 *Seint Poule . . . fuit*. 1 Cor 15: 10.

C1/19 *fynall pease*. See 397n.

C1/22–3 *holdeth of . . . of God*. The instructions given to English ambassadors attending peace negotiations in Calais in 1439 specified that Normandy and other lordships should be held 'al immediately of God and in no wyse of eny erthly creatur': *Proceedings and Ordinances*, ed. Nicolas, v. 390.

C1/25 *noterily*. See 90n.

C1/25 *feruientlier*. Sp. with medial ⟨i⟩ is not rec. in *OED*, *fervently, adv.*, or *MED*, *ferventli, adv.*, and is perhaps an error from minim confusion.

C1/25–7 *to obteyne . . . enheritaunce*. 2 (non-finite v.) phrases in grammatical apposition, a feature of WW's style as well: see Introduction, pp. lxxx–lxxxiii. Recurrence here suggests it was, or came to be, recognized as a feature of style, not a repeated error.

C1/34 *my pore fadyr William Worcestre.* The only explicit atrribution of *BkNob.* to WW. The phrase suggests that WW has died, i.e. before the end of the reign of Richard III on 22 Aug. 1485 (see C1/1–2n.). The prologue's author calls himself *lege-man* C1/31, so the author was not Worcester's daughter, but which son is unclear: a letter by one son signing himself 'R' mentions a brother and sister (Cambridge, Corpus Christi College, MS 210, pp. 39, 41–2, printed in *Itinerar-ies*, 386). *ODNB, s.n.* Worcester [Botoner], William, and C&A, 33 n. 115, suggest that the Codicil's prologue is by a son called William, but the forename cannot be confirmed.

C1/35–6 *he exercised . . . .xliiij^{ti} yeris.* Despite the pron. *he*, this is a non-finite clause describing Fastolf (= 'him having exercised . . .'). On Fastolf's service, see 2353–5n.

C1/37 *this boke.* See Introduction, p. l.

C1/38 *your . . . predecessoure* = Edward IV, brother of Richard III, to whom WW dedicated *BkNob.* itself (see 2n., 55n., etc.).

C1/40–2 *Renatus Vegesius . . . Tree of Batayles.* Publius Flavius Vegetius Renatus, *Epitoma rei miltaris*; Sextus Iulius Frontinus, *Stratagemata*; Honoré Bouvet, *L'Arbre des batailles.* None were WW's sources for *BkNob.*, but all were sources for Christine de Pizan's *Livre des faits d'armes* on which WW drew heavily, wrongly calling her work *The Tree of Batailles* (152, see n.) and ascribing her words to *Vegecius* (850–5, see n.). WW also elsewhere falsely claims to cite Vegetius directly (614–24, see n.). But WW does credit *Dame Cristen* as his source (151, 163, 165, 789, 875, 878, 903, 930, 1666, 1670), and when giving biographical information in a siden. (see 1666n.). WW's son is ignorant of or ignores her role.

C1/43–4 *experiense . . . conduyte . . . polecye.* The terms occur repeatedly (e.g. 1988, 2057, 2321) and once in close proximity (777–81) in *BkNob.*, as does the contrast of *auctours* (and *auctorite* C1/33) and *experiense* (25 and n.).

C1/44–5 *as wele . . . the lande.* Echoes the close of *BkNob.*: *keping the see as well as the londe* 2577–8.

C1/46 *vndre . . . correccion.* See 23–4n., 2580n., C2/42, etc.

C1/46–7 *[I] submytt me . . . that.* While *submytt* could be a pa. p. premodifying the subject *I* C1/47, the conj. *that* C1/47 introduces a subclause, which requires a preceding main clause, which a finite refl. v. *I submytt me* (as emended) can best supply.

C1/48 *Codicelle* = 'appendix to a will or legal document' (*MED, codicil, n.*; *OED, codicil, n.*), as used in Fastolf's will, in Gairdner, no. 385, and by others (e.g. *PL*, no. 1042, ll. 4, 8, 9). That sense confirms that the Codicil was seen as an appendix to something else, i.e. *BkNob.*

C1/49–56 *conduyte of . . . decease.* Introduces the governance of John, duke of Bedford, as subject of the Codicil, as of much of *BkNob.*

C1/52 *of your partie obidience* = 'of the obedient group under your jurisdiction': collocation not recorded in *OED, party, n.,* but cf. *MED, parti(e, n.,* 5(b), '~adversarie' and '~contrarie': see also *BkNob.* 1450 *partie contrarie*; Codicil, C2/62 *party aduersarie*; *PL,* nos. 509, ll. 26–7, 'partie contrarie'; 518/29–30, 'partye contrarye'; 1049/64, 'partie aduersary'.

C1/55 *.xiij. yeres.* Precisely echoes 478, 1357.

C1/62 *.xxxiiij^{ti} yeres.* Echoes 1218–19 and 1481 (see nn.).

C1/65–7 *Herry the Vte . . . . .xv. days.* Precisely echoes 425 (see n.), 1233.

C1/65 *named kyng.* See 56n., etc. and C1/79 below.

C1/68 *trespasemente.* Precisely echoes 1232–3. See also 292 (and n.), 1317.

C1/68 *aftir that.* Recapitulates *aftir his trespasemente.*

C1/69 *grene age.* Echoes reference to Henry VI's minority at 1373 (see n.), and see also 1349, 1911, 2314–15, 2331.

C1/70–1 *by the statutes . . . realme.* In an ordinance of Aug. 1374, Charles V specified that the age of majority for kings of France was 14: *Ordonnances des roys de France de la troisième race,* vi, ed. D. F. Secousse (Paris, 1741), 26–32 (at 31). The ordinance is mentioned in *GCF,* Charles V, ch. 'Du commencement du roy Charles sisiesme' (*Chron-Jean-Charles,* iii. 384).

C1/75–6 *desired to leue . . . Roon.* Echoes 1360–1.

C1/81 *reuaylyng.* See 64n.

C1/84 *noble* [*line*]. Some word is missing after *noble.* Perhaps *line* has enough of the same letters as *noble* to cause eyeskip. Compare e.g. *noble lynage* 1324.

C1/88–90 *in this boke . . . commytted.* Summarizing Codicil, ff. 8^{r}–11^{r} (Appendix 1 below). The *names* C1/89 evokes the opening word *Nomina* (Appendix 1/4). WW's son's ensuing summary largely follows the reordering of the quires of the Codicil, as evident from the second set of 15th-c. leaf signatures: see Introduction, pp. lxix–lxx. Throughout that summary C1/87–C1/90, C1/112–83, C1/192–222 (ff. 3^{v}–6^{v}), the late 16th- or early 17th-c. hand annotating, perhaps that of the contents list on f. 7^{r–v} (see C1/1–2n.), marks each new item summarized with underlining and/or a trefoil in the margin; the same or another hand in a thinner nib then adds a reference to the late 16th- or early 17th-c. foliation of the Codicil (i.e. excluding this prologue). See Introduction, p. xli. (We have not included these subsequent markings in the textual notes.)

C1/95 *quene ys . . . Dame Iaques.* Jacquetta de Luxembourg (*c.*1416–72), duchess of Bedford and Countess Rivers, mother of Elizabeth Woodville, wife of

Edward IV. This suggests that a version of the prologue to the Codicil was first written for Edward IV and then revised incompletely for Richard III.

C1/97-112 *in this writyng . . . hesteyng.* Summarizes much of the Codicil, but adding reference (as at C1/14) to the *cardinall* virtues, which are not otherwise mentioned in the largely documentary sources in the Codicil.

C1/107 *ablementes of werre.* Set collocation: see e.g. describing Fastolf's arming his household, *PL*, no. 692, ll. 31–2, 46.

C1/107 *arterie* = 'implements of war' (not necessarily guns): see *MED*, *artelrie*, *n.*, where the majority of citations have a sp. without medial ⟨l⟩, as in *OED*, *artry*, *n.*

C1/113-15 *what pencyon . . . councelloures.* Summarizing Codicil, ff. 13ᵛ–14ᵛ (*Wars in France*, ii. 534–6): *pencyon, fees and wages* < 'Pensionum . vadiorum . Regardorum' in the title on f. 13ᵛ.

C1/115-20 *astate of . . . accustomed.* Summarizing Codicil, ff. 14ᵛ–15ᵛ (*Wars in France*, ii. 536–8).

C1/115, 118 *officers royall.* Adj. postposed, as *royall* often is: see Introduction, pp. xc–xci, and *OED*, *royal*, *adj.*, etymology.

C1/117 *procu[rat]ours* = 'legal officials' (*MED*, *procuratour*, *n.*). *Wars in France*, ii. 525, conjects 'procutour'. Fees to 'Aduocato Procuratori Regis' are listed in Codicil, f. 15ʳ (*Wars in France*, ii. 537), the section being summarized here (see C1/115–20n.). How the MS error *procubours* arose is unclear, unless by attraction to **b** in 'Cambiatoris' above 'Procuratori' on Codicil, f. 15ʳ.

C1/120-35 *substaunce of . . . regencye.* Summarizing Codicil, ff. 20ʳ–27ᵛ (*Wars in France*, ii. 547–65).

C1/121 *profites ordinarie* = 'customary profits' (cf. *MED*, *ordinari*, *adj.*, 1.(a), a common collocation to describe profits from the lands in France. See also Lat. 'Soluciones ordinarie' (Codicil, f. 21ʳ; *Wars in France*, ii. 548) and 'Recepta ordinaria' (Codicil, ff. 12ᵛ–13ʳ; *Wars in France*, ii. 532–3).

C1/122 *demaynes.* Common in Eng. but < 'le Demaynes de Normandie', in Fr. among the Lat., in Codicil, f. 20ᵛ (*Wars in France*, ii. 547).

C1/124 *Mayne* = Codicil, ff. 21ᵛ–23ʳ (*Wars in France*, ii. 549–53).

C1/125-9 *Harecourte . . . Newborough.* Place names taken, in slightly different order, from Codicil, f. 23ʳ⁻ᵛ (*Wars in France*, ii. 553–4). Several recur in lists of the regent's titles in Codicil, ff. 8ʳ, 59ᵛ (Appendix 1/8–10, Appendix 3/10–13).

C1/125 *Harecourte.* Harcourt, *département* of Eure.

C1/125 *Dreux. Département* of Eure-et-Loir.

C1/126 *vecounte.* Antedates by 120 years the 1st citation in *OED*, *viscounty*, *n.*, 2 = 'territory' of a viscount, but *MED*, *viscountie*, *n.*, has one citation, earlier.

C1/126 *Ellebeff.* Elbeuf, *département* of Seine-Maritime.

C1/126 *Lyslebone.* Lillebonne, *département* of Seine-Maritime.

C1/127 *Beamount.* Beaumont-le-Roger, *département* of Eure.

C1/127 *baronyes de La Ryuere-de-Tybovyle.* One barony, La Rivière-Thibouville, *département* of Eure, though pl. *baronyes* suggests confusion by WW's son. A list of receipts in Codicil, f. 23ᵛ (*Wars in France*, ii. 554), gives as one entry 'Item receptum de la Ryvere de Thibovile', but the title to the list names it as only 'Tybovile' (f. 23ʳ, *Wars in France*, ii. 553).

C1/128 *Dauvers.* Error for Auvers, *département* of Manche. Error occurs elsewhere in Codicil, e.g. Appendix 3/12.

C1/129 *Newborough.* Le Neubourg, *département* of Eure.

C1/130-1 *taylles . . . gabelle . . . quaterismes.* < Codicil, f. 21ᵛ (*Wars in France*, ii. 550).

C1/132 *t'h'reddis for prysoners.* < 'de tercia parte valoris Prisonarium', Codicil, f. 21ᵛ (*Wars in France*, ii. 550).

C1/134 *tuycion and sauegard.* Common collocation in Codicil, e.g. 'salua Custodia et tuicione' (ff. 21ʳ, 22ᵛ; *Wars in France*, ii. 548, 551).

C1/135 *bethyn.* Rare form favoured also by WW: see e.g. 52n.

C1/136-50 *in this boke . . . Yorke.* Summarizing Codicil, ff. 28ʳ-31ʳ (Appendix 2 below).

C1/140 *secunde viage.* Echoing *secundi viagij*, in WW's longer heading, later crossed out, to the text here summarized, viz. Appendix 2/1-3, textual note. The phrase was conventional (e.g. *second voyage* C3/6).

C1/142-3 *truxe . . . Charlys the VIJᵗʰᵉ.* < *treuga . . . Carolum Septi'mum'* (Appendix 2/10-11) or *tempore treugarum . . . Carolum . VIJ.*, in WW's longer heading later crossed out (printed in Appendix 2/1-3, textual note).

C1/144 *archers.* Perhaps because he has overrun into the marg., the scribe omits ⟨e⟩ and adds a large abbreviation, usually that for medial ⟨m⟩, above the word.

C1/145-7 *whiche was afore . . . was expired* = As events afterwards, during the governorship of Richard, duke of York, showed (*shewed aftir*), Normandy had hitherto (*afore*) been poorly (*nakedly*) provisioned; and *after hys terme exspired*, the governorship was *commytted* to Edmund, duke of Somerset. See C4/2-6n. For other unusual senses of *nakedly*, see *PL*, nos. 604, l. 52, and 888, l. 26, on which see Davis, 'Epistolary', 265.

C1/151-8 *abrygement . . . kyng.* Summarizing Codicil, ff. 51ʳ-55ʳ, edited from a slightly longer text, with collation of variants from Codicil, as 'Documents

Relating to the Anglo-French Negotiations', ed. Allmand, 135–9. Codicil omits Allmand's antepenultimate paragraph of *c.* 280 words ('Item, toutes lesquelles choses . . . passer dela la mer', 138–9) and the final subscription, and places Allmand's penultimate paragraph ('Fait et apointe . . . lan mil CCCC xxxix', 139) last.

C1/151 *abrygement.* Technical legal term widely used in *PROME* and other documentary contexts: *OED, abridgement, n.; MED, abbreg(g)ement, n.* Codicil's text of the peace proposals was also slightly abridged (see C1/151–8n.).

C1/154–8 *present . . . kyng.* Long absolute clauses, listing those present at the peace negotiations at Calais in 1439, incl. Henry Beaufort (d. 1447), bishop of Winchester and cardinal, and Charles (d. 1465), duke of Orléans.

C1/156 *beyng . . . prysonere .xxiiij. yere.* Charles, duke of Orléans, had been a prisoner in England since his capture at the battle of Agincourt in 1415.

C1/158 *kyng.* An eras. before this word (see textual note) was perhaps *called* or *named* as in *BkNob.* before references to Henry VI: see 56n., etc.

C1/158–61 *Whiche petycions . . . Arras.* Adds that the proposals at Calais in 1439 were similar to (*accordyng to*) those at the congress of Arras, held between 5 Aug. and 21 Sept. 1435.

C1/161 *duryng by* = 'continuing for'. See *OED, by, prep.* and *adv.,* A.III.20, 'for'; *MED, bi, prep.,* 4.(c).

C1/161–5 *the seide cardinall . . . partye.* Long absolute clauses listing those present at the congress of Arras.

C1/163–4 *ij. cardinallys . . . Cypres.* Niccolò Albergati (d. 1443), cardinal priest of Santa Croce, and Hugues de Lusignan (d. 1442), known as the cardinal of Cyprus. The two epithets are joined without a conjunction in grammatical apposition, as in WW's style: see Introduction, pp. lxxx–lxxxiii.

C1/165–6 *in the tyme of . . . deceasid* = 'around the time when' John, duke of Bedford, died (i.e. around 14 Sept. 1435).

C1/166 *and in the dissoluyng of the forsaide conuencion.* Clarifying that Bedford died (14 Sept. 1435) during (*and in*) the process of *dissoluyng* the congress of Arras (ending 21 Sept. 1435).

C1/177–83 *oppynyons and . . . conduyte.* Summarizing Codicil, ff. 38ʳ–43ᵛ (printed as text C2). On the order of texts in the Codicil when Worcester's son wrote the summary in C1, see Introduction, pp. lxix–lxx.

C1/182 *after.* Conj.; = 'as'. See 1812 (and n.).

C1/184 *the case . . . chaunged.* WW also made an autograph comment in the Codicil conceding that information about the 1420s, 1430s, and 1440s was not a perfect guide to the 1470s: f. 32^r (*Wars in France*, ii. 565). See Wakelin, *Humanism*, 109.

C1/191 *reason vaylable.* For the postposed adj., see Introduction, p. xci.

C1/192–9 *certeyne avertisementis . . . councellyd.* Summarizing Codicil, ff. 44^r–47^r (printed as text C3). After the first reordering of quires, this text straddled two quires signed *E* (like the text summarized in C1/176–83) and *F*.

C1/202 *more rypliere.* Davis, 'Epistolary', 262–3, notes that a double comparative adv. construction is common in WW's own language, and that this phrase occurs in *PL*, no. 535, l. 18.

C1/206–9 *inuentorie . . . Roone.* Summarizing Codicil, ff. 32^r–37^r (*Wars in France*, ii. 565–74). After the first reordering of quires, this quire had the leaf signature *G*.

C1/210 *Maunce, Mayn.* Both the city of Le Mans (*Maunce*) and its county of Maine: see 531–2n.

C1/210 *Sent-Zusan.* Sainte-Suzanne, *département* of Mayenne.

C1/212, 221 *ducdom.* See 21–2n.

C1/214–22 *certeyn articles . . . chauntithe.* Summarizing Codicil, ff. 47^v–50^r (printed as texts C4 and C5). At this point, WW's son stops following the order of the Codicil after first reordering and jumps back to part of the quire with the leaf signature *F* at the time that he was writing. *Also . . . ys made mencyon* might suggest that this is an afterthought.

C1/222 *chauntithe*='makes clear' (?). *MED*, *chaunten*, *v.* (1), does not record this figurative, intransitive sense, which is akin to, and antedates, the 1st citation in *OED*, *chant*, *v.*, II.5.a ('to harp on about something').

TEXT 2: SIR JOHN FASTOLF'S ARTICLES RELATING TO THE CONGRESS OF ARRAS, 1435

C2/1–24 *Here folowen . . . Herry VJth.* WW adds this heading in space left blank on the top two-thirds of the page, then continues (from *graunt* 20) down the left margin in the gutter, alongside the main scribe's copying of C2/25 ff.

C2/3 *graunt maister.* Antedates 1st citation in *OED*, *grand master*, *n.*; not in *MED*, under *graunt*, *adj.*;<Fr. *grand maistre*, 'chief official of a household or military unit'.

C2/10 *trux generalle.* For the postposed adj., see Introduction, p. xci.

C2/11–20 *renounce . . . graunt or condecend.* WW sometimes translates, sometimes paraphrases, the French demands of 1439, which restated those of 1435; they are in Codicil, f. 51^{r-v}, 'Lun touchant la renonciaction . . . ont contredit plainnement' (printed from a different MS in 'Documents Relating to the Anglo-French Negotiations', ed. Allmand, 135).

C2/13 *second poynt*. The 1st point was *the condicion* C2/11. WW's French source makes the enumeration clearer with 'Lun . . . Et lautre' (Codicil, f. 51^r; 'Documents Relating to the Anglo-French Negotiations', ed. Allmand, 135).

C2/17 *homage lyege*. *lyege* can function as an adj.='feudal' (*MED*, *lege*, *adj.*, 3.(a); *OED*, *liege*, *adj.* and *n.*, A.2), i.e. here postmodifying *homage*, but *liege homage* was a technical status in feudal law, recorded in *OED*, *liege*, *adj.* and *n.*, Compounds, and in one citation in *MED* under both *homage*, *n.*, 1.(a), and *lege*, *adj.*, 3(a) from *PROME*, itself reporting the French demands of 1439 'en foy et hommaige lige ressort et souuerainete' (Codicil, f. 51^r; 'Documents Relating to the Anglo-French Negotiations', ed. Allmand, 135), which doublets WW echoes here (*yn feyth and yn homage lyege, ressort and souuereynte*).

C2/17 *paree one of the pares*. The emendation of *paree one* in *Wars in France*, ii. 575, 'parceone', is cited in *MED* as a misspelling ('[read: parceonere]') of *par-cener*, *n.*, 1.(c),='fellow' or 'partner'; see similarly *OED*, *parcener*, *n*. But in the MS two words *paree one* are split over a line break and not marked with any hyphen as the next line break is ('deman-|des'), and double *ee* is clear. Trans. < French demands of 1439 in Codicil, f. 51^r, 'en parrie comme les aultres pers de france'. See *DMF*, *parrie*, *n.*, 'Dignité de pair attachée à un grand fief relevant immédiatement de la couronne'. This calque of the Fr. word seems not to be included in *MED* or *OED*.

C2/19 *yn kyng ys behalf*. *MED*, *bihalve*, *n.*, and *OED*, *behalf*, *n.*, cite *behalf* preceded only by a limited range of possessive nouns, viz. *emperor's* and *God's*; *kingis behalue* recurs at C2/30.

C2/30 *It is thought them*='it seems to them' (*OED*, *think*, *v.*^{1}).

C2/31 *vndere . . . correccion*. See 23–4n., 258on. Here and at the start of subsequent articles (e.g. C2/42, C2/47, C2/65, etc.), this phrase refers not to the historical figures described but to the author of these articles, expressing humility before the king or his council as he presumes to advise his superiors. It usually follows the phrase introducing the advice in impersonal terms e.g. *(h)it semyth* up to C2/64, or *yt is thought* from C2/86 onwards, or *it may be ordeined* C2/208. Such use occurs in Lat. proposals gathered into WW's notebook, Arundel, f. 333^r ('Sub correccione atque benigne supportacione').

C2/47 *vndere . . . correccion*. See C2/31n.

C2/48–59 *diuers treties . . . auauntage*. For such treaties, see 1001–1187 and nn. The Treaty of Amiens (*Amyenx* C2/52–4) between John, duke of Bedford, Philippe le Bon, duke of Burgundy, and Jean, duke of Brittany was signed on 17

Apr. 1423 (Richard Vaughan, *Philip the Good: The Apogee of Burgundy* (London, 1970), 9).

C2/52 *pees finall.* See 397n.

C2/56–7 *notwithstonding . . . othes, sacramentes or promises.* Same formula in *BkNob.* 1180–1.

C2/59–61 *and the kingis men . . . bothe.* A new absolute clause: = 'and the men of the [English] king and of the king of Navarre [having been] put out of France and Normandy'.

C2/64 *etc.* This alludes to some assumed knowledge, perhaps of the broken truces enumerated in *BkNob.*

C2/65–72 *And therfore . . . disherite hymsilf* = 'Henry VI should *not* (C2/68) pay attention (*rewarde*) either to *clamour* from people who (*which* C2/69) naturally love his enemy *nor* (C2/70) to (*for* C2/70) the destruction of the land, which is preferable to losing that land; nor (*ner* C2/71) must he give up his title the land.'

C2/65 *vndere . . . correccion.* See C2/31n.

C2/73 *assignacion.* Antedates 1st citation in this sense (= 'allocation' of property to others) in *OED, assignation, n.,* senses 1 or 2; but *MED, assignacioun, n.,* has many 15th-c. citations, which, though not parsed thus, have this sense in context.

C2/78–80 *which, though . . . contrarie—that God defende!—his name . . . wolde abide* = 'which fortune sent by God [*it,* referring back to *aduenture* C2/77], even if (*though*) it is against the king—God forbid!—nonetheless his name etc. would abide. For the interj., see also C2/101–2, etc.

C2/83 *soche on goode day . . . that* = 'one such good day . . . when', i.e. *among many* bad days: see *OED, such, adj.* and *pron.,* V.28.b.

C2/98 *myghtly.* See 198n.

C2/105–6 *that . . . that.* The 3nd *that* is recapitulative, after the intervening subclause (see next n.).

C2/105–6 *aftere that the case stondith now* = 'as the situation stands now'.

C2/106 *con[d]ui[t]e[d].* MS *contuideth,* with *h* over an unerased letter; but syntax in this doublet requires a pa. p. We parse the medial sp. with ⟨t⟩ then ⟨d⟩ as a misspelling of *conduited* = PDE *conducted,* a sp. recorded in *OED, conduct, v.,* Forms, and *MED, conduiten, v.,* where it antedates the 1st citation in this sense in *OED, conduct, v.,* II.6. This sense is not recorded in *MED, conduiten, v.,* though a related sense is in *MED, conducten, v.*

C2/111 *to conquest.* Antedates 1st citation in *OED, conquest, v.,* but *MED, conquesten, v.,* has earlier citations.

C2/129 *Crotay.* Le Crotoy, port on the northern coast of France.

C2/131 *Vermandoys.* Vermandois, a historic county in eastern Picardy around Saint-Quentin.

C2/132 *Lannoys.* The Laonnois, the area around Laon on the border of Picardy and Champagne.

C2/132 *Bourgoyne*=Burgundy. The 2nd syllable is abbreviated as superscript **ne**; our expansion here and at C2/236 follows the full spelling in WW's addition at C2/54.

C2/138 *them thinke it.* The impersonal v. (='it seems to them').

C2/140 *an[c]ien.* MS *anoien* could be related to *MED, avouen, v.* (1), or *MED, vouen, v.* (1),='sworn' (enemy), but more likely is a miscopying of **c** as **o**, from 'ancien', often sp. without final ⟨t⟩ (e.g. *auncien* C2/218). France was commonly described as the 'ancien enemye' in e.g. *PROME* (and see *auncien aduersaries* 107), though *OED, ancient, adj.* and *n.*¹, A.II.5.a, attests this sense only from 1579.

C2/142 *reke nere shame*='care nor be ashamed' (i.e. to be a traitor). The MS runs *reke nere* together, perhaps misreading as *OED, recover, v.*¹. But sp. ⟨reke⟩ is attested (*OED, reck, v.*), and sp. 'nere' for *nor* recurs in these articles (e.g. C2/27, C2/217).

C2/143–4 *willful [h]edi[ne]s.* MS *ediens* is inexplicable. It perhaps miscopies the uncommon *headiness*, as in WW's phrase *after his owne wilfulnesse and hedinesse* in 2393–4, and 'willes ande hedynes' in his revisions to Scrope, *Dicts*, 38, l. 21. *MED, hedinesse, n.*, is commonly collocated with *will*. *Wars in France*, ii. 580, emends to '[disob]ediens', which makes sense in context, but how such a scribal error would arise is hard to explain.

C2/146 *borders.* MS *borderers* seems to be dittography; *MED, bordure, n.*, 1.(b), cites this from *Wars in France*, ii. 580, as a variant sp., but with no other citations; *OED, border, n.*, does not cite it. The much later *OED, borderer, n.*, does not refer to a place.

C2/147 *Chartraine.* The area around Chartres in central France, south-east of Maine.

C2/147 *Britayne*=Brittany.

C2/147 *suggestion. OED, suggestion, n.*, 7, and *MED, suggestioun, n.*, 3, list this sp. from *Ipomedon* as 'Misused' for *OED, subjection, n.*, I.1, and *MED, subgeccioun, n.*; but *MED* also cites Scrope, *Dicts*, 309, l. 27, and the recurrence suggests that this was an acceptable sense and sp. in WW's milieu.

C2/151 *appatise*='exact tribute from'. This sp. not in *OED* or *MED*. By date of composition, not of MS, *appatise* would antedate by one year the 1st citation in

OED, patise, v., MED, patisen, v. See also *patised* 2219n. and the n. *apatismentis* C4/60n.

C2/159 *bith* = 'are'. For the ⟨th⟩ inflection in the 3 pl. pr., see Introduction, p. xcvi, and *beth* C2/117.

C2/163 *noote of tirannye.* Echoed in 223.

C2/166 *prince* = 'capture' or 'exactions (i.e. in war)'. A calque on Fr.: see *DMF, prise, n.*[1], with frequent forms sp. with ⟨n⟩ (*prinse*), which are not recorded in *OED, prise, n.*[2], or *MED, prise, n.* (1).

C2/169 *be.* The subject (= the *aduersaries* C2/168) is not repeated, though this is a main clause.

C2/173 *ribaudekyns.* By date of composition, not of MS, this antedates 1st citation (1443) in *OED, ribaudequin, n.,* and *MED, ribaudekin, n.*

C2/173 *culueryns.* By date of composition, not of MS, this antedates 1st citation (1443) in *MED, culverin, n.,* and (1466) in *OED, culverin, n.*

C2/175 *of necessarie* = 'necessary'. Construction is not recorded in *OED, necessary, adj.* and *n.,* or *MED, necessarie, n.* Perhaps a scribal error for *of necessite* (found at C2/187).

C2/175 *conduyt.* By date of composition, not of MS, this antedates the 1st citation (1454) in this sense (= 'management') in *MED, conduit, n.,* 5, or *OED, conduct, n.,* II.6.a, from *PL,* no. 509, l. 25, by Fastolf and in WW's handwriting.

C2/177 *prenable.* 1st citation in *OED, prenable, adj.,* but *MED, prenable, adj.,* has one doubtful earlier citation.

C2/190 *amongis.* The 3rd syllable is abbreviated in the MS, and no preferred sp. in full occurs in scribe B's work; we expand following the scribe of *BkNob.,* who prefers *amongis.*

C2/202 *whereas there* = 'where there is'. Implying 'where they have' (and *there* = perhaps PDE pron. *their*). Perhaps *as* is a scribal error for *is,* but sense is clear otherwise.

C2/209 *myghtelie.* Cf. 198n.

C2/213 *faren with foule.* Common phrasal v. (*MED, faren, v.,* 8.(a), = 'treated'), often collocated as *fare foul with,* = 'treat badly' (recorded in *OED, fare, v.*[1], II.4.c, and 2 citations in *MED, foule, adv.,* under 3.(a) and 4.(a)), so we emend to remove inflectional *-d* as a scribal error, caused by the MS's l. break after *fou* and eyeskip with *distroied.*

C2/215–16 *cours of marchaundice* = 'free movement of trade'.

C2/216 *Scluse.* Sluis, now in the Netherlands.

C2/232 *Iene*=Genoa.

C2/234 *outeraunce*. 1st citation in *MED, outraunce, n.*; by date of composition, not of MS, antedates by one year 1st citation in *OED, utterance, n.*[1]. (N.B. different from *OED, outrance, n.*)

C2/234–5 *well-helpen and strenghted*. Still governed by modal v. *shall* C2/233; auxiliary v. *be* is understood. The form of the pa. p. *helpen* is rare, perhaps an error for *holpen*.

C2/236 *Duke Burgoyne*=Philippe le Bon. See 490–1n. For the sp., see C2/132n.

C2/238 *feith*. By date of composition, not of MS, this v. (as it must be after the modal *shuld*) slightly antedates the 1st citation in *MED, feithen, v.*, and *OED, faith, v.*, from Margery Kempe's *Boke* (dated *c*.1438). The exact sense here='give one's pledge to' (?), is not captured in *MED* nor quite in *OED*, though it is closer to later senses 2 and 4 there.

C2/242 *outrecuidaunce*. 1st citation in *MED, outrecuidaunce, n.*, and 1st by date of composition, not of MS, in *OED, outrecuidance, n.*

C2/244 *And which thing*='leaving alliances', for whatever reason.

C2/245 *day[li]e*. MS *day be* probably confused **li** for **b**; compare the visually similar *dailie* at C4/40 (f. 48ʳ). For this emendation, see *Wars in France*, ii. 584.

C2/252 *scaling*. Antedates 1st citation of *OED, scaling, n.*, but *MED, scaling, ger.*, has citations from earlier MSS and texts.

C2/259 *but as the chois*='unless [this is the] choice'.

C2/260 *[be] famyn be fayne*. As at C2/199, the articles recommend famine to drive the enemy to surrender. As such, the prep. *be*, the usual sp. for PDE *by*, is needed. Perhaps omitted by confusion with the subsequent *be fayne* with a similar sequence of letters.

C2/272 *bi [them] speciallie*. The MS prep.+adv. is probably an error, perhaps for *by speciality*,='in particular' (see *MED, specialte*, 1.(a); *OED, specialty, n.*, P1), but better sense is given by supplying a pron. *them*, referring to the *Englisshemen* of C2/270–1, whose advice is contrasted with *Frenshe* counsel.

TEXT 3: ARTICLES OF THE COUNCIL OF RICHARD, DUKE OF YORK, 1440

C3/1–10 *Here folowen . . . xlv*. WW adds in the top margin in 2 stints with different colours of ink. The 2nd stint starts at *toke the charge* and continues in the right margin, much of it from *the ij. day* to *yere of* over erasure.

C3/6-8 *at hys second . . . Hery the .VJ.* Arrangements were still being made for York's *second voyage* in May 1441 (*Proceedings and Ordinances of the Privy Council*, ed. Nicolas, v. 145, 146), and he did not arrive in Normandy until late June 1441, almost a year after his appointment. A letter from the council at Rouen, complaining of the delay, is copied into the Codicil (ff. 57ʳ and 58ʳ⁻ᵛ; *Wars in France*, ii. 603–7). These articles are not otherwise dated; earlier ones are alluded to at C3/11-12, C3/28, C3/36, C3/118-19. Lines C3/82-3, C3/88 refer to the *letting and empeschement of the vitailing of Hareflewe* and to the possibility that York might be asked to lay siege to Harfleur; that implies that the town, taken by the English in late Oct. 1440 (see 835–7n.), is still under French control, suggesting a date before then for some of these articles. In the prologue to the Codicil WW's son describes the present text (C3) as *taken and wretyn oute of the writyng of many othir grete articles and auertisementis at the seide tyme devised and councellyd* (C1/197-9), so this text may combine different sets of articles. York's articles are referred to in *Proceedings and Ordinances of the Privy Council*, ed. Nicolas, v. 133 (13 Feb. 1441), 145 (16 May 1441), 159 (17 Nov. 1441). For discussion of these and the terms of York's appointment, see Griffiths, *Henry VI*, 459–61; P. A. Johnson, *Duke Richard of York, 1411-1460* (Oxford, 1988), 35–8.

C3/8-10 *toke the charge . . . Mˡ. iiijᶜ. xlv.* As WW's heading correctly states, York's 2nd lieutenancy ran from 2 July 1440 until Michaelmas 1445 (see 1235–40n.).

C3/11 *my.* Throughout C3, York's council speaks in the first person singular, referring to York in the third person (e.g. *my saide lorde* C3/13), presumably because the instructions were composed by a single member of that council, perhaps Fastolf.

C3/11-12 *vppon . . . late.* An allusion to a previous set of articles.

C3/12-13 *my lordis . . . lordis, counseile* = 'my lords of the king, our sovereign lord's, council'.

C3/13 *my said lorde.* See C3/11.

C3/18-19 *goode publique.* Here and at C3/152 = a translation of Lat. *res publica*, differing from the three Eng. translations found in *BkNob.*: see 3n., etc., and for the concept generally in *BkNob.*, 1731–1842, 2055–8.

C3/28 *othere of my said lordes articles.* See C3/11-12, C3/36.

C3/30 *hym* = 'the duke of Brittany', who can be called to aid York's army.

C3/31 *like as he* = 'just as he, the duke of Brittany' can reciprocally call on York's army.

C3/32 *as for.* Continues, after the parenthetical *like as he . . . lorde*, describing how York *myght call hym* (= 'the duke of Brittany' C3/30) for help *as for* (= 'on behalf of') *the king.*

C3/36 *other articles.* See C3/11–12, C3/28.

C3/39–42 *the somme . . . to be . . . deliuered and paid.* An absolute clause with inf. v. *to . . .* dependent on *yt hath liked* C2/36, adding York's remuneration to his appointment.

C3/40 *entretenement.* 1st citation, in any sense, in *OED, entertainment, n.,* I.1.a, and only citation in *MED, entertenement, n.*

C3/44 *desireth.* Introduces a long list of York's requirements, each introduced with *that*+a clause or *to*+inf., in different eventualities (*in cas that,* etc. C3/46, C3/50–1, C3/53).

C3/52 *as he can*='so that he can'.

C3/55 *socours.* Sp. with final ⟨s⟩ is common in 15th-c. Eng.: see *OED, succour, n.,* Forms.

C3/64 *Item.* Here onwards the MS marks each new paragraph or 'article' with a red paraph.

C3/67 *Maideston stone.* Kentish ragstone, quarried near Maidstone, was used to make cannonballs in the 15th c.: Clifford J. Rogers, 'Gunpowder Artillery in Europe, 1326–1500: Innovation and Impact', in Robert S. Ehlers Jr., Sarah K. Douglas, and Daniel P. M. Curzon (eds.), *Technology, Violence, and War: Essays in Honor of Dr. John F. Guilmartin, Jr.* (Leiden, 2019), 37–71 at 49–50.

C3/67 *foulers.* Antedates 1st citation in *OED, fowler, n.,* 3, and the 1st citation, apart from macaronic accounts, in *MED, fouler, n.*

C3/68 *fournysshe.* If these articles are datable to 1440, this antedates the 1st citation of 1442 in *OED, furnish, v.,* and *MED, furnishen, v.* Given the novelty of the borrowing, the uninflected pa. p. *fournysshe* without final ⟨d⟩ might not be a scribal error. See also *furnysshid* C4/46 datable to 1448.

C3/68 *last.* The exact measurement of a *last* varies but for gunpowder (of which *saltpetire* is the main ingredient) it came to be 2,400 lb: see *OED, last, n.*[2], II.2.a.

C3/71 *maistre gonners.* 1st citation in *OED, master gunner, n.;* only citation in *MED, maistre, n.,* 1.(f), ~*gonner.*

C3/71–2 *yemen gonners.* By date of composition, not of MS, antedates 1st and only citation in *OED, yeoman, n.,* C.2, *yeoman gunner;* 1st citation in *MED, yeman, n.,* 1.(c), ~*gonner.*

C3/73–4 *speres-shaftes.* Neither *OED, spear-shaft, n.,* nor *MED, spere-shaft, n.,* record forms where the first element (as edited) has a pl. inflection, so this is perhaps a mistaken double ⟨ss⟩ medially; but the MS's word division and punctus *speres . shaftes* suggest the first ⟨s⟩ is understood as part of the 1st element.

C3/74 *.CC. groos.* As a *groos* is 12 dozen, this=28,800 bowstrings. The *groos* is a common unit of measurement for bowstrings in military accounts: see *MED*, *grose, n.*

C3/75 *paueis of ordonnaunce*='large shields [for defence] of military equipment'.

C3/82–3 *for letting . . . Hareflewe*='for the impeding and obstruction of the victualling of Harfleur'. See C3/6–8n. For the sp. of Harfleur, see 426–56n.

C3/83–4 *for the seure . . . Rouen.* By contrast with blockading French-controlled Harfleur, the navy will ensure supplies reach English-controlled Rouen.

C3/85 *Diepe.* Dieppe, *département* of Seine-Maritime, then, as this article says, a major fishing port. Taken by the French in 1435.

C3/92–3 *myght be the comaundement . . . lande. be*=PDE 'by'; *lande*=a v. in a triplet with *acompaignie* and *strenght*.

C3/95 *tarie.* Not scribal confusion of **c** and **t** in an exemplar; more likely is some sense='retain, impound', a sense not quite recorded in, but close to, *OED, tarry, v.*, 2, or *MED, tarien, v.* (1), 2.(b) or 2.(a).

C3/116 *lorde good grace. lorde*='lord's', an unmarked possessive.

C3/119 *king.* MS *king lord* could be omitting an epithet *our sovereign* (used 3 times in C3) or *our said sovereign* (used 4 times), but more likely seems repetition by attraction of *lord* nearby.

C3/125 *king . . . goode lordship.* See similarly C3/116n.

C3/131–2 *the first halue-yere . . . expired.* An absolute clause with a pa. p.:='the 6 months being finished'.

C3/134 *lay.* i.e.='encamp': see *MED, leien*, 12.(d).

C3/138 *capitaineries.* 1st citation in *MED, capitainerie, n.*; antedates 1st citation in *OED, captainry, n.*

C3/139 *retrait.* 1st citation in *OED, retrait, adj.*,='reserved for'. *MED* parses as the pa. p. of the v. *retraien*, 1.(b), but that does not seem correct in this context.

C3/152 *goode publique.* See C3/18–19n.

C3/163 *seuirte.* The minims *ui* could equally be *iu*; neither sp. is common, but *MED, seurte, n.*, records the same sp. printed by Blayney, 4, l. 27, 192, l. 3, and see likewise *seuirly* 12, l. 20.

C3/165 *lieuten[aunt].* MS *lieutene* seems an error, perhaps prompted by the l. break. This form without the syllable ⟨a(u)nt⟩ is not recorded in *OED, lieutenant, n.*; this is the only citation in *MED, lieutenaunt, n.*

C3/170 *my said lord, the duke, charge.* Both *lord* and *duke* are unmarked possessives (see C3/116n., C3/125), here with *the duke* as an epithet in grammatical apposition clarifying which *lord* is referred to (i.e. York, not Henry VI), as at C3/172.

C3/172-3 *deuoure*. Not minim confusion of **u** for **i**; the sp. ⟨our⟩ is common and captured the likely pronunciation: see *OED*, *devoir*, *n.*, Forms.

C3/177 *Grete and Priue Seales*. The Great Seal was used by the Chancellor, the Privy Seal by the king.

TEXT 4: SIR JOHN FASTOLF'S INSTRUCTIONS TO EDMUND BEAUFORT, DUKE OF SOMERSET, MARCH 1448

C4/2-6 *Edmond . . . Harry the Sexte*. Edmund Beaufort, duke of Somerset, was appointed *lieuetenaunt and gouuernour generall* on 24 Dec. 1446 for a term of three years, to begin on 1 Mar. 1447. M. K. Jones dates these instructions to 30 Mar. 1448. Somerset had arrived in Rouen by 22 Apr. 1448: Jones, 'The Beaufort Family', 191, 202-3, 208.

C4/8 *First*. In the MS a paraph precedes this and the next 2 articles only (C4/17, C4/22).

C4/8 *goode correcion*. See 23-4n., 258on., C2/31, etc.

C4/14-15 *yff any charge . . . ayenst you*. For similar concerns about future accusations, see C3/126-9, C3/163-75.

C4/16 *can or dare*. See C4/36-7.

C4/16 *done for you* = 'act [*done*: inf.] on your behalf'.

C4/17-18 *It is thought . . . to be made* = 'It is thought (necessary) to establish'.

C4/17 *correccion beforesaide*. See C4/8.

C4/18 *conueieng*. Either = 'contracting' or = 'communicating'.

C4/19-20 *appointement breking*. For this construction, see Introduction, pp. lxxxvii–lxxxviii, and C4/37 (see n.), etc.

C4/24-5 *rightwiselie*. MS separates as *right wiselie*. The chancellor should be *wise* as well C4/22, but this adv. describes executing *iustice*, so PDE *righteously* seems correct. *MED*, *rightwisli*, *adv.*, records the sp. as frequent, including in Blayney, 72, l. 23.

C4/26-7 *that there may . . . confourme them to* = 'who there may act in conformity with'. For *there*, *Wars in France*, ii. 593, prints 'theie', but the MS is unambiguous; *there* = 'on the duke of Somerset's council'.

C4/33 *sene too* = 'provided for'.

C4/36–41 *oppressours ner extorcioners . . . abbregging her souldeours wages.* Concerns, and some vocabulary, shared in 877–910, there from Christine de Pizan, and 2168–251 on *oppressions* (2189, 2202) by English *extorcion* (909, 2189) of the locals in Normandy due to *abbregging* (908, 2173) of soldiers' wages.

C4/36–7 *can and dare.* See C4/16.

C4/37 *iustice-keping.* Common phrase in *BkNob.*: see 1328, 1621, etc. For the construction, see Introduction, pp. lxxxvii–lxxxviii.

C4/42–5 *ordinaunce . . . require.* See similarly C5/60–4.

C4/44 *ridbawdkyns.* See C2/173.

C4/45 *that parties.* See also C4/64. Common in *BkNob.*: see 89–90n.

C4/50 *furnysshid.* See C3/68n.

C4/51 *Pounthorson, Aueraunshes.* Pontorson and Avranches, *département* of Manche, on the border of Normandy and Brittany.

C4/53 *places.* Pl. inflection is abreviated in the MS. Scribe B prefers the sp. ⟨is⟩ on this word, but only in text C4 uses ⟨es⟩ on this word, so we expand here contrary to his preference elsewhere.

C4/59 *[a]fer[r]aunt.* The scribe probably misreads a short **r** of secretary script in his exemplar as **u** and elides the initial vowel with the article. *MED, afferaunt, n.* = 'proportion' (i.e. according to the size): see similarly *after the quantite and afferaunt* in *BkNob.* 1305–6 and in OMA, FP 47, 'after the afferaunt of there degree'. *Wars in France*, ii. 594, prints 'theferante'.

C4/60 *apatismentis.* 1st citation in *MED, apatisment, n.*; not in *OED*; and cf. 2219n. See also *appatise* C2/151.

C4/64 *to that parties.* See C4/45n.

C4/68 *forsean . . . that* = 'provided . . . that'.

TEXT 5 : SIR JOHN FASTOLF'S ADVICE ON
RELIEVING THE DUKE OF SOMERSET, 1450

C5/12 *beyng beseged at Caen.* The siege of Caen took place in June 1450. The list of places lost 'durant la charge et gouuernance du duc de Somerset', in Arundel, f. 287ᵛ, states that the siege lasted until the vigil of St John (23 June).

C5/14 *auertisment "were" not kept.* WW, correcting, perhaps misread the pl. inflection *-ys* on the noun *auertismentys* as the pr. 3 sg. *ys* and replaced it with a subjunctive *were*. This turns a typical absolute clause, with a participle, into a subclause with a finite v., but WW does not accordingly adjust the prep. *of* to a conj. (e.g. *that*).

C5/14–16 *Ser Thomas Kyriell . . . Fermynye*. Battle of Formigny, 15 Apr. 1450: see 1264–71 and n.

C5/15 *made for the feelde* = 'appointed for this campaign'. Antedates 1st citation in this wider sense in *OED, field, n.,* 6.d; not recorded in *MED, feld, n.,* 6.a, but close to 6.c. or 7.

C5/15 *infortune*. Adj. not recorded in *OED* (nor in *infortune, v.,* e.g. as pa. p.); only citation in *MED, infortune, adj.*

C5/18 *pety capteyns*. Cited in *OED, petty captain, n.* Depending on the date of WW's revisions to the Codicil (which this term is part of), possibly antedating *OED*'s other 1st citation dated to 1475, which is also in *MED, peti, adj.,* 1.(b). See also 1268.

C5/23 *vnder . . . correccion*. For similar formulae, see C2/31 (and n.), etc.

C5/34–5 *as the avice of . . . counceile*. *Wars in France* emends *as* to *at*, but *as* loosely introduces the advice of the king's council.

C5/36 *Item*. Here onwards the MS marks each new 'article' with a paraph.

C5/55 *marchal*. MS abbreviation to *mar^{al}*. *OED* and *MED, marshal, n.,* record both two-syllable and three-syllable forms, as in *mareshall* 380, 420, and *marchall(e)* 490, 523, 2153; the expanded abbreviation here follows the commoner form, as collocated in *BkNob.* with *conestable or marchalle* 2153.

C5/60–4 *ordynaunces for the felde . . . parties*. Precisely echoes C4/42–4.

C5/64 *into parties*. Variant (perhaps an error?) for the idiom *in that parties* as in the related passage C4/45.

C5/65–74 *admiralles . . . redie*. Same general point as C4/66–71, including the same list of ports and some of the same vocabulary.

C5/66 *streitlie*. This sense (= 'firmly'?) not recorded in *OED, straightly, adv.,* or *MED, streightli, adv.*; antedates two citations in *MED, strictli, adv.,* which sense seems related.

C5/82 *Explicit . . . opusculum*. WW adds a colophon, but this is the end only of the collection of articles in English; the Codicil continues.

GLOSSARY

The Glossary includes words obsolete in Present Day English, words which are used at some points in senses obsolete in Present Day English, or words in confusing spellings. For comparison, some familiar senses or spellings are glossed alongside the unfamiliar ones. In most cases *OED* is used to adjudicate what is obsolete. The Glossary lists variant spellings of words here glossed, except for variation between vocalic ⟨i⟩ or ⟨y⟩ and consonantal ⟨u⟩ or ⟨v⟩. It usually lists line references only for the first three instances of most words, senses, or spellings.

Alphabetization follows spelling in the manuscripts and, where variant spellings occur, usually the spelling that would come earliest in the alphabet (including where spellings occur both with and without initial ⟨h⟩). However, the manuscripts' uses of ⟨i⟩ or vocalic ⟨y⟩ and ⟨u⟩ or ⟨v⟩ are alphabetized by the modern equivalent spelling, and where the manuscripts' consonantal ⟨i⟩ would in modern spelling become ⟨j⟩ (on which see Introduction, pp. c–ci) it is alphabetized under ⟨j⟩. This includes creating sets of entries under ⟨j⟩ and ⟨u⟩.

Line references without a prefix are to *The Boke of Noblesse* itself; those prefixed with C1, C2, etc., are to the extracts 1, 2, etc., of the Codicil. The Appendices, largely in Latin, are not included in the Glossary.

ABBREVIATIONS

1/2/3 sg./pl. first, second, third person singular/plural
adj. adjective
adv. adverb
comp. comparative
conj. conjunction
gen. genitive
impers. impersonal (verb)
indecl. indeclinable
infin. infinitive
interj. interjection
n. noun
pa. past

pa. p. past or passive participle
pl. plural
pr. present
pr. p. present participle
prep. preposition
pron. pronoun
refl. reflexive
sg. singular
subj. subjunctive
superl. superlative
v. verb
vbl. n. verbal noun (gerund)

A

A *interj.* Ah 1281, 2273, 2487
abandonned *pa. p.* sacrificed 1445, 2134; **habandonned** 2520, **haboundonned** 2555–6
abated *pa. p.* reduced 1515
abbregging *n.* reducing 908, C4/41
abill *adj.* able C4/53, C5/49, **habill** 2475, **hable** 2071; **abillere** *adj. comp.* more able C4/47
abillementis *n. pl.* equipment C3/64,

ablementes C1/107, **habillementis** C2/116
abreggement *n.* reduction 2173
accepted *pa. p.* considered 862, 863, received 2259
according *n.* proof 1278
accordyng *adj.* corresponding C1/158–9, C3/69
accordithe *pr. 3 sg.* agrees 1739; **accorden** *pr. 3 pl.* agree 1530
accustomed *pa. 3. pl.* were accustomed 2341; **accustomed** *pa. p.* calculated

to owe in tax 539, allocated C1/120, **accustumed** made customary 2367

acyn *adv.* similar, akin 1319

acompt *n.* financial reckoning C3/110

acquitaile *n.* carrying out of duties C2/42

act *n.* deed 558, 568; **actis** *pl.* deeds 256, 309, 979, etc., narratives 1819

admynestred *pa. p.* supplied C2/4

admonestementis *n. pl.* admonishments 2391

adnullyng *vbl. n.* putting an end to C1/179

aduaileable *adj.* beneficial C5/33

aduenture *n.* chance C2/77, **auentur** danger 1967, **auenture** chance 981, danger 288, 1260, 1438, etc., venture 1972; **in auenture** at risk C2/75; *see also* **auenture**

aduersaire *n.* adversary 746

aduersarily *adv.* by misfortune 1532

aduerse *adj.* opposing 198, 220, 454, etc.

aduertised *pa. p.* informed 2201, advised C2/48, C3/131; **aduertisyng** *pr. p.* advising C5/22

aduertisement *n.* information 1331, **auertisment** advice C2/2, C5/14; **aduertisementis** *n. pl.* warnings 2391, **aduertysmentys** instructions, C3/1, C4/1, **aduertissmentys** C5/1, **avertisementes** C1/193, **auertisementis** C1/198, C1/199, **auertismentys** C2/21

advice *inf.* advise C1/104, **aduise** 2533, **auise** 1871, C1/202, find out C2/58; **auised** *pa. 3 pl.* advised 1841; **aduised** *pa. p.* recommended C2/203, C2/247, C3/88, etc. **avysed** C2/1, C3/2

aduis *n.* advice C2/48, C3/37, C3/119, **auise** 1757, 1914, 2438, consideration 2040; **avises** *n. pl.* recommendations C2/23

aduisement *n.* consideration 2045–6, **avysement** 1966

aduitailing *n.* provision of supplies C3/86, **aduitailling** C2/136

aferraunt *n.* size, proportion C4/59 (see n.), **afferaunt** 1305

affermithe *pr. 3 sg.* agrees 740

affiaunce *n.* faith 1242

afoote *adv.* on foot 1886

afore *adv.* beforehand C1/146

afore *prep.* in front of 369, before C5/55

after *adv.* afterwards 33, 38, 128, etc., **aftir** C1/146

after *conj.* after 698, 1072, 1270, etc., as 1812, C1/182

after *prep.* after 214, 258, 287, etc., according to 1259, 1305, 1815, etc., following 96, 630, because of 101, **aftir** after C1/68, C1/149, according to C1/39, C1/118; **after that** according to what 2481

agreithe hym *pr. 3 sg. refl.* assents 753

aiel *n.* grandfather 1039

aleyed *adj.* laid out with paths 2107

alleway *adv.* always 862, 1008, **allweies** C2/160, **alway** 843, 1182, 1257, etc.

allied *pa.* married 471, allied 1209, 1214, 1508

allowed *pa. p.* praised 790

alonlie *adv.* 2276, **alonly** 1301, C2/74, C2/167

ambassyade *n.* deputation C2/7–8, **anbassiat** C1/160

amercie *inf.* fine 2359

and *conj.* if 1506, 1644, 1697, etc., who indeed 2075 (see n.)

angures *n. pl.* auguries 1814 (see n.)

antecessour *n.* predecessor in a title or office 436, 957, 2340, etc., **antecessoure** 55

apatismentis *n. pl.* tributes exacted from territory C4/60

appaise *inf.* appease 2532

apparteynithe *pr. 3 pl.* are appropriate 2403

appatise *inf.* exact tribute from C2/151

appointement *n.* pact, agreement C2/25, C2/43, C2/53, etc., **appoyntment** C2/95; **appointementis** *n. pl.* agreements C3/118

approued *adj.* experienced 1757, 1782

approuethe *pr. 3 sg. impers.* is proven 116; **approued** *pa. p.* proven 1403

approwementis *n. pl.* efficient management (of land) 1986

apropred *pa. p.* thought appropriate for 2341

apt *adj.* fit, prepared, qualified 2321, 2332, **apte** 619

aray *n.* battle formation 969, **arraie** clothing 2413

archedenes *n. pl.* archdeacons 2257

arraiementis *n. pl.* adornments 2418, **arraymentis** 2420

arterie *n.* implements of war C1/107
assignacion *n.* allocation 880, 2173,
C2/73; **assignacions** *n. pl.* allocations
C3/44
astate *n.* rank 1032, 1386, 1419, etc.,
condition 1251, 1759, C1/115, noble
condition C1/80, C4/23, powerful person 1612, social group C3/17; **astates**
n. pl. ranks 1298, powerful people
C1/162, C1/164, **astatis** ranks 2266,
2353, powerful people 1208, 2529,
2534, social groups represented in
parliament 1028, **Astates** Estates of
the French kingdom C1/80
astonyed *pa. p.* daunted 48, 951, 2323
astrologien *n.* astrologer 1550
atwix *prep.* between 808, 1022, 1224,
etc., **atwixen** 745, **atwixt** 1003, C5/76
auctorised *pa. p.* given legal force 739,
proven 1300, appointed 1862
auctour *n.* inventor 2334, **auctoure**
author C1/42, **autor** authority, source
1961, 2062, 2332; **auctours** *n. pl.*
authorities 2273, C1/43
auncestries *n. pl.* ancestors 2328, 2386,
auncestres C1/29
auncien *adj.* ancient 107, 230, 533, etc.,
aged 1757, 1782, 1869, etc., **auncient**
ancient 28, 30, 32, etc., aged 1765,
1768
auaile *n.* benefit 1795, 2293, C4/59
auaunce *inf.* promote 2091, 2508;
auaunce hem/vs *inf. refl.* put them-
selves/ourselves forward 105, **auaunce
hym** move into battle 1970-1;
auauncyth hym *pr. 3 sg. refl.* puts
himself forward 1966; **auaunce hym**
subj. 3 sg. refl. put himself forward
1969; **auauncyng** *pr. p.* promoting
3, C1/8, C1/83, **auaunsing** 1615,
1725, 1770, stirring 632; **auaunsing
hymsilfe** *pr. p. refl.* putting himself
forward 1950; **auaunced** *pa. 3. sg.*
promoted 1417; **auaunced** *pa. 3 pl.*
put forward 2129; **auaunced hym** *pa.
3 sg. refl.* put himself forward 407,
2035, **auaunsid hym** 1953, **auaunsid
hymsilfe** 1940; **auaunsid hem** *pa.
3. pl. refl.* put themselves forward
1407; **auaunced** *pa. p.* promoted
873; **auaunced hem** *pa. p. refl.* put
themselves forward 574

auauncement *n.* promotion 67, 1818,
1887-8, etc., **auauncemente** C1/107,
C1/181, **auaunsment** 1729
auaunted *pa. 3 pl. refl.* boasted 2282
auauntgard *n.* vanguard of an army 408
aueyn *n.* oats 2081
auenture *n. see* **aduenture**
auenture *inf.* take a chance 854
ayen *adv.* again 23, 49, 204, etc., **ayene**
777, C2/254, C3/114, etc.
ayen *prep.* against 2467, 2518, **ayens**
2008, C2/101, C2/142, etc., **ayenst**
106, 124, 198, etc.

B

baillies *n. pl.* bailiffs C2/222
baleese *n. pl.* scourges 1653
banerettis *adj.* above the rank of
knight-bachelor 382
barnage *n.* barony 1691
batellous *adj.* warlike 1930
be, *prep.* by 25, 41, 45, etc., **bie** C2/264,
by 9, 25, 43, etc.
be *inf.* be 8, 19, 49, etc., **bee** 9, 1841,
2489, **bene** 2165, C4/31; **be** *pr. 1 pl.*
are 1717, 2302, **bee** 1707; **be** *pr. 2
pl.* are C1/25, **ben** 42, 863, **bene** 658,
709; **is** *pr. 3 sg.* is 7, 9, 37, etc.; **be** *pr.
3 pl.* are 174, 754, 851, etc., **bee** 2092,
ben 24, 48, 153, etc., **bene** 39, 166,
228, etc., **beth** C2/117, **bith** C2/159;
be *subj. 2 pl.* be C4/34; **be** *subj. 3
sg.* be 225, 631, 912, 914, etc., **bee**
C3/171; **be** *subj. 3 pl.* be 1262, C1/6,
C4/52, etc., **bee** C4/38; **being** *pr. p.*
being 89, 116, 287, etc.; **were** *pa. 2 pl.*
were 238, 861, 1459; **was** *pa. 3 sg.* was
32, 84, 128, etc.; **were** *pa. 3 pl.* 37,
131, 299, etc., **werre** 870; **where** *pa.
subj. 3 sg.* were 2534; **be** *pa. p.* been
64, 145, 234, etc., **bee** 298, **ben** 1180,
1244, etc., **bene** 843, 845, 1034, etc.
becom *inf.* become 1845, **become** 1161,
1680, 1856; **become** *pr. 3 pl.* go to
2322
behapped *pa. 3 sg.* happened C3/164
behofe *n.* benefit 2432
behofefull *adj.* needful 1779, **behofull**
C1/203, **behouefull** C3/178
beneurte *n.* happiness 2121
beoffes *n. pl.* cattle (as meat) 2065

bere out *inf.* put on (an appearance) 2348

bereffe *inf.* steal 603; **bereued** *pa. p.* stolen 966, 1494

besied hem *pa. 3. pl. refl.* occupied themselves 2013

besinesse *n.* anxiety 74, 2348, 2364, **be-synesse** labour 2119, **bysnes** eagerness 95 (see n.)

bestaile *n.* livestock C2/134

bethyn *prep.* within 52, 112, 426, etc.

bethout *prep.* without 192, 221, 223, etc., **bethoute** 2062, **bethat** 176 (see n.); **bethout** outside 1639

beting *vbl. n.* dashing (of waves) 2494

billis *n. pl.* curved blades C2/174

birthe *n.* rank 121, 609, 1507, etc., birth 28

blandisshing *adj.* charming 1639

blode *n.* kinship 701, genealogy 1299, blood C1/84, C1/93, **bloode** kinship 147, C1/51, C2/32, race 28, 30, 40, etc., genealogy 43, 229, 543, etc., aristocracy 342, 505, 2506, blood 144, 150, 632

bobauncees *n. pl.* fine trappings 2419

bonchief *n.* prosperity 618

boundemen *n. pl.* slaves 2507

bowes *n. pl.* bowmen 2068, bows C3/74, C4/43, C5/61

brede *n.* breadth C2/125

bren *inf.* burn C2/192; **brent** *pa. p.* burnt 1581, **brente** C2/189; **brennyng** *vbl. n.* burning 142, 158, C2/132

bretherin *n. pl.* brothers 84, 1320, 2011, **brethern** 1325, **bretherne** 88

Breton *adj.* ancient British 35, 1572, 1585, etc., Breton 412

bring to mynde *phr. v.* remember 5, 265, 1602, etc.

Brutes *n. pl.* ancient British peoples 30, **Brutis** 229

burgeis *n. pl.* townsfolk 2469, **burgeises** 332, 2086

but *adv.* only 59, 174, 193, etc.

but *conj.* unless 215, 2368, C2/178, but 69, 151, 188, etc.; **but if** *conj.* unless 2448, C2/176

C

can *inf.* know how to 2316; **can . . . thanke** *phr. v.* express thanks C2/227

capitaineries *n. pl.* captaincies C3/138, C3/146, **capitaneries** C3/154, C3/159

capitall *n.* chapter 1551

capitall *adj.* deadly 2148

carekkis *n. pl.* carracks, warships 466, **carekys** 434, 437, 445, **carrakes** 814, 1352

Cartages *n. pl.* Carthaginians 1502, 2008

cast *inf.* calculate 1194

casuelte *n.* chance occurrence 1534

cause *n.* condition 1517, cause 162, 167, 181, etc.; **causes** *n. pl.* matters 1915, causes 166, 177, 180, etc., **causis** 1619, 1831, 2187, undertakings 597

cautel *n.* trick 133

cenatoure *n.* senator 10, 69, 1603, etc., **senatoure** 1525, 1865, 1889, etc.; **cenatours** *n. pl.* senators 1608, 1702, 1833, 1866, **senatours** 1602, 1637, 1794„ etc.

centaurus *n. pl.* centaurs 606

certein *n.* certainty 886

certez *adv.* certainly 2205

chafed *pa. p.* enraged 631

charge *n.* burden 115, 565, 2436, responsibility 486, 1381, 1688, etc., moral importance 148, cost C2/180, office C3/8, C3/154, accusation C4/14; **charges** *n. pl.* charges 552, taxes 2192, 2220, responsibilities C1/189, offices C3/165, **chargis** charges C1/134, C1/137, offices C3/146, C3/156, C3/159, etc., burdens 2526

charge *inf.* tax 2182, appoint C3/79; **charging** *pr. p.* being a burden C4/40; **charged** *pa. p.* taxed 897, appointed C5/81, attacked 782, 1951, accused C4/64

chargeable *adj.* grave 2299

chariottes *n. pl.* wagons 965

chauncelere *n.* senior administrative official C1/115, **chaunceller** C4/23

chaungers *n. pl.* money-changers 2561

chauntithe *pr. 3 sg.* makes clear C1/222

cheualerous *adj.* adhering to codes of knightly behaviour 929, **cheualrous** 2274, 2333, **cheualrouse** C1/43

cheualier *n.* knight 428, C1/35; **cheualers** *n. pl.* knights 1124, **cheualiers** 537, 1761–2

cheualrie *n.* knightly behaviour 592, 926, 1305, etc., body of mounted

armed men 406, 414, 856, etc., **cheualry** C1/64, **cheualrye** C1/87,
C1/137
chevetaine *n.* military leader C5/46–7,
C5/51, C5/76, **cheueteyn** 886, 903,
C5/10, **cheveteyne** C5/59, **chieftein**
879, 907, 954, etc., **chiefteyne** 1687,
1945, **chieueteyne** 1672, 2153,
C5/58, etc.; **cheueteins** *n. pl.* military
leaders 816, 893, **chieftains** C2/123,
C2/151, C2/172, etc., **chiefteins**
824, 834, 2170, **chiefteynes** C1/100,
chieueteyns 882, 1445, 2281, etc.
chief *n.*, **in chief** directly (from an
authority) 1486, C1/22
chier *n.* generous attitude 1385, 2104
chosen *adj.* noble 251, 1397, 2373
ciuile *adj.* concerning Civil Law 1915,
2347
clepid *pa. p.* called 270, 280, 358, etc.,
clept 1056; **cleping hym** *pr. p.* calling
himself 521, **cleping hymsilf** 547
clerk *n.* author 736, 1745, 2132; **clerkis**
n. pl. authors 1731, pupils 1639, 1653,
scholars 1826
clymethe *pr. 3 pl.* climb 1781
Codicelle *n.* appendix C1/48, C1/176,
C1/214
cohercion *n.* compulsion 2188, 2261
coherted *pa. p.* compelled 1160, 2078–9
coyne-money *n.* coinage 2560
colour *n.* cover 723, 1078, 1113, etc.,
pretended reason 2172, **coloure** cover
54, 109, 744, etc.; **colours** *n. pl.* deceptions 2371, colours 2110
colourable *adj.* fraudulent 137, 1110
colourid *adj.* fraudulent C2/57
comen wele *n.* common good 1557,
comon wele 622, 1793, 1818, etc.,
comyn wele 1616
comynalte *n.* people of a nation 1601
comyng on *n.* attack 755
comissarie *n.* royal official 1133; **comissaries** *n. pl.* royal officials 1137, 1153
comitte *inf.* commission C4/160; **comytted** *pa. p.* commissioned 2561,
C3/42, granted 1689, committed 2377,
commytted 1687, 2246, C1/90, etc.
commyn profit *n.* common good 1795,
comon profit 1729, 1756, 1758, etc.,
comon profite 1692, 1725, **comyn
proffyt** 1766–7, **comyn profit** 1606,
1627, 2056

comon publique *n.* common good 1690,
1917, C1/8, **comyn publique** 3, C1/86
comons *n. pl.* common people 2203,
2525, 2528, etc., **comyns** 206, 1611,
2076, etc., **Comyns** the House of
Commons 1033
compassid *pa. p.* planned 2113
complisses *n. pl.* allies 1187
composicion *n.* agreement 1468–9
comprehendid *pa. p.* included 852, 1095
conclude *subj. 3 sg.* decide upon C2/85,
C2/104; **concluded** *pa. p.* determined
C2/169, concluded 1782
condecend *inf.* agree C2/20, **condescende** 740, 2000
conduit *pa. p.* guided 1896, governed
1896, **conduyt** conducted C1/184,
C5/11, **conduyte** C1/183, **conduyted**
C1/110, C2/106 (see n.)
conduit *n.* guidance 182, 781, 1875,
etc., conduct 884, 919, 1916, etc.,
conduyte C1/44, C1/49, C1/57
confunded *pa. p.* defeated 2489
connyng *n.* learning 1579, 1829, C1/39
conquest *inf.* conquer C2/111
conseruacion *n.* preservation C1/9,
C1/141
consumed *pa. p.* destroyed 456, used up
C2/113
contenaunce *n.* behaviour 2350–1, 2378
contenting *pr. p.* compensating 900;
content *pa. p.* compensated 2177,
contentid 2514
contrauersye *n.* disagreement C5/17
corage *n.* intention 1844, 2301, valour
872, 1284, 1408, **courage** 857, 1473–4,
1953, etc., spirit 142, 590, 2470, etc.;
corages *n. pl.* intentions 975, valour
239, 1313, **courages** 96, 753, 1856,
etc., **couragis** 230
corage *inf.* encourage 26, **courage** 7,
608; **couraged** *pa. 3 sg.* encouraged
1863; **couraged** *pa. p.* encouraged
1472
corageouser *adj. comp.* braver 873
corone *n.* the crown C2/36, C2/67,
coroune 1455, C1/85, C2/90, **corowne**
C1/171, C2/12, C2/16
cosins-germains *n. pl.* cousins 377,
1325, 1392
cost *n.* expense 115, 565, 1382, etc.,
coste C2/269; **costis** *n. pl.* expenses
552, 912, C1/133, etc.

coste *n.* coast C3/89; **costis** *n. pl.* coasts 1779

costius *adj.* expensive 2418, **costues** 2420

cote-armes *n. pl.* men entitled to wear heraldic arms 506

counceile *n.* advice 69, 182, 218, etc., policy 957, group of advisors 1908, council 127, C3/18, C3/120, etc., **concelle** C2/24, C2/30, **counseile** C2/32, C2/203, C2/273, etc.; **counseiles** *n. pl.* councils C2/270

counceile *inf.* confer 2532; **counceilithe** *pr. 3 sg.* advises 614, 875, 877; **counceiled** *pa. 3 sg.* advised 209, 959, 1841, etc., **concellid** 1834; **counceiled** *pa. p.* recommended 2286, **counseiled** advised C2/45, C2/272; **counseiling** *vbl. n.* discussion 2570

counceile-yeuyng *n.* advising 1924

count *n.*, **set no count of** did not regard as valuable 936

courtis-halding *n. pl.* court-sessions 2348

couthe *pa. 3 pl.* could 363, 1490

couenable *adj.* suitable 238, 2244, 2286

couetice *n.* greed 263, 869, 1571, etc., **couetise** 923, 927, 939, etc.

covyn *n.* confederacy 1650

croiserie *n.* crusade 271, 292

culueryns *n. pl.* guns C2/173

cure *n.* care, attention 1694, 1809

curtesie *n.* courtliness 2338, **curtesyie** favour 2172

D

daunger *n.* mercy 1613; **dangers** *n. pl.* dangers 1779

day *see* **monithe, yere**

debate *n.* conflict 2449, C5/77; **debates** *pl.* conflicts 1171

debitees *n. pl.* deputies 2180

Decade *n.* subdivision of Livy's *Ab urbe condita* 1625, 2516

deciplyne *n.* instruction C1/42

dedis *n. pl.* accounts of deeds 1819, deeds 9, 75, 102, etc.

defalcacion *n.* withholding (money) 2173

defalke *inf.* withhold (money) 2181, 2434; **defalking** *vbl. n.* withholding (money) 908

defaut *n.* lack 441, 871, 1060, etc., **defaute** 757, 865, 894, etc., fault 760, 1700, 2038; **yn deffaut of** due to the failure of C5/13

defende *inf.* resist 222, defend 259, 738, 1439, etc.; **defend** *subj. 3 sg.* forbid 1496, C5/36, **defende** 749, 1277, C2/79, etc.; **defending** *pr.p.* defending 1334, 1358, 1475, etc.; **defended** *pa. 3 sg.* defended 430, **defendid** 258, 281, 314, etc.

deformite *n.* defectiveness (in law) 1302

defoule *inf.* trample down 169

degre *n.* rank 1032, 1728, 2551, **degree** 1512, 2049, 2450, etc.

delites *n. pl.* pleasurable vices 600, 625, 627, etc.

delyuer *inf.* deliberate C1/202

deliuer *inf.* give 1638, 1645, release 1994, 2000, accept combat offered by 2324; **delyuered** *pa. 1 sg.* gave 919; **deliuerid** *pa. 3 pl.* gave 1663; **deliuerid** *pa. p.* released 128, 1998-9, given 1062, 1687, C2/14

deliuer *adj.* agile 2319

deliueraunce *n.* release 1992

demains *n. pl.* demesne, inherited territories 2218, **demaynes** 1031, C1/122

deme *inf.* judge 872, imagine 1553, 2205; **demed** *pa. p.* judged C2/34, C2/40, C2/64

demened *pa. p.* managed C2/106, C5/33, conducted C2/273, C4/32

demenyng *n.* conduct C4/31

denyed *pa. 3 sg.* refused 1997

depart *inf.* part with 870, 2470, **departe** give up C2/71, C2/90, leave C3/124; **departethe** *pr. 3 pl.* leave 890; **departed** *pa. p.* divorced 702-3, left 337, 432, 2149

descomfit *pa. 3 sg.* defeated, routed 338, **descomfited** 797, **desconfited** 254, **discomfited** 1990; **descomfit** *pa. p.* defeated 403, 2140, **descomfited** 812, 814, 818, etc., **discomfit** 246-7

descomfiture *n.* defeat 773, 1080, victory 519, 1520, **discomfiture** defeat 784, victory 368-9, 468, 1525, etc.; **discomfitures** *n. pl.* defeats 1281

desert *n.* desolation 1898

despende *pr. 3 pl.* spend 2433; **despendid** *pa. p.* spent 65, 596, 1605, etc.

desport *inf.* play 1639

desteined *pa. p.* dishonoured 230
destrussed *pa. p.* defeated 1968, C5/15
deuoire *n.* duty C2/226, **deuoure**
C3/172-3; **put hym in (his) deuoire**
inf. refl. do his best 1724-5, 1728, **put
yow in youre deuoire** do your best
223-4
dew *adj.* morally right 160, 1029, due
869, 990, 1143, etc.
died vpon *pa. 3. sg.* died from 2008
disclayme *n.* renunciation (of legal title)
1042
disclayme *inf.* renounce C2/11
discomfit *n.* defeat 766
discomfort *inf.* discourage 748
discorage you *inf. refl.* be disheartened
861; **discoragethe them** *pr. 3 pl. refl.*
are disheartened 888
discrecion *n.* judgement 1966, C3/162;
yeris of discrecion *n. pl.* age of legal
capability 698
discrete *adj.* prudent 2438, C2/86,
C2/123, etc.
disgising *n.* fantastical style of clothing
2420
disherite *inf.* disinherit C2/72; **disheriting** *vbl. n.* disinheriting C2/81
dispoilid *pa. p.* stripped 1652
dispose *inf.* make arrangements 2571;
disposed hym *pa. 3 sg. refl.* readied
himself 1088, 1436
dispositiflie *adv.* as a tendency 1542
disseasid *pa. p.* deprived of seisin 720
disseising *n.* deprivation 1462
dissimilacion *n.* deception 111, 1223-4;
dissimilacions *n. pl.* deceptions 108,
C2/57
dissimiled *pa. p.* pretended 892, 1244,
1247
distresse *n.* adversity 1406, 2016, **distrusse** control C2/103
distributif *adj.* freely giving 2576
diuers *n. pl.* diverse means 1560
doctour *n.* learned author 1528; **doctours** *n. pl.* learned authors 1301
doctrined *pa. p.* taught 2337
dolorous *adj.* sorrowful 19, 57, 339, etc.
Dolphin *n.* Dauphin 566
domes *n. pl.* fates 1552
donion *n.* fortress C2/253, **donioune**
335

doubt *inf.* fear 2466; **doubted** *pa. 3 sg.*
doubted 1934, 1936; **doubte** *imp.* fear
2406
doubt *n.* fear C5/6, **doubte** 304, 1710,
doubt 1248; **doubtes** *n. pl.* dangers
C4/47
doubtable *adj.* feared 1580-1
drawen *pa. p.* composed C1/215;
drawen *adj.* educated 1909 (see n.);
drawen forthe *adj.* educated 2315
dryuen *pa. p.* herded C2/134-5, C2/135,
C2/136
duche *n.* duchy 51, 86, 245, **duchie** 51,
349, 458, etc.; **duchees** *n. pl.* duchies 1030, 1334, 1463, **ducheez** 21,
113 (see n.), 283, etc., **duchiees** 1468,
duchies 689, 1329, **duchiez** 1125 (see
n.)
duke *n.* military leader 251, 1622, 1918,
etc., duke (aristocrat) 264, 285, 343,
etc.; **dukes** *n. pl.* dukes (aristocrats)
89, 342, 469, etc., **dukis** 76, 1393,
1761, etc.
dured *pa. 3 sg.* continued, endured 201,
1108
duryng *adj.* continuing C1/161
dutee *n.* debt 2435; **deutees** *n. pl.* debts
2434, **duteis** 2430

E

easye *adj.* insignificant C1/200, **esie**
2379; *see also* **esy**
easily *adv.* meagrely 870
effectuall *adj.* successful C1/191, **effectuelle** zealous 1229
effectuelly *adv.* successfully C1/167
egall *adj.* impartial C4/24
egallie *adv.* equitably 623, 2380
eide *n.* aid 88, 478, 493, etc.
elect *pa. p.* chosen, elected 262, 1766,
electe 1957, C1/51, C1/196
embatailed *pa. p.* arrayed for battle 933,
968, **embatilled** 1429
embrace *inf.* prejudice a jury 2350
empeschement *n.* hindrance C3/82,
accusation C3/126, **empeshement**
hindrance 1054
empeschid *pa. p.* hindered C3/104
employ *n.* task 2484 (see n.)
empressid *pa. p.* formed 95
enacted *pa. p.* entered into official
record 691, 1122, 1301, written 591

endentid *pa. p.* contracted C5/25

endenting *n.* contracting C3/35

endite *inf.* indict 2359

enfamyned, *pa. p.* starved 363

enforce *inf.* strengthen 1500, 1516; **enforcethe** *pr. 3 pl.* oblige 980; **enforced** *pa. 3 sg.* encouraged 2423; **enforced** *pa. p.* encouraged 1472, obliged 2213

enhardid *pa. p.* emboldened 778

enheriter *n.* heir 698, 1067; **enheriteris** *n. pl.* heirs 1121

enseled *pa. p.* sealed 920

entend *inf.* intend 1971, **entende** attend 1696; **entendyth** *pr. 3 sg.* intends 234; **entende** *subj. 3 pl.* attend C3/81; **ententid** *pa. 3. sg.* attended to 295, intended 1441

entendement *n.* understanding 587

entirprise *n.* martial endeavour C2/255, **entreprise** 180, 568, 884, etc.; **entreprinses** *n. pl.* martial endeavours 161, 609, 855, etc., **entreprises** 207, 352, 809, etc., **entreprisez** 842, **entreprinses** daring tasks 597, 601

entitled *pa. p.* written down 7, entitled 658, 661

entreprennoure *n.* adventurer 1939

entretenement *n.* maintenance C3/40

entretid *pa. p.* treated 125, 2245, persuaded C3/16, C3/114, **intretid** appointed C5/46; **entretide with** *pa. p.* negotiated with C3/52

er *adv.* before 982

ering *vbl. n.* ploughing 2119

erledom *n.* county 22, 267, 685, etc.

erst *adv.*, **at erst** *adv. phr.* for the first time 141

erthe-tiliers *n. pl.* agricultural workers 2089

escarmisshes *n. pl.* battles, military engagements 359–60

escuiers *n. pl.* squires 1125

especiall *adj.*, **in especiall** *adv. phr.* in particular 1731, 2300, 2422, etc., **in especialle** 576, 613, 615

estate *n.* financial provision C3/57, C3/62

esy *adv.* scarcely 2193; *see also* **easye**

eured *pa. p.* favoured 1447, C2/39; **ewred** *pa. p.* had good fortune 1312 (see n.)

euereche *adj.* every one C3/17, C3/178

euill *adv.* evilly 2399, **euille** poorly 887

example *inf.* set an example 2450

excersise *inf.* practise 2306, 2341, **exercise** C1/108; **excersised** *pa. 3 sg.* trained 2330; **exercised** *pa. 3. pl.* practised 777; **excercised** *pa. p.* trained 786, **excersised** 805, 2315, **exercised** 846, 853, experienced C1/35, C1/43; **excersising** *vbl. n.* practising 1307, 1867, 2194, etc.

exclusyfe *adj.* completely 1232

exercise *n.* practice 747, 757, 761, etc., training 849

exercitacion *n.* practice 619

exercited *pa. p.* trained 792

extendid *pa. p.* assessed in value 769

expert *pa. p.* trained 774, 796, 1910, etc., **experte** C1/201, **expertid** 1830

expert *adv.* expertly 1908

eyen *n. pl.* eyes 1307

F

facultees *n. pl.* branches of knowledge 2379–80, **faculteez** skills 2345

fadere *n.* father C1/196, C2/51, **father** 266, 306, 390, etc., **fathir** 1657; **faderis** *n. pl.* fathers 1644

fayn *adj.* glad 2434, **fayne** 1443, C2/158, C2/260

fall *inf.* happen C2/99, C3/164, C4/21, **falle** 1541, 1817, 2155, fall 1563, 2003; **fallithe** *pr. 3 sg.* happens 1553, 1597, falls 1596; **fallithe** *pr. 3 pl.* happen 1534; **fall** *subj. 3 sg.* happen C3/48, C3/128, C3/169, etc.; **falling** *pr. p.* happening 1825; **fille** *pa. 3. sg.* descended 663, fell 784, happened 2072, 2207, 2399, etc.; **fille** *pa. 3 pl.* happened, 989, fell 781; **fill** *pa. subj. 3 sg.* happened 1401, **fille** 620; **falle** *pa. p.* happened 981, 1246, 1554, **fallen** 743, 982, 1264, etc., **felle** 1615, 2059

faren with foule *pa. p.* treated badly C2/213 (see n.)

faute *n.* lack 364, 2249

fauten *pr. 3 pl.* are lacking 1827; **fauted** *pa. p.* erred 2298

febled *pa. 3 sg.* weakened 1850; **febled** *pa. p.* weakened 1280, 1523

fedde *pa. 3 sg.* fedde . . . forthe deceived 1640

feeld *n.* battle 544, 1402, 1423, etc., **feelde** 339, , 404, 503, etc., victory in

battle, 189, 198, field, 147, 391, 1785,
background for a coat of arms 660,
felde battle 1967, 1968, C1/111, etc.;
feeldis *n. pl.* fields 1640
feernesse *n.* bravery 106, 584
feers *adj.* warlike 38, 100, 241, **feerse**
2047; **feerser** *adj. comp.* more eager
872
feerslie *adv.* in a warlike fashion 2145,
feersly eagerly 1775
feersnes ferocity 239, **feersnesse** 96, 97
feith *inf.* give one's pledge to C2/238
fell *adj.* fierce 1942; **fellir** *adj. comp.*
fiercer 1948
felouship *n.* body of armed men 839,
904, 1342, etc., **felyshyp** 1968, 1972,
2078
fenied *adj.* feigned 723
feruientlier *adv. comp.* more ardently
C1/25
fet *n.* activity 2346 (see n.); **fette of
werre** *n.* martial exploits C1/59
feute *n.* fealty 1121; **feutees** *n. pl.* feal-
ties 1138
figure *n.* literary form 608
figured *pa. p.* represented, narrated 598
finaunce *n.* ransom 393, 551, 1982,
money 237, 871, 991, etc.; **finaunces**
money C2/114, C2/203
folehardiesse *n.* foolhardiness 1910–11
forasmoche *adv.* because 2539, C1/12
forbere *imp.* spare 2471; **forborn** *pa. p.*
spared C3/114
force *n.* fortitude C1/10, C1/15, C1/33,
etc., force 84, 171, 756, etc.
fordone *pa. p.* destroyed 1271
forging *pr. p.* fabricating 137
formost *adj.* most advanced in military
position 1408
forsean . . . that *conj.* provided that
C4/69
fortyfe *inf.* fortify C1/190
fortune *n.* fortune 64, 751, 942, etc.;
fortunes *n. pl.* unlucky events 2238
fortune *inf.* happen 1650, make fortu-
nate 776; **fortune** *subj. 3. sg.* happen
C3/103, C4/39; **fortuned** *pa. 3 sg.*
happened 1632, 2074, 2146, etc.
foule *see* **faren with foule**
foulers *n. pl.* light cannons C3/67
furnisshe *inf.* supply 1987; **fournysshe**
pa. p. supplied C3/68, **furnisshed** 791,
911–12, 1469, etc., **furnysshid** C4/46

frank *adj.* free (from captivity) 1996
frankis *n. pl.* francs (French currency)
C3/61, C3/62
fraunchise *n.* (legal) freedom 2141,
2463, **frauncheis** 2501; **fraunchises**
(legal) privileges 1807
fredom *n.* freedom C3/123; **fredoms**
n. pl. (legal) privileges 2463
fronture *n.* frontier territory C4/59;
frontures *n. pl.* frontier fortresses
C4/50, C4/51–2, C4/54, **frountours**
frontier territories C4/56
fructufull *adj.* fruitful 1702
fruit *n.* fruit 2120, **fruyte** C2/134;
fructis *n. pl.* fruits 2107

G

gabelle *n.* French salt tax C1/131
galeis *n. pl.* seagoing ships with both
sails and oars, used in warfare 1353,
galeyes 434
garners *n. pl.* granaries 2126
garnesons *n. pl.* groups of troops
C2/187, **garnisons** garrisons C2/148,
C2/188, C3/70
gentiles *n.* noble behaviour 2342 (see
n.)
gentiles *n. pl.* members of the gentry
381, 405
good *n.* (*indecl.*) wealth 893, 1605, 2486,
etc., **goode**, 2433, 2442, 2465, etc.;
goodes *n. pl.* material goods 171, 237,
562, etc., **goodez** 934, 992, **goodis**
946, 950, 970, etc.
goodis *n. pl.* (pagan) gods 1878
gouernaunce *n.* control 1166, conduct
1448, 1556, 2289, etc., government
1304, 1630, 1677, etc., management
1132, 1688, **gouuernaunce** government 1789, C4/62, management 2057,
C3/164, conduct C4/32
gouernoure *n.* ruler 170, 1758, 1791,
etc., military leader 1521, 1920, 2141,
ship's captain 1776, governor 478,
1354, 1673, **gouuernour** C4/3, C5/32,
gouuernoure 1355; **gouernours**
n. pl. rulers 1643, 1654, 1755, etc.,
gouuernours 1634, military leaders
2263
gouuernaunt *n.* governor 1239, C3/4,
gouuernaunte C1/139, C1/147,
C1/149, etc.

grace *n.* divine grace 6, 953, 1448, etc., luck 264, forgiveness 216, 2087, C2/261, favour 905

graunt maister *adj.* chief officer C2/3

graunt-oncle *n.* great-uncle 562

gree *n.* goodwill 2409

grene age *n.* youth 1349, 1373, 1911, etc.

groos *n.* unit of twelve dozen C3/74

grounde *n.* basis 1735, C3/137, ground 1946, 1951; grounde maters *n. pl.* bases C1/180

grounded *pa. p.* established 1095, educated 1827

groundly *adv.* thoroughly, fully 305

grugged *pa. 3 pl.* grumbled 2528

gulis *n.* red (in heraldry) 660

H

hab– *see under* ab–

hable *subj. 3 sg.* give resources to C4/63

hald *inf.* have possession of C2/15, halde 1486, holde 654, 1046, 1120, etc., have allegiance 103, keep C3/135; holdeth *pr. 3 sg.* has possession C1/22, holdithe continues 643; halden *pr. 3 pl.* have possession 2218, 2384, haldyn remain 1594; halding *pr. p.* having allegiance (to) 107, 507–8, holding 492, 967, continuing C2/130; heelde *pa. 3. sg.* had possession 1014, continued 1054, 1173; halde *pa. p.* reputed 1777, 1967, halden 1301, 1511, 1928, etc., holden 98, 1923, 2378, kept C3/45, C4/20; holdeth hym *pr. 3 sg. refl.* remains C3/60; holde theym *pr. 3 pl. refl.* behave 1248; holding vp *pr. p.* supporting 1335

halithe *pr. 3 pl.* haul 1774, 1781

happithe *pr. 3 sg. impers.* happens 977

harde-hert *adj.* hard-hearted 2002

hardely *adv.* bravely 854

hardy *adj.* foolhardy 1965, hardye 1964

harneis *n.* armour 934; stode . . . to harneys *pa. 3 pl.* took up arms 2076–7

haunten *pr. 3 pl.* are accustomed to use 99; haunting *pr. p.* practising 78; haunting *vbl. n.* practising 155, 156, 186, etc.

hauen tounes *n. pl.* seaports C2/207

hauyoure *n.* wealth 2551, 2559

He *interj.* Oh 1410, 1492, 2223, Heh 1241

heire *n.* air 1830

hem *pron.* him 1615, hym 36, 214, 215, etc.

hem *pron.* them 74, 394, 503, etc.; hem *refl. pron.* themselves 105, 386, 405, etc., hemsilfe 624, 1106, 1948, etc., hemsilffe C3/39; *see also* thaym

her *pron.* her 702, hir 1670

her *pron.* their 678, 682, 952, etc., here 8, 95, 137, etc., hir 1516, hire 2179; *see also* their

herbers *n. pl.* pleasure gardens 2105, 2109, 2113

heriter *n.* heir 82, 1040

hertis wille *n.* deepest desire 1161

hesteyng *vbl. n.* attacking C1/112

hethyn *adj.* pagan 1613

hethynesse *n.* territory inhabited by non-Christians 1387

hymsilf *refl. pron.* himself 94, 547, 611, etc., hymsilfe 1940, 1950, 2049

hir *see* her

hire *inf.* hear 2393; hiring *pr. p.* hearing 2241

hire *see also* her

his *separated genitive* 785, is 123, 306, 343, etc., ys 293, 440, 541, etc.

historiall *adj.* historical 692

historied *pa. p.* recounted 348, 575, 1984

historier *n.* historian 724, 1295, 1570

hold– *see* hald

hole *adj.* sole 697, all 1156, complete 993, 1162, whole 298, C1/67

holsom *adj.* beneficial 1866

holy *adv.* wholly 2430

homage *n.* performance of homage 1061, 1119, 1140, etc.; homages *n. pl.* performances of homage 1136, 1138, 1141, etc.

homage lyege *n.* liege homage C2/17

homager *n.* vassal 1142; homagieris *n. pl.* vassals 1123, homagiers 1155, 1161

honoure *n.* honour 391, 573, 723, etc., onure 2569; *see also* ounere

hoost *n.* army 1919, 2508, hooste 2148, C5/55, C5/57, etc., host 403, 492, 916, hoste 1342, 2028, oost 785, 804, 807, etc., ooste 1521, 1694, 2142, etc., ost

911; **hostes** *n. pl.* armies 1977, **oostis**
912, 1676, 1916, **ostes** 958, 1945
hors-met *n.* fodder for horses 2081,
hors-mete 899
hostied *see* **oostay**
hubes *n. pl.* caps (?) 2069 (see n.)

I

i– *see headnote*
if *conj.* if 161, 185, 215, etc., **yef** C2/101
imperiall *adj.* civil (law) 739, **imperialle**
1029
importable *adj.* unbearable 2217
importune *adj.* grievous 742
importunyte *n.* difficulty 2444
incontinent *adv.* right away 1436, 1443,
2406, etc.
inconuenient *adj.* immoral 2401
inconuenient *n.* trouble 981, 2437,
C2/100, etc.; **inconuenientis** *n. pl.*
troubles 1197, 1246, 2155, etc., crimes
1559, 2206
indigence *n.* destitution 2425, need
2497
indigent *adj.* destitute 2441
inducid *pa. p.* influenced 2399, 2402
infortune *adj.* unfortunate C5/15
infortune *n.* misfortune 742, 1283, 1532
inordynat *adj.* immoral 927
inordinatlie *adv.* immorally 2290
inposicion *n.* taxation levy C1/130; **imposicions** *n. pl.* taxation levies 2216,
2519
intentif *adj.* diligent 2119
into *prep.* until 46, 1232, 1595, into 95,
271, 326, etc.
intretid *see* **entretid**
intrusion *n.* invasion, attack 111, 580,
719, etc.; **intrusions** *n. pl.* invasions,
attacks 1496, 1517
irnesse *n. pl.* irons 141 (see n.)
is *see* **his**

J

j– *see headnote*
ioing *inf.* join C2/148
ioly *adj.* vigorous 1901
iorney *n.* battle 1425, C5/16, **iournay**
808, 818, 1269, **iourney** 500, 842,
1430, etc.; **iorneys** *n. pl.* battles 840,

iourneis 1231, 1350, 1805, itineraries
1153, **iurneyse** battles C1/57
yoie *see under* **y–**
ioieust *adj. superl.* causing most joy
2110
iubardie *n.* danger 1947, 2130, **iubardy**
2135, **iubardye** C5/5, **iupardie** 923,
1446, 1460, etc.; **iubardies** *n. pl.*
dangers 2354
iudiciell *adj.* astrological 1829, 1831
iuellis *n. pl.* jewels 2100, 2439, 2512,
iuelx 940, 960, 961
iust *inf.* joust 1886
iust *adj.* just 80, 156, 162, etc., **iuste**
C1/180; **iuster** *adj. comp.* more just
637
iusticer *n.* ruler 39
iustice *n.* justice 154, 167, 184, etc.;
iustices *n. pl.* judges 1755, 1762,
2362, etc.
iustis *n. pl.* jousts 2316

K

kepe hym *inf. refl.* be on guard 214–5;
kept hem *pa. 3 pl. refl.* were on guard
336
kepe *n.* attention 893
knighthode *n.* chivalric ethical code
579, 723, 852, etc.
knyghtly *adv.* bravely 1952
knouyng them *pr. p. refl.* being know-
ledgeable in C2/271

L

labourage *n.* cultivation (of land) 2091,
2119, 2125; **labouragis** *n. pl.* cultivation (of land) 1986
largelie *adv.* generously 2470, 2520,
2535, etc.
largesse *n.* generosity 894, 2573, 2576
last *n.* a measure of 2400 lb. C3/68
late *adj.* recent 85, 108, 475, etc.
late *adv.* recently 55, 60, 109, etc.
laten *pa. p.* rented out C3/147
lawreat *adj.* distinguished (of a poet)
976
leefe *inf.* live C5/56, **lyue** 909, 1663,
1707, etc.; **lyue** *pr. 1 pl.* live 2226;
lyued *pa. 3 sg.* lived C1/166; **lyued**
pa. p. lived 1388

left *adj.* adverse 864, **lift** 1533
legeaunce *n.* allegiance C1/7, **ligeaunce** 2244, C2/143, C5/81
lege-man *n.* loyal subject C1/31; **liegemen** *n. pl.* loyal subjects 72, **liegesmen** 122
leiethe *pr. 3 sg.* cites 1671
lekis *n. pl.* leagues C2/125
lerne *inf.* learn 1744, 1814, 2346, etc., teach 1635; **lernithe** *pr. 3 pl.* teach 978; **lerned** *pa. p.* learned 2358, taught 778, 786, 792, etc., **lernid** 846; **lerned theym** *pa. 3 pl. refl.* learned 2355
lerning *n.* lesson 974
lessing *pr. p.* lessening 857; **lessid** *pa. p.* lessened 754
lette *inf.* prevent C3/84; **lettid** *pa. p.* prevented C3/104, C5/37; **letting** *vbl. n.* preventing C3/82, C3/99
leuable *adj.* recoverable 2174
libarde *n.* leopard 711; **libardis** *n. pl.* leopards 660, 712
liberallie *adv.* freely 2512
licence *n.* leave to depart 889, 890, permission 1878, C3/95
liege-people *n. pl.* loyal subjects 2160, **liege-peple** 346, 1159, 1235, etc.
lifelode *n.* income 947, 1895, **lyuelode** 1493, 2210, 2262, etc.
lift *see* left
ligeaunce *see* legeaunce
ligneallie *adv.* lineally 2396
like *inf.* be pleased C2/78; *subj. 3 sg.* please C3/65, C3/78, C3/89, etc.; **liked** *pa. p.* pleased C3/36
lyu- *see* leefe
lyue-daies *n.* lifetime 2012
lyuerey *n.* uniform 2069
lyuing *n.* life 737
liures *n. pl.* pounds C3/39; **liures sterlinges** *n. pl.* pounds 375, 542; **liures turneis** *n. pl.* coins used in France 948
loggeyns *n. pl.* defensive positions 2085
long *inf.* pertain 1672, C5/63; **longeth** *pr. 3 sg.* pertains C2/27, **longith** pertains C4/43, C5/61; **long** *subj. 3. sg.* pertain 2476; **longing** *pr. p.* pertaining 2342; **longid** *pa. 3 pl.* pertained 2568
lose *adj.* unencumbered C2/186
lucre *n.* gain C2/152, C3/147

lust *pr. 3 sg.* wishes 610, 776, 1220, etc.; **lust** *pr. 3. pl.* wish 2351
lyes *n.* leash 454

M

magnifie *inf.* glorify 1557; **magnifiethe** *pr. 3. sg.* praises 2088; **magnified** *pa. p.* renowned 1579, 1582, 1665, etc.
maynteyn *inf.* protect 2246, 2362, **maynteyne** 1606, support 2091, conduct (a war) 165, **meinteine** protect 925, 2253; **maynteyned** *pa. 3 pl.* maintained 1418, protected 1612; **mainteyned** *pa. p.* supported 2227, **meyntened** 160, protected 2382, **meynteyned** 1390, kept in good order 174; **meintenyng** *vbl. n.* conducting (a war) 153, 159
maister *n.* ship captain 1776, household officer C2/3, schoolteacher 1638, **maistre** 1637; **maistres** *n. pl.* rulers 1654, **maistris** 1909, 2263, 2567, etc., masters 1544
maister of sciencis *n.* schoolteacher with MA degree 1632
maisterdom *n.* victory in battle 190
maistre gonners *n. pl.* chief gunners C3/71
maistrie *n.* strength 189; **maistries** *n. pl.* skills 2331, 2341
male-infortuned *adj.* unlucky 499
malles *n. p.* warhammers C4/44, C5/62
manassed *pa. p.* menaced 2211
manhod *n.* dignity 124–5, bravery 1448, 1650–1, 1655, etc., virtue 1988, 2357, **manhode** bravery 460, 872, 2505, virtue 1863, C1/98
manyfolde *adj.* many 1243
manlinesse *n.* bravery 96, 239, 1403
manly *adj.* brave 38, 1474, 1963, etc., **manlie** 1865, 1963, 2042
manly *adv.* bravely 360, 463, 611, **manlie** honourably 405
mantelle . . . yow *inf. refl.* protect yourself 581
marc *n.* (*indecl.*) Continental monetary unit of uncertain weight 948, **mark** English marks 1379
marcher *n.* territory 1371
marches *n. pl.* territories 2219, C4/50, C4/57, **marchis** 1339, 2263
marques *n. pl.* marquises 1761

masle *adj.* male 683, 694

masty hound *n.* hunting dog 454

meintenaunce *n.* maintenance (i.e. abuse of law) 2381

memoriall *n.* remembrance 1405, memorial C1/73, C1/92

menage *n.* household 2052

mene *n.* means 2166, C2/76, C2/194; meenez *n. pl.* means 2288, menes 1649, C4/26

meoue *inf.* start (a war) 215, moeue 209; moeuithe *pr. 3 sg.* proposes 163; meoued *pa. 3. sg.* prompted 1639, entailed 1648; meoued *pa. p.* proposed 26, 148, 151, started (a war) 220

mesuage *n.* farmstead 2057

mete *n.* food 899, 2499, 2504

meueable *adj.* movable 1494, 2521, 2576

mightifull *adj.* mighty 1323, 1713, 1791, etc.

might- *see* myght-

mildewis *n. pl.* attacks of crop blight 2051

mynistre *inf.* administer 2267, 2380

ministrours *n. pl.* clergymen 2257, legal officers 2382

mynussed *pa. p.* diminished 754, mynusshed 1515, 1523

mischief *n.* harm 885, 2291

mischieued *pa. 3 pl.* harmed 2212; myscheuid *pa. p.* harmed 1244

mysspende *inf.* waste 2370; misspendid *pa. p.* sinfully indulged 991

mo *adv.* more 441, C2/240, moo 586, 1451, C5/26

moenys *see* moyen

moeu- *see* meoue

mondeyn *adj.* earthly 2117, mondeyne 2121

monithe *n.* month 720, 997, 1011, etc., month 392, C4/5; monethis *n. pl.* months C1/70, monithes 53; monithes day months 1154

mortalite *n.* loss of life 299, 1292

mote *pr. 3 sg.* might 2496

mow *inf.* be able to 2053

moyen *n.* means 1063, 1499, 2564, etc., moyene 225; moenys *n. pl.* means 639

mure *adj.* mature 1889

muys *n. pl.* bushel (?) 1522 (see n.)

myghtelie *adv.* powerfully C2/209, mightilie 1442, myghtly 198, 1452, C2/98, myghtlye 2084

N

naked *adj.* unarmed 2070

nakedly *adv.* poorly C1/146

ne *conj.* nor 59, 65, 155, etc., ner C2/28, C2/36, C2/71, etc., nere C2/27, C2/62, C2/93, etc., no 626, nor 2303, C2/35, C2/41, etc.

nedill *n.* compass 1778

nere *see* ne

nere *adj.* closely related 501, 701, 1392, etc.

nerenesse *n.* close kinship C1/92

new *adj.*, of the new *adv. phr.* anew 444, 446

nighe *inf.* collect 2434

nighe *adv.* nearly 2212

no *see* ne

noblesse *n.* nobility 588, 592, 625, etc., people of noble rank 1383, 1688, C1/82

noie *inf.* harm 1527, noy 2489

noise *n.* slander C3/166

noised *pa. p.* rumoured C2/34

nombre *inf.* count 2563; nombred *pa. p.* recounted 853, calculated 1451

nom-power *n.* inability 900

none *adj.* no 639, 655, 727, etc.

none *adv.* by no means C2/43

noote *n.* accusation 2062, C2/163, note reputation 223, 1302

noterily *adv.* famously C1/25, notorily 90, infamously 218–19, 665

nother *conj.* nor 793, 1973, C1/91, etc.; nothere neither C2/35, neither 231, C1/189, C1/221, neithere C3/107, C4/64, nether 60, 755, nethere C3/70

nouches *n. pl.* items of jewellery 940, 2546

O

obeisaunce *n.* rule 473, 910, 1152, etc., obeissaunce 896, 1796, 2224, etc.

obeisaunt *adj.* obedient 58, 1235, 1444, obeisauntes 541, obeissauntes 895

obeisauntes *n. pl.* subjects 2186, obeissauntes 894, obeissauntis 2182, 2249

occupie *inf.* take part in 2348, 2379; occupied *pa. 3 sg.* spent 1480, occupied 1866, 1867; occupied *pa. p.* spent 65, undertaken 2367

office *n.* job, position, 1689, 1866, 1867, etc.; **offices** *n. pl.* jobs, positions 1771, 1861, C1/89, etc., duties C1/14

often-sithis *adv.* often 1989–90

onure *see* **honoure**

oolesse than *conj.* unless C2/96

oost *see* **hoost**

oostay *inf.* wage war C2/125, C2/127; **osteyng** *pr. p.* encamping 298; **hostied** *pa. 3 sg.* waged war 350

opyn *adj.* widely known 641, 2431, public 2543

opteyne *inf.* obtain 1409

or *conj.* before 128, 1155, 1208, etc.

ordenaunce *n.* ordnance, military supplies 868, 1442, 1470–1, etc., **ordonaunce** C3/64, **ordonnaunce** C3/75, **ordynaunce** C1/207, **ordinaunce** command C2/89, C5/32, arrangement C5/79; **ordenaunces** *n. pl.* commands C5/57, military supplies 2568, **ordinaunces** C1/106, C2/116, C2/172, etc.

ordinarie *adj.* customary C1/121

ordonne *inf.* appoint C3/161; **ordene** *subj. 3. sg.* arrange C5/59

oriflamble *n.* banner of the kings of France 372

ost *see* **hoost**

osteyng *see* **oostay**

other *conj.* or C5/79

ouer *prep.* after 1372

ouerhand *n.* victory 1449, 2237, **ouerhande** 494, 932, 1409, **ovyrhand** 1971

ouerleid *pa. 3 sg.* defeated 461; **ouerleid** *pa. p.* defeated 240

ouermore *adv.* furthermore 311, 533, 2156, etc.

ouerthrow *pa. p.* defeated 525, 980, 1261, etc., **ouerthrowen** 2034

ouerthrow *n.* defeat 505, 989, 1265, etc., **ovyrthrow** 200; **ouerthrowes** *n. pl.* defeats 1584

ounere *inf.* honour 776; *see also* **honoure**

outeraunce *n.* sale C2/234

outrecuidaunce *n.* arrogance C2/242

P

paast *n.* events in the past 139

payne *n.* fine 914

paynemys *n. pl.* non-Christians 275

paynym *adj.* pagan 2274

parauenture *adv.* perhaps C2/82

parcellis *n. pl.* parts 1233

parciall *adj.* unfair C4/24

paree *n.* dignity of a peerage held directly from the Crown C2/17

pares *n. pl.* peers C2/17

parfit *adj.* righteous 1792, proven 666; **parfiter** *adj. comp.* more righteous 637, more correct 1820

parfitelie *adv.* fully 1827

parson *n.* physical body 2115, person C1/67, **parsone** 514, 1031, 2468, etc., **person** physical body C5/5–6, **persone** person C4/30; **parsones** *n. pl.* physical bodies 2129, C3/149, people 129, 1492, 2377, etc., **persones** C2/28

parsonelly *adv.* personally 1230

partie *n.* side in a dispute, battle 54, 100, 108, etc., section (of text) 1670, 1803, C1/192, part 1751, 2120, C3/138, etc., region 1587; **parties** *n. pl.* region 90, 1081, 1475, etc.

passage *n.* river-crossing C2/178, right of navigation C3/99, C5/68

passe *adv.* past 1097, 1481

passed *adj.* past 687

passing *pr. p.* surpassing 1305

passions *n. pl.* torments 74, 94, 1283

patised *pa. 3 pl.* made payments 2219

paueis *n. pl.* shields C3/75

peas *n.* truce 1000, 1022, 1048, etc., peace 2456, **pease** truce 397, 1044, 1064, etc., peace 222, 639, 727, etc., **pees** truce C3/48, peace C2/27, C2/45, C2/52

peasibly *adv.* peaceably 1046, **pesibly** 130

peine hem *inf. refl.* strive 926; **peyned theym** *pa. 3 pl. refl.* strove 1661

peised *pa. p.* considered C3/142

pellure *n.* fur trimming 2419

penons *n. pl.* knights bachelor 409

persecucion *n.* affliction 2053; **persecucions** *n. pl.* afflictions 1493, 2201

pesible *adj.* peaceful C2/166

pesyn *n. pl.* peas 2081

pety capteins *n. pl.* officers below a captain 1268

pille *inf.* plunder C5/53

piller *n.* plunderer 2198; **pilleris** *n. pl.* plunderers 928

pilours *n. pl.* pillars 1326

piteous *adj.* pitiful 19, 57, **pitous** feeling pity 2205

pitouslie *adv.* pitifully 2019, **pitously** 147

plaine batell *n.* pitched battle 652

pledours *n. pl.* advocates 1909

plenerlie *adv.* completely 1119

plesaunce *n.* satisfaction 2288

poesy *n.* fiction 608, **poesye** 602

polecye *n.* policy C1/44, **polesye** C1/103, **policie** 781, 1969, 1988, etc.

policie *adj.* politic 1910

possessid *pa. p.* given possession 718, 1189, 1484, etc., possessed 687

pouder *n.* spice 626

pouresshid *pa. p.* impoverished C2/236

pourueie *inf.* provide C3/90, **purueie** C4/15, **puruey** 2533, C3/66, **puruoie** 2523; **purueyed** *pa. 3. sg.* provided 2069; **purueied** *pa. p.* provided 2048, 2287-8, 2568, etc.

power *n.* power, 106, 178, 187, etc., army, armed force 297, 304, 431, etc., **powere** C2/41, C3/23, C3/27, power C2/66, C2/236, C2/258, etc.

practik *n.* business 2345, 2366, 2370, practice 2376, **practique** 2346

praies *n. pl.* spoils of war 934, 960

precedent *n.* president (of French parliament) C1/116

preferryng *n.* promotion 3, C1/8, **proferring** 1834

prenable *adj.* vulnerable to capture C2/177

prese *n.* crowd 2562

prestis *n. pl.* loans to the monarch 2428, 2430

pretendid theym *pa. 3. pl. refl.* professed to be 2209

price *n.* reputation 768, 864, 2487, price 2128, **prise** value 936

prince *n.* capture C2/166

principales *n. pl.* essential elements (of academic subjects) 1827-8

print money *n.* stamped coinage 2544

priuacion *n.* loss 993-4, 1162, 1542, etc.

priue *adj.* secret 2261

processe *n.* narrative 305, **proces** process C2/141

procuratours *n. pl.* legal officials C1/117 (see n.)

proferring *see* **preferryng**

profound *adj.* learned 1826

progenitoure *n.* ancestor 1204; **progenitours** *n. pl.* ancestors 576, 658, 717, etc., **progenitoures** 664, 860, 1003

propre *adj.* personal 1031, 1038, 2546, etc.

prouidence *n.* foresight 979, 989-90, 1977, etc., provisioning 2064

prouision *n.* provisioning 236, 2248, C3/54, planning 1826, 2056, C2/216, etc., foresight 2287; **prouisions** *n. pl.* provisions 867

puissantly *adv.* forcefully C2/198, successfully C2/97, C2/180, **puissauntlie** 2464, forcefully 1421, **puissauntly** successfully 1376-7

puissaunce *n.* army 610, 762, C2/41, etc., force C2/61

puissaunt, *adj.* powerful 43, 89, 241, etc.

purpose *inf.* propose 1513; **purposing** *pr. p.* intending C1/25; **purposed** *pa. 3 sg.* proposed 1853, C1/159-60, **purposid** 1657, 1844, intended 326; **purposed** *pa. p.* proposed C2/7, **purposid** 26

purueaunce *n.* provision 1212, preparations C5/39, **purueiaunce** 783

purueie *etc.*, *see* **pourueie**

purveours *n. pl.* officers in charge of provisioning 2063

put out *inf.* pay out 2535, 2556

put out *inf.* expel 1435, **put oute** C2/194; **put out** *pa. p.* expelled 53, **put oute** 578, C2/60

Q

quaiers *n. pl.* booklets 2392

quarters *n. pl.* units of measurement, multiples of bushels (?) 770 (see n.)

quaterismes *n. pl.* 25% tax on wine C1/131

querel *n.* quarrel 193, **querelle** cause 1263

quite *adj.* acquitted 1996

quyte hem *inf. refl.* acquit themselves C4/12; **quite hem** *pa. 3 pl. refl.* acquitted themselves 405

R

racountre *n.* military engagement 1970, **recountre** 1269, 1341; **recountres** *n. pl.* hostile attacks 755, 840

raise *n.* military expedition 1217

rampanyng *pr. p.* standing erect 634

rappyne *n.* robbery, plunder 924, **rapyn** 909, 2188, **rapyne** 928

rather *adv.* sooner 902, 1638, C1/25, rather 186, 328, 329, etc., **rathere** C2/77, rather than C2/89, **rathir** rather 1411, 1557, 1614, etc.

raunsom *n.* ransom 1292, **raunson** 128, 374, 393, etc.

raunsone *inf.* ransom C2/151; **raunsonyng** *vbl. n.* ransoming 945

rauynes *n. pl.* robberies 2202

realme *n.* realm C1/20, C1/50, C1/71, etc., **reaume** 23, 35, 51, etc., **reyaume** C1/197, **roiaum** 564, **roiaume** 250, 290, 459, etc., **royalme** C4/16; **roiaumes** *n. pl.* realms 187, 569, 1054, etc., **roymes** C1/9

rebuked *pa. p.* driven back 232, 1075, C2/98, **rebukid** 1707, reproved 1832

recomforting hem *pr. p. refl.* recovering their spirits 1954

recordacion *n.* memory 75

recountre *see* **racountre**

recouere *n.* recovery (of territory) 68, 748, **recuere** 2166, 2474, C1/19, **recuuerey** 727

recouueraunce *n.* recovery C3/136

redoubted *pa. p.* revered C1/12, C1/38

regalite *n.* jurisdiction 2207

regencie *n.* sovereignty 1304, role as regent C1/56, C1/58, C1/79, etc.

registred *pa. p.* recorded 1170, 1301

registres *n. pl.* record books 1122

reignithe *pr. 3 pl.* continue, persist 924, 1598, 1659, etc.; **regnyng** *pr. p.* continuing, persisting 2230, **reigning** 299, 869, 1569, etc., ruling 2199; **reigned** *pa. 3 sg.* ruled 214, 1218, 2454, etc., continued, persisted 1796; **reigned** *pa. p.* continued, persisted 1600, 1716

reke *inf.* care C2/142

relacion *n.* statement 700

relese *n.* surrender 1027, 1035, 1036, etc.

relese *inf.* surrender 1023, 2435; **relesid** *pa. 3 sg.* granted (property rights to) 653

releue *inf.* relieve C2/148, **relief** 238, 1210, 1439, etc., **relyeff** C5/11, **relyeve** 200; **releued** *pa. 3 sg.* 2501

religiouste *n.* religious life 2476

remeue *inf.* abandon 969

rengid *pa. p.* laid out 2108, 2113

renne *inf.* ride on horseback 2316, run 1886; **rennythe** *pr. 3 sg.* flows 2494, is prevalent 2162; **rennen** *pr. 3 pl.* run 1781; **renne** *pa. 3. sg.* ran 2145; **rennyng** *vbl. n.* running 2318

renome *n.* renown 1386, **renomme** 91, 99, 320, etc., **renommee** 1323, 1658, 1808

rentis-paieng *n.* payment of rent 2217

repaire *n.* gathering C3/58

repairing *n.* recovering 49, 62, putting right 580

repaired *pa. p.* repaired C4/52, **repared** put right 1498, 2573

require *inf.* require 726, 1510, 2179, etc.; **requirithe** *pr. 3 sg.* requires 184; **required** *pa. 3 sg.* requested 1854, 1877, 1933, etc., required C3/27

rered *pa. p.* levied 898

rescow *inf.* defend C2/264, **rescue** relieve (from a siege) 444; **rescued** *pa. 3 sg.* relieved (from a siege) 1377; **rescowed** *pa. p.* defended C2/253

rescue *n.* relief of a siege 832, 838, 1276; **rescous** *n. pl.* reliefs of sieges C3/92, **rescues** C1/57, **rescuse** 842

resort *n.* right of legal appeal to 655, **ressort** 1143, C2/17

resort *inf.* defer 1121, **resorte** come C3/58

respit *n.* delay 1376

rethoricien *n.* rhetorician 1739

retrait *pa. p.* reserved C3/139

reualed *pa. p.* diminished 64, 292, 2258, **reualid** 230; **realyng** *pr. p.* dismissing C1/179; **reuaylyng** *vbl. n.* diminishment C1/82

reuolucion *n.* rotation (of years) 1797

rewarde *n.* payment 2172, 2181, reward 2020, regard 1635, C2/69, C2/228; **rewardes** *n. pl.* payments 1385, **rewardis** 945, 1558, 2264

ribaudekyns *n. pl.* wheeled cannons C2/173, **ridbaudekins** C5/62, **ridbawdkyns** C4/44

ricchesse *n.* wealth 1682, 2103, 2121, **richesse** 562; **ricchesses** *n. pl.* riches 2101

rightwiselie *adv.* with justice C4/24–5

rightwisnes *n.* justice C2/82, **rightwisnesse** 1610, 1720

riote *n.* moral dissipation 626

ripe *adj.* (intellectually) well-prepared C1/168; **rypare** *adj. comp.* (intellectually) better prepared C1/175

rypliere *adv. comp.* more preparedly C1/202

ryte *n.* habit 2417

roiaum(e) *see* **realme**

royame-warde *n.+suffix* towards (your) realm 124

rothir *n.* rudder 1778

S

sacrement *n.* solemn oath 1180; **sacramentes** solemn oaths *n. pl.* C2/56, **sacramentis** 1105, **sacrementis** 1488

sacred *pa. p.* consecrated 110

sadde *adj.* serious C4/15, C4/24

safegard *n.* security C4/7, C5/2, **saufegarde** protection 296, 1692, 2014, etc., **sauffegarde** C3/163, C5/39, **sauffgard** C3/136, **sauffgarde** C3/156, **saufgarde** C5/42, C5/45, **sauegard** C1/134, **sauuegarde** C3/40

sak *n.* sack (as measurement) 1212

salux *n. pl.* French gold coins 552

scaling *n.* escalade C2/252

scant *adv.* scarcely 1108

scapyth *pr. 3 sg.* escapes 1967

science *n.* intelligence 617, academic knowledge 1830; **sciencis** *n. pl.* academic subjects 1635; **vij. sciences** *n. pl.* the seven liberal arts 1379; *see also* **maister of sciencis**

scomfited *pa. p.* defeated 758

scout-wach *n.* guard 453

scutis *n. pl.* French *ecu* coins 394, 395

seased *pa. 3 sg.* seized 1060

seased *pa. p.* given possession 718, 1189, 1484, **seised** 676, **seisid** invested as 674

season *n.* time 237, 755, 869, etc., **seson** 980, 1461; **ceasons** *n. pl.* seasons

1815, **seasons** 1824, 2495, **sesons** seasons C2/200, C2/205

seche *inf.* seek C2/158, C2/260, **seke** C4/45, C5/63; **seke** *subj. 3 sg.* seek 216

secretaire *n.* secretary 733

secretis *n. pl.* hidden workings (of God) 1561

segyng *pr. p.* besieging 337

seigniour *n.* feudal overlord 1143

seigniorie *n.* lordship 173, **seigniourie** 1691, 2096; **seigniouries** *n. pl.* lordships 690, 1485–6, **seignories** 170–1

seles *n. pl.* seals (on documents) 1488

semblable *adj.* similar 936, 1071, 1882, etc.

semblabelie *adv.* similarly C3/73, **semblabely** C2/55, **semblably** C3/68

semlinesse *n.* attractiveness 2115

senatoure *see* **cenatoure**

seneschalcie *n.* French territory administered by a seneschal 1137, 1145, 1146, etc.

seruage *n.* servitude 1644, 1879, 2009, etc.

set . . . be *inf.* value 959; **set . . . by** *pa. 3 sg.* valued 798, 1800, **set . . . by** *pa. 3 pl.* valued 950

set . . . of *pa. 3 sg.* care about 2044–5; **set of** *pa. p.* esteemed 2353

sethe *see* **sithe**

seuerte *n.* safety C2/166, C3/40, C3/50, etc., **seuirte** C3/163, **suerte** 1692, 2078; **seuerteis** *n. pl.* legal protections C3/44, **seurtees** 396–7

sew *inf.* pursue 1257

sewre *adj.* assured 880, C4/18

shame *inf.* be ashamed C2/142

sharpe *adj.* harsh 302, 840, C2/139, etc., sharp 1653

sharping *n.* sharpening, improvement 975

shire-day *n.* session of the shire-court 2359

shiris-halding *n. pl.* sessions of the shire-court 2349

siege *n.* encampment of people laying siege 1641

simple *adj.* lowly 2350, simple 586, 901; **simpler** *adj. comp.* lowlier 2489; **simplest** *adj. superl.* lowliest 864

singuler *adj.* personal 193, selfish, 263, 869, 1558, etc., for personal profit 2345, 2366, C3/146, **singulere** 2370

singulerly *adv.* in particular 882
sithe *conj.* because 7
sithe *conj.* since 1190, **sithen** 1585,
   sethe 1410, **sethen** since 566
sithe *prep.* since 1317, 1393
sithe *adv.* since 85, 1821, **sethe** 113
sithe *adv.* then, afterwards 424, 1372,
   1503, etc., **sithen** 40, 132, 253, etc.,
   sethe 1354
sitteth *pr. 3 sg.* befits C2/28
skermyssh *n.* battle 1970
slommering *adj.* slumbering 144
socour *inf.* relieve 1210, C5/11, **socoure** C2/250, C4/65; **socoured** *pa.
   p.* relieved 2214
socoure *n.* assistance 66, 363, 553, etc.,
   socours C3/55
sogett *n.* servant C1/35; **sogettes** *n. pl.*
   subjects C1/7, **subgectis** 58, 141, 359,
   etc., **subgeitis** 1185, 1235, 1356, **subgettis** 173, 493–4, 541, etc., **sugettis**
   C2/120, C3/30, **suggettis** C3/157
solasse *n.* leisure 1962
soote *adj.* sweet 2109
sore *adv.* badly 48, 1365, 1850, etc.
sore-fought *adj.* hard-fought 1090
soude *n.* wages 901; **men of soude** *n. pl.*
   paid soldiers 907, 2168
soude *inf.* pay (i.e. wages) 992, **soulde**
   871; **soulde** *pa. 3 sg.* paid 1212;
   souded *pa. p.* employed 881
soudeyng *n.* paying of wages 868, **souding** 2511
soudeours *n. pl.* soldiers 441, 886, 899,
   etc., **souldeours** 2181, C4/41, C4/71,
   etc. **sowdieris** 876, 880, 967
soune *inf.* lead 1545; **sounethe** *pr. 3 pl.*
   lead 1531
souereyn *n.* master 1552, **souuerayn**
   lord C2/92, **souuereyn** 1460, C1/22
souereyn *adj.* noble 2279, **souereyne**
   ruling 1704, **souuerain** noble 573,
   C3/99, C3/151, **souueraine** C3/13,
   C3/16, C3/103–4, etc., **souuereyn**
   C1/94, C2/143, **souuereyne** 1377,
   C3/116, C3/125
souereinte *n.* sovereignty 1120, 1143,
   souuereinte 654, C2/17, **souuereynte**
   self-mastery 1547
sped *pa. p.* brought to fruition C1/60;
   sped hem *pa. 3. sg. refl.* succeeded
   C5/19
spede *n.* success 884, C2/121

spedlye *adv.* speedily C5/19
speris *n. pl.* spears 1886, spearmen
   1133, 2068, C1/143, etc.
spirituell *adj.* ecclesiastical 1380, 1724,
   2266, etc.; **Lordis Spirituell** *n. pl.*
   Churchmen in the House of Lords
   561, **Lordis Spirituelle** 1033
spoused *pa. p.* married 697
stappis *n. pl.* footsteps 964, **steppis** 589,
   1836, 2010
statis *n. pl.* powerful people 2545
stere *imp.* stir 2452
sterlinges *see* liures
sterne *n.* steering gear of a ship 1778
stifly *adv.* resolutely 1421
store *inf.* equip 1987, 2049; **stored** *pa. p.*
   equipped 791, supplied 2080
straunge *adj.* foreign 176, 233, 241,
   etc., unusual 851, 2050, 2054, etc.;
   straunge frome unrelated to 2346
straungiers *n. pl.* foreigners 1383, visi-
   tors 2266
strecchithe *pr. 3. sg.* extends 1744–5
streightes *n. pl.* narrow passes 783
streit *adj.* narrow 415
streitlie *adv.* firmly C5/66, C5/81
strenght *n.* stronghold C2/264, strength
   106, 240, 610, etc.; **streynghtis** *n. pl.*
   strongholds C2/267
strenght *inf.* strengthen C3/93;
   strenghted *pa. p.* made safe C2/235
succede *v.* follow 1309, succeed (to an
   inheritance) 2396, C1/85
sueng *adj.* following 1077
suerte *see* seuerte
suffraunce *n.* permission (of God) 1560
suffre *inf.* allow 1648, 1711, 1998, etc.,
   endure 1283; **suffre** *imperative* allow
   229, 2255; **suffrethe** *pr. 3 sg.* allows
   1258, **suffrithe** 1254; **suffring** *pr. p.*
   allowing 896, 1558, 1706, etc., endur-
   ing 1492; **suffred** *pa. 3. sg.* allowed
   36, 1345, 1573, etc., submitted 1612,
   1980, endured 1953, **suffrethe** endured 1289–90; **suffred** *pa. p.* allowed
   162, 626, 1561, etc., endured 973,
   1293
suggestion *n.* subjection C2/147
supportacion *n.* support C4/13
surcharge *pr. 3 pl.* overburden 2268–9;
   surcharged *pa. p.* overburdened 2215;
   surchargeyng *vbl. n.* overburdening
   2260

surmountethe *pr. 3 sg.* overcomes 792–3

T

tailed *adj.* entailed (in law) 1025

tailes *n. pl.* taxes 2519, **tailis** 898, 2216, **taylles** C1/130

tarie *inf.* retain C3/95, delay 2570; **taried** *pa. 3 sg.* delayed 1273; **taried** *pa. 3 pl.* delayed 1270; **tarieng** *vbl. n.* delay 1376

tasque *n.* forced payment 2478, 2531; **tasques** *n. pl.* forced payments 2216, 2519, C1/130, **taskis** 898

telle *inf.* count 2563

temperat *adj.* self-restrained 2374

temporell *adj.* secular 2266, 2289–90, 2477, **temporelle** 1724; **Lordis . . . Temporell** *n. pl.* secular members of the House of Lords 561, **Lordis . . . Temporelle** 1033

tendring *pr. p.* taking care of 1616; **tendred** *pa. 3 sg.* took care of 1876; **tendred** *pa. p.* taken care of 2464, **tendrid** considered 59

tenementis *n. pl.* lands held in tenure 947, 1236

termes *n. pl.* words 10, 1739, (legal) terms C3/158, C4/20, **termys** words 734, 1737

terrien *adj.* earthly 2096

testament *n.* (legal) will 212, 2453, 2459

than *adv.* then 229, 336, 688, etc., **then** 56, 228, 427, etc.

than *prep.* than 28, 586, 637, **then** 787, 871, 1845, etc.

thaym *pron.* them C2/223, **thayme** C2/159, C2/222, C3/141, etc., **them** 61, 166, 179, etc., **theym** 66, 101, 782, etc., **theyme** 776, 1285; **thaym** *refl. pron.* themselves C2/189 (?), **theym** 855, 1248, 1661, etc., **theyme** 782, **themsilfe** C2/153, C2/188, **theymsilf** 1412; *see also* **hem**

the *pron.* thee 2489; **the** *refl. pron.* thyself 2489

then *see* **than**

theire *pron.* their 27, 67, 79, etc., **there** C1/89, C2/31, C2/37, etc., **theyr** 198, 969, C1/89; *see also* **her**

therto *adv.* in addition 367, 898, 1420, etc., to that place 690, to that purpose 1209

these *adj.* these 10, 1164, 1179, etc., **this** 641, 742, 809, etc., **thys** 734

they *conj.* although, though 177, 857, **though** C2/79, **thoughe** 861, 1248, 1262, etc.

theym *see* **thaym**

think *inf.* seem fitting 725; **thinke** *subj. 3 sg.* seem fitting C2/138

think *inf.* think 1514, C3/162; **think** *subj. 3 sg.* think 2476

this *see* **these**

this *adv.* thus 578, 1706, 1715, **thus** 102, 1002, 1496, etc.

tho *pron.* those 32, 36, 88, etc., **thoo** C5/42

thought *n.* care 1809, 1887, anxiety 2364, **thoughte** 73

thraldom *n.* servitude 2478

threddis *n. pl.* thirds (of income) C1/132

tissue *n.* rich cloth 2116

title *pr. 1 sg.* write down 448

to *adv.* too 159, 841, 861, etc., **too** 2262, 2527, C4/33

tofore *prep.* in the presence of 1844, 1853

tombed *pa. p.* entombed C1/77, **tombid** 1361

tomorne *adv.* tomorrow 2543

tone *pron.* one C2/129

tooke vppon theyme *pa. 3 pl. refl.* behaved, acted 782

tormentrie *n.* mistreatment 2228

tothere *pron.* other C2/130

toure *n.* fortress C2/253, tower 1577

trespasemente *n.* death C1/68, **trespassement** 292, 1232–3, 1317

trewes *n.* truce 114, 117, 723, etc., **trux** 1044, 1056, 1076, etc., **truxe** C1/142; **trewes** *n. pl.* truces 998, 1005, 1007, etc.; **trewes-keping** *n.* truce-keeping 1243; **trewes-taking** *n.* truce-making 1185

trouth *n.* oath C4/14, faithfulness C2/63, C4/13, **trouthe** 124, 578, 723, etc., truth 1538, 1621; **trouthis** *n. pl.* oaths C2/31, C2/160

trux *see* **trewes**

tuycion *n.* protection C1/134

turneis *see* **liures**

U

u– *see headnote*

vmbre *n.* shadow (figurative), cover 54, 109, 131, etc.

vnfoughten *pa. p.* without having fought 1429

vngoodelie *adv.* wickedly 2245, vn-goodely 125

vnyoned *pa. p.* united 685

vnkonnyng *adj.* unskilful 2323

vnmanly *adj.* inhuman 1462

vnware *n.* unwariness 782

vsage *n.* custom 1813, 2475, practice 619, 1885, 2316, vsaige 747, use 2419

vse *inf.* behave 2413, take part in 165, pursue 179, 905, 2455, use 183, 613, 615, etc.; vsithe *pr. 3 pl.* are accustomed 100; wysng *pr. p.* following 2363; vsed *pa. 2 pl.* were accustomed C2/224; vsed *pa. 3 sg.* used 957, 1378, pursued 1655; vsed *pa. 3 pl.* used 616, 2415, pursued 1661; vsed *pa. p.* used 1197, 1572, 1719, etc., accustomed 2376

vsurpe *inf.* rise up 1704; vsurpen *pa. 3 pl.* took wrongly 2260; vsurped *pa. p.* wrongly taken 172

vtteraunce *n.* extreme degree 2325

vttering *vbl. n.* selling C2/233

vtterly *adv.* outright 1119, utterly 1278, 1997, C2/169, etc.

vttermost *adj.* extreme 232, 1852, 2135, etc.

V

v– *see headnote*

vaileable *adj.* useful 2193–4, vaylable C1/191

vaillauntnesse *n.* bravery 1309

vailliaunce *n.* bravery 1677

vallente *n.* will 167 (see n.), voulente 2555

vapour *inf.* rise 104

vayneglorie *n.* pride 1801, 1808, vaynglory 2062

vecount *n.* territory under the authority of a viscount C1/126, vecounte C1/126, vicounte C1/126

venged *pa. p.* avenged 175, venge 193

vengeable *adj.* vengeful 511

verailie *adv.* truly 2204, veraly C2/154, verralie 1514, 1872

verdure *n.* flourishing growth 2107

verray *adj.* true 50, 106, 689, etc.

verray *adv.* very, completely 58, 78, 730, etc.

vessell *n.* plate 935, 2439, 2547, vesselle 960, 966

viage *n.* military expedition 329, 462, 463, etc., voiage 442, 881, 1266, etc., voyage *n.* pilgrimage 294, 694; viages *n. pl.* military expeditions C1/59, voiages 1238

viegnes *n. pl.* vines C2/133, C2/174

viellars *n. pl.* old men 1936

vileyned *pa. p.* insulted 2258

visit *inf.* afflict 2397

vitaile *n.* food 364, 915, 1471, etc., vitaille 2064, 2082; vitailes *pl.* supplies 912, vitailis 2430, vitailles C3/96

vitailers *n. pl.* suppliers of provisions 913, vitaillers C3/83

vitailing *n.* provisioning 831, C3/83, C3/97–8

vitailled *pa. p.* supplied with food 439, 446

vocatis *n. pl.* advocates C1/117

voiage *see* viage

voide *inf.* abandon, leave 1402, 1443, avoid 2437; voydith *pr. 3 sg.* abandons 1968; voided *pa. 3 sg.* cleared 403, abandoned 1429; voided *pa. p.* abandoned 1423

voulente *see* vallente

vulgarilie *adv.* commonly 1692

W

wach and ward *n.* guard duty 452 (see n.)

wage *inf.* pay 238, 987, employ 992; waged *pa. p.* paid 197, employed 199, 302, 326, etc.

wagyngys *n. pl.* wages 871

wanhope *n.* despair 2242–3

warde *inf.* protect 2326; wardithe *pr. 3 sg.* protects 794

ware *adj.* cautious 2466

waste *pr. 3 pl.* harm 2268, wastithe 2192, wastyn waste 2347; wastid *pa. 3 pl.* wasted 2210; wasted *pa. p.* wasted 1903, C2/113, devastated

C2/71, **wastid** 300, destroyed 2507;
wasting *vbl. n.* devastating C2/70
wele *n.* welfare 1601, 1807, 2293, etc.,
    well 1419, 1658, 1877, etc.; *see also*
    comen wele
wele-brethed *adj.* exercised 2319
wele-defensid *pa. p.* having strong
    defences 1134
well-ensured *pa. p.* trusted C5/55
welle-willeris *n. pl.* supporters 141
welthe *n.* wealth 1816, happiness 2297
wered *pa. p.* worn out 1981, **werid** 1505
werre *inf.* wage war 328, 735, 1647, etc.;
    werreied *pa. 3 sg.* waged war 274,
    werrid 1349, 1849; **werred** *pa. 3 pl.*
    1502
wete *inf.* know, understand 1736; **that is
    to wete** i.e. 616–17, 683–4, 1020, etc.
wethirs *n. pl.* kinds of weather 2050
what *adj.* whatsoever 1401, 2322,
    2506, etc.
where *see* **be**
wight *n.* importance 148, **wighte** C1/200
wilfull *adj.* wilful C2/143, voluntary
    2150, **willfull** 1973
wilfullie *adv.* voluntarily 1980, **wilfully**
    2015, 2035, C2/72, etc.
wyntris *n. pl.* winters, as reckoning of
    years 1387
wise *n.* manner 286, 595, 632, etc.;
    wises *n. pl.* ways 897, 2433

wited *pa. p.* blamed 1700
withdrawers *n. pl.* people retreating
    1410
witholden *pa. p.* prevented from acting
    C3/107
woo *interj.* woe 1241
worship *n.* honour 5, 91, 92, etc.
worship *inf.* show respect to 2253, 2277,
    2546
worshiplie *adv.* honourably 1341, 2102
wysng *see* **vse**

Y

ye *pron.* you 42, 72, 74, etc.
yeede *pa. 3 sg.* went 1354
yeer day *n. (indecl.)* years 202, **yere day**
    years 595, 866, 2185, etc.
yef *see* **if**
yeft *n.* gift 649, **yefte** C1/123
yelde *inf.* give 2510, **yelden** surrender
    1679; **yelding** *pr. p.* submitting 2225;
    yeldid *pa. 3 pl.* surrendered 364;
    yolden *pa. p.* surrendered 297, 473,
    532, submitted 895, 910, subdued 235
yelding-vp *vbl. n.* giving up 2232
yen *n. pl.* eyes 2003
yoie *n.* joy 1440 (see n.); *see also* **ioieust**
    under **j–**
ys *see* **his**

INDEX OF PROPER NOUNS

As *The Boke of Noblesse* and the sections from its Codicil printed here have many proper nouns, a full Index of them is desirable. For *The Boke* and English extracts from the Codicil, the respective Explanatory Notes gloss more fully all proper nouns, including problematic cases. For the Appendices, this Index supplies the only gloss, in giving current forms of names or dates of death for identifiable people there mentioned.

The Index alphabetizes by spellings recognizable from current scholarship, rather than by spellings in the primary texts, to allow comparison with Stevenson's *Wars in France*, which this edition overlaps with and complements. Like the Explanatory Notes, the Index gives names in the current language of the person or place concerned (e.g. *Anjou, Foulques, count of*, not *Fulk* ...), unless it would be eccentric to do so (e.g. *St Augustine*, not *Aurelius Augustinus Hipponensis*).

Where the primary text differs confusingly from the currently recognized name, the Index supplies the former in bold to gloss the latter and supplies a separate cross-reference (e.g. *The Hagge* for *Saint-Vaast-la-Hougue*), unless that cross-reference would be closely adjacent. The index includes Worcester's references to people which turn out to be incorrect (e.g. his erroneous citations from Vegetius).

Aristocrats and ecclesiastics are indexed under the place name of their best-known title (*Bedford, John, duke of*), unless they are more commonly known now by a surname (e.g. *Beaufort, Henry*, not *Winchester, Henry Beaufort, bishop of*). Other place names in titles are not indexed separately (e.g. the many other titles of John, duke of Bedford, in Appendix 3/9–14). However, places to which people were appointed in temporary military offices are indexed.

The Index gives the date of death, where we know it, the date of battles, and, for a few small places, the French *département*.

Some identifications and dates are drawn from *OCD*; *ODNB*; the AHRC-funded *The Soldier in Later Medieval England Online Database*, www.medievalsoldier.org; *The Gascon Rolls Project (1317–1468)*, www.gasconrolls.org; Adrian R. Bell, Anne Curry, Andy King, and David Simpkin (eds.), *The Soldier in Later Medieval England* (Oxford, 2013); *English Suits before the Parlement of Paris, 1420–1436*, ed. C. T. Allmand and C. A. J. Armstrong, Camden Society, 4th ser., 26 (1982); Linda Clark (ed.), *The House of Commons 1422–1461*, 7 vols. (Cambridge, 2020).

al-Malik al-Zahir Rukn al-Din Baybars al-Bunduqdari, sultan of Egypt and Syria (d. 1277) 300–1

al-Muazzam Turanshah, sultan of Egypt (d. 1250) 1291

Acre 296

Actovyle, Raulyn *see* Anquetonville, Raoulet d'

Aemilia Paulla Tertia 1838

Africa 289, 1502, 2519

Agamemnon 593, 1918, 1920, 1932, 1935

Agenais 1021, 1145

Agincourt, battle of (1415) 468, 812, 958, 1365

Ajax (**Ayax**) 1926, 1928, 1931

Albon, W. App. 3/58

Albret, Arnaud-Amanieu, lord of (d. 1401) 1124

Alençon App. 1/46, App. 1/59, App. 2/67, App. 3/16

Alençon, Charles II, count of (d. 1346) 343

Alençon, Jean II, duke of (d. 1476) 521, 547, App. 3/32

Alexander the Great 176

Alfonso VII, king of Castile-León (d. 1157) 704

Amiens (**Amyenx, Amyeus**) 1045, C2/53

Anglesey 1574

Angoulême (**Engwillom**) 1148

Saint-Cloud (**Seynt-Clow**), battle of (1411) 196, 200

St George 1163, 1395–6

Saint-James de Beuvron (**Saynt-Iaques de Beverton**) (Manche) App. 1/38–9

Saint-Jean-d'Angély (**Saint-Iohn-Euangelist**) 351

St Jerome 2295

Saint-Laurent-des-Mortiers (**Laurens-Martire**) (Mayenne) App. 1/57

Saint-Lô 1370, App. 2/86

St-Lo, Henry App. 3/59

St Paul C1/17

St Paul's Cathedral 680

Saint-Sauveur-le-Vicomte (**Saint-Savire de Ive, Seynt-Sauour-Vicount**) App. 1/73, App. 1/75

Sainte-Suzanne (**Sent-Zusan, Seyn-Suzan**) C1/210, App. 1/51, App. 1/90

Saintonge 1149

Saint-Vaast-la-Hougue (**The Hagge**) 330

Salisbury Cathedral 2283

Salisbury, William Aiscough, bishop of (d. 1450) C3/20

Salisbury, Thomas Montagu, earl of (d. 1428) 483, 489, 536, 823, 826, App. 1/15, App. 1/146, App. 3/40

Salm, Simon I, count of (**Fennes, erle of**) 345

Salvain (**Salveyne**), Sir John App. 1/54

Sancerre, Louis II, count of (d. 1346) 345

Santa Croce (**Seint Crosse**), Niccolò Albergati, cardinal priest of (d. 1443) C1/163

Santiago de Compostela (**Seint Iames**) 694

Sardis (**Sardes**) 2100

Scales, Thomas, Baron Scales (d. 1460) 536, App. 1/31, App. 2/95, App. 3/43

Scipio, Cornelius, fictional character (**Kayus son**) 10

Scipio Aemilianus Africanus, Publius Cornelius (d. 129 BCE) 1874, 1902, 1908, 1912

Scipio Africanus Maior, Publius Cornelius (d. 183 BC) (**Scipion Affrican**) 1822, 2007, 2011, 2015

Scipio Asiagenes, Lucius Cornelius (d. after 183 BCE) (**Scipion Asian**) 1822, 2012, 2018, 2022

Scotland; see also Marches (of Scotland) 313, 523, 528

Scluse see Sluis; Sluys, battle of (1340)

Seine, river C3/82

Seine-Head (**Seyn-Hede**) 438

Seine, battle of the (1416) 437–8, 814, 1352

Selby App. 3/63

Senlis 1426, 1430, 1432

Sens, Guillaume de Melun, archbishop of (d. 1376) 378

Sens, Hugues de Toucy, archbishop of (d. 1168) 699

Sent-Zusan, Seyn-Suzan see Sainte-Suzanne

Shardelow, Sir John (d. 1432) App. 1/119

Shorthose, Sir Gadifer App. 1/163

Shrewsbury, battle of (1403) 526

Shrewsbury, John Talbot, earl of (d. 1453) 833–4, 837, App. 1/24

Sicily 2536

Sigismund of Luxembourg, king of the Romans (d. 1437) 447–8

Sirie see Syria

Sluis (**Scluse**) C2/216

Sluys (**Scluse**), battle of (1340) 316, 322, 1073

Socrates 2095

Solomon (**Salamon**) 2278

Somerset 418

Somerset, Edmund Beaufort, duke of (d. 1455) 833, 836–7, C1/148–9, C1/216, C4/2, C5/4, C5/19–20,

Somerset, John Beaufort, duke of (d. 1444) 836

Spain 401, 416, 434, 1315, 1414, 2335

Spencer, Hugh App. 2/107

Stafford, Sir Humphrey (d. 1442) App. 3/34

Stafford, William (d. 1450) App. 3/34

Stanlowe, John App. 2/109

Stourton, Sir John II (d. 1462) C3/21

Strangways, Sir John App. 1/164

Suffolk, William de la Pole, duke of (d. 1450) 490, 826, 1367, App. 1/19, App. 3/41

Surienne, Sir François de (d. 1462) App. 1/78

Syria (**Sirie, Surie**) 279, 296, 1314

Tairs see Tours